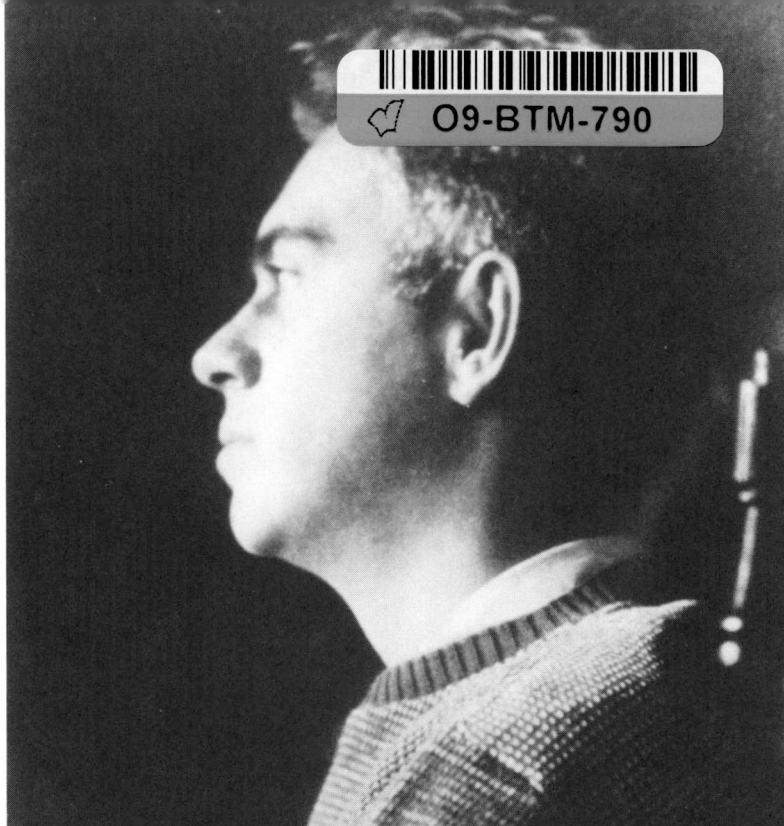

Dictionary of Literary Biography • Volume Forty-eight

American Poets, 1880-1945
Second Series

Dictionary of Literary Biography

Documentary Series

Yearbooks

Dictionary of Literary Biography • Volume Forty-eight

American Poets, 1880-1945
Second Series

Edited by
Peter Quartermain
University of British Columbia

A Bruccoli Clark Book
Gale Research Company • Book Tower • Detroit, Michigan 48226

Advisory Board for
DICTIONARY OF LITERARY BIOGRAPHY

Louis S. Auchincloss
D. Philip Baker
John Baker
William Cagle
Patrick O'Connor
Peter S. Prescott

Matthew J. Bruccoli and Richard Layman, *Editorial Directors*
C. E. Frazer Clark, Jr., *Managing Editor*

Manufactured by Edwards Brothers, Inc.
Ann Arbor, Michigan
Printed in the United States of America

Library of Congress Cataloging-in-Publication Data

American poets, 1880-1945, second series.

(Dictionary of literary biography; v. 48)
"A Bruccoli Clark book."
Includes index.
1. Poets, American—20th century—Biography—
Dictionaries. 2. Poets, American—19th century—Biog-
raphy—Dictionaries. I. Quartermain, Peter. II. Series.
PS129.A546 1986 811'.009 [B] 86-7550
ISBN 0-8103-1726-5

For Webster and Seville

Contents

Contents

Plan of the Series

The advisory board, the editors, and the publisher of the *Dictionary of Literary Biography* are joined in endorsing Mark Twain's declaration. The literature of a nation provides an inexhaustible resource of permanent worth. It is our expectation that this endeavor will make literature and its creators better understood and more accessible to students and the literate public, while satisfying the standards of teachers and scholars.

To meet these requirements, *literary biography* has been construed in terms of the author's achievement. The most important thing about a writer is his writing. Accordingly, the entries in *DLB* are career biographies, tracing the development of the author's canon and the evolution of his reputation.

The publication plan for *DLB* resulted from two years of preparation. The project was proposed to Bruccoli Clark by Frederick G. Ruffner, president of the Gale Research Company, in November 1975. After specimen entries were prepared and typeset, an advisory board was formed to refine the entry format and develop the series rationale. In meetings held during 1976, the publisher, series editors, and advisory board approved the scheme for a comprehensive biographical dictionary of persons who contributed to North American literature. Editorial work on the first volume began in January 1977, and it was published in 1978.

In order to make *DLB* more than a reference tool and to compile volumes that individually have claim to status as literary history, it was decided to organize volumes by topic or period or genre. Each of these freestanding volumes provides a biographical-bibliographical guide and overview for a particular area of literature. We are convinced that this organization—as opposed to a single alphabet method—constitutes a valuable innovation in the presentation of reference material. The volume

plan necessarily requires many decisions for the placement and treatment of authors who might properly be included in two or three volumes. In some instances a major figure will be included in separate volumes, but with different entries emphasizing the aspect of his career appropriate to each volume. Ernest Hemingway, for example, is represented in *American Writers in Paris, 1920-1939* by an entry focusing on his expatriate apprenticeship; he is also in *American Novelists, 1910-1945* with an entry surveying his entire career. Each volume includes a cumulative index of subject authors and articles. The final *DLB* volume will be a comprehensive index to the entire series.

With volume ten in 1982 it was decided to enlarge the scope of *DLB* beyond the literature of the United States. By the end of 1985 twenty-one volumes treating British literature had been published, and volumes for Commonwealth and Modern European literature were in progress. The series has been further augmented by the *DLB Yearbooks* (since 1981) which update published entries and add new entries to keep the *DLB* current with contemporary activity. There have also been occasional *DLB Documentary Series* volumes which provide biographical and critical background source materials for figures whose work is judged to have particular interest for students. One of these companion volumes is entirely devoted to Tennessee Williams.

The purpose of *DLB* is not only to provide reliable information in a convenient format but also to place the figures in the larger perspective of literary history and to offer appraisals of their accomplishments by qualified scholars.

We define literature as the *intellectual commerce of a nation:* not merely as belles lettres, but as that ample and complex process by which ideas are generated, shaped, and transmitted. *DLB* entries are not limited to "creative writers" but extend to other figures who in this time and in this way influenced the mind of a people. Thus the series encompasses historians, journalists, publishers, and screenwriters. By this means readers of *DLB* may be aided to perceive literature not as cult scripture in the keeping of cultural high priests, but as at the center of a nation's life.

DLB includes the major writers appropriate to each volume and those standing in the ranks immediately behind them. Scholarly and critical counsel has been sought in deciding which minor figures to include and how full their entries should be. Wherever possible, useful references will be made to figures who do not warrant separate entries.

Each *DLB* volume has a volume editor responsible for planning the volume, selecting the figures for inclusion, and assigning the entries. Volume editors are also responsible for preparing, where appropriate, appendices surveying the major periodicals and literary and intellectual movements for their volumes, as well as lists of further readings. Work on the series as a whole is coordinated at the Bruccoli Clark editorial center in Columbia, South Carolina, where the editorial staff is responsible for the accuracy of the published volumes.

One feature that distinguishes *DLB* is the illustration policy—its concern with the iconography of literature. Just as an author is influenced by his surroundings, so is the reader's understanding of the author enhanced by a knowledge of his environment. Therefore *DLB* volumes include not only drawings, paintings, and photographs of authors, often depicting them at various stages in their careers, but also illustrations of their families and places where they lived. Title pages are regularly reproduced in facsimile along with dust jackets for modern authors. The dust jackets are a special feature of *DLB* because they often document better than anything else the way in which an author's work was launched in its own time. Specimens of the writers' manuscripts are included when feasible.

A supplement to *DLB*—tentatively titled *A Guide, Chronology, and Glossary for American Literature*—will outline the history of literature in North America and trace the influences that shaped it. This volume will provide a framework for the study of American literature by means of chronological tables, literary affiliation charts, glossarial entries, and concise surveys of the major movements. It has been planned to stand on its own as a vade mecum, providing a ready-reference guide to the study of American literature as well as a companion to the *DLB* volumes for American literature.

Samuel Johnson rightly decreed that "The chief glory of every people arises from its authors." The purpose of the *Dictionary of Literary Biography* is to compile literary history in the surest way available to us—by accurate and comprehensive treatment of the lives and work of those who contributed to it.

The *DLB* Advisory Board

Foreword

"And what do I care if yellow and red are Spain's riches and Spain's good blood. Here yellow and red mean simply Autumn!"—William Carlos Williams (1919)

In 1835 Sir William Rowan Hamilton devised a revolutionary algebra (he called it "Quaternions") in which *ij* is not equal to *ji* but to *-ji*. In 1867 Karl Marx, in *Das Kapital,* argued that *"20 yards of linen = 1 coat"* is not necessarily the same as *"1 coat = 20 yards of linen."* The astonishing revolution of thought and art which we think of as modern, which questioned and often overthrew the commonsense assumptions of an earlier age, has its roots in the nineteenth century (and, indeed, before): Darwin proposed in 1859 that we are descended from apes; Freud proposed throughout a long career, which began in 1885-1886, that the springs of behavior lie in our unconscious, that our casual or mistaken utterances are more meaningful than our deliberate ones, that dreams have meaning, that we are not, after all, reasonable or rational creatures; Jane Ellen Harrison in *Prolegomena to the Study of Greek Religion* (1903) demonstrated that ancient Greek religion and mythology originated in dark and sometimes bloody rituals, not in reasonable thought or fiction, and that Dionysus, the principle of irrationality, is as important in Greek thought and life as is Apollo, the principle of reason. Sir James G. Frazer, in his comparative study of the beliefs and institutions of mankind, *The Golden Bough* (1890-1915), helped establish the idea that folklore and myth embody ways of looking at the world and ways of thinking about it, and gave impetus on one hand to anthropological studies which gradually dispelled the notion that certain men and societies are "primitive" or "savage" and on the other to studies of language and symbolism. Meanwhile, studies of Homer and of oral poetry began to undermine orthodox grammar and conventional verbal logic by setting paratactic syntax alongside hypotaxis as a legitimate structure for the sentence. The discovery of cave paintings at Altamira in 1879 and at Pair-non-pair and La Mouthe in the last decade of the century gradually led to the recognition of archaic or paleolithic man as intelligent, artistic, and possessed of a culture, while the study of these paintings and of aboriginal art from Africa, the Americas, and Australasia con-tributed in the early years of the twentieth century to the breakdown of perspective and verisimilitude and of the picture plane in painting. Cézanne, in any case, showed that paintings are not pictures but *paint,* and Mallarmé told Degas that "poetry is not written with ideas but with words." In the twentieth century Werner Heisenberg learned (through Willard Gibbs) how to use Hamilton's quaternions in quantum analysis: the world of quantum physics defies rationality, since light is *both* wave *and* particle, since (in the words of Niels Bohr) "an independent reality in the ordinary physical sense can neither be ascribed to the phenomena nor to the agencies of observation," since every observation of phenomena introduces uncontrollable elements, since space and time cannot be distinguished, and thus cause and effect cannot be discerned. As J. Robert Oppenheimer put it, "If we ask . . . whether the position of the electron remains the same, we must say 'No'; if we ask whether the electron's position changes with time, we must say 'No'; if we ask whether it is in motion, we must say 'No.' "

In March 1914, when T. S. Eliot was a student at Harvard Graduate School working on the philosophy of F. H. Bradley, Bertrand Russell, who was then one of his teachers, summed it all up in a lecture on *Our Knowledge of the External World* to the Lowell Institute in Boston: "The immense extension of our knowledge of facts in recent times," he said, has—as it did in the renaissance—"made men distrustful of the truth of wide, ambitious systems: theories come and go swiftly, each serving, for a moment, to classify known facts and promote the search for new ones, but each in turn proving inadequate to deal with the new facts when they have been found. Even those who invent the theories do not, in science, regard them as anything but a temporary makeshift. The ideal of an all-embracing synthesis, such as the Middle Ages believed themselves to have attained, recedes further and further beyond the limits of what seems feasible. In such a world, as in the world of Montaigne, nothing seems worthwhile except the discovery of more and more facts, each in turn the deathblow to some cherished theory; the ordering intellect grows weary, and becomes slovenly through despair." A world, then, of uncertainty and ambiguity and contradictions; a world without unity, and unknowable; a world in which the solid security of shared (and perhaps unspoken) assumptions and traditions is no longer available; a world in which masterpieces are no longer recognizable and works of art no longer identifiable; the modern struggle is the struggle to make sense of the world by defective means, to discover how to live amid disorder. The story of modern American poetry is of those poets who do indeed have one thing in common: their perception of the world as fragmented and uncertain (and it is among them that the battlelines are drawn). It is in their attitudes toward that world, the assumptions they bring to bear, the devices and strategies that they adopt, the resources they exploit or reject, that modern American poets can be characterized, and it is in this context that their work can be read: "To be modern," Marshall Berman has observed, "is to experience personal and social life as a maelstrom, to find one's world and oneself in perpetual disintegration and renewal, trouble and anguish, ambiguity and contradiction; to be part of a universe in which all that is solid melts into air." The variety of responses among modern writers is diverse indeed, ranging from the sort of acceptance Berman's "to be part of a universe" suggests (as in the work of William Carlos Williams) through a hard-fought and uneasy compromise (as in the work of Eliot) to a complete rejection of this modern vision in favor of a more traditional perception of the universe (as in the work of William Ellery Leonard or Robert P. Tristram Coffin).

The perception of irony as a characteristic modern device or mode gave rise to a whole school of American modernist writers who, following Eliot in their poetic practice, in their theoretical work established the New Criticism, an approach and methodology that prevailed in the universities and outside them from the late 1920s through the 1940s and beyond. Viewed through the lens of the New Criticism a number of nineteenth-century writers seem strikingly modern in the ways in which they handle their disillusionment, in their adoption of irony not simply as a mask through which to view the world but as a strategy of survival. But it is not the only strategy available, nor is it the only perspective. The major issues in twentieth-century American poetry, issues which had a profound canonical effect, appear fairly early in the century, most obviously in the work of Ezra Pound, T. S. Eliot, and William Carlos Williams.

The opening poem of Pound's *Hugh Selwyn Mauberley* (first part written in 1919) has not without reason acquired a reputation for complexity and obscurity, what with its puns, its allusions, its rhymes out of one language into another, its shifts of literary reference from one culture into another, its vocabulary, its syntax, its use of Greek. Yet what the poem is *about* is quite straightforward: bankruptcy. Bankruptcy experienced, sensed—and its accompanying frustration. The poet, aesthete perhaps, is himself bankrupt; society, indeed the whole culture, is bankrupt; there is no way at the present time in which it is possible to be a poet at all (without, at any rate, writing what the English poet Basil Bunting later called "Overdrafts"). Viewed one way, the poem is a sum of the individual life, the poet's. Viewed another, it has representative value, a summing up and a summoning up of the culture in which the poet is: its miscellaneousness, its lack of direction, its instability, its lack of focus. It is a culture too amorphous to be worked against, and the artist in any case has no idiom in that culture, nor any form in which that idiom can express itself; it is a world uncongenial to the artist, and the artist is uncongenial to the world—save in fragments, perhaps. The complexity of the poem is a complexity of surface, and what makes for the greatest difficulty is the multiplicity of the voices—just how does the poem sound? Who is the speaker? Is it Pound himself? Some clubby London literary pundit? This is the central question, and Pound deliberately leaves it not only unanswered but unanswerable—the multiplicity of voices sound *at once*, simultaneously. The reader is left in ambiguity, able to identify no voice as dominant, and unable as a result to decide what attitude to take (sympathy? hostility? approval? rejection?) toward either Mauberley or the culture in which Mauberley finds himself—and of which the reader himself is a part. Holding all judgment in abeyance then, the reader holds all the voices, the conflicts, the contradictions, the ambiguities, in mind at once; in thus accepting the multiplicity and ambiguity of the world of this opening poem, the reader discovers the complexity of his own responses to the world and of his feelings about it.

Leaving the question open in this way is what sets Pound in marked contrast to Eliot. *The Waste Land* (1922) is a very different sort of poem. Eliot himself, in the *Paris Review* interview in 1959, said he wrote it to get something off his chest, and in a lecture at Harvard he called it "the relief of a personal . . . grouse against life; it is just a piece of rhythmical grumbling." Unlike the first poem of *Hugh Selwyn Mauberley*, it is a complaint about the decline of Western culture. A cry of rage and despair, *The Waste Land* is a quest for unity in a fragmented and isolating world, using history as a means to judge the present, holding up tradition as a measure of loss; if it is at all possible to restore order—or a sense of order—it is not in the world as a whole, but only in one's personal life. The main thrust of the poem is not simply toward establishing a sense of unity (the poem has a remarkable singleness of purpose in its sequential multiplicity of voices), but toward changing the modern world, or at least shoring up the ruins. The poem is a cry against the modern world, and a resistance to it. Where Pound accepts the fragmented world and determines to build with what there is, Eliot is hungering for the world that's gone. In Canto 85 Pound notes that there are "No classics,/no American history,/no centre, no general root,/no *prezzo giusto* [that is, just price] as core," and thereby identifies *The Cantos* as an attempt to provide them. In *The Waste Land* Eliot, in saying "These fragments I have shored against my ruins," resists the modern condition.

Eliot's influence on American poetry, like Pound's, has been inescapable and far-reaching; indeed, it was Eliot, not Pound, who came to rule informed taste in America. The central issue in twentieth-century American poetics is discernible in the difference between the two poems; it is, in the long run, the difference between unity and diversity, singularity of meaning and multiplicity of meaning, monotheism and polytheism, closed form and open form. When William Carlos Williams, looking back in his *Autobiography* in 1951, called *The Waste Land* "the great catastrophe to our letters," he both enlarged and more clearly defined the terms of the disagreement among poets (and still he acknowledged "the blast of Eliot's genius which gave the poem back to the academics"): "Critically Eliot returned us to the classroom just at the moment when I felt that we were on the point of an escape to matters much closer to the essence of a new art form itself—rooted in the locality which would give it fruit." When *The Waste Land* appeared Williams was working on *Spring and All* (1922)—a book which Louis Zukofsky would carry around in his pocket until it was virtually tattered, a book which never achieved wide circulation and was extremely difficult to find until it was reprinted in *Imaginations* by New Directions in 1970 alongside the equally scarce *Kora in Hell* (1920). In 1918 Williams wrote the prologue to *Kora in Hell* and attacked Pound and Eliot for running off to Europe. He called Pound "the best enemy U.S. verse has" for doing so (though he would always hold up the essential value of Pound's poetry) and accused Eliot

not simply of being "a subtle conformist" to European (and more specifically English) tradition, an "archbishop of procurors to a lecherous antiquity": he called his work "rehash, repetition . . . of Verlaine, Baudelaire, Maeterlinck" and imagined an international congress of poets having "parodies of the middle ages, Dante and *langue d'oc* foisted upon it as the best in United States poetry." In a 1919 essay called "Belly Music," which appeared in *Others*, he flatly asserted that "the mark of a great poet is the extent to which he is aware of his time and NOT . . . the weight of liveliness in his metres. . . . It is NOT true that we can sing the old songs. The old poetry will NOT do." Williams rejects the tradition and the learning he associates with Eliot and Pound as harmful to the American poem: all his life he insisted on two points which most clearly set out his opposition to them. These are, as he phrased them in a talk at Dartmouth College in 1936, first, that "all art begins in the local and must begin there since there only will the senses find their material"; second, that "American poetry is not written in English but American. The two languages are in many ways diametrically opposed to each other though using mostly the same words. The effect on poetry in the two is fundamental. English verse connotes a past which largely governs it. It is bound up with the English language. In America we speak a new, swiftly evolving tongue unlike English in poetic connotations. . . . Without such an understanding there can be no superlative excellence in this place so far as poetry is concerned."

It is an argument over language, culture, symbolism; it is an argument about the nature of tradition, about the materials of poetry and what a poem is. Eliot seeks to connect the world of the present and the work of the present to the work of great artists and thinkers of the past, and invokes tradition, history, and religion as powers—"the poet must develop or procure the consciousness of the past . . . and he should continue to develop this consciousness throughout his career," he said in "Tradition and the Individual Talent" (1919); Pound invokes culture and seeks in books such as *How to Read* (1929) and *Guide to Kulchur* (1938) to make the reader "dig out the vital spots" in the culture of the past, and bring them to the present; Williams invokes the power of the individual to discover and rediscover his world and lift to the imagination "those things that lie under the direct scrutiny of the senses, close to the nose." In 1942 in an essay titled "The Invisible University" he said that he envied much of what Eliot had: "I long for what I presume to be his knowledge of Greek and Latin and I pine for his reading which I never got. What, I say, should I not be able to do with them if I could only have done those things. What revolutions, what revelations! I wonder. But that is what I think. If only I had the sound and knowledge of the Greek in my head how I could put it to use today. But maybe I couldn't. I might become just as they are, helpless with it." When, four years later, he called his long poem *Paterson* (1946) "a reply to Greek and Latin with the bare hands" he meant that in that poem he was doing (he hoped) what he saw the ancient Greeks and Romans (the first poets) doing: translating the actual immediate world into the world of the poem, making it new. In insisting that poetry be made out of the local and sensible, Williams necessarily insisted that it be the spoken (American) word, not the (bookish) written one; that it be immediate in and to the world (that things be seen for what they are, not freighted with symbolic or other significance or meaning—which in the prologue to *Kora in Hell* he called "an easy lateral sliding"). He insisted, too, that the poet be inseparable from the man. Eliot, on the other hand, argued (in "Tradition and the Individual Talent" and elsewhere) that "what happens [to the poet] is a continual surrender of himself as he is at the moment to something which is more valuable. The progress of an artist is a continual self-sacrifice, a continual extinction of personality. . . . The more perfect the artist, the more completely separate in him will be the man who suffers and the mind which creates." Eliot sees the poet as creating, and what he creates is masterpieces; Williams sees the poet as perceiving, and what he writes is testimony.

The difference is crucial, for a concern for masterpiece rests on a consideration of the means by which something called "nature" becomes something called "art," and the notion of what constitutes "art" is necessarily preconditioned by a set of rules, stated or not, which exists prior to the work and to which the work must conform. The predilection for rules which the notion of masterpiece fosters separates the poem from the outside world, demands that it conform to abstract criteria. In separating the work of art from the work of nature the artist separates himself from his work, and his work from his life; the work of art is seen as immutable, and even as Absolute. A concern for testimony leads the poet to anchor the poem firmly in his life, in the process of composition, in the world of experience, in the personal. If, as Williams wrote to Harriet Monroe in 1913, "life is above all

things else at any moment subversive of life as it was the moment before—always new, irregular," then the poem must incorporate that irregularity and indeterminacy into its structure by whatever means come to hand, including, say, the poet's own errors, the mistakes in writing; it might even abandon unity (one of the classic rules): the poem must be true to its own history, the history of its own composing. The opposition between the two views has frequently been called the opposition between the classic and the romantic, but it is perhaps more accurate to view it as an opposition between singleness and multiplicity of vision. It is possible to write bad work either way, of course, just as it is possible to write good. Pound, Eliot, and Williams are all great poets.

The issue was rarely (if ever) as clear-cut as this brief description suggests, however. In "Pounding Fascism," which appeared in *Sulfur* in spring 1985, Charles Bernstein has suggested that Ezra Pound himself, who stands at the wellhead of twentieth-century American poetry, is in the form of *The Cantos* releasing the unified voice and consciousness toward a multiplex and polyphonous world and work, nomadic and fragmentary, while at the same time his desire is for a hierarchical and ordered structure. Even though Pound says (in the *New Age*, 10 January 1918) that "the monotheistic temperament has been the curse of our time," his desires and habits of thought are monotheistic: hence his fascism. The contention which is at the heart of *The Cantos* is a contention at the heart of modern American poetry, and one of the sources of its great energy in the first half of this century; few indeed are the poets whose attitudes are as clearcut as those of Eliot and Williams. Eliot and Pound enabled renaissance English or medieval Italian or modern French (or Dante, Confucius, the *Upanishads*) to enter an *American* poem; Williams, in his intense localism, posed the authenticity of American speech against their literariness, against their internationalism, and brought the colloquial and insistent rhythms of nongrammatical speech into the American poem.

Furthermore, in the late years of the nineteenth century a number of strongly individualistic writers, growing up in a nonacademic or at any rate nonliterary climate, perforce created their own poetry: Edwin Arlington Robinson (born 1869), Robert Frost (1874), and Wallace Stevens (1879), as well as William Carlos Williams (1883), Ezra Pound (1885), and T. S. Eliot (1888). The Robinson-Frost streams have not, in this century, been influential—though both poets enjoyed a wide readership and are clearly major writers. Wallace Stevens's influence has been pervasive and varied (writers as diverse as John Ashbery, Robert Creeley, and Theodore Roethke, for example, are considerably indebted to him), but historically he has not founded a tradition; there is no Stevens "school." And although Williams, Pound, and Eliot are the dominant figures in the first sixty-or-so years of the century, they were not of course working alone. What was accomplished was accomplished over a number of years, through a series of poetic generations which the organization of these three volumes of the *Dictionary of Literary Biography* seeks to reflect by grouping poets according to the years of their births. Volume 45 covers poets born in 1885 through 1897. This volume covers poets born in 1898-1916, and a final volume will deal with those born in 1842-1884. Needless to say, the generations are not clear-cut and inevitably there are omissions: we know virtually nothing about such writers as Alanson Hartpence, Orrick Johns, and Billy Saphier, for example, yet they are important in the history of early modernist writing in America. And there are several complicating factors. First and foremost of these is the American language itself.

Of the nearly 28 million immigrants to the continental United States in the period 1820-1910, 63.5% of them (that is, nearly 18 million) arrived during the thirty-one years 1880-1910, and 31.5% of them (more than 8.75 million) arrived in the first eleven years of the twentieth century at an average rate of more than 2,400 a day (in 1907 they came at a rate of more than 3,500 a day). Not many of them spoke English. In 1854, one of the peak immigration years, 50% of 427,833 immigrants spoke German, and 37% spoke English; in 1882, 32% of 788,922 immigrants spoke German, and 22% English; in 1907, 29% of 1,285,349 immigrants spoke German, and 8.9% spoke English. The Census Bureau reported that in 1900 more than 12 million (16.4%) of a total population of 76.3 million were foreign born, and roughly 16 million (21.4%) were native born of foreign parents; that is to say, 37.8% of the population were either foreign born or native born of foreign stock. Since the census only recorded statistics for the white population, the figures are conservative, but even if 30% of these were native speakers of English (and that estimate is surely high) then just under 20 million (26%) of the 1900 population learned English as a second language—if they learned it at all. The 1910 census reported that of the more than 32 million Americans of foreign

white stock, over 22 million of them (or about 24% of the white population) were from non-English-speaking stock. It seems reasonable to estimate that somewhere between one person in four and one person in five in the continental United States in 1910 learned English as a second language, or did not know it at all. Further, immigrants to the United States tended to cluster in New England, the Middle Atlantic states (New York, New Jersey, Pennsylvania, and Delaware), and the Midwest, and to avoid the South. In 1900 only 7.9% of the white population of the South was foreign born or native born of foreign stock (as compared to 37.8% for the continental United States), a *decline* from the figures for 1870, the earliest year in which such a count was made. In 1850, 45% of the population of the Middle Atlantic states was foreign born (655,929 of them in New York, the bulk of them presumably in New York City), while only 14% of the population of New England was foreign born (and many of them Irish). In *A Century of Population Growth From the First Census to the Twelfth 1790-1900* (1909) the Census Commissioners reported that "In both New England and the Middle States, more than half of each 1,000 of the white population in 1900 were of foreign parentage. It appears, moreover, . . . that in these two sections of the country the proportion is increasing with great rapidity." The effect of all this on the American language— and on American poetry—has been profound. Southern writing, for example, is linguistically as well as culturally distinct from that of the rest of the nation, and it is surely significant that three major innovators among twentieth-century American writers learned English as a second language: Gertrude Stein spoke German as a small child; William Carlos Williams, Spanish (though he may have learned both languages from the very beginning); and Louis Zukofsky's first language was Russian Yiddish.

Of the large number of German-speaking immigrants who entered the United States in the 1850s and the 1880s (as many as English speakers, if not more), many were both articulate and politically active. They brought with them habits of thought attendant on a language which combines and compounds words with great (and perhaps to an English ear almost pedantic) precision and concreteness (hydrogen, for instance, is *wasserstoff*); a language which reflects an almost singular taste for large abstractions for which there is in English no precise equivalent (like, say, *weltanschauung*); a language which in addition to its penchant for polysyllabic words habitually delays the verb to the end of the sentence. Such linguistic habits fed a native American taste for rhetoric (Alexis de Tocqueville observed as early as the 1820s that Americans go to speeches where Europeans go to plays); fed into a culture which, increasingly urbanized and industrialized, increasingly needed technical terms and fairly high-order abstractions in order to cope with increasing social complexity; and fed into a literary and artistic culture which had acquired from romanticism (more specifically from Coleridge and Kant) a taste for Neoplatonic abstractions and Latinisms. The language which the immigrants learned (often, perhaps, from a grammar and/or a dictionary) had already been deracinated, and hence rendered abstract, almost from the very foundation of American colonies. The earliest settlers may have thought of themselves as Englishmen, and as far as they could they educated their children along English lines or even sent them to England for their schooling, but at the same time, willy-nilly, the fact of exile not simply from English culture but from the English landscape divorced the language from the world: William Carlos Williams observed that "they saw birds with rusty breasts and called them robins" when "what they saw were not robins. They were thrushes"; much of the language Americans used, certainly, had no visible antecedents as they walked down the street. In important respects, the American language is history-less.

It was also in important respects at the turn of the century a dead language. The history of American writing (and especially poetry) in the twentieth century can be read as the history of a language gradually acquiring native speakers, when there were none before; a dead language, reversing all customary patterns, returning to life. A dead language is a language that exists without its surrounding and supportive culture, a culture which defines the things to which the language refers. Classical Latin is a dead language because the groups of people who understood the culture that gave rise to the language are gone: as they vanished, so did the world embodied in the words set forth by them, and the history of the language, at some profound level apprehended, felt in the language by its speakers, became forgotten, and that language became a special territory reserved for special functions. Those millions of Americans who learned English as a second language through books rather than through speech rarely came to feel the kinship of words, what I. A. Richards called "the interanimation of words." But the abstractness, the thin-ness, of the America language was

not confined to immigrants. Matthew Arnold observed of Emerson's poetry in 1884 that "he is not plain and concrete enough. . . . A failure of this kind goes through almost all his verse, keeps him amid symbolism and allusion and the fringes of things"; in 1901 William Butler Yeats complained of Longfellow that "no words of his borrow their beauty from those that used them before, and one can get all that there is in story and idea without seeing them as if moving before a half-faded curtain embroidered with kings and queens, their loves and battles and days out hunting, or else with holy letters and images of so great antiquity that nobody can tell the god or goddess they would commend to an unfading memory." It is almost a commonplace among twentieth-century American writers to notice, as Gertrude Stein did in her 1935 lectures on narration at the University of Chicago, that in American writing words "began to detach themselves from the solidity of anything"; elsewhere she told an audience that the American language exhibits a "lack of connection" with material daily living. Many things conspired to lay an English vocabulary over an American landscape, and Malcolm Cowley was by no means the only American of his generation to complain bitterly that in school "our studies were useless or misdirected, especially our studies in English literature: the authors we were forced to read, and Shakespeare most of all, were unpleasant to our palate; they had the taste of chlorinated water." Thus, when Williams calls *Paterson* "a reply to Greek and Latin with the bare hands" he is identifying his poem as an attempt to end the divorce between the American and his speech, between American speech and American culture and landscape, between American speech and American writing. In the context of the state of the American language, Malcolm Cowley and Slater Brown's remark in the last issue of *Broom* that "Eliot believes in tradition, form, everything dead" is both poignant and urgent.

Some other complicating factors can be fairly briefly outlined. The widespread adoption as textbooks in American colleges and universities of *Understanding Poetry* by Cleanth Brooks and Robert Penn Warren (1938, fourth edition 1976), and of anthologies such as *Modern American Poetry: An Introduction,* edited by Louis Untermeyer (1919, seventh edition 1950), had a profound effect upon the nature of American poetry, and on the shape of the canon, for they established an orthodoxy that defined both what sort of thing a poem is and (as corollary) who the worthwhile poets are. *Understanding Poetry* is perhaps the most influential textbook ever to have been published in the field; at least one generation of poets and possibly two formally studied poetry through this book (between 1938 and 1976 the book went through four editions and over fourteen printings; in 1986 it is still in print): writers as different as John Berryman and Robert Lowell learned to write—or in their schooling were encouraged to write—the kind of poetry that the book fostered. *Understanding Poetry* derived its tenets from the New Criticism as established and practiced in the United States by Brooks, Warren, John Crowe Ransom, and Allen Tate (perhaps Eliot's most astute American followers). A cardinal principle of the book is that in the long run the meaning of a poem cannot be stated at all (except by repeating the poem) but can only be perceived, understood, and appreciated; it teaches the explication of poems through the analysis of relationships between elements in the poem, but especially through the examination of irony and paradox; imagery and ambiguity are fundamental in the consideration of tone, theme, and structure, and it is through these means that the student is shown how to attempt the explication of meaning. *Understanding Poetry* discusses "intention and meaning" and works from the assumptions, first, that "the unity of a poem, like that of any work of art, is a unity of final meaning," and second, that the poet "shapes and uses" language—that the poet is, in other words, the author, the creator of the poem, and is in control. Following Eliot's lead, the book exhibits a marked preference for the work of John Donne and the English metaphysicals over that of Ben Jonson or Sir Thomas Wyatt, and sees poetry as expressive and/or communicative in its aims. As Cleanth Brooks put it in 1947 in *The Well Wrought Urn*, a poem is "a structure of meanings, evaluations, and interpretations; and the principle of unity which informs it seems to be one of balancing and harmonizing connotations, attitudes, and meanings. . . . [The unity is] an achieved harmony." Critics of the book were fond of remarking that *Understanding Poetry* taught difficulty as a virtue and lucidity as of dubious value in poetry; cynics accused the book of serving the interests of professors who, if all good poems are difficult poems, thus have something to profess. The year after the book first appeared, Basil Bunting complained in a letter that "the age of poems for commentators returns."

Understanding Poetry and its host of imitators did much to establish modern writing against the at-times-virulent conservatism of such traditionalists as A. E. Housman in England, and Stanton A.

Coblentz, Max Eastman, Robert P. Tristram Coffin, and John G. Neihardt in America. James Laughlin (later to become not only an accomplished poet himself but the most important single figure in the publishing of poetry in the United States) recorded in an interview in 1981 that when he was an undergraduate at Harvard in 1934 "You couldn't mention Pound's or Eliot's name in [Robert] Hillyer's class or you'd be sent out of the room," and there is no question at all that critics such as Brooks, Warren, Ransom, Tate, Edmund Wilson, and Yvor Winters (and Eliot himself, of course) made possible an American readership for modern British and American poets such as W. H. Auden, Hart Crane, E. E. Cummings, Robert Frost, Archibald MacLeish, Louis MacNeice, Wallace Stevens, Dylan Thomas—and, later, Richard Eberhart, Randall Jarrell, Robert Lowell, Theodore Roethke, Delmore Schwartz, Karl Shapiro, Richard Wilbur, and others. With the exception of Frost and Stevens, the diversity of this list is more apparent than real, for these writers constitute a poetic generation that, consciously influenced by Eliot's criticism, wrote in an ironic and formal mode. But in thus establishing an orthodoxy of received opinion, many British and American poets were also (to a greater or lesser degree) *excluded* from the modern canon and to all intents and purposes driven underground, becoming more or less invisible (at least to "serious critics" and trade publishers). Among these are such writers as Basil Bunting, Hilda Doolittle (H. D.), David Jones, Mina Loy, Robert McAlmon, Hugh MacDiarmid, Thomas Merton, Marianne Moore, Lorine Niedecker, Charles Reznikoff, Kenneth Rexroth, Laura Riding Jackson, Gertrude Stein, William Carlos Williams, and—later—Robert Creeley, Robert Duncan, Roy Fisher, Allen Ginsberg, Ronald Johnson, George Oppen, Charles Olson, Jeremy Prynne, Jack Spicer, John Wieners, and Jonathan Williams. Some of these writers died with their work out of print or even unpublished (H. D., Marianne Moore, Mina Loy, Lorine Niedecker), or, if it was in print, published and kept in print by James Laughlin's New Directions (Thomas Merton, Kenneth Patchen, Ezra Pound, Kenneth Rexroth, William Carlos Williams). Others first published their work outside the United States (Robert Creeley, Charles Olson, Ezra Pound, Louis Zukofsky) or privately (Lorine Niedecker, Charles Reznikoff, William Carlos Williams). H. D. at her death was remembered, if at all, for her earliest poems; it was not until twenty years later—after her long poems later published as *Hermetic Definition* had circulated in xeroxes of the manuscripts—that her *Collected Poems* were published by New Directions. The strength of the canonical tradition of modern American poetry is reflected in the reputation of Kenneth Rexroth, whom James Dickey dismissed in 1980 as "one of the worst" of American poets while Eliot Weinberger (poet, translator, and editor) only two years later would call him "America's great Christian poet" and suggest that "postwar American poetry is the 'Rexroth Era' as much as . . . the earlier decades are the 'Pound Era.'" One of the great ironies in the history of modern reputations is that William Carlos Williams, who complained that the publication of *The Waste Land* in 1922 "set me back twenty years," not only had to wait twenty-five or twenty-six years for recognition within the universities and by the general public, but achieved that recognition through the publication in 1946 of Randall Jarrell's review of *Paterson I* in *Partisan Review* and in June 1948 of Robert Lowell's review of *Paterson II* in the *Nation*. In 1948 Williams was sixty-five years old, Jarrell was thirty-four, and Lowell was thirty-one. Yet Cleanth Brooks remarked in a 1964 lecture, later printed in *A Shaping Joy*, that Williams's "The Red Wheelbarrow" remains "quite inert. I see the white chickens and the raindrops glazing red paint. But I have to take on faith the author's statement that 'so much depends' on this scene." Robert Lowell, describing the nature of his indebtedness to Williams and looking back on his education at Kenyon College in the late 1930s under John Crowe Ransom, recalled in 1961 that "My own group, that of Tate and Ransom, was all for the high discipline, for putting on the full armor of the past, for making poetry something that would take a man's full weight and that would bear his complete intelligence, passion and subtlety," that "for us Williams was part of the revolution that had renewed poetry, but he was a byline. Opinions varied on his work. It was something fresh, secondary, and minor, or it was the best that free verse could do." Yet although he is "a model and a liberator," he confessed, "the difficulties I found in Williams twenty-five years ago are still difficulties for me. Williams enters me, but I cannot enter him." The difficulty is instructive and derives in part from a predilection to read poems for the unity of their final meaning rather than for the play of possible meanings, to read them for the controlled play of ambiguity and irony rather than for the play of syntax and language per se. One view explains it as the difference between seeing life as a self-improvement course and life as an adventure.

The difference between the two camps was never perhaps as simple as this discussion suggests, but it is nevertheless true that trade publishers tended to favor poets blessed by the university and, often, teaching in it, and that poets outside the universities had to make do with fugitive publication in little magazines, by small private presses, or overseas. The history of the politics of poetry publishing in the United States has yet to be written, but it is closely related to the fortunes of the two traditions; the central texts in the academic tradition were Eliot's two essays "Tradition and the Individual Talent" and "Hamlet and his Problems," both widely anthologized; outside the academy, they were Williams's *Kora in Hell* and *Spring and All*, both extremely difficult to find, both enjoying a substantial underground reputation and influence. The effect of the two camps on the poet, and the complexity of their interrelationship, is perhaps best shown in Robert Duncan's description of *his* education in 1935 or 1936 (he is two years younger than Robert Lowell): "Books had opened in childhood imaginations of other lives in which the idea of our own lives dwelling took on depths and heights, colors and figures, a new ground beyond self or personality in the idea of Man. But this prescribed thing was different, books became materials for examinations. English Literature with its reading lists, its established texts, its inquisitions, was to map our compulsory path in what had seemed before an open country. Work by work, author by author, the right roads were paved and marked, the important sights were emphasized, the civic improvements were pointed out where the human spirit had successfully been converted to serve the self-respect of civil men, and the doubtful, impulsively created areas were deplored. If we, in turn, could be taught to appreciate, to evaluate as we read and to cultivate our sensibilities in the ground of other men's passions, to taste and to regulate, to establish the new thing in the marketplace, we were to win some standing in the ranks of college graduates, and educated middle class, urbane and professional, as our parents had done before us." Against that orderly and ordered world Duncan sets an order of poetry "that seemed to contain a personal revelation," in which the poem is "not demanding a response but testing for an affinity," in which the reader submits to the poem as the poet is seen to submit to the language: it is writing as discovery. Such a view of the poem rejects the notion of the poet as controlling his work. It is a crucial distinction, and one that not only complicates the relations between the two traditions but confuses and blurs the boundaries: a poet like

Wallace Stevens, for example, can in poems like "A Clear Day and No Memories" write a short lyric of great beauty which works through a concentrated play of irony and paradox, and whose beauty rests in large degree upon not simply the poet's control over his materials but the reader's recognition of that control (in this he is very like Frost), but he also, in other poems, submits to the language, submits to the poem—relinquishing, one might say, conceptual as well as perceptual control—though he keeps tight hold on the *form.*

The apparently simple distinctions between the two camps, the academic and nonacademic, had by the 1960s begun to blur, and with the wisdom of hindsight it became apparent that the distinctions had probably always been blurred. Yet that blurring first became visible, probably, in 1948, with the publication not of Williams's *Paterson II* (nor of Olson's seminal book on Melville, *Call Me Ishmael,* 1947), but of Pound's *Pisan Cantos,* which won the Bollingen Prize (the fact that Allen Tate was one of the judges who awarded the prize to Pound suggests the complexity of this picture). Pound's central position in the history of modern American poetry rests in part on the fact that his early poetry (up to and through the complete *Hugh Selwyn Mauberley*) served as a model for the academic tradition, the university poets, while his *Pisan Cantos* and the early *Homage to Sextus Propertius* (1919) served as model or inspiration for such later poets as Robin Blaser, Robert Creeley, Robert Duncan, and Charles Olson, who fought that tradition vehemently and who at least were able to emerge from the underground if not come into prominence in the 1950s. With the publication in 1960 of Donald Allen's catalytic and crucial anthology *The New American Poetry 1945-1960* that underground was provided with its own college and university textbook and itself started an orthodoxy; the central critical document for the group, Charles Olson's *Projective Verse* (1950), at last achieved wide circulation. And Pound was seen to be, in his career as a whole, a seminal figure in both traditions.

It is only, then, with that complexity in mind that the following extremely oversimplified summary can be read at all: there are two traditions, or rather *camps* (for they are indeed at war); there are two ways of looking at the world, and they exist side-by-side, perhaps in the same person; they seem to have been endemic to American writing throughout its history. In his extraordinary book *All That Is Solid Melts Into Air* (1982) Marshall Berman suggests that "to be a modern*ist* is to make oneself somehow at home within the maelstrom, to

make its rhythms one's own, to move within its currents in search of the forms of reality, of beauty, of freedom, of justice, that its fervid and perilous flow allows." In that search, however, there is a difference between a man's emotions and intellections giving value to what he sees as an otherwise valueless universe and world—where the meaningfulness of experience is a construct, more or less deliberate and conscious, of the individual's; where traditional values are invoked, perhaps overtly projected onto a seemingly indifferent or impenetrable cosmos—and a man's experience of the world as the experience of a world of signs—where things and events are seen as striving to speak, where to evoke an image is to receive a sign (whose meaning may be obscure indeed), where the cosmos is experienced as potential meaning, striving to be seen and to be declared, where the act of writing is an act of translation, bringing "into human language a word or phrase in which the universe itself is written" (the phrase is Robert Duncan's). It is the difference between singleness of vision and multiplicity of vision; between the belief that the universe is knowable, and that it is essentially and perdurably ambiguous, mysterious; between making things meaningful, and working toward an awareness of meaning. Heidegger commented in *What is Called Thinking?* that "multiplicity of meanings is the element in which thought must move in order to be strict thought" precisely because the fleeting, the confused, the dim, and the uncertain are the elements of experience which best exhibit reality; in these terms, intellectual certainty is precarious if not delusory.

For the poem, the difference is telling. For in one case, form is given to or imposed on experience (the poet bringing to his experience a set of preconceptions and assumptions)—in which case the poem becomes a poetry of *content,* and the critical apparatus brought to bear upon the poem insists upon "form" and "content" as distinct aspects of the work. In the other, form is found in experience, and content is discovered in *matter* ("no ideas but in things," wrote Williams in *Paterson*). When form is given to experience, poets write poems which are closed forms; often, perhaps asserting an absolute, or in quest of one; always, in the long run, reducible to a single unity of meaning or interpretation; monotheistic in their belief and desire, such poets write poems which have a point, have something to say. And when form is discovered in experience, poets write poems which are open forms, processes rather than products, poems of possibility and possible meanings: the poet does not know what it is he wants to say, and indeed in the course of writing discovers what it is that the poem says, for if form is discovered in experience, that experience includes the experience of language, especially the language in which the poem is written, and to which the poet is necessarily obedient. Such poems may or may not be open to a single interpretation, and, although they have (perhaps) an ending, they are not necessarily complete. Hence Williams when he died was working on book six of *Paterson* (which he originally planned in four books), and Pound, when he died, was still working on *The Cantos*, originally designed to end at Canto 100.

In the history of American writing, the dominance of one of these attitudes over the other seems to run in cycles. The early struggles of the imagists (first under Pound's aegis, then under Amy Lowell's) for recognition and dominance pushed the *Others* group (Maxwell Bodenheim, Alfred Kreymborg, Mina Loy, Marianne Moore, and others) to one side; in the 1930s the sheer prominence of Eliot (in 1932-1933 as Charles Eliot Norton Professor of Poetry at Harvard University he delivered the lectures which became *The Use of Poetry and The Use of Criticism*) pushed to one side the objectivist group (George Oppen, Carl Rakosi, Charles Reznikoff, William Carlos Williams, and Louis Zukofsky)—who have come to recognition and influence if not dominance in the 1980s—and contributed to the utter neglect of such political poets as Norman Macleod and Lola Ridge. The essential contention between the two attitudes is the great source of energy for modern American poetry, and accounts in large part for its great diversity and power, as does the increasing confidence through the century of the American poet with a native American idiom. When the American army (in the form of six soldiers) arrived in the French village of Culoz on 1 September 1944, Gertrude Stein was there to welcome them and, as she tells us in *Wars I Have Seen* (1946), was reminded of an earlier liberation, at the end of World War I, twenty-seven years earlier, by an American army whose soldiers spoke English, who spoke American English, but yet who were not native speakers: "[In 1944] they had a poise and completely lacked the provincialism which did characterize the last American army, they talked and they listened and they had a sureness, they were quite sure of themselves, they had no doubts or uncertainties and they had not to make any explanations. The last army was rather given to explaining, oh just anything, they were given to explaining, these did not explain, they were just conversational. . . . I think of the Americans of the last war, they had their language but they were not yet in possession of it, and the children of the depression as that generation called itself was beginning to possess its language but it was still struggling but now the job is done, the G. I. Joes have this language that is theirs, they do not have to worry about it, they dominate their language and in dominating their language which is now all theirs they have ceased to be adolescents and have become men." The story of modern American poetry to World War II is the story of successive generations of writers increasingly gaining familiarity in and security with the American idiom, increasingly gaining confidence in the possibility of being *American* poets without having to turn to Europe for models or for approval, or having to turn deliberately away from Europe. It is instructive, then, to group poets in short "generations" as these volumes of the *Dictionary of Literary Biography* do, for the complexity of the pressures on the writer, of the patterns of literary history of which he is a part, are then emphasized.

—*Peter Quartermain*

Acknowledgments

This book was produced by BC Research. Karen L. Rood, senior editor for the *Dictionary of Literary Biography* series, was the in-house editor.

Art supervisor is Patricia M. Flanagan. Copyediting supervisor is Patricia Coate. Production coordinator is Kimberly Casey. Typesetting supervisor is Laura Ingram. The production staff includes Rowena Betts, David R. Bowdler, Deborah Cavanaugh, Kathleen M. Flanagan, Joyce Fowler, Ellen Hassell, Pamela Haynes, Judith K. Ingle, Judith McCray, Mary Scott Sims, Joycelyn R. Smith, and Lucia Tarbox. Jean W. Ross is permissions editor. Joseph Caldwell is photography editor. James Adam Sutton and Joseph Matthew Bruccoli did photographic copy work for the volume.

Walter W. Ross and Rhonda Marshall did the library research with the assistance of the staff at the Thomas Cooper Library of the University of South Carolina: Lynn Barron, Daniel Boice, Connie Crider, Kathy Eckman, Michael Freeman, Gary Geer, David L. Haggard, Jens Holley, Marcia Martin, Dana Rabon, Jean Rhyne, Jan Squire, Ellen Tillett, and Virginia Weathers.

American Poets, 1880-1945
Second Series

Dictionary of Literary Biography

Léonie Adams
(9 December 1899-   )

Tony N. Redd
The Citadel

BOOKS: *Those Not Elect* (New York: McBride, 1925);
High Falcon & Other Poems (New York: John Day, 1929);
This Measure (New York: Knopf, 1933);
Poems: A Selection (New York: Funk & Wagnalls, 1954).

OTHER: *The Lyrics of François Villon,* edited and translated by Adams and others (Croton Falls, N. Y.: Limited Editions Club, 1932);
Yvan Goll, *Jean sans terre/Landless John,* translated by Adams and others (San Francisco: Grabhorn, 1944);
"Conrad as Master," in *The Contemporary Poet as Artist and Critic: Eight Symposia,* edited by Anthony Ostroff (Boston: Little, Brown, 1964), pp. 121-127.

Léonie Adams has written some of the finest lyrics of the twentieth century, poetry in the tradition of the great English romantics, with influences from the seventeenth-century metaphysicals, Yeats, and the later French symbolists. Her great intellect is manifested in her verse not as intellectuality but as the ordering power of an acute sensibility.

The fifth of sixth children, Léonie Fuller Adams was born on 9 December 1899, in Brooklyn, New York, to Charles Frederic and Henrietta Rozier Adams, parents whose forebears had settled in Maryland as early as the seventeenth century. Charles F. Adams, however, had been born in Santiago, Cuba, where his father had sugar and banking interests; his mother was Venezuelan. He

Léonie Adams

received his formal education in New England and evidently passed along to his daughter some of his own passion for literature. Although Léonie Adams formed several deep friendships at school, she seems to have had a rather sheltered and lonely childhood. So strict was her upbringing, that she

3

was not allowed to travel on the subway until she went to Barnard College; and then, although she was eighteen, her lawyer-father usually accompanied her.

At Barnard Adams wrote her first poems in secret. While she was still an undergraduate, in 1921, her "April Mortality" appeared in the *New Republic.* This poem, in which an individual's bitter bones "lecture" his hopeful heart on the subject of the mortality of all natural beauty, provided clear evidence of the kind of contemplative lyric and chiaroscurist perception that would later become hallmarks of Léonie Adams's art:

> And if thou dreamest to have won
>> Some touch of her in permanence,
> 'Tis the old cheating of the sun,
>> The intricate lovely play of sense.
>
> Be bitter still, remember how
>> Four petals, when a little breath
> Of wind made stir the pear-tree bough,
>> Blew delicately down to death.

In 1922 Adams received an A.B. degree magna cum laude from Barnard College and began to earn a rather sketchy living, first as a staff editor at Wilson Publishing Company (1922-1926) and later as an editorial assistant at the Metropolitan Museum of Art (1926-1928). A Barnard friend, Marian Smith, showed some of her poems to Louis Untermeyer, who recommended them to Max Eastman and Ridgely Torrence. Another friend, Raymond Holden, took her first collection of poetry, *Those Not Elect*, to Robert M. McBride and Company, which published the volume in 1925.

In his review of *Those Not Elect* for the *Nation* (3 March 1926), Allen Tate located Léonie Adams's literary ancestors with precision: "Her sensibility, metaphysical in Johnson's sense, has isolated a world somewhere between eighteenth-century decoration and the fresh intensity of a lyric by Thomas Heywood or Greene. For all her aptness in certain early sixteenth-century conventions . . . the fusion of her qualities brings her closer to Carew than to any other poet." Tate concluded his appraisal of this fifty-page volume on a note of high praise: "There are perhaps five poems in this book of almost ultimate perfection."

One of these five poems may have been "Death and the Lady," the best of several subjective dialogue poems found in *Those Not Elect.* Its diction, music, and irony are reminiscent of "Here Lies a Lady" and "Antique Harvesters," poems by John

Crowe Ransom, the poet whom, among her contemporaries, Léonie Adams perhaps most closely resembles. In Adams's poem Death tries to strike a bargain with a Lady, who "to dancing-measures still/Would move, while beauties on her lay," and the poet asks,

> Tell me, Lady,
> If in your breast the lively breath
> May flicker for a little space,
> What ransom will you give to death.

The lady is not willing to entertain Death until the sweet substance of her youth has become the stuff of dreams and memory. Yet when, as a "Ghostly Lady," or mere ghost of her former self, she petitions an end, Death balks: "Beauties I claim at morning-prime/ . . . the lack-luster in good time." Such irony is not a mere property of Adams's poetry; it is so strong a force in the habit of her thought that it designs the very contexture of her perceptions.

Those Not Elect convinces a reader of Léonie Adams's mastery of the sonnet form. "Discourse with the Heart" exhibits passages as flawlessly beautiful as some of Shakespeare's best lines:

> Since now most precious mines can give no gold
> So absolute but it's made metaphor,
> And richer by its shining told;

but perhaps the sonnet which most clearly illustrates the genius of the poet's peculiar sensibility is "Thought's End." The only other writer this poem even vaguely brings to mind with its interesting and precise personification, "heft" of the music of repetition, and chiaroscuro suggestiveness is Emily Dickinson. As is so often the case in an Adams poem the speaker, almost always the poet, is contemplating the effect of nightfall on her consciousness. As she watches, "the hills drink the last color of light,/All shapes grow bright and wane on the pale air," and, as is also frequently true in an Adams lyric, the intimations received are rather terrifying:

> Be self no more against the flooding dark:
> There thousandwise sown in that cloudy blot
> Stars that are worlds look out and see you not.

In his review of *Those Not Elect* (*Bookman*, December 1925) Louis Untermeyer observed: "Where Miss Adams is least successful she fails on a high plane. Among the emerging lyricists none leads us to expect—or demand—more." She did not disappoint her admirers with her second volume,

For Louis Untermeyer

" Rebellion shook an ancient dust,
And bones bleached dry of rottenness,
Said, 'Heart, be bitter still, nor trust
The earth, the sky in their bright dress.

Heart, heart, dost thou not break to know—
This anguish thou wilt bear alone,—
We sang of it an age ago,
And traced it dimly upon stone.'
Until all the drifting race of men,
Thou also art begot to mourn
That she is crucified again,
The lovely beauty yet unborn.
And if thou dreamest to have won
Some touch of her in permanence,
'Tis the old cheating of the sun
The intricate lovely play of sense.

Be bitter still, remember how
Four petals when a little breath
Of wind made stir the pear-tree bough
Blew delicately down to death. "

                                        Léonie Adams

September   1925

Fair copy of "April Mortality," first published in the New Republic *in 1921 while Adams was still an undergraduate (by permission of the author; courtesy of the Lilly Library, Indiana University)*

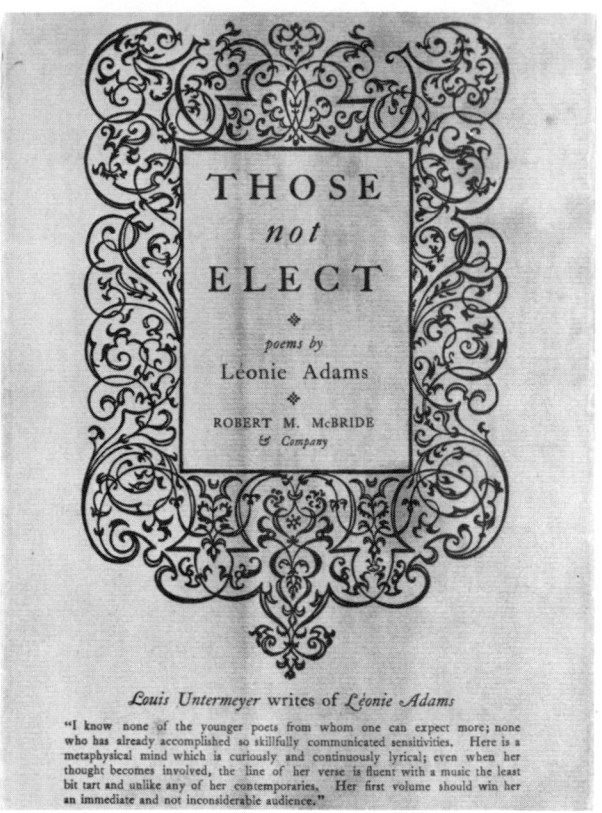

Dust jacket for Adams's first book, in which Allen Tate found "five poems . . . of almost ultimate perfection" (courtesy of the Lilly Library, Indiana University)

which was published four years later while she was living in Paris.

In 1928 Adams became one of the first poets to receive a Guggenheim Fellowship and left New York "for a first taste not of Paris but of the literary life and to get together a second book." En route to France, she paused in Oxford, where she joined forces with Allen Tate, also the recipient of a Guggenheim Fellowship in 1928, and his wife, the novelist Caroline Gordon. In Paris Adams shared a flat in the Hôtel de Fleurus with the Tates and their young daughter, often accompanying them on Thursday afternoon visits to Gertrude Stein at 27, rue de Fleurus. Certainly, though, the parties held in Ford Madox Ford's apartment on Saturday evenings were more interesting and, perhaps, instructive. As Allen Tate remembered, "in the autumn of 1929 the soirées became much more literary and tyrannously competitive. We were commanded to play a difficult French parlor game called bouts-rimés. Ford passed around pencils and paper and assigned us the rhyme words of a Shakespeare sonnet or of a sonnet by 'my aunt Christina Rossetti,

a beautiful poet.' Everybody had to use the assigned rhymes, and the winning sonnet was graded on both its quality and the speed of its composition."

During her two years in France (1928-1930), Adams achieved both of the goals she had set for herself: she received a taste of literary life, and she collected the material for her second book of verse, *High Falcon & Other Poems*, which appeared in 1929.

Although virtually the same length as *Those Not Elect*, *High Falcon & Other Poems* contains at least twice as many truly distinguished poems. *Development* in the sense of successful experimentation is not a term that yields much meaning in discussing Adams's career. With each succeeding volume she came into fuller mastery of the themes and techniques which had always been hers.

One master whose influence can be clearly seen in this second volume is the later Yeats. As the following lines from "Windy Way" illustrate, Adams seems to have learned from him a way of hurrying straight speech into verse and of straining the line by a syllable:

It was my life, or so I said,
And I did well, forsaking it,
To go as quickly as the dead.
For more than every traveller wise,
They're off before their dawdling kin
Can drop the pennies on their eyes,
Knowing it would be vain to tell,
Who have so vast a leave in mind,
If all night long a fare you well.

In *High Falcon & Other Poems* Adams often elucidates (but never disfigures) the idea by means of the natural and practicable image, a technique which would make her poems seem at home in the world of Henry Vaughan, Thomas Traherne, Richard Crashaw, and Robert Herrick. But her images are, on the whole, free from remote astronomical and supernatural references, adhering instead to the details of rural landscape and weather almost to the point of specialty. Nor do her poems contain the religious themes associated with metaphysical poetry. Instead they testify more obliquely, but just as pervasively, to the sacred character of poetry, to the ancient idea that nature is numinous, and that each event in a human life and each object of nature signifies something else. Poetry thus defined illuminates and explores. In "Sundown," for example, one finds large truths suggested in the poet's perception of an oak's experience in an autumn sunset. First, it is a surprise to learn that the strong tree can look so frail in the autumn wind:

> Now shall you see pent oak gone gusty and frantic,
> Stooped with dry weeping, ruinously unloosing
> The sparse disheveled leaf, or reared and tossing
> A dreary scarecrow bough in funeral antic.

But then comes the comfort of the penultimate stanza's reminder that the tree's seasonal reduction is a part of the sacredness of the natural process, as is a sunset:

> This is the immortal extinction, the priceless wound
> Not to be staunched. The live gold leaks beyond,
> And matter's sanctified, dipped in a gold stain.

In several poems in *High Falcon & Other Poems* Adams makes effective use of symbolism but nowhere more successfully than in "The Mount," where Time is figured as a steed of light, and in "The Horn," where tribute is paid to the redemptive power of poetry:

> In coming to the feast I found
> A venerable silver-throated horn,
> Which were I brave enough to sound,
> Then all as from that moment born
> Would breathe the honey of this clime,
> And three times merry in their time,
> Would praise the virtue of that horn.

The best poems in *High Falcon & Other Poems* are perhaps "The Figurehead," with its near perfect use of visual imagery and cadence; "Kennest Du Das Land," which is a haunting and delicate elegy in memory of the most beautiful features of the landscape of life; "Twilit Revelation," which deserves to stand in the company of John Crowe Ransom's "The Equilibrists" as one of the best metaphysical love poems written in this century; and "Caryatid," a powerful meditative lyric. In the poem's four sentences, Léonie Adams has written brilliantly about a theme which Keats developed in some of his greatest poems, such as "On Seeing the Elgin Marbles for the First Time"—that is, the relationships among art, the artist, the lover of art, and Time. As the poet contemplates a caryatid surrounded by the ruins of the temple she had once adorned, he (the lover of art) observes that this marble priestess (the work of art), although harmed by time ("There is no clasp which stays beauty forever./Time has undone her, from porphyry, from bronze."), shall continue forever as a tribute to "the

white Athenian wonder overthrown" and as proof of the sculptor's genius.

In 1930 Adams returned to New York from France and managed to secure a teaching position at Washington Square College of New York University, where she remained through 1932. It was there that she met the critic William E. Troy, whom she married on 3 June 1933. Also in 1933 her excellent poem *This Measure*, with illustrations by George Plank, appeared as number 7 in The Borzoi Chap Books series published by Alfred A. Knopf. The speaker in the poem compares, or measures, the seasonal transformations in her life against those of trees, with the hope of detecting a clear parallel:

> How many seasons I have watched the boughs,
> The first are happy-tongued and happy-leaved,
> Then bleed, as though an autumn were the last,
> While that great life was with them undeceived,
> Which all a wintering world seals home more fast.

But like the speaker in Gerard Manley Hopkins's "Thou Art Indeed Just, Lord," the individual in Adams's poem decides that the "measure" of vernal music buried deep in her wintry world is too small to renew her and that she must have, deserves to have, in fact, the redemptive touch of an outside force.

During the 1933-1934 academic year Adams taught at Sarah Lawrence College in Bronxville, New York, and in 1935 she and Troy went to Bennington College in Bennington, Vermont, where Adams taught in 1935-1937 and 1941-1944. In 1945 Troy took a position at the New School for Social Research in New York City, where he remained until the year before his death in 1961. Adams taught at New Jersey College for Women in 1946-1948, and in 1947 she became a lecturer at Columbia University, where she remained until 1968. Beginning in 1934 she and Troy spent as much time as they could at an old house they had bought in Connecticut.

Except for rare appearances of her poems in *Poetry* and the *New Republic*, Adams remained virtually silent as a poet from 1933 until 1954. Perhaps the only light she shed on the reason for this silence was her statement in Fred B. Millett's *Contemporary American Authors* (1940): "I sometimes feel that poetry at present like other things is about to undergo the kind of variation that amounts to the leap to a new genus. I was first preoccupied with sound patterns—that took me to the seventeenth century—then I recognized the necessity for the more modern preoccupation with images which should not be gathered along the way of discourse or meditation, but assumed before starting out, like apparel, or entered into as a world. I have been silent a long time because I am now grappling with the limitations of the lyric."

During the twenty-five years between the publication of *High Falcon & Other Poems* in 1929 and the publication of *Poems: A Selection* in 1954, Adams's handful of admirers remained loyal. It was devoted readers, such as Allen Tate and Louis Untermeyer, who elected her to the Chair of Poetry at the Library of Congress in 1948 and to membership in the National Institute of Arts and Letters in 1949. During her tenure at the Library of Congress (1948-1949), she began to arrange the material which would later appear in *Poems: A Selection*, published in 1954. For this volume she was awarded Yale University's Bollingen Prize in Poetry in 1955, a recognition which she shared with her friend Louise Bogan, a writer with whose work critics had been comparing Adams's poetry for almost thirty years.

Poems: A Selection opens with twenty-four poems written after 1929, continues by reprinting nearly the whole of *High Falcon & Other Poems* (thirty-seven poems), and concludes by selecting twenty-four poems out of nearly forty in Adams's first volume, *Those Not Elect* (1925). The proportion is right: *High Falcon & Other Poems* shows her work consistently at its best. Some of the longer pieces in the first section of the selected poems seem to suffer from incoherence, primarily because of faulty punctuation and unclear pronoun reference; also they are often too "poetic," too full of terms like "else-wending," "rime-bedabbled," and "enduskings." But among these twenty-four poems there are also some masterpieces, such as "Goodbye Those Children," which re-creates the evanescent summers of every childhood, until they fade away into stones and a starfish kept as mementos:

> And in the box, amongst its eery smell,
> Mortal and stiff the starry arms were rayed,
> That reached reminding from some other time
> And this, how fallen a thing can lie, still much
> As first, odd fossil flower or monster, still
> Singular, crusted with itself, as when
> Its thorns curled shrinking from the wondering
>   touch.

Adams's post-1929 poems remind the reader that she is a nature poet in the sense that she in-

terprets nature more than man (there are almost no people in her poems) and that she is a very private poet in the sense that she is moved not so much by what happens as by what her subtle and exquisite mind makes of it. She depicts not with implication, but by rich suggestion. The sonnet "Alas, Kind Element!" illustrates all of these characteristics. In this poem the speaker by means of an extended simile compares her life to a tree (the wood is Adam's most familiar setting), first in winter:

> Then I was sealed, and like the wintering tree
> I stood me locked upon a summer core;
> Living, had died a death, and asked no more.

Then, after the "kind element" of a spring breeze begins to stir the leaves,

> the wishful leaves have thronged the air.
> My every leaf leans forth upon the day;
> Alas, kind element! which comes to go.

The speaker finds a correspondence to the truth of her condition in the world of nature, but exactly what that truth is remains sealed beneath suggestion.

Léonie Adams has perhaps written some of the most brilliant poems in American poetry on the season of autumn. Three of the finest works in *Poems: A Selection* deal with this season of ultimate revelation—including "The Runner with the Lots," "For Harvest," and "Words for the Raker of Leaves." The last of these poems memorably succeeds in extracting the very essence of the temporal, or in articulating the tragic undertones of autumn:

> Clime of two climes
> Seems here in time straying,
> Its whisperer within sun,
> Where in warm musing is stood;
> And light to the cheek of flesh
> All without sifts cool
> Upon the sun-warmed one.
> Nearer eared than the heard,
> The silences beneath
> Of pathos without cry.

In the two decades following the publication of *Poems: A Selection*, Adams continued her active career as a teacher. She was a Fulbright Lecturer in France (1955-1956), a staff member at the Bread Loaf Writers' Conference (1956-1958), and a visiting professor at the University of Washington,

Seattle (1969-1970) and at Purdue University (1971-1972). She also continued to win prizes during this period: a Fellowship from the Academy of American Poets (1959); a sabbatical grant from the National Commission on Arts (1966-1967); and the Brandeis University Poetry Medal (1969).

In 1961 William Troy, Adams's husband of twenty-eight years, died of cancer. Following his death Adams performed the important task of compiling a collection of his essays, which was edited by Stanley Edgar Hyman and published by Rutgers University Press in 1967. This brilliant volume, *William Troy: Selected Essays*, received the 1968 National Book Award in Arts and Letters.

Although Léonie Adams has not published a book of poetry in more than twenty-five years, four or five of her poems, such as the marvelous landscape poem "Country Summer," are fairly well known to readers because of their frequent appearances in anthologies. There is a danger, however, that the greater part of the distinguished body of her work may be ignored precisely because a piece or two remain in high favor.

Léonie Adams's reputation was solidly estab-

lished in the 1920s and the integrity, soundness, discipline, and exciting sensibility manifest in her poetry have enabled her work to survive a number of revolutions in literary taste, theory, and practice. Certainly she is among the four or five American women who have produced poetry of high distinction in the twentieth century.

References:
Babette Deutsch, *Poetry in Our Time* (Garden City: Doubleday, 1963), pp. 235-238;
Horace Gregory and Marya Zaturenska, *A History of American Poetry, 1900-1940* (New York: Harcourt, Brace, 1946), pp. 291-299;
Allen Tate, Review of *Those Not Elect, Nation,* 122 (3 March 1926): 237-238;
Yvor Winters, Review of *High Falcon & Other Poems, Hound and Horn,* 3, no. 3 (1930): 454-461.

Papers:
There are collections of Adams's papers at Yale University, the Library of Congress, and the University of Delaware.

Stephen Vincent Benét
(22 July 1898-13 March 1943)

John Griffith
University of Washington

See also the Benét entry in *DLB 4, American Writers in Paris, 1920-1939.*

BOOKS: *Five Men and Pompey: A Series of Dramatic Portraits* (Boston: Four Seas, 1915);
The Drug Shop, Or Endymion in Edmonstoun (New Haven: Yale University Press, 1917);
Young Adventure: A Book of Poems (New Haven: Yale University Press, 1918; London: Oxford University Press, 1919);
Tamburlaine the Great, adapted by Benét and Monty Woolley from Christopher Marlowe's play (New Haven: Yale University Press, 1919);
Heavens and Earth: A Book of Poems (New York: Holt, 1920);
The Beginning of Wisdom (New York: Holt, 1921; London & Sydney: Chapman & Dodd, 1922);

Young People's Pride: A Novel (New York: Holt, 1922);
King David (New York: Holt, 1923);
Jean Huguenot (New York: Holt, 1923; London: Methuen, 1925);
The Ballad of William Sycamore, 1790-1880 (New York & New Haven: E. B. Hackett, Brick Row Book Shop, 1923);
Tiger Joy: A Book of Poems (New York: Doran, 1925);
Spanish Bayonet (New York: Doran, 1926; London: Heinemann, 1926);
John Brown's Body (Garden City: Doubleday, Doran, 1928; London: Heinemann, 1928; London: Oxford University Press, 1944);
The Barefoot Saint (Garden City: Doubleday, Doran, 1929);

Gale International Portrait Gallery

The Litter of the Rose Leaves (New York: Random House, 1930);

Ballads and Poems 1915-1930 (Garden City: Doubleday, Doran, 1931; London: Heinemann, 1933);

A Book of Americans, by Benét and Rosemary Carr Benét (New York: Farrar & Rinehart, 1933);

James Shore's Daughter (New York: Doubleday, Doran, 1934; London: Heinemann, 1934);

Burning City (New York: Farrar & Rinehart, 1936; London & Toronto: Heinemann, 1937);

The Devil and Daniel Webster (Weston, Vt.: Countryman Press, 1937);

Thirteen O'Clock: Stories of Several Worlds (New York & Toronto: Farrar & Rinehart, 1937; London & Toronto: Heinemann, 1938);

The Headless Horseman, libretto by Benét and score by Douglas Moore (Boston: Schirmer, 1937);

Johnny Pye & the Fool-Killer (Weston, Vt.: Country

Man Press, 1938; London & Toronto: Heinemann, 1939);

My Favorite Fiction Character (N.p.: Ysletta Press, 1938);

The Ballad of the Duke's Mercy (New York: House of Books, 1939);

The Devil and Daniel Webster, libretto by Benét and score by Douglas Moore (New York: Farrar & Rinehart, 1939);

Tales Before Midnight (New York: Farrar & Rinehart, 1939; London & Toronto: Heinemann, 1940);

The Devil and Daniel Webster: Play in One Act (New York: Dramatists Play Service, 1939);

Nightmare at Noon (New York & Toronto: Farrar & Rinehart, 1940);

We Stand United: A Declaration (New York: Council for Democracy, 1940);

A Summons to the Free (New York & Toronto: Farrar & Rinehart, 1941; London: Oxford University Press, 1941);

Listen to the People (New York: Council for Democracy, 1941);

Tuesday, November 5th 1940 (New York: House of Books, 1941);

Selected Works of Stephen Vincent Benét, 2 volumes (New York: Farrar & Rinehart, 1942);

They Burned the Books (New York & Toronto: Farrar & Rinehart, 1942);

Dear Adolf (New York: Farrar & Rinehart, 1942);

A Child Is Born: A Modern Drama of the Nativity (Boston: W. H. Baker, 1942);

Western Star (New York & Toronto: Farrar & Rinehart, 1943; London: Oxford University Press, 1944);

America (New York & Toronto: Farrar & Rinehart, 1944; London & Toronto: Heinemann, 1944);

O'Halloran's Luck and Other Short Stories (New York: Penguin, 1944);

Prayer. A Child is Born (New York & Toronto: Farrar & Rinehart, 1944);

We Stand United and Other Radio Scripts (New York & Toronto: Farrar & Rinehart, 1945);

The Last Circle: Stories and Poems (New York: Farrar, Straus, 1946; London & Toronto: Heinemann, 1948);

Selected Stories (Dublin & London: Fridberg, 1947).

PLAY PRODUCTIONS: *Nerves*, revision of John Farrar's play, by Benét and Farrar, New York, Comedy Theatre, 1 September 1924;

That Awful Mrs. Eaton, by Benét and Farrar, New York, Morosco Theatre, 29 September 1924.

SCREENPLAYS: *Abraham Lincoln,* adaptation by Benét, continuity and dialogue by Benét and Gerrit Lloyd, United Artists, 1930;

Cheers for Miss Bishop, adaptation by Benét, based on Bess Streeter Aldrich's novel *Miss Bishop,* United Artists, 1941;

All That Money Can Buy, screenplay by Benét and Dan Tothroth, based on Benét's short story "The Devil and Daniel Webster," RKO, 1941.

Between the years 1928 and 1943, Stephen Vincent Benét was one of the best-known living American poets, more widely read than Robert Frost, T. S. Eliot, William Carlos Williams, or Wallace Stevens and as well respected in book review columns. He was a rarity among twentieth-century authors, a poet whose books sold in the tens of thousands and who was honored in the poetry workshops and lecture halls of prestigious universities. Since that time, his reputation has declined steeply among literary sophisticates to the point where his poetry is seldom included in college literary anthologies and his name is often neglected in literary histories; but his poems and several of his short stories remain steadily in print, finding a sizable audience among general readers year after year.

Benét was the youngest of the three children of James Walker Benét, U.S. Army, a literate and humane career officer who presided over a household which Benét remembered as unfailingly warm and happy and alive with the most varied intellectual activity. James W. Benét "was interested in everything from the Byzantine Emperors to the development of heavy ordnance," Stephen wrote in 1940, "and was the finest critic of poetry I have ever known." He was Benét's lifelong hero. Benét's mother, Frances Neill Rose Benét, was also an avid reader and the author of occasional verse; his sister Laura, fourteen years his senior, and his brother William, twelve years his senior, were both poets and authors as well.

Benét grew up in a series of army-base homes that introduced him to several regions of the United States: he was born in Bethlehem, Pennsylvania, and spent his first five years in Watervliet, New York, a year in Illinois, six years in Benicia, California, and four years in Augusta, Georgia. He entered Yale at the age of seventeen. Encouraged by his family, he was from the beginning a precocious reader and writer of fiction and verse, immersing himself in William Makepeace Thackeray, Joseph Conrad, Rudyard Kipling, William Morris,

Christina and Dante Gabriel Rossetti, G. K. Chesterton, and dozens of lesser lights—and in the traditions of American military history. Although a traumatic year at Hitchcock Military Academy in Jacinto, California, in 1910-1911, showed him that military life could be mean and brutal, Benét basically loved and applauded the principles of honor, courage, duty, and patriotism which he found embodied in his father's career. From his earliest years, Benét developed a taste for romantic, melodramatic, and heroic fiction and poetry, a sympathetic observer's interest in America's regional cultures, and an old-fashioned devotion to domestic and patriotic values.

His success as a writer came early and continued all through his life. He won his first poetry prize from *St. Nicholas Magazine* at thirteen, sold his first poem to *New Republic* two months before his seventeenth birthday, and had his first volume of poetry, *Five Men and Pompey,* published in winter 1915. He followed his brother William to Yale in September 1915 and quickly became a major con-

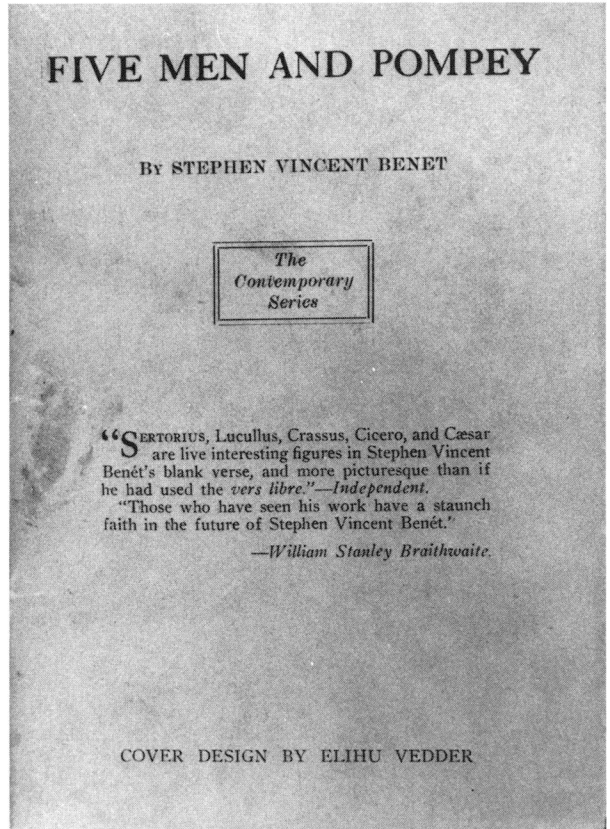

Dust jacket for Benét's first book, published during his freshman year at Yale (courtesy of Thomas Cooper Library, University of South Carolina)

tributor to the *Yale Literary Magazine,* a member of its editorial board in 1916, and its chairman in 1918. He also contributed to the *Yale Record,* the undergraduate humor magazine, and served as one of its editors in 1918. He continued to sell poetry to national magazines, publishing *The Drug Shop, Or Endymion in Edmonstoun* (1917). Well before he enlisted in the army in April 1918 (he finagled his way in despite his poor eyesight and was discharged three days later when the extent of his myopia was discovered), his renown as a poet had spread beyond the Yale campus. Benét found work with the State Department in Washington, D.C. in August 1918. His third book, *Young Adventure: A Book of Poems,* was published that October and in December of the same year he returned to Yale, where he was awarded a B.A. in June 1919.

After three months of working for a New York advertising agency, Benét returned to Yale for graduate study in English, earning an M.A. in June 1920. During the 1919-1920 school year he and Monty Woolley, a young faculty member who later became a successful actor, prepared an acting version of Christopher Marlowe's *Tamburlaine the Great* (1590), which was published by Yale University Press in 1919. In addition to having his poems and short stories published in national magazines, he contributed to *S4N,* a New Haven little magazine founded by Dudley Fitts that provided a vehicle for a number of young poets, including Benét, Ramon Guthrie, and Fitts himself. Benét was considerably less diligent in his class work than in his extracurricular writing, but he earned an M.A. in June 1920, submitting, instead of a traditional thesis, a group of poems that was published as *Heavens and Earth* by Holt in 1920.

He began his first novel in the summer of 1920 and had finished and published it by September of 1921. *The Beginning of Wisdom* is Benét's "flaming youth novel," the genre of autobiographical fiction which flourished in the 1920s, of which F. Scott Fitzgerald's *This Side of Paradise* is the best-known example. Benét made his first trip to Paris in 1920-1921 on a Yale traveling fellowship, worked on poetry and fiction there, and met Rosemary Carr, whom he married in Chicago on 26 November 1921—partly on the strength of his initial successes in writing fiction for a commercial market.

His already remarkable reputation as a young poet took a quantum jump forward with *The Ballad of William Sycamore,* published in the *New Republic* in 1922 and as a pamphlet in 1923. This poem is Benét's first thorough-going achievement with the

subject matter and technique that were to produce his most significant poetry: the rendering of gracefully idealized popular or mythic American character types in craftsmanlike, broadly entertaining rhymed verse. Benét's genius was for intelligent, affirmative, easily accessible, somewhat sentimental American portraiture of the sort that popular fiction and the movies sometimes exploited. In *The Ballad of William Sycamore,* Benét mythicizes the pioneer-scout type (Davy Crockett, Daniel Boone, Kit Carson) whose identifying marks are readily familiar: "a coonskin cap," a log cabin, "long, straight squirrel-rifles," fiddle music, a powder horn, a leather shirt. Economically enough, Benét's poem alludes to classic elements in the schoolroom mythology of preindustrial America: the buffalo, the unfenced land, the westering wagon trains, "the Bloody Ground of Kentucky," Johnny Appleseed, the Alamo, Custer's Last Stand. Even old seafaring New England is represented in Sycamore's wife, who reminds him of "a Salem clipper." The poem's force lies in the authority with which Benét incorporates these familiar images into the precisely rhymed, recitable stanzas of his ballad:

> My father, he was a mountaineer,
> His fist was a knotty hammer;
> He was quick on his feet as a running deer,
> And he spoke with a Yankee stammer.

The poem celebrates the rugged individualism of the fictional William Sycamore, who "could not live when they fenced the land." And yet it is neither angry nor critical about the movement of American history; Sycamore's passing is of the noble and necessary sort that gives modern America its sturdy roots in an honorable past:

> Now I lie in the heart of the fat, black soil,
> Like the seed of a prairie thistle;
> It has washed my bones with honey and oil
> And picked them clean as a whistle.

Such images of abundance and fertility, such wholesomely enriched soil, implicitly guarantee the strength of Benét's America.

His penchant for choosing images and expressive details from the ready stock of popular stereotypes assured, of course, that Benét's poetic achievement would eventually be derided by critics who valued original, experimental, or esoteric styles. Benét's verse was conventional in that his mind was fundamentally in accord with mainstream American culture and worked naturally

The editorial board for the Yale Literary Magazine, *1919: (seated) Donald M. Campbell, Stephen Vincent Benét, and Frank P. Heffelfinger; (standing) Robert M. Coates, J. J. Schieffelin, and Thornton Wilder*

within the framework of characters and stories already familiar to his audiences, as his next big poetic success, *King David,* further demonstrated. A two-hundred-line ballad in six parts, published in the *Nation* in 1923, *King David* won that magazine's annual poetry prize and was published as a pamphlet the same year. It also drew some letters protesting the poem's perceived irreverence toward the Bible. In fact, his poem does virtually nothing but retell the story of David and Bathsheba as it appears in 2 Samuel, lightly embroidered with lines from David's elegy for Saul and Jonathan and a few similes from the Song of Solomon. Benét's poem calls attention to the irony of the Lord's favoring David despite his committing adultery and murder and his casual repentance for those transgressions (this lack of sincerity is apparently what offended some readers); but the biblical account, in its more solemn way, also calls attention to that irony. The main impact Benét effected was the intellectual shock of seeing a story that is normally bathed in the halo-light of canonized scripture, presented in a cheerfully jazzy modern manner. If the story were not a familiar one, no such effect would be possible.

Another of Benét's early successes with the ballad, "The Mountain Whippoorwill" (published in *Century* magazine, 1925), tells the heroic come-

from-behind victory of an unknown youth over the reigning lords of the community—or, as Benét's subtitle puts it, "How Hill-Billy Jim Won the Great Fiddlers' Prize" away from Old Dan Wheeling, Big Tom Sargent, and Little Jimmy Weezer (big wheels, sergeants, and weasels) at the game they think is their own. The poem has a good deal in common with Benet's best-known short story, *The Devil and Daniel Webster* (published in the 24 October 1936 issue of the *Saturday Evening Post* and as a book in 1937), in which a folk artist sways a difficult audience by releasing the emotional and imaginative power latent in his grass-roots origins. In some respects, *The Mountain Whippoorwill* is little more than a pastiche of phrases and motifs from tall-tale and dialect humor of the sort Thomas Bangs Thorpe, Mark Twain (Samuel Clemens), and Joel Chandler Harris had made current generations before: "Everythin's as lazy as an old houn' dog"; "He could fiddle down a possum from a mile-high tree"; "Go down, Moses, set my people free"; "Hell's broke loose in Georgia." Benét develops some symbolic intention around the idea of the whippoorwill. The whippoorwill reminds Hill-Billy Jim of his home in the Georgia mountains; he speculates whimsically that his mother may have been a whippoorwill; he calls his fiddle his little whippoorwill. His fiddling is a kind of rustic American version of the roman-

Benét at the time of his marriage to Rosemary Carr

tics' music of the Aeolian harp, voicing as it does the primal powers and meanings of nature. The idea may be stock bardic romanticism, but Benét's language is colloquial Southern American, and the poem became one of his most popular and most-often republished.

The Ballad of William Sycamore and "The Mountain Whippoorwill" almost immediately achieved status as modern American classics and appeared in a number of anthologies. But Benét's struggle to earn a living was not significantly eased by the prestige that accrued to them. The years between the publication of "The Mountain Whippoorwill" (1925) and *John Brown's Body* (1928) were filled, for Benét, with the frantic efforts of a young man trying to support himself and his family (his daughter Stephanie Jane was born in 1924) entirely from the sale of his writing. He engaged in a patchwork of belletristic enterprises, piecing out a barely adequate income: he wrote formula short stories for magazines; he reviewed books and plays; he collaborated with John Farrar on two unsuccessful

stage dramas, *Nerves* and *That Awful Mrs. Eaton* (both produced in 1924); he wrote romantic fiction for serialization.

In 1925, he approached the Guggenheim Foundation with a proposal for a long historical poem on the Civil War, requesting a grant of $2,500 to support himself while he researched and wrote it. The foundation gave him his grant, and he set out for Paris, where he and his family could live more cheaply while he worked on the poem which, he thought, might "take about 7 years to write & I'd have to read an entire library first." (The Benéts' second child, Thomas Carr, was born in Paris in 1926.)

Supported by his fellowship and the fees for a few magazine short stories, Benét actually completed his 15,000-line panorama of the Civil War in less than two years, a monumental outpouring of sustained effort that left him exhausted for months afterward. Measured by almost any standard, the result was worth the investment. *John Brown's Body* (1928) was the magnum opus that elevated Benét's status from that of a promising young poet-storyteller to that of a national hero and a prodigy of popular success unknown among American poets, surpassing even the tremendous sales of Henry Wadsworth Longfellow's *The Song of Hiawatha* (1855) and *Evangeline* (1847) of the previous century. The recently organized Book-of-the-Month Club adopted it as one of its selections. In its first two years, the poem sold more than 130,000 copies. It has since gone through dozens of printings and remains a steady seller year after year.

The poetry reviewers immediately and understandably began to call it an epic, though Benét himself was shy of that honorific term and referred to it instead as his "cyclorama." *John Brown's Body* brought to fruition the young Benét's admiration for heroism, his patriotic love of the United States as a vital complex of culturally distinct regions and heritages, and his talent for clear, graceful, and accessible narrative verse.

Before anything else, *John Brown's Body* is a history of the Civil War—in some respects, Bruce Catton has said, the best single book ever written on the subject. Each section is based on different characters' experiences in various battles and campaigns. The poem "begins shortly before John Brown's raid upon Harper's Ferry," Benét noted. Its action is continuous, ending "just after the close of the war and Lincoln's assassination." Each of the poem's eight books features at least one major military event: book one—Harper's Ferry; book two—

the firing on Fort Sumter and the first Battle of Bull Run; book three—Shiloh; book four—the campaigns in eastern and western Virginia; book five—Antietam and the hard winter of 1862; book six—the Wilderness Campaign, Grant and Sherman at Vicksburg; book seven—Gettysburg; book eight—Sherman's march to the sea and the surrender at Appomattox. Included in this chronology are numerous other major public occurrences—the hanging of John Brown, the election of Lincoln, the formation of the Confederate cabinet, the appointment and dismissal of various generals, the death of Stonewall Jackson, the death of Lincoln.

Upon this historical skeleton Benét applied the flesh of the personal experiences of dozens of historical and fictional characters, participants in the vast conflict. For some of his material, Benét drew on letters and diaries of actual Civil War soldiers; for some, he studied the careers of great leaders such as Lincoln, Lee, Grant, and Jackson and projected himself into their minds, giving them soliloquies such as this one for Lincoln:

> We can fail and fail,
> But, deep against the failure, something wars,
> Something goes forward, something lights a match,
> Something gets up from Sangamon County ground
> Armed with a bitten and blunted axe
> And after twenty thousand wasted strokes
> Brings the tall hemlock crashing to the ground.

Throughout the poem, Benét meticulously selects and constructs his cast of characters to represent various types of Americans involved in the war. Primarily he sees a conflict between the bourgeois-Puritan New England temper and the aristocratic-romantic South. Most of his Southern characters are connected, in one way or another, with the Wingate family of Georgia, reputed descendants (through an illegitimate connection) of England's Charles II: Clay Wingate, the family scion, a dashing young cavalryman; his mother, Mary Lou Wingate, "as slightly made/And as hard to break as a rapier-blade"; Cudjo and Aunt Bess, the loyal slaves; Spade, the runaway slave; the coquette Lucy Weatherby; the slightly wild, barely respectable Sally Dupré; and an assortment of young gallants who attend soirées at Wingate Hall and ride with the Wingates in the fictional Black Horse Troop (based on the Black Horse Cavalry). Other Southern types are more briefly sketched: Luke Breckinridge, a Tennessee hillbilly, ignorant, superstitious, a hard-eyed feuder and a sure shot

with his long rifle; and Sophy, a poor white, "scared chambermaid in Pollet's Hotel."

Benét dramatizes the New England temper primarily in young Jack Ellyat of Connecticut, in the impressionistically sketched slave-trading Yankee skipper in the prelude (" 'I get my sailing orders from the Lord.' He touched the Bible"), the "lady" abolitionists of the North, and the poeticized words of John Brown:

> And if we live, we free the slave,
> And if we die, we die.
> But God has digged His saints a grave
> Beyond the western sky.

Benét includes two other Northern types: Ellyat's comrade-in-arms Bailey, a fiercely provincial, tough-talking Illinoisian, and Jake Diefer of Pennsylvania, a stolid German peasant who goes to war, loses an arm, and comes home to his farm again. The Border States and the West, according to Benét's foreword, are represented in the poem by John Vilas, a romantic individualist, wanderer, and noncombatant, whose daughter marries Jack Ellyat at the end of the poem.

Benét's view of the war is basically a nationalistic, broadly tolerant and conciliatory one. There are no major villains in his story; the Confederates and Unionists depicted in any detail are treated with respect and sympathy, their motives seen as decent ones. Lincoln is a hero; so is Lee. Clay Wingate's reasons for going to war are expressed this way:

> *Why were they all going out to war?*
> He brooded a moment. It wasn't slavery,
> That stale red-herring of Yankee knavery
> Nor even states-rights, at least not solely,
> But something so dim that it must be holy.
> A voice, a fragrance, a taste of wine,
> A face half-seen in old candleshine,
> A yellow river, a blowing dust,
> Something beyond you that you must trust.

In his invocation, Benét forthrightly announces his intention to make *John Brown's Body* an all-American expression, reflecting its author's background and the spirits of America's various regions.

> This flesh was seeded from no foreign grain
> But Pennsylvania and Kentucky wheat,
> And it has soaked in California rain
> And five years tempered in New England sleet
>
> To strive at last, against an alien proof

And by the changes of an alien moon,
To build again that blue, American roof
Over a half-forgotten battle-tune[.]

In pursuit of his objective, Benét frankly exploits the popular romantic auras surrounding Lincoln, Lee, Grant, the antebellum South, the stern and sturdy New England Puritans, the great American war. There is almost something of the newsreel announcer in Benét's terse, dramatic evocation of the great names and events of his subject:

Thus they were marshalled and drilled, while Spring
    turned Summer again,
Until they could stumble toward death at gartersnake-
    crooked Bull Run.
He had been through Chancellorsville and the whis-
    tling wood,
He had been through this last day. It is well to sleep
After such days.

And yet—each road that you take,

Each dusty road leads to Appomattox now.

Benét's father died in 1927, just as Benét was finishing work on *John Brown's Body*. His admiration for the kind of steady martial strength he associated with his father permeates Benét's great poem, as in this description of Grant:

You see him standing,
Reading a map, unperturbed, under heavy fire.
You do not cheer him as the recruits might cheer
But you say "Ulysses doesn't scare worth a darn.
Ulysses is all right. He can finish a job."
And at last your long lines go past in the Grand Review
And your legend and his begin and are mixed forever.

The impact of *John Brown's Body* on the reading public was instantaneous, confirming once again Benét's judgment of his talents and his audience. True to Benét's vision of the poem as a transregional statement of American sentiments, it found admirers in every section of the country, who sent Benét fan letters by the thousands.

Despite the poem's unprecedented popular success, Benét's struggles to support his family on the proceeds of his writing did not end (he lost a good deal of money in the stock market crash of 1929), really, until the end of his life. The Benéts' third child, Rachel Carr, was born in 1931. All during his career, he continued to write short stories aimed calculatingly at popular magazines such as the *Saturday Evening Post, Country Gentleman,* and *Good Housekeeping.* He did a stint of screenwriting

in Hollywood for three months in 1929-1930, turning out the script of *Abraham Lincoln* for D. W. Griffith. He hated the Hollywood system of writing by committee.

In 1930 Benét suffered the first debilitating attacks of arthritis of the spine, an ailment which, with its complications, rendered most of the final thirteen years of his life a time of great physical discomfort. At the same time, the United States was entering the depths of the Great Depression; Benét, living in New York City, witnessed poverty and demoralization on every level of society. His first reaction was bitter disillusionment with two-party politics, evidenced by his announcement that he voted for the Socialist Norman Thomas in 1932. Within a very few years, though, he had come to admire Roosevelt's New Deal programs and became one of Roosevelt's staunchest defenders among the New York intelligentsia.

The combined traumas of his own physical and financial difficulties, the collapse of the American economy and its counterparts in the rest of the world, and the rise of fascism in Europe and such quasi-fascist stirrings in the United States as the emergence of Father Charles Coughlin and Huey Long, elicited from Benét a series of angry, sometimes apocalyptic vision or nightmare poems, most appearing in 1935 and 1936, and many, including "Nightmare, with Angels," "Litany for Dictatorships," "Ode to the Austrian Socialists," and "1936," were collected in *Burning City* (1936). "Nightmare for Future Reference" and "Nightmare at Noon," written in 1940, likewise cover a range of large-scale disasters, some political, some technological, some moral. "Litany for Dictatorships" chants a roll of the victims of political oppression; "Ode to the Austrian Socialists" recounts, impressionistically, the massacre of socialist communitarians in 1934. "Metropolitan Nightmare" is a futuristic story of a change of weather that brings tropical heat and a newly evolved steel-eating termite to New York. "Nightmare Number Three" describes the revolt of machines against their human masters. The poem "1936" envisions an army of skeletons marching into a war that Benét believed was imminent. "Nightmare for Future Reference" envisions a third world war, during which the whole human race gradually finds itself sterile. "Nightmare at Noon" (1940) is the monologue of a nervous American, trying to reassure himself that the war in Europe will not engulf the United States as well. "Nightmare, with Angels" catalogues a number of theories about how, if just this or that little flaw were corrected, humanity could achieve

Page from a draft for "Litany for Dictatorships" (by permission of the Estate of Stephen Vincent Benét; courtesy of the Clifton Waller Barrett Library, University of Virginia)

Benét outside the Killingworth, Connecticut, studio where he wrote most of Western Star. *He rented the property from Henry Seidel Canby, one of the founders of the* Saturday Review, *in the summers of 1937, 1938, and 1940 so that he could be near Yale for historical research.*

Utopia, then ends with the appearance of a sinister angel, "his mask ... the blank mask of Ares, snouted for gas-masks," who says:

> You will not be saved By General Motors or the pre-
> fabricated house.
> You will not be saved by dialectic materialism or the
> Lambeth conference.
> You will not be saved by Vitamin D or the expanding
> universe.
> In fact, you will not be saved.

Yet it was also during this period that Benét collaborated with his wife Rosemary on *A Book of Americans* (1933), a series of lighthearted and affirmative poems for children about such figures from the past as Thomas Jefferson, Daniel Boone, Cotton Mather, and John James Audubon. And it

was during this period, too, that his short-story writing culminated in the tales for which he is now remembered—*The Devil and Daniel Webster* (1937) *Johnny Pye & the Fool-Killer* (1938), "By the Waters of Babylon" (collected in *Thirteen O'Clock*, 1937).

Eminent among American men of letters, Benét branched out into a number of areas. In 1933 he accepted the editorship of the Yale Series of Younger Poets, a demanding job which he took very seriously, reading, analyzing, and commenting on dozens of book-length manuscripts each year. He lectured widely and appeared at writers' conferences, wrote book reviews for the *New York Herald Tribune* and the *Saturday Review of Literature,* was active in both the National Institute of Arts and Letters (to which he had been elected in 1929) and the American Academy of Arts and Letters (to which he was elected in 1938). Perhaps no one since William Dean Howells had occupied so central and influential a position in the industry of American letters as Benét did during the 1930s.

With the outbreak of World War II in Europe, Benét threw himself unsparingly into the enterprise of building American national morale, devoting himself increasingly to what he frankly called propaganda for the Allied cause. He worked for the Council for Democracy, wrote speeches, radio scripts, *America* (1944, a 40,000-word history of the United States for worldwide distribution), and much else in similar veins. In 1942 President Roosevelt read his poem "Prayer" at the United Nations.

All during these years Benét drove himself brutally, and his fragile health gave way. He was first hospitalized for several weeks in 1939 with nervous exhaustion. Four years later, on 13 March 1943, he suffered a heart attack and died in his wife's arms.

Western Star (1943), book one of a projected nine-book narrative poem about the settlement of America upon which Benét had begun work in 1928, was published soon after his death and was awarded the Pulitzer Prize for Poetry in 1944. The completed portion of *Western Star* is some 5,000 lines long, mostly unrhymed verse in five- and six-beat lines, with occasional departures into rhyme, often ballad forms. It tells the story of the first English settlements in Virginia and New England.

Benét's historiographical approach to the westering movement in *Western Star* is essentially the same as it was to the Civil War in *John Brown's Body:* he tells the interwoven stories of real and representative fictional characters, drawing back from time to time to discuss the significance of the events in the voice of a modern commentator. Lacking the sensational popular appeal of legendary heroes such as Lincoln, Lee, and John Brown, and the celebrated names and places of the Civil War, *Western Star* has never had the popular impact of Benét's earlier opus. The verse throughout is more modest and sedate, its emotional objectives less pronounced and melodramatic than in the Civil War poem. If there had been no *John Brown's Body*, *Western Star* probably would have attracted little critical or popular attention. It is more of a footnote to Benét's career than the capstone he had hoped it would be.

Benét would probably be worth remembering for a handful of his ballads and vision poems, and for the best of his short stories. The measure of his achievement, however, is indisputably *John Brown's Body*, a poem whose naîveté and conventionality in themes, techniques and viewpoints are raised, by the greatness of its subject and Benét's devoted craftsmanship, to the level of high folk art. In trying to weigh the ultimate value of this work, one is tempted to compare Benét to Longfellow: both wrote graceful (some would say facile) narrative and lyric verse that treated popular historical subjects and expounded solid, safe moral and social values. Both were highly praised and embraced by general readers and literary establishments alike, and both fell from favor with the literary tastemakers in the generations that followed their deaths.

In the final analysis, though, it is more in-structive to group Benét with writers such as Carl Sandburg, Vachel Lindsay, and Edgar Lee Masters—poets of considerable force and vitality whose verse drew from American lore and history a stock of ideas, feelings, and images that occasionally excited popular audiences to a degree that subtler, more fastidious poets can only dream of doing.

Letters:

Selected Letters of Stephen Vincent Benét, edited by Charles A. Fenton (New Haven: Yale University Press, 1960).

Bibliography:

Gladys Louise Maddocks, "Stephen Vincent Benét: A Bibliography," *Bulletin of Bibliography,* 20 (September 1951): 142-146; 20 (April 1952): 158-160.

Biography:

Charles A. Fenton, *Stephen Vincent Benét: The Life and Times of a Man of Letters, 1898-1943* (New Haven: Yale University Press, 1958).

Reference:

Parry Stroud, *Stephen Vincent Benét* (New York: Twayne, 1962).

Papers:

Benét's papers are in the Beinecke Library at Yale University.

John Berryman

John Haffenden
University of Sheffield

BIRTH: McAlester, Oklahoma, 25 October 1914, to Martha Little and John Allyn Smith.

EDUCATION: B. A., Columbia University, 1936; B. A., Clare College, Cambridge, 1938.

MARRIAGES: 24 October 1942 to Eileen Patricia Mulligan (divorced). 1956 to Elizabeth Ann Levine (divorced); child: Paul. 1 September 1961 to Kathleen Donahue; children: Martha, Sarah Rebecca.

AWARDS AND HONORS: Euretta J. Kellett Fellowship, 1936; Charles Oldham Shakespeare Scholarship, 1937; Rockefeller Foundation research fellowship, 1944, 1945; *Kenyon Review*— Doubleday short-story prize for "The Imaginary Jew," 1945; Guarantors Prize (*Poetry*), 1949; Shelley Memorial Award (Poetry Society of America), 1949; Levinson Prize (*Poetry*), 1950; Guggenheim Fellowship, 1952, renewed 1953; Rockefeller Fellowship in poetry, 1956; Harriet Monroe Poetry Award, 1957; Brandeis University Creative Arts Citation, 1960; Ingram Merrill Foundation award, 1963; Russell Loines Award (National Institute of Arts and Letters), 1964; Pulitzer Prize for *77 Dream Songs,* 1965; Guggenheim Fellowship, 1966; Academy of American Poets Fellowship, 1966; National Endowment for the Arts Grant, 1967; National Book Award for *His Toy, His Dream, His Rest,* 1969; Bollingen Prize in Poetry, 1969; D.Litt., Drake University, 1969; Regents' Professor of Humanities, University of Minnesota, 1969; Senior Fellowship, National Endowment for the Humanities, 1971.

DEATH: Minneapolis, Minnesota, 7 January 1972.

BOOKS: *Poems* (Norfolk, Conn.: New Directions, 1942);
The Dispossessed (New York: William Sloane, 1948);
Stephen Crane (New York: William Sloane, 1950; London: Methuen, 1950; with additional material, Cleveland & New York: World, 1962);
Homage to Mistress Bradstreet (New York: Farrar, Straus & Cudahy, 1956);
His Thought Made Pockets & the Plane Buckt (Pawlet,

John Berryman (courtesy of Eileen Simpson)

Vt.: Claude Fredericks, 1958);
Homage to Mistress Bradstreet and Other Poems (London: Faber & Faber, 1959; New York: Farrar, Straus & Giroux, 1968);
The Arts of Reading, by Berryman, Ralph Ross, and Allen Tate (New York: Crowell, 1960);
77 Dream Songs (New York: Farrar, Straus, 1964; London: Faber & Faber, 1964);
Berryman's Sonnets (New York: Farrar, Straus & Giroux, 1967; London: Faber & Faber, 1968);
Short Poems (New York: Farrar, Straus & Giroux, 1967);
His Toy, His Dream, His Rest (New York: Farrar, Straus & Giroux, 1968; London: Faber & Faber, 1969);

The Dream Songs (New York: Farrar, Straus & Giroux, 1969);

Love & Fame (New York: Farrar, Straus & Giroux, 1970; revised edition, London: Faber & Faber, 1971);

Delusions, Etc. (New York: Farrar, Straus & Giroux, 1972; London: Faber & Faber, 1972);

Selected Poems 1938-1968 (London: Faber & Faber, 1972);

Recovery (New York: Farrar, Straus & Giroux, 1973; London: Faber & Faber, 1973);

The Freedom of the Poet (New York: Farrar, Straus & Giroux, 1976);

Henry's Fate & Other Poems 1967-1972, edited by John Haffenden (New York: Farrar, Straus & Giroux, 1977; London: Faber & Faber, 1978).

OTHER: "Twenty Poems," in *Five Young American Poets* (Norfolk, Conn.: New Directions, 1940);

Answers to "The State of American Writing, 1948: Seven Questions," *Partisan Review*, 15 (August 1948): 856-860;

"Three and a half years at Columbia," in *University on the Heights*, edited by Wesley First (Garden City: Doubleday, 1969), pp. 51-60.

John Berryman is associated with a group of poets who have become known as the "Middle Generation," a group that includes Delmore Schwartz, Randall Jarrell, Theodore Roethke, and Robert Lowell. It is a critical convenience to label much of the work of Berryman and Lowell, along with that of Sylvia Plath, as "confessional," but the tag is certainly belittling. It suggests a poetry which indulges in vulgar self-exposure, and neglects to note, for example, that Berryman's poems—even in *The Dream Songs* (1969) and *Love & Fame* (1970), which are supposedly his most confessional volumes—are in fact the products of sustained imagination and craft. Berryman and his contemporaries certainly had highly disturbed lives, with elements of self-victimization, but the poems should not be mistaken for the lives. Literary historians must eventually evaluate those lives from the perspectives both of individual psychology and of cultural context. Robert Lowell worried the question in an 18 March 1963 letter to Berryman "What queer lives we've had even for poets! There seems something generic about it, and determined beyond anything we could do." In view of the fact that this generation reached adulthood just before World War II, they had also to wonder, as Lowell later put it, "Were we uncomfortable epigoni of Frost, Pound, Eliot, Marianne Moore, etc? This bitter pos-

sibility came to us at the moment of our *arrival*."

Faced with such great antecedents, Berryman had to serve a long apprenticeship as a poet, burdened by influence, which lasted until the late 1940s. "Berryman's earlier work," Kenneth Connelly has observed, "is often that of a very self-conscious, sometimes too respectful scholar sweating in the poet's academy, with results, as Dudley Fitts noted long ago, which were marred by 'an aura of contrivance' " (*Yale Review*, Spring 1969). But the apprenticeship paid off, for his major works, *Homage to Mistress Bradstreet* (1956) and *The Dream Songs*, are sui generis, unprecedented long poems of humane interest and high literary art, not of unmediated expressiveness or merely confessional interest. As Denis Donoghue observed of *The Dream Songs*, "the poem is all perception, surrounded by feeling. The feeling is not on show, on parade; it comes into the lines only because it attends upon perceptions which could not appear without that favour." Berryman's life is at the center of his best poetry, and his poetry is a function of his obsessions. He in fact experienced the whole gamut of obsessions—emotional, psychological, philosophical, religious—which a modern man might endure, but he managed to stand outside himself in his poems by means of personae. "His poems are so close to a sense of life, an imparting of truth complete with the bias of technique and personality, that they have the true flavour of fiction," Douglas Dunn has written. "An enormously comprehensive and unsentimental pathos slips out of his work, complicated and perplexing. We realize that although it may all be about ordinary Berryman, it generalizes itself, it has compass."

Berryman suffered from mismatched parents. His father, John Allyn Smith, had migrated from the family home in Minnesota and worked in the banking business in Oklahoma, where he met and married a young schoolmistress, Martha Little. It is evident that honor came before passion in their marriage, for Martha soon realized her incompatibility with her husband; she was snobbish, capable and ambitious, while Smith seems to have been a decent but unstriving character. After ten years in Oklahoma, Smith resigned from the bank, and the family, including a second son, Robert Jefferson (born in 1917), moved to Florida to try their business prospects. But the Florida boom collapsed in the mid-1920s; Smith's professional hopes foundered and he became depressed and withdrawn. In addition, perhaps because he had come to feel emotionally dispossessed by his wife's strong, exclusive love for the children, Smith showed every sign of being dangerously unstable and fickle in his behavior. He committed suicide by shooting himself on 26 June 1926.

Berryman often regarded that event, which took place in his twelfth year, as the trauma of his life, and in later years he was obsessed with grief, self-identity, and psychological dislocation, as well as with questions of temporal and religious destiny, all of which infused his major poetry. His cast of mind construed affliction as a creative stimulant. Burdened by his mother's influence and dominance, he continually worried the neurotic conflict he believed his father's suicide had triggered. From time to time, in an effort to rationalize the tribulations which fed his poetry, he quizzed his mother for the truth about his father, but most of what she told him characterized Smith as a man deeply aliennated, at a point of existential crisis, and irremediably selfish. Although Berryman often reckoned with the fact that his mother must have contributed to the sense of rejection Smith experienced, he mostly suppressed his own feeling of disaffection for her and so perpetuated the self-divisions which charged his best poetry. While self-dramatization galvanized his mature creative output—as late as 1970, he claimed that he retained "enough feelings" about his father to "dominate" *The Dream Songs*—he struggled through his personal life in a state of continual disequilibrium, rage and remorse, relieved only by periods of exultation.

In Florida the Smiths had been befriended by a man named John Angus McAlpin Berryman. Late in 1926 he married Martha Smith, and the family presently moved to New York City. Young John, who duly adopted his stepfather's surname, attended the newly founded "jock" school, South Kent School in Connecticut, where he boarded for four years from 1928. At that time the school set the highest value on excellence in competitive sports, much more than on academic accomplishments, and it is clear that Berryman, who had all too little aptitude for the playing field, was grievously misplaced. He was subjected to an emotionally confusing existence which forced him to separate his natural abilities from his pretended ambitions and interests. Although he attained high academic success he had to do so while affecting self-disparagement and in the face of what amounted to the school's depreciation. He suffered from a certain amount of bullying, which provoked him to one suicide attempt on 7 March 1931, but his studiousness and cleverness, much encouraged by his mother, at last worked to his good: he was the first boy in the history of the school to bypass

the sixth form and to go straight from the fifth into college.

At Columbia College of Columbia University in New York, he spent two years compensating to himself by becoming a great social success and a lion among the coeds, but his failure in one examination shocked him so much that he soon made steadier academic progress. His mother played an enormously influential part in fostering his intellectual and creative talents, but it was the example and guidance of Mark Van Doren, who became a fatherly mentor, which finally fixed his ambitions. Berryman credited Van Doren as being "the presiding genius of all my work until my second year, when I fell under the influence of W. B. Yeats," and characterized his teaching as "strongly structured, lit with wit, leaving ample play for grace and charm. . . . It stuck steadily to its subject and was highly disciplined. . . . If during my stay at Columbia I had met only Mark Van Doren and his work, it would have been worth the trouble. It was the force of his example, for instance, that made me a poet." For his part, Van Doren remembered Berryman as "first and last a literary youth: all of his thought sank into poetry, which he studied and wrote as if there were no other exercise for the human brain. Slender, abstracted, courteous, he lived one life alone, and walked with verse as in a trance." Berryman published several poems and reviews in the *Columbia Review,* and studied so hard that the dean of Columbia College eventually considered him "conspicuously qualified . . . for academic distinction."

He finally won the distinction of becoming Kellett Fellow, which enabled him to study for two years (1936-1938) at Clare College, Cambridge, where he worked under George Rylands and won the prestigious Oldham Shakespeare Scholarship in his second year. He met W. H. Auden in England, befriended Dylan Thomas, whom he "half-adored" for "his intricate booms & indecent tales/ almost entirely untrue" (*Delusions, Etc.,* 1972), and received an audience with his hero W. B. Yeats, who left him, as he recorded at the time, with "an impression of tremendous but querulous force, a wandering intensely personal mind which resists natural bent (formal metaphysics by intuition, responsible vision) to its own exhaustion." Also in England, he became engaged to a young woman, who visited him in New York when he returned there for the academic year 1938-1939, but the relationship could not last when she decided to stay in England for the duration of World War II.

While in England Berryman had determined

Berryman with his mother soon after his return from England in 1938 (courtesy of Eileen Simpson)

to become a teacher, but he failed to gain a job on returning to New York and spent one year in a state of considerable nervous stress, writing poems (some of them were published in *Southern Review*), abortive plays, and book reviews for *New York Herald Tribune Books*. In 1939 he became for one year part-time poetry editor of the *Nation,* and took up an appointment as instructor in English at Wayne University in Detroit (now Wayne State University), where he lived and worked with a charismatic young friend, Bhain Campbell. A poet and Marxist, Campbell strove to inject some social and political consciousness into Berryman's apprentice poetry, but Berryman's early work manifests a concern with the craft of poetry—the dynamics of style, form, metrics—to the extent of neglecting content. The strain of his year at Wayne caused Berryman to suffer from exhaustion and from attacks which were diagnosed as petit mal epilepsy. Furthermore, Bhain Campbell contracted cancer and died late in 1940, an event which caused Berryman a profound grief which he associated with the death of his father. In 1940 he began work as an instructor in English at Harvard University, and in 1942 he married his first wife, Eileen Patricia Mulligan, whose love and moral support for his work and whose

sufferance of his increasingly bizarre neurotic drives kept them together for a period of more than ten years.

Berryman's earliest poems were first brought together, along with poems by Mary Barnard, Randall Jarrell, W. R. Moses, and George Marion O'Donnell, in *Five Young American Poets* (1940), and then in a slim volume of his own, *Poems* (1942). Most of the items in those first collections were written in 1939, and have been well characterized by Joel Conarroe as "ominous, flat, social, indistinctly allusive, exhausted . . . an echo chamber." Well schooled and crafted, infused with a sense of loss and unlocated portentousness, they mostly fail to synthesize personal feeling and reflection, and have pretensions to the meditative poise Berryman valued in the poetry of Yeats's middle period. Too much in them is labored and realized only through rhetoric, so that even poems which figure sociopolitical subjects (prompted by Berryman's association with Bhain Campbell) bury the contemporary ills and evils they treat in specious gestures and solemn style. Conrad Aiken, R. P. Blackmur, Allen Tate, Oscar Williams, and John Crowe Ransom spotted the promise of Berryman and of Randall Jarrell in the group volume of 1940, and indeed

Eileen Mulligan, 1942 (courtesy of Eileen Simpson)

certain poems, such as Berryman's "Winter Landscape," deserve their reward as anthology pieces. However, Berryman recognized at an early stage that he had been beguiled by literary influences, Yeats, Auden, and Delmore Schwartz being chief among them, and that both the forms and attitudes of his first published poems derived as much from works of literature as from subjects of real personal concern. "Desires of Men and Women," for example, might have been entitled "Variation on a Theme by Delmore Schwartz"; Berryman once pointed out that "the first line is a variant of his 'Tired and unhappy, you think of houses.'" (Likewise, what really interested Berryman about "The Animal Trainer," a poem in two parts completed by March 1940 but published four years later, was that its form derived from poems by Conrad Aiken and Bhain Campbell.) Berryman struggled to find his own voice throughout the 1940s, trying all the while to break away from the dominant influence of Yeats on what he called "the compositional base" of his poems. Since he protractedly worried the

claims of literature over life—he once wondered "what day of mere living presents so rich & complicated an experience" as the life of literature?—it is ironic that his greatest achievements as a poet finally came from fashioning the literature of life.

In 1943 he started teaching as an instructor in English at Princeton University, where he worked under another of his heroes, Richard Blackmur, and numbered among his talented students W. S. Merwin, Frederick Buechner, and William Arrowsmith. Berryman showed great respect and affection for Blackmur, Frederick Buechner recalls: "Blackmur seemed an old gull drying his wise wings in the sun, Berryman a sandpiper skittering along the edge of the tide." Princeton was Berryman's home for the next decade, and his circle of friends expanded markedly during that time. After his initial period of teaching, in 1944 he undertook a two-and-a-half-year stretch of independent research in Shakespearean textual criticism (supported by a Rockefeller Foundation research fellowship, he virtually completed an edition of *King Lear* which has never been published) before he was again appointed to the teaching faculty in 1946. He was successively associate in creative writing, resident fellow in creative writing, and Alfred Hodder Fellow and became a conspicuously successful teacher with a charisma that awed his students. Those students and other friends who were closest to him nonetheless discerned the psychological pressure and pain under which he labored, a restlessness of the spirit coupled with a deep despair of himself. At Harvard University from 1940 to 1943 he had suffered a more oppressive intellectual climate, from much of which (unlike his colleague Delmore Schwartz) he had shielded himself, only to indulge in increasingly morbid and paralyzing self-appraisal. At Princeton long hours of isolated study caused him to brood more and more. His tolerance for personal and professional setbacks became lower than ever, and by the late 1940s he assumed a sort of a second nature, a guise in which to face what he believed to be the overwhelming demands of his work and society. Many of his acquaintances saw his public role as that of an eccentric, a combination of braggart, womanizer, unpredictable drinker, and formidable—sometimes savagely assertive or dismissive—intellectual. In fact, whether intimidating or endearing, his behavior was often just the superficial aspect of a temperament that was all too often tormented by acute insecurity, self-recrimination, and self-exaction. To a degree, after 1947, Berryman came to hide his fears in drink. His diaries from the 1940s

The sun rushed up the sky, the taxi flew.
There was a kind of fever on the clock
. That morning. We arrived at Waterloo
With time to spare and couldn't find my track.

The bitter coffee in a small café
Gave us our conversation. When the train
Began to move I saw you turn away
And vanish, and the vessels in my brain

Burst, the train roared, the other travellers
In flames leapt, burning on the tilted air
Cur si Cruccia. I heard the devils curse
And shriek with joy in that place beyond prayer.

Fair copy of "Parting as Descent," from Five Young American Poets, *published by New Directions in 1940 (from* Homage to Mistress Bradstreet and Other Poems *copyright © 1968 by John Berryman; reprinted by permission of Farrar, Straus & Giroux, Inc.; courtesy of Thomas Cooper Library, University of South Carolina)*

give the impression of a man stricken by neurosis and self-analysis, paradoxically sustaining himself by greater demands on the self, and too little evidence of the many happy times he enjoyed with his wife.

In 1948 William Sloane Associates published *The Dispossessed,* a volume of rhymed stanzaic poems burdened by feelings of hopelessness and confusion, wielding abstruse images and torturing syntax in an unrewarding fashion. It was characteristic of Berryman's desolated attitude during the early and mid-1940s that he should have followed in some verses the example and tone of Louis Aragon, especially as in *Le Crève-Coeur* (1941; Berryman later complained that he had been "conned" by Aragon), where a bitter sentimentality and sense of personal defeatism vis-à-vis World War II harmonized with Berryman's sense of affairs. He tended to see his own inner conflicts mirrored in the European holocaust. Some of the poems of *The Dispossessed,* milling with inflated sentiment and opaque image, are virtually incomprehensible in whole or in part. The title poem, for instance, begins with a quotation from Luigi Pirandello and leads into a surrealistic assemblage of images; it is easy to miss the point that the poem actually concerns the dropping of the atomic bomb on Hiroshima—"an evil sky (where the umbrella bloomed)/twirled its mustaches." Joel Conarroe properly comments: "The humorless, abstract, often bloodless quality of much of the early work, inhibited even in an age of arid art, gives evidence of the price Berryman paid for rejecting the validity of his own sensory experience. . . . Berryman succeeds less well with the social-ironic speculative poem, by way of Auden, than with the personal lyric . . . that has its source in his own feelings." Contemporary reviewers understandably felt they could find little to praise in the collection, though a number of them expressed hopes for Berryman's future. While Randall Jarrell reasonably discovered "raw or overdone lines side by side with imaginative and satisfying ones" (*Nation*, 17 July 1948), Yvor Winters taxed Berryman's "disinclination to understand and discipline his emotions. Most of his poems appear to deal with a single all-inclusive topic: the desperate chaos, social, religious, philosophical, and psychological, of modern life, and the corresponding chaos and desperation of John Berryman" (*Hudson Review*, Fall 1948). However, one group of nine dramatic monologues, "The Nervous Songs" (which are to some extent influenced by Rainer Maria Rilke), stand out as psychologically vibrant dramas which prefigure Berryman's mature work. As Conarroe has written, "In its form, the three six-line stanzas with flexible rhyme schemes, and in its mood of intense auto-revelation, the sequence is an important forerunner of *The Dream Songs*."

The year 1947, however, had finally brought contingent reality directly into the center of Berryman's creative life. He had an illicit affair with a woman to whom he gave the pseudonym Lise and wrote a running commentary on its progress in the form of a sequence of sonnets which were published only twenty years later as *Berryman's Sonnets* (1967). The sonnets use a Petrarchan rhyme scheme, much archaic or antic diction, and dislocated syntax (which at best reflects the turbulence of the poet's moods and at worst draws attention to itself as factitious and gauche). The sequence in some ways corresponds to a traditional and perhaps artificial scheme—moving from hope and anxiety through dangerous and guilty fulfillment to withdrawal and reproach—but that paradigmatic design was in fact fortuitous, for the sequence at all stages logs the actuality of the affair. *Berryman's Sonnets* provides an inventory of the poet's being, mind, and moods, at stages on a blind road. Berryman quickly assumed the role of a spectator of his own drama, and the sonnets served appetite as much as satisfaction. He became at once obsessively "in love" with his mistress and self-consciously withdrawn, exercising a double consciousness which left a discrete gap between the man who experienced and suffered and the writer who evaluated and composed emotion into a literary artifact.

Since circumstances kept Berryman and Lise apart for much of the summer, he was often compelled to fashion an image of her, a myth, drawing on imaginative invention and on literary analogues. Accordingly, the sonnets sometimes fall short of what Roy Pascal has called a "correlative in the outer world" (*Design and Truth in Autobiography*, 1960). Berryman leaned toward literature to find models of his love, sometimes with a consequent excess of self-regard. In sonnet 75, he compares himself to Petrarch, in 29 to Honoré de Balzac, in 21 to David in relation with Bathsheba; sonnet 16 was suggested by Philip Sidney's second sonnet to Stella. In other words, by comparing himself to well-known precursors in the role of adulterer or sonneteer, he was drawn to behold himself in the role of poet and to diminish attention to the lady. His literary self-consciousness is marked even in the first sonnet of the sequence—"I wished, all the mild days of middle March/ . . . your blond good-nature might/(Lady) admit . . ./Me to your story"—which alludes to Stéphane Mallarmé's poem "M'introduire dans ton histoire"; the first four lines of sonnet 102 (a poem, Berryman recorded in his journal, written on "15 August in the morning after my worst nightmare for months: a killer, mad") are a loose imitation of the first four lines of Tristan Corbière's poem "Heures"; sonnet 105 is a virtuoso performance prompted by a reading of the Grimms' tale "The Duration of Life." Likewise, the final line of sonnet 52 includes a slightly mistranscribed quotation from the last line—"Da ist meiner Liebsten Haus"—of Wilhelm Müller's "Wasserflut" ("The Water's Flow"), set to music, as part of *Winterreise*, by Franz Schubert: it is one of many private references in the sequence, for Berryman and Lise loved playing recordings of Schubert's song cycle together. A good deal of the obscurity and inscrutability of the sonnets may be attributed, not only to the necessity of subterfuge and secrecy, but to the fact that much of their content and thematic linkage was the product of the poet's isolation from his love, compelling him to be self-conscious and literary. Many of the sonnets, he knew, were authentic in impulse but made insincere by artistic devices.

On the other hand, perhaps just as many were written in direct response to the lover, and they include the best of all the sonnets, which are fully charged with personal emotion, anguish, and poignancy, and communicate it to the reader. They served, like Jonathan Swift's *Journal to Stella* or Laurence Sterne's *Journal to Eliza*, as a way of imparting his feelings to Lise. In that sense the most accomplished sonnets were a form of homage, poems about as well as to his love. Berryman's journal entry for 16 July 1947, for instance, includes the sincere comments: "(. . . she is my *conscience* as well as my inspiration); four new sonnets, and even better (what I couldn't get peace for earlier) four old ones perfected—still I die of longing: if I hadn't faith in her I don't know what I would do." Milton Gilman points to the cold surface texture of many of the allusive sonnets, and perceptively argues that Lise "is, in a sense, the creative agent of every poem, the source of tone, rhythm, image, and theme." She is "a provisional deity. . . . The real center of interest is the increasingly complex psychological state of the speaker. . . . the *illicit* nature of the affair is so important in the Sonnets, providing an opportunity to release all kinds of feeling: lust, longing, scorn, guilt, pity, fatigue, despair, fear, impatience, joy."

Reviewers of *Berryman's Sonnets*, when they at last appeared in 1967, highlighted the importance of their style as laying the ground for Berryman's use of disrupted syntax in his major works, *Homage to Mistress Bradstreet* and *The Dream Songs*, where style—what Anthony Thwaite called in a review for the *New Statesman* (17 May 1968) the "awful spasmodics" of *Berryman's Sonnets*—is integrated with subject, functional and not gratuitous. But what is perhaps equally important about the achievement of *Berryman's Sonnets* is that they showed him the way to marry his creative gift to his life. The essence of Berryman's art and his literary success lay in his ability to tap and impart the deepest reaches of the human personality and consciousness.

Berryman's desire and guilt over the affair of 1947, and over other illicit affairs in the late 1940s, immediately charged the theme and form of his first major work, *Homage to Mistress Bradstreet*, which he began in 1948 and finished in 1953. A long poem of fifty-seven stanzas, with a complex metric and sophisticated rhyme scheme, it succeeds both as lyric and as drama, and has been called by Edmund Wilson "the most distinguished long poem by an American since *The Waste Land*." Berryman himself declared that he "set up the *Bradstreet* poem as an attack on *The Waste Land:* personality, and plot—no anthropology, no Tarot pack, no Wagner." He deplored Eliot's notion of the impersonality of the poet, and rather professed the "passionate sense of identification" he found in Walt Whitman.

Homage to Mistress Bradstreet employs an apparently objective scheme of two voices—the voice of Anne Bradstreet, the first poet of New England, and that of the "poet" who both conjures up the heroine and appears to be conjured up by her (since the poem largely follows the putative expe-

riences of her life). Berryman's Bradstreet is rendered as an alienated, creative woman, rebellious against husband, father, and God. She registers a sense of spiritual and domestic displacement, bears a child, momentarily succumbs to the seductive blandishments of the "poet" who figures as a sort of demon lover, but then withdraws from him and moves forward into her declining years and death. The poem ends with a sense of historical quietus and fatalism. Much of the poem draws on the facts of the life of the real Anne Bradstreet, some of which are distorted, even perverted, for imaginative purposes which justifiably serve the work's major themes—religious apostasy, adulterous inclination, creative stultification, guilt, retribution, remorse—all of which match Berryman's personal obsessions. Berryman's own marriage and adulteries are sublimated in the poem, so that its fictive form actually speaks directly for the poet's passionate concerns. In depicting a relationship beyond space and time, Berryman deploys a conceptual device which transcends and encompasses subjective utterance and accordingly succeeds on a multiplicity of structural and thematic levels. In a sense *Homage to Mistress Bradstreet* does offer a personal confession and an exploration of its subject, but in a form which transfigures self-exhibition through art.

It may be fair, as John Frederick Nims wrote in a 1958 review, to judge that the poem stresses "a sort of depressing propaganda for the view that the flesh is evil," but it needs to be said that the poem is stylistically far more flexible (moving swiftly, for example, between moments of tenderness, triumph, hysteria, and pathos) than the limits Nims sets: "In Berryman's stanza everything is tense, numb, shivering, painful. . . . Throughout the poem I find this alternation of strength, gravity, even nobility with a shrill hectic fury, a whipped-up excitement, a maudlin violence of *mal protesi nervi*." (Berryman himself reasonably explained, "I was taking chances at the time of my poem. I had to get a language that was not hers, but not mine, but would *not be pastiche*, like Ben Jonson's projection of Spenser.") Nims's comments are as just as those by any other adverse critic of the poem (compare, for instance, the severely critical long essay "The Life of the Modern Poet," in the 23 February 1973 issue of the *Times Literary Supplement*), where the anonymous reviewer perceptively argues that "purportedly concerned with Anne Bradstreet, [Berryman's] poem is really about 'the poet' himself, his romantic and exacerbated personality, his sense of loneliness, his need for a mistress, confi-

HOMAGE TO MISTRESS BRADSTREET

(Born 1612 Anne Dudley, married at 16 Simon
Bradstreet a Cambridge man steward to the
Countess of Warwick & protege of her father
Thomas Dudley secretary to the Earl of Lin-
coln. Crossed in the <u>Arbella</u>, 1630, under
Governor Winthrop.)

The Governor your husband stayed so long
Moved you not, restless, waiting for him? Still,
You were a patient woman.--
I seem to see you pause here still:
Sylvester, Quarles, in moments odd you pored
Before a fire at, bright eyes on the Lord,
All the children still.
'Simon..' Simon will listen while you read a Song.

Outside the New World winters in grand dark
White air lashing high thro' the virgin stands
Foxes down foxholes sigh,
Surely the English heart quails, stunned.
I doubt if Simon than this blast, that sea,
Spares from his rigour for your poetry
More. We are on each other's hands
Who care. Both of our worlds unhanded us. Lie stark,

Thy eyes look to me mild. Out of maize and air
Your body's made, and moved. I summon, see,
From the centuries it.
I think you won't stay. How do we
Linger, diminished, in our lovers' air,
Implausibly visible, to whom, a year,
Years, over interims; or not;
To a long stranger; or not; shimmer and disappear.

Rot jaw-ript with its wisdom, terrible then,
Then not. When the master dies, who misses you?
Your master never died.
Simon ah thirty years past you----
Pockmarkt & westward staring on a haggard deck
It seems I find you, young. I come to check,
I come to stay with you,
And the Governor, & Father, & Simon, & the huddled men.

Pages from the typescript for Homage to Mistress Bradstreet *in the Allen Tate papers (from* Homage to Mistress Bradstreet
*copyright © 1956 by John Berryman; reprinted by permission of Farrar, Straus & Giroux, Inc.; courtesy of Princeton
University Library)*

Homage 3

Women sleep sound. I was happy once...
(Something keeps on not happening. I shrink?)
These minutes all their passions and powers sink
And I am not one chance
For an unknown cry or a batting of unknown eyes.

Chapped souls ours, by the day Spring's strong winds swelled,
Jack's pulpits arched, more glad. The shawl I pinned
Flaps like a shooting soul
Might in such weather Heaven send.
Succumbing to a faith-shed yellow sash
I prod the fascinating succotash—
I must be disciplined,
In arms, against that one and our dissidents and myself.

Versing, I shroud among the dynasties,
Quaternion on quaternion, tireless I phrase
Anything past, dead, far,
Sacred, for a barbarous place.
--To please your wintry father? all this bald
Abstract didactic rime I read appalled
Harrassed for your fame
Mistress neither of fiery nor velvet verse, on your knees,

Hopeful & wretched, chaste, laborious, odd,
Whom the sea tore.--The damned roar with loss,
So they hug & are mean
With themselves, and I cannot be thus.
Why then do I repine, sick, wicked, and long
After what must not be? I lie wrong
Once more. For at fourteen
I found my heart more carnal and sitting loose from God,

Vanity and the follies of youth took hold of me;
Then the pox blasted, when the Lord returned.
That year for my sorry face
So-much-older Simon burned,
So father smiled, with love. ~~Their~~ _their will be_ ~~was not~~ done.
God to me ill lingeringly, learning to shun
A bliss, a lightning blood
Vouchsafed, what did seem life. I kissed his mystery.

Drydust in God's eye the aquavivid skin
Of Simon snoring lit with fountaining dawn
When my eyes unlid, sad.
John Cotton shines on Boston's sin
Shaming: ~~And~~ I am drawn, in pieties that seem
The weary drizzled of an unremembered dream.
Women have gone mad
At twenty-~~four~~ _one._ I listen to something high & thin.

dante, confessor"; but his conclusion that Berryman "has too little human reality to sustain his myth" may be disputed by emphasizing the transcendent imaginative richness of the achievement.

Homage to Mistress Bradstreet, as one or two critics have pointed out, has some likeness to Robert Lowell's poem *Lord Weary's Castle* (1946), but any comparison necessarily fails in essentials: Berryman's poem is peculiar to himself in both style and concerns. He was undoubtedly correct when he observed, "In the Bradstreet poem, as I seized inspiration from [Saul Bellow's novel *The Adventures of Augie March,* 1953], I sort of seized inspiration, I think, from Lowell, rather than imitated him." Berryman had befriended Lowell as early as 1944, and enthusiastically reviewed *Lord Weary's Castle* in 1947.

Lowell himself recalled that Berryman "was humorous, thrustingly vehement in liking . . . more adolescent than boyish. . . . Hyperenthusiasms made him a hot friend, and could also make him wearing to friends—one of his dearest, Delmore Schwartz, used to say that no one had John's loyalty, but you liked him to live in another city. . . . John could quote with vibrance to all lengths, even prose, even late Shakespeare, to show me what could be done with disrupted and mended syntax. This was the start of his real style."

There is no doubt that Berryman managed to be both fiercely loving and very competitive toward Lowell and other poets, but he invariably gave his love and kept the rivalry to himself. On the whole, he felt that his own achievements as a poet came second to Lowell's, as he wrote in an undated, not necessarily disingenuous letter to his mother shortly after Robert Frost's death in 1963: "Frost's going puts—as you wouldn't think it would—a problem to me. I have never wanted to be king. . . . I've been comfortable since 1946 with the feeling that Lowell is far my superior. . . ."

Berryman's obsessional self-inquisition and his growing dependence on alcohol (he first began to drink heavily in 1947) put undue strains on his private life, but it enabled him to develop a strong sense of identification with what he discovered to be (in a sometimes willful and not always strictly scholarly way) the psychological problems of Stephen Crane. Reviewers received *Stephen Crane* (1950), his critical biography, respectfully but on the whole skeptically, for a number shared Graham Greene's criticism of the book's "tortured prose" and of Berryman's dubious use of depth psychology as a mode of literary criticism. Morgan Blum, on the other hand, considered it a "flawed but distinguished book"—distinguished in its treatment of the intersections between Crane's life and work.

Berryman's bravura teaching continued to flourish: he taught at the University of Washington in early 1950, and spent a most successful semester as Elliston Professor of Poetry at the University of Cincinnati in Spring 1952. His endeavors as a Shakespearean scholar (which at many stages of his life he valued as highly as his work in poetry) and his poetry writing were equally rewarded with a Guggenheim Fellowship for critical study and for creative writing, which enabled him to complete *Homage to Mistress Bradstreet.* But his psychological disturbances compelled him to seek the help of a psychiatrist, whom he consulted at length in the late 1940s and early 1950s, and he also spent some time in group therapy. Moreover, the stresses of his drinking, his anguished disposition, and his increasingly wayward conduct caused his first wife to leave him at the end of a hectic summer in Europe in 1953. Eileen Berryman Simpson has recently published two books of her own, a worthy novel, *The Maze* (1975), which is, according to one reviewer, "quite transparently the story of the marriage's breakup. . . . less satisfying as fiction than as biography," and a memoir, *Poets in Their Youth* (1982).

Berryman then taught in the Writers' Workshop at the University of Iowa in spring 1954 and at Harvard University during that summer. ("He taught by exemplitude," Edward Hoagland, who studied under him at Harvard, has recalled. "He talked mostly about books he had loved with a fever that amounted to a kind of courage"). He returned to the University of Iowa that fall, but he was obliged to resign after a drunken altercation with his landlord which resulted in a night's imprisonment. (His students in the Writers' Workshop included W. D. Snodgrass, Donald Justice, William Dickey, and Jane Cooper.) Allen Tate, whom he had regarded as a master since they first met at Columbia in 1935, saved the situation by inviting him to Minneapolis ("Site without history!" Berryman ironically invoked the city in one of his late poems, "Mpls, Mother"), where he started teaching courses in humanities in 1955. It was in Minneapolis that Berryman became fast friends with Saul Bellow, whom he always looked to as a model of literary style and energy. In 1956 he married Elizabeth Ann Levine, who bore him a son, Paul, the following year, but the relationship fared badly and ended in divorce in 1959.

Berryman's sense of personal dereliction led him to undertake a long period of dream analysis

Alister Cameron and John Berryman in Cincinnati, 1952 (courtesy of Eileen Simpson)

on his arrival in Minneapolis, and to embark upon the greatest work of his career, *The Dream Songs,* first published in two parts, *77 Dream Songs* (1964) and *His Toy, His Dream, His Rest* (1968).

"I set up *The Dream Songs* as hostile to every visible tendency in both American and English poetry," Berryman later declared. "The aim was . . . the reproduction or invention of the motions of a human personality, free and determined. . . ." *The Dream Songs* is a long poem of 385 sections, each (with small exceptions) being composed of three six-line stanzas, which deal with the multitudinous preoccupations and adventures, notions, and emotions, of a persona named Henry (alias Henry Pussycat, Henry House, Mr. Bones). Henry is now and then challenged and ineffectually corrected by an unidentified friend, his interlocutor. It is neither a narrative nor a philosophical poem, but a poem to which Berryman opened his entire mind and being, acts and eventualities, high thoughts and dark obsessions. Berryman once announced that poetry aims "at the reformation of the poet, as prayer does. In the grand cases—as, in our century—Yeats and Eliot—it enables the poet gradually, again and again, to become almost another man. . . ." He therefore declared that Henry was not himself, the poet, but "a white American in early middle age sometimes in blackface, who has suffered an irreversible loss and talks about himself sometimes in the first person, sometimes in the third, and some-

times even in the second." The shifting pronominal identification of Henry (who *is* obviously, to all intents and purposes, Berryman himself) became a function of Berryman's self-exploration, an ironic device which throws character and attitude free of solipsism or egotism. Berryman told Jane Howard that "the various parts of [Henry's] identity are fluid. They slide, and the reader is made to guess who is talking to whom. Out of this ambiguity arises richness. The reader becomes more aware, is forced to enter into himself."

The device of splitting facets of himself into dramatis personae owed much to Freud's analysis of ego and id, and to the classical opposition of alazon and eiron (the egoistic and pretentious man confronted by an ironic man who staggers self-possession), but also to an insight which Berryman independently perceived but later found rehearsed by W. H. Auden in "Balaam and His Ass" (*The Dyer's Hand,* 1963): "To present artistically a human personality in its full depth, its inner dialectic, its self-disclosure and self-concealment, through the medium of a single character is almost impossible."

In an interview dating from 1963, Berryman said, "I have an anti-hero in [*The Dream Songs*] who's a character the world gives a hard time to." The poem is often obscure and abstruse, especially in *77 Dream Songs,* with private references and arcane allusions; it also uses daring and lively syntax, and a mixed diction including what the poet himself

Elizabeth Ann, John, and Paul Berryman, 1957 (courtesy of Princeton University Library)

called "coon talk." Such a motley style owes much to a tradition which reaches back through the ethos, rhythms, and attitudes of the blues to the minstrel tradition. Berryman himself pinpointed one source of his inspiration in the figure of Thomas Dartmouth Rice, a white actor of the early-nineteenth century who mimicked a black—"Jim Crow"—so finely that he managed to transform painful dispossession into art. Berryman identified with the social and spiritual underdog, and his Henry in a black mask expresses his own pain and pathos in a mode which extends beyond egotism and embraces other outcasts. Minstrelsy, as William Wasserstrom has written, "represents the climactic and synoptic solution to the poet's 'long, often back-breaking search for an inclusive style, a style that could use his erudition,' Robert Lowell says, and 'catch the high, even frenetic, intensity of his experience, disgusts and enthusiasm.' "

The Dream Songs, which Berryman called an epic, is a poem as ambitious as Walt Whitman's *Song of Myself,* William Carlos Williams's *Paterson,* or Hart Crane's *The Bridge,* but unlike *Song of Myself,* for instance, it proposes no system. It contains and

bodies forth a personality, and philosophical and theological notions, but it is above all a pragmatic poem, essaying ideas and emotions, love, lust, lament, grief. Several of the finest poems are elegies for fellow poets—Delmore Schwartz, Randall Jarrell, Theodore Roethke, Sylvia Plath—and certain key songs compass Berryman's ambivalent feelings for his dead father. "Always," Kenneth Connelly has written, "Henry stands above his 'father's grave with rage,' resentful, compassionate, jealous, accusing, finally gaining the courage to spit upon it. (The mystery of a careless earthly father modulates inevitably into Henry's analogous broodings over the Heavenly Father and his family, provoking some of the most brilliant religious poems of our time.)" Through the persona of Henry, Berryman, as Wasserstrom expresses it, "synthesizes all fragments of the self [and] helps the self to mediate, accommodate, comply and in this way avoid all menace of extinction."

Berryman believed that feelings might be imaginatively controlled in the order of art, and hoped that *The Dream Songs* might be as useful to the reader as to himself. "These Songs are not meant to be understood, you understand./They are only meant to terrify & comfort." He felt that Whitman's *Song of Myself* was a poem that "will do good to us," and the same may be true of *The Dream Songs,* which is by turns highly comic and savagely painful. It also has inevitable weaknesses and faults, one of which is perhaps not unlike the fault Berryman found in *Song of Myself* when he described it as "too idiosyncratic, like *Paradise Lost,* to rank with the very best poems. . . ." A number of critics have objected to Berryman's "abuse" of syntax, the whirligig of his demotic and literary diction (Robert Lowell found himself "rattled" by "mannerisms"), and what Denis Donoghue has called his "hotspur materials." However, a larger area of unrest, which Berryman always shared, concerns the shape and structure of *The Dream Songs,* epic or otherwise. Berryman continually attempted to model his poem on traditional epic structures, including Dante's *Divine Comedy,* the liturgy of the Bible, and the *Iliad,* and included a group of poems in which the hero dies and visits the underworld (book 4, the opus posthumous sequence which occupies the middle section of the poem, many critics consider to be among the finest of the songs; Robert Lowell told Berryman he considered book 4 "the crown of your wonderful work, witty, heartbreaking, all of a piece. . . . one of the lovely things in our literature"), but the nature of the songs entirely depended on the plotless fortunes of Berryman's own life during the thirteen years of writing. The "individual human soul under stress" to which he referred in a 1970 conversation with Richard Kostelanetz is that of Berryman as Henry; Berryman could no more map the poem to a prefigured narrative or philosophical conclusion than he could forecast the luck of his own life, as he virtually acknowledged in an interview for the *Paris Review:* "I was what you might call open-ended. That is to say, Henry to some extent was in the situation that we are all in in actual life—namely, he didn't know and I didn't know what the bloody fucking hell was going to happen next. Whatever it was he had to confront it and get through."

Song 311 gives us both the poet's predicament and his procedure:

> Hunger was constitutional with him,
> women, cigarettes, liquor, need need need
> until he went to pieces.
> The pieces sat up & wrote. They did not heed
> their piecedom but kept very quietly on
> among the chaos.

The dissociated "pieces," as Denis Donoghue has explained, go to make up the whole of the man and his work: "This is not Whitman's way. Whitman's aesthetic implies that the self is the sum of its experiences, not the sum of its dissociated fragments. . . ." In a 29 April 1962 letter to Robert Lowell, Berryman worried that the songs "are partly independent but only if . . . the reader is familiar with Henry's tone, personality, friend, activities; otherwise, in small numbers, they seem simply crazy . . . ," but many good critics have demonstrated not only the folly of accusing the poem of confessional self-indulgence and disorder but also that what Berryman thought a weakness is actually a strength. Adrienne Rich, for instance (in a review Berryman called "the most serious study any large area of my work's ever had"), observed "first of all, the presence through the book of an effective unifying identity, and second, the power of that identity to define its surroundings so accurately. . . . a truly original work, in the sense in which Berryman has made one, is superior in inner necessity and by the force of a unique human character."

Berryman fought hard to finish *The Dream Songs,* and incorporated into it all the adventures, observations, and vicissitudes of his life. In 1957, for instance, he undertook a successful but exhausting lecture tour of India, which gave him acute insights into a foreign culture. At home in Minneapolis the disestablishment of the department of inderdisciplinary studies in 1958 sustained his sense that his professional life would always be hapless and harrowing. He nonetheless fully committed himself (for the rest of his life, as it turned out) to teaching in the humanities program at the University of Minnesota, and developed a spectacular pedagogical style, ardent and terrified, and accentuated by the problems of alcoholism. The *Minneapolis Star* reported after his death: "In the classroom, Berryman was electrifying. . . . When he was wrapped up in a lecture—and he usually was, whatever the specific topic—he would stalk from one side of the room to the other, now whispering, now bellowing, invariably trembling with emotion and perspiring freely." His academic career reached a peak in 1969, when he was appointed Regents' Professor of Humanities, a distinction which left him far more humbled than conceited, and Drake University conferred on him an honorary doctorate. He also became a formidably successful performer in the role of public bard, and in his last decade he gave many campus readings at which his voice was by turns thick with drink, engagingly bombastic, and even menacing. His audiences found him thrilling, alarming, exhilarating, ripe with quips and asides. Jane Howard's profile of the poet (*Life,* 21 July 1967) served as much as any other report of the 1960s to sell Berryman in an image reminiscent of Dylan Thomas; she perfectly reflected the eccentric style—sensational, temperamental, learned—he had encouraged in his conduct. William Heyen, Berryman's host at a visit to the Brockport Writers Forum in 1970, likewise described him as "Charming, disputatious, dominating, brilliant." Like Samuel Johnson, however, Berryman always felt the anxieties of fame, and sustained himself with equal parts of arrogance, self-irony, and terror.

He gained much happiness and a focus for his personal life when he married his third and last wife, Kathleen (Kate) Donahue, in 1961. Three years later they managed to buy a modest house, the first and last home Berryman ever owned, on Arthur Avenue in Minneapolis. The couple had two children, Martha in 1962 and Sarah Rebecca in 1971. In 1966-1967 the family lived on a Guggenheim Fellowship in Dublin, where Berryman passed long hours drinking but finally assembled *The Dream Songs.* The conclusion of that poem after thirteen years of work could not but be a great loss to him, for reasons he might have known when he recalled (in "A Tribute," *Agenda,* 4, 1965) how he had once pressed T. S. Eliot to urge Ezra Pound

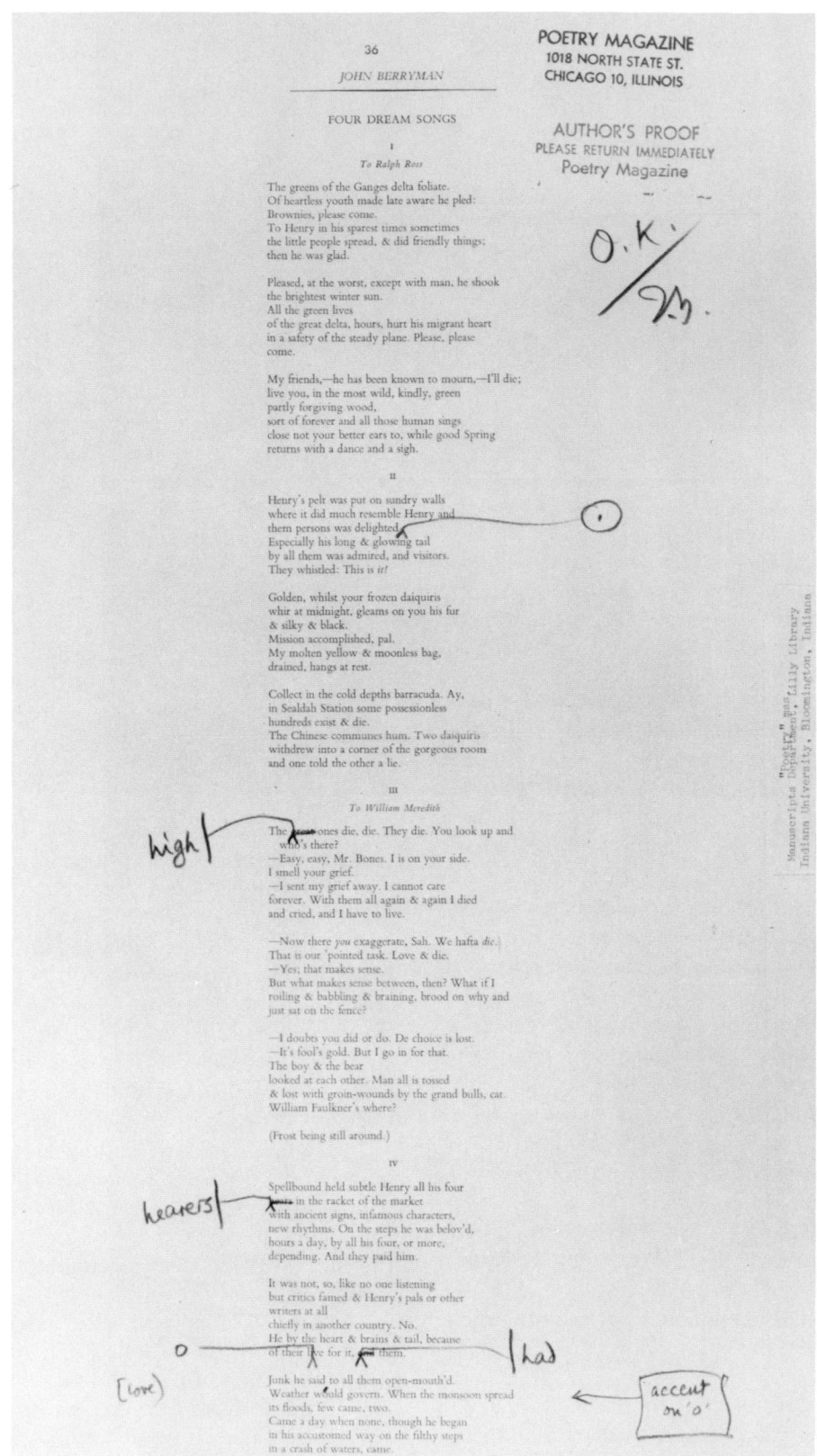

Corrected proof for "Four Dream Songs," published in the October 1962 issue of Poetry *magazine. They appear in* 77 Dream Songs *(1964) as poems 27, 16, 36, and 71 respectively (from* 77 Dream Songs *copyright © 1968 by John Berryman; reprinted by permission of Farrar, Straus & Giroux, Inc.; courtesy of the Lilly Library, Indiana University).*

John Berryman (photograph by Michael Chikiris)

to finish *The Cantos:* " 'Oh no,' Eliot said gravely, 'I could never do that. That would be the end of him. He would have nothing to do.' I did not then like this attitude but it was right and I was wrong."

The consensus of critical opinion on Berryman's next volume of poetry, *Love & Fame* (1970), is that it marks a falling off in inspiration and technique, an unfortunate return to the lyric form. Wistful for the ambition and scope of his major works, even Berryman registered the inevitable limits of his latest venture: "if I keep on writing lyric poems, that's all I'll be doing, I'm going to run out sooner or later." Half of *Love & Fame* consists of autobiographical poems, which Robert Lowell considered "profane and often in bad taste, the license of John's old college dates recollected at fifty." Quite apart from the question of "bad taste" (which several reviewers impugned), the lyrics are in fact compellingly accessible, witty, and often ironic. The volume acquired a fortuitously ironic structure when Berryman ended it with "Eleven Addresses to the Lord," a group of lyrics which reaffirm a querulous and ambiguous religious faith—"I only as far as gratitude & awe/confidently & absolutely go"—and require the reader to measure the secular and lubricious poems which pre-

cede them only in the context of the book as a whole. One reviewer, Walter Clemons, gave this perceptive and generous construction of *Love & Fame:* "Some of those poems are very hard to take. Behind a coarse jocularity, a desperate man was trying to cheer himself up, I thought when I first read and disliked them. I now think he was deliberately caricaturing, in bold poster colors, the bumptious, lost eagerness of his youth." However, no reader can afford to overlook the cautionary irony of Robert Lowell's comment that Berryman may have found his autobiographical excursions "too inspiring and less a breaking of new ground than he knew."

As with all Berryman's major works, the writing of *Love & Fame* ran in tandem with the experience of his life. He recovered his faith in Christ while undergoing treatment for alcoholism in 1970. He had suffered from alcoholism for more than twenty years, and first took steps to recover in 1969. The lessons he learned during two courses of treatment at St. Mary's Hospital, Minneapolis, in 1970, which included his conviction that a "God of rescue" had interceded in his life, established him as a recovering alcoholic but also left him feeling perilously self-exposed. He tried hard to take a stable view of his anguished sensibility and of his disturbed career (which he too often insisted on dating back to his father's suicide), but years of sickness and waste of spirit had taken their toll. Berryman's "late conversion," Douglas Dunn has saliently written, "proves the honesty of his anguish at the cruelty of the world, the competition without kindness. Yet it derives from fatigue."

Berryman drafted an autobiographical novel about the process of becoming a recovering alcoholic, but most critics have judged that the unfinished *Recovery* (1973) stands as an extraordinary and readable document about Berryman himself rather than as a fully realized work of literary art. He also completed a last book of poems, *Delusions, Etc.* (1972), but it fails on the whole to embody the passionate intensity of his best work, despite the undoubted success of certain poems—the idiosyncratic relish, for example, of "Beethoven Triumphant" and "Scholars at the Orchid Pavilion," the fierce identification of "Drugs Alcohol Little Sister" and "Tampa Stomp," and the poignant lament of "He Resigns." As the anonymous author of "The Life of the Modern Poet" (*Times Literary Supplement*, 23 February 1973) has written, "The last books have an intense but narrowly documentary appeal," and represent "the brave valediction of a man who chose his own way to die." In 1971 Berryman won a Senior Fellowship from the National Endowment for the Humanities in order to complete a critical biography, "Shakespeare's Reality," but he would not live to do so. He found that he no longer had the patience or energy for persevering with his writing, and ultimately that his capacity had failed; he committed suicide by jumping from the Washington Avenue Bridge in Minneapolis on 7 January 1972.

Berryman spent himself in his dedication to the work of poetry, as Daniel Hughes, who witnessed him at his desk in the early 1960s, observes: "I have never seen before or since such concentration. . . . I felt the presences of his terrible cost and commitment, and I loved him." When an interviewer asked him in 1965 to state the most important elements of good poetry, he replied, "Imagination, love, intellect—and pain. Yes, you've got to know pain." In at least one other interview Berryman seemed to find self-gratification in his "overdevelopment of sensibility"—"It's the price we pay," he announced. But whatever strain of misplaced and painfully ironic complacency that observation contains need not condition our reading of his best creative work, in which he found a dynamic form and style to make art of his life and obsessions. *Homage to Mistress Bradstreet* offers a remarkably imagined and densely achieved drama, with conceptual vigor and intricate execution, and deserves the praise it received from Edmund Wilson, Conrad Aiken, and Robert Lowell. That poem and *The Dream Songs* survive as the supreme achievements of a poet who believed that the essence of poetry is "the expression of emotion in action," and that "Art is created out of ordeal and crisis." Despite its vaunted difficulty and occasional weakness—local incoherence, word thickness, stylistic obscurity—*The Dream Songs* is a richly imagined and moving work. Berryman also merits attention as one of the most notable religious poets of recent years. In addition, what many of his last poems do fulfill is Berryman's own prescription that "Some of the best writing is really transparent. . . . The artist just says what he thinks, or says how he feels. . . . The art comes just in placing, pure syntax."

It is worth emphasizing the word *heroic* in Robert Lowell's claim that *The Dream Songs* is "the single most heroic work in English poetry since the War, since Ezra Pound's *Pisan Cantos*." Any discussion of literary history since World War II will also need to take account of the fact that *The Dream Songs* manifestly inspired Lowell to emulate Berryman's achievement with his own *Notebook* (1969), a work he subsequently refashioned and (according to some critics) weakened by imposing on it an overtly chronological and possibly lame form in its revised version, *History* (1973).

Interviews:

Jonathan Sisson, "My Whiskers Fly: An Interview with John Berryman," *Ivory Tower*, 14 (3 October 1966): 14-18, 34-35;

Jane Howard, "Whiskey and Ink, Whiskey and Ink," *Life*, 63 (21 July 1967): 67-68, 70, 73-76;

Elizabeth Nussbaum, "Berryman and Tate: Poets Extraordinaire," *Minnesota Daily*, 9 November 1967, pp. 7, 10;

John Plotz and others, "An Interview with John Berryman," *Harvard Advocate*, 103 (Spring 1969): 4-9;

Richard Kostelanetz, "Conversation with John Berryman," *Massachusetts Review*, 11 (Spring 1970): 340-347;

Martin Berg, "A Truly Gentle Man Tightens and Paces: An Interview with John Berryman," *Minnesota Daily* (University of Minnesota), 20 January 1971, pp. 9, 10, 14-15, 17;

Peter A. Stitt, "The Art of Poetry XVI: John Berryman 1914-1972," *Paris Review,* 14 (Winter 1972): 176-207;

William Heyen, "John Berryman: A Memoir and an Interview," *Ohio Review,* 15 (Winter 1974): 46-65.

Bibliographies:

Richard J. Kelly, *John Berryman: A Checklist* (Metuchen, N. J.: Scarecrow Press, 1972);

Ernest C. Stefanik, Jr., *John Berryman: A Descriptive Bibliography* (Pittsburgh: University of Pittsburgh Press, 1974);

Gary Q. Arpin, *John Berryman: A Reference Guide* (Boston, Mass.: G. K. Hall, 1976).

Biographies:

John Haffenden, *The Life of John Berryman* (London & Boston: Routledge & Kegan Paul, 1982);

Eileen Simpson, *Poets in Their Youth* (New York: Random House, 1982; London: Faber & Faber, 1982).

References:

Conrad Aiken, "A Letter," *Harvard Advocate,* 103 (Spring 1969): 23;

Jack V. Barbera, "Shape and Flow in *The Dream Songs,*" *Twentieth Century Literature,* 22 (May 1976): 146-162;

John Bayley, "John Berryman: A Question of Imperial Sway," in *Contemporary Poetry in America,* edited by Robert Boyers (New York: Schocken, 1974), pp. 59-77;

Edward Butscher, "John Berryman: In Memorial Perspective," *Georgia Review,* 27 (Winter 1973): 518-525;

Walter Clemons, "Man on a Tightrope," review of *Delusions, Etc., Newsweek,* 79 (1 May 1972): 113-114;

Joel Conarroe, "After Mr. Bones: John Berryman's Last Poems," review of *Delusions, Etc., Hollins Critic,* 13 (October 1976): 1-12;

Conarroe, *John Berryman: An Introduction to the Poetry* (New York: Columbia University Press, 1977);

Kenneth Connelly, "Henry Pussycat, He Come Home Good," review of *His Toy, His Dream, His Rest, Yale Review,* 58 (Spring 1969): 419-427;

Martin Dodsworth, "John Berryman: An Introduction," in *The Survival of Poetry,* edited by

Dodsworth (London: Faber & Faber, 1970), pp. 100-132;

Denis Donoghue, "Berryman's Long Dream," review of *The Dream Songs, Art International,* 13 (20 March 1969): 61-64;

Douglas Dunn, "Gaiety & Lamentation: The Defeat of John Berryman," *Encounter,* 43 (August 1974): 72-77;

Milton Gilman, "Berryman and the Sonnets," review of *Berryman's Sonnets, Chelsea,* 22/23 (June 1968): 158-169;

John Haffenden, *John Berryman: A Critical Commentary* (London: Macmillan, 1980; New York: New York University Press, 1980);

Alan Holder, "Anne Bradstreet Resurrected," *Concerning Poetry,* 2 (Spring 1969): 11-18;

Lewis Hyde, "Alcohol and Poetry," *American Poetry Review,* 4 (September 1975): 7-11;

Randall Jarrell, "Verse Chronicle," *Nation,* 168 (17 July 1948): 80-81;

"The Life of the Modern Poet," *Times Literary Supplement,* 23 February 1973, pp. 193-195;

J. M. Linebarger, "A Commentary on *Berryman's Sonnets,*" *John Berryman Studies,* 1 (January 1975): 13-24;

Linebarger, *John Berryman* (New York: Twayne, 1974);

Robert Lowell, "For John Berryman," *New York Review of Books,* 6 April 1972, pp. 3-4;

Lowell, "The Poetry of John Berryman," *New York Review of Books,* 28 May 1964, pp. 2-3;

William J. Martz, *John Berryman* (Minneapolis: University of Minnesota Press, 1969);

Edward Mendelson, "How to Read Berryman's *Dream Songs,*" in *American Poetry since 1960,* edited by Robert B. Shaw (Cheadle Hulme, Cheshire: Carcanet Press, 1973), pp. 29-43;

John Frederick Nims, "Homage in Measure to Mr. Berryman," review of *Homage to Mistress Bradstreet, Prairie Schooner,* 32 (Spring 1958): 1-7;

Sergio Perosa, "A Commentary on *Homage to Mistress Bradstreet,*" *John Berryman Studies,* 2 (Winter 1976): 4-25;

Adrienne Rich, "Mr. Bones, He Lives," review of *77 Dream Songs, Nation,* 198 (25 May 1964): 538, 540;

Ernest C. Stefanik, "A Cursing Glory: John Berryman's *Love & Fame,*" *Renascence,* 25 (Summer 1973): 115-127;

Valerie Trueblood, Reply to Lewis Hyde's "Alcohol and Poetry," with a rejoinder by Hyde, *American Poetry Review,* 4 (November 1975): 46-47;

William Wasserstrom, "Cagey John: Berryman as

Medicine Man," review of *His Toy, His Dream, His Rest, Centennial Review,* 12 (Summer 1968): 334-354;

Yvor Winters, "Three Poets," *Hudson Review,* 1 (Autumn 1948): 404-405.

Papers:
The John Berryman Papers are owned by University of Minnesota Libraries.

Arna Bontemps
(13 October 1902-4 June 1973)

Minrose C. Gwin
Virginia Polytechnic Institute and State University

BOOKS: *God Sends Sunday* (New York: Harcourt, Brace, 1931);

Popo and Fifina: Children of Haiti, by Bontemps and Langston Hughes (New York: Macmillan, 1932);

You Can't Pet a Possum (New York: Morrow, 1934);

Black Thunder (New York: Macmillan, 1936);

Sad-Faced Boy (Boston: Houghton Mifflin, 1937);

Drums at Dusk (New York: Macmillan, 1939; London: Harrap, 1940);

The Fast Sooner Hound, by Bontemps and Jack Conroy (Boston: Houghton Mifflin, 1942);

They Seek A City, by Bontemps and Conroy (Garden City: Doubleday, 1945); revised and enlarged as *Anyplace But Here* (New York: Hill & Wang, 1966);

We Have Tomorrow (Boston: Houghton Mifflin, 1945);

Slappy Hooper, the Wonderful Sign Painter, by Bontemps and Conroy (Boston: Houghton Mifflin, 1946);

Story of the Negro (New York: Knopf, 1948; enlarged 1955);

George Washington Carver (Evanston, Ill.: Row, Peterson, 1950);

Chariot in the Sky: A Story of the Jubilee Singers (Philadelphia: Winston, 1951);

Sam Patch, the High, Wide & Handsome Jumper, by Bontemps and Conroy (Boston: Houghton Mifflin, 1951);

The Story of George Washington Carver (New York: Grosset & Dunlap, 1954);

Lonesome Boy (Boston: Houghton Mifflin, 1955);

Arna Bontemps in August 1939, photograph by Carl Van Vechten (by permission of Joseph Solomon, the Estate of Carl Van Vechten)

Frederick Douglass: Slave, Fighter, Freeman (New York: Knopf, 1959);

100 Years of Negro Freedom (New York: Dodd, Mead, 1961);

Personals (London: Breman, 1963);

Famous Negro Athletes (New York: Dodd, Mead, 1964);

I Too Sing America, by Hughes and Bontemps (Dortmund: Verlag Lambert Lensing, 1964);

Mr. Kelso's Lion (Philadelphia: Lippincott, 1970);

Free At Last: Life of Frederick Douglass (New York: Dodd, Mead, 1971);

Young Booker: Booker T. Washington's Early Days (New York: Dodd, Mead, 1972);

The Old South: "A Summer Tragedy" and Other Stories (New York: Dodd, Mead, 1973).

PLAY PRODUCTIONS: *St. Louis Woman*, by Bontemps and Countee Cullen, New York, Martin Beck Theatre, 31 March 1946;

Free and Easy, Amsterdam, Theatre Carré, 15 December 1949.

OTHER: *Father of the Blues: An Autobiography by W. C. Handy*, edited by Bontemps (New York: Macmillan, 1941);

Golden Slippers: An Anthology of Negro Poetry for Young Readers, edited by Bontemps (New York & London: Harper, 1941);

The Poetry of the Negro, 1746-1949, edited by Bontemps and Langston Hughes (Garden City: Doubleday, 1949; revised and enlarged as *The Poetry of the Negro, 1746-1970*, Garden City: Doubleday, 1970);

The Book of Negro Folklore, edited by Bontemps and Hughes (New York: Dodd, Mead, 1958);

James Weldon Johnson, *The Autobiography of an Ex-Colored Man*, introduction by Bontemps (New York: Hill & Wang, 1960);

American Negro Poetry, edited by Bontemps (New York: Hill & Wang, 1963; revised, 1974);

"The Negro Renaissance: Jean Toomer and the Harlem Writers of the 1920's," in *Anger, and Beyond*, edited by Herbert Hill (New York: Harper & Row, 1966), pp. 20-36;

Hold Fast to Dreams: Poems Old and New, edited by Bontemps (Chicago: Follett, 1969);

Great Slave Narratives, edited, with an introduction, by Bontemps (Boston: Beacon, 1969);

Saint Louis Woman, in *Black Theater*, edited by Lindsay Patterson (New York: Dodd, Mead, 1971);

The Harlem Renaissance Remembered: Essays, edited, with a memoir, by Bontemps (New York: Dodd, Mead, 1972).

PERIODICAL PUBLICATIONS:

POETRY

"Spring Music," *Crisis*, 30 (June 1925): 93;

"Dirge," *Crisis*, 32 (May 1926): 25;

"Holiday," *Crisis*, 32 (July 1926): 121;

"Tree," *Crisis*, 34 (April 1927): 48.

FICTION

"A Summer Tragedy," *Opportunity*, 11 (June 1933): 174-177, 190;

"Barrell Staves," *New Challenge*, 1 (March 1934): 16-24.

NONFICTION

"Who Recreates Significant Moments in History," *Opportunity*, 22 (Summer 1944): 126-139;

"Two Harlems," *American Scholar*, 14 (April 1945): 167-173;

"Langston Hughes," *Ebony*, 2 (October 1946): 19-23;

"White Southern Friends of the Negro," *Negro Digest* (August 1950): 13-16;

"Buried Treasures of Negro Art," *Negro Digest* (December 1950): 17-21;

"How I Told My Child About Race," *Negro Digest* (May 1951): 80-83;

"Chesnutt Papers at Fisk," *Library Journal*, 77 (1952): 1288;

"Facing a Dilemma," *Saturday Review*, 35 (16 February 1952): 23 + ;

"Bud Blooms," *Saturday Review*, 35 (20 September 1952): 15 + ;

"Harlem Renaissance," *Saturday Review*, 36 (28 March 1953): 15-16;

"Three Portraits of the Negro," *Saturday Review*, 36 (28 March 1953): 15-16;

"New Black Renaissance," *Negro Digest* (November 1961): 52-58;

"Evolution of Our Conscience," *Saturday Review*, 44 (9 December 1961): 52-53;

"Minority's New Militant Spirit," *Saturday Review*, 45 (14 July 1962): 30;

"Harlem: the Beautiful Years: A Memoir," *Negro Digest* (January 1965): 62-65;

"Why I Returned," *Harper's*, 230 (April 1965): 176-182;

"Harlem in the Twenties," *The Crisis*, 73 (October 1966): 431-434 + ;

"Langston Hughes: He Spoke of Rivers," *Freedomways*, 8 (Spring 1968): 140-143.

"Time," wrote Arna Bontemps in his sixty-sixth year, "is not a river. Time is a pendulum." Certainly this black writer's voluminous contributions in literature and history support that theory and are informed by it. Bontemps's histories of the black experience, his biographies of notable black Americans, his novels and short stories, his children's fiction, his anthologies of works by black writers, and particularly his poetry explore the relationship between the past and present and its bearing on the inheritors of the black experience. In Bontemps's writings the assassination of Martin Luther King, Jr. in 1968 is presented as a repetition of the squelching of nineteenth-century slave uprisings. The Harlem of the 1920s echoes the primitivism and freedom of African jungles. All is of a piece. Bontemps's importance as literary artist and historian hinges upon his efforts to show black Americans that their own past is rich and various, and that their yearning for freedom, both in the past and present, is an essential common bond grounded in a proud heritage. Yet, to the white reader as well, Bontemps is an important voice—both as an American writer and as a powerful spokesman for a humanistic society. An important figure in the Harlem Renaissance, Bontemps's sense of black heritage, his artistry, and his humanistic concerns are intensely felt in the small body of poetry published between 1924 and 1931, and collected in 1963 in *Personals*. As Kenneth Burke has suggested, "we are nearest to the center of the essential Bontemps in his poetry."

There is indeed a vibrant, emotional quality in Bontemps's poetry, which may stem both from his youth and sense of self-realization found, as he put it, in being "twenty-one, sixteen months out of college, full of golden hopes and romantic dreams." The poetic intensity of these early verses comes also from the place and time. "There was something special about being young and a poet in Harlem in the middle 'twenties," wrote Bontemps in the preface to *Personals*. As part of the burgeoning sense of excitement during the Harlem Renaissance, the "New Negro" artists were setting out to redefine the black past, "to recapture this definite, though sometimes dim, quality in poetry, painting and song." Like the other writers of the Harlem Renaissance, Bontemps felt, "Through us, no less, America would regain a certain value that civilization had destroyed." Bontemps's poetry is characterized by an intoxicating gusto, a sense of excitement, of self-discovery, of release from inhibition. All of these qualities are perhaps reactions against a middle-class, fundamentalist Christian background—one with no emphasis on roots, art, or racial heritage.

Bontemps was born Arnaud Bontemps in Alexandria, Louisiana, the son of Marie Caroline Pembrooke and Paul Bismark Bontemps, a strong-willed brick mason who would eventually become a lay minister in the Seventh Day Adventist Church. After being forced off the sidewalk by two drunk white men on a Saturday night, the elder Bontemps moved his family to a Los Angeles neighborhood where, Bontemps recalled, "we were the only colored family. . . . The people next door and up and down the block were friendly and talkative, the weather was perfect, there wasn't a mud puddle anywhere, and my mother seemed to float about on the clean air." The most significant influence upon the young Bontemps may have been his exuberant great-uncle rather than his austere father. After Bontemps's mother died, he lived with his grandmother in the California countryside; and Uncle Buddy, who had also followed the family to the West Coast, became for his twelve-year-old great-nephew a repository of black culture. Despite disapproval from Bontemps's father, Uncle Buddy loved minstrel shows, dialect stories, signs, charms, and mumbo jumbo. Bontemps recalled the old man's sneering retort upon being told that there were no such things as ghosts: "That's pure nonsense. I seen one just last night. He was standing up yonder by the gate." In contrast, Bontemps's father sent his adolescent son to San Fernando Academy, a predominantly white boarding school, with the admonition, "Now don't go up there acting colored." As he grew older, Bontemps found his parents' antipathy to their own blackness echoed, as Sandra Alexander suggests, "by educators, historians, writers, and others in sympathy with the philosophy of assimilationism who he felt conspired, either consciously or unconsciously, to deprive the black man of knowledge about his cultural and historical past." His father's and great-uncle's opposing attitudes toward their racial roots made Bontemps aware of a conflict which most American blacks must face: to "embrac[e] the riches of the folk heritage," or to make a clean break with the past and all it represents. Bontemps found that integrated schools relegated black history to "two short paragraphs: a statement about jungle people in Africa and an equally brief account of the slavery issue in American history." He would devote his life to rectifying the omissions.

His careers as literary artist, historian, editor, critic, and as head librarian and public-relations director at Fisk University were all directed toward the goal of establishing a social and intellectual environment in which the Afro-American heritage, literature, and sense of self could be nurtured. Having earned a B. A. from Pacific Union College in 1923, he taught in private schools in New York as he began his writing career. His poetry began to be published in literary magazines in 1924 and he soon found recognition. His poems "Golgotha Is a Mountain" and "The return" won the Alexander Pushkin Award for Poetry offered by *Opportunity: Journal of Negro Life* in 1926 and 1927. *The Crisis* magazine awarded "Nocturne at Bethesda" a first prize in 1927.

By the early 1930s the Depression had cut drastic inroads into the Black Renaissance and into its spirit of optimism, which had buoyed Bontemps's early verse. Having married Alberta Johnson on 26 August 1926, Bontemps was now a family man with two children (they eventually had six), and to support them, he was forced to go south in 1931 to teach at Oakwood Junior College, a black Seventh Day Adventist school in Huntsville, Alabama. The college discouraged its students from developing racial awareness, and eventually Bontemps was accused by the administration of harboring subversive racial ideas and ordered to burn his books. He resigned in 1934, packed his family into an old Ford, and took them to California, much as his father had years before.

His first novel, *God Sends Sunday* (1931), was followed by two others, *Black Thunder* (1936) and *Drums at Dusk* (1939). Of these, *Black Thunder*, the fictional version of the 1800 slave rebellion led by Gabriel Prosser, is best known. The novel became, as Richard Barksdale and Keneth Kinnamon point out, "a significant 'first' in this particular genre of Black literature."

From 1935 to 1938 he taught at the Shiloh Academy in Chicago. The Caribbean flavor of some of his writing may be traced to his travel in the Caribbean, subsidized by the Julius Rosenwald fellowship for creative writing that he was granted in 1938. (He received another Rosenwald fellowship in 1942, for work on the Negro in Illinois project in Chicago.) Upon receiving a masters of library science from the University of Chicago in 1943, Bontemps was appointed head librarian at Fisk University in Nashville, Tennessee, where he remained until 1965. During this period Bontemps not only received two Guggenheim Fellowships (1949, 1954) for creative writing but also expanded his interest in black history, collecting and editing volumes of literature, folklore, and autobiography.

Throughout his career he also wrote novels and biographies for children, including *You Can't Pet a Possum* (1934), *Story of George Washington Carver* (1954) and *Lonesome Boy* (1955). During the 1940s, Bontemps wrote two plays: *St. Louis Woman*, a musical comedy adapted from *God Sends Sunday*,

with Countee Cullen (produced on Broadway in 1946), and *Free and Easy* in 1949. His introductions to anthologies often provide definitive, scholarly comments on folk materials as the foundation for the richness of black literary heritage. Volumes such as *Poetry of the Negro, 1746-1949*, edited with Langston Hughes (1949); *Book of Negro Folklore*, also edited with Hughes (1958); *American Negro Poetry*, (1963), *Great Slave Narratives* (1969), and *The Harlem Renaissance Remembered: Essays* (1972), stand as important contributions to American literature. A posthumous collection of short fiction, *The Old South*—including such poignant stories as "A Summer Tragedy," as well as Bontemps's biographical essay "Why I Returned," an account of a black man's search for his Southern roots—appeared in 1973.

In 1969 he renewed his ties with Chicago by taking a teaching position at the University of Illinois at Chicago Circle. In 1969 he became curator of the James Weldon Johnson Memorial Collection at Yale University, an important holding of original Afro-American materials from the Harlem Renaissance. By 1971 he was back at Fisk as writer-in-residence, remaining there until his death on 4 June 1973.

Bontemps's fiction, histories, and anthologies have been widely recognized for their influence in increasing interest in black literature and culture. *Personals*, however, his collection of twenty-three poems of the 1920s, remains a moving artistic record of a young black artist who was exercising his imagination for the first time in the milieu of Harlem's turbulent literary and social excitement. In later years Bontemps inscribed Jack Conroy's copy of the book as "these vestiges of the Twenties."

Personals is an apt title for the slender volume. The poems radiate what Charles Nichols has called "an almost Wordsworthian sense of wonder—the freedom, joy and love of a beholden soul in the face of the awesome infinity of the universe." In these poems of his youth, Bontemps's is a personal wonder—that of a young man whose spirit is surging with the enormous possibilities of self-definition and self-acceptance through art. In his introduction to *American Negro Poetry* (1963) Bontemps commented on the importance of the Harlem artistic experience, particularly the significance of its poetry: "In the Harlem Renaissance of the twenties poetry led the way for the other arts. It touched off the awakening that brought novelists, painters, sculptors, dancers, dramatists, and scholars of many kinds to the notice of a nation that had

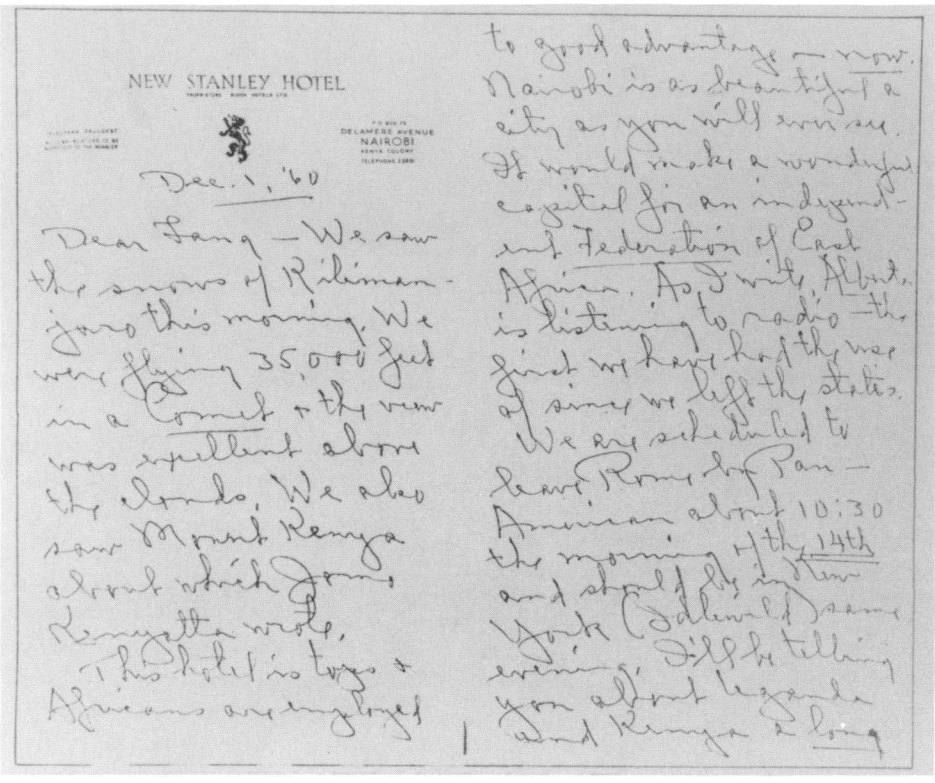

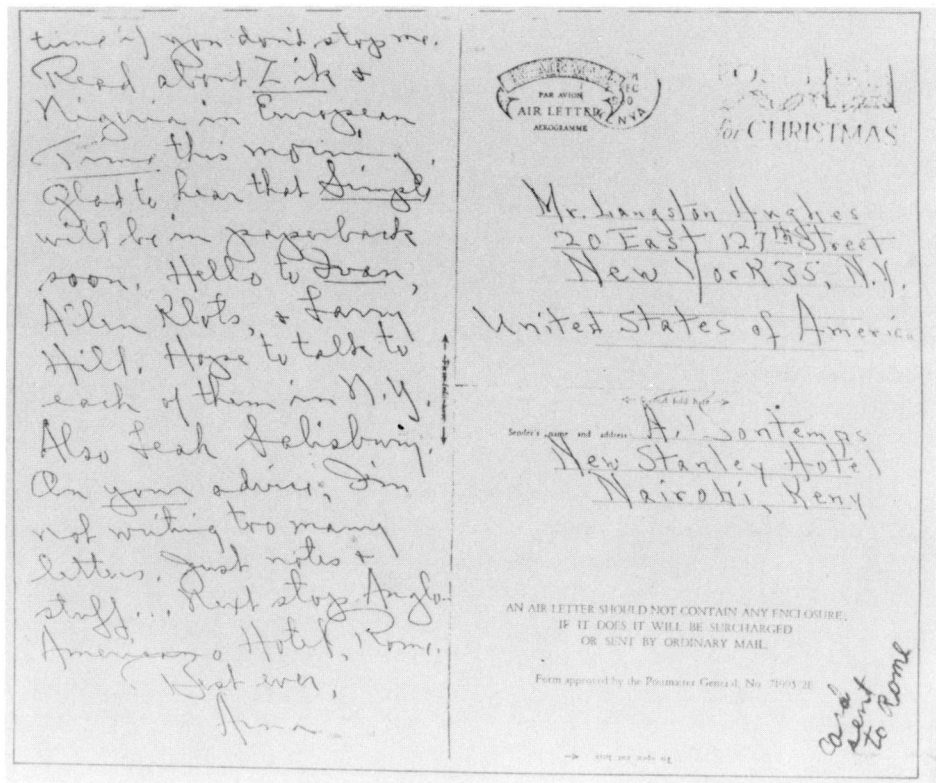

A letter to Langston Hughes written while Bontemps was on a speaking tour in Uganda and Kenya (by permission of Alberta Bontemps, the Estate of Arna Bontemps; courtesy of the James Weldon Johnson Collection, Beinecke Library, Yale University)

nearly forgotten about the gifts of its Negro people."

Certainly Bontemps was surrounded with poetry and poets during this period. A chorus of new voices led by Claude McKay, Jean Toomer, Langston Hughes, and Countee Cullen made the decade a golden age of black art. In 1922 McKay's *Harlem Shadows* became the first collection of new poems by a black published by a major American publisher in a decade. A summer-school student at UCLA at the time, Bontemps picked up a copy of the McKay poems in the public library on the way home, read it on the "yellow Pacific Electric streetcar that day and a second time that night, then began telling everybody I knew about it." Bontemps was conscious of such McKay poems as "If We Must Die" and "Harlem Dancer" when he headed for New York two years later.

In New York Bontemps quickly became fast friends with Hughes, Cullen, and other black artists. Hughes's 1926 manifesto on black art became Bontemps's as well: "We younger Negro artists who create now intend to express our individual dark skinned selves without fear or shame. If white people are pleased we are glad. If they are not, it doesn't matter. We know we are beautiful. And ugly too. The tom-tom cries and the tom-tom laughs. If colored people are pleased we are glad. If they are not, their displeasure doesn't matter either. We built our temples for tomorrow, strong as we know how, and we stand on the top of the mountain free from within ourselves."

In his prize-winning poem, "The return," published a year later, Bontemps renders the throb of the tom-tom with great lyrical intensity, and, like many of Bontemps's poems, "The return" synthesizes racial consciousness and personal emotion:

> Darkness brings the jungle to our room:
> the throb of rain is the throb of muffled drums.
> ....
> ... This is a night of love
> retained from those lost nights our fathers slept
> in huts; this is a night that must not die.

In this poem also is a theme which reappears in all of Bontemps's work—the attempt to return to original sources, to move back in time to unleash racial memory: "Let us go back and search the tangled dream." While the poet knows the necessity of such an attempt, and he also acknowledges that, though such a return in consciousness may be ultimately sustaining, only a moment of intense insight is possible before the vision flees in the gray light of reality: "Our walls close about us we lie and listen/to the noise of the street, the storm and the driven birds." In "Reconnaissance" as well, the young poet looks to the past for revelation, embarking on "the starry descent into time," where again the ultimate source is found in a return to the natural rhythms of the jungle:

> Alone with the shore and the harbor,
> the stems of the cocoanut trees,
> the fronds of silence and hushed music,
> we cried for the new revelation
> and waited for the miracles to rise.

The young Bontemps expresses personal anguish in such poems as "Homing" and "My heart has known its winter." Both poems are intense renderings of despair, alienation, or loneliness. As Arthur Davis has pointed out, there is a "sad, brooding quality" about the poems in *Personals*. In "Homing" loneliness seems to be the result of a strong sense of homelessness, of an inability to return to the "Sweet timber land" of one's early memories, where "strong black men/hew the heavy log!" The poet asks,

> must I always be
> a wild bird
> riding the wind
> and screaming bitterly?

In "My heart has known its winter," personal emotion is hidden from the external world so that "men will never think this wilderness/was barren once when grass is over all."

Though during his Harlem period Bontemps was concerned with primitivism as a means through which the "New Negro" could recapture "a certain value that civilization had destroyed," his poems also reflect the traditional Christianity of his youth. In "Gethsemane," he uses the religious implications of the title as a framework for the expression of personal despair; in the garden of his poem,

> A tree bent down and dew dropped from its hair.
> ....
> I stretched full-length upon the grass and there
> I said your name but silence answered me.

Uncharacteristically, "Miracles" is uplifting, as if biblical wonders are possible in the presence of love on a spring day:

> A jug of water in the sun
> will easy turn to wine

if love is stopping at the well
and love's brown arms entwine.

Yet in "Golgotha is a mountain," Bontemps links Christ's agony to the suffering of blacks everywhere. African blacks dig gold and precious stones in mountains which "should be ours." Mountains themselves become sinister smothering threats, which "get big in time and people forget/what started them at first." The inability of traditional Christianity to make the suffering of the black race meaningful occupies Bontemps in "Nocturne at Bethesda": "This ancient pool that healed/a host of bearded Jews is now lifeless and powerless." Now "no Saviour comes/with healing in His hands." Blacks can find no solace under heaven:

The golden days are gone. Why do we wait
so long upon the marble steps, blood
falling from our open wounds? And why
do our black faces search the empty sky?

Again Bontemps's answer lies in the power of racial memory:

I may pass through centuries of death
with quiet eyes, but I'll remember still
a jungle tree with burning scarlet birds.
There is something I have forgotten, some precious
    thing.
I shall be seeking ornaments of ivory,
I shall be dying for a jungle fruit.

In "Nocturne at Bethesda" and in other poems as well, Bontemps joins McKay, Cullen, Hughes, Hurston, and others in creating the archetypal black consciousness as a suffering but indomitable self. This black self becomes a symbol of endurance in the face of the dark despair of the slavery years, which is so graphically described in Bontemps's "Southern mansion" as echoing the "chains of bondmen dragging on the ground." It is this black self, the self that Bontemps and other black artists of the Harlem awakening were artistically growing toward, which gives many of Bontemps's poems their strength and resonance and makes *Personals* a significant reflection of the growth of black American literature during the 1920s. In much of his poetry, Bontemps links the black self to the cycle of the seasons and a closeness to natural rhythms. "A black man talks of reaping," the last poem in this collection, moves slowly and powerfully to the conclusion that it is unnatural and disastrous for human beings not to reap what they themselves sow. The persona of the poem rep-

Arna Bontemps (Gale International Portrait Gallery)

resents the black race forever planting but never reaping. Just as Cullen's "From the Dark Tower" advises the white world that blacks "shall not always plant while others reap," and Hughes threatens that continual deferral of dreams may result in explosion, Bontemps ends "A black man talks of reaping" with an implied threat:

Yet what I sowed and what the orchard yields
my brother's sons are gathering stalk and root;
small wonder then my children glean in fields
they have not sown, and feed on bitter fruit.

Yet, on the whole, Bontemps's poems speak more about the persistent will of blacks to endure to a better day. "The day-breakers" reflects black strength and determination not "to waste the life" yet also an insistence upon acknowledgment: "Yet would we die as some have done:/beating a way for the rising sun."

Surely Bontemps's importance as a poet lies in his own "beating a way for the rising sun" of black art. Though he accomplished much as librarian, historian, editor, critic, and novelist, his poetry gives him a significant place in the awakening of the black literary consciousness—the Harlem Renaissance. Still his poetry speaks with lyrical intensity to listeners of all races. It speaks of the search for heritage, for love, and for fairness, certainly themes which evoke powerful and universal responses. It is the power and universality of his poetry, as well as his other valuable contributions to black literature and history, which support the growing critical realization recently articulated by R. Baxter Miller: "Bontemps deserves more appreciation."

Letters:

Arna Bontemps-Langston Hughes Letters, 1925-1967, edited by Charles Nichols (New York: Dodd, Mead, 1980).

Bibliographies:

James A. Page, *Selected Black American Authors: An Illustrated Bio-Bibliography* (Boston: G. K. Hall, 1977), p. 19;

Robert E. Fleming, *James Weldon Johnson and Arna Wendell Bontemps: A Reference Guide* (Boston: G. K. Hall, 1978).

References:

Sandra Carlton Alexander, "The Achievement of Arna Bontemps," Ph. D. dissertation, University of Pittsburgh, 1976;

Richard Barksdale and Keneth Kinnamon, eds., *Black Writers in America* (New York: Macmillan, 1972), pp. 628-630;

Sterling Brown, *The Negro in American Fiction* (Washington, D. C.: The Associates in Negro Folk Education, 1937), pp. 74-75;

Jack Conroy, "Memories of Arna Bontemps, Friend and Collaborator," *American Libraries,* 5 (December 1974): 602-606;

Arthur P. Davis, "Arna Bontemps," in *From the Dark Tower: Afro-American Writers, 1900-1960* (Washington, D. C.: Howard University Press, 1974), pp. 83-89;

R. Baxter Miller, Review of *Arna Bontemps-Langston Hughes Letters, 1925-1967, Black American Literature Forum,* 15 (Fall 1981): 113-116;

Eugene B. Redmond, "Minor, or Second-Echelon, Poets of the Renaissance," in his *Drumvoices: The Mission of Afro-American Poetry* (Garden City: Doubleday, 1976), pp. 197-200;

Roger Whitlow, *Black American Literature: A Critical History* (Totowa, N. J.: Littlefield, Adams, 1974), pp. 100-103.

Papers:

Several oral history audiotapes, interviews, correspondence, photographs, and manuscripts are located in the Fisk University Library Special Collections. The Bontemps-Hughes letters are located in the James Weldon Johnson Collection at Yale University.

Kay Boyle

(19 February 1902-   )

Joanne McCarthy
Tacoma Community College

See also the Boyle entries in *DLB 4, American Writers in Paris, 1920-1939,* and *DLB 9, American Novelists, 1910-1945.*

BOOKS: *Short Stories* (Paris: Black Sun Press, 1929);

Wedding Day and Other Stories (New York: Cape & Smith, 1930; London: Pharos Editions, 1932);

Plagued by the Nightingale (New York: Cape & Smith, 1931; London & Toronto: Cape, 1931);

Landscape for Wyn Henderson (London: Curwen Press, 1931);

A Statement (New York: Modern Editions Press, 1932);

Year Before Last (London: Faber & Faber, 1932; New York: Harrison Smith, 1932);

The First Lover and Other Stories (New York: Smith & Haas, 1933; London: Faber & Faber, 1937);

Gentlemen, I Address You Privately (New York: Smith & Haas, 1933; London: Faber & Faber, 1934);

Kay Boyle, 1930

My Next Bride (New York: Harcourt, Brace, 1934; London: Faber & Faber, 1935);

The White Horses of Vienna and Other Stories (New York: Harcourt, Brace, 1936; London: Faber & Faber, 1937);

Death of a Man (London: Faber & Faber, 1936; New York: Harcourt, Brace, 1936);

Monday Night (New York: Harcourt, Brace, 1938; London: Faber & Faber, 1938);

A Glad Day (Norfolk, Conn.: New Directions, 1938);

The Youngest Camel (Boston: Little, Brown, 1939; London: Faber & Faber, 1939);

The Crazy Hunter and Other Stories (London: Faber & Faber, 1940); republished as *The Crazy Hunter: Three Short Novels* (New York: Harcourt, Brace, 1940);

Primer For Combat (New York: Simon & Schuster, 1942; London: Faber & Faber, 1943);

Avalanche (New York: Simon & Schuster, 1944; London: Faber & Faber, 1944);

American Citizen Naturalized In Leadville, Colorado (New York: Simon & Schuster, 1944);

A Frenchman Must Die (New York: Simon & Schuster, 1946; London: Faber & Faber, 1946);

Thirty Stories (New York: Simon & Schuster, 1946; London: Faber & Faber, 1948);

1939 (New York: Simon & Schuster, 1948; London: Faber & Faber, 1948);

His Human Majesty (New York, London & Toronto: Whittlesey House/McGraw-Hill, 1949; London: Faber & Faber, 1950);

The Smoking Mountain: Stories of Postwar Germany (New York, London & Toronto: McGraw-Hill, 1951; London: Faber & Faber, 1952);

The Seagull on the Step (New York: Knopf, 1955; London: Faber & Faber, 1955);

Three Short Novels (Boston: Beacon, 1958);

The Youngest Camel Reconsidered and Rewritten (New York: Harper, 1959; London: Faber & Faber, 1960);

Generation Without Farewell (New York: Knopf, 1960; London: Faber & Faber, 1960);

Collected Poems (New York: Knopf, 1962);

Breaking the Silence: Why a Mother Tells Her Son About the Nazi Era (New York: Institute of Human Relations Press, American Jewish Committee, 1962);

Nothing Ever Breaks Except the Heart (Garden City: Doubleday, 1966);

Pinky, the Cat Who Liked to Sleep (New York: Crowell-Collier/London: Collier-Macmillan, 1966);

Pinky in Persia (New York: Crowell-Collier, 1968);

Being Geniuses Together, 1920-1930, by Robert McAlmon, revised with supplementary chapters by Boyle (Garden City: Doubleday, 1968; London: Joseph, 1970);

Testament For My Students and Other Poems (Garden City: Doubleday, 1970);

The Long Walk at San Francisco State and Other Essays (New York: Grove, 1970);

The Underground Woman (Garden City: Doubleday, 1975);

Fifty Stories (Garden City: Doubleday, 1980);

Words That Must Somehow Be Said: The Selected Essays of Kay Boyle, 1927-1983 (Berkeley: North Point Press, 1985).

OTHER: Gladys Palmer Brooke, *Relations & Complications, Being the Recollections of H. H. The Dayang Muda of Sarawak,* ghostwritten by Boyle (London: John Lane/Bodley Head, 1929);

Ernest Walsh, *Poems and Sonnets,* anonymously edited by Boyle (New York: Harcourt, Brace, 1934);

365 Days, edited by Boyle, Laurence Vail, and Nina Conarain (London: Cape, 1936; New York: Harcourt, Brace, 1936);

Bettina Bedwell, *Yellow Dust,* ghostwritten by Boyle (London: Hurst & Blackett, 1937);

Fourteen of Them, includes a memorial chapter on Anthony John Rizzi by Boyle (New York & Toronto: Farrar & Rinehart, 1944);

The Autobiography of Emanuel Carnevali, compiled, with a preface, by Boyle (New York: Horizon Press, 1967);

Enough of Dying! Voices for Peace, edited by Boyle and Justine Van Gundy, with an introduction and three selections by Boyle (New York: Laurel, 1972);

"Report from Lock-Up," in *Four Visions of America,* by Boyle, Erica Jong, Thomas Sanchez, and Henry Miller (Santa Barbara: Capra Press, 1977).

TRANSLATIONS: Joseph Delteil, *Don Juan* (New York: Cape & Smith, 1931);

René Crevel, *Mr. Knife, Miss Fork* (Paris: Black Sun, 1931);

Raymond Radiguet, *The Devil in the Flesh* (Paris: Crosby Continental Editions/New York: Harrison Smith, 1932; London: Grey Walls Press, 1949).

PERIODICAL PUBLICATIONS: "Monody to the Sound of Zithers," *Poetry,* 21 (December 1922): 125;

"Morning," *Broom,* 4 (January 1923): 121-122;

"Old Burden," *Forum,* 69 (January 1923): 1097;

"Summer," *This Quarter,* 1 (Spring 1925): 40-44;

"Harbor Song," *Poetry,* 25 (February 1925): 252-253;

"Depart," "To a Seaman Dead on Land," and "Portrait," *Poetry,* 29 (February 1927): 250-251;

"To America," "For an American," "O This Is Not Spring," and "Carnival 1927," *This Quarter,* 3 (Spring 1927): 108-117;

"A Sad Poem," *transition,* no. 10 (January 1928): 109;

"Career," *Nation,* 132 (15 April 1931): 414;

"Flight of Fish," *Nation,* 137 (16 August 1933): 190;

"Flying Foxes and Others," *Nation,* 137 (18 October 1933): 444.

Kay Boyle's poetry is often relegated to a minor footnote in her distinguished literary career, for she is better known for her fiction, which includes fourteen novels and ten short story collections. Two of her stories, "The White Horses of Vienna" and "Defeat," were named O. Henry Memorial Award winners in 1935 and 1941. However, as she told a 1964 interviewer, "I started out

as a poet and I wrote many, many volumes of poetry when I was a child." Her first published work was poetry. She adds that "William Carlos Williams, who was one of my very dearest friends, got very angry if anyone called me a prose writer. He always referred to me as a poet, and he said that it was just by mistake I had written prose."

The daughter of Howard and Katherine Evans Boyle, Kay Boyle was born into an affluent family in St. Paul, Minnesota, but spent her early years traveling in Europe and the United States, with homes in Philadelphia, Atlantic City, the Poconos, and Cincinnati. She had little formal education; though she studied briefly at Miss Shipley's School in Bryn Mawr, Pennsylvania, she was for the most part tutored by her mother, who imparted to her a lasting and passionate love of literature, music, and social justice. In *Being Geniuses Together* (1968), Boyle writes: "Because of my mother, who gave me definitions, I knew what I was committed to in life; because of my father and my grandfather, who offered statements instead of revelations, I knew what I was against." She dedicated her first published novel, *Plagued by the Nightingale* (1931), to her mother "and her undying flame."

In 1916 the family moved to Cincinnati, where Boyle studied violin at the Cincinnati Conservatory of Music (and became concertmeister). She attended Ohio Mechanics Institute for two years in 1918-1920, hoping to become an architect; then for more than a year she worked as a switchboard operator and cashier in her father's office while attending secretarial school at night. In 1922 she went to New York City, taking with her a packet of poems in a black oilskin briefcase. Her sister Joan, a designer at *Vogue,* managed to place her as a secretary to fashion writer Margery Welles. Boyle was joined by Richard Brault, a young French engineer whom she had met in Cincinnati and who had just graduated from the University of Cincinnati. After they were married at city hall on 24 June 1922 Brault began work as a meter inspector for the New York electric company and Boyle found a job closer to her heart, in the offices of *Broom* magazine.

Broom, which Boyle called "probably the handsomest and arty-est of any literary publication of its time," was edited from Europe by Harold Loeb (the model for Robert Cohn in Ernest Hemingway's 1926 novel, *The Sun Also Rises*). Australian poet Lola Ridge headed its New York office, and became the second major influence on Boyle, who writes: "Her work expressed a fiery awareness of social injustice. . . . Lola's causes became mine, and when I wrote my poems now I borrowed from her conscience and her poetic vocabulary." Through Ridge's weekly open houses at *Broom,* Boyle met such literary figures as Marianne Moore, Elinor Wylie, Edwin Arlington Robinson, and William Carlos Williams. Later she was to remember: "If I was certain of anything in life then it was that everyone who wrote possessed a singular piece of knowledge from which I had been excluded. I believed that everyone—and writers in particular—had been given information . . . which endowed them with their marvelous authority." Yet, despite her deferential view of more-established writers, Boyle was beginning to have her own poems published. "Monody to the Sound of Zithers" appeared in a 1922 issue of *Poetry* and "Morning" was published in the January 1923 issue of *Broom.*

In June 1923 the Braults left New York with borrowed money to spend the summer with his family in Brittany. Boyle planned to begin a novel and to finance their way home with a publisher's advance. Instead, Boyle earned nothing from her writing, the meeting with Brault's conservative family was disastrous, and after a miserable summer his sister gave them enough money to get to Paris so that he might find work. There Boyle made her first real contact with American expatriates through Loeb, who introduced her to poet and publisher, Robert McAlmon, who became a lifelong friend. Many years later Boyle revised his memoirs, *Being Geniuses Together: 1920-1930,* adding chapters on her own life.

The stay in Paris was brief. Brault found a job in Le Havre, and in spring 1924 was transferred to Harfleur. On the surface Boyle's life appeared very domestic, although she did not stop writing. She had finished one novel (but the manuscript was later lost), had begun a second and a third, and continued to publish poetry.

In 1925 Ernest Walsh, a young Irish-American expatriate, poet, and editor, who had seen Boyle's work in *Broom* and *Poetry,* invited her to contribute to the first issue of *This Quarter,* which he would publish with Ethel Moorhead. The issue, dedicated to Ezra Pound, featured the work of McAlmon, William Carlos Williams, Gertrude Stein, Hemingway, and James Joyce. When Boyle became seriously ill with what was suspected to be tuberculosis in February 1926, it seemed imperative that she go to the south of France. Walsh and Moorhead welcomed her to their villa at Grasse, where after regaining her health she helped to edit *This Quarter* and fell in love with Walsh.

Walsh was ill with tuberculosis, although he joked that he was good for another five years, but his condition became critical in September 1926, and he was finally taken to a Monte Carlo hospital, where he died on 16 October 1926. Boyle stayed on in Nice until after she gave birth to Walsh's daughter, Sharon, and then in April 1927 she returned to Brault, who had refused to divorce her and was by then working in England. At this time she wrote several moving poems (later collected in *A Glad Day,* 1938) inspired by Walsh's death: "To America," "For an American," "And Winter," "O This Is Not Spring," and "Carnival 1927."

While Boyle was still in the south of France, Eugene Jolas sent her a telegram from Paris, asking her to contribute to a new magazine, *transition,* which he and Elliot Paul would edit. Nearly all of the writing Boyle had published from 1927 until 1929 appeared in the pages of this influential little magazine. In spring 1928, her marriage effectively over, Boyle went to Paris at the urging of English poet Archibald Craig, who arranged for her to help his sister, the Dayang Muda of Sarawak, write her memoirs. Together Boyle and Craig enthusiastically planned a yearbook of "living poetry," an anthology which, although they advertised it, was never published. (McAlmon, who did not share Boyle's enthusiasm for the surrealist writing published in *transition,* ridiculed their proposal in a Paris bar, jerking the announcement off the wall and shredding it. Boyle retorted by throwing a beer stein at him.)

As her friend Caresse Crosby described her in Paris, her appearance was striking: "Kay is built like a blade—to see her clearly you must look at her from one side and then from the other; both are exciting." She indulged her passion for large earrings, and walked the streets of Paris in a tight black dress, a red scarf wound dramatically around her shoulders, her eyes smeared with burnt cork because she could not afford makeup. In Paris she met most of the celebrated figures of the time, including Joyce, Stein, and Raymond Duncan.

After she completed the Dayang Muda's memoirs, Boyle joined Duncan's pseudo-Greek colony and worked in his Paris shop, selling hand-woven rugs and tunics. Eventually she became disenchanted with Duncan and tried to leave, but the colony would not allow her to take her daughter Sharon. McAlmon engineered their escape in December 1928 to the country home of Harry and Caresse Crosby. A fictionalized description of Duncan's colony and her escape to the Crosby's house appears in Boyle's novel *My Next Bride* (1934).

It is interesting to note that during her stay

The Countess of Polignac, Laurence Vail, Kay Boyle, Hart Crane, and Caresse Crosby, 1929

in Paris Boyle became fast friends with two very different, very influential men in the world of literature—McAlmon and Eugene Jolas. McAlmon had the reputation of being willing to do anything to help other writers, but he had strong beliefs about the nature of art and, Boyle writes, an "almost pathological mistrust of the subconscious." One of her poems, "Dedicated to Guy Urquhart," was actually written for McAlmon, and suggests the complexity of this man, whom she describes elsewhere as "coldly and bitterly skeptical of contemporary values." (Urquhart was a pseudonym under which McAlmon once submitted some poems to *transition* to avoid the prejudice against his name and views held by the *transition* group. The poems were published, though the same issue also contained two jingles denigrating McAlmon.)

Jolas was familiar with German and French poetry and psychology, and, in Boyle's words, fascinated by the "graphing of the night-mind and his concept of it as a marvelously unexplored territory." When Jolas published his manifesto, "Rev-

olution of the Word," in the June 1929 issue of *transition,* its signers included Boyle, the Crosbys, Hart Crane, and American artist and poet Laurence Vail. This treatise declared that a revolution in language had in fact occurred, that the writer had "the right to use words of his own fashioning and to disregard existing grammatical and syntactical laws," and concluded emphatically: "The writer expresses. He does not communicate. The plain reader be damned." Boyle later declared, "Our revolution . . . was against all literary pretentiousness, against weary, flowery rhetoric, against all the outworn literary conventions." This kind of experimentation, strongly influenced by Walsh, as well as Jolas and other *transition* writers, is evident in Boyle's *Short Stories* (1929), published in Paris by the Crosbys' Black Sun Press; *Wedding Day and Other Stories* (1930); and *A Glad Day* (1938), her first book of poems.

Having acquired a divorce from Brault, Boyle married Laurence Vail on 2 April 1932 and had three daughters by him. The family lived in southern France and Austria, and later in the French Alps. In 1934 Boyle received a Guggenheim Fellowship to work on an epic poem on flight (still unfinished).

The title poem of *A Glad Day,* rich with lush sounds and images, alternates accentual poetry with the language of the prose poem:

> Here people and stock and vegetation breathed
> air not rarer but laid the nostril wide like
> silver rings set one upon another in. Dark
> was the day the flock came close for comfort
> asking sirup to soothe devouring shears to
> travel through their fleece.

In addition to the influence of Jolas's revolution of the word, one can hear in these cadences that tendency of Boyle's which McAlmon irritably called "going Irish-twilighty." In other poems Boyle continues to experiment with language close to stream of consciousness. Her lyric poems on the death of Walsh are also included in the volume. The book was politely received, although Reuel Denney, writing in *Poetry,* called it "symbolist melodrama."

In the late 1930s Boyle met Joseph von Franckenstein, an Austrian baron who had resisted the Nazi takeover of his country. A scholar of classical languages and culture, he tutored the Vail children. When the family fled France in August 1941, he also came to the United States. Boyle married him in 1943 after her divorce from Vail; they had a daughter and a son. Franckenstein became an American citizen, trained in Colorado, and returned to France as an OSS officer. He is the central figure in Boyle's long poem, *American Citizen Naturalized in Leadville, Colorado* (1944), but the poem's success depends too much upon the reader's knowing that fact. Without such a key, the poem becomes cryptic and didactic. Boyle's meditation on war and life is earnest but disappointing, although she has treated similar themes with great effectiveness in her fiction.

After World War II, Boyle returned tò Europe as a foreign correspondent for the *New Yorker,* living with her husband in occupied Germany, where he worked for the state department until 1953. During the McCarthy investigations of the 1950s, Boyle was accused of communist sympathies. In spite of her denial, she was blacklisted, and Franckenstein lost his government job. For a time she wrote and taught at various American schools, including the Thomas School in Rowayton, Connecticut. In 1958 she was named to the National Institute of Arts and Letters (and in 1978 to

the American Academy). In 1961 she received a second Guggenheim Fellowship, followed by fellowships from Wesleyan University in 1963 and Radcliffe Institute for Independent Study in 1965.

Boyle published her *Collected Poems* in 1962. In addition to previously uncollected poems, the volume includes *A Glad Day* and most of *American Citizen Naturalized in Leadville, Colorado* and is dedicated to William Carlos Williams. Some changes in Boyle's style are evident in the new poems. For example, in simple, perfect poems such as "October 1954" and "Print from a Lucite Block," she seems to be moving closer to traditional poetic forms. Still, she continues to experiment. "A Winter Fable" is an interesting work, juxtaposing a "crystal palace" in Salzburg with the ladies' room of Grand Central Station at Christmastime. The anecdote of the black woman and the cat "with the head of a male ballet dancer," trained to select "the nicest-looking lady in the place," is put into prose narrative, but the poem ends with a blowzy chorus of bag ladies, huddled together for warmth.

This collection is her best, with enough representative work to acquaint the reader with her themes, range, and frequently brilliant images. Yet critical reception was varied. Reviewing the book for the *New Republic,* David Ray dismissed it as "only a projection of the poet as sentimental woodswalker," but others were more generous. Richard Howard, writing in *Poetry,* noted that "her landscapes . . . are made into emblems of the wild heart," but deplored her "do-it-yourself punctuation, the slack and period rhythms."

Shortly after Boyle's 1963 appointment as professor of English at San Francisco State College, Franckenstein died of lung cancer. San Francisco during the 1960s was a breeding ground for unrest. In 1968 Boyle served thirty-one days in Santa Rita Prison after her second arrest during a sit-in at the Oakland Induction Center, in protest against the Vietnam draft. Typically, she was at the center of the campus upheaval in 1968-1969, her strong political idealism leading her to march with her students, who were demanding changes in the administration. She also fought to sponsor black poet Sonia Sanchez at the college. Acting upon her belief that "the writer must recognize and must accept his commitment to his times," Boyle wrote two books about this period: *The Long Walk at San Francisco State* (1970), essays detailing the 1968 student protests, and *Testament for My Students and Other Poems* (1970).

Testament for My Students and Other Poems is perhaps Boyle's most impassioned volume, but that

Janet Flanner, Berenice Abbott, Kay Boyle, and Lillian Hellman at the Rutgers University "Women and the Arts in the Twenties" conference, 8 April 1978

passion is also its chief flaw. Its concerns are primarily social and political, and the messages frequently overwhelm the poetry. When Boyle writes of human rights and political injustice, a shrill note creeps into her poetry. Her essays are under much tighter control. Her political convictions are absolutely sincere, but in this case they mar her art. *Testament for My Students and Other Poems* does contain a scattering of lyric poems that, as always, retain her strengths.

In 1980 Boyle was awarded a National Arts Endowment Fellowship for "extraordinary contribution to American contemporary literature over a lifetime of creative work." She has received honorary doctorates from Columbia College, Chicago (1971); Skidmore College (1977); and Southern Illinois University (1982). She is currently working on a history of Irish women.

In an interview Boyle once remarked that a writer needs two qualities: "an acute awareness of words, of language, . . . almost a disease in itself," and "an awareness of life, so pressing, so keen that it threatens with every instant to absorb all the time

and energy which rightly should be given by the writer to the writing itself." Kay Boyle's own writing, in poetry and prose, mirrors this conviction, as does her life.

Interview:

Charles F. Madden, ed., *Talks with Authors* (Carbondale: Southern Illinois University Press, 1968), pp. 215-236.

Bibliography:

Roberta Sharp, "A Bibliography of Works By and About Kay Boyle," *Bulletin of Bibliography & Magazine Notes*, 35 (October 1978): 180-189, 191.

Reference:

Sandra Whipple Spanier, *Kay Boyle: Artist and Activist* (Carbondale & Edwardsville: Southern Illinois University Press, forthcoming 1986).

Papers:
Most of Boyle's manuscripts and other papers are at the Morris Library, Southern Illinois University, Carbondale.

John Malcolm Brinnin
(13 September 1916-   )

Philip L. Gerber
State University of New York College at Brockport

BOOKS: *The Garden is Political* (New York: Macmillan, 1942);

The Lincoln Lyrics (Norfolk, Conn.: New Directions, 1942);

No Arch, No Triumph (New York: Knopf, 1945);

The Sorrows of Cold Stone: Poems, 1940-1950 (New York: Dodd, Mead, 1951);

Dylan Thomas in America: An Intimate Journal (Boston: Little, Brown, 1955; London: Dent, 1956);

The Third Rose: Gertrude Stein and Her World (Boston: Little, Brown, 1959; London: Weidenfeld & Nicolson, 1960);

Arthur, The Dolphin Who Didn't See Venice (Boston: Little, Brown, 1961);

Selected Poems of John Malcolm Brinnin (Boston: Little, Brown, 1963; London: Weidenfeld & Nicolson, 1963);

William Carlos Williams (Minneapolis: University of Minnesota Press, 1963);

Skin Diving in the Virgins, and Other Poems (New York: Delacorte, 1970);

The Sway of the Grand Saloon: A Social History of the North Atlantic (New York: Delacorte, 1971; London: Macmillan, 1972);

Sextet: T. S. Eliot & Truman Capote & Others (New York: Delacorte/Seymour Lawrence, 1981);

Beau Voyage: Life Aboard the Last Great Ships (New York: Congdon & Lattès, 1981).

OTHER: *Modern Poetry: American and British*, edited by Brinnin and Kimon Friar (New York: Appleton-Century-Crofts, 1951);

Emily Dickinson, edited by Brinnin (New York: Dell, 1960);

A Casebook on Dylan Thomas, edited by Brinnin (New York: Crowell, 1960);

The Modern Poets: An American-British Anthology, edited by Brinnin and Bill Read (New York: McGraw-Hill, 1963); enlarged as *Twentieth-Century Poetry (1900-1970): An American-British Anthology* (New York: McGraw-Hill, 1970).

Although he is most deservedly known for his poetry, John Malcolm Brinnin's broad range of literary activities stamps him as a man of letters. Besides producing six volumes of verse, he has earned reputations as editor, anthologist, social historian, and literary biographer.

John Malcolm Brinnin was born in Halifax, Nova Scotia, to American parents, John Thomas and Frances Malcolm Brinnin, but the family moved to Detroit when he was four years old. For a brief time he attended Wayne State University, later transferring to the University of Michigan, where he was a classmate of the young playwright Arthur Miller. By the time of his graduation in 1941 Brinnin was publishing poems regularly in periodicals and was well on the way toward a literary reputation, having won three consecutive Avery Hopwood Awards in Ann Arbor as well as, in 1939, the Jeanette Sewell Davis Prize given by *Poetry* magazine for a group of poems by a young poet. Brinnin won for his poems "Prague" and "Cadillac Square."

In 1941-1942 Brinnin studied at Harvard University and in 1942 published his first collection of verse, *The Garden is Political*, reflective in part of his coming of age during the Great Depression of the 1930s. Sharp tensions between capital and la-

John Malcolm Brinnin at Bowen's Court, Elizabeth Bowen's estate in County Cork, Ireland, 1952

bor, for instance, dominate "Cadillac Square: 1933":

> In early spring this heartlike acre shines:
> Canyoned streets, carlines
> Flow with violence of union, men
> Learn faith in fathers then;
> The butcher from the suburb and the clerk
> Hear the organizers speak
> The echoing language of the pioneer,
> And in that press they cheer
> With such a swirling and reproachless voice
> The city swims in noise;

strife on a larger scale, as the world moves toward global war, concerns the title poem of this first book:

> The whole beguiling summer burns
>
> With guilty pleasures, gaily burns,
> Waltzes and rounds before
> The glimmering imminence of guns.

The Garden is Political received enthusiastic reviews as a work of uncommon promise. Babette

Deutsch, an early champion of the younger poet, called attention to a "durable toughness" which characterized even his occasional verses: "Here is a young man aware at once of his world and of the instrument with which he calibrates it." In 1942 also, Brinnin's earlier, thirty-two-poem cycle, *The Lincoln Lyrics,* appeared in the New Directions Poet of the Month series to mixed reviews. Written entirely in four-line stanzas of blank verse, *The Lincoln Lyrics* ran the risk of monotony; Babette Deutsch found the poet to have "not quite achieved his ambitious task."

At this time Brinnin began his career as a teacher, serving first on the faculty at Vassar College (1942-1947), as a poet-in-residence at Stevens College (1947), and then as an associate professor at the University of Connecticut, Storrs (1951-1962). From 1948 to 1950 he was an associate editor with Dodd, Mead, and on three occasions (1954, 1956, and 1961) he acted as a U.S. State Department lecturer and delegate in Europe.

It was apparent to critics of Brinnin's early work that among his mentors were T. S. Eliot and W. H. Auden; his debts to them seemed obvious to reviewers of his third book, *No Arch, No Triumph*

(1945), a collection devoted to exploring the experience of the average, urban man, particularly in time of war:

> It is always there, rattling the teacups at four,
> Tilting the sea gull on his favorite perch,
> Twitting his gaudy eye. But in the town,
> Well used to it, bread is delivered as usual.

These lines from "Gunnery Practice" perhaps epitomize what F. C. Flint described as Brinnin's typically "level style, intellectualized phrasing and effects of a thoughtful speaker uttering disturbing observations calmly"; Flint compared the poem favorably to Auden's "Dover." Brinnin himself has said that he was a member by birth of "the Auden generation" and that, along with many others his age, he had necessarily to define himself vis-à-vis Auden's overpowering influence, which dominated his day as no day since has been dominated.

In *Poetry* (April 1945), Jeremy Ingalls said that Brinnin belonged "securely in the present tradition which requires of a poet an exact and lucid line operating in a manageable and analyzable form." Brinnin periodically has confirmed the "very formalist streak" in his verse: "My poetry is composed." As a signal of Brinnin's poetic direction, that interest in, and command of, form was discernible from the beginning. Although he is equally at home in the free-verse tradition which has dominated American poetry in the twentieth century, Brinnin's free verse has never pretended to a spontaneous pouring-out of emotion on the page. Rather, his free verse is much like Eliot's, always tightly controlled, explicitly cadenced, and more often than not moving to the tune of sporadic unpatterned rhymes. "I believe in technique," says Brinnin, explaining that for him technique "really amounts to knowing what possibilities are available to you." Along the way, Brinnin has experimented widely in the major lyric forms and mastered most of them. He actively enjoys revision, an essential component of the composing process, and produces fifty to a hundred versions of almost all of his poems.

As Brinnin, through his publications, defined himself as a poet, his fascination with form became increasingly evident, often expressing itself in varieties of play. For instance, his fourth collection, *The Sorrows of Cold Stone* (1951), included a sheaf of acrostic poems devoted to friends such as Mary Walker, Truman Capote, Bill Read, and Theodoros Stamos, illustrator of the volume. Brinnin began these poems not with the intent to create portraits, but merely as linguistic experiments. He hoped, he said, "to get into a subliminal stage of my mind, nonlogical, and see what would happen, using the acrostic as the key to turn it." But ultimately, Brinnin admitted to defeat in his aim, in that many of the poems did turn out to be portraits: "I simply wanted to see what would happen if some little clue were given by which my mind could range and still organize a poem that was technically tight. This was important for a short period."

Brinnin's command of form rather naturally found expression in parody as well. Aside from making their own statements, his parodies serve well to reveal the total understanding with which Brinnin comprehended the characteristic styles and techniques employed—often invented—by his contemporaries, Auden not omitted. The best of these parodies, such as "Twelve or Thirteen Ways of Looking at Wallace Stevens" and "A Thin Facade for Edith Sitwell," are often anthologized. Another parody, equally adept, begins thus:

> Marianne Moore's

> not an attitude
> but a climate—
>   native rivers
>   where light, pale but successful, spots
>   a lank destroyer stopped in a gorgeous calm,
>   or a sharklike sloop.

In 1955 the Poetry Society of America awarded Brinnin its Gold Medal for Distinguished Service to Poetry, and, following publication of his *Selected Poems* in 1963, Brinnin was awarded the Centennial Medal for Distinction in Literature by his alma mater, the University of Michigan.

Of steadily increasing significance has been Brinnin's role as a literary biographer. *Dylan Thomas in America* (1955) relates directly to Brinnin's extended service as director of the New York City YM-YWHA Poetry Center, beginning in 1949. One reason for accepting that appointment, he has said, was the opportunity it provided of inviting Dylan Thomas to read his poems in an American setting. This accomplished, Brinnin and the self-destructively alcoholic Welshman became fast friends. He found himself largely in charge of Thomas during the poet's various tours of America, and he was present when Thomas died in New York. To be forced to observe the physical and emotional disintegration Thomas underwent and yet be helpless to prevent it exhausted Brinnin him-

John Malcolm Brinnin, Dylan Thomas, and Frances Steloff at Steloff's Gotham Book Mart, 1952 (photograph © G. D. Hackett)

self, and in 1956 he resigned his directorship of the poetry center.

Some years later, Brinnin told Cleveland Amory, "For twenty years I lived a concentrated literary life. I went everywhere and knew everyone. But after Dylan's death that changed . . . I'm not a recluse, but I'm reclusive . . . I don't do any talk shows or lectures. I'm not that kind of person."

In 1970 Brinnin brought out a volume of new poems. In reviewing his first book of verse, Babette Deutsch had noted that "some of the finest passages deal with airports and travel by plane," and the title of this volume, *Skin Diving in the Virgins, and Other Poems*, is indicative of the growth of the travel poem as a major genre for Brinnin, who has become something of a professional traveler himself. Some of these verses are of a highly personal, even intimate, nature. "Letter from an Island" is a call from the heart to a loved one left behind on the mainland and sorely missed:

> You'd like the way this island seems to sail.
> I think you'd like its blowzy innocence;
> the mornings full of notices, the nights
> striated by steel bands, and the sort of scratch

> cantatas in which roosters and wild dogs
> make their concordances.

These calm and smoothly cadenced lines typify the reflective stance which has grown more and more to be a hallmark of Brinnin's verse. A representative poem in *Skin Diving in the Virgins* might find the poet removed to a sleepy tropical island, aboard an airplane en route overseas, lingering in a remote Italian hill town—anywhere far removed in time and space from the active life left behind, escaped from, or abandoned temporarily at "home." Having achieved a modicum of tranquillity at last amid the torpor of Caribbean heat, Brinnin, alone now, can contemplate the personal tragedy of Dylan Thomas's death in "Journal Entries":

> Palm trees, dreamy as giraffes,
> munch the dead air.
> My room is shuttered, small, pistachio.
> A rainy old mirror tries, but I
> have given my last interview.
> *"Let him die!"* . . . Why, asks the light bulb,
> rocking the dim room. *"Because he's dead."*

Travel stimulates consideration of events of

Brinnin and Truman Capote in Portofino, Italy, 1953 (photograph by Bill Read)

world-wide importance, as in "Dachau," which Brinnin visited sometime long after the events that produced its infamy:

> Families out from Munich—slouch hats,
> plus fours, pigtails & reptile shoes—
> come crunching the loud path.
> Their voices—gentle, almost lyrical—
> reach through my dark. *"Er ist ein Jude,"*
> a woman whispers, perhaps to a child,
> *"er weint für alle Juden."*

As his poetry attests from beginning to end, Brinnin's travels have been many and frequent; he has crossed the Atlantic more than sixty times, at first in liners great and small, later in jets. These experiences shaped the basis not only for a number of travel articles but for a most readable history of the North Atlantic steamers, *The Sway of the Grand Saloon* (1971), a volume replete with legendary names from *Great Eastern* and *Titanic* to *Normandie* and *Queen Mary*.

Recently, Brinnin has published biographical sketches of other writers, some of whom he met in connection with his post at the poetry center. Included in the volume *Sextet* (1981) are reminiscences of Truman Capote, a friend of twenty-five years, whom Brinnin met at Yaddo, the artists community in New York State, where Capote was working on *Other Voices, Other Rooms* (1948); Henri Cartier-Bresson, with whom Brinnin took an extended and ultimately disappointing collaborative journey through the United States for a proposed volume that would have combined a hundred Cartier-Bresson photographs with a text by Brinnin; Elizabeth Bowen, visited at her great country home in Ireland, Bowen's Court, while her husband, Alan Cameron, lay dying upstairs; a series of encounters during the 1950s with Edith, Osbert, and Sacheverell Sitwell, British poets, aristocrats, and idiosyncratics; Alice B. Toklas, whom he met in Paris while he worked at completing his biography of Gertrude Stein, *The Third Rose* (1959); and T. S. Eliot, whom he was able to entice into giving a reading at the New York Poetry Center because Eliot needed the money and was not allowed to take funds out of England, then still under certain wartime restrictions. Based upon journals which Brinnin began to keep in 1942, *Sextet* provides unique views into the lives of these literary figures. Hope that other volumes might follow is sustained by Brinnin's declaration that "there's plenty more where that came from."

Urbane, sophisticated, literate, witty, contemplative, formalist—any and all of these terms suit the talents of John Malcolm Brinnin, both in prose and in verse. His generally high reputation as a poet can best be summed up in the phraseology of Raymond Holden. In evaluating his achievement in 1951, Holden found Brinnin possessed of "an ear and a voice which rank him high among American poets." Brinnin's later career only serves to confirm that judgment. Currently retired from Boston University, where he began teaching in 1962, Brinnin continues his peregrinations with a relaxed agenda—Cambridge in the spring, Venice in the summer, Key West in the winter—and he continues to write, relatively free of pressures. "I'm one of those people who don't write a poem unless something urges them to do it," Brinnin says of himself. He could write a poem in a day or a poem every day, "but I've been a poet long enough to know you have to be urged from inside. You don't write a poem until there's a poem to write."

Interviews:

Cleveland Amory, "Trade Winds," *Saturday Review,* 55 (29 January 1972): 12;

Philip L. Gerber and William Heyen, "A Kind of Exorcism: A Conversation with John Malcolm Brinnin," edited by Gerber and Robert J. Gemmett, *Prairie Schooner,* 48 (Fall 1974): 201-221;

Robert Dahlin, "John Malcolm Brinnin," *Publishers Weekly,* 220 (11 December 1981): 6-7.

References:

Milton Crane, "A Violence Not Cold," review of *The Sorrows of Cold Stone, New York Times Book Review,* 22 July 1951, p. 12;

Babette Deutsch, "Of Our Own Time," review of *The Garden is Political* and *The Lincoln Lyrics, Nation,* 155 (1 August 1942): 97;

F. Cudworth Flint, "New Books of Verse," review of *No Arch, No Triumph, New York Times Book Review,* 25 February 1945, p. 10;

Raymond Holden, "Inner Echoes of Word Sounds," review of *The Sorrows of Cold Stone, Saturday Review,* 34 (29 December 1951): 10;

Jeremy Ingalls, "Scripture on Observation Hill," review of *No Arch, No Triumph, Poetry,* 66 (April 1945): 32-35;

John Frederick Nims, "Through a Gloss Darkly," review of *The Garden is Political* and *The Lincoln Lyrics, Poetry,* 61 (February 1943): 622-626.

Sterling Brown
(1 May 1901-   )

Don Wood
State University of New York at Buffalo

BOOKS: *Outline for the Study of the Poetry of American Negroes* (New York: Harcourt, Brace, 1931);

Southern Road (New York: Harcourt, Brace, 1932);

The Negro in American Fiction (Washington: Associates in Negro Folk Education, 1938);

Negro Poetry and Drama (Washington: Associates in Negro Folk Education, 1938);

The Last Ride of Wild Bill and Eleven Narrative Poems (Detroit: Broadside Press, 1975);

The Collected Poems of Sterling A. Brown, edited by Michael S. Harper (New York: Harper & Row, 1980).

OTHER: "The Negro in Washington," in *Wash-*

Sterling Brown (photograph by Roy Lewis)

ington City and Capital, Federal Writers' Project (Washington, D.C.: U.S. Government Printing Office, 1937);

The Negro in Virginia, edited by Brown, The Writers' Program (New York: Hastings House, 1940);

The Negro Caravan, Writings by American Negroes, edited by Brown, Arthur P. Davis, and Ulysses Lee (New York: Dryden Press, 1941);

"Athletics and the Arts," in *The Integration of the Negro into American Society,* Papers of the Fourteenth Annual Conference, Division of Social Sciences, Howard University, edited by E. Franklin Frazier (Washington, D.C.: Howard University Press, 1951), pp. 117-147;

Entries on Matthew Arnold, Charles Baudelaire, Emily Brontë, Robert Burns, Emily Dickinson, Ralph Waldo Emerson, Benjamin Franklin, Robert Frost, Heinrich Heine, A. E. Housman, Thomas Jefferson, Abraham Lincoln, Henry Wadsworth Longfellow, Herman Melville, *Moby-Dick,* Edgar Allan Poe, Henry David Thoreau, Mark Twain, and Walt Whitman, in *The Reader's Companion to World Literature,* edited by Lillian D. Hornstein, G. D.

Percy, and others (New York: New American Library, 1956).

PERIODICAL PUBLICATIONS: "Roland Hayes," *Opportunity,* 3 (June 1925): 173-174;
"Our Literary Audience," *Opportunity,* 7 (February 1930): 42-46;
"Negro Character As Seen by White Authors," *Journal of Negro Education,* 2 (April 1933): 179-203;
"The Negro Writer and His Publisher," *Quarterly Review of Higher Education Among Negroes,* 9 (July 1941): 7-20;
"Spirituals, Blues and Jazz—The Negro in the Lively Arts," *Tricolor,* 3 (April 1945): 62-70;
"Negro Folk Expression," *Phylon,* 11 (Autumn 1950): 318-327;
"Negro Folk Expression: Spirituals, Seculars, Ballads and Work Songs," *Phylon,* 14 (Winter 1953): 45-61;
"A Century of Negro Portraiture in American Literature," *Massachusetts Review,* 7 (Winter 1966): 73-96.

Poet, critic, scholar, teacher, folklorist, and consummate yarn-spinner, Sterling Brown has been among the most influential and, until recently, one of the most neglected black American writers of the twentieth century. Hailed by everyone from W. E. B. Du Bois to Stokely Carmichael for his contributions to Afro-American culture, Brown is perhaps best known for his depictions of rural black America in poems that are based on such folk forms as blues and spirituals and that incorporate a brilliant use of dialect. His poetic output has not been prolific. Yet, while some have pointed to what Arthur P. Davis has called his "perfectionist tendencies" as an explanation, they fail to take note of the fact that "No Hiding Place," his follow-up to his first book of poetry, *Southern Road* (1932), was rejected and was not published until his collected poems came out in 1980. Although Brown is often considered a poet of what came to be known as the Harlem Renaissance, and his poem "When de Saints Go Ma'chin' Home" did in fact win first prize in the 1927 *Opportunity* contest, his major work did not begin to appear until the 1930s, well after that movement had run its course. As Brown himself would say years later, "The New Negro is not to me a group of writers centered in Harlem during the second half of the twenties. Most of the writers were not Harlemites; much of the best writing was not about Harlem, which was . . . no more Negro America than New York is America."

Sterling Allen Brown was born in Washington, D.C., where his father, the Reverend Sterling N. Brown, was professor of religion at Howard University. Sterling A. Brown attended Dunbar High School, where he edited a school magazine and began writing poetry. In 1918 he enrolled at Williams College, was elected to Phi Beta Kappa in 1921, and graduated with a B.A. in 1922. In 1923 he took his master's degree at Harvard University. He taught successively at Virginia Seminary and College in Lynchburg (1923-1926), where he met his wife, Daisy Turnbull; at Fisk University in Nashville, Tennessee; and at Lincoln University in Missouri. It was during these years in the South that Brown came into close contact with the Afro-American folklore which would have such a profound impact upon his poetry. In 1929 he became professor of American literature at Howard University, an institution with which he has been associated for more than half a century. In addition, he has served as visiting professor at Atlanta University, New York University, the University of Minnesota, Vassar College, and the University of Illinois.

Brown's first book of poetry, *Southern Road* (1932), appeared to great acclaim. In his introduction James Weldon Johnson, who had previously dismissed dialect poetry on the grounds that it was too limited, having "only two stops—pathos and humor," saw fit to reverse his previous stance. Calling Brown's work "fine" and "unique," he pointed out that Brown's language is not the "conventionalized dialect" of the minstrel tradition, but is "the common, racy, living speech of the Negro in certain phases of *real* life." Brown is not merely a literary writer, nor is he simply transcribing folk poetry, Johnson said: "he has deepened its meanings and multiplied the implications. He has actually absorbed the spirit of his material, made it his own; and without diluting its primitive frankness and raciness, truly re-expressed it with artistry and magnified power."

Southern Road is divided into four sections. In the last Brown uses no dialect and employs the sonnet and other traditional literary forms with varying degrees of success. It is, however, as Johnson points out in his introduction, "in his poems whose sources are the folk life that he makes, be-

Sterling Brown, Dorothy Maynard, and W. E. B. Du Bois at Fisk University, 1941

yond question, a distinctive contribution to American Poetry." Unlike Langston Hughes, whose best work also relies on folk material, and with whom he is often compared, Brown focuses primarily upon rural subjects. Also, the alien-and-exile theme prevalent among the Harlem Renaissance writers is not found in Brown's work. His farmers, preachers, prisoners, prostitutes, and itinerant workers are as at home in their surroundings as they are intensely involved in the business of survival. Their tragedies and triumphs, their folly as well as their dignity, are treated with a straightforwardness which allows the lives of rural blacks to be revealed in their own words:

> Lemme be wid Casey Jones,
>   Lemme be wid Stagolee,
> Lemme be wid such like men
>   When Death takes hol' on me,
>   When Death takes hol' on me. . . .

Presented in ballad form, the "Odyssey of Big Boy" raises its wandering protagonist to the mythic proportions of the black folk heroes whose exploits are celebrated in ballads central to oral black culture. The first poem of *Southern Road,* Big Boy's song sets the stage for the rest of the collection's characters to present their own odysseys through the small towns and back roads of black America.

Brown has at times been referred to as a "protest" poet, and it is true that many of his poems deal with the injustices suffered by blacks, particularly in the South. In "Sam Smiley," for example, Brown presents the story of a World War I veteran who arrives home to find his woman in prison for having killed the child she has had by a rich white man during Sam's absence:

> The whites had taught him how to rip
>   A Nordic belly with a thrust
> Of bayonet, had taught him how
>   To transmute Nordic flesh to dust.
> . . . .
> He stopped buckdancing when he reached
>   The shanties at his journey's end;
> He found his sweetheart in the jail,
>   And took white lightning for his friend.

Upon the woman's death, Sam murders the white man and is subsequently lynched. The joyful buckdancing Sam had engaged in on his way home is given a grotesquely ironic twist in the final stanza:

> The Oaken leaves drowsed prettily,
>   The moon shone down benignly there;

> And big Sam Smiley, King Buckdancer,
>   Buckdanced on the midnight air.

The fact that the concerns of this poem remained important to Brown over the years is shown by its inclusion, under the title "Sam Yancey," in *The Last Ride of Wild Bill and Eleven Narrative Poems* (1975) more than forty years later.

The majority of Brown's poems remain free of the stridency expressed by a later generation of black poets in the 1960s. Although there is certainly an undercurrent of righteous—and justified—anger in his poetry at the outrages perpetrated upon his people, for the most part Brown presents the harsh, often tragic existence of rural blacks without overt commentary, letting the situations, and the people involved in those situations, speak for themselves. One of the major devices used by all people as a means of coping with adversity is humor, the ability to laugh at, and through, hard times and circumstances. Brown uses this device to great advantage, and it prevents his poetry from falling into mere pathos or rampant rage. An excellent example of Brown's skillful use of humor can be seen in the "Slim Greer" series of poems, in which the hero "Passed for white," although he is "no lighter/ Than a dark midnight." He keeps company with a white woman, but is discovered when a "Hill Billy" hears him "a-tinklin'/Some mo'nful blues. . .":

> The cracker listened
> An' then he spat
> An' said, "No white man
> Could play like that. . . ."

Slim narrowly escapes only to have a brief fling with employment in Arkansaw in "Slim Lands a Job?" In order to hire Slim, his prospective employer proposes to fire "a slow nigger," whereupon we see him, at work:

> A noise rung out
>   In rush a man
> Wid a tray on his head
>   An' one on each han'
>
> Wid de silver in his mouf
>   An' de soup plates in his vest
> Pullin' a red wagon
>   Wid all de rest. . . .

In "Slim in Atlanta," leaving Arkansaw and gainful employment behind, Slim discovers that:

> Down in Atlanta
>   De whitefolks got laws

For to keep all de niggers
    From laughin' outdoors.

Hope to Gawd I may die
    If I ain't speakin' truth
Make de niggers do deir laughin'
    In a telefoam booth.

This state of affairs strikes Slim as being so hilarious that he rushes past "a hundred shines" waiting their turn, thrusts out the occupant of the booth, and proceeds to laugh for four straight hours. When he comes up for air, he sees "*Three* hundred niggers there/In misery." This situation sets Slim to laughing so hard that an ambulance is sent for and "De state paid de railroad/To take him away." Despite all the laws of the land, both written and unwritten, which prevent blacks from being truly open in public view, Slim Greer is able to slip between the cracks of the white man's barriers and have a good laugh at the state's expense.

Another element which is clearly reflected in Brown's poetry is his sense of pride in the strength of his people and in their ability to survive, and sometimes even thrive, in spite of the wretched conditions in which they are forced to live. The stoicism of American blacks is amply displayed in "Memphis Blues":

Memphis go
By Flood or Flame
Nigger won't worry
All de same—
Memphis go
Memphis come back,
Ain' no skin
Off de nigger's back.
All dese cities
Ashes and rust. . . .
De win' sing sperrichals
Through deir dus'.

Through hard times and worse times the people's will to survive endures. Brown finds the source of some of that strength in his beautiful homage "Ma Rainey":

O Ma Rainey,
Sing yo' song;
Now you's back
Whah you belong,
Git way inside us,
Keep us strong. . . .

Like Casey Jones and John Henry, like Brown's own characters Big Boy and Slim Greer, Ma Rainey embodies the will of a people to keep on in spite of it all, to sing in the face of adversity, and to make the very act of survival an act of heroism. As Brown declares in "Strong Men,"

One thing they cannot prohibit—
    The strong men . . . coming on
    The strong men gittin' stronger.
Strong men. . . .
Stronger. . . .

From 1936 to 1939 Brown served as editor on Negro Affairs in the Federal Writers' Project of the WPA, was awarded a Guggenheim Fellowship for 1937-1938, and in 1939 was a staff member for the Carnegie-Myrdal Study of the Negro. Two works of criticism, *The Negro in American Fiction* and *Negro Poetry and Drama,* were published in 1938. In 1941 his landmark anthology, *The Negro Caravan,* was published. Reprinted often since its initial publication, it has been, and continues to be, an indispensable source book on black poetry from 1760 to 1941. As Julius Lester states in his introduction to the 1969 reprint of the book, "It comes as close today as it did in 1941 to being the most important single volume of black writing ever published."

Brown has been as influential as a critic as he has been as a poet. In *The Negro in American Fiction* he traces the depiction of the Negro in American fiction from his earliest appearance in the late eighteenth century to 1937. Brown's critical insights on fiction from William Hill Brown to William Faulkner are, in the words of Arthur P. Davis, "valuable because he is looking steadily at his material and seeing it whole—not through the perspective of some stereotype." *Negro Poetry and Drama* also examines both black and white authors and is thus able to show the development of black artists within the context of American writing as a whole, beginning with Jupiter Hammon and Phillis Wheatley and moving on to such writers as Vachel Lindsay and Richard Wright. Because of its broad scope, the book is more ambitious than any previous work on the subject, and it stands as a pioneering effort, which still holds a secure place in the critical history of the black in American literature.

Through the years Sterling Brown has contributed a large number of articles to such periodicals as *Opportunity,* the *Journal of Negro Education, Journal of American Folklore, Phylon, Black World,* the *Massachusetts Review,* the *Christian Register,* and the *New Republic.* His short stories and sketches have been published in *South Today,* the *Record Changer,*

Phylon, and the anthology *American Negro Short Stories* (1966). In addition to his ground-breaking essays on black literature, Brown has written on a number of other areas of black culture, particularly jazz, a subject to which he brings, in the words of Arthur P. Davis, "a deep interest and thorough knowledge." His most thorough exploration of the subject is contained in "Athletics and the Arts," an article which he contributed in 1951 to *The Integration of the Negro into American Society,* the Papers of the Fourteenth Annual Conference of the Division of Social Sciences, Howard University. In 1956 Brown contributed a number of entries for *The Reader's Companion to World Literature* on a wide array of authors ranging from Charles Baudelaire and Heinrich Heine to Matthew Arnold and Walt Whitman.

In 1975 Brown's second volume of poetry, *The Last Ride of Wild Bill and Eleven Narrative Poems,* was published. The centerpiece of the book is the long title poem, in which Wild Bill, a numbers operator, again a character of mythic dimensions, does battle with the insidious chief of police. A hero to the people, Bill is eventually defeated by the chief after a series of mock-heroic clashes and chases, and ends up in hell, where the ungodly throng gathers to greet him with shouts of "Give us the number,/Wild Bill,/Tell us/What fell!" The collection is full of "unsung" heroes such as "Crispus Attucks McKoy," "Stepson of Garvey,/Cousin of Trotter,/Godson of DuBois," who is literally torn to pieces by a mob of "Thirty-five thousand/Nordics and Alpines,/Hebrews and Gentiles," but whose soul "Goes marching on." The themes of black endurance and heroism, and the humor which both arises from and helps to alleviate the plight of blacks remain central to Brown's poetry forty-three years after the appearance of *Southern Road.* Things have not changed much in America in the intervening years. That the violence and oppression have increased is reflected in the violence which pervades the collection. The humor is darker and seems more bitter, and the heroes, with few exceptions, end up dead. But the heroism is also of a much more active and defiant variety. Unlike Slim Greer, who slips out of town, Brown's later heroes, Wild Bill, Crispus Attucks McKoy, Big Jess, and Joe Meek, all stand up proudly and bravely against the "crackers" who try to push them around. It is thus very apt that the book should republish as "Sam Yancey," the poem about Sam Smiley, the former G.I. who is lynched for actively avenging his woman's death in *Southern Road;* he finds many kindred souls in *The Last Ride of Wild Bill.*

Over the last ten years Sterling Brown has finally begun to receive the recognition he deserves. Important studies of Afro-American poetry, most notably Arthur P. Davis's *From the Dark Tower* (1974) and Jean Wagner's *Black Poets of the United States* (1973), have devoted substantial space to a study of Brown's work and his place in the history of black American letters. Indeed, Wagner's book is dedicated to "Sterling and Daisy Brown in lasting friendship and gratitude." Wagner goes on to state that Brown "would have much more competently written this book." Another indication of this overdue recognition was the publication of his collected poems in 1980, including his rejected book of poems, "No Hiding Place." As Michael S. Harper says in his preface to the collection, "Sterling Brown is a trustee of consciousness, and a national treasure; he will die with *that* hammer in his hand. His poems now belong to us all."

Sterling Brown has been recognized as a "national treasure" not only for his poetry and criticism, but also for his role as a teacher and as a living repository of the rich folk traditions which inform his poetry, and as a wellspring of information and tall tales which he is more than happy to impart to any willing listener. As Hoyt Fuller, editor of *Black World,* put it, "Settle him down, loosen his tie, provide him with some congenial and intelligent company, and turn him on. The stories flow. Out of his fascinating past, a life filled with both raw and genteel adventures in that mad, rich, vibrant world on the mellow sidelines of America, he serves up a living history of the past forty years." Brown himself is somewhat more modest in describing his role as oral historian: "I am a long talker. And I remember vividly, and I'm in two traditions. One is the tradition of Mark Twain. I remember vividly what happened and also a large number of things that did not happen, but sound good. I am the best yarnspinner at Howard University. I am the best liar at Howard University, in the Mark Twain tradition. I can outlie Ralph Bunche, who was a great liar."

A vital part of the very folk tradition which he celebrates in poetry and criticism, Sterling Brown, as Jean Wagner has written, "is not satisfied, as Hughes had been, to borrow only the forms of his verse from the storehouse of folk poetry. He imbues himself with its spirit, its practical philosophy, its humor, and its speech—which, for him, have lost none of their validity, and have permitted him to handle present-day themes with undeniable originality." Brown has managed to impart that spirit to his peers and successors, and to be a major influence upon and inspiration to at least three generations of poets, critics, and educators.

Bibliography:
Robert G. O'Meally, "An Annotated Bibliography of the Works of Sterling A. Brown," in *The Collected Poems of Sterling A. Brown,* edited by Michael S. Harper (New York: Harper & Row, 1980), pp. 243-255.

References:
Arthur P. Davis, *From the Dark Tower: Afro-American Writers 1900-1960* (Washington, D.C.: Howard University Press, 1974), pp. 125-135;

Genevieve Ekaete, "Sterling Brown, a Living Legend," *New Directions,* 1 (Winter 1974): 4-11;

Blyden Jackson and Louis D. Rubin, Jr., *Black Poetry in America* (Baton Rouge: Louisiana State University Press, 1974), pp. 58-62;

Vera M. Kutzinski, "The Distant Closeness of Dancing Doubles: Sterling Brown and William Carlos Williams," *Black American Literature Forum* (Spring 1982): 19-25;

Margaret Perry, *Silence to the Drums, A Survey of the Literature of the Harlem Renaissance* (Westport, Conn.: Greenwood Press, 1976), pp. 142-148;

Mary Strong, "Poetry Corner," *Scholastic,* 36 (29 April 1940): 25, 27;

John Edgar Tidwell and John S. Wright, introductions to "Sterling A. Brown, Afro-American Poet: A Special Section," *Callaloo: A Black South Journal of Arts and Letters* (February-May 1982): 11-105;

Jean Wagner, *Black Poets of the United States: From Paul Laurence Dunbar to Langston Hughes,* translated by Kenneth Douglas (Urbana & Chicago: University of Illinois Press, 1973);

James O. Young, *Black Writers of the Thirties* (Baton Rouge: Louisiana State University Press, 1973), pp. 151-158, 181-187.

Stanley Burnshaw

(20 June 1906-   )

Peter Revell
Westfield College, London

BOOKS: *Poems* (Pittsburgh: Folio Press, 1927);

A Short History of the Wheel Age (Pittsburgh: Folio Press, 1928);

The Great Dark Love (New York: Privately printed, 1932);

The Iron Land: A Narrative (Philadelphia: Centaur Press, 1936);

The Bridge: A Play (New York: Dryden Press, 1945);

The Revolt of the Cats in Paradise: A Children's Book for Adults (Gaylordsville, N. Y.: Crow Hill Press, 1945);

The Sunless Sea: A Novel (London: Davies, 1948; New York: Dial, 1949);

Early and Late Testament (New York: Dial, 1952);

Caged in an Animal's Mind (New York: Holt, Rinehart & Winston, 1963);

The Hero of Silence (Lugano, Switzerland: Lugano Review, 1965);

The Seamless Web: Language-Thinking, Creature-Knowledge, Art-Experience (New York: Braziller, 1970; London: Allen Lane/Penguin, 1970);

In the Terrified Radiance (New York: Braziller, 1972);

Mirages: Travel Notes in the Promised Land (Garden City: Doubleday, 1977);

The Refusers: An Epic of the Jews, a Trilogy of Novels Based on Three Heroic Lives (New York: Horizon, 1981);

My Friend, My Father (New York: Oxford University Press, 1985);

Robert Frost Himself (New York: Braziller, forthcoming, 1986).

OTHER: Van Wyck Brooks, Alfred Kreymborg, Lewis Mumford, and Paul Rosenfeld, eds.,

photograph by Chris Corpus

The American Caravan, includes poems by
  Burnshaw (New York: Macaulay, 1927);
André Spire and his Poetry: Two Essays and Forty Trans-
  lations (Philadelphia: Centaur Press, 1933);
Two New Yorkers: Fifteen lithographs, paintings, and
  etchings by Alexander Kruse with fourteen lyrics by
  Alfred Kreymborg, edited by Burnshaw (New
  York: Humphries, 1938);
The Poem Itself: Forty-Five Modern Poets in a New
  Presentation, edited, with an introduction, by
  Burnshaw (New York: Holt, Rinehart & Win-
  ston, 1960; Harmondsworth: Penguin, 1964);
Varieties of Literary Experience: Eighteen Essays in
  World Literature, edited, with a contribution,
  by Burnshaw (New York: New York Univer-
  sity Press, 1962; London: Owen, 1963);
The Modern Hebrew Poem Itself, from the beginnings to
  the present: sixty-nine poems in a new presentation,

edited by Burnshaw, T. Carmi, and Ezra
  Spicehandler (New York: Holt, Rinehart &
  Winston, 1965).

PERIODICAL PUBLICATIONS: "Turmoil in the
  Middle Ground," review of *Ideas of Order* by
  Wallace Stevens, *New Masses,* 17 (1 October
  1935): 41-42;
"Wallace Stevens and the Statue," *Sewanee Review,*
  69 (Summer 1961): 355-366.

Stanley Burnshaw is probably best known as
the author of *The Seamless Web* (1970), a study of
the ontology of poetry and a defense of its importance in human life, which James Dickey, reviewing
the book for the *New York Times Book Review* (24
September 1972), judged to be "the most exciting,
releasing book on the nature of poetry since *Bio-
graphia Literaria.*" His own work as a poet, extending over more than fifty years, is not so widely
known to the general reader. It admirably exemplifies his theoretical dicta, that poetry is "the
expression of the creator's total organism" and that
its role, when "the war against Nature has been
confidently waged and won," is to answer the question "Now that man is victorious, how shall he stay
alive?" Briefly during the 1930s, Burnshaw uneasily shared some of the Marxist assumptions that
seemed an answer to the time's dismay, but the path
he took in his search for answers to fundamental
questions has always been uniquely his own. Seen
in retrospect, his work stands apart from the fashions and movements of its time. As Louis Untermeyer remarked in his *Poetry* magazine review of
Caged in an Animal's Mind (1963), "Burnshaw derives from no one; he is his own mentor."

Burnshaw was born on 20 June 1906 in New
York City. His father had recently been appointed
director of a home for Jewish orphans. Both parents had immigrated to the United States from eastern Europe to escape the oppression of Jews that
followed the Czarist pogroms of the 1880s. Burnshaw movingly tells his father's story in "My Friend,
My Father," the third in his trilogy of novels, *The
Refusers* (1981), which is also the best source of information on his own early life, presented through
the eyes of his father. (*Commentary* magazine
praised "My Friend, My Father," predicting that it
would be widely anthologized. In fact, Oxford University Press has recently published a paperback
edition of this novel with a preface by Leon Edel.)
His mother's terrified flight, as a young girl with
her family, from the imminent danger of arrest by
the police in St. Petersburg, is the subject of Burn-

shaw's poem "House in St. Petersburg" (collected in *Caged in an Animal's Mind*), which subtly borrows the phrasing of the *Dayenu* passage in the Passover service to link terror with the cause.

America had been almost a reluctant choice of destination for Burnshaw's father, who considering himself a child of the Enlightenment, had wanted to go to France or Germany but had heeded the advice of his fellow immigrants on what he might find in these countries. In America he had flourished and eventually gained a Ph.D. in philology from Columbia University, promising an outstanding teaching career. Instead he found himself, at first almost reluctantly, serving the Jewish community in support of its destitute children.

In 1912 the family moved from New York City twenty miles north to Pleasantville, New York, where Burnshaw's father re-established the orphanage on a cottage-home basis, attracting as a result of its success, nationwide attention and a visit from President Taft. The son spent his later childhood in these rural surroundings and was, by his own account, more interested in baseball than in books, in the countryside than the classroom. Yet he intensely admired his father and over many years came to inherit his intellectual preoccupation, though with a literary and humanistic emphasis rather than the father's scholarly and humanitarian dedication. The polymath and polylinguist Stanley Burnshaw became owed a great debt to his father's early teaching.

Burnshaw enrolled as a student at Columbia University in 1924 but transferred to the University of Pittsburgh when the family moved to that city. He gained his B. A. in 1925, already intent on a career as a teacher and writer, but took a job as an apprentice advertising copywriter with the Blaw-Knox Steel Corporation in Blawnox, Pennsylvania, to support himself and to save the money for a year of graduate study in Europe. He had begun to write poetry as a student and continued to do so in his limited spare time. Some of this work was published in little magazines, such as the *Midland, Voices,* the *Echo,* and *Palms,* and in volume one of *The American Caravan* (1927), an influential anthology of avant-garde writing edited by Van Wyck Brooks, Alfred Kreymborg, Lewis Mumford, and Paul Rosenfeld. Burnshaw also started his own magazine, *Poetry Folio,* in 1926, setting the type himself, and in 1927 published his *Poems,* a slim volume of ten short poems in an edition of sixty copies, from his own Folio Press. His two years with Blaw-Knox were not congenial but his spare-time activity was important in establishing the style and direction of his life,

the interest in typography, printing, and design preparing him for his later successful career in publishing. The daily contact with the harsh realities of industrial life, even though through the eyes and mind rather than the hands, also established the attitudes toward industrial society which set the course of his life in the 1930s and informed much of his later work as a poet. His most ambitious project during these years was a book-length series of poems in which he attempted to work out these attitudes and their relation to his talent as a poet; five sections of the poem sequence were accepted for publication in the first volume of *The American Caravan* anthology. With this mark of recognition from a major avant-garde publication to encourage him, he set off for Europe in May 1927.

Though he attended classes at the University of Poitiers and later at the Sorbonne, probably the most important event of Burnshaw's year in Europe was his meeting with the French poet André Spire. The results appeared in 1933, when *André Spire and his Poetry,* Burnshaw's first full-length volume, was published. The two essays and forty translations that make up the book provide impressive evidence of the range and scholarly grasp of his knowledge of European literature, while some of his comments on Spire in the introductory essay indicate the extent of the French poet's influence on him.

In his own poetry, Burnshaw has employed traditional forms, including the sonnet, blank verse, stanzaic poems, and couplets, but his most characteristic mode is what Robert Frost called "loose iambic," utilizing some rhymes and half-rhymes and an intermittent pattern of stresses, held together by its dramatic impulse. This allegiance to form is different from the structure of Spire's vers libre, but Burnshaw's poems, like Spire's, are frequently constructed on a series of rhetorical questions or invocations. They have the same quality of eloquent speech and their strong verbal line is sustained through an often sinewy syntax which gives the poem as a whole a kind of fibered strength. For Burnshaw the poem is above all a living structure.

For Spire, Burnshaw further comments, "Nature is inevitably 'the enemy' and in a poem by that title, [he], like Robert Frost and very few other poets, recognizes that the law in nature is war." The central argument of all Burnshaw's work concerns man's relation with nature, his struggle to master it through a relentlessly developing technology and his fatal reluctance to admit that he is part of it. Mind and matter are one, Burnshaw asserts in *The Seamless Web* for " ' The body makes the mind'—

what else could make it? Yet men have been splitting themselves into two for thousands of years." The germ of this belief can be seen, with a somewhat Lawrentian coloration, in his second small and privately printed collection of nine poems, *The Great Dark Love* (1932). Though most of these poems have been included in later and more accessible collections they have never reappeared as a group, regrettably, since the philosophical impulse behind them is significant as a stage in Burnshaw's work. In a prose note at the end of the book he explains that his "vision of existence" is: "founded on the belief that life upon earth is one phase of a plane of infinite existence having neither beginning nor end in time. The divine principle of this present phase is a profound harmony born of the surface conflicts of the natural law. . . . In its early condition the natural earth-world lived by means of a non-intellectual consciousness—a blood-stream consciousness common to all living creatures, from which state the human being, for one, diverged into an intellectual consciousness."

At this period, however, Burnshaw was becoming increasingly preoccupied with the surface conflicts of the struggle between labor and capitalism in America, though he never lost sight of the deeper issues. On returning from Europe in 1928 he had found a post as advertising manager with the Hecht Company in New York, which left him enough time and energy for some literary journalism, as a contributing editor for *Modern Quarterly,* and to continue work on the poem sequence begun in Pittsburgh. He also continued his graduate study at New York University and then, against all advice, resigned from the Hecht Company in 1932 to begin a year's postgraduate work at Cornell, taking his master's degree the following year. He married his second wife, Madeline, in 1934 and, unable to find an academic teaching position, looked to derive his income from journalism. What he had witnessed of human misery and degradation in Pittsburgh, together with the rapid economic decline as the Depression took hold caused his outlook to take an increasingly political direction. After part-time work for the New York leftist weekly, the *New Masses,* he took up a full-time post with them in 1933, as drama critic and occasional contributor of articles, poems, and reviews, which he held until 1936. His review of Wallace Stevens's *Ideas of Order* (1935), entitled "Turmoil in the Middle Ground," in which he charged Stevens with confusion, contradiction, and irrelevance in face of the social disasters of the time, prompted Stevens's poetical reply, "Mr. Burnshaw and the Statue." The

dispute remains a minor topic in Stevens criticism, to which Burnshaw himself contributed some twenty-five years later in a retrospective essay published in the *Sewanee Review* (Summer 1961).

His departure from *New Masses* ironically almost coincided with the publication of *The Iron Land* (1936), his long poem sequence on the Pittsburgh years, which he describes in *The Refusers* (1981)—using his father's words—as a "Communist-Conservationist epic." It was an ambitious attempt, much in the current of the times, to depict the day-to-day life of a steel mill and the local community that serves it. The workers, men and women, are seen as the tormented victims of the economic bondage imposed by their bosses, who appear in an intermittent allegory as the despotic rulers of "Cassanod," the tyrannical empire of twentieth-century capitalism. The Marxist frame of reference is explicitly stated in only a few poems, notably "New Youngfellow" and "Das Kapital," but the condemnation of the capitalist system is clearly stated throughout, most effectively in such poems as "I, Jim Rogers," "Morning Song: New Style," and "The Crane-Driver," which recall some of the graphically descriptive footnotes that underpin the theorizing of Marx's work. Many of the meditative and philosophical lyrics of Burnshaw's two earlier collections of poetry are reprinted in the poem sequence, appropriately, since it was in this industrial setting that they were written. They appear here as evidence of the poet's deepening sense of man's inner life, emerging slowly in his experience of the harsh diurnal round and leading him to condemn the destructive technology of modern society, which bends, breaks, and destroys nature without regard for the consequences.

As he ruefully admitted many years later, Burnshaw had himself become confused by the intensely pragmatic view of literature held by the *New Masses.* Yet *The Iron Land* was not to be his last political poem. After two years (1937 and 1938) as editor-in-chief for The Cordon Company in New York, he established in January 1939 his own firm, the Dryden Press, for which he functioned as president of and editor-in-chief until the firm was merged with Holt, Rinehart and Winston in 1958. He published little of his own work between 1939 and 1945 but marked his return to the literary scene with *The Bridge,* which appeared under the Dryden Press imprint in 1945.

The Bridge is Burnshaw's only attempt at verse drama—surprisingly, in view of the fondness, apparent in his poetry as a whole, for the vocative and interrogative—but it shows considerable skill in its handling of dramatic structure and the presentation of a complex ideological message. This message bears some relation to that of *The Iron Land*, but the conflict between capital and labor is here presented in symbolic terms, as a project to build The Strip, a causeway "to the future" which is directed by Graves, a labor leader, and Miller, his black foreman. The project is continually observed, attacked, harassed, and undermined by Dumond, a capitalist boss and city official, with help from Haines, his fascist-style chief of police. The contending parties are supported by Skinner, Dumond's destructively insane technical planner, and by Carver, the idealistic designer who wants to make of The Strip a vaulting arc into a visionary future as The Bridge, which has at the bridgehead a symbolic figure of a woman firmly planted on the banks of the Future. She reaches out to the banks of the Present to bring mankind forward from where it is now into the Future with her:

Our bridgehead leans toward the far horizon
To mix with a far light flooding. Look, the arms
Reach out to greet the future: outstretched arms
On whose young strength we hang our road
Till tomorrow also stands with outstretched arms
That the two bridgeheads may meet, the old and the
    new
Join hands to close the ocean.

One theme of the drama is the perversion of technology by greed; there is a relation to Hart Crane's poem *The Bridge* (1930) in that Carver's role represents in part the power of art to inspire human society and redeem its technology. But the point is not ideological; as the play states clearly, to reach the future we must become the Future—we must change ourselves from the limitations of the Now to the possibility of Tomorrow.

Burnshaw's comic-satiric poem *The Revolt of the Cats in Paradise*, also published in 1945, marks his total rejection of communism and its curtailment of individuality. His search for new ground in the moral vacuum of the immediate postwar years is perhaps best studied in his brilliantly sardonic novel, *The Sunless Sea* (1948), a progressively manic tale of book publishing and marital complications in New York which offers several levels of meaning, the deepest an often hilarious allegory of the soul and its impatience to transcend the material world in a search for religious panaceas.

Early and Late Testament (1952), Burnshaw's first major collection of poems, was not a wholly successful attempt to consolidate the new ground

he felt he had won in his postwar transitional period. The long title poem reworks much of the material of *The Iron Land*, stripping it of its realist and political elements so that only the philosophical bones are left, to which further philosophical sections are appended. The poem's theme—the inadequacy of depending on "the strength of singleness" in coping with the problems of modern existence—is clearcut. Yet, the result is obscure and tedious as a long poem, although individual sections, including some that first appeared separately in his earliest collections, still retain their appeal. The most valuable parts of *Early and Late Testament* are two moving poems of love and praise, "Poetry: The Art," an apostrophe to Walt Whitman and a celebration of the unity of body, mind, and spirit in his art, and "The Hollow River," a lament for a dead child. Most important in terms of Burnshaw's development is the central section of twelve odes that signals, in "Random Pieces of a Man" and "In a Museum," the emergence of his later style, a poetry that is both personal and abstract, informed

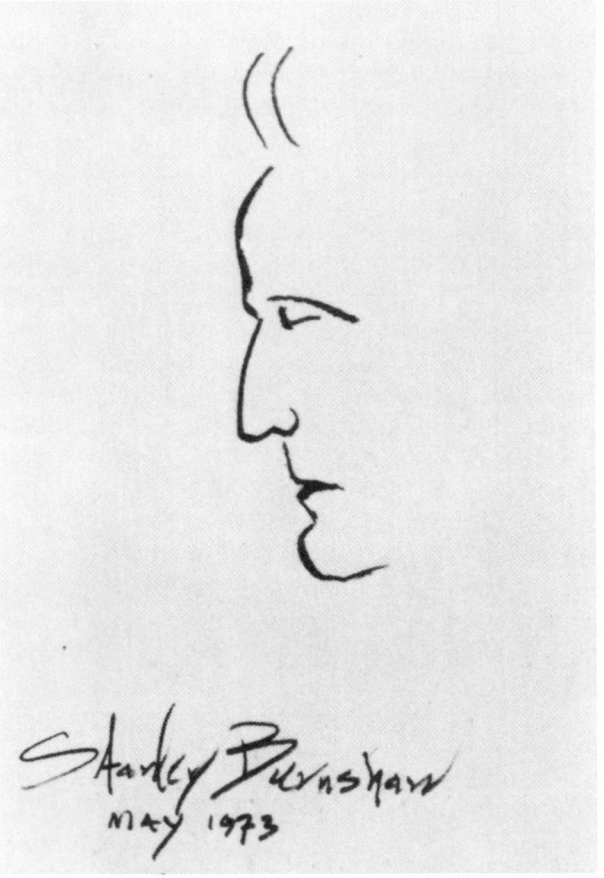

Drawing from Self-Portrait *(1976), compiled by Burt Britton (by permission of Stanley Burnshaw)*

by a sense of the antiquity of humankind, the multiplicity and complexity of its past experiences and imaginings, and the desolation of its godlessness. This later poetry is far from being without hope, since it asserts with compelling lyricism the beauty and strength of a nature in which humanity is irretrievably involved, but it offers no easy meanings nor any easy answers. Its message, and that of *Caged in an Animal's Mind,* is "trust to the forces of life." To borrow the argument of *The Seamless Web,* nature makes the mind and the mind cannot unmake nature. The implications of the poetry are agnostic, and there is no trace of pantheism, anthropomorphism, or nature-sentiment, but the form of optimism that underlies it is larger than the absurd hope of existentialism.

The learned frame of reference and the wide-ranging intellectual curiosity of this later work were the fruit of a settled and happy life and the opportunity to devote more time to study and to teaching. His second marriage having ended in divorce, Burnshaw married Lydia Powsner in 1942. He lectured at New York University in the years 1958 to 1962 and edited *Varieties of Literary Experience* (1962), a distinguished collection of "Eighteen Essays in World Literature" which includes his own essay "The Three Revolutions of Modern Poetry." In 1960 he had edited, with others, *The Poem Itself,* an original attempt to develop an alternative mode of understanding poetry in languages other than English. The usual method of recreating the poem in English as a new poem, at best approximating the original meaning and language, is replaced by an analytical essay which presents a literal version and a gloss which elucidates idioms, ambiguities, and ironies. The method was highly praised, by Herbert Read and Lionel Trilling among others, as the most satisfactory yet found to bring the poetry of other languages to the English-speaking reader. Burnshaw has, from the time of his book on Spire to the present day, produced many excellent verse translations from European poetry according to the conventional method, but he also persevered with the new method in *The Modern Hebrew Poem Itself* (1965).

After the merger of Dryden Press with Holt, Rinehart and Winston in 1958, he was at last able to devote the larger part of his time to writing and research, though he remained a vice-president and consultant to the house until 1968. *The Seamless Web,* his major contribution to theoretical literary criticism, published in 1970, was based on years of research in psychology, linguistics, biochemistry, anatomy, aesthetics, as well as "conventional" literary criticism to discover the name and nature of poetry in the context of modern knowledge and its undiminished importance as a human activity. The poet (and all humankind) is a part of nature—in the words of the title poem of his 1963 collection, he is *Caged in an Animal's Mind* with "No wish to be more or less/Than I am," yet with an unassuageable will

> To range the inhuman storm,
> Follow wherever it lead
> And answer—whether I hear
> A Voice or only the voices
>
> Of my own self-answering scream
> In a void of punishing calm.

His most recent collection, *In the Terrified Radiance* (1972) continues to move, though with much also that is direct and tender, in "this eden/that flows from the terrified radiance of our minds." The collection also includes *The Hero of Silence,* a poem sequence on the life of Mallarmé, published in the *Lugano Review* and as a separate pamphlet in 1965. The elemental universe of many of these poems later found its logical counterpart in modern Israel, the setting of Burnshaw's most recent poem, *Mirages* (1977), subtitled *Travel Notes in the Promised Land.* This poem, some fifty pages in length, was later included as an epilogue to *The Refusers.* This trilogy of novels connects his father's life, and thus his own, with the long tradition of Jewish free-thinking, which the first part of the trilogy traces back to Moses, who is depicted more as the pragmatic leader of enslaved Hebrews than the divinely inspired monotheist. In this land of old gods and old wars made new, the mirages of man's hopes and fears rise before the poet figure in a search that is endless, "leading us out of our nights/Into untroubled wakefulness."

Burnshaw, who now lives on Martha's Vineyard, continues to teach, lecture, give poetry readings, and write. In 1983 he was awarded an honorary doctor of humane letters degree by Hebrew Union College—Jewish Institute of Religion. In late 1986 George Braziller will publish Burnshaw's *Robert Frost Himself,* which Leon Edel has called "a moral lesson for all biography." He is currently preparing a *Stanley Burnshaw Reader,* which is scheduled for publication in 1987, with an introduction by Denis Donoghue.

Burnshaw's most-recent poetry is an impressive departure in an altogether new direction, but the central body of his work is, like Robert Frost's, concerned with a dark and ambiguous universe. That it lacks Frost's saving touch of homeliness and simplicity has limited its audience, but its strengths, since they are an appeal to the deepest strengths of our human nature, are likely to endure.

References:

Agenda, special Burnshaw issue, 21/22 (Winter 1983/Spring 1984);

Robert Alter, "Paradoxes of Belief," review of *The Refusers, New York Times Book Review*, 4 April 1982, pp. 18-19;

Germaine Brée, "The Poet is Always Present," *American Scholar*, 39 (Summer 1970): 522-524;

Peter Dale, Review of *The Seamless Web, Agenda*, (1971): 32-39;

James Dickey, "In the Terrified Radiance," review of *The Seamless Web, New York Times Book Review*, 24 September 1972, p. 4;

Dickey, "The Many Ways of Speaking in Verse," review of *Caged in an Animal's Mind, New York Times Book Review*, 22 December 1963, p. 4;

D. J. Enright, "O Altitudo!," review of *The Seamless Web, New York Review of Books*, 15 (3 September 1970): 34-35;

Herbert Read, "On Translating Poetry," *Poetry*, 98 (April-September 1961): 56-59;

Peter Revell, "Poets 5," *Alphabet*, no. 7 (1963): 85-87;

André Spire, review of *The Great Dark Love, Mercure de France*, série moderne, 248 (1 December 1933): 303-309;

Wallace Stevens, "Mr. Burnshaw and the Statue," in *The New Caravan*, edited by Alfred Kreymborg, Lewis Mumford, and Paul Rosenfeld (New York: Norton, 1936), pp. 72-77;

Lionel Trilling, "The Poem Itself," *Mid-Century* (August 1960);

Ruth R. Wisse, "Jewish Dreams," review of *The Refusers, Commentary*, 73 (March 1982): 45-48.

Malcolm Cowley
(24 August 1898-)

Peter Revell
Westfield College, London

See also the Cowley entries in *DLB 4, American Writers in Paris, 1920-1939* and *DLB Yearbook: 1981.*

BOOKS: *Racine* (Paris: Union, 1923);

Blue Juniata: Poems (New York: Cape & Smith, 1929; London: Cape, 1929); revised and expanded as *Blue Juniata: Collected Poems* (New York: Viking, 1968);

Exile's Return (New York: Norton, 1934; London: Cape, 1935; revised edition, New York: Viking, 1951; London: Bodley Head, 1961);

The Dry Season (Norfolk, Conn.: New Directions, 1941);

The Literary Situation (New York: Viking, 1954; London: Deutsch, 1955);

Black Cargoes: A History of the Atlantic Slave Trade, 1518-1865, by Cowley and Daniel P. Mannix (New York: Viking, 1962; London: Longman, 1963);

Van Wyck Brooks, by Cowley and R. D. Oakes (N. p., 1963);

The Faulkner-Cowley File: Letters and Memoirs, 1944-1962 (New York: Viking, 1966; London: Chatto & Windus, 1966);

Think Back on Us . . . A Contemporary Chronicle of the 1930s, edited by Henry Dan Piper (Carbondale & Edwardsville: Southern Illinois University Press, 1967);

A Many-Windowed House: Collected Essays on American Writers and American Writing, edited by Piper (Carbondale & Edwardsville: Southern Illinois University Press, 1970);

A Second Flowering: Works and Days of the Lost Generation (New York: Viking, 1973; London: Deutsch, 1973);

—And I Worked At the Writer's Trade (New York: Viking, 1978);

The Dream of the Golden Mountains: Remembering the 1930s (New York: Viking, 1978);

Malcolm Cowley, circa 1930

The View from 80 (New York: Viking, 1980).

OTHER: S. Foster Damon and Robert Hillyer, eds., *Eight More Harvard Poets*, includes poems by Cowley (New York: Brentano's, 1923);

Pierre MacOrlan, *On Board the Morning Star*, translated by Cowley (New York: A. & C. Boni, 1924);

Joseph Delteil, *Joan of Arc*, translated by Cowley (New York: Minton, Balch, 1926; London: Allen & Unwin, 1927);

Paul Valéry, *Variety*, translated, with an introduction, by Cowley (New York: Harcourt, Brace, 1927);

Adventures of an African Slaver, Being a True Account of the Life of Captain Theodore Canot, Trader in Gold, Ivory & Slaves on the Coast of Guinea: His Own Story as Told in the Year 1854 to Brantz Mayer . . ., edited, with an introduction, by Cowley (New York: A. & C. Boni, 1928; London: Routledge, 1928);

Marthe Lucie Bibesco, *Catherine-Paris*, translated,

with an introduction, by Cowley (New York: Harcourt, Brace, 1928);

Raymond Radiquet, *The Count's Ball*, translated by Cowley (New York: Norton, 1929);

Bibesco, *The Green Parrot*, translated by Cowley (New York: Harcourt, Brace, 1929; London: Selwyn & Blount, 1929);

Maurice Barrès, *The Sacred Hill*, translated, with an introduction, by Cowley (New York: Macaulay, 1929);

After the Genteel Tradition, edited, with contributions, by Cowley (New York: Norton, 1937; revised edition, Carbondale: Southern Illinois University Press, 1964);

Books That Changed Our Minds, edited by Cowley and Bernard Smith (New York: Doubleday, Doran, 1939);

André Gide, *Imaginary Interviews*, translated, with an introduction, by Cowley (New York: Knopf, 1944);

The Viking Portable Library Hemingway, edited, with an introduction, by Cowley (New York: Viking, 1944);

Aragon, Poet of the French Resistance, edited by Cowley and Hannah Josephson, with translations by Cowley and others (New York: Duell, Sloan & Pearce, 1945); republished as *Aragon Poet of Resurgent France* (London: Pilot, 1946);

The Portable Faulkner, edited, with an introduction, by Cowley (New York: Viking, 1946; London: Macmillan, 1961; revised and enlarged edition, New York: Viking, 1967); republished as *The Essential Faulkner* (London: Chatto & Windus, 1967);

The Portable Hawthorne, edited, with an introduction and notes, by Cowley (New York: Viking, 1948; revised and enlarged, 1969); republished as *Nathaniel Hawthorne: The Selected Works* (London: Chatto & Windus, 1971);

The Complete Poetry and Prose of Walt Whitman, 2 volumes, introduction by Cowley (New York: Pellegrini, 1948); republished as *The Works of Walt Whitman*, 2 volumes, with a new introduction in volume 1 and a new prefatory note in volume 2 by Cowley (New York: Funk & Wagnalls, 1968);

"To a Girl I Dislike," "An Old Fellow to His Friends," and "To a Dilettante Killed at Vimy," in *The Harvard Advocate Anthology*, edited by Donald Hall (New York: Twayne, 1950), pp. 151-153;

The Stories of F. Scott Fitzgerald, edited, with an introduction, by Cowley (New York: Scribners, 1951);

F. Scott Fitzgerald, *Tender is the Night: A Romance
. . . with the Author's Final Revisions,* edited, with
a preface, by Cowley (New York: Scribners,
1951);

*Three Novels of F. Scott Fitzgerald: The Great Gatsby,
Tender Is the Night (With the Author's Final Revision), The Last Tycoon,* edited, with introductions, by Cowley and Edmund Wilson (New
York: Scribners, 1953);

Writers at Work: The Paris Review Interviews, first se-
ries, edited, with an introduction, by Cowley
(New York: Viking, 1958; London: Secker &
Warburg, 1958);

Walt Whitman, *Leaves of Grass, The First (1855) Edi-
tion,* edited, with an introduction, by Cowley
(New York: Viking, 1959; London: Secker &
Warburg, 1960);

The Bodley Head F. Scott Fitzgerald . . . Short Stories,
volumes 5 and 6, selected, with an introduction, by Cowley (London: Bodley Head,
1963);

"A Theme with Variations," "To a Dilettante Killed
at Vimy," and "Nantasket," in *Harvard Advocate Centennial Anthology,* edited by Jonathan
D. Culler (Cambridge: Schenkman, 1966),
pp. 109, 111, 113;

Fitzgerald and the Jazz Age, compiled by Cowley and
Robert Cowley (New York: Scribners, 1966);

*The Lessons of the Masters: An Anthology of the Novel
from Cervantes to Hemingway,* edited by Cowley
and Howard Hugo (New York: Scribners,
1971);

Paul Valéry, *Leonardo Poe Mallarmé,* translated by
Cowley and James R. Lawler (Princeton:
Princeton University Press, 1972; London:
Routledge & Kegan Paul, 1972).

PERIODICAL PUBLICATIONS: "Writer's
Choice," *Horizon,* 16 (Summer 1974): 106-
109;

"The Red Wagon," *Sewanee Review,* 84 (Spring
1976): 219-220.

Malcolm Cowley is best known as a critic and
literary historian whose sound judgment, understanding, and polished prose have earned him in
a long lifetime of working "at the writer's trade,"
a place beside Van Wyck Brooks and Edmund Wilson as one of the foremost professional literary
critics in twentieth-century America. His work as a
literary historian and critic has been especially concerned with chronicling the activities and interpreting the works of the American writers who
came to maturity during and after World War I, a

group of which he was part and which was named,
in a chance remark by Gertrude Stein, the lost generation. In the words of Philip Young, "the commentary on which [Cowley] spent so many years
no longer seems . . . just a history of its writers but
a part of what was written." The discernment and
understanding apparent in his criticism, which is
characterized by broad generalization and close
analysis equally, certainly owe much to the fact that
he has himself written poetry. His first book, *Blue
Juniata* (1929), is a collection of poems, and he has
continued to write poetry all his life, though his
output in verse has not been large. His work is not
widely represented in the anthologies, but he has
a genuine reputation as a poet and the best of his
poems convey a vital sense of sharply delineated
individual experience which becomes a part of the
reader's imagination.

The son of William and Josephine Hut-
macher Cowley, Malcolm Cowley was born in a
farmhouse near Belsano, in Cambria County,
Pennsylvania, on the western slope of the Alleghe-
nies. His father was a homeopathic physician; he
had a sister who died young but who is poignantly
evoked in several of his poems. The family, apparently a loving one (Cowley dedicated both of
his full-length collections of his poetry to his parents), moved to Pittsburgh and Cowley attended
high school there, but they contrived to spend the
summers near Belsano, which came to seem in retrospect his real home since "it is difficult to feel
nostalgia for Pittsburgh." Yet, in an article for *Horizon* (Summer 1974), he remembered, "As a little
boy in pyjamas, lying next to the radiator on winter
mornings, I had raced through most of those
twenty-five closely printed volumes [of the Wav-
erley novels] in their maroon cloth bindings. That
was in my father's Pittsburgh waiting room, where
patients seldom came before five o'clock and then
not many." He met Kenneth Burke, later well
known as a literary critic and theoretician, when
Burke was five, and, as he told Diane Eisenberg in
a 1979 interview, in high school they became close
friends, beginning to exchange "a huge number of
letters in which we would talk at times about ourselves and what we were doing and what we had
read. At other times we talked about literary problems and in this case that exchange has gone on
down until yesterday."

Cowley's belief that reading and writing are
an inescapable part of living and his penchant for
cultivating literary friends and acquaintances continued at Harvard, which he entered as a freshman
in the fall of 1915. The poems he contributed to

the *Harvard Advocate* are uncollected except for two included in *Eight More Harvard Poets*, (1923), edited by S. Foster Damon and Robert Hillyer, and four others included in the *Harvard Advocate* anthologies edited by Donald Hall in 1950 and Jonathan D. Culler in 1966. These poems already display the directness, clarity, and knowledgeability that are among his special virtues as both a critic and a poet. The first of these poems, "To Certain Imagist Poets," appeared in the *Advocate* for 31 March 1916; the last, "Eighteenth-Century Sonnet," was published in the 1 April 1920 issue. The titles might imply sympathy with the attitudes of the Harvard aesthetes, who had flourished at Harvard just before Cowley's time. But Cowley's "The Last of Lyric Poets" (*New Republic*, 27 January 1932; collected in *Think Back on Us . . .*, 1967), an essay on E. E. Cummings, the best poet of that group, makes clear his lack of sympathy with the posturing and fantasizing of the aesthetes.

Cowley's undergraduate studies were interrupted by World War I, and he sailed for France as a member of the American Field Service in April 1917. He had volunteered for noncombatant service as an ambulance driver but found himself instead driving munitions trucks for the French army. The experience reflected in the poems with titles such as "To a Dilettante Killed at Vimy" and "Bayonet Drill," which he continued to contribute to the *Advocate*, left no room for fantasy. After returning from France in fall 1917, he entered the U.S. Army and spent the remainder of the war at an artillery officers' training school. On his release from service he married his first wife, Marguerite Frances (Peggy) Baird, on 12 August 1919 and earned his A.B. (cum laude) from Harvard in 1920, "as of the class of 1919."

Cowley and his wife set up house in a cold-water flat in Greenwich Village, subsisting on the modest income derived from occasional book reviewing and a job as an advertising copywriter for *Sweet's Architectural Catalogue*. In 1921 he was awarded an American Field Service scholarship which enabled him to travel to France with his wife and follow a postgraduate program in French literature at the Université de Montpellier, where he earned a diploma in French studies in 1922. After the fellowship was extended for a further year of study, the Cowleys went to live in Giverny, also spending time in Paris, where Cowley met members of the Dadaist movement—including Tristan Tzara, André Breton, and Louis Aragon. His first published books were translations of works by contemporary French writers, including Paul Valéry,

Pierre MacOrlan, and Raymond Radiguet, which appeared between 1924 and 1929.

Though Cowley participated in the American literary exodus to France, his status as a student on a scholarship put him in a somewhat different category and encouraged a spectatorial attitude. At this time he considered himself primarily a poet, as his poems had by then appeared in some of the leading magazines, including the *Dial*, the *Little Review*, the *Pagan, Broom*, and Harriet Monroe's *Poetry*. During his years in France he met such American expatriates as Ernest Hemingway and Ezra Pound (the meeting with Pound is described in a 1922 poem "Ezra Pound," later titled "Ezra Pound at the Hotel Jacob"), but he spent more time and was on closer terms with the French writers whose work engaged his interest more closely. His studies in French literature fostered the objectivity which became an essential part of the critical reviews and essays he produced abundantly in the 1930s and 1940s. There is also an eloquently French strain in some of Cowley's poetry of the 1920s and later, expressed most clearly in the agonized seeking after truth of depiction and emotion in a poem such as "Coal Town" (*North American Review*, August 1922), collected in *Eight More Harvard Poets* as "Mine No. 6." The first of his poems to be printed by the *Little Review* (July 1919), "Sunday Afternoon (After Jules Laforgue)," is an imitation of Jules Laforgue's "Complainte des Pianos," but Cowley's characteristic verse style, then and later, is plain and direct, without Laforgue's obliqueness and attenuated emotion. The same poetic style is apparent in Cowley's translations of poems written by Louis Aragon during World War II and collected in *Aragon, Poet of the French Resistance* (1945). One of these, "The Time of Crossword Puzzles," also included in the revised and expanded edition of Cowley's *Blue Juniata* (1968), is an example of Cowley's admirably lean and direct style as a translator.

Returning to live in Greenwich Village in 1923, Cowley took up his old job for *Sweet's Architectural Catalogue* and continued to contribute reviews and articles to the magazines. In 1925 he left his job at *Sweet's* and depended for a living on freelance writing and translating. For a brief period in 1928 he coedited *Broom* with Matthew Josephson.

Cowley identified himself closely with the postwar generation of American writers, which he felt to be separated from its own past and the nation's, by its early knowledge of death and destruction in World War I. Cowley's friends in the Village, who included Matthew Josephson, Allen Tate and his wife Caroline Gordon, Hart Crane, John Brooks Wheelwright, Robert M. Coates, and Peter Blume, were all near-contemporaries and nourished the sense of a shared outlook, which they possessed even more than most generations. In "Hart Crane: A Memoir," collected in *A Second Flowering* (1973), Cowley described his visit with Tate to Crane's room overlooking Brooklyn Bridge, after which, "We left his room, all three of us talking excitedly, and wandered through the streets lined with brick-red warehouses until we came to the end of a scow at the end of a pier at the Brooklyn end of the bridge. There we sat talking, more slowly now, while we looked across the river at an enormous electric sign—WATERMAN'S FOUNTAIN PENS—and all those proud towers beyond it with the early lights flashing on. Suddenly we felt—I think we all felt—that we were secretly comrades in the same endeavor: to present this new scene in poems that would reveal not only its astonishing face but the lasting realities behind it. We did not take an oath of comradeship, but what happened later made me suspect that something vaguely like that was in our minds."

It was in large part Hart Crane's interest and enthusiasm that led Cowley to compile his first book of poems, *Blue Juniata: Poems,* published in 1929 by Cape & Smith in New York and in London by Jonathan Cape. Crane had worked through the poems with Cowley in the summer of 1928, and when it seemed that an American publisher could not be found, he took Cowley's manuscript to Paris in 1929 (a trip ostensibly to arrange the publication of his own poem, *The Bridge,* 1930). He had almost persuaded Harry Crosby of the Black Sun Press to publish it, when he heard from Cowley that Harrison Smith of Cape & Smith was to publish the book in America. Cowley's and Crane's letters about the book have been collected in *Robber Rocks* (1968), a selection of letters and memoirs of Crane brought together by Susan Jenkins Brown, another of their Greenwich Village friends.

Blue Juniata: Poems (1929) collects a substantial part of Cowley's published work to that date (the earliest poem is "Young Kuppenheimer Gods," which first appeared in the November 1919 issue of the *Harvard Advocate* as "Nantasket") as well as a group of four previously unpublished poems. The collection is structured chronologically and divided into five sections, to express the poet's experiences both as an individual and as a representative of his generation, with its sense of uniqueness. Cowley's first literary memoir, *Exile's Return* (1934, revised 1951), covers much of the

same ground in the dimension of literary history. Some of the subtitles for its chapters pick up the titles from the sections of *Blue Juniata,* so that parts of *Exile's Return* can be read as prose glosses on the poems. The title poem for the book and the first section, "Blue Juniata," introduces a hauntingly evocative group of poems that celebrates less the sweetness of the past than its inescapable burden, focusing on the poet's childhood as a country boy near Belsano, not his city boyhood in Pittsburgh. The Juniata, Cowley explains in a prose note, is a river in west-central Pennsylvania, while "Blue Juniata" is the title for a sentimental ballad, popular in the middle years of the nineteenth century, which the old people of his childhood still hummed, having forgotten the words except for the first lines: "Wild roved an Indian girl/Bright Alfarata,/Where sweep the waters/Of the blue Juniata." The wistful irony in this note echoes through the whole collection. Cowley's poems depict a hard and unsentimental environment, which the child and later the man begin to understand. The Indians have been killed off, the forests cut for tanbark and burned over, the hills scoured and scarred by abandoned mines. The poet commemorates, almost grudgingly, the hard men of the place ("Empty Barn, Dead Farm," revised as "Overbeck's Barn" for the 1968 edition), those hard enough to bring the thin soil to fruition ("Hickory Cove," revised as "Poverty Hollow," and "The Hill above the Mine"), and hard enough to have their will and damn the rest ("Dan George," "Laurel Mountain"). "Day Coach," near the end of this section, describes the journey each man takes to the knowledge of his own past, and is the first appearance of the Doppelgänger image in which Cowley shows an abiding, disquieted interest.

The second section of the book, "The Adolescent," collects poems arising from life in Greenwich Village after college and the war. The setting of grimy tenements matches the mood of the new arrivals, who enjoyed themselves while "Our college textbooks and the complete works of Jules Laforgue gathered dust on the mantlepiece among a litter of unemptied ashtrays." "Valuta," the third section, depicts the rootless life of expatriate Americans in Europe "following the dollar, ah, following the dollar" in that continent of "old hierarchies and values" which "had ceased to have any values whatever; it had only prices, which changed from country to country." "The City of Anger," the fourth section, tells of the hard realities of the life they found on their return, when "the exiles straggled

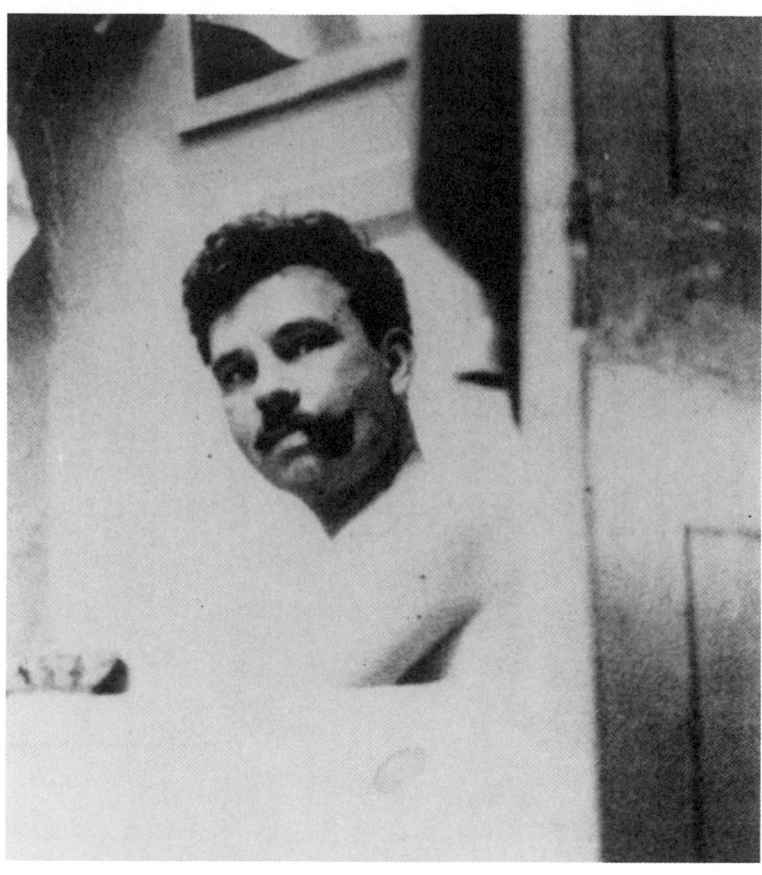

Malcolm Cowley in the bathtub at the studio apartment he rented near the offices of the New Republic, *where he went to work in 1929 (by permission of Malcolm Cowley)*

home at last, with no official committee of welcome."

A number of the poems in these two sections are the classic expressions, succinct and final, of the mood of those times. "The Lady from Harlem (In Memory of Florence Mills)" epitomizes the brave but fragile charm of the jazz age, its self-destructing innocence. "Ten Good Farms," for his Greenwich Village friend Slater Brown, is an apocalyptic vision of a New York finally brought to ruin by its own corruption—"no, in our lifetime, we could never make out of/Manhattan Island ten good farms." "Buy 300 Steel," dedicated to Matthew Josephson, who was by then working in a broker's office, taps at the foundations on which the whole tottering economic system was based. "The Flower in the Sea," a strangely prophetic poem dedicated to Hart Crane and written while Crane was still working on *The Bridge,* captures Crane's visionary tone perfectly and exemplifies the affinities between their work at this time.

The final section of *Blue Juniata: Poems,* "Old Melodies: Love and Death," shows, to use Crane's description of it in a letter to Cowley, "the eloquent and more abstract matter mounting to a kind of climax toward the end." "William Wilson," which borrows its title and Doppelgänger theme from Edgar Allan Poe's 1839 short story, pleased even Yvor Winters, who reviewed the book for *Hound and Horn* magazine. Death is the theme of many of these poems, a subject often close to the thoughts of a generation who had seen so much of it. The final poem, "The Urn," is Cowley's major statement of the idea that every American (and every human being) carries with him some part of the soil of his childhood that is both the ground of his birth and the emblem of his mortality, like the dust in an urn.

This excellent poem, later included in the first chapter of *Exile's Return* and much anthologized, won for Cowley in 1927 the Helen Haire Levinson prize from *Poetry* magazine, where it had been published in November 1926. Part of the $100 prize served as the down payment on a back-road farmhouse in western Connecticut, which became a

Malcolm Cowley and Robert Penn Warren, 1933 (by permission of Malcolm Cowley)

weekend base for the Cowleys into the early 1930s. Many of their Greenwich Village friends had similarly found temporary retreats in the Tory Hill area, just over the New York State line. In 1929, as Cowley's work as a poet seemed sure to attain full fruition, his career became firmly set in the direction of literary journalism when he became literary editor of the *New Republic* to succeed Edmund Wilson, who had recommended him. He held the post until 1944. The editorial grind, graphically described by Cowley in "Adventures of a Book Reviewer" (in *Think Back On Us . . .*) was the ideal foundation for his later work as a literary historian, but not ideally conducive to poetry.

His marriage to Peggy Baird having ended in divorce, Cowley had married Muriel Maurer on 18 June 1932, and in 1936 they and their son Robert moved to a farmhouse in Sherman, Connecticut. This house has remained his home base during his active career as a critic, as editor of literary texts, and as visiting professor at many universities in America and England.

Seventeen poems, mostly written between 1935 and 1941, were collected in Cowley's second collection of verse, *The Dry Season* (1941). The dryness is partly that of "August, the dry season of your life" (in the title poem), that time when business, or busy-ness, leaves little scope for feeling or reflection. The reference is also in part to the dry

and gritty decade of the 1930s, coming after (as it came to appear in retrospect) the rich flowering of the 1920s. One poem in this collection, "The Long Voyage," perhaps the simplest statement of Cowley's recurrent theme of exile and homecoming, exerted a particular appeal in years of World War II and was included in a number of anthologies. Another, "The Last International," written in 1935, is an impassioned statement about the plight of the dispossessed during the Depression, seen as a nightmare vision of a living dead, "their unbreathing armies/marching against the Capitol in ranks." This poem, and others such as "Roxane," "The Firstborn," and the magnificent "Tomorrow Morning," which expresses with mingled conviction and regret the radical view of America in the 1930s, are the poetical counterpart of much of Cowley's work, in speech and written prose, for the left-wing League of American Writers, which he helped to found in 1935.

While acting as literary editor for the *New Republic*, Cowley served in 1942 as a staff member of the Office of Facts and Figures in Washington, D.C. After the war, in 1948, he began his long and fruitful association with Viking Press as a literary adviser. His residence in 1950-1951 as a visiting professor at the University of Washington in Seattle was the first of a series of visiting professorships, at Stanford University (1956-1957, 1959-1961); the University of Michigan (1957-1958); the University of California (1962-1963); Cornell University (1964-1965); Hollins College (1968-1969, 1970-1971); and the University of Minnesota (1971-1972). In 1973 he taught at Warwick University, in England, where, in 1975, he was awarded an honorary Litt.D.

During this period he was active not only as a writer but also in public affairs: beginning in 1948 he served for twenty-three years as chairman of the zoning board in Sherman, Connecticut, for example, and in 1956-1959 and again in 1962-1965 he served three-year terms as president of the National Institute of Arts and Letters. He was Chancellor of the American Academy of Arts and Letters from 1967-1976. He received, then, considerable honors and recognition. And in 1968, Cowley put the seal on his reputation as a poet with the revised and expanded *Blue Juniata: Collected Poems*. This volume includes all but six of the poems from his first collection, many revised and sometimes retitled, as well as all the poems from *The Dry Season*. Although it retains the basic autobiographical form of the first collection, even the prose notes (also much revised), this volume is essentially a new

Malcolm Cowley

The Lost People

The bedroom on the courtyard, and the tree
of heaven that brushed our window there, we slept
and loved and slept all the long afternoon;
the quiet in the streets and twilight still
at ten o'clock, the sidewalk tables crowded,
the Arab selling rugs, and we moved south,
south with the end of summer to a shore
that looked toward Africa, and fleshly white
sea-lilacs died in the sand.

Then north again with spring, the wooden inn
dry-rotting under the Heiterwand, the major
without a pension, fragile and polite,
full-breasted Rosa singing to the starved
and pederastic poet, these were broken
wax figures in a war-pale landscape. We
were new, invincible, we paid our bills
and then moved on. A moment to admire
the glister of decay, and we moved on
brightly among the ruins.

Late, late in youth we heard the market wagons
roll in the streets, the blind violinist play,
but did we hear the shamble of the waiter
coming to count our saucers, did we hear

First page of the typescript for "The Lost People" in the R. P. Blackmur papers. The poem was first collected in The Dry Season
(by permission of the author; courtesy of Princeton University Library).

The Bollingen Prize Committee for 1953: W. H. Auden, Richard Eberhart, Louise Bogan, Malcolm Cowley, and Leonard Bacon.
They awarded the prize to Marianne Moore.

book, containing nineteen "superb additions" (as Kenneth Burke called them in a review) including three poems written in the year of the book's publication, which are among the finest Cowley has written. "Boy in Sunlight" and "The Pyre" evoke the happiness and sorrows of his childhood years with unforgettable poignancy, and the poem with a Whitmanesque title, "Here with the Long Grass Rippling," with its allusions to the Vietnam War, presents a sober and somber meditation on the state of the nation in an era of high technology. Only the title is ironic in this poem. The wish for a better world, the hope

> to greatly love a few;
> to love the earth, to be sparing of what it yields,
> and not to leave it poorer for my long presence

exemplify the directness, simplicity, and honesty that are the most valued qualities in all of Cowley's work. These poems also show his continuing command of the craft of writing in verse. Though he has written in regular stanzas, in couplets, even in sonnets, the great part of his poetical work is in

free verse that (to use the words of Allen Tate in a review of the first *Blue Juniata*) "move[s] with the loose orderliness of highly conscious prose—without any falling off in the poetry." No better example of this quality could be found than "The Pyre," which describes the selling of his childhood home in what might be the words of a letter to a cousin, but which carries an immense charge of emotion that seems to sweep the words aside though they remain the more eloquent for their plainness.

Cowley has remarked that he has an affinity for writing memoirs, that he is happiest when he is piecing together a critical commentary from the life he has known, and his later years have been an astonishing second flowering in his creativity as a literary historian. Yet, though it has been less appreciated, his power as a poet has also continued unabated. The poems themselves have continued to be few in number, but of memorable quality. He has continued to publish them since the second *Blue Juniata*. "The Red Wagon" (*Sewanee Review*, Spring 1976; republished in *The View from 80*), is a startling view of early childhood, seen through the eyes of an old man, that moves from the warm glow of tender reminiscence to the chilling fearfulness of a ghost story. Malcolm Cowley is an example of that rare phenomenon, a poet who has continued to produce his best work in old age.

Bibliography:
Diane U. Eisenberg, *Malcolm Cowley: A Checklist of His Writings, 1916-1973* (Carbondale & Edwardsville: Southern Illinois University Press, 1975).

References:
Susan Jenkins Brown, *Robber Rocks: Letters and Memories of Hart Crane, 1923-1932* (Middletown, Conn.: Wesleyan University Press, 1968);
Kenneth Burke, " 'I dipped my finger in the lake and wrote,' " review of *Blue Juniata: Collected Poems, New York Times Book Review,* 17 November 1968, pp. 8, 76;
Diane U. Eisenberg, "A Conversation with Malcolm Cowley," *Southern Review,* new series 15 (Spring 1979): 288-299;
Lewis P. Simpson, "Malcolm Cowley and the American Writer," *Sewanee Review,* 84 (Spring 1976): 221-247;
Allen Tate, "A Regional Poet," review of *Blue Juniata: Poems, New Republic,* 60 (28 August 1929): 51-52;
Yvor Winters, "The Poetry of Malcolm Cowley," review of *Blue Juniata: Poems, Hound & Horn,* 3 (October-December 1929): 111-113;
Philip Young, "For Malcolm Cowley: Critic, Poet, 1898- ," *Southern Review,* new series 9 (Autumn 1973): 778-795.

Papers:
The major collection of Cowley's papers is in the Newberry Library, Chicago.

Hart Crane

Joseph Miller

See also the Crane entries in *DLB 4, American Writers in Paris, 1920-1939* and *DLB Yearbook: 1981.*

BIRTH: Garrettsville, Ohio, 21 July 1899, to Clarence A. and Grace Hart Crane.

AWARD: Guggenheim Fellowship, 1931.

DEATH: At sea, 27 April 1932.

BOOKS: *White Buildings* (New York: Boni & Liveright, 1926);
The Bridge (Paris: Black Sun Press, 1930; New York: Liveright, 1930);
The Collected Poems of Hart Crane, edited by Waldo Frank (New York: Liveright, 1933);
The Complete Poems and Selected Letters and Prose of Hart Crane, edited by Brom Weber (Garden City: Doubleday/Anchor, 1966; London: Oxford University Press, 1968);
Seven Lyrics (Cambridge, Mass.: Ibex Press, 1966);
Ten Unpublished Poems, edited by Kenneth Lohf (New York: Gotham Book Mart, 1972).

The years immediately preceding World War I saw the introduction of international modernism to America, and the years immediately following saw American artists in all the arts adopting and adapting the new ideas and grafting them onto a distinctly American consciousness. By 1923 Hart Crane was writing *The Bridge* (1930), in which he endeavored to unite the style of modernism, the heritage of the symbolists and postimpressionists, with the spirit of American romanticism, the heritage of Ralph Waldo Emerson and Walt Whitman. *The Bridge* is Crane's longest and most ambitious work, and he saw its problematic nature even as he wrote it. "At times the project seems hopeless, horribly so," he wrote to a friend, "and then suddenly something happens inside one, and the theme and

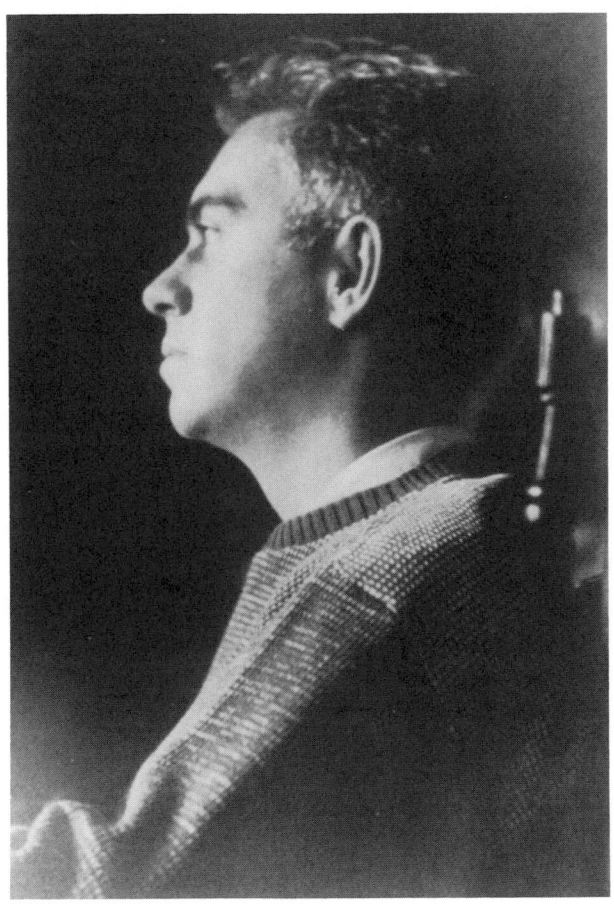

Hart Crane, summer 1931 (photograph by William Wright)

the substance of the conception seem brilliantly real, more so than ever! At least, *at worst*, the poem will be a *huge* failure!" Apart from questions of its ultimate success or failure, *The Bridge* retains its character as a monumental experiment, and as such stands as a landmark in twentieth-century American poetry. In the truest sense the poem came from "inside" the poet, and indeed Hart Crane's entire life and career can be seen as a grand experiment: a projection of the ever-expanding, all-absorbing, all-consuming optimism of Emerson upon the cold cruel realities of modern life.

He was born Harold Hart Crane in Garrettsville, Ohio, on 21 July 1899, the only child of Clarance A. and Grace Hart Crane. Both the Cranes and the Harts were old mercantile families, and the poet's father, known as C. A., built up for himself a large fortune in the manufacture and sales of chocolate candy. The style and values of the Cranes' life were quintessentially bourgeois: they lived in comfort, and they maintained a certain superficial culture without any serious commitment to the arts. The marriage of C. A. and Grace Crane was a thoroughly unhappy one, and they made one another miserable from the day of their wedding in 1898 until long after their divorce in 1917. Grace Crane was famously beautiful and profoundly neurotic. She was terrified of sex, and spent her life alternately in suffering from psychosomatic illnesses and in undergoing Christian Science therapy. She smothered her son with affection, involved him in all her marital quarrels, turned him against his father, and established with him a bond of mutual dependence. Hart Crane found this bond stifling, but for all his life he could free himself from it only sporadically and with difficulty. C. A. Crane was an ambitious, unromantic man, generous and well-meaning, but unable by nature to cope with his unhappy wife or to understand his oversensitive, bookish, homosexual son. After the divorce, C. A. Crane was married twice again, both times happily, first to a woman who died in 1928, and then to one who survived him. He died in 1931, after a reconciliation with his son, who was drowned at sea the following year. Grace Crane, who had been alienated from her son for some time as the result of a dispute over his inheritance from his grandmother, survived his death by fifteen years, during which time she devoted herself to his memory and to his reputation as a poet, assisting his editors and biographers. She lost her money and her beauty, and she, who had been raised in wealth and innocence, always sheltered and always something of a snob, was reduced in her last years to poverty, making her living as a charwoman. She met old age, loneliness, and poverty with a stoic dignity completely unknown in her earlier life, which had been characterized more by hysterical fits and sentimental blackmail.

Both the strengths and weaknesses of Hart Crane as a poet are evidenced in his character as a man, which is inexplicable apart from the atmosphere of emotional turmoil in which he lived his life. His was a volatile personality, excitable and exuberant, and not notably stable. He was given to passionate enthusiasms and to intense attachments to people, who, finding themselves overwhelmed by his attentions, invariably withdrew and disappointed him. Euphoric delight was followed by gloom and anger, followed by another passion. Although from an early age he was a dedicated and hard-working poet, he wrote with bursts of inspiration and suffered, when there was no inspiration, from fears that his gift had evaporated. He never achieved a calm detachment from his poetry any more than he did from his family.

Grace Hart Crane

Clarence A. Crane

When Hart Crane was four years old, the family moved to Warren, Ohio, where C. A. Crane founded a syrup factory, and in 1908, while Grace Crane was in a private sanatorium recovering from a nervous breakdown, Hart moved from Warren to Cleveland to live with his maternal grandmother, whose house served thereafter as the family home. It was a big three-story frame house with a pair of turrets on the front, in one of which Hart maintained his own private "ivory tower," complete with books, a Morris chair, a phonograph and records, and a Corona portable typewriter. Here as an adolescent he began his serious involvement in poetry. He took piano lessons from his Aunt Alice and remained all his life an avid, if undisciplined, amateur pianist, and it was Aunt Alice's collection of standard editions—Emerson, Whitman, Victor Hugo, Robert Browning—that inspired in him an admiration for great literature. She later remembered him at ten: "Once he stood there looking at all the books. 'This is a wonderful collection, Aunt Alice,' he said. He ran his fingers through his hair—he had a habit of doing that—and then he turned to me, very seriously: 'This is going to be

my vocation,' he said. 'I'm going to be a poet.'" Hart Crane had a long apprenticeship ahead of him, but he seems never to have wavered in his decision to become a poet.

In 1914 Hart Crane entered East High School, which was then one of the showplaces of the Cleveland educational system, with high academic standards and a record of successful graduates. Here he studied the "Classical" program, which emphasized English literature and composition, mathematics, and languages. He was a good student and learned easily, but his academic record was complicated by frequent and excessive absences from school, caused by upheavals in the family. There was a long and, as far as school was concerned, disastrous winter vacation in 1915 on the Isle of Pines (now the Isle of Youth) south of Cuba, where Mrs. Hart, the poet's grandmother, had a house, and twice Hart made long trips around the country with his mother. In 1916 they toured the West, including San Francisco, Yellowstone National Park, and the Canadian Rockies. Hart kept up with his school work as best he could, but most of his real learning was done on his own.

In the provincial metropolis of Cleveland he could indulge his passions for art and music and the theater, and in the "ivory tower" he pursued a course of private reading in literature that could only be called ambitious and precocious, including such writers as Plato, Plutarch, Honoré de Balzac, Voltaire, and Boccaccio. He read Nathaniel Hawthorne, Oscar Wilde, and Edgar Allan Poe, and in poetry Percy Bysshe Shelley and Algernon Swinburne. His earliest poems were long rhapsodies in the manner of Swinburne, full of gods and goddesses. He haunted Richard Laukhuff's literary bookshop in downtown Cleveland, where he read all the newest avant-garde journals and little magazines. Hart Crane was by temperament and practice essentially an autodidact, and one is inclined to think that the style and content of his mind would not have been greatly different had he finished high school or attended a university. In 1916, following his parents' separation, Hart, a very green, very idealistic seventeen-year-old, was allowed to go to New York and make his mark on the world.

The plan was originally that Hart would study with a tutor toward passing the examination that would allow him to enter Columbia University without a high-school diploma, but this proved from the beginning to be little more than a pretense that permitted him to stay in New York. He was far too eager to become a successful poet immediately to be willing to spend four more years in school. While still in Cleveland he had made the acquaintance of Harriet Moody, widow of William Vaughn Moody, shown her his poems, and solicited her patronage. In September of 1916 he had actually published a poem in a New York journal called *Bruno's Weekly*, and, now that he was in New York, he lost no time in following up on every possible connection he could muster. He was never shy about pressing himself and his poems upon anyone who might prove useful, and because of his youth and guileless charm he seldom failed to make them his friends. Carl Schmitt, a painter he had known in Cleveland, became his first mentor in New York, introduced him to a wealth of modernist ideas about art and literature, and served as a critic and sounding board for his early poems. Schmitt introduced Crane to Padraic and Mary Colum. "Really," he wrote his mother, "as I expected, I am right in the swing. Tomorrow I call on the noted Irish poet & dramatist, Padraic Colum. Then I shall meet Frank Harris, editor of 'Pearsons,' and friend-biographer of Oscar Wilde. . . . Within a few weeks I expect to be printed in the columns of the 'New York Eve-

Hart Crane, in 1916, shortly before he went to New York

ning Sun.' Fine, isn't it." It was the Colums who gave him Arthur Symons's book on the symbolist movement and introduced him to the poetry of Charles Baudelaire, Arthur Rimbaud, and Paul Verlaine.

At this time, almost simultaneously, Crane came under the influence of two very different, but perhaps complementary, spheres of literary activity. One was that of the *Little Review*, which Margaret Anderson had brought from Chicago to New York in 1917. It was the champion of the English and French modernist circles. Ezra Pound was the *Little Review*'s "foreign editor," and he filled its pages with the works of writers he admired, especially T. S. Eliot, W. B. Yeats, Wyndham Lewis, and James Joyce. Crane was excited about these writers; the offices of the *Little Review* became his second home in New York; and he worked there off and on, never with much success, selling advertisements. The other important sphere of influence centered upon the journal *Seven Arts*, founded in 1916 by Waldo Frank, Van Wyck Brooks, James

Oppenheim, and Paul Rosenfeld. This group was the American school, whose guiding spirit was Walt Whitman. The editors of *Seven Arts* promoted writers such as Theodore Dreiser, Sherwood Anderson, and Robert Frost, and anyone whom they felt to be in the great tradition of Emerson, Thoreau, Melville, Whitman, and Emily Dickinson. Crane was a friend and enthusiastic admirer of Sherwood Anderson, and Waldo Frank became a kind of spiritual older brother to Crane and later edited his first *Collected Poems*. Crane moved freely between these two circles and drew upon them both. Although his was essentially a magpie's attitude toward ideas and theories, the synthesis Crane effected between these two very dissimilar sources is an important part of his contribution to modern American literature.

Hart Crane's life in New York was not easy. He was not interested in any kind of occupation apart from writing poetry, and so he was often short of money, especially when the strained communications between his parents caused his allowance to be delayed. Hart sided totally with his mother in the divorce disputes, but as a result her emotional demands on him were greater than ever. She went to Florida to socialize and forget, but she insisted nonetheless upon daily letters from her son and telegraphed him if they were late. She wrote him: "You, in my trouble, have been able to pay me for all the care & anxiety I have had for you since you came to me nearly eighteen years ago— I am expecting great things from you & when we see each other again we can talk over our plans which look very beautiful to me now. I am asking you to send me your love every day as I shall you." And in another letter: "So I am asking you to write me often Harold because your letters even though short are a stimulus to me, & surely you love me enough to do what you can to help me fight my way back to peace, happiness, & health. . . . Do not allow yourself to become an egotist & unmindful of others—But just remember that true happiness is largely due to service & no matter how rich your day may have been in opportunities, it is not entirely complete unless you have done or thought of someone else—Please write me often." Hart was completely in his mother's thrall and had no defenses whatsoever against such manipulation until years later, and then only by breaking with her. After Grace Crane returned from Florida, she brought her mother to New York, where they lived with Hart in a one-bedroom apartment on Gramercy Park. From here Mrs. Crane negotiated an abortive reconciliation with her husband, and oth-

erwise spent her time in bed with fits of "nerves," nursed by her mother with Christian Science and by her son with sympathetic attention. It is a wonder that Hart could write anything under such conditions, but it is during this time that he wrote some of his best early poems, such as "Annunciation" and "Fear," and these poems as well as several others were published within the year in Joseph Kling's the *Pagan*, a Greenwich Village journal. Hart Crane's earliest poems are interesting now primarily as a prelude to what was to follow. They were never reprinted during his lifetime, and Waldo Frank included them in *The Collected Poems of Hart Crane* (1933) as an appendix.

Hart Crane found friendship and encouragement among the New York literati, but the presence of his mother only prolonged his childhood. She moved restlessly back and forth between New York and Cleveland, always on the brink of a nervous collapse or hoping to recover from one. Hart depended upon his parents for money, and early in 1918 C. A. Crane became increasingly difficult about money and threatened to withhold Hart's allowance unless his son produced some evidence of being employed or even of seriously seeking employment. The entrance of the United States into World War I added further uncertainty to the young man's life. He looked upon the army as a possible escape from his family, but when he tried to enlist he was turned away because he was still a minor. Instead he worked for a time in a munitions plant in Cleveland as a contribution to the war effort.

When the war had ended Hart Crane took a job as a reporter for the *Cleveland Plain Dealer*. He left the *Plain Dealer* in February 1919 to return to New York and become "advertising manager" of the *Little Review* for four months. In August, on the recommendation of his father, Hart got a job with Rheinthal and Newman in New York, the firm that supplied the Crane company with the Maxfield Parrish reproductions that they featured on their candy boxes. He began as a shipping clerk and finished as a shipping clerk three months later. He then returned to Ohio to work for his father, first in Akron, then in Cleveland, until father and son had a violent argument on 20 April 1921, whereupon Hart quit his job and broke decisively with his father. He worked briefly for an advertising firm in Cleveland, writing copy, and then went back to New York to work briefly for the J. Walter Thompson Company, an advertising agency. This job was followed by others in advertising and sales, always brief, and indeed he never held a job with any success. In 1925 and again in 1927 the financier and philanthropist Otto Kahn gave Hart Crane money, which somewhat alleviated his poverty, but it was nonetheless a persistent discouragement to him to be unable to keep a job, especially in the prosperous and optimistic environment of the 1920s. This condition was in part a result of his restless nature and in part a result of his uncompromising dedication to poetry, which kept him from giving himself wholeheartedly to any other enterprise.

During these years Hart Crane's love relationships were no more stable or longlasting than his jobs, characterized as they were by the peaks of elation and the depths of despair. He had a penchant for merchant sailors, the nature of whose work occasioned sad partings and jealous separations. He suffered attacks of "homesickness" for the security of his childhood family, but from a distance he felt too strongly the emotional greed of his mother ever to succumb to her again by returning to Cleveland. If he neglected his letters to her, she could write, "I wish you to realize that you treat me very badly indeed. . . . It isn't fair at all to me, Hart . . . dead silence for two weeks. . . . Now I won't *have* such neglect—and I won't love you at all any more if you ever repeat such indifference." Yet Hart Crane was not morbid or melancholy by nature. On the contrary, he was full of vitality and eager for experience and for success, had an abundance of friends, and was widely regarded as very good company. But peace and fulfillment eluded him, as though his stars were crossed.

One might say that Hart Crane sought to discover in poetry what he found lacking in life. As early as 1919, at the precocious age of twenty, he had already begun the poems of his early maturity, which would be collected eventually and published in his first volume of verse, *White Buildings*, in 1926. With "My Grandmother's Love Letters" and "Garden Abstract" Crane establishes the connection between his poetry and his personal experience, in the one between his poetry and his family, in the other between his poetry and his sexuality. "My Grandmother's Love Letters" is a wistful poem in which the poet seeks in vain to reconstruct from old letters, "brown and soft,/And liable to melt as snow," the emotional life of his grandmother, Elizabeth Belden Hart, with whom he spent much of his childhood. There is pathos in this attempt to reassemble the shards of a broken family, but the poem ends on a note of self-protective irony: "And so I stumble. And the rain continues on the roof/With such a sound as gently pitying laughter"—as

if to ward off any charges of sentimentality. "Garden Abstract" is a personal poem of a very different sort. In it the poet projects his own homosexual impulses upon the figure of a young girl, who is experiencing an erotic surrender to the larger forces of nature: "The apple on its bough is her desire," and "She is prisoner of the tree and its green fingers." The sexual symbolism of this garden, that of male sexuality to be precise, was not lost on its first readers, at a time when Freud was fad and fashion, although there is no evidence that Crane ever read any of the works of Freud. The girl's ravishment by the forces of nature is, however, more than merely sexual. Crane called the poem a piece of "pure pantheistic aestheticism," and indeed in "Garden Abstract" the beginnings of Crane's visionary aspirations are apparent, as he seeks through the materials of his own life some archetype of unity, beauty, and escape from self-consciousness. At the end of the poem, "She has no memory, nor fear, nor hope/Beyond the grass and shadows at her feet."

In "Praises for an Urn," within the strict conventions of the English elegy, Crane transforms the grief and sense of loss experienced upon the death of a friend into a reflection upon the inviolability of art. His friend was Ernest Nelson, a Norwegian immigrant, a well-read and intelligent man and a would-be poet and painter, who lived in Cleveland and died in autumn 1921. Crane sees him as the type of the artist-victim who is pitted against the vulgarity and materialism of an uncaring society. "He was one of the many," he wrote to a friend, "broken against the stupidity of American life in such places as here." Together Ernest Nelson and the poet had speculated upon the immortality of the soul, and now one of them is dead and the other is left to confront the "insistent clock," which is "perched in the crematory lobby." The poet refuses to mourn, but scatters his verses instead, like ashes, like seeds perhaps, upon the world and succeeds thereby in robbing the sun of its triumph over the moon, that is, in robbing the world of facts of its triumph over the world of imagination. In "At Melville's Tomb," also an elegy of sorts, it is the sea—always an important symbol for Crane— that is the all-emcompassing element which reconciles the tormented artist to the tribulations of life and death: "Then in the circuit calm of one vast coil,/Its lashings charmed and malice reconciled,/Frosted eyes there were that lifted altars;/And silent answers crept across the stars."

The religious image of the "lifted altars" is continued in "Lachrymae Christi," one of Crane's most overtly religious poems and one of his most difficult. There is no logic in this poem but for the logic of metaphor and the link and association of sounds and connotations, moving elusively around a central theme: again redemption and serenity achieved through suffering. The power of the imagination (the moon) transforms the cruel world of mills and machinery into a pastoral spring. In nature perhaps there is a hope of renewal for the poet who has lost his way, a kind of baptism that will "Anoint with innocence,—recall/To music and retrieve what perjuries/Had galvanized the eyes." His theme is now "Not penitence/But song, as these/Perpetual fountains, vines,—/Thy Nazarene and tinder eyes." The abundance and extravagance of images in this poem is reminiscent of Richard Crashaw's "St. Mary Magdalene, or The Weeper," and in the parenthesis that directly follows the lines quoted above, the poet interjects a note upon his own experience of the cleansing power of tears and suffering—like benzine, a liquid both flammable and caustic, which in line two rises "from the moon." In the end of the poem the redemptive sacrifice of Christ is associated with the death and regeneration of nature, as personified in Dionysus, and with the renewal of poetry, symbolized by the "grail." "Lachrymae Christi" is an excellent example of Crane's stretching and straining language in order to suggest if not wholly to express some phenomenon that is utterly mysterious: the triumph of grace over the cruelties of nature. In the end the "Unmangled target smile" of Christ/Dionysus is held up as a goal, a target, in contrast to the "unyielding smile" of the "sure machinery," that is, of the mangle itself, the world of vulgar commercialism.

In "Lachrymae Christi" the suffering is the suffering of a poet, and the redemption is the renewal of his song. He is recalled "To music," "Not penitence/But song," and the "sphinxes from the ripe/Borages of death have cleared my tongue/Once and again." This theme of suffering as the source and occasion of poetry and of poetry as the release from suffering is a central one in Hart Crane's verse, as it was in his life. The poem "Legend," for example, which he placed significantly at the opening of *White Buildings* (1926), is, as it were, the legend of these poems, the story of their origins and a key to reading them. The poet is confronted by the chaotic flux of the world: "As silent as a mirror is believed/Realities plunge in silence by." But rather than lose himself in repentance and vain regrets and be destroyed like the moth in the flame, he approaches life as a lover. Order and meaning

in the chaotic world can be grasped "only by the one who/Spends out himself again," and it is he who will see some "bright logic" in it, however unarticulated, "Unwhispering," experienced directly and immediately, "as a mirror/Is believed." This knowledge is not necessarily comforting: it is called "This cleaving and this burning," "the smoking souvenir,/Bleeding eidolon!" It is the price the poet pays for his art: "Then, drop by caustic drop, a perfect cry/Shall string some constant harmony,—/Relentless caper for all those who step/The legend of their youth into the noon." There is a suggestion in the third and fourth stanzas of "Legend" that the reader must also share the poet's burden, become a lover, and spend himself again and again, if he is to arrive at the poet's bright logic.

The agony of the creative life and the poet's problematic acceptance of it are also the theme of "Passage." The poet seeks to escape his destiny, again in a pastoral setting: "In sapphire arenas of the hills/I was promised an improved infancy." (Little could have appealed to Hart Crane more than an improved infancy.) But this flight involves leaving memory "in a ravine," and while the abandonment of memory means the loss of pain, it also means a loss of all the pleasures that memory and the imagination have to offer. The boon is not worth the sacrifice, he decides, and "So was I turned about and back, much as your smoke/Compiles a too well-known biography." He returns, retrieves his stolen book of memory, and proposes "To argue with the laurel," when he is immediately granted a vision of some esoteric Egyptian mystery, which baffles him. The poet does not achieve any certainty or lasting satisfaction, but here at least in the world of visions is an intensity of life that far surpasses the vegetable state of forgetfulness.

In "Black Tambourine" the poet compares his own plight in life to that of "The Black man, forlorn in the cellar," shut off from society by "the world's closed door." In this life he "Wanders in some mid-kingdom" between the heaven of art, "his tambourine," and death, "a carcass quick with flies."

The comic aspects of this position of the poet at odds with society did not escape Hart Crane. Early on he saw himself as a bit of a clown, and the lines: "The everlasting eyes of Pierrot/And, of Gargantua, the laughter," which in "Praise for an Urn" he employs to describe Ernest Nelson, he wrote originally to characterize himself. Crane wrote "Chaplinesque" in October 1921, shortly after seeing Charlie Chaplin's film *The Kid,* of which he wrote to Gorham Munson that "comedy . . . has never reached a higher level in this country before." He called Chaplin a "dramatic genius." The spirit of the age and the medium of the silent film were perfectly matched in Charlie Chaplin, whom the French adopted as their own, nicknaming him "Charlot," because they saw in him a reincarnation of Pierrot, that favorite of the French and Italian stage, who has his origins in the commedia del l'arte of the renaissance. Crane saw in Chaplin the archetype of the poet in the modern world, a combination of clown, Everyman, and fool, rueful, witty, and self-deprecating, evading with a sidestep and a smirk the "inevitable thumb" of the police? of death? of a cruel world? "And yet these fine collapses are not lies," he says, if they permit the clown to preserve "the heart." By way of paraphrase Crane wrote to Gorham Munson: "I have made that 'infinitely gentle, infinitely suffering thing' of Eliot's into the symbol of the kitten. I feel that, from my standpoint, the pantomime of Charlie represents fairly well the futile gesture of the poet in U.S.A. today, perhaps elsewhere too. And yet, the heart lives on." In the last stanza of "Chaplinesque" the moon—again the poetic imagination—transforms "an empty ash can" into "a grail of laughter," which suggests that while the pursuit of poetry, especially amid the rejected debris of the world, is ludicrous and clownish, it is at the same time very serious, even sacred.

The idea of the poet as wry comedian is characteristic of the euphoric postwar period, the Jazz Age, the 1920s—an idea that found its fullest expression in Wallace Stevens's long quasi-autobiographical poem "The Comedian as the Letter C" (1923)—but it is from Jules Laforgue (1860-1887), particularly through the mediation of Ezra Pound and T. S. Eliot, his greatest disciples, that the hesitant, mocking, ironical manner of melancholy comedy came into the English poetry of this century, Eliot's "The Love Song of J. Alfred Prufrock" (1917) being the most notable example. In 1886 Laforgue published twenty-three "Pierrot poems" in his *L'Imitation de Notre Dame La Lune*, a volume that Hart Crane ordered from Paris in the fall of 1920. The following summer Crane translated three of the "Locutions des Pierrots" into English, but in his translations of Laforgue he dilutes the ironic spirit considerably and substitutes a more robust, more typically American style of braggadocio, more characteristic of his own nature than the irony of Laforgue, and closer to the broad humor of Whitman than to the urbane wit of Eliot.

It is instructive to note that after "Chaplinesque" Crane never again attempted a poem in the ironic manner of Laforgue, and in this respect

"Chaplinesque" marks a decisive point in his career. He could still be ironical when he chose, as in the second section of "For the Marriage of Faustus and Helen," which he wrote early in 1922 and which appeared in the January 1923 issue of *Broom* as "The Springs of Guilty Song." Here there is a certain detachment and a jazzy smartness in the images and in the rhythms, but Crane soon found himself repelled by the mordant humor, the alienation, and the increasing pessimism of Eliot and his followers. He wrote to Allen Tate at this time: "The poetry of negation is beautiful—alas, too dangerously so for one of my mind. But I am trying to break away from it. Perhaps this is useless, perhaps it is silly—but one *does* have joys." He had no doubt already experienced too much misery in his life to wish to pursue it in his poetry, and he was by temperament an optimist. Crane found sympathy and encouragement in his optimism among his friends of the *Seven Arts* camp, who called themselves "Young America" and were intent upon humanizing and revitalizing American civilization through the arts, restoring the optimism of Emerson and Whitman, and defeating the cruel powers of materialism. Waldo Frank, for one, was an avowed idealist in the style of the New England transcendentalists, and professed such things as: "The essence of all reality lies in the Ideal," and "America is a mystic Word. We go forth to seek America." It was in the spirit of Young America, in reaction to Eliot's *The Waste Land*, published in 1922, that Hart Crane envisaged "For the Marriage of Faustus and Helen," which he finished the following year. "There is no one writing in English who can command so much respect, to my mind, as Eliot," he explained. "However, I take Eliot as a point of departure toward an almost complete reverse of direction.... I would apply as much of his erudition and technique as I can absorb and assemble toward a more positive, or ... ecstatic goal.... I feel that Eliot ignores certain spiritual events and possibilities as real and powerful now as, say, in the time of Blake."

"For the Marriage of Faustus and Helen" was Crane's longest and most ambitious poem to date. It is presented as a prothalamion—that most affirmative kind of poem—to celebrate the union of Faustus, "the poetic or imaginative man of all times," and Helen, "the symbol of this abstract 'sense of beauty.'" To underscore his affirmation of the existence of ideal love and ideal beauty in the modern world, Crane couches his myth aggressively in modern, urban, and technological images. In section one Faustus pursues his vision of

Helen even while riding a streetcar: "Then I might find your eyes across an aisle,/Still flickering with those prefigurations." He ends the section by praying that Helen accept his adoring eye, "One inconspicuous, glowing orb of praise." Praise of an ideal as yet unattained, perhaps unattainable, is his theme. The second section is less strong than the other two, lapsing from mystic reverence to a tone almost of condescension, and it seems somewhat incongruous in the context. The scene is a jazz club on a roof garden, and the beautiful young woman—she is not called Helen by name—is less a goddess than a flapper. In section three Crane presents Helen as the ideal of beauty that survives the carnage and devastation of war. Of it he wrote to Waldo Frank, "This last part begins with *catharsis*, the acceptance of tragedy through destruction (The Fall of Troy, etc., also in it). It is Dionysian in its attitude, the creator and the eternal destroyer dance arm in arm, etc., all ending in a restatement of the imagination as in Part I." On the strength of this catharsis Faustus can say, "Let us unbind our throats of fear and pity." The combat pilot is called "religious gunman," and "eternal gunman," to suggest the liberating and religious function of material destruction when the ideal remains intact. The poem ends with a plea for praise rather than blame of "the years," the modern era, because of the triumphs it has witnessed of the imagination over despair. It is a blatant plea for optimism. Upon completing "For the Marriage of Faustus and Helen" Crane wrote to Gorham Munson that he felt himself "quite fit to become a suitable *Pindar* for the dawn of the machine age, so called. I have lost the last shreds of philosophical pessimism during the last few months. O yes, the 'background of life'—and all that is still there, but that is only three-dimensional. It is to the pulse of a greater dynamism that my work must revolve. Something terribly fierce and yet gentle." It was in this spirit of buoyancy and idealism that Crane conceived his first plans for *The Bridge*, a project that would occupy him intermittently for the next seven years.

The background of life was, indeed, still there, and Crane did not cease to write lyrics inspired by the tribulations of his private life just because he was also intent upon creating a larger, more impersonal myth of affirmation. Such poems as "Possessions" and "Recitative" call up the same tensions between aspirations and fulfillment as "For the Marriage of Faustus and Helen," and each ends with a similar call to optimism. Around Easter 1923, just weeks after finishing "For the Marriage of Faustus and Helen," Crane left Cleveland for

good and settled in New York. There he caught up with old friends and made new ones, hoping to find "some kind of community of interest . . . something better than a mere clique," only to find, as the months passed, "factions, gossips, jealousies, recriminations, excoriations," a good many of which were instigated by Crane himself. He disliked his job at J. Walter Thompson, he was beset with problems from Cleveland, and a mutilated version of his "For the Marriage of Faustus and Helen" was published in the journal *Secession*. In October he wrote to his mother, "My state of nerves and insomnia here due to the mad rush of things, and the noisy nights around the place I am obliged to live in, make it imperative that I get away before I have a real breakdown." He first intended to spend the winter on the Isle of Pines, but he decided instead to stay with his friends Edward Nagle and Slater Brown, who had rented a house near Woodstock, New York. This stay in the country was one of the happiest times in Hart Crane's life. To one friend he wrote: "I really am happy to hear the wind in the boughs, use the axe and saw, and even enjoy the bit of cooking which I share in doing. There is not much time for other things except on rainy days like the last, when I sat reading the Golden Bough. . . ." And to another he wrote: "To speak briefly, I have never felt so fine in my life before. So quiet it is here! No cats fighting, people quarrelling or subways beneath you to make the ground tremble." Two years later Crane enjoyed a similar winter pastoral as the guest of Allen and Caroline Gordon Tate in Patterson, New York, while he was doing the "research" and first drafts of *The Bridge*.

There is a hint of an "appalling tragedy"—presumably sexual—that took place the evening before he left New York for Woodstock, of which he wrote to a friend, "It keeps coming to me, though, in a kind of terrible rawness. . . . It does cry for words, however,—and I'm wondering if I am equal to such an occasion, such beauty and anguish, all in one." Such is the background of "Possessions" and "Recitative," which he brought back with him from Woodstock shortly after the new year. Both poems deal with the anguish of lust and the abiding hope for some kind of fulfillment in love. "Possessions" presents a "Record of rage and partial appetites," followed directly by the flat statement that "The pure possession, the inclusive cloud/Whose heart is fire shall come." "Recitative" presents a vivid and haunting picture of man as a creature divided against himself, "Janus-faced," "Twin shadowed halves," like someone looking in

Hart Crane, Allen Tate, and William Slater Brown in a Times Square photographer's gallery, February 1925

a mirror, "Borne cleft to you, and brother in the half." But when the sun rises, "The bridge swings over salvage," the morning bells are heard, "All hours clapped dense into a single stride," and the poet addresses his doppelgänger, his alienated self: "Forgive me for an echo of these things,/And let us walk through time with equal pride." It is significant that in neither "Possessions" nor "Recitative" is there any resolution or fulfillment beyond a tenacious determination to avoid despair. Even that determination is a kind of grace, an intimation of something positive. Of "Recitative" he wrote to Allen Tate: "Against this paradoxical DUALITY is posed the UNITY, or the conception of it (as you got it) in the last verse." And to his mother in the same month he wrote: "I have a revived con-

fidence in humanity lately, and things are going to come very beautifully for me—and not after so very long, I think. The great thing is to Live and NOT Hate. (Christian Science, in part, I think; and a very important doctrine of belief. Perhaps the most important.)"

Perhaps the strongest statement of this doctrine of belief in the face of unsatisfactory personal experience, and Crane's profoundest expression of his striving for unity and perfection in love, is to be found in "Voyages," a suite of love poems that he wrote in the fall of 1924 and included in *White Buildings* (1926). The summation and crowning achievement of the volume, these six poems doubtless contain some of Crane's finest lyric poetry, firmly rooted as they are in the facts of his own life and aimed at a visionary resolution strictly within the context of his own emotional and imaginative existence.

Shortly after returning to New York from Woodstock Crane fell in love with a young man called Emil Opffer and in April 1924 moved with him into an apartment at 110 Columbia Heights in Brooklyn, "in the shadow of that bridge," as he wrote to Waldo Frank. The relationship seems to have been a passionate friendship, based on affection and mutual understanding and intensely heightened by eroticism. Opffer worked as a ship's writer, sailing out of New York for periods of eight weeks at a time followed by the same amount of time or less with Crane in Brooklyn. For Crane this experience was "Heaven and Hell." Of the heaven he wrote to Frank: "I have seen the Word made Flesh. I mean nothing less, and I know now that there is such a thing as indestructibility. In the deepest sense, where flesh became transformed through intensity of response to counter-response, where sex was beaten out, where a purity of joy was reached that included tears." The hell of separation from Opffer involved Crane in states of "almost hysterical despair," fits of jealousy, fears of venereal disease, and binges of drinking and carousing. The relationship cooled into a casual friendship within the year, but while it lasted it offered Crane the material out of which he forged "Voyages."

Much of the success of "Voyages" is the result of Crane's happy use of the sea as a symbol of human love, its overwhelming grandeur, its beauty, its dangers, and its power to transport a person beyond what is familiar. Crane associated his own experience of love with the sea, as he wrote in the same letter to Frank: "I think the sea has thrown itself upon me and been answered, at least in part, and I believe I am a little changed—not essentially, but changed and transubstantiated as anyone is who has asked a question and been answered." "Voyages I," borrowing a theme from Melville, presents the sea (and love) as something dangerous: "there is a line/You must not cross nor ever trust beyond it," because "The bottom of the sea is cruel." It is something larger than man, beyond his control. In "Voyages II" the poet calls the sea "this great wink of eternity," a glimpse of the perfection of love in a timeless sphere, where "sleep, death, desire,/Close round one instant in one floating flower." In part three the poet continues "this tendered theme" of the sea, of the "Infinite consanguinity it bears," in a realm "through black swollen gates," where the lover surrenders himself totally,

"and where death, if shed,/Resumes no carnage, but this single change,—/Upon the steep floor flung from dawn to dawn/The silken skilled transmemberment of song." In part four the lovers, having surrendered themselves totally to one another, are separated, but the sea is now the medium of a spiritual union between them, overcoming the limitations of space as it has those of time. And the communication between the parted lovers is one of song; "No stream of greater love advancing now/Than, singing, this mortality alone/Through clay aflow immortally to you." This vision of unity despite separation, "in mingling/Mutual blood, transpiring as foreknown," fills the poet with hope of a complete spiritual fulfillment in love, of a "pure possession": "In this expectant, still exclaim receive/The secret oar and petals of all love." Part five marks the death of the love that had once bridged the sea, and now "The cables of our sleep so swiftly filed,/Already hang, shred ends from remembered stars." The faithless lover takes the poet's gift of total love and sails away with it: "No,/In all the argosy of your bright hair I dreamed/Nothing so flagless as this piracy." Crane does not leave the poem with an image of love sundered and pirated. He was candid about his own failure to find satisfaction in love, but the vision of the possibility of perfect love was also a part of his experience, and ultimately the most important part. In "Voyages VI," beyond the stormy sea of mundane love, is a celestial sphere, of "rivers mingling toward the sky," in which "Creation's blithe and petalled word" is addressed to Venus, the goddess of love, "the lounged goddess when she rose/Conceding dialogue with eyes/That smile unsearchable repose—" intimating a possible fulfillment in Love. The goddess is then replaced by the image of an island, Belle Isle, which is called "Still fervid covenant," and "white echo of the oar," an echo, that is, of "The secret oar and petal of all love." In the last stanza this mystery is called "the Word": "The imaged Word, it is, that holds/Hushed willows anchored in its glow./It is the unbetrayable reply/Whose accent no farewell can know." "The imaged Word" is the poet's final name for his vision, "the Word made Flesh." Crane is borrowing, of course, St. John's expression for God's revelation of himself to mankind in the flesh of Jesus Christ, and suggesting at the same time the "imaged word" of poetry, the medium by which the poet's vision is made available to his readers. The vision is a vision of faith in the possibility of a sublime fulfillment in love—"a very important doctrine of belief"— and not a mystical experience of that fulfillment,

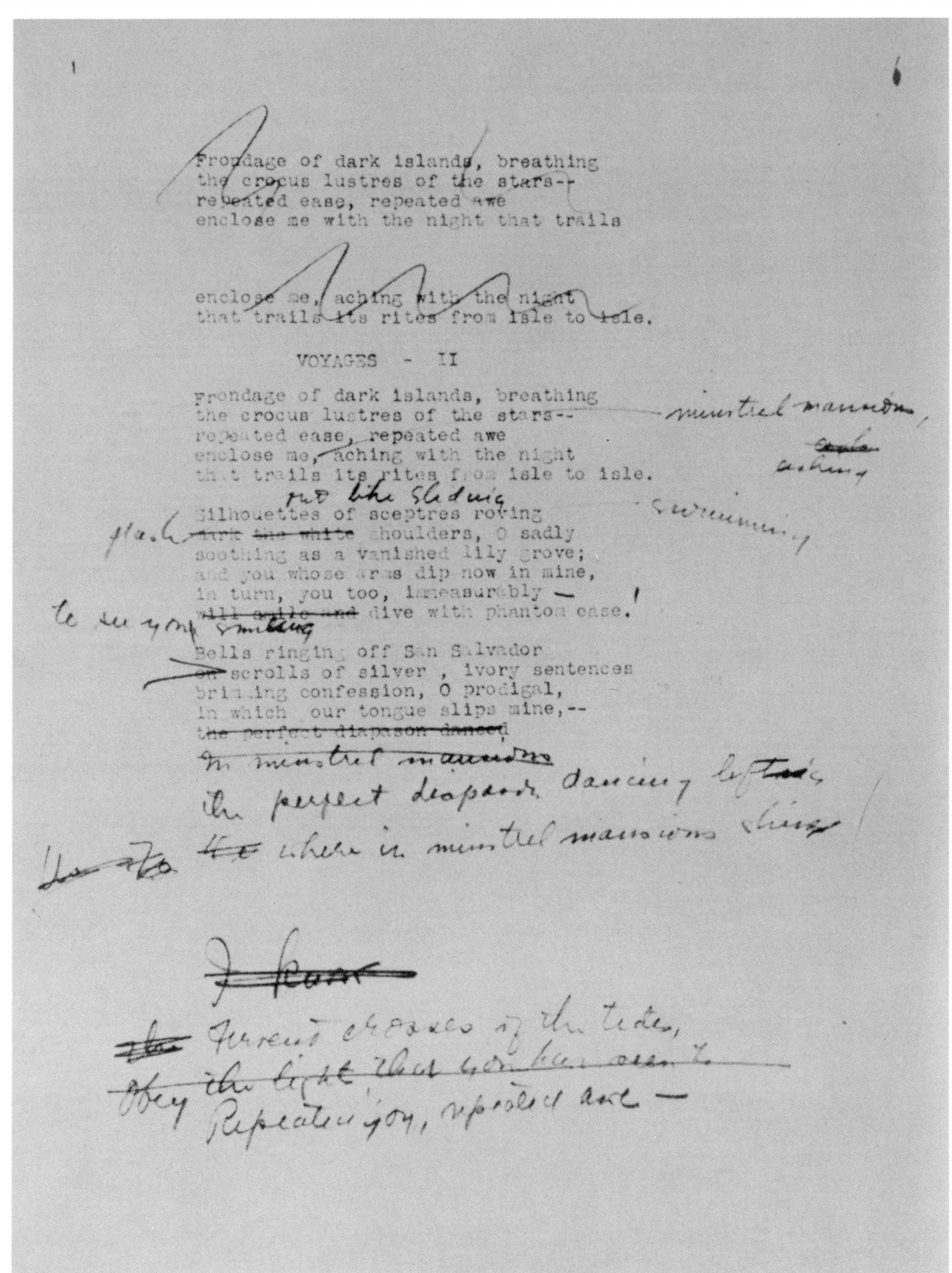

Drafts (circa autumn 1924) for a portion of "Voyages II," collected in White Buildings *(courtesy of the Rare Book and Manuscript Library, Columbia University)*

and it is Crane's humility in not extending the poem beyond what he had himself seen and felt that accounts for the authenticity of "Voyages."

The final image in "Voyages," of the poet-voyager sailing to a Belle Isle of the imagination, firmly establishes Hart Crane in the symbolist tradition, and it is not without justice that Carl Sandburg called him "the Cleveland Rimbaud." But there was too much of Cleveland in Crane—too much of modern industry and commerce and too much of the expansive optimism of the American heartland—to allow him to accept the isolation and alienation from society that comes with the role of *poète maudit*. Emerson, in his essay "Art," says that the artist of genius must "find beauty and holiness in new and necessary facts, in the field and roadside, in the shop and mill," and "raise to divine use the railroad, the insurance office, the joint stock-company." Crane, in his essay "Modern Poetry" (1930) says, "For unless poetry can absorb the machine, i.e., *acclimatize* it as naturally and casually as trees, cattle, galleons, castles and all other human associations of the past, then poetry has failed of its full contemporary function." It was Crane's ambition to build upon the spiritual illuminations of his private life and extend them into an optimistic vision of all America, acclimatizing the industrial world to all the human associations of its past, that informs his longest and most ambitious work, *The Bridge*. His model and mentor was not Rimbaud but Whitman.

As noted above, the initial idea for *The Bridge* came to Crane directly upon his finishing "For the Marriage of Faustus and Helen," while he was still living in Cleveland. In February 1923 he wrote to Gorham Munson: "I am ruminating on a new longish poem under the title of *The Bridge* which carries on further the tendencies manifest in 'F and H.' " He intended it originally to be "something of equal length" to "For the Marriage of Faustus and Helen," and he expected to finish it for inclusion in a first volume of his poems, but as he worked on *The Bridge* its scope and length expanded. The project was begun with great enthusiasm and announcements far and wide of his ambitious plans, but in fact very little of *The Bridge* had yet been written in the winter of 1926, when Crane had his *White Buildings* published by Boni and Liveright (without *The Bridge*) and returned to *The Bridge* after an interval of two years. Then came a brief period of prodigious creativity, between April and November 1926, when Crane retired to the Isle of Pines, thanks to the grant from Otto Kahn, and wrote ten of the fifteen sections of *The Bridge*. The

following year he saw most of these sections published separately in various periodicals. It was not until 1929, however, stimulated by a promise from Harry and Caresse Crosby to publish it in Paris, that Crane actually finished his poem, and *The Bridge* was finally published by the Crosbys' Black Sun Press in February 1930, and by Horace Liveright in New York in April. The order of the separate parts of the poem as it was published bears no relation to the order of their composition, and at one point (in August 1926) Crane wrote, "I skip from one section to another now like a sky-gack or girder-jack." Despite the seven years of its gestation, the singleness of its inspiration and the simultaneous composition of many of its parts contributed greatly to a sense of organic unity in *The Bridge* as a whole.

Again T. S. Eliot's *The Waste Land* offers a useful focus of comparison and contrast to Crane's intention and achievement in *The Bridge*. Structurally and stylistically there are considerable similarities: both poets are thoroughly eclectic, drawing upon a wide range of cultural and historical ma-

Hart Crane at Harry and Caresse Crosby's country retreat in Ermenonville, France, spring 1929

terial and assimilating it in a nonnarrative, thematic web of associations and allusions. Even the "gloss notes" were suggested by Eliot's notes for *The Waste Land*. After *The Bridge* was published Crane wrote to a sympathetic but confused reviewer (Herbert Weinstock) to suggest that "with more time and familiarity with *The Bridge* you will envisage it more as one poem with a clearer and more integrated unity and development than was at first evident. . . . It took me nearly five years, with innumerable readings to convince myself of the essential unity of [Eliot's *The Waste Land*]. And *The Bridge* is at least as complicated in its structure and inferences as *The Waste Land*—perhaps more so." But Crane's admiration of *The Waste Land* was more for its style than for its ideas. When it first appeared he was "rather disappointed," and found it "good, of course, but so damned dead." And later he wrote, "I tried to break loose from that particular strait-jacket [the fashionable pessimism of T. S. Eliot], without however committing myself to any oppositional form of didacticism. . . . [*The Bridge*], as a whole, is, I think, an affirmation of experience, and to that extent is 'positive' rather than 'negative' in the sense that *The Waste Land* is negative."

Both Eliot and Crane were mythologizing poets, and it is precisely in their use of myth that they are at the same time so similar and so different. Crane in all probability read T. S. Eliot's review of Joyce's *Ulysses* in the *Dial* (November 1923), where Eliot wrote: "In using the myth, in manipulating a continuous parallel between contemporaneity and antiquity, Mr. Joyce is pursuing a method which others must pursue after him. . . . It is simply a way of controlling, of ordering, of giving a shape and significance to the immense panorama of futility and anarchy which is contemporary history." In outlining his project for *The Bridge* to Otto Kahn in 1927, Crane wrote: "What I am after is an assimilation of this experience, a more organic panorama, showing the continuous and living evidence of the past in the inmost vital substance of the present." These words explain how Crane adopted the method propounded by Eliot and adapted it to idealistic purposes.

Unlike Eliot, Crane seems to have known very little about mythology or history, but he did have a strong intuitive sense of the mythic or symbolic qualities in persons, places, and things, be they contemporary, historical, or fictional. Brooklyn Bridge itself, the controlling symbol of the poem, with which it begins and ends, is at the same time a historical object, a work of art, a product of modern technology, and a perfect metaphor for the desire,

the spiritual ambitions, and the unifying and reconciling aspirations of American idealism. In the "Ave Maria" section Crane introduces Christopher Columbus, a man whose courage and faith led him to discover a New World. It was Columbus who forged the union of European culture and religion with the native soil of Pocahontas, "Powhatan's Daughter." For Crane Rip Van Winkle represented a man who carries the past around with him in his experience of modern life. The Land, the vast American continent drained by the Mississippi, is celebrated in "The River" section, the Sea in "Cutty Sark," and the Air in "Cape Hatteras," where the Wright brothers once again manifest that spiritual urge to transcend time and space, to fly. In "The Dance" the mythic material of America is invested with mystery and eroticism. At every turn in *The Bridge* it is the visionary trend in the American experience that inspires Crane to praise and poetry.

"The Dance" can be seen as the high point or turning point in this visionary celebration; and vision is indeed the very lock and key of *The Bridge*, but Crane was too honest as an observer of modern life to claim that the visionary experience in America is, or ever has been, an easy one. The powers of darkness—materialism and vulgarity—are too great to ignore. In "National Winter Garden," for example, Love, the very basis of idealism, is cheapened and compromised by lust and commercialism, combined in the burlesque theater. In "Quaker Hill" the once sacred New England landscape—the Promised Land and New Jerusalem of the Puritan Fathers—is now nothing but real estate, golf courses, and antique auctions. And in "The Tunnel"—the tunnel that goes under the East River where the Brooklyn Bridge flies over it—is a kind of modern Hades, a mockery of everything that has gone before. It is only in "Atlantis," the last section of the poem but the first to be written, that a balance is restored, but this balance is achieved only by the transformation of the bridge into a spiritual reality, a spiritualization and interiorization of the entire myth and history of America. The epigraph from Plato—"Music is then the knowledge of that which relates to love in harmony and system"—indicates that the fulfillment of this journey toward idealism is ultimately in the world of ideas, where music is not sound but knowledge. The bridge becomes "Love" and "Answerer of all," and the poet dedicates himself and his song to it: "So to thine Everpresence, beyond time,/Like spears ensanguined of one tolling star/That bleeds infinity—the orphic strings,/Sidereal phalanxes, leap and converge:/—One Song, one Bridge of

Drafts for parts of "The River" and "Van Winkle" sections of The Bridge *(courtesy of the Rare Book and Manuscript Library, Columbia University)*

Fire!" In the end it is Fire, that sanguine element, that transcends Earth, Air, and Water.

Crane was well aware of the contradiction existing in a vision that never gets beyond the mind of the visionary. In June 1926 he wrote to Waldo Frank: "The validity of a work of art is situated in contemporary reality to the extent that the artist must honestly anticipate the realization of his vision in 'action' (as an actively operating principle of communal works and faith), and I don't mean by this that his procedure requires any bona fide evidences directly and personally signalled, nor even any physical signs or portents. The darkness is part of his business. It has always been taken for granted, however, that his intuitions were salutary and that his vision either sowed or epitomized 'experience' (in the Blakeian sense)." Hart Crane's confidence in "what has always been taken for granted" was entirely emotional and not at all intellectual. In the same letter he said, "Emotionally I should like to write *The Bridge;* intellectually judged the whole theme and project seems more and more absurd.... These 'materials' were valid to me to the extent that I presumed them to be (articulate or not) at least organic and active factors in the experience and perceptions of our common race, time and belief. The very idea of a bridge, of course, is a form peculiarly dependent on such spiritual convictions. It is an act of faith besides being a communication. The symbols of reality necessary to articulate the span—may not exist where you expect them, however. By which I mean that however great their subjective significance to me is concerned—these forms, materials, dynamics are simply non-existent in the world. I may amuse and delight and flatter myself as much as I please—but I am only evading a recognition and playing Don Quixote in an immorally conscious way."

Here Hart Crane is placing himself precisely at the center of the essential dilemma of romanticism. Not only did he feel that the values and vision he found in the past seem to have evaporated in the twentieth century, but even in the present the values and vision he felt within himself appear to have no necessary connection to the world outside the self. Crane seems never to have resolved this dilemma—indeed resolution is not possible without recourse to some transcendent absolute—but he did, within a few months following this letter, go on to write the greater part of *The Bridge,* presumably trusting that what has always been taken for granted can safely be taken for granted again. In this trust he had a considerable weight of authority from the nineteenth century behind him, in the

romantic poets, and especially in Thomas Carlyle and Emerson. Carlyle advocated a blind leap of the will, a pronouncement of the "Everlasting Yea" to the validity of personal experience. Emerson, in his essay "The Poet," claimed that the products of the poetic imagination have "a certain power of emancipation and exhilaration for all men.... We are like persons who come out of a cave or cellar into the open air. This is the effect on us of tropes, fables, oracles and all poetic forms. Poets are thus liberating gods. Men have really got a new sense, and found within their world another world, or nest of worlds; for the metamorphosis once seen, we divine that it does not stop.... [The poet] unlocks our chains and admits us to a new sense." It is this blind faith in the creative, transforming, revivifying power of the individual imagination that is the spiritual heritage of Whitman. In the same letter to Waldo Frank quoted above, Crane wrote, "If only America were half as worthy today to be spoken of as Whitman spoke of it fifty years ago there might be something for me to say—not that Whitman received or required any tangible proof of his intimations, but that time has shown how increasingly lonely and ineffectual his confidence stands." How much more lonely and ineffectual did Hart Crane's confidence seem to many of his first readers in the wasteland of the Depression era.

Unlike Crane, T. S. Eliot had no such confidence; he trusted the intellect more than the emotions, and he rejected the romantic theory of visionary imagination. In this he was the guiding spirit of an entire generation of literary critics who were essentially antipathetic to Hart Crane's poetry. For many years the consensus of opinion on *The Bridge* was roughly that which Elizabeth Drew expressed in 1936, that "Structurally, on both spiritual and formal planes, the poem remains a muddle." In 1939 F. R. Leavis wrote that "Crane's symbolism amounts to nothing more than a turgidly rhetorical 'shall'.... The poem is wordy chaos, both locally and in sum ... I cannot see that, apart from his conviction of genius and his confidence, he had any relevant gift." Two of the severest indictments of Crane came finally from two of his greatest admirers, Allen Tate and Yvor Winters. Both felt in the 1920s that Crane was a poet of genius, but with the further development of their critical ideas, and in light of Crane's demise, they both came to think that his lack of a system of knowledge or of rational means for defining his experience was the cause of the failures in both his life and his art and offered proof of the self-destructiveness inherent in romanticism. Tate wrote (in the 1930s): "Far from 'refuting' Eliot, his whole career is a vindication of Eliot's major premise—that the integrity of the individual consciousness has broken down.... The poet did not face his first problem, which is to define the limits of his personality and to objectify its moral implications in an appropriate symbolism. Crane could only assert a quality of will against the world, and at each successive failure of the will he turned upon himself." Winters wrote (in 1947): "The Emersonian doctrine, which is merely the romantic doctrine with a New England emotional coloration, should naturally result in madness if one really lived it; it should result in literary confusion if one really wrote it. Crane accepted it; he lived it; he wrote it." For Tate and Winters, as for other proponents of the New Criticism, such as Kenneth Burke, John Crowe Ransom, and R. P. Blackmur, it was the entire romantic tradition that was on trial: Hart Crane was only their monitory example. Both Tate and Winters had lost their enthusiasm for *The Bridge* even before it was finished, and when it appeared Winters wrote an unfavorable review of it in *Poetry* (June 1930), which Crane interpreted as a personal attack and the bitterest betrayal.

The generally hostile, bewildered, or indifferent reactions to his great poem were only one of the many reversals that Hart Crane met with in the last few years of his life. In 1928 there was the permanent break with his mother and the death of his grandmother, followed in 1930 by the death of his father, to whom he had been warmly reconciled. Largely to escape his mother's emotional demands, Crane took his small inheritance from his grandmother and sailed to Europe, where he spent the first six months of 1929. In Paris, which he called "the most interesting madhouse in the world," he met scores of prominent people in the arts, but the endless partying and drinking took its toll both on his health and on his spirits, and he got very little writing done. His European sojourn ended with a fracas with the police in a Paris café and a stint in jail. Harry Crosby, with whom Crane spent most of his time in France, shot his mistress and himself in New York in December 1929, and it was Crane who bore the bad news to Crosby's wife and mother. By far the most serious grief for Crane was what seemed like the failure of his powers as a poet. After 1927 he wrote next to nothing but for two brief periods (in the summer of 1929 and the winter of 1932), and what he did write, he realized, was far inferior to his best early work. Most of his time was spent in drunkenness and debauchery. In March 1931 he received a Guggenheim Fellowship for the purpose of studying "European culture, classical and romantic, with especial reference to contrasting elements implicit in the emergent features of a distinctive American poetic consciousness"; but, if indeed he ever had any serious intention of pursuing such a study, he promptly abandoned it and went instead to Mexico, where he gave himself up extensively to alcoholic and sexual intemperance.

Crane did, however, take an interest in Mexican culture—architecture and religious rituals in particular—and he had a love affair, his only heterosexual attachment, with Peggy Baird, an old friend from New York who was at the time married to Malcolm Cowley. He had periods of hopefulness about his writing, and in one of those periods, in the winter of 1932, he wrote his last and one of his finest poems, "The Broken Tower." "The Broken Tower" is a poignant recapitulation of his entire career as the "sexton slave" of the "antiphonal carillons" of poetry: "The bells, I say, the bells break down their tower." He "entered the broken world/ To trace the visionary company of love." He poured out his words without knowing whether they were "cognate, scored/Of that tribunal monarch of the air" or "cleft to despair." He looks forward to building a new tower, "a tower that is not stone/(Not stone can jacket heaven)," a spiritual tower that will join earth and heaven, so that "the commodious, tall decorum of that sky/Unseals her earth, and lifts love in its shower." This is the same private vision of love and perfect union that we find at the end of "Voyages," and this vision is the most essential and authentic motive in all of Hart Crane's life and work. He sought to reunite what had been sundered—his parent's marriage, or the broken world—through the power of love and poetry. His failure to connect this vision with the world outside himself does not invalidate the desire, but whenever he wearied and the force of his will could not hold out against the unhappy facts of reality, he was in despair. His was not generally thought to be a suicidal personality, but it was in such a period of despair, after a night of riotous behavior on board ship, around noon on 27 April 1932, that he leapt to his death from the deck of the *Orizaba*, on which he and Peggy Baird were sailing back to New York.

The report of his suicide fueled the legend of Hart Crane the tragic-romantic poet-hero driven to an early death, like Keats, by hostile critics, and that legend together with the antiromantic position of the New Critics served for many years to prevent any just evaluation of Crane's poetry. And yet, Har-

Peggy Baird Cowley and Hart Crane in Mexico, 1932

old Bloom has said that in the 1930s, "when I was eleven years old," it was the poetry of Hart Crane that "cathected me onto poetry, a conversion or investment fairly typical of many of my generation." Crane's world view is considered to have had a significant influence upon such later poets as Charles Olson and Robert Creeley, but it has been only since the 1960s, when the New Criticism began to give way to a more sympathetic, or at least more historical and objective, view of romanticism, that Hart Crane has come into his own. The difficulties and obscurities of his poems and the problems of pattern and structure in *The Bridge* have been solved by works of scholarly explication, most notably those by L. S. Dembo and R. W. B. Lewis. Any questions that could have been left by the earlier biographies by Philip Horton and Brom Weber have been more than answered in John Unterecker's encyclopedic biography *Voyager* (1969). There is now an abundance of learned studies of Crane's

life and work, and the interest that he continues to inspire among poets and readers of poetry today is enough to justify Allen Tate's original opinion (1925), that "Hart Crane's poetry, even in its beginnings, is one of the finest achievements of this age."

Letters:

The Letters of Hart Crane, 1916-1932, edited by Brom Weber (New York: Hermitage House, 1952);

Letters of Hart Crane and His Family, edited by Thomas S. W. Lewis (New York & London: Columbia University Press, 1974).

Bibliographies:

Kenneth A. Lohf, *The Literary Manuscripts of Hart Crane* (Columbus: Ohio University Press, 1967);

Joseph Schwartz, *Hart Crane: An Annotated Critical*

Bibliography (New York: David Lewis, 1970);

Schwartz and Robert C. Schweik, *Hart Crane: A Descriptive Bibliography* (Pittsburgh: University of Pittsburgh Press, 1972);

Schwartz, *Hart Crane: A Reference Guide* (Boston: G. K. Hall, 1983).

Biographies:

Philip Horton, *Hart Crane: The Life of an American Poet* (New York: Norton, 1937);

Brom Weber, *Hart Crane: A Biographical and Critical Study* (New York: Bodley Press, 1948);

Susan Jenkins Brown, *Robber Rocks: Letters and Memories of Hart Crane, 1923-1932* (Middletown, Conn.: Wesleyan University Press, 1969);

John Unterecker, *Voyager: A Life of Hart Crane* (New York: Farrar, Straus & Giroux, 1969).

References:

Joseph J. Arpad, "Hart Crane's Platonic Myth: The Brooklyn Bridge," *American Literature*, 39 (March 1967): 75-86;

R. W. Butterfield, *The Broken Arc: A Study of Hart Crane* (Edinburgh: Oliver & Boyd, 1969);

David R. Clark, ed., *Critical Essays on Hart Crane* (Boston: G. K. Hall, 1982);

Clark, ed., *The Merrill Studies in "The Bridge"* (Columbus, Ohio: Merrill, 1970);

Stanley K. Coffman, Jr., "Symbolism in *The Bridge*," *PMLA*, 66 (March 1951): 65-77;

Malcolm Cowley, "A Preface to Hart Crane," *New Republic*, 62 (23 April 1930): 276-277;

Cowley, "Two Views of *The Bridge*," *Sewanee Review*, 89 (Spring 1981): 191-205;

L. S. Dembo, *Hart Crane's Sanskrit Charge: A Study of The Bridge* (Ithaca: Cornell University Press, 1960);

Dembo, "Hart Crane's 'Verticalist' Poem," *American Literature*, 40 (March 1968): 77-81;

Waldo Frank, "The Poetry of Hart Crane," *New Republic*, 50 (16 March 1927): 116-117;

Gordon K. Grigsby, "Hart Crane's Doubtful Vision," *College English*, 24 (April 1963): 518-523;

Allen Grossman, "Hart Crane and Poetry: A Consideration of Crane's Intense Poetics with Reference to 'The Return,'" *ELH*, 48 (Winter 1981): 841-879;

Alfred Hanley, *Hart Crane's Holy Vision: "White Buildings"* (Pittsburgh: Duquesne University Press, 1981);

Samuel Hazo, *Hart Crane: An Introduction and Interpretation* (New York: Barnes & Noble, 1963);

Barbara Herman, "The Language of Hart Crane,"

Sewanee Review, 58 (January-March 1950): 52-67;

Maurice Kramer, "Hart Crane's 'Reflexes,'" *Twentieth Century Literature*, 13 (October 1967): 131-138;

Herbert A. Leibowitz, *Hart Crane: An Introduction to the Poetry* (New York: Columbia University Press, 1968);

R. W. B. Lewis, *The Poetry of Hart Crane: A Critical Study* (Princeton: Princeton University Press, 1967);

Deena Posy Metzger, "Hart Crane's Bridge: The Myth Active," *Arizona Quarterly*, 20 (Spring 1964): 36-46;

Helge Normann Nilsen, *Hart Crane's Divided Vision: An Analysis of The Bridge* (Oslo: Universitetsforlaget, 1980);

Thomas Parkinson, "Hart Crane and Yvor Winters: A Meeting of Minds," *Southern Review*, 11 (July 1975): 491-512;

Parkinson, *Hart Crane and Yvor Winters: Their Literary Correspondence* (Berkeley, Los Angeles & London: University of California Press, 1978);

Sherman Paul, *Hart's Bridge* (Chicago: University of Illinois Press, 1972);

Donald Pease, "Blake, Crane, Whitman, and Modernism: A Poetics of Pure Possibility," *PMLA*, 96 (January 1981): 64-85;

Robert L. Perry, *The Shared Vision of Waldo Frank and Hart Crane* (Lincoln: University of Nebraska Press, 1966);

Vincent G. Quinn, *Hart Crane* (New York: Twayne, 1963);

Roger Ramsey, "A Poetics of *The Bridge*," *Twentieth Century Literature*, 26 (1980): 278-293;

Sidney Richman, "Hart Crane's 'Voyages II': An Experiment in Redemption," *Wisconsin Studies in Contemporary Literature*, 3 (Spring-Summer 1962): 65-78;

Joseph Riddel, "Hart Crane's Poetics of Failure," *ELH*, 33 (December 1966): 473-496;

Richard H. Rupp, "Hart Crane: Vitality as *Credo* in 'Atlantis,'" *Midwest Quarterly*, 3 (April 1962): 265-275;

Joseph Schwartz, "A Divided Self: The Poetic Sensibility of Hart Crane with Respect to *The Bridge*," *Modernist Studies*, 3 (1979): 3-18;

Bernice Slote, "The Structure of Hart Crane's *The Bridge*," *University of Kansas City Review*, 24 (March 1958): 225-238;

Slote, "Transmutation in Crane's Imagery in *The Bridge*," *MLN*, 123 (January 1958): 15-23;

Monroe K. Spears, *Hart Crane* (Minneapolis: University of Minnesota Press, 1965);

Allen Tate, "The Self-made Angel," *New Republic*, 129 (31 August 1953): 17-21;

Alan Trachtenberg, ed., *Hart Crane: A Collection of Critical Essays* (Englewood Cliffs: Prentice-Hall, 1982);

M. D. Uroff, *Hart Crane: The Patterns of His Poetry* (Urbana, Chicago & London: University of Illinois Press, 1974).

Papers:

The major collection of Hart Crane's manuscripts is in the library of Columbia University.

Caresse Crosby

(20 April 1892-24 January 1970)

Melody M. Zajdel
Montana State University

See also the Harry and Caresse Crosby entry in *DLB 4, American Writers in Paris, 1920-1939.*

BOOKS: *Crosses of Gold* (Paris: Privately printed, 1925; enlarged edition, Paris: Messein, 1925);

Graven Images (Boston & New York: Houghton Mifflin, 1926);

Painted Shores (Paris: Editions Narcisse, 1927);

The Stranger (Paris: Editions Narcisse, 1928);

Impossible Melodies (Paris: Editions Narcisse, 1928);

Poems for Harry Crosby (Paris: Black Sun Press, 1931);

The Passionate Years (New York: Dial, 1953; enlarged edition, London: Redman, 1955).

OTHER: Harry Crosby, ed., *Anthology*, includes poems by Caresse Crosby (Paris: Privately printed, 1924);

"The Stranger," *transition*, no. 18 (November 1929): 96-101;

47 Unpublished Letters from Marcel Proust to Walter Berry, edited and translated by Harry Crosby and Caresse Crosby (Paris: Black Sun Press, 1930).

Although only a minor poet in her own right, Caresse Crosby had a significant impact on modern literature. With her husband, Harry Crosby, and later on her own, she published and promoted many of the early modernists. The Crosbys' Black Sun Press produced works by D. H. Lawrence, Kay Boyle, Ezra Pound, James Joyce, and Hart Crane, and in the 1930s, Caresse Crosby established Crosby Continental Editions to print inexpensive paperback editions of American and French novels. As editor and publisher of *Portfolio: An Intercontinental Review* (1945-1948), Crosby fostered the continued exchange of ideas between writers and artists in France and America. In addition to her publishing ventures, Crosby also supported avant-garde art through her sponsorship of individuals, through exhibits at her Crosby Gallery of Modern Art in Washington, D.C., during the 1940s, and through her establishment of an artists' colony in Rocca Sinibalda, Italy, in the early 1950s. Her final energies were devoted to the world-peace movement. She helped found Citizens of the World and Women Against War, and in the 1960s she purchased a mountaintop in Cyprus, where she intended to build a world-peace center. All her undertakings were notable for the tireless vitality she brought to them. Caresse Crosby was an activist who made ideas concrete, for both herself and others.

The daughter of William and Mary Phelps Jacob, she was born into a socially prominent New York family, what she called "a crystal chandelier background." Mary Phelps (Polly) Jacob—only later self-styled Caresse—was educated at private schools and, as was expected in her social class, debuted at Sherry's and was formally presented at

Caresse Crosby, 1929

the Court of St. James's. Little in her early life indicated her future rebelliousness, although her high spirits were evident from the beginning. While in school she began a neighborhood newspaper, for which she wrote both poetry and local news. However, at this period of her life, her inventiveness took less a literary turn than a fashion one. In 1913 she invented and patented a "backless brassiere," to be worn instead of a corset. Light and risqué, its unconventionality was the harbinger of her future life-style. She produced about a hundred before selling the patent for $1,500.

In January 1915 Polly Jacob married Richard Rogers Peabody, a young Boston banker. Although Crosby felt somewhat dislocated in Boston society, she was relatively happy and had two children, Billy and Polly, before Peabody was called to serve in World War I. On Peabody's return, his increasingly serious alcoholism and her newfound interest in a young Harvard war hero, Harry Crosby, led to their divorce. She had met Henry Grew Crosby, six years her junior, while chaperoning a social out-

ing. Within a few weeks the two were lovers. The difference in their ages, her marital status, and their flagrant and impassioned courtship scandalized proper Boston society. Although the Peabodys' divorce was final in December 1921, familial and social pressures on the couple forestalled an immediate marriage. Only after a separation and transcontinental romance (he was in Paris, she in New York City), were they married. Two days after the ceremony on 9 September 1922, the Crosbys and her two children sailed for Paris.

For the next seven years, Caresse and Harry Crosby lived out the advice given in one of Caresse's poems, "Wisdom of the East": "You must live before you can write. . . ." These seven years were frenetic, hedonistic, exuberant, and a total break with the "polite society" in which both had grown up. Living first in Paris, then in the suburb of Ermenonville, in a restored mill they called Le Moulin du Soleil, the Crosbys partied with artists and socialites, met with writers, studied literature, and

The Crosbys in Paris, September 1922

began to both write and publish. In 1924 Caresse officially changed her name from Polly to Caresse and began in earnest her career as a writer. Her poems had two primary themes: the romanticizing and immortalizing of her relationship with Harry Crosby, and her quest for Love and Beauty (the ideals) in modern life. Her first five books (the bulk of her poetic career) appeared in rapid succession and varied only minimally in form, theme, and quality.

Caresse's first book, *Crosses of Gold,* printed privately in 1925, was typical of her poetry. It was a collection of love lyrics in conventional form. Although she supported avant-garde writers and later signed Eugene Jolas's "Revolution of the Word" manifesto, her own works remained doggedly conventional. Her modernism was confined to her open references to the physical nature of love rather than to a concern with form.

Her second volume of poems, *Graven Images,* appeared a year later. Harry Crosby's cousin, Walter Berry (a friend of Edith Wharton and Henry James), suggested that America needed a second Amy Lowell, so Crosby sent a manuscript to Lowell's publishers, Houghton Mifflin, in Boston. They accepted the volume, although with considerably less expectation that it would supersede Lowell's poetry, and Crosby's book became the only volume of poetry by either Harry Crosby or herself not initially published at their own expense.

Painted Shores (1927) was Crosby's poetic roman à clef of her elopement to Paris with Harry Crosby and the succeeding five years. More skillfully crafted than those in the previous two books, the poems were carefully arranged to trace the path of her own love story from the departure of two lovers from New York, to their arrival in France, to the woman's recognition of betrayal, to the decision of the lovers to remain together even after that betrayal, in recognition of the intensity of their original passion.

Crosby's fourth volume, *The Stranger,* published in 1928, was her epic, addressed to the three men in her life: her father, her husband, and her son. In it she identifies with her father as the source of her "indestructible idealism." It, along with *Impossible Melodies* (1928), focuses on the many kinds of love that the individual experiences—parental, familial, passionate, sexual, and platonic—throughout life.

As both Caresse and Harry Crosby began to write, they needed a means to get into print. Their solution was their own press. The couple first started publishing under the imprint Editions Nar-

cisse (named for their black whippet) but soon changed the name to Black Sun Press. Once underway, Black Sun Press published original works by other writers, including Joyce, Lawrence, Hart Crane, Proust, and Pound. Caresse Crosby was in charge of the day-to-day business of the press. Although they had a master printer, Roger Lescault, it was she who designed the colophon, chose the paper, set margins, and planned the layout of pages. She also illustrated several of the works, including her *Painted Shores* and Harry Crosby's *The Sun* (1929). Her detailed attention to material and the printing process made the volumes from Black Sun Press exceptionally well crafted.

In November 1929 the Crosbys returned to the United States on a semiannual visit. In the seven years of their marriage, Harry and Caresse had explored individual as well as common interests. However, progressively, Harry's obsession with an egocentric sun mythology and worship was leading him to suicide. On this visit, he had a tryst with Josephine Rotch Bigelow, one of his lovers, who had agreed to join him in a suicide pact, which Harry saw as the ultimate act of love and art. On 10 December 1929 Harry Crosby failed to meet Caresse Crosby and his mother at an appointment with his uncle, J. P. Morgan, Jr. When he later failed to meet them for dinner, Caresse Crosby asked their escort, Hart Crane, to look for him. Crane discovered the bodies of Harry Crosby and Bigelow, both dead of gunshot wounds. Shaken by the murder-suicide, Caresse Crosby stayed in the United States only long enough to have Harry Crosby's body cremated, and then returned to Paris.

In Paris, Crosby continued the work of Black Sun Press. However, her publication of *Poems for Harry Crosby* (1931) marked the end of her career as a poet. The volume, again a collection of love poems, reasserted Crosby's belief that the love between her and Harry Crosby was so strong, so central a passion in each of their lives, that even after death the two were fated "Forever to be Harry and Caresse." She spent the next two years in another, equal labor of love: the reprinting of Harry Crosby's poetry in a series of four volumes—each with a preface or afterword (by T. S. Eliot, Stuart Gilbert, D. H. Lawrence, and Ezra Pound)—and publishing his *War Letters* (1932). She also edited and published Hart Crane's *The Bridge* (1930), Ezra Pound's *Imaginary Letters* (1930), and Archibald MacLeish's *New Found Land* (1930).

In 1931 Caresse expanded her publishing venture by founding, with Jacques Porel, Crosby

Continental Editions. The function of Crosby Continental Editions was to provide inexpensive paperback reprints of works by important modern writers. The publication list compiled by Crosby and Porel featured both French and American authors. Among those whose books were reprinted were William Faulkner, Ernest Hemingway, Kay Boyle, Antoine de Saint-Exupery, and Alain-Fournier. They also brought out *Indefinite Huntress and other Stories* (1932), a previously unpublished collection by Robert McAlmon. Although paperback editions had become popular in Europe, they were not in America; the press, not economically successful, soon ceased publication.

In the mid-1930s Caresse returned to the United States to live. In 1936 she purchased Hampton Manor, an estate near Fredericksburg, Virginia. Here, the visiting Salvador Dali would create art by suspending a piano in one of the garden trees. While restoring Hampton Manor, Caresse met Selbert (Bert) Young and married him on 24 March 1937 (they were divorced in the early 1940s). Throughout the late 1930s and the 1940s, Crosby turned her attention to promoting the visual arts. In the early 1940s she opened the Crosby Gallery of Modern Art in Washington, D.C. Her final publishing venture combined her continuing interest in literature with her recent business of exhibiting art. *Portfolio: An Intercontinental Review* was a true mixed-media quarterly, designed to "present to an imaginative public, lively and varied examples of work by modern authors." The list of contributors to the journal is impressive: Kay Boyle, Karl Shapiro, Robert Lowell, Stephen Spender, Jean-Paul Sartre, Albert Camus, Gwendolyn Brooks, Anaïs Nin, Henri Matisse, Pablo Picasso, and Henry Moore were all included. Innovative in form as well as content, the drawings and writings were each "a movable unit, to carry away or to have bound or to frame upon the wall." Although shorter lived than other Black Sun Press publishing ventures (only four issues), the quarterly was critically well received.

In 1953, urged by friends such as Henry Moore and Malcolm Cowley, Crosby published her last book, *The Passionate Years*, an anecdotal memoir of her life. The book was recollection, not research, and not perfectly reliable in dates and places. Many of the remembrances were of short personal encounters with major figures, such as F. Scott Fitzgerald intentionally dropping his gloves in her stateroom, hoping to accompany her abroad, and Hemingway irately responding to being called

Caresse Crosby, early 1950s

"precious." As a record of ambiance and personalities, it is a useful resource.

In the final decade and a half of her life Crosby published books by poets Sy Kahn and Bill Barker under the imprint Castle Continental Editions in the 1960s, and she became increasingly active in the international peace movement, founding and supporting both Citizens of the World and Women Against War. She purchased various sites, settling finally on a hilltop in Cyprus, where she planned to build a peace center. Plans for the construction by Buckminster Fuller of a geodesic dome were halted, however, at Crosby's death on 24 January 1970.

Crosby's own poetry was considerably less impressive than the works she so tirelessly promoted in her presses. But her exuberance assisted numerous modern writers and painters and created ways to give their works needed public exposure. Both personally and professionally she lived by her motto: "The answer to the challenge is always 'Yes.'"

Bibliography:
George Robert Minkoff, *A Bibliography of the Black Sun Press*, introduction by Caresse Crosby (Great Neck, N.Y.: Minkoff, 1970).

References:

Jane Baltzell, "The Answer Was Always 'Yes!,'" *Brumonia* (January 1955): 5-9;

Millicent Bell, "The Black Sun Press to the Present," *Books at Brown,* 17 (January 1955): 2-24;

Kay Boyle, "The Crosbys: An Afterword," *ICarbS,* 3 (Spring-Summer 1977): 117-125;

Shelley Cox and Carolyn Moe, *The Black Sun Press* (Carbondale: Friends of Morris Library, 1977);

Hugh Ford, *Published in Paris: America and British Writers, Painters and Publishers in Paris, 1920-1939* (New York: Macmillan, 1975), pp. 168-230;

Harry T. Moore, "The Later Caresse Crosby. Her Answer Remained 'Yes,'" *ICarbS,* 3 (Spring-Summer 1977): 127-134;

Anaîs Nin, *The Diary of Anaîs Nin, 1955-1956* (New York: Harcourt Brace Jovanovich, 1976);

Geoffrey Wolff, *Black Sun: The Brief Transit and Violent Eclipse of Harry Crosby* (New York: Random House, 1976).

Papers:

The Black Sun Press Archives are at the Morris Library, Southern Illinois University, Carbondale, Illinois.

Harry Crosby

(4 June 1898-10 December 1929)

Melody M. Zajdel
Montana State University

See also the Harry and Caresse Crosby entry in *DLB 4, American Writers in Paris, 1920-1939.*

BOOKS: *Sonnets for Caresse* (Paris: Privately printed, 1925; enlarged edition, Paris: Privately printed, 1925; enlarged again, 1926; revised edition, Paris: Editions Narcisse, 1927);

Red Skeletons (Paris: Editions Narcisse, 1927);

Chariot of the Sun (Paris: At the Sign of the Sundial/Cour Du Soleil D'Or, 1928);

Shadows of the Sun (Paris: Black Sun Press, 1928);

Transit of Venus (Paris: Black Sun Press, 1928; enlarged edition, Paris: Black Sun Press, 1929);

Mad Queen (Paris: Black Sun Press/Editions Narcisse, 1929);

Shadows of the Sun, second series (Paris: Black Sun Press, 1929);

The Sun (Paris: Black Sun Press, 1929);

Sleeping Together (Paris: Black Sun Press, 1929);

Shadows of the Sun, third series (Paris: Black Sun Press, 1930);

Aphrodite in Flight (Paris: Black Sun Press, 1930);

Torchbearer (Paris: Black Sun Press, 1931);

War Letters (Paris: Black Sun Press, 1932);

Shadows of the Sun: The Diaries of Harry Crosby, edited by Edward Germain (Santa Barbara, Cal.: Black Sparrow Press, 1977).

OTHER: *Anthology,* edited by Crosby (Paris: Privately printed, 1924);

Oscar Wilde, *The Birthday of the Infanta,* foreword by Crosby (Paris: Black Sun Press/Editions Narcisse, 1928);

47 Unpublished Letters from Marcel Proust to Walter Berry, edited and translated by Harry Crosby and Caresse Crosby; republished in French as *47 Lettres Inedites de Marcel Proust a Walter Berry,* edited by Harry Crosby and Caresse Crosby (Paris: Black Sun Press, 1930).

PERIODICAL PUBLICATIONS: "Why Do Americans Live in Europe?," by Crosby and others, *transition,* no. 14 (Fall 1928): 97-119;

"Hail: Death," *transition,* no. 14 (Fall 1928): 169-170;

"Suite: Aeronautics; the Sun," *transition,* no. 15 (February 1929): 19-24;

"The New World," *transition,* no. 16/17 (June 1929): 30;

"Observation-Post," *transition,* no. 16/17 (June 1929): 197-206;

Harry Crosby

"Dreams 1928-1929," *transition,* no. 18 (November 1929): 32-36;

"For a protection," *transition,* no. 18 (November 1929): 47;

"Short Introduction to Words," *transition,* no. 18 (November 1929): 206-207;

"Illustrations of Madness," *transition,* no. 18 (November 1929): 102-103;

"Sleeping Together," *transition,* no. 19/20 (June 1930): 233-238.

For literary scholars, Harry Crosby has been an extreme example of the rebellious and dissipated American expatriate of the 1920s. His life more than his writings has gained him a place in literary history. Revealing influences from nineteenth-century romanticism to symbolism, Dadaism and surrealism, his works demonstrate, in microcosm, the course of modernist literary thought and form. His strongest impact was as a publisher: as founders of the Black Sun Press, he and his wife, Caresse Crosby, published modernist writers such as James Joyce, D. H. Lawrence, Archibald MacLeish, Kay Boyle, Hart Crane, and Ezra Pound.

Harry Crosby was the epitome of the well-bred, well-connected Bostonian. Though he was born Henry Sturgis Crosby, his parents soon changed his middle name to Grew. From his parents, Stephen Van Rensselaer Crosby and Henrietta Marion Grew Crosby, he inherited his patrician good looks and his awareness that he was expected to manage well his capital and his personal affairs. Little in his happy and unexceptional youth indicated that his entire adulthood would be spent rebelling against this background. He attended private schools, finishing preparatory work at St. Mark's School in Southborough, Massachusetts. Graduated from St. Mark's in 1917, Crosby was caught up in the excitement of America's entrance into World War I. Like many young men, he seemed equally motivated by patriotism and a desire for glory, but his naively romantic view of war was shattered quickly and irreversibly through personal experience.

In June 1917 Crosby joined the American Field Service Ambulance Corps, and the next month he sailed to France, determined to prove his valor and win a medal. His letters to his family, posthumously published as *War Letters* (1932), present his war experiences with a touching mixture of jingoism, naive enthusiasm, and realistic descriptions of the living conditions at the front. In September 1917, after the American Field Service ambulance sections had become part of the U.S. Army, Crosby enlisted in the army as a private and continued to serve as an ambulance driver. His experiences at the Battle of Verdun marked him for life. On 22 November 1917, while he was waiting to carry wounded soldiers to the back lines, Crosby's ambulance was destroyed by a shell that burst within ten yards of it, leaving Crosby unharmed, but seriously injuring a close friend, Way Spaulding. So profound an impression did this narrow escape from death have upon him that, after the war, Crosby remembered this encounter with death annually, commemorating its anniversary, calling it his death day. Just as a birthday records entrance into the world of the living, Crosby's death day came to symbolize his obsession with death. For him, life and death were equally powerful and capricious forces, both to be shaped by the individual's hand, if possible. Both Malcolm Cowley and Geoffrey Wolff, who differ on the extent to which Crosby was representative of his generation, pinpoint this experience as the start of Crosby's determination to choose the "right" time and way to die. Having cheated Death at Verdun, he would seek to make his own death an act of conscious art. Later in his life, Crosby linked death symbols to all his intense psychological and emotional experiences, comparing them to this moment of most intense feeling. At the time, however, he was grateful for his life, writing home, "I thank God with all my heart for saving me."

Crosby remained in France after the Armistice, into March of 1919. His recognition of the futility and monumental waste of the war became increasingly apparent in his letters home. Sounding much like the poets he would later admire, Crosby described the battlefields as a modern wasteland: "Shell-gutted ravines, pock-marked hillocks, frightful roads, masses of debris, dead horses, smashed, overturned wagons, vegetation and general ghastliness pervade the whole ungodly, awful scenery," he wrote on 14 November 1917. Although his perceptions of heroism in war were modified, his ambitions were not. Before returning home, Crosby jubilantly achieved his original intent of winning a medal, announcing his achievement to his parents in a boyishly exuberant wire: "Saturday, March 1, 1919. Won oh Boy!!!!!!! THE CROIX DE GUERRE. Thank God."

The young man who returned to Boston in April 1919 was a changed person: he began drinking heavily and rebelling against the upper-class mores of proper Boston. Almost immediately he entered Harvard, as expected; but then he scandalized his family by falling in love with a married woman six years his senior, Mary Phelps Jacob Peabody (nicknamed Polly, though she and Harry Crosby later changed her name to Caresse). Meeting on 4 July 1920, they were instantly attracted, and within weeks they had become lovers. Crosby's new impetuosity and intensity became apparent in a characteristically dramatic form when he began in spring 1921 to threaten suicide if he could not marry Polly Peabody. In June 1921 Crosby was granted a B.A., *honoris causa* (a "war degree" that allowed returned veterans to graduate early), and the next month he began working for the Shawmut National Bank in Boston. Meanwhile Polly Peabody, formally separated from her husband, moved with her two children to New York City. The two lovers continued to write and meet, but the courtship was stormy, and Polly hesitated to marry Harry even after her divorce was finalized in December 1921.

Crosby's mother, hoping to prevent the marriage, arranged for him to work for his uncle J. P.

Morgan at the Paris bank, Morgan, Harjes et Cie. In spring 1922 Crosby left for Paris, but Polly had preceded him. She stayed for several months, returning to New York in July. Within weeks, Harry had proposed by telegram and followed her to New York. They were married on 9 September in the chapel of the Municipal Building in New York City and returned to Paris, with her children, just two days later. The wedding and emotions of this period are poetically described in a sonnet sequence that Caresse Crosby later included in *Painted Shores* (1927). Although their courtship and marriage did not elicit a similar burst of poetry by Crosby, it was during this time (starting in January 1922) that he began to keep diaries that chronicled his emotional and intellectual growth, later published in three series as *Shadows of the Sun* (1928-1930).

For the next seven years, until his suicide in 1929, the Crosbys were fixtures in the American community in Paris. Their wealth, enthusiasm, and genuine interest in modern art and literature, as well as their publishing enterprise, gained them introduction to numerous writers and artists. Sylvia Beach found them "two of the most charming people" she had met in Paris. Their wild entertainments, traveling, gambling, drinking, opium eating, and flagrant affairs seemed designed to attract attention and to shrug off the restraints of conventional middle-class American social values.

In late 1923 Crosby met his cousin Walter Van Rensselaer Berry, an international lawyer and a close friend of Edith Wharton and Henry James. Having already started with Polly Crosby on an extensive and eclectic reading program, Crosby was encouraged in his dream of becoming a poet by Berry, who advised him to give up banking if he wished to become a writer. On 31 December 1923 Crosby quit Morgan, Harjes et Cie.

In 1924 Crosby extended his artistic concerns by branching into publishing. His privately published *Anthology* is a collection of poems by his favorite poets, from Poe to Mallarmé to Polly Crosby (whose name they now changed to the more euphonious Caresse). In 1925 Crosby went on to publish the first book of his own poetry, *Sonnets for Caresse*. Over the next two years, the book would go through three more revised and enlarged editions totaling only 196 copies. As is obvious from the number of copies, the poems were published from a desire for personal expression rather than as a public declaration of his vocation as poet. Crosby's poetry mixed convention and experimentation, both in forms and themes. The poems in this volume are predominantly love poems, recollec-

Way Spaulding, Philip Shepley, Harry Crosby, George Richmond Fearing, and Stuart Kaiser wearing their war decorations on Armistice Day, 1919. Each had won the Croix de Guerre.

tions of war, and childhood memories, all permeated with Crosby's dark vision of life and his preference for the macabre, morbid, and morose. Love is torture, lost childhood is remembered elegiacally, and war is the agent of death. The romantic and symbolist influences are clear.

As both Crosbys began to write more, they needed an outlet for their works. In 1927 they decided to start their own press, Editions Narcisse (which they later called Black Sun Press). Although Roger Lescault (previously a specialist in printing announcements and certificates) was the master printer, the Crosbys personally designed all the books printed under their two imprints, choosing paper, setting margins, commissioning original artwork for illustrations and frontispieces. To inaugurate Editions Narcisse the Crosbys published two books: the fourth edition of Crosby's *Sonnets for Caresse* and his *Red Skeletons*.

In *Red Skeletons*, which he called his "swan song to the decadent," Crosby intertwines images of the war, death, and the sun. Twenty-four of the thirty-four poems in this volume had appeared in

Sonnets for Caresse, but they are reordered for effect. Along with ten new poems, they present, in increasingly dark and cryptic sun imagery, the despairing vision of their author. The themes of madness, suicide, and evil become part of Crosby's obsession with death. Characteristic of his tone was his choice of Hungarian artist Alastair (the Baron Hans Henning von Voight) to illustrate this volume. *Red Skeletons* marks the end of Crosby's use of conventional poetic form. After its publication, Crosby moved on to avant-garde forms, including surrealistic free verse and trance, or automatic, writing.

Even as he was carving out his self-designated role as poet, Crosby was busily living the frenetic life which was his most conscious work of art. With a seemingly insatiable desire for experience, he traveled extensively in 1925-1927 through Europe and North Africa and began his extensive use of opium and other drugs to alter his perception and sensations. He partied compulsively and indulged in a series of love affairs, some platonic, most not. Still, in 1926 and 1927, Crosby began to meet and

*Harry Crosby's favorite photograph of himself and Caresse
Crosby, Etretat, France, 1925*

interact with other writers. Through contacts that
included Berry and Beach, Crosby became acquainted with Ezra Pound, Archibald MacLeish,
Ernest Hemingway, and Eugene Jolas. Works by
Pound and MacLeish would be published by Black
Sun Press, while his relationship with Jolas led to
his becoming an associate editor and contributor
to *transition*.

In October 1927 Walter Berry died. Crosby,
who became executor and residual legatee of the
estate, inherited Berry's library, a collection of almost eight thousand volumes of "every kind of
book imagined from the oldest Incunabula down
to the most recent number of transition. . . ." A
misunderstanding over Edith Wharton's rights to
part of the library caused ill feelings, but ended
with Crosby retaining most of the collection. As he
recorded in his journal, the inheritance prodded
Crosby to further study and experimentation in
literature.

Crosby articulated his theory of sun worship
throughout his works, particularly the tirades and

dreams published in journals such as Eugene Jolas's
transition. Crosby met Jolas in fall 1927, after of-
fering to sponsor a $100 award to the best poet
published in the first twelve volumes of *transition.*
At roughly the same time, Crosby showed Jolas his
diaries. Portions of the diaries, along with dream
records, began to appear in *transition* regularly
thereafter. These publications dealt cryptically,
sometimes in a hallucinatory manner, with his affairs, his sun worship, his readings and thoughts
on modern literature and society, and his dreams.
Within a year, he was listed as a contributing editor
and had signed Jolas's "Revolution of the World"
proclamation, a manifesto that was essentially surrealist in nature.

The year 1928 brought the extension of two
important phases of Crosby's life: he increased his
publishing activities, and he continued to become
more and more obsessed with sun worship in his
poetry and his life. In 1928 the Crosbys published
twelve books, including *Sun,* by D. H. Lawrence;
Git Le Coeur by Lord Lymington (Gerard Vernon
Wallop Lymington, ninth Earl of Portsmouth); an
edition of Edgar Allan Poe's *The Fall of the House
of Usher; Letters of Henry James to Walter Berry* (compiled from the inherited Berry library); *Hindu Love
Book,* an erotic manuscript the Crosbys found in
Damascus; two volumes of poetry by Caresse
Crosby (*The Stranger* and *Impossible Melodies*); and
three volumes by Harry Crosby (*Chariot of the Sun,
Shadows of the Sun,* and *Transit of Venus*). Many of
the poems in *Chariot of the Sun* were written early,
between 26 January and 24 March 1928, while the
Crosbys and his mother were on an extended journey in the Middle East. While in Egypt Crosby read
Lawrence's *The Plumed Serpent* (1926) and found,
so he believed, a kindred sun worshipper. After
reading Lawrence's book, Crosby started a correspondence which would lead to the publication of
Lawrence's *Sun* (1928) and the personal meeting
of the two men. In 1929 Black Sun Press would
also publish an author-illustrated edition of Lawrence's *The Escaped Cock.* Although each man was
intrigued by the other, their relationship did not
develop into closeness. Lawrence could appreciate
Crosby's passion for experience and his reliance on
his unconscious. He could not forgive what he saw
to be a lack of artistry. Crosby could admire Lawrence's art in general but he rejected Lawrence's
explicit sexuality. When Lawrence offered to let
him publish *Lady Chatterley's Lover,* Crosby called it
"disgusting." The key that Crosby hoped would
unite them—their seemingly shared sun mythology
and imagery—was too different to be a common

grounding. In Crosby's egocentric mythology, the sun was a symbol of unconscious creative force. Day and night paralleled life and death; both sides of each pair of opposites were part of the sun's cyclic power and both were creative. Crosby's jumbled and contradictory system eventually led to his belief that suicide was the ultimate creative act. If the sun is both life and death, and simultaneously the source of all creativity, then death can be a return to the center of life, a creative return to the unconscious. Thus, suicide becomes an act of creativity, a work of art.

In 1928, as Crosby's writings became increasingly dominated by his personal death imagery, he began to talk with Caresse Crosby and various lovers about joint suicide as the completion of love in its most artistic form. He and Caresse went so far as to pick a date (years in the future) when they would die together. Although Caresse would later deny that their conversations were serious, Crosby's writings suggest, in retrospect, the literalness of his intent. All his love poems in the three volumes published in 1928, but especially those in *Transit of Venus*, link love and death. Murder and suicide have become more frequent than images of the sun and making love. While Caresse Crosby ignored or refused to take seriously the suicide request, on 9 July 1928 Crosby met someone not so reluctant to be part of what he perceived as his final act of poetry: Josephine Rotch. Henceforth, the Mad Queen (Rotch) frequently replaced the Cramoisy Queen (Caresse) in Crosby's love poetry.

Crosby's poetry was also becoming more widely known. His poetry, diary excerpts, and articles appeared in several small journals: *transition*, the *Morada, Pagany*, and *Blues*. Archibald MacLeish and Kay Boyle were taking his vocation as poet seriously, as evidenced in their discussions of his poetry in their correspondence with Crosby. Even T. S. Eliot (retrospectively, in an introduction to a 1931 republication of the enlarged edition of *Transit of Venus*, 1929) noted that during this period Crosby was legitimately experimenting in his poetic form, "Aware of a direction, and ignorant of the destruction. . . ." The energy of Crosby's writing was evident to even his harshest critic. Simultaneously, with the increased recognition accorded his poetry, Crosby's dissipations, despair, and destructiveness were becoming more widely known as well. At the New Year's Eve party at Le Moulin du Soleil in 1928 Robert McAlmon surveyed the participants and noted to Kay Boyle, "They're all wraiths, all of them . . . God knows what they've done with their realities." It was becoming clearer and clearer in

Josephine Rotch, the "Mad Queen" of Crosby's late love poetry

Crosby's writings that the reality was fading in the opium/hashish/alcohol vision of artist as madman, seer, and "assassin" of self and of culture.

In January 1929, through Jolas, Crosby met Hart Crane, and within four days of their meeting, Crosby agreed to publish Crane's *The Bridge* (1930) upon its completion. Until his death Crosby was Crane's primary benefactor. Urging Crane to complete his poem, he secluded Crane at his country house, Le Moulin du Soleil, for most of February 1929, during which time Crane roughed out the "Cape Hatteras" portion of *The Bridge*. In July 1929 Crosby bailed him out of jail, where he had been taken after an argument over a bar bill, and loaned him money to return to New York. Although their self-destructiveness might have seemed a common bond, Crane's appeared uncontrollable while Crosby's was almost always calculated, part of his role as poet-madman and worshipper of *Sol niger*.

Crosby's final year, 1929, was marked by an explosion of activity. In the first three months,

Crosby met not only Hart Crane and D. H. Lawrence, but, most exciting for him, James Joyce. In February 1929 Crosby noted in his diary that he and Caresse Crosby went to Shakespeare and Company to ask Sylvia Beach "if Joyce would be willing to let us edit a fragment of his *Work in Progress.*" The Crosbys met with Joyce twice in March, signed an agreement with him on 6 April, and worked out the contract details with Beach. Their work on Joyce's book demonstrates the care that went into the publications of Black Sun Press. They contracted to print 600 copies (100 of them signed) of *Tales Told by Shem and Shaun,* a collection of three stories ("The Maddest Thick That Ever Heard Dump," "The Mookse and the Gripes," and "The Ondt and the Gracehoper") already published in *transition.* Their generous stipend to Joyce was $2000. Although Picasso declined to do the frontispiece, Brancusi accepted and did two drawings. The first, while acceptable to Beach and Joyce (it was later hung in Shakespeare and Company), was not modern enough for the Crosbys. The second drawing, an abstract of four lines, was the frontispiece they selected. To meet Joyce's request that a scientist write the introduction, they found C. K. Ogden, the creator of Basic English. Like all Black Sun publications, the bindings, boxes, and ribbons were made from expensive materials by Babont. In addition to Joyce's stories, Black Sun increased its output dramatically in 1929, publishing Kay Boyle's first book, *Short Stories,* Archibald MacLeish's *Einstein,* Eugene Jolas's *Secession In Astropolis,* Bob Brown's *1450-1950,* Lawrence's *The Escaped Cock,* Lord Lymington's *Spring Songs of Iscariot,* editions of Laurence Sterne's *A Sentimental Journey* and of *The Rubaiyat of Omar Khayyam,* and four volumes by Crosby: *Mad Queen, Shadows of the Sun* (second series), *The Sun,* and *Sleeping Together.*

Much of Crosby's writing in 1929 was influenced by his association with Jolas. The pathological obsession with suicide remained his own, but his desire for radical change and his reliance on dreams, his acceptance that the poet "must call for the barbaric catastrophe of the spirit and for an eternal anarchy" (as Jolas wrote in "Transatlantic Letter"), and his personal surrender to "the rhythmic 'hallucination of the word,'" reflected the affinity between the two men's aesthetics. In his first book of the year, *Mad Queen,* Crosby explored this spiritual anarchy in his dreams and his tirades. Linking orgasm to death, destruction to creativity, Crosby sought to loose the Dionysian dynamism and subconscious power of the poet on the modern wasteland. As his diaries chronicled, he was ob-

sessed with reversing, at least personally, T. S. Eliot's vision of the world's ending in a whimper. The poet, at least, should end his world with a bang, should "explode (suns within suns and cataracts of gold) into the frenzied fury of the Sun. . . ." In his most telling poem in this volume, "Assassin," Crosby envisioned himself the destroyer of the world, the one who would by death and chaos clear away hypocrisy and sterility.

Jolas's influence is further evidenced in *Sleeping Together,* a collection of Crosby's dreams. Many had appeared already in *transition.* Jolas reported dreams in *transition* as expressions of the poets' unconscious, believing that dreams would link the intuitive to the real and that examinations of them would reveal the true creative process. Crosby's dreams seemed less immediate and intense than his poetry, but the demarcation was becoming increasingly blurred. The lower level of intensity of this volume might well have been caused by Crosby's detachment. Crosby's biographer, Geoffrey Wolff, posits that Crosby was only playing with the dream form, that he "first read Freud and Jung, and then created conundrums for their theories to solve." Certainly this volume was less gripping than Crosby's contemporaneous poetry.

The year 1929 was not just the close of a decade, but, as Crosby said, the "end of Europe." Moreover, Crosby had reached the conclusion to his own artistic philosophy. The only art left to be perfected was his death. Although he seemed to consider several possibilities (including flying a plane into the sun), he settled on joint suicide with his Mad Queen and Fire Princess. After the Crosbys arrived in New York City on 22 November 1929 for a visit with their families, Harry Crosby spent several days in early December with Josephine Rotch in Detroit. They made plans to meet one last time before he returned to France. On 7 December Hart Crane threw a going-away party in Brooklyn for the Crosbys. The guests included many of Crosby's favorite American writers, among them E. E. Cummings, William Carlos Williams, Malcolm Cowley, and Matthew Josephson. Three days later, when Crosby failed to join Crane, Caresse Crosby, and his mother for dinner and the theater, Crane was sent to locate him. He was found dead in Stanley Mortimer's studio. With him was Josephine Rotch, whom he had shot prior to shooting himself. Crosby's body was cremated 12 December 1929.

In 1930 Caresse Crosby published two previously unpublished volumes by her husband: *Shadows of the Sun* (third series) and *Aphrodite in Flight.* The first is the final, unrevised volume of

Crosby's diaries; the second is a love manual purporting to be based on the principles of aerodynamics. *Torchbearer* (1931) was Crosby's final book of poetry. It was published as part of a series of four volumes called *Collected Poems*, which also included the new editions of *Chariots of the Sun, Transit of Venus,* and *Sleeping Together.* For each volume Caresse Crosby commissioned a preface or afterword. D. H. Lawrence's preface appeared in *Chariots of the Sun,* T. S. Eliot wrote the preface for *Transit of Venus,* Stuart Gilbert's tribute from *transition* prefaced *Sleeping Together,* and Ezra Pound provided the afterword to the *Torchbearer.* The poems in *Torchbearer* move beyond the dream records of *Sleeping Together,* becoming almost automatic or trance writing. Lawrence, Eliot, Gilbert, and Pound praised Crosby's vitality more than his creations. The final Black Sun publication of a book by Crosby was his *War Letters* (1932), edited by Caresse Crosby and prefaced by Henrietta Crosby, his mother.

The posthumous response to Crosby focused on his life, more than his work. His literary associations more than his images were remembered, and his publishing the works of others had more impact on modern literature than his poems. Though he had wanted to thwart mortality both literally (by committing suicide) and figuratively (by leaving one enduring work behind), it was his death which drew the most attention. His death emblematically sealed a decade in American letters and made him the dark image of the American expatriate experience between the wars.

Bibliography:

George Robert Minkoff, *A Bibliography of the Black Sun Press,* introduction by Caresse Crosby (Great Neck, N.Y.: Minkoff, 1970).

Biography:

Geoffrey Wolff, *Black Sun: The Brief Transit and Violent Eclipse of Harry Crosby* (New York: Random House, 1976).

References:

Kay Boyle, "The Crosbys: An Afterword," *ICarbS,* 3 (Spring-Summer 1977): 117-125;

Malcolm Cowley, *Exile's Return,* revised edition (New York: Viking, 1951), pp. 246-288;

Caresse Crosby, *The Passionate Years* (New York: Dial, 1953; enlarged edition, London: Redman, 1955; Carbondale: Southern Illinois University Press, 1968);

Noel Riley Fitch, *Sylvia Beach and the Lost Generation* (New York: Norton, 1983), pp. 284-287;

Edward B. Germain, "Harry Crosby His Death His Diaries," *ICarbS,* 3 (Spring-Summer 1977): 103-110;

Frederick J. Hoffman, *The Twenties: American Writing in the Postwar Decade,* revised edition (New York: Free Press, 1962);

"In Memoriam: Harry Crosby," memorials by Kay Boyle, Hart Crane, Stuart Gilbert, Eugene Jolas, Archibald MacLeish, and Phillippe Soupault, *transition,* no. 19/20 (June 1930): 221-232;

Sy M. Kahn, "Hart Crane and Harry Crosby: A Transit of Poets," *Journal of Modern Literature,* 1 (1970): 45-56;

Robert McAlmon, *Being Geniuses Together 1920-1930,* revised edition, with additional material by Kay Boyle (Garden City: Doubleday, 1968);

Sasha Newborn, "Harry Crosby's Sun Code," *ICarbS,* 3 (Spring-Summer 1977): 111-116.

Papers:

The unpublished notebooks, letters, and memorabilia of Harry Crosby are in the Black Sun Press Archives at the Morris Library, Southern Illinois University at Carbondale.

Countee Cullen
(30 May 1903-9 January 1946)

Shirley Lumpkin
Marshall University

See also the Cullen entry in *DLB 4, American Writers in Paris, 1920-1939.*

BOOKS: *Color* (New York & London: Harper, 1925);

The Ballad of the Brown Girl: An Old Ballad Retold (New York & London: Harper, 1927);

Copper Sun (New York & London: Harper, 1927);

The Black Christ and Other Poems (New York & London: Harper, 1929);

One Way to Heaven (New York & London: Harper, 1932);

The Medea and Some Poems (New York & London: Harper, 1935);

The Lost Zoo (A Rhyme for the Young, But Not Too Young) (New York & London: Harper, 1940);

My Lives and How I Lost Them (New York & London: Harper, 1942);

On These I Stand: An Anthology of the Best Poems of Countee Cullen (New York: Harper, 1947).

PLAY PRODUCTION: *St. Louis Woman,* by Cullen and Arna Bontemps, New York, Martin Beck Theatre, 31 March 1946.

OTHER: *Caroling Dusk: An Anthology of Verse by Negro Poets,* edited, with contributions, by Cullen (New York & London: Harper, 1927);

St. Louis Woman, by Cullen and Arna Bontemps, in *Black Theatre,* edited by Lindsay Patterson (New York: Dodd, Mead, 1971).

PERIODICAL PUBLICATIONS: "Poet on Poet— *The Weary Blues," Opportunity,* 4 (February 1926): 73;

"The Dark Tower," *Opportunity,* 4 (December 1926): 388; 5 (February 1927): 53-54; 5 (March 1927): 86-87; 5 (April 1927): 118-119; 5 (May 1927): 149-150; 5 (June 1927): 180-181; 5 (July 1927): 210-211; 5 (August 1927): 240-241; 5 (November 1927): 336-337; 5 (December 1927): 373-374; 6 (January 1928): 20-21; 6 (February 1928): 52-53; 6 (March 1928): 90; 6 (April 1928): 120; 6 (July 1928): 210; 6 (September 1928): 271-273.

Countee Cullen

Countee Cullen became a central figure in the Harlem or New Negro Renaissance and in American poetry in general with the publication of his first book, *Color* (1925), which black and white critics hailed as both beautiful and promising. While his reputation for writing beautiful lyrical poetry remained high throughout his poetic career, which was cut short by his untimely death in 1946, critics began to question how well he fulfilled his poetic promise. Many came to believe that his education was something of a handicap, leading him to exclude from his poetry a wide range of feelings and ideas, and any hint of vernacular or musicality, in favor of traditional American and English versification and such standard romantic subjects as love and death. Nonetheless, Cullen was a bright star of the New Negro Renaissance. As one of the primary figures in the development of Negro literature, he was well acquainted with all the major writers in the New Negro Movement and Negro literature in general, from the older James Weldon Johnson, Charles S. Johnson (editor of *Opportunity*), W. E. B. Du Bois (editor of *Crisis*), and Alain Locke, to his contemporaries, including Langston Hughes and Arna Bontemps.

Despite the waning of his reputation and perhaps of his muse, Cullen continued to be known for poems characterized by beauty and nobility, filled with his favorite image for the goodness and promise of life, spring. While he insisted that he should be considered a poet, rather than a Negro poet, black and white critics commented rather acidly that, whatever Cullen thought, his best poetry was informed by racial experience. His ambivalence about what he was to call the Christian and pagan values struggling for dominance in his art and in his life led to suggestions that he could not create a sustained worldview or that he romanticized and failed to understand the African experience. Yet his carefully crafted poems, especially those in *Color,* had tremendous influence. Langston Hughes called "Heritage" the most beautiful poem he knew. Other readers responded to Cullen's brief ironic epitaphs, his tension-laden sonnets (such as "Yet Do I Marvel" and "From the Dark Tower"), or his lyrical celebrations of the sensuous and painful love of brown boys and girls. His work came to be identified with the best of the academic or traditional versification of the New Negro Renaissance, and it has been praised for expressing some of the most painful and ironic archetypal experiences of black people. In his time, Cullen was as much a sensation on the American poetry scene as Edna St. Vincent Millay. Yet later generations of white Americans have been less familiar with his work than black Americans. Perhaps his race, more than his failure to sustain his early promise and his tendency to use conservative versification and poetic clichés, is partly responsible for this partial eclipse. Until recently his poems were anthologized primarily in black poetry anthologies rather than in more general collections of American poetry.

Popular and appreciated for his gentleness and selfless concern for others, Countee Porter Cullen was shy and not particularly open about his life, even with his closest friends. He once re-

marked in a letter to Claude McKay that he did not see why a poet's life should be an open book for the public, and Cullen's certainly is not. His exact birth date was questionable for a number of years, although 30 May 1903 is now firmly established. There is still some uncertainty about the place of his birth. His second wife, Ida Mae Roberson Cullen, said he was born in Baltimore; Langston Hughes and his longtime best friend Harold Jackman said Louisville, Kentucky; and Cullen himself is reported to have said New York. Such confusion about the details of Cullen's life is related to the deliberate silence Cullen maintained about the painful experiences in his life. In his reticence about the date and place of his birth, for example, Cullen seemed to be obscuring his lack of contact with his mother, Mrs. Elizabeth Lucas of Louisville, Kentucky, who neither raised nor even got in touch with her son from the time of his birth until he became well known in the 1920s. Cullen helped his mother financially after she contacted him, and, when she died in Louisville on 28 October 1940, he attended her funeral—actions suggesting a complex set of feelings he never wished to share with the general public or even his close friends. Cullen was raised by another woman, possibly his grandmother, a Mrs. Porter, who had brought him to New York City when he was about nine years old. They settled in an apartment near Salem Methodist Episcopal Church; and when Mrs. Porter died in 1918, the Reverend and Mrs. Frederick Cullen of this same church adopted Cullen as their son. While the adoption was informal, Cullen considered this couple his mother and father and was devoted to them. The conflicting emotional currents in his feelings about his childhood were not subjects Cullen desired to explore in conversation or in poetry, and he never did so.

Countee Cullen began writing poetry during his distinguished career at DeWitt Clinton High School, publishing "I Have a Rendezvous with Life (with apologies to Alan Seeger)"—which became a popular and prize-winning poem—in the January 1921 issue of the school's well-known literary magazine the *Magpie*. Cullen was one of the few Negroes at the school, but one of several prominent Afro-American graduates. In his later years he was to be interviewed for the *Magpie* by another DeWitt Clinton student, James Baldwin.

After graduating from DeWitt Clinton in January 1922, Cullen entered New York University the same year and continued to write poetry which appeared in *Opportunity, Crisis,* the *Bookman, Poetry, Harper's,* and the *American Mercury.* During his un-

The DeWitt Clinton High School Class of 1922. Cullen is third from right in the front row (photograph from the 1921 yearbook; courtesy of the Schomburg Center for Research in Black Culture, the New York Public Library, Astor, Lenox and Tilden Foundations).

dergraduate years, Cullen spent his summers working as a waiter in Atlantic City to help defray the costs of his education. He began entering poetry contests and winning prizes in them, gradually becoming known within the black and white literary communities. In 1923 he won second prize in the Witter Bynner undergraduate poetry contest with his "Ballad of the Brown Girl," which was published in 1927. In 1924 he again won second prize in the Witter Bynner contest, and in 1925 he won first prize. *Poetry*'s John Reed Memorial Prize was awarded him in 1925 for "Threnody for a Brown Girl." Significantly, that same year he was second in the *Opportunity*-sponsored poetry contest with the poem "To One Who Said Me Nay" (first prize went to Langston Hughes for "The Weary Blues," a poem in a vernacular, jazz, blues-based poetic language which was the polar antithesis of the style and the subject matter of Cullen's work). The two poles of New Negro poetry, the literary, individualistic lyricism of Cullen and the folk-derived people's voice of Langston Hughes, were thus established.

In 1925, the year Cullen was elected to Phi Beta Kappa and earned a B.A. from New York University, Harper and Brothers published *Color*, which won the Harmon Foundation Literary Award and received praise from black and white critics alike. Although Mark Van Doren suggested that, because some of the poems in *Color* seemed too long for their content, the young poet should not hurry his next book and William Stanley Braithwaite, almost alone among black or white critics, deplored what he called the racial content or flavor, Walter White and Alain Locke, leaders of the New Negro Movement, were enthusiastic about both the racial flavor and the style of writing.

The poems in *Color*, written during his undergraduate years, are Cullen's enduring work, and the grouping of the poems was one Cullen was to follow in later books. *Color* is divided into three sections: one group titled "Color," on the beauty of brown boys and girls and the bitter ironies and cruelties inflicted on brown people by the color line; one group on love, "For Love's Sake"; and one group on death, "Varia." All the poems are carefully constructed, employing a wide range of traditional versification forms, including sonnets, quatrains and epitaphs. Neither his themes, nor his admiration for the great romantic poets such as John Keats, nor his being, in his words, "a rank conservative, loving the measured line and the skillful rhyme" were to change throughout his poetic career. The amount of poetry he wrote and the number of poems he wrote on the theme of color—both on its beauty and on the horrifying effects of racism—was to diminish, but his theme did not significantly change. As Cullen wrote for *Twentieth Century Authors* (1942): "Most things I write I do for the sheer love of the music in them. Somehow I find my poetry of itself treating of the Negro, of his joys and sorrows—mostly of the latter—and of the heights and depths of emotion I feel as a Negro."

Always motivated by a powerful love of poetry and the ideal of being a poet, Cullen attended Harvard and studied literature and poetry writing with Robert Hillyer, among others, earning an M.A. in 1926. Known as an omnivorous reader with a taste for the classics and the romantics, Cullen was not unacquainted with the oral tradition of song, dance, speech, and religion in the Afro-American community. Since he loved to dance, he loved jazz and other Afro-American and Afro-Caribbean dance music. He certainly heard, responded to, and possibly participated in the shouting church services and the chanted sermon of the black Protestant Christian church. He was also aware of the imagists and of the New Poetry movement; for during his many lectures and readings in his tuned and musical voice, Cullen made many contemporary contacts and by 1925 and 1926 had met Harriet Monroe, Edwin Arlington Robinson, and Robert Frost, and had had many poems published in Monroe's *Poetry* magazine, as well as in black magazines such as *Crisis* and *Opportunity*. He had a wide range of acquaintances among black writers, such as Hughes, who were deliberately using free verse, the vernacular, jazz rhythms and phrasing, blues, and the concentrated concrete images of black life in their work. He never lost his taste, however, for Tennyson, Millay, Keats, and other traditional versifiers; nor did he, while he freely and modestly admitted that other poets were more innovative and experimental in style, ever become convinced that the oral folk tradition of black (or any other) people should be the basis for or should appear in poetry unrefined by conventional versification. Thus in his February 1926 *Opportunity* review of Langston Hughes's *Weary Blues*, Cullen wrote that he considered the jazz poems interlopers among the "truly beautiful poems" because such

poems "move me along with the frenzy and electric heat of a Methodist or Baptist revival meeting" and such "chills and fevers of emotion" are not really spiritual, nor do they seem to belong "to the dignified company, that select and austere circle of high literary expression which we call poetry."

In addition to his selective love of refined poetic versification, Cullen believed that poetic themes should be "austere" and chose the dignified styles of the sonnet, metered couplets, or brief ironic epitaphs because he sought controlled emotion to express his conception of beauty in his poetry. When he wrote about himself and selected poems from his own works for inclusion in his 1927 anthology of poetry by black poets, *Caroling Dusk*, Cullen explained more fully why he chose control in poetry, explaining that "his chief problem has been that of reconciling a Christian upbringing with a pagan inclination" and that "his life so far has not convinced him that the problem is insoluble." This issue, rather than whether to write about color, was the one he thought was central in his poetry; and to reconcile the Christian and the pagan he needed effective formal control.

The issue of color was continually raised, however, sometimes by Cullen himself, as he did in his anthology when he reiterated, with what he admitted might be "sickening" frequency, that he wished "no racial consideration" to bolster the reputation of his poetry. Acting upon his idea that "poet" was a more important category than "Negro," he called his anthology, one of several anthologies of black poetry to appear in the 1920s, *Caroling Dusk: An Anthology of Verse by Negro Poets* rather than "An Anthology of Negro Poetry" because he stated in the foreword he believed that Negro poetry "must emanate from some country other than this in some language other than our own." Since he argued Negro poets like himself used the heritage of the English language and were more individuals than men of the same color (what he called "the individual diversifying ego" transcending "the synthesizing hue"), he felt that Negro poets' work did not represent any "serious aberration from the poetic tendencies of their times." Selecting his own and other Negro poets' poems on that basis, he rejected the plantation-dialect of Dunbar and others, because of what he called "certain sociological considerations and the natural limitations of dialect for poetic expression" and because of the times' condemnation of artificiality. Although he praised the folk vernacular and musically based styles of James Weldon Johnson and Langston Hughes, he never looked to the oral tradition or to free verse for his own poetry about colored folk and tended to exclude Hughes's and other black poets' most vernacular, jazz, blues, and free-verse work from his anthology. For example, he chose Fenton Johnson's earlier work written in traditional versification, over his more powerful, free-verse poems of urban despair, such as "Tired," for his *Caroling Dusk* anthology.

This emphasis on conservative versification and exclusion of disrupting emotions or new styles marked his 1927 books, *The Ballad of the Brown Girl* and *Copper Sun*. Although *The Ballad of the Brown Girl* may have had its origin in a ballad that Cullen said he heard in Kentucky in 1915, the poem is essentially Cullen's rewriting of the black folk ballad in the form of an English literary ballad in quatrains. His changes make the motivations of the black girl, who is queenly and wishes to avenge the insult hurled at her blackness by a white woman, different enough to change the flavor of the story. *Copper Sun* has the same divisions that he had used in *Color*, but the "color" section is much shorter, including only "From the Dark Tower," "Threnody For a Brown Girl," and a small number of other poems on the beauty and pain of color. The longest sections are "The Deep in Love," poems about the pains and joys (more pains than joys) of love, and "Varia," poems about death and memorials to fallen poets, especially romantic ones. Two other short sections, "At Cambridge," containing the poems Cullen wrote as exercises in different verse forms for Robert Hillyer's class, and the poems "Juvenalia," are lighter in tone and consciously less serious poems, although love and its loss figure prominently in them. While critics such as Lyman Kittredge were enthusiastic about *The Ballad of a Brown Girl*, reactions to *Copper Sun* were mixed. E. Merrill Root in *Opportunity* and *New York Times* book reviewer Herbert S. Gorman applauded *Copper Sun*, but others such as Emanuel Eisenberg in the *Bookman* were negative. The critics generally enjoyed *Copper Sun* but agreed that the book was slighter and less intense than *Color*. Perhaps critical reaction would have been less mixed if *Copper Sun* had been the first, rather than the second, of Cullen's books. As it was, critics such as Harry Alan Potamkin, in the *New Republic*, were beginning to remark on Cullen's lack of growth.

Cullen's personal life during the period 1926-1928 had the same combination of ups and downs, successes and shadowy hints of failure or at least a loss of vigor, as his literary career. A successful assistant editor and columnist in his "From the Dark Tower" column for *Opportunity*, which was

edited by Charles S. Johnson in 1926-1928, Cullen was able to review books and write on subjects of interest to blacks, gather material for his anthology, and write. As a result of his literary achievements he won a Guggenheim grant in 1928 to study in France for a year. Before he departed for France he married W. E. B. Du Bois's daughter, Yolande Du Bois, whom he had known since the summer of 1923, on 9 April 1928. Their wedding was a glittering social affair, drawing Afro-Americans from all circles. Cullen's relationship with Yolande is shrouded in the same kind of mystery as the circumstances of his birth and intimate family relationships. He and Yolande traveled together after the wedding, but she did not accompany Cullen when he left for France on 30 June 1928 with his father, Reverend Frederick Cullen, and his intimate personal friend Harold Jackman. Yolande joined him in France for July 1928, but returned to the United States and to her job. The marriage was apparently over. While many of the poems Cullen wrote during this period and published in *The Black Christ and Other Poems* (1929) explore the bitterness and pain caused by disappointment over the character of a beautiful beloved and by the agony of lost love, the exact reasons for his break with Yolande remain obscure. Certainly her father, W. E. B. Du Bois, harbored no bitterness toward Cullen; Cullen's family and friends never mentioned his situation.

After his fellowship was extended, Cullen remained in France a year longer than he had originally planned, writing poems he published in *The Black Christ and Other Poems* and a series of articles for the *Crisis*. Upon his return to the United States in 1930, he and Yolande were divorced.

Cullen loved France, and he returned there, especially to Paris for vacations until 1939. He savored his study at the Sorbonne, speaking French, dancing madly in the music halls, partying with sculptors, poets, and writers. He savored the freedom to write. Feeling released in France from the self-consciousness, the restraints and the cruel horrors of Jim Crow racism, Cullen was also at home among the artifacts of French civilization.

What was invigorating for Cullen did not seem to have such a happy effect upon his poetry. *The Black Christ and Other Poems* was one of his least successful books with critics. Composed of a long "Varia" section and a short "color" section, with an "interlude," a group of poems that were primarily ironic and bitter in tone, the book had as its centerpiece the "color" poem "The Black Christ," which was considered one of Cullen's weakest

Countee Cullen, 1941 (photograph by Carl Van Vechten; by permission of Joseph Solomon, the Estate of Carl Van Vechten)

works. Written in couplets, the poem attempts to fuse the dramatic story of two Southern black brothers—one of whom is lynched—with an allegorical representation of Christ's crucifixion and resurrection and the romantic image of the tragic death of spring. This attempted merger was ambivalently received by a critical community clearly divided over the success of such a combination. More than half the critics considered the poem's style inappropriate, its content ambiguous, confused, and unrealistic, and the work as a whole lacking in the ability to confront or re-create the horrifying and concrete truth of lynching. Ironically, the "color" section also contains Cullen's response to critics who wanted him to write more poems on racial subjects and in a particular style. An angry and ironic work, "To Certain Critics" opens with the well-known lines: "Then call me traitor if you must,/Shout treason and default!" Cullen replied to the stinging accusation of treason to his race by saying, "I'll bear your censure as your

praise,/For never shall the clan/Confine my singing to its ways/Beyond the ways of man." Cullen insisted, in no uncertain terms, upon maintaining the high calling of a true poet who could not be confined to the tastes of a single group.

While Cullen had no doubts that being a poet was a sacred calling, he seemed to have many doubts about what he should do to earn a living, to sort out his personal life, and to keep his muse alive. During the 1930s he wrote and published *One Way to Heaven* (1932), a novel about Harlem, its classes and religion, but poetry and a definite means of earning his living did not seem to come. Since he was well known and associated with the best of New Negro poetry and literature, as well as well educated, Cullen was offered a position in the Department of English Literature at Dillard University in New Orleans in 1934. Although his appointment was announced in the New York newspapers, Cullen decided not to accept this offer, nor the others he apparently received, to teach in Southern schools. One of the main reasons for his refusal was that he had received offers only from Southern schools. Cullen wanted to stay in the North partly to be near his family, but mostly to enjoy the opportunities afforded blacks and to avoid the humiliating day-to-day contacts with a Jim Crow society which had made his trips to the South so galling, and which had made his attitude toward life in the United States and toward white people so bitter and angry at times. Trying to earn a living and to preserve his muse, he became a junior-high-school French teacher and eventually taught creative writing at Frederick Douglass Junior High School, an all-black school with a primarily white staff in New York. Joining the staff in 1934, Cullen remained there until his death in 1946.

During his twelve years as a full-time schoolteacher, Cullen continued to write, to read his poetry and lecture, and to serve his community. He worked on the education committee for the 1935 commission that investigated the causes of the New York riot. In 1943 he wrote to the newspapers about the lamentable repetition of the 1935 riot's causes, which precipitated the 1943 riot in New York. While reading at Fisk University in Nashville in 1944, he was offered the Chair of Creative Literature there, but once again he turned down employment in the South to remain at his New York post. In 1945 he collaborated on a play with Arna Bontemps, *St. Louis Woman*, an adaptation of a Bontemps novel, *God Sends Sunday* (1931).

Cullen wrote less poetry during this period. He was continually active, and on 27 September

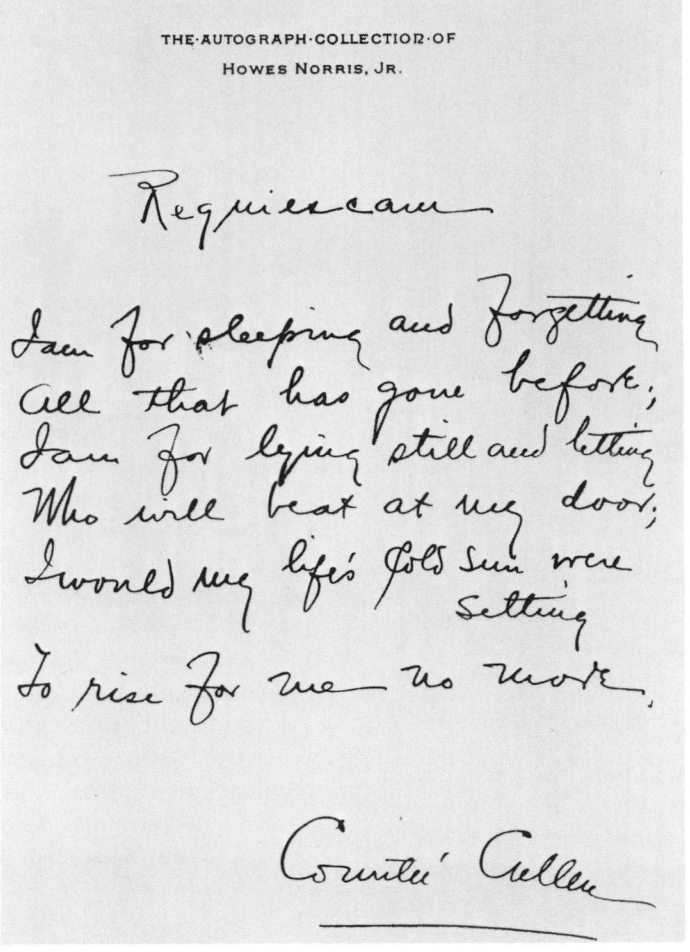

THE·AUTOGRAPH·COLLECTION·OF
HOWES NORRIS, JR.

Fair copy of "Requiescam" (by permission of the Estate of Countee Cullen; courtesy of the Clifton Waller Barrett Library, University of Virginia)

1940 he married Ida Mae Roberson, a woman he had known since 1930, and settled happily with her. Lack of time and energy, probably resulting from the amount of work he did teaching school and from his development of high blood pressure, might have contributed to the decline in poetry writing, but his interests seemed to have changed as well. In 1935 he published *The Medea and Some Poems,* consisting primarily of his translation of Euripides' *Medea,* which had favorable reviews, although it was not as widely noticed as his previous books. In 1940 he published a book of poems for children, *The Lost Zoo,* and in 1942 a book of stories for children, *My Lives and How I Lost Them.* According to Cullen these works were written in collaboration with his feline friend Christopher Cat, who told him the stories that he recounted poetically. *The Lost Zoo* tells stories of the animals who did not get on the ark, although they had been

invited, and hence passed out of the world. The animals' names such as "The Snake-That-Walked-Upon-His Tail," "The Ha-Ha," the "Squililigee," and the humorous, ironic stories show no diminution of Cullen's imagination. Nor has his verse lost its music, as the opening lines indicate: "You've heard, no doubt, of the Dinosaur/The Dodo bird, and the African Roc;/But the Wakeupworld, shaped like a clock,/And the lazy Sleepamitemore,/The Pussybow that could mew and barks,/The lonely Squililigee,/The Treasuretit that loved the dark,/Nobody's heard of these but me." Delightful, yet full of subtle criticism of human behavior, the poetry in *The Lost Zoo* is well suited to an audience of older children, but is in no way slight.

Cullen obviously considered this poetry as fine as his earliest, for just before his death from high blood pressure and uremic poisoning in 1946 he had completed his selection of the poetry by which he wanted to be known. From *Color* to *The Lost Zoo*, he culled the poems which were the essence of his vision of poetry and of his lyrically tuned ear for traditional verse for *On These I Stand: An Anthology of the Best Poems of Countee Cullen* (1947). In this collection, published posthumously, Cullen gathered his "Heritage" (with its Christian and pagan conflict expressed in vibrant colorful images), his sonnets, his ironic epitaphs, such as "For a Lady I Know" ("She even thinks that up in heaven/Her class lies late and snores,/While poor black cherubs rise at seven/To do celestial chores"), "To Certain Critics" and the unpopular "The Black Christ," poems praising France and cats from *The Medea and Some Poems*, *The Ballad of the Brown Girl*, and poems from *The Lost Zoo*, such as "The Wake-up-world." Choosing poems written according to the method that had been at once his strength and his weakness—conservative versification coupled with exclusion of emotions he considered inappropriate for poetry—Cullen included what he believed was his best work in *On These I Stand* and clearly revealed the character of what Gwendolyn Brooks was to call his "careful talent."

His death, unlike his birth, was an event of public note and his funeral was an occasion for public participation and mourning. While critics may have felt that the "careful" talent revealed in the whole body of his poetry was less than what had been promised in his early work, Cullen created a rich heritage of brown beauty in verse for what Gwendolyn Brooks called "every lover of lyrical richness." If the body of poems was small and, ironically, anthologized more in collections of black poetry than in volumes of American poetry, Cullen's life and art represented, as his friend Owen Dodson said, "the noblest way" of expressing the urge to lyrical song and the hope for a day when color would not limit human achievement.

Bibliography:

Margaret Perry, *A Bio-Bibliography of Countee P. Cullen* (Westport, Conn.: Greenwood Press, 1971).

References:

Owen Dodson, "Countee Cullen (1903-1946)," *Phylon,* 7 (January-March 1946): 19-20;

Blanche Ferguson, *Countee Cullen and the Negro Renaissance* (New York: Dodd, Mead, 1966);

Nathan I. Huggins, *Harlem Renaissance* (New York: Oxford University Press, 1971), pp. 206-210;

Margaret Perry, *Silence to the Drums: A Survey of the Literature of the Harlem Renaissance* (Westport, Conn. & London: Greenwood Press, 1976), pp. 31-56;

J. Saunders Redding, *To Make a Poet Black* (College Park: McGrath, 1968), pp. 108-112;

Eugene B. Redmond, *Drumvoices: The Mission of Afro-American Poetry* (Garden City: Anchor/ Doubleday, 1976), pp. 179-185;

Beulah Reimherr, "Countee Cullen: A Biographical and Critical Study," M.A. thesis, University of Maryland, 1960;

Darwin Turner, *In a Minor Chord: Three Afro-American Writers and Their Search for Identity* (Carbondale: Southern Illinois Press, 1971), pp. 60-88;

Jean Wagner, *Black Poets of the United States From Paul Laurence Dunbar to Langston Hughes*, translated by Kenneth Douglas (Urbana, Chicago & London: University of Illinois Press, 1973), pp. 283-347.

Papers:

Cullen's papers are at the libraries of Atlanta University and the University of California, Berkeley, and in the James Weldon Johnson Collection at the Beinecke Library, Yale University.

E. E. Cummings

Jenny Penberthy
University of Cape Town

BIRTH: Cambridge, Massachusetts, 14 October 1894, to Edward and Rebecca Haswell Clarke Cummings.

EDUCATION: A.B., 1915; A.M., 1916; Harvard University.

MARRIAGES: 19 March 1924 to Elaine Orr Thayer (divorced); child: Nancy. 1 May 1929 to Anne Minnerly Barton (divorced). 1934 (common law) to Marion Morehouse.

AWARDS AND HONORS: *Dial* award, 1925; Guggenheim Fellowships, 1933, 1951; Levinson Prize (*Poetry* magazine), 1939; Shelley Memorial Award, 1945; Academy of American Poets Fellowship, 1950; Harriet Monroe Poetry Award, 1950; Eunice Teitjens Memorial Prize (*Poetry* magazine), 1952; Charles Eliot Norton Professor of Poetry (Harvard University), 1952-1953; National Book Award Special Citation for *Poems 1923-1954*, 1955; Bollingen Prize in Poetry, 1958; Oscar Blumenthal Prize (*Poetry* magazine), 1962.

DEATH: Madison, New Hampshire, 3 September 1962.

BOOKS: *Eight Harvard Poets,* by Cummings and others (New York: Gomme, 1917);
The Enormous Room (New York: Boni & Liveright, 1922; London: Cape, 1928);
Tulips and Chimneys (New York: Seltzer, 1923; enlarged edition, Mount Vernon, N.Y.: Golden Eagle Press, 1937);
& (New York: Privately printed, 1925);
XLI Poems (New York: Dial Press, 1925);
Is 5 (New York: Boni & Liveright, 1926);
Him (New York: Boni & Liveright, 1927);
Christmas Tree (New York: American Book Bindery, 1928);
[No Title] (New York: Covici-Friede, 1930);
CIOPW (New York: Covici-Friede, 1931);
ViVa (New York: Liveright, 1931);
Eimi (New York: Covici-Friede, 1933);
No Thanks (Mount Vernon, N.Y.: Golden Eagle Press, 1935);
Tom (New York: Arrow Editions, 1935);
1/20 (London: Roger Roughton, 1936);
Collected Poems (New York: Harcourt, Brace, 1938);
50 Poems (New York: Duell, Sloan & Pearce, 1940);
1 x 1 (New York: Holt, 1944; London: Horizon Press, 1947);
Anthropos—The Future of Art (Mount Vernon, N.Y.: Golden Eagle Press, 1944);
Santa Claus—A Morality (New York: Holt, 1946);
Puella Mea (Mount Vernon, N.Y.: Golden Eagle Press, 1949);
XAIPE: Seventy-One Poems (New York: Oxford University Press, 1950);
i: six nonlectures (Cambridge: Harvard University Press, 1953);

E. E. Cummings, 1920s (photograph by J. Sibley Watson)

Poems 1923-1954 (New York: Harcourt, Brace, 1954);

E. E. Cummings: A Miscellany, edited by George Firmage (New York: Argophile Press, 1958; enlarged edition, New York: October House, 1965; London: Owen, 1966);

95 Poems (New York: Harcourt, Brace, 1958);

100 Selected Poems (New York: Grove Press, 1959);

Selected Poems, 1923-1958 (London: Faber & Faber, 1960);

Adventures in Value (New York: Harcourt, Brace & World, 1962);

73 Poems (New York: Harcourt, Brace & World, 1963; London: Faber & Faber, 1964);

Fairy Tales (New York: Harcourt, Brace & World, 1965);

Complete Poems 1923-1962, edited by George Firmage (2 volumes, London: MacGibbon & Kee, 1968; 1 volume, New York: Harcourt Brace Jovanovich, 1972);

Poems 1905-1962, edited by Firmage (London: Marchim Press, 1973);

Tulips & Chimneys: The Original 1922 Manuscript with the 35 Additional Poems from &, edited by Firmage (New York: Liveright, 1976).

PLAY PRODUCTION: *Him,* New York, Provincetown Playhouse, 18 April 1928.

OTHER: Louis Aragon, *The Red Front,* translated by Cummings (New York: Contempo, 1933).

E. E. Cummings's experimentation with form and language places him among the most innovative of twentieth-century poets. His style eludes specific association with any one modern line. He was applauded by such various poets as Ezra Pound, William Carlos Williams, Marianne Moore, Robert Graves, Laura Riding, Allen Tate, Theodore Roethke, and Louise Bogan, but he remained peripheral to contemporary poetic movements. He was one of the earliest modern poets (Guillaume Apollinaire and Mina Loy preceded him) to introduce typographical eccentricities into writing. His dazzling linguistic risk taking was in fact painstakingly measured to control sound—pacing, syllable stress, juncture—and sight. The intricate spatial patterning led Marianne Moore to describe his poems as "a kind of verbal topiary-work." The strong visual character of Cummings's writing owes much to his parallel development as a painter. Indeed, his dismemberment of syntax derived from the advances in contemporary European visual art, particularly cubism.

However modern the stimulus for and the superficial appearance of his writing may have been, much of it arises from a nineteenth-century romantic reverence for natural order over man-made order, for intuition and imagination over routine-grounded perception. His exalted vision of life and love is served well by his linguistic agility. He was an unabashed lyricist, a modern cavalier love poet. But alongside his lyrical celebrations of nature, love, and the imagination are his satirical denouncements of tawdry, defiling, flat-footed, urban and political life—open terrain for invective and verbal inventiveness. He trained his ear on the rhythms of American speech: he attacked the inauthentic and the manipulative; he twisted overused words into punning submission; he mimicked familiar public slogans in despairing but vigorous poems, such as the justly celebrated "next to of course god america i/love you land of the pilgrims' and so forth . . . ," and, from "POEM, OR BEAUTY HURTS MR. VINAL":

take it from me kiddo
believe me
my country, 'tis of

you,land of the Cluett
Shirt Boston Garter and Spearmint
Girl With The Wrigley Eyes(of you
land of the Arrow Ide
and Earl &
Wilson
Collars)of you i
sing: land of Abraham Lincoln and Lydia E. Pinkham,
land above all of Just Add Hot Water And Serve—
from every B.V.D.

let freedom ring[.]

Edward Estlin Cummings grew up in a Cambridge, Massachusetts, household which resounded with the verbally adroit and sententious speech of his self-made, civic-minded father, a Harvard professor and Unitarian clergyman, Edward Cummings. Family diaries provide copious documentation of young Estlin's early years and his resolve to become a poet. Rebecca, his mother, endorsed this ambition and orchestrated a delightful round of writing games and improvised theatrics to keep the young writer's imagination alert. In her long life, Cummings's devotion was constant—"if there are any heavens my mother will (all by herself) have/one." His Cambridge youth was happy, protected, homogenous. The family spent each summer on their property, Joy Farm, near

The poet's mother, Rebecca H. Cummings, in 1892 (portrait by Charles Hopkinson; courtesy of the Massachusetts Historical Society)

Silver Lake in New Hampshire. Cummings would return to it nearly every summer of his life. Allusions to the idyll of childhood recur through his work, as in the early and much anthologized poem from *Tulips and Chimneys* (1923), "in Just-/spring":

> and eddieandbill come
> running from marbles and
> piracies and it's
> spring
>
> when the world is puddle-wonderful
>
> the queer
> old balloonman whistles
> far   and   wee
> and bettyandisbel come dancing
>
> from hop-scotch and jump-rope and [.]

These years saw the beginnings of his abiding delight in mime, theater, and particularly the circus, which came to signify for him a devoted and pure artistry.

Between the ages of eight and twenty-two, Cummings wrote close to a poem a day. In his earnest application he imitated a wide variety of poetic forms—the ballad, the heroic couplet, the heroic quatrain, the rondeau, the rondel, the sonnet, the Spenserian stanza, and the triplet. The Cambridge tradition, as defined especially by Henry Wadsworth Longfellow, claimed his first allegiance. After he had entered Harvard in September 1911, John Keats and then Dante Gabriel Rossetti took precedence. Cummings was, of course, a superb mimic, but his grasp of the poetic potential of language was more than superficial. In the spring of his sophomore year, he joined the editorial board of the literary magazine the *Harvard Monthly* and through this association began important friendships with S. Foster Damon, John Dos Passos, Schofield Thayer, J. Sibley Watson, and Stewart Mitchell: all conversant with new developments in the arts. Thayer and Watson, who had each inherited great wealth, would in the 1920s become joint owners of the *Dial,* with Mitchell as managing editor. Besides publishing his poems, they were to provide generous support for Cummings's painting and poetry.

The literary influence of these new friendships and the contact they provided with modern literature did not immediately alter Cummings's style. He continued to work doggedly within rigid, imposed forms. In his senior year, 1915, he wrote his first highly successful poem, a ballad which succeeds by its flaunting of discipline:

> All in green went my love riding
> on a great horse of gold
> into the silver dawn.
>
> four lean hounds crouched low and smiling
> the merry deer ran before.
>
> Fleeter be they than dappled dreams
> the swift sweet deer
> the red rare deer.
>
> Four red roebuck at a white water
> the cruel bugle sang before.

The first clear indication of his affinity with a modern sensibility occurs in a term paper, "The New Art," which Cummings revised and presented as an address at the June 1915 Harvard com-

Elizabeth and E. E. Cummings with their father, Edward Cummings (courtesy of the Houghton Library, Harvard University)

mencement ceremony, where he received his A.B. "magna cum laude in literature especially Greek and English." This descriptive and impressionistic piece covered a range of avant-garde activities in the arts: developments from realism to cubism; overlaps between the visual arts and music and literature; achievements of artists such as Paul Cézanne, Marcel Duchamp, Igor Stravinsky, Arnold Schönberg, and Gertrude Stein. Cummings's introduction to the liberties of modern art prompted in his own conduct a new daring much opposed to the middle-class, high-minded ethos of his father-dominated home. Accompanied by his new friends, he became acquainted with the saloons and burlesque theaters of Boston, with popular arts and performers—clowns, acrobats, tap dancers, chorus girls—and with the drunks and prostitutes among their clientele. This was a magical netherworld for the sheltered Cambridge youth. The conservative Harvard style he had adopted in early work that Thayer referred to as "mortuary pieces" was gradually undermined. But through this early work Cummings had achieved a solid grounding in traditional verse forms against which he would bounce his teasing, acrobatic modernity. Many of his best poems allude with irony to traditional diction or

form, often in amusing combinations of archaic with modern vocabulary and syntax:

(ponder,darling,these busted statues
of yon motheaten forum be aware
notice what hath remained [.]

Eight Harvard Poets (1917)—accepted for publication in fall 1916, after Cummings had earned his A.M. from Harvard the previous June—features the work of the Harvard Poetry Society—an informal group of poets associated with the *Harvard Monthly*, who met to read one another's work. Also including poems by Damon, Dos Passos, Robert Hillyer, Mitchell, William A. Norris, Dudley Poore, and Cuthbert Wright, *Eight Harvard Poets* contains eight poems by Cummings, all of which bear traces of his mature style and give evidence that he has heeded Pound's injunction against excessive verbiage. The poems are stark, and their staggered arrangement on the page draws attention to the densities of single words. In his earliest published experiments in subverting the conventions of punctuation, capitalization, and syntax, he aimed to uncover, beneath the mantle of custom and habit, a more-interesting, more-essential

E. E. Cummings, 1915

preferred the vicissitudes of the life of full-time artist and poet.

Mounting war fever offended his pacifist leanings, but on 7 April 1917, the day after the United States entered the war, Cummings volunteered for the Norton-Harjes Ambulance Service, a frequent choice among young antimilitarist intellectuals. On board ship he met William Slater Brown with whom he was to share much of his war experience and many subsequent years of friendship. The two men arrived in Paris to find that they had been separated from the rest of their unit, who had all gotten off the train at the wrong station. The bureaucratic muddle that ensued gave them a five-week holiday in Paris, enough to establish Cummings's lasting devotion to that city—"a divine section of eternity." Parisian low life provided him with endless entertainment and a brimming source of poetry.

But the ambulance service caught up with them, and on 13 June Cummings and Brown arrived at Section Sanitaire XXI, in the village of Germaine between St. Quentin and Ham. During three frustrating, idle months of service, boredom

mechanism and dynamism of language. The poems are also quite clearly conceived as visual objects—they are typographic novelties. One poem from this period, which he excluded from the final selection for the book, required the reader to read back and forth across the page (for example: "I will wade out/srewolf gninrub ni depeets era shgiht ym llit"). The poem "Crepuscule" marks the beginning of his use of the lowercase first-person singular pronoun, which would become a Cummings trademark. (Though the *i's* were capitalized when the poem appeared in *Eight Harvard Poets* because a copy editor decided they were typographical errors and "corrected" them.) The lowercase *i* suggests the somewhat contradictory impulse toward humility *and* uniqueness of his persona.

On 1 January 1917 Cummings moved to New York, where, he later recalled, "I also breathed: and as if for the first time." He worked at the mail-order book business for P. F. Collier, but the tedium of office work drove him to resign from the only regular job he ever held on 25 February. He

William Slater Brown, 1917

and disgust with their compatriots drove them to seek company among the ordinary French soldiers of nearby units. These actions raised suspicions that had already been alerted by Cummings's and particularly Brown's flagrant attempts to outwit and provoke the censors in letters home. (In one letter to his parents Cummings wrote that he was in "a place hardly *germain* to my malcontent.") On 23 September 1917 they were detained on suspicion of treason and sent, after questioning, to a Dépôt de Triage in the Normandy town of La Ferté-Macé, where aliens suspected of espionage and undesirable activities were detained. Three months of internment in a large chapel-like room in the Dépôt de Triage provided the material for Cummings's first literary success, *The Enormous Room* (1922). At first he and Brown enjoyed the change of scene, the release from their inept compatriots, and the solidarity among the foreign prisoners. "I'm having *the time of my life!*" he told his parents. Indeed, it was not a typical prison experience; the confinement was intended more as a precaution than as a punishment. Cummings wrote poetry, kept notebooks, read Shakespeare with Brown—"days spent with an inimitable friend in soul stretching probings of aesthetics, 10 hour nights (9 pm—6.45 am) and fine folk to converse in five or six languages beside you—perfection attained at last." He wanted no intercession on his behalf. Even so, his father was outraged and interfered to secure his son's release. His father's correspondence with officialdom forms the preface to *The Enormous Room*. Cummings was freed on 19 December and returned undernourished to his parents' home. Over the next three years, he wrote his prose account of the experience.

At the end of February 1918, he returned to New York to resume the bohemian life he had had in Paris and to share a studio with Brown, who arrived in April. Cummings gave most of his time to painting, which at that time presented greater challenges to him than poetry. Inspired by sights in Paris, particularly Pablo Picasso's sets for the ballet *Parade*, he worked at perfecting cubist technique. Schofield Thayer commissioned paintings and urged Cummings's poems on Martyn Johnson, editor of the *Dial*. In July 1918 his Greenwich Village artist's routine was interrupted; he was drafted for service in the U.S. Army and sent for training to Camp Devens, about forty miles west of Cambridge. He refused an opportunity to enter a training school for officers and NCO's, stubbornly holding to the nonheroic role of the *i*. Without the companionship of Brown's intelligent mind, he re-

E. E. Cummings on leave from Camp Devens in 1918 (courtesy of the Houghton Library, Harvard University)

sented his curtailed freedoms and found no fascination in the heterogenous assortment of men in his barracks. One of the abiding contradictions in his position of romantic individualism was his simultaneous admiration and scorn for ordinary people.

During his six months at Camp Devens, he produced many of the poems that appeared in his next three published volumes, and a number of essays on theory of art and literature. He was especially interested in the finer discriminations of a reader's or viewer's senses, what he called "organic sensation"—kinesthetic experience of weight or resistance, subtle varieties of pressure or pain, a certain balance in the inner ear, and so on. How, he wondered, do the arts summon, mix, or muddle these sensations? Experimenting with his own poetry he compiled extensive lists of rhyming or alliterating words and then composed from this palette of sounds. Many of these forays are indistinguishable from contemporary Dadaist or Surrealist jottings: "the Bar.tinkling luscious jigs dint of ripe silver with warmlyish wetflat splurging smells waltz the glush of squirting taps. . . ." Cummings dabbled in several of the -isms of early-twentieth-century art. He was attracted to futurism because of its dedication to movement. The adjective "alive" ranks in his vocabulary as the highest praise—it combines notions of being and becoming with movement, vigor, engagement, and delight.

In the spring of 1918, Schofield Thayer's wife, Elaine, had started to engage Cummings's own faculties of vigor, movement, and delight. Their growing attachment and subsequent affair were entirely sanctioned by Thayer. Elaine was a beauty, open to idealization by a romantic like Cummings. John Dos Passos remembered "Those of us who weren't in love with Cummings were in love with Elaine." Scores of Cummings's best erotic

Elaine Orr, late 1920s (courtesy of Nancy T. Andrews)

poems, such as "i like my body when it is with your/ body," were written for Elaine. In 1919, shortly after Cummings was discharged from the army, Elaine became pregnant and Cummings was, without doubt, the father. Nancy, born on 20 December 1919, was given Thayer's surname.

After his discharge in January 1919 Cummings had returned to Greenwich Village to share a studio with Brown and to settle again into serious painting. He entered two works in the spring 1919 show of the New York Society of Independent Artists. By October 1920 he had finished *The Enormous Room* and, after finding little interest among New York publishers, left the manuscript in his father's resourceful hands.

The following year Cummings and Dos Passos toured Europe together, arriving in Paris, the final point of their journey, in mid-May 1921. There Cummings began his lifelong friendship with Ezra Pound, whom he described to his parents as "altogether, for me, a gymnastic personality." Elaine and Schofield Thayer were also in Paris for the July divorce that would unite Cummings with Elaine and his daughter, Nancy. He lived cheaply on money provided by Elaine's generous purse and by his father—family money would continue to supplement his meager earnings throughout his life. He drew and painted and, evidently, enjoyed Parisian cuisine: "I eat snails almost daily, oysters biweekly, mussels weekly, mermaids once a month."

Boni and Liveright accepted *The Enormous Room*, which appeared in May 1922 and was well received, even in the popular press. The *Boston Sunday Globe* gave their review the headline: "Harvard Man, Son of Prominent Preacher, Reveals His Terrible War Experience Involving High Officials." Like his poetry, this prose work (it is neither a novel nor a conventional memoir) subverts expectations: it is a high-spirited account of injustice and imprisonment in a freewheeling linguistic style that darts in and out of French and English in an unprecedented manner, as in the following excerpt: "lest the ordinarily tantalizing proximity of *les femmes* should not inspire *les hommes* to deeds which placed the doers automatically in the clutches of himself, his subordinates, and *la punition*, it was arranged that once a week the tantalizing proximity aforesaid should be supplanted by a positively maddening approach to coincidence. . . ." At the end, Cummings prevents his readers from seeing his release as a conventional resolution. The central focus of the book is, after all, romantic individualism. He attacks all attributes of government, believing that authority tramples on the development and expression of the individual being. His early fondness for Rossetti's allegorical mode resurfaces in a series of allusions to John Bunyan's *Pilgrim's Progress* (1678). These accumulated allusions elevate and focus the narrative.

Since his imprisonment Cummings had been writing poems. He had already tried unsuccessfully to place a manuscript he called *Tulips & Chimneys*, and, living in Paris in 1922, he revised the manuscript, removing several sexually explicit sonnets but leaving a remarkable collection of 152 poems which would not see publication, as a collection, during his lifetime. Between 1923 and 1925 the contents were scattered over three volumes of his poems. Only in 1976 was the complete manuscript finally published as Cummings had intended, under its original title, including the ampersand he preferred.

In April 1923 Cummings heard that Boni and Liveright would publish a condensed version of his manuscript, as *Tulips and Chimneys* (1923)—the tulips are free-verse lyrics and the chimneys are sonnets written in response to a sordid urban world. The collection opens with a number of his college poems, his formal declamatory "Epithalamion" written for the wedding of Elaine and Schofield Thayer in 1916 and his more sophisticated "Puella Mea" written for Elaine in 1919. His mature work is grouped under "Impressions," "Portraits," "Post Impressions," and the three sections of sonnets— "realities," "unrealities," and "actualities"—under the heading "Chimneys." The poems take liberties with poetic convention and public taste, as in his farewell to Cambridge morality: "the Cambridge ladies who live in furnished souls." But many are romantic invocations which exploit archaic language:

> spring omnipotent goddess thou dost
> inveigle into crossing sidewalks the
> unwary june-bug and the frivolous angleworm
> thou dost persuade to serenade his
> lady the musical tom-cat, thou stuffest
> the parks with overgrown pimply
> cavaliers and gumchewing giggly
> girls and not content
> Spring, with this
> thou hangest canary-birds in parlor windows[.]

The poem continues to mock its own grandiose manner though it never loses sight of its celebration of sensation and new life. In this early collection, Cummings introduces an attitude that remains consistent throughout his work, an attitude that, in

condemning mankind while idealizing the individual, is the basis for his portraits and his satires. The sarcastic

> Humanity i love you
> because you would rather black the boots of
> success than enquire whose soul dangles from his
> watch-chain which could be embarrassing for both—

ends with the statement, "Humanity/i hate you" (the poem was first collected in *XLI Poems*, 1925).

Portrait-poems held a strong appeal for Cummings the painter. *Tulips and Chimneys* includes his well-known "Buffalo Bill's" and others that take their subjects from the demimonde. Many of these poems employ the dialect of the lowbrow café dweller—a quasi-phonetic, comic approximation of their speech: "eet smeestaire steevensun/kum een, dare ease Bet, an LeeLee, an dee beeg wun" from "when you rang at Dick Mid's Place."

The proportion of sonnets in the volume, and indeed in all of Cummings's poetry, is high. He thrived on the disjunction of its formal constraints and his irreverent content. He liked to follow the rhyme scheme of the Petrarchan sonnet to which he added, in the final couplet, the characteristic Shakespearean modifying twist. The device could transform an initially romantic poem into a satire. In general, he reserved the sonnet or metrical forms for his more serious poems which embody a complex, transcendent vision. The looser, more experimental poems, on the other hand, aim to communicate concrete sensations and perceptions in all their existential immediacy. He shuns conventional syntax and punctuation as based on an arrangement of thoughts, feelings, and sensations already completed. His concern is with the instantaneous: "suddenly" is among his favorite words. Typography performs a dynamic function by approximating visually the actual object or experience that gave rise to the poem as in "breathing Spring twi (after rain) light."

Back in New York, Elaine and Cummings were married on 19 March 1924, and Cummings legally adopted Nancy on 24 April. Then four, she was a delight to him. He composed stories for her (some of which were published years later in *Fairy Tales,* 1965), and took her to the zoo and the circus as he had done in Paris. Life with Elaine was a pleasure too, with its round of restaurants, clubs, theaters, and friends' apartments. Dos Passos remembered, "After a couple of brandies on top of wine Cummings would deliver himself of geysers of talk. I've never heard anything that remotely approached it. It was comical ironical learned brilliantlycolored intricatelycadenced damnably poetic and sometimes just naughty."

Cummings continued to paint and to relish his role as experimental poet and iconoclast. *Tulips and Chimneys* was met by a number of hostile reviews, but this first major collection found more sympathy and interest than much of his subsequent work. In a review for *Poetry,* under the title "Flare and Blare," Harriet Monroe objected to his eccentricities of punctuation and typography; yet, she added, "He is as agile and outrageous as a faun, and as full of delight over the beauties and monstrosities of this brilliant and grimy old planet. There is a grand gusto in him. . . ." Edmund Wilson in the *New Republic* took accurate aim: "Cummings's style is an eternal adolescent, as fresh and often as winning but as half-baked as boyhood. A poet with a real gift for language, for a melting music a little like Shelley's, which rhapsodizes and sighs in soft vowels disembarrassed of their baggage of consonants, he strikes often on ethereal measures of a singular purity and charm—his best poems seem to dissolve on the mind like the flakes of a lyric dew; but he never seems to know when he is writing badly and when he is writing well. He has apparently no faculty for self-criticism."

The Dial Press sifted through the poems remaining from the original *Tulips & Chimneys* manuscript and selected forty-one for a volume entitled *XLI Poems* (1925). Cummings then arranged for a private printing of the remainder of the manuscript plus some new poems. His title was *&* for the ampersand that he regretted was missing from Boni and Liveright's *Tulips and Chimneys.* The two additional volumes are distinguished from the first by a larger number of erotic poems.

In May 1924, two months after the Cummings's marriage, Elaine left for Europe to settle the estate of her deceased sister, Constance. In June she wrote that she'd fallen in love with an Irish fellow passenger, Frank MacDermot, and wanted a divorce. The forlorn Cummings did all he could to dissuade her and, after he failed, he entered into an extended custody battle over Nancy. But he was defeated and until 1948, when she heard the news directly from him, Nancy had no knowledge that he was her father.

Although 1925 was a year of great personal distress, it was also a year of literary achievement. *XLI Poems* and *&* both appeared and were well received. In a *Dial* review of *XLI Poems* Marianne Moore called him "fanciful, yet faithful to that verisimilitude of eye and of rhetoric which is so im-

portant in poetry," adding that he "shapes the progress of poems as if it were substance; he has 'a trick of syncopation Europe has,' determining the pauses slowly, with glides and tight-rope acrobatics, ensuring the ictus by a space instead of a period, or a semi-colon in the middle of a word, seeming to have placed adjectives systematically one word in advance of the words they modify, or one word behind, with most pleasing exactness." She went on to say, "The physique of the poems recalls the corkscrew twists, the infinitude of dots, the sumptuous perpendicular appearance of Kufic script; and the principle of the embedded rhyme has produced . . . some sublimely Mohammedan effects."

Cummings was earning a steady if small income by writing comic sketches for *Vanity Fair*— mock interviews, parodies of theater reviews, letters to the editor—a job which he despised. At the end of 1925 he won the *Dial* award "for distinguished service to American letters." The prize of $2000 equaled a full year's livelihood. He was a regular contributor to the *Dial,* which in ten years published thirty-seven of his poems, several critical articles, parts of his play *Him* (1927) and numerous drawings and paintings. The editors considered him their discovery among the moderns.

Encouraged by his success, Boni and Liveright contracted with Cummings early in 1926 for a volume of poems that would include a brief introductory reader's guide. He wrote to his mother about his choice of title: "IS FIVE (short for Twice Two Is Five, hasten to add.) But even so, how will M. et Mmme. Everyone compwehend?—such is the curse of awithmetic." The explanatory introduction became a characteristic statement about the superiority of process over product: "If a poet is anybody, he is somebody to whom things made matter very little—somebody who is obsessed by Making." The implication is that "making" is process and life-giving, whereas "made" is stasis and death. The poems in *Is 5* (1926) mark no striking advance on the mature poems of *Tulips and Chimneys.* There is a larger proportion of satirical poems, particularly antiwar pieces such as the exasperated though gentle critique of American civilian concern—

my sweet old etcetera
aunt lucy during the recent

war could and what
is more did tell you just
what everybody was fighting

for,
my sister

isabel created hundreds
(and
hundreds)of socks . . .

—or such as the Siegfied Sassoon-type diatribe of
"the season 'tis, my lovely lambs":

braving the worst,of peril heedless,
each braver than the other,each
(a typewriter within his reach)
upon his fearless derrière
sturdily seated—Colonel Needless
To Name and General You know who
a string of pretty medals drew

(while messrs jack james john and jim
in token of their country's love
received my dears the order of
The Artificial Arm and Limb)[.]

As with all his books of poetry thus far, sales of *Is
5* were minimal.

Interest in drama and the theater was running high during the 1920s, and Cummings was
drawn into Greenwich Village discussions of European and American dramatic expressionism. Out
of this excitement he wrote the play *Him*, a somber,
overcomplex Strindbergian drama, an ambitious
effort to enact Freudian ideas. The play is a series
of vignettes with circus sideshows, vaudeville skits,

Anne Barton Cummings

burlesque sketches, and Dada nonsense representing the unconscious. The main character, Him, is
another manifestation of the nonhero, the lowercase *i*, the Everyman, the Anybody, but also the
artist and playwright. Again, Cummings's identity
is barely concealed. However, the play represents
one of his few extended attempts to make a considered composition out of the responses which
constitute the poetic sensibility. Marianne Moore,
managing editor for the *Dial,* recommended they
print excerpts from *Him,* noting, "Some of it seems
to me as imaginative and expert as anything of his
I have read; and some of it to the contrary." The
excerpts appeared in the August 1926 issue with a
photograph of Cummings's painting *Noise Number
13.* Boni and Liveright's publication of the play
prompted the Provincetown Playhouse to stage it.
Under James Light's direction, it opened on 18
April 1928 to an amazed and fascinated audience.
Cummings had written a "Warning" for the program: "Relax and give the play a chance to strut
its stuff—relax, stop wondering what it's all
'about'—like many strange and familiar things, Life
included, this Play isn't 'about,' it simply is. Don't
try to enjoy it, let it try to enjoy you. DON'T TRY
TO UNDERSTAND IT, LET IT TRY TO UN-
DERSTAND YOU." The play ran to full and delighted houses for twenty-seven performances.

On 1 May 1929 Cummings married Anne
Barton, and together they departed for Europe.
During the next two years they spent a great deal
of time in Europe, probably because it was less expensive to live there than in the United States.

Cummings's book with no title, published by
Covici-Friede in 1930, is an assemblage of nine
nonsense stories, each preceded by an amusing line
drawing. A narrative manner without narrative
purpose or direction mingles, over sixty-three
pages, clichés, epigrams, slogans, and puns: "Once
upon a time, boys and girls, there were two con-
genital ministers to Belgium, one of whom was insane whereas the other was six-fingered. They met
on the top of a churchsteeple and exchanged with
ease electrically lighted visiting cards and the one
who was not steering picked a rose and handed it
to the waitress with the remark: 'Urinoir gratuit.' "

Another book followed in January 1931. The
single published collection of his artwork, it was
titled *CIOPW,* an acronym formed from the initial
letters of the words *charcoal, ink, oil, pencil, water-
color.* Its subject is autobiographical, drawing on
treasured features of Cummings's world: acrobats,
burlesque dancers, Chaplin, a merry-go-round,

portraits of his family, landscapes of Paris and of Joy Farm in New Hampshire.

With the demise of the *Dial* in 1929, few of Cummings's poems appeared in periodicals. However, in the early 1930s *This Quarter*, "a magazine of left-bank activities" edited by Edward Titus in Paris, published several of his poems, including those which reflect his troubled second marriage, which would end in 1932:

> nothing is more exactly terrible than
> to be alone in the house, with somebody and
> with something)
>
>   You are gone. there is laughter
> and despair impersonates a street[.]

Such poems also appeared in *ViVa*, published in October 1931. The book contains seventy poems. Of the first sixty-three poems every seventh one is a sonnet, and the last seven poems are all sonnets. (Thus the book contains fourteen sonnets for the fourteen lines of the sonnet form.) Otherwise the development is similar to that in all his books of poetry since *Is 5*, a tendency that Cummings described as "to begin dirty (world: sordid, satires) & end clean (earth: lyrical, love poems)." The collection indulges in the familiar linguistic manipulations. There are the by now predictable attacks on modern mass thinking; and a variety of portraits, many of them spoken in the subject's dialect. Play with language, such as the spoonerisms of poem twenty-one, "helves surling out of eakspeasies per(reel)hapsingly," tends to turn serious, bitter, or occasionally strident. Among the satires is a poem which draws on his experience at Camp Devens, "i sing of Olaf glad and big/whose warmest heart recoiled at war:/a conscientious object-or." As these lines suggest, it is one of Cummings's most trenchant antiwar pieces:

> but—though all kinds of officers
> (a yearning nation's blueeyed pride)
> their passive prey did kick and curse
> until for wear their clarion
> voices and boots were much the worse,
> and egged the firstclassprivates on
> his rectum wickedly to tease
> by means of skilfully applied
> bayonets roasted hot with heat—
> Olaf(upon what were once knees)
> does almost ceaselessly repeat
> "there is some shit I will not eat"
>
> our president,being of which

> assertions duly notified
> threw the yellowsonofabitch
> into a dungeon,where he died [.]

Olaf is an early type of the individual in a number of Cummings's poems. "Mostpeople" follow orders, do their duty; the individual is true to himself.

The mood of the volume is often affectionate: the poem for his mother, "if there are any heavens . . . ," the celebrations of his favorite phenomena—stars, birds, flowers, twilight—and the love poems such as "somewhere I have never traveled, gladly beyond/any experience."

In May 1931 Cummings had left Anne Cummings behind in Paris and traveled to the Soviet Union. American intellectuals, especially those—like Cummings and his friends—who expressed socialist ideals, had been quick to approve government sponsorship of art and literature in the Soviet Union and to note the optimistic reports on the current Soviet Five-Year Plan at a time when the West reeled under economic depression. Cummings's dissatisfaction with American culture predisposed him to enjoy his trip, yet his philosophy of individualism surely made him suspicious of collectivist ideology. During his stay he began to conceive of Russia as another Enormous Room, empty of laughter, fun, color, and spirit—an "uncircus of noncreatures." The travel diary he kept from 10 May to 14 June 1931 was much expanded for *Eimi*, published in 1933. The title, "I am" in Greek, asserts, once again, the individual against the collective. Within the mythic structure a journey to the Underworld—replete with allusions to Dante's *Inferno*—made by one Comrade Kem-min-kz (the Russian pronunciation of his name), the book traces various events that occurred on Cummings's journey, in their correct sequence. It is written in the same highly personal and mannered style of his poetry. In the following passage, for example, he is leaving Russia: "USSR a USSR a night-USSR a nightmare USSR home for the panacea Negation haven of all(in life's name)Deathworshippers hopper of hate's Becausemachine(U for un- & S for self S for science and R for -reality)how it shrivels:how it dwindles withers;how it wilts diminishes wanes;how it crumbles evaporates collapses disappears—the verily consubstantial cauchemar of premeditated NYET." In the more than sixty reviews of *Eimi* in newspapers and magazines, reviewers expressed almost unanimous bafflement and impatience.

During the writing of *Eimi*, Cummings's antagonism to the Soviet Union became an obsession.

Working drafts for "somewhere i have never traveled . . . ," collected in ViVa *(by permission of Nancy T. Andrews, the Estate of*
E. E. Cummings; courtesy of the Houghton Library, Harvard University)

*Marion Morehouse Cummings (photograph by
Edward Mueller)*

He grew to despise both Communists *and* liberals. During the Roosevelt-Truman era his loathing for American culture grew, and his conservatism turned into reactionary bitterness. Before *Eimi* he had been regarded as a voice from the left because of the antiauthoritarian demeanor of the poems and *The Enormous Room*. He lost friends and the once unquestioning support of a literary world now increasingly sympathetic to literature fueled by a social conscience.

In 1932 while his divorce was being negotiated, Cummings met Marion Morehouse, a generous spirit who would remain his companion and common-law wife (it appears they never married) until his death. She was, like Elaine and Anne, a great beauty. Cummings's persistent financial worries lifted when, in the spring of 1933, he was awarded a Guggenheim Fellowship on the strength of the briefest proposal for "a book of poems."

At about the same time Lionel Kirstein, editor of the *Hound and Horn*, persuaded Cummings to compose a ballet scenario; at Marion's suggestion, he adapted *Uncle Tom's Cabin*. *Tom* was published in 1935, but not staged even though David Diamond completed the score in 1936. Both Diamond and Kirstein were among a number of young people who became close friends of Cummings's. He enjoyed preaching his doctrine of individualism and devotion to art. These new friendships filled the gap left by the deaths and disaffections of older friends.

Meanwhile Cummings could find no publisher for his new collections. Fourteen houses turned him down, partly because of the Depression economy and partly because his recent sales (for *Is 5*, *ViVa*, *[No Title]*, *Eimi*) had all been low. At last, *No Thanks* (1935), dedicated to the publishers who had rejected the book—their names arranged on the page in the shape of a funeral urn—was published by the Golden Eagle Press. Cummings's mother subsidized the printing. As with all his books, the poems are carefully assembled in a symbolic schema. In *No Thanks*, the seventy poems are arranged in a pattern of three poems followed by a sonnet; with a cluster of three sonnets at the halfway point. Cummings visualized the book in the shape of a V: moving from two "moon" poems, descending to "earth" poems at the center of the book, and then rising to two "star" poems at the conclusion. His selection presents a fully developed view of life: his reverence for the instinctive self and the world of feeling against his contempt for the analytical mind and its imprisoning intellectual systems. Early in the collection "sonnet entitled how to run the world" offers the advice, "don't." Another attacks a man who "does not feel because he thinks" or, worse, one who "does not have to think because he knows." American culture takes its usual beating, as does "progress":

o pr
gress verily thou art m
mentous superc
lossal hyperpr
digious etc i kn
w & if you d[,]

and the slaves of the totalitarian state:

kumrads die because they're told)
kumrads die before they're old
(kumrads aren't afraid to die
kumrads don't
and kumrads won't
believe in life)and death knows whie[.]

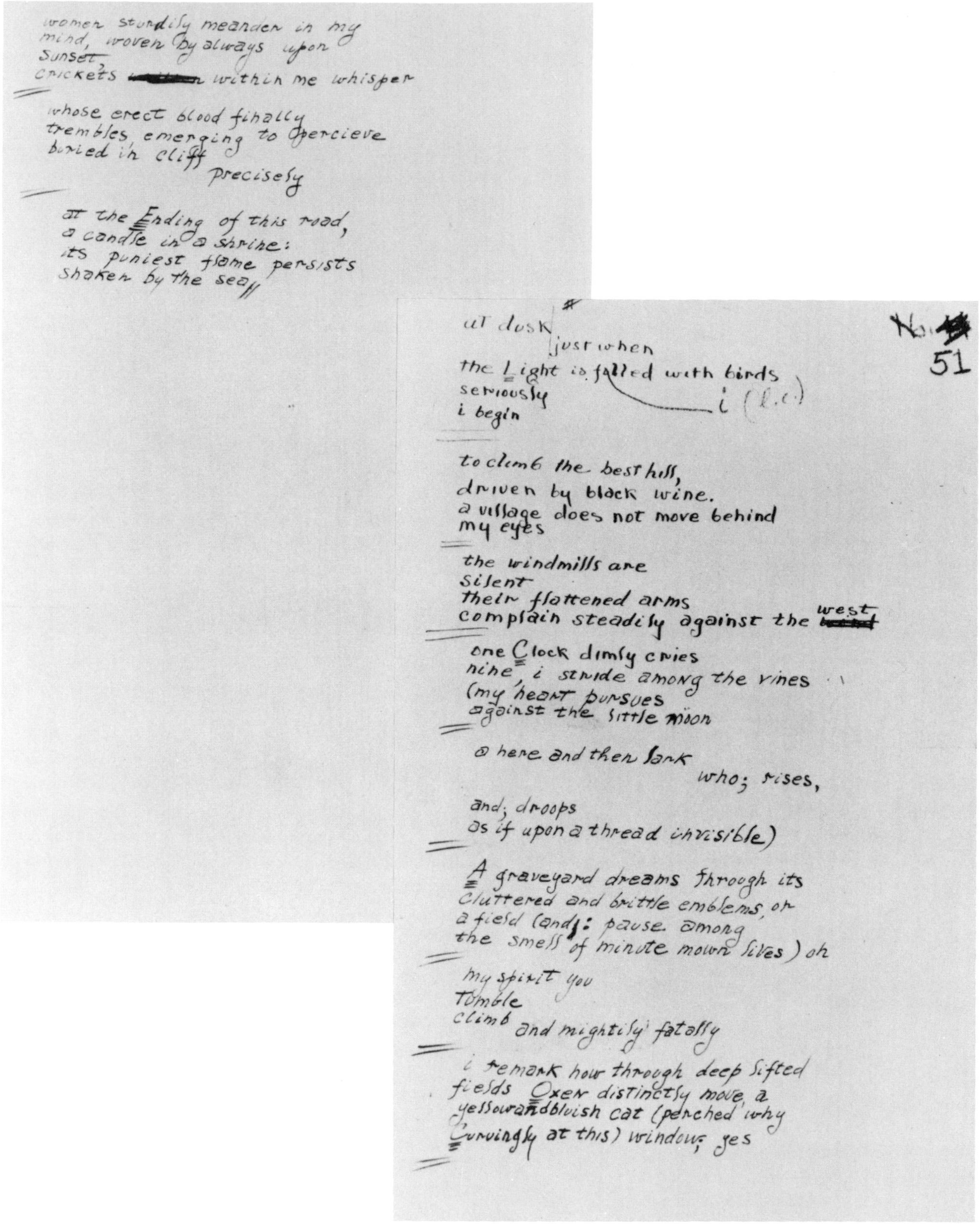

women stundily meander in my
mind, woven by always upon
Sunset,
Crickets ~~within~~ within me whisper

whose erect blood finally
trembles, emerging to ~~p~~ercieve
buried in cliff
                precisely

at the Ending of this road,
a candle in a shrine:
its puniest flame persists
shaken by the sea//

at dusk #
            just when
the Light is falled with birds,
seriously   i (l.c)
i begin

to climb the best hill,
driven by black wine.
a village does not move behind
my eyes

the windmills are
silent
their flattened arms   west
complain steadily against the ~~east~~

one Clock dimly cries
nine, i stride among the vines
(my heart pursues
against the little moon

& here and then lark
                    who; rises,

and; droops
as if upon a thread invisible)

A graveyard dreams through its
cluttered and brittle emblems, or
a field (and): pause among
the smell of minute mown lives) oh

my spirit you
Tumble
climb and mightily fatally

i remark how through deep sifted
fields Oxen distinctly move, a
yellowandbluish cat (perched why
curvingly at this) window; yes

Final draft for a poem published in No Thanks *(by permission of Nancy T. Andrews, the Estate of E. E. Cummings; courtesy of the Clifton Waller Barrett Library, University of Virginia)*

These cantankerous poems are matched by open, more felicitous tributes to the natural world, to the promise of beginnings, of spring and of love.

Certain words in Cummings's vocabulary carry a rather full evaluative cargo—apart from his special veneration for the word "alive," he pays tribute to "is" ("Is will still occur" despite threats from "knowings" and "credos"), "guess," "dare," "open," "dream," and "yes." Words singled out for loathing are "same," "reason," "shut," "numb," and "mostpeople." "Who" is the acceptable relative pronoun since it always refers to an individual; "which" is despicable since, in his usage, it refers to a depersonalized human being, a nonperson. Nikita Khrushchev, for instance, is "a which that walks like a who." In *No Thanks*, Cummings takes his customary liberties with word forms. He is specially fond of the prefix "un-" which, placed before any noun, deprives it of its essence, its "thingness." Furthermore, in an effort to steer language away from abstraction, he constructs nouns out of verbs, adjectives, or adverbs, thereby suggesting motion where conventional language would suggest stasis and mere function. His polymorphous use of ordinary words extends their range of connotations and their capacity to become metaphors.

The two "star" poems which end the volume introduce a religious tone that is new in Cummings's work. Words such as "holy," "miraculous," "lifting hopes and hands," and an aspect of humble wonder before a higher force suggest that his father's Unitarian message had left its mark after all.

Because *No Thanks* was not published by a major house it had little promotion and very few notices. In 1938 Harcourt, Brace decided to gather Cummings's scattered work into a *Collected Poems*. It was more widely reviewed and better received than any of his other books, but sales were still slow. At the publisher's request, Cummings included a preface which reiterates his values:

> The poems to come are for you and for me and are not for mostpeople—it's no use trying to pretend that mostpeople and ourselves are alike. Mostpeople have less in common with ourselves than the squareroot-ofminusone. You and I are human beings; mostpeople are snobs. . . .
>
> Life,formostpeople,simply isn't. Take the socalled standardof living. What do mostpeople mean by "living"? They don't mean living. Theymean the latest and closest plural approximation to singular prenatal passivity which science,in its finite but unbounded wisdom,has succeeded in selling their wives. If

science could fail, a mountain's a mammal. Mostpeople's wives can spot a genuine delusion of embryonic omnipotence immediately and will accept no substitutes. . . .

> Miracles are to come. With you I leave a remembrance of miracles: they are by somebody who can love and who shall be continually reborn,a human being; . . .

Vitriol churns beneath the intimate, chatty surface and raises questions about the snobbery and elitism that Cummings wanted to repudiate. It is an abstract notion of humanity that Cummings hates.

There were 315 poems in the book, including twenty-two new ones. Among them, Yvor Winters found too much evidence of "infantile exhibitionism"; and Horace Gregory found too little evidence of development over the years. Yet Dudley Fitts wrote for the *Saturday Review of Literature:* "With all its failures and beauties, its clashing styles, its brainsmashing complexities and moving simplicities, this is the poetry of a man of complete artistic integrity."

During World War II, in 1940, *50 Poems* appeared. They are more compact and philosophical

E. E. Cummings, summer 1939 (photograph by Marion Morehouse Cummings)

but otherwise not strikingly different from the usual collection of syntactically daring satires and love poems. The volume contains such frequently anthologized pieces as his small myth of a secret self, "anyone lived in a pretty how town," and the poem for his father, "my father moved through dooms of love." In retrospect, Cummings regarded this poem for his father as the start of a new development where he began to speak with a morally responsible voice and with greater concern for others.

Critics attacked the book for its now over-familiar style and subject matter. A wartime publication, it made no mention of the contemporary global crisis. Babette Deutsch wrote a scathing review for the *Nation* (17 May 1941) in the form of a pastiche letter-poem addressed to Cummings, parodying his manner and pointing to, among other things, the formulaic ease of his method:

```
;but
it is
nineteenfortyone mrcummings
,and you must forgive us
if we sometimes
y
      aaaw
            n
 . . . . . . . . . . . . . . . . . . . . . . . . . . . .
. . . we are not asking you for
something new ,simply
few
and (er
)or better
?poems
```

Sales were slow but steady; his reputation continued to grow, gradually, until by the 1960s the book was earning him $400 per year in royalties.

The entry of the United States into the war did not escape Cummings's notice. His revulsion against the growing hatred for the Japanese prompted him to write a skillfully patterned satire on incoherent, racist anger:

```
ygUDuh

   ydoan
   yunnuhstan

   ydoan o
   yunnuhstan dem
   yguduh ged

   yunnuhstan dem doidee
   yguduh ged riduh
```

ydoan o nudn[.]

In 1941 Cummings began to have pains in his left leg and back and was diagnosed as having osteoarthritis of the spine, which caused him pain for the rest of his life. He wore an uncomfortable metal corset, which he referred to as "the iron maiden," and unrelenting physical discomfort made him moody and irascible.

In 1944, with the publication of *1 x 1*, Henry Holt and Company became Cummings's publisher for what would be the peak years of his career. *1 x 1* is his most important volume of poems. The selection reflects universal concerns and a greater joy in life; it has less bitterness and fewer satires. Looking back on this period he said, "The 2nd 'world war' finds me trying to cheer up my native land; I feel responsible to certain anonymous-or-otherwise admirers."

1 x 1 is divided into three parts and progresses from dark to light, a schematic orderliness that is familiar from earlier collections. Section one opens with an imagistic piece about a dull November day, the sky a "nonsun blob" and moves on in "it's over a (see just," to a modern rendering of man's fall from grace:

```
then over our thief goes
(you and i)
has pulled(for he's we)
such fruit from what bough
that someone called they
made him pay with his now.
```

A few dark poems are clustered in this first section: "ygUDuh," "a salesman is an it that stinks Excuse," "a politician is an arse upon," "pity this monster manunkind/not." At the end of the section Cummings strikes the theme implicit in the title—oneness and love, the means (one times one) whereby oneness is reached. Variations on the theme occur throughout the book, as in the following lines reminiscent of Donne:

```
one's not half two. It's two are halves of one:
which halves reintegrating,shall occur
no death and any quantity;but than
all numerable mosts the actual more[.]
```

Section two ("X") contains some of his more compact and obscure poems, and also some of his more fragmented:

```
old mr ly
fresh from a fu
```

ruddy as a sun
with blue true two

man
neral
rise
eyes[.]

His memorable elegy for Sam Ward, the handyman at Silver Lake, is here too:

rain or hail
sam done
the best he kin
till they digged his hole

:sam was a man[.]

In Section three ("l") Cummings's manner is lyrical and optimistic. Oneness in the natural world moves to oneness in human life with poems about the growth of a flower, the approach of dawn, the shock of spring, and on to love poems (some of which are very sentimental). He places his dedication to Marion Morehouse at the emotional high point of the book, the end.

1 x 1 was well received by a war-weary country. Theodore Spenser called it "a poetry of joy, that seeks for joy and, perhaps at the cost of wearing blinkers, finds and succeeds, to our great delight, in expressing it." William Reisen in the *Cincinnati Enquirer* wrote of the change in the poems: "Cummings, whose lower case poems were once regarded as the 'dernier cri' in modernism, has developed beyond mere sensationalism into a sincere and responsible artist although he still clings to his forms." For *1 x 1* Cummings received the Shelley Memorial Award from the Poetry Society of America. It was published in Great Britain in 1947, the second British edition of his poetry. *1/20* (1936) was the first.

In 1945 he made an exception to his rule of avoiding causes and, with William Carlos Williams, Karl Shapiro, Conrad Aiken, and others, he published a statement in the newspaper *PM*, 26 November 1945, in defense of Ezra Pound. His argument was: "Every artist's strictly illimitable country is himself." (Later he would use the same argument against charges of anti-Semitism in his own work.) He also gave money he could ill afford in order to help pay for Pound's medical treatment.

In 1946 the *Harvard Wake* published a special Cummings number, which contained his new play *Santa Claus* (subtitled *A Morality*), a fairy tale, and a poem as well as several tributes by other writers. William Carlos Williams praised Cummings's lin-

Nancy and E. E. Cummings, 1950s (photograph by Marion Morehouse Cummings)

guistic achievement and the moral quality with which he addresses the private consciences of his readers. Other leading writers who contributed to the issue were Marianne Moore, Theodore Spenser, Lionel Trilling, Jacques Barzun, Paul Rosenfeld, and John Dos Passos.

Santa Claus, published separately by Henry Holt before Christmas in 1946, was a hybrid morality play and children's pantomime. Its archetypal characters and its action, which includes sudden reversals, derive from the tradition of the marionette theater.

In 1950 Oxford University Press published a collection of poems called *XAIPE*, pronounced *Ky-ereh* and meaning in Greek "Rejoice." Its seventy-one poems begin with a sunset and end with a new moon, "luminous tendril of celestial wish." There are elegies for friends such as Paul Rosenfeld and Peter Munro Jack, satires, and these lines in a sonnet about the atom bomb:

whose are these(wraith a clinging with a wraith)[.]

ghosts drowning in supreme thunder?ours
(over you reels and me a moon,beneath,

bombed the by ocean earth bigly shudders)

XAIPE and the fellowship given to Cummings by
the American Academy of Poets after its publication became the center of accusations of anti-Semitism in the following lines:

a kike is the most dangerous
machine as yet invented
by even yankee ingenu
ity(out of a jew a few
dead dollars and some twisted laws)
it comes both prigged and canted[.]

His publishers had tried to persuade him to drop
the poem but he resisted all interference, saying,

it is more than most kind of thee, mon-
sieur, to warn me of le public's reaction to 2
Wild Words (see how they run). And yet the
(however painful) fact that America is not a
free country doesn't, I feel, justify anyone's
behaving like a slave or three or (in the lines
of the Bad Bald Poet) steady
there once was a cuntry of owe
such lofty ideals that know
man ever could mension
(imagine the tention)
what might have offended jane dough
selah[.]

Seven out of thirty-two essays in the first collection
of Cummings criticism, S. V. Baum's *EETI: eec:
E. E. Cummings and the Critics* (1962), are devoted
to the question of anti-Semitism in his poetry.

In February 1952 Cummings was invited to
be the Charles Eliot Norton Professor at Harvard
for the academic year 1952-1953. He accepted
somewhat reluctantly since Harvard seemed to him
a center of misguided intellectualism, and he found
Harvard politics too lax. To his sister, he wrote:
"Have yet to encounter anybody in any manner
connected with Harvard who isn't primevally
pink." He chose, however, to keep his support for
Joseph McCarthy and Eisenhower-Nixon Repub-
licanism to himself, and he accepted the position,
which required only that he deliver six lectures in
return for a salary of $15,000.

His six lectures were published by Harvard
University Press in 1953 in two forms: a printed
text of the lectures and the readings he gave at the
end of each as well as a full set of recordings made
during the lectures. *i: six nonlectures* also includes
selected key passages from his own work as well as
an idiosyncratic selection of what he considered the
best poems of Western literature. The lectures are
autobiographical rambles. The first two describe
his father and mother, his childhood home, his
early friends and books. (Robert Graves found
these lectures too "corny," preferring the poet's
"Old Carnality.") Lecture three is a reminiscence
about Harvard, New York, and Paris:

Thus thru an alma mater whose scholastic
bounty appeared the smallest of her bless-
ings—and by way of the even more magnificent institutions of learning, New York and
Paris—our ignoramus reaches his supreme
indebtedness. Last but most, I thank for my
self-finding certain beautiful givers of illimitable gladness
whose any mystery makes every man's
flesh put space on;and his mind take
off time[.]

The last three lectures—"i & you & is," "i & now
& him," and "i & am & santa claus"—present his
stance as a writer. A large proportion of each lecture contains quotations from his writing. He concluded the series as follows:

I am someone who proudly and humbly affirms that love is the mystery-of-mysteries,
and that nothing measurable matters "a very
good God damn:" that "an artist, a man, a
failure" is no mere whenfully accreting
mechanism, but a givingly eternal complexity—neither some soulless and heartless ul-
trapredatory infra-animal nor any un-
understandingly knowing and believing and
thinking automaton, but a naturally and miraculously whole human being—a feelingly
illimitable individual; whose only happiness
is to transcend himself, whose every agony
is to grow.

Ecstasy and anguish, being and becoming; the immortality of the creative imagination and the indomitability of the human
spirit—these are the subjects of my final poetry reading: which (I devoutly hope) may
not wrong a most marvellous ode by Keats,
and the magnificent closing stanzas of Shelley's Prometheus Unbound.

The nonlectures were a popular success
among undergraduates and visitors, but graduate
students and faculty were disappointed. David Per-

kins, a graduate student, reported, "I thought them elegantly phrased and delivered but empty of content. This was the general response of students and faculty." By all accounts Cummings's delivery was masterful.

In the 1950s Cummings began to draw an income through his poetry readings. He had become a superb reader of his own work and possibly one of the best readers of his time. Across America, he attracted capacity audiences. He read slowly and precisely registering every nuance that typography indicated. His agent, Betty Kray, arranged a schedule each fall and spring at colleges, museums, and art centers, and she supervised payment, travel, and other details, such as "There will be no provision for autographing books, attending dinners, receptions, and other social functions as part of the total reading engagement. . . . there will be no commentary with the reading." Despite his physical discomfort ("a casually dressed elderly man . . . stifflegged, with one shoulder raised as though bearing a chip of contention") he continued performing—he enjoyed his own accomplishment and also the applause and adulation of his audiences.

The first full collection of Cummings's poems, *Poems 1923-1954* (1954), was met, on the whole, with enthusiasm and with the respect accorded to one of the country's foremost poets. In 1957 he accepted the role of Festival Poet at the Boston Arts Festival (three previous Festival Poets had been Robert Frost, Carl Sandburg, and Archibald MacLeish). Required to compose a festival poem, Cummings violated the expectations of his audience and the benign mood of the festival by reading his savagely satiric "THANKSGIVING (1956)." The ironical title reflects the anger and grief felt by Americans at the invasion of Hungary on their day of national celebration. Cummings had written to his daughter, Nancy, in a "shaggyblack chasm of shame & anger created by UNamerica's absolute D'abord encouragement & utter ensuite abandonment of that handful of humanbeings who did the bravest thing since Finland." The poem begins:

a monstering horror swallows
this unworld me by you
as the god of our fathers' fathers bows
to a which that walks like a who

but the voice-with-a-smile of democracy
announces night & day
"all poor little peoples that want to be free
just trust in the u s a"

suddenly uprose hungary

and she gave a terrible cry
"no slave's unlife shall murder me
for i will freely die[.]"

In 1958 he won the Bollingen Prize for Poetry, $1000, from Yale University and published a collection of prose pieces, *E. E. Cummings: A Miscellany,* which included his early Harvard commencement speech, "The New Art," and essays written for the *Dial* and *Vanity Fair.* In 1965 George Firmage revised and expanded the book to include other prose pieces. *95 Poems,* also published in 1958, was the last book of new poems to be published in Cummings's lifetime. It was as youthful in outlook as his earlier work. The sixty-four-year-old poet could still assert:

Time's a strange fellow;
                    more he gives than takes
(and he takes all)nor any marvel finds
quite disappearance but some keener makes
loser,gaining
          —love!if a world ends

more than all worlds begin to(see?)begin[.]

As Betty Kray remembered his last years in New York, "every night around ten o'clock he would come by, tap on my window, and I would go with him on a long prowl through the Village streets. We walked and I listened and he talked about himself, about the world, about the things he loved. I disagreed with much of his political belief but held my tongue; he was quite vulnerable during this period. . . . He would disprove over and over again the critics' charge that neither his poems nor his paintings showed 'development'; that was the most intolerable of all the criticism."

He and Marion spent their summers and falls on Joy Farm taking close interest in raccoons, deer, a red fox who chased crickets, a gray fox, a porcupine, woodchucks, and chipmunks. Birds and flowers were his special delight: "Hummingbirds, a robin, phoebes, an indigo bunting, thrushes, a purple finch, swallows—buttercup, vetch, iris, sweet rocket & wild roses—backed by our seven mountains—what more could any human creature ask?"

Cummings collapsed at Joy Farm on 2 September 1962 and died the following day from a brain hemorrhage. He was sixty-seven. That summer he had been preparing another book of poems. George Firmage and Marion Morehouse assembled *73 Poems* for publication by Harcourt, Brace and World in 1963. It is a peaceful register

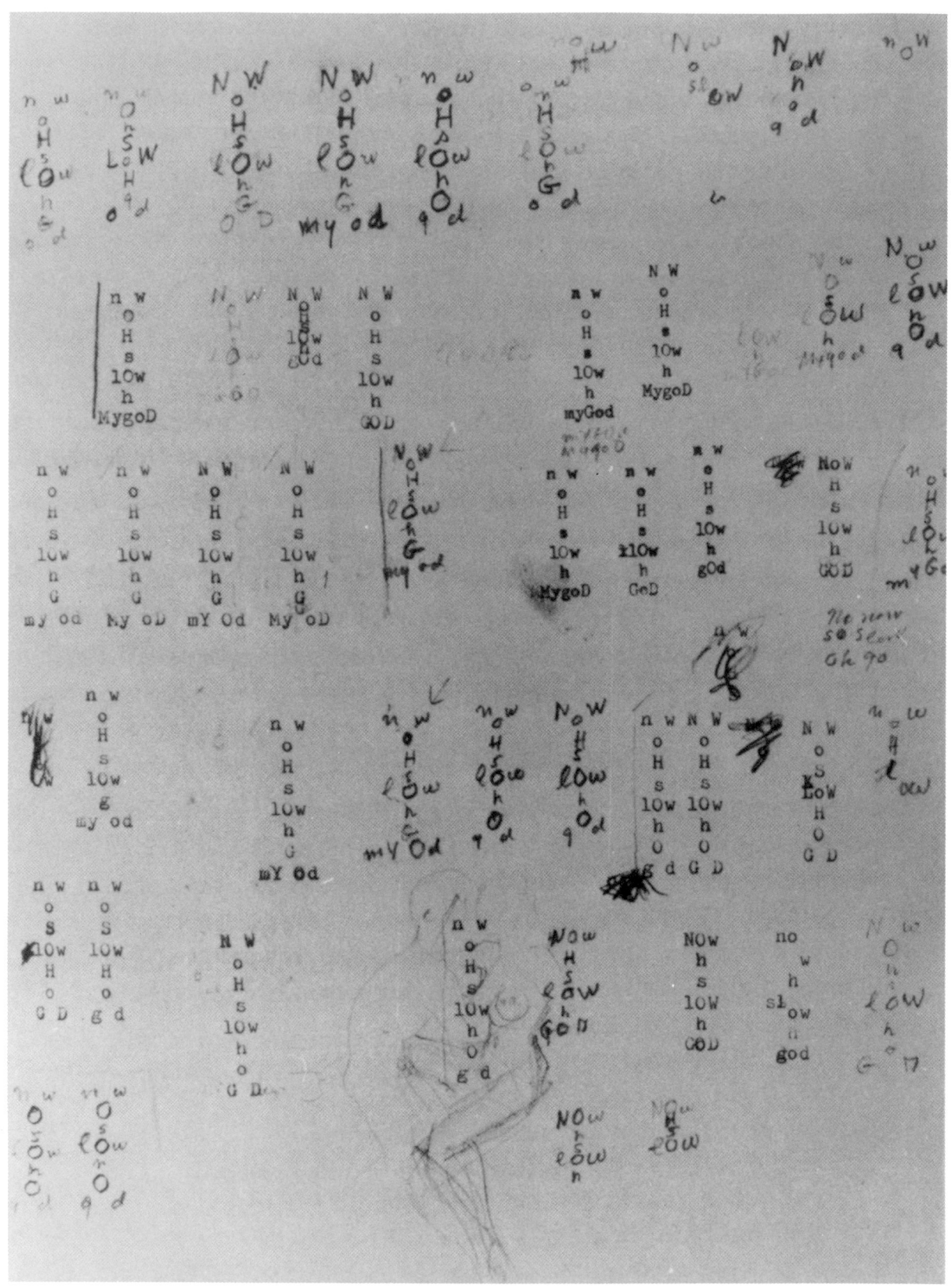

Working drafts for "n.w.," written in 1962 (by permission of Nancy T. Andrews, the Estate of E. E. Cummings; courtesy of the Houghton Library, Harvard University)

of the birds, flowers, stars, springtimes and church-bells of the Joy Farm of his youth and old age.

From midcareer onward, Cummings's poetry had been criticized for its lack of development. There are certainly no identifiable, discrete periods in his work as there are with other modern poets such as Yeats, Pound, and Eliot. He said of people and poetry: "There are two types of human beings children & prisoners. Prisoners are inhabited by formulae. Children inhabit forms. A formula is something to get out of oneself, to rid oneself of—an arbitrary emphasis deliberately neglecting the invisible and significant entirety. A form is something to wander in, to loose oneself in—a new largeness, dimensionally differing from the socalled real world." Cummings's own wanderings within a form led, regrettably, to a formula. But he did perfect his style and through beautifully calibrated readings, brought a love of poetry to many followers of the arts. In the 1950s he became one of the best-known poets in the country, particularly to college students. He was equally popular in the 1960s, since he spoke, in an antiauthoritarian language, for the expression of impulse and emotion. Reliably a maverick, he might well have shied away from the generation of imitators he unintentionally spawned (but, as Babette Deutsch proved in her "review," his style was easy to copy).

Relatively little critical attention has been given to his work, which does not lend itself to detailed academic study. But his poems themselves are still widely available and never fail to appear in anthologies of modern or American poetry.

Cummings's achievement deserves acclaim. He established the poem as a visual object (he can be seen, in fact, as a forerunner of concrete poetry); he revealed, by his x-ray probings, the faceted possibilities of the single word; and like such prose writers as Vladimir Nabokov and Tom Stoppard, he promoted sheer playfulness with language. Despite a growing abundance of second-rate imitations, his poems continue to amuse, delight, and provoke.

Letters:
Selected Letters of E. E. Cummings, edited by F. W. Dupee and George Stade (New York: Harcourt, Brace & World, 1969).

Bibliographies:
George J. Firmage, *E. E. Cummings: A Bibliography* (Middletown, Conn.: Wesleyan University Press, 1960);
Guy L. Rotella, *E. E. Cummings: A Reference Guide* (Boston: G. K. Hall, 1979).

Biographies:
Charles Norman, *E. E. Cummings: The Magic Maker* (New York: Macmillan, 1958; revised edition, New York: Duell, Sloan & Pearce, 1964);
Bethany K. Dumas, *E. E. Cummings: A Remembrance of Miracles* (London: Vision Press, 1974);
Richard S. Kennedy, *Dreams in the Mirror: A Biography of E. E. Cummings* (New York: Liveright, 1980).

References:
S. V. Baum, ed., *EETI:eec: E. E. Cummings and the Critics* (East Lansing: Michigan State University, 1962);
Irene Fairley, *E. E. Cummings & Ungrammar; a Study of Syntactic Deviance in His Poems* (Stamford, Conn.: Windmill Press, 1975);
Norman Friedman, *E. E. Cummings: The Art of His Poetry* (Baltimore: Johns Hopkins Press, 1960);
Friedman, *E. E. Cummings: The Growth of a Writer* (Carbondale: Southern Illinois University Press, 1964);
Friedman, ed., *E. E. Cummings: A Collection of Critical Essays* (Englewood Cliffs, N.J.: Prentice-Hall, 1972);
Journal of Modern Literature, special Cummings issue (April 1979);
Rushworth Kidder, "E. E. Cummings, Painter," *Harvard Library Bulletin,* 23 (April 1975): 117-138;
Wake, special Cummings issue (Spring 1976).

Papers:
The Cummings collection in the Houghton Library at Harvard University contains nearly all the papers that were in Cummings's possession at the time of his death. Other important collections are in the Humanities Research Center at the University of Texas, Austin; the Clifton Waller Barrett Library at the University of Virginia; and the National Archives, in Washington, D.C.

Edward Dahlberg

(22 July 1900-27 July 1977)

Larry R. Smith
Firelands College, Bowling Green State University

BOOKS: *Bottom Dogs* (London: Putnam's, 1929; New York: Simon & Schuster, 1930);

Kentucky Blue Grass Henry Smith (Cleveland: White Horse Press, 1932);

From Flushing to Calvary (New York: Harcourt, Brace, 1932; London: Putnam's, 1933);

Those Who Perish (New York: John Day, 1934);

Do These Bones Live (New York: Harcourt, Brace, 1941); republished as *Sing O Barren* (London: Routledge, 1947); revised as *Can These Bones Live* (New York: New Directions, 1960);

The Flea of Sodom (London: Nevill, 1950; Norfolk, Conn.: New Directions, 1950);

The Sorrows of Priapus (Norfolk, Conn.: New Directions, 1957);

Truth Is More Sacred, by Dahlberg and Herbert Read (New York: Horizon, 1961; London: Routledge & Kegan Paul, 1961);

Because I Was Flesh (Norfolk, Conn.: New Directions, 1964; London: Methuen, 1965);

Alms for Oblivion (Minneapolis: University of Minnesota Press, 1964; London: Oxford University Press, 1964);

Reasons of the Heart (New York: Horizon, 1965);

Cipango's Hinder Door (Austin: University of Texas Press, 1966);

The Edward Dahlberg Reader, edited, with an introduction, by Paul Carroll (New York: New Directions, 1967);

The Leafless American, edited, with an introduction, by Harold Billings (Sausalito, Cal.: Roger Beacham, 1967);

The Carnal Myth: A Search into Classical Sensuality (New York: Weybright & Talley, 1968; London: Calder & Boyars, 1970);

The Confessions of Edward Dahlberg (New York: Braziller, 1971);

The Olive of Minerva (New York: Crowell, 1976);

Bottom Dogs, From Flushing to Calvary, Those Who Perish, and Hitherto Unpublished and Uncollected Works (New York: Crowell, 1976).

OTHER: "Fascism & Writers," in *American Writers' Congress,* edited by Henry Hart (New York:

Edward Dahlberg, 1968 (photograph by Bernard Gotfryd)

International Publishers, 1935), pp. 26-32;

Kenneth Fearing, *Poems,* introduction by Dahlberg (New York: Dynamo, 1936), pp. 11-14;

The Gold of Ophir: Travels, Myths and Legends in the New World, edited, with an essay, by Dahlberg (New York: Dutton, 1972).

PERIODICAL PUBLICATIONS: "The Beginnings and Continuations of Lorry Gilchrist," *This Quarter,* no. 4 (Spring 1929): 61-80;

"The Orphanage: Herman Mush Tate," *This Quarter,* no. 4 (Spring 1929): 80-101;

"November Blues," *This Quarter*, no. 4 (Spring 1929): 193-195;

"New York," *This Quarter*, no. 4 (Spring 1929): 196-197;

"Ariel in Caliban," *This Quarter*, no. 4 (Spring 1929): 258-263;

"Hitler's Power Over Germany: The Nazi Strength Analyzed," *New York Times*, 9 April 1933, p. 3;

"Bitch Goddess: Notes on a Novel," *Signature* (Spring 1936): n. pag.;

"Robert Graves and T. S. Eliot," *Twentieth Century*, 166 (August 1959): 54-58;

"Essays & Poems: A Miscellany," *Massachusetts Review*, 5 (Spring 1964): 462-475;

"Hart Crane," *New York Review of Books*, 5 (20 January 1966): 19-22;

"Dahlberg on Dreiser, Anderson and Dahlberg," *New York Times Book Review*, 31 January 1971, pp. 2, 30-31.

A poet, an aphorist, a novelist, a mythographer, an astute and caustic critic, a literary cult figure, an astounding autobiographer, Edward Dahlberg has proven himself a writer on diverse subjects in protean forms. His daring originality and personality mark his treatment of the mythic and personal, the political and spiritual sides of the American experience. Dahlberg brought his own approach to the modernist goal of recreating a historical tradition through his works. His chief formal innovations are directed toward a recasting of the genres of poetry, fiction, and autobiography to include elements of one another. An expatriate writer of the 1920s, a proletarian novelist of the 1930s, a prophetic spokesman for a fundamental humanism in the 1940s, he worked anthropological, autobiographical, and classical roots in later years, making a radical shift from naturalist to classicist, from Marxist to humanist. Dahlberg is a rare American poet of mythography as well as lyric personal verse. His extraordinary prose style is at times of erudite obscurism, and at others the personal and poetic.

All his life a maverick from the commercial and academic marketplace, Dahlberg became a literary figure in the 1960s as a spokesman for a collective yet individual humanism. As he explained in 1966, "I propose to go along as I always have done, sowing dragon's teeth when necessary, and seeding affections in the souls of my unknown readers if I can." Alternately called a Midwestern Ishmael, a lamenting Whitman, and a curmudgeon of American literature, Dahlberg explained him-self with graphic and characteristic humor, "As for myself, I'm a medievalist, a horse and buggy American, a barbarian, anything, that can bring me back to the communal song of labor, sky, star, field, love." While his fierce defiance of the patterns of success often brought failure upon himself and in his writing, it earned him the much-deserved title of American original. In Edward Dahlberg the writing is the man, and there is much in the experience of that life to make his work tragically, comically, even beautifully unique.

Claiming a Slavic and Polish heritage, with "as many Catholics as Jews among my ancestors," Dahlberg explained in his brilliant autobiography *Because I Was Flesh* (1964) that his maternal grandfather was a traveling timber merchant from Warsaw. His mother, Lizzie, fled this domineering household to a New York ghetto, where she found work in a button factory. At sixteen her brother arranged a marriage for her with a stocky fur merchant whose "only virtue was that he had no conspicuous vices." Soon with three sons and a heart full of loneliness, Lizzie turned for attention to Saul Gottdank, the barber. Through his mother's memories, Dahlberg describes this man who was to be his father, "He had the soft, crooked locks of Absolom and vain white teeth which he showed her; he wore a dude's vest the color of deep brown eider . . . he had a quick, teasing manner, clever and nimble rather than jolly." His mother's affair with Gottdank culminated in Edward's birth on 22 July 1900, in a charity hospital in Boston, where his mother had fled. As he explained later, "She gave me her father's name [Dahlberg] to hide the fact that I was as illegitimate as the pismire, the moth or a prince." However openly declared, his illegitimacy haunted Dahlberg for most of his adult life. Despite the close emotional bond between mother and son, he said of his young adult life, *"Who is my father?* was my continual liturgy."

In both *Because I Was Flesh* and his novel *Bottom Dogs* (1929), Dahlberg colored his early childhood with an aura of despair, "My mother and I were luckless souls"; "I was born incontent"; "My mother had two miserable afflictions, neither of which was she ever to overcome: her flesh—which is my own—and the world, that cursed both of us." Following a London trip to claim an inheritance that never materialized, Lizzie and young Edward returned to the United States. They traveled to Dallas, Texas, with Gottdank where he taught her to be a barber, then stole her money and abandoned her, an act repeated again after they were briefly reunited in Memphis and New Orleans. Lizzie and Edward, like a wandering Ishmael and Hagar, tried Louisville, then Denver, and finally settled in Kansas City, a warm and open town. As she became the successful proprietor-operator of the Star Lady Barbershop, he began to find a sense of himself in the Kansas City of 1905.

Kansas City is clearly an important part of Edward Dahlberg's personal mythography, as he returned to it in later life and as he described it in his writings: "Kansas City was my Tarsus; the Kaw and the Missouri Rivers were washpots of joyous Dianas from St. Joseph and Joplin. It was a young, seminal town and the seed of its men was strong. Homer sang of many sacred towns in Hellas which were no better than Kansas City as hilly as Eteonus and as stony as Aulis."

Despite this newfound sense of location, it was clearly not an easy life which he and his mother made: "Kansas City was the city of my youth and the burial ground of my poor mother's hopes; her

The Jewish Orphan Asylum in Cleveland, where Dahlberg's mother sent him in 1912

blood, like Abel's, cries out to me from every cobblestone, building, flat and street." While his mother went through an endless series of entanglements with men, Edward was enrolled in a Catholic school in Kansas City in 1907. Lizzie continued to lose her money to men, first to a Jewish baker named Harry Cohen, then in a short, disastrous marriage to an opportunistic jeweler named Popkin, and finally through an attachment to a retired ship's captain, Henry Smith. Smith's most profound effect on the family was to split it apart by urging Lizzie to send young Edward to an orphanage. Fearing Edward's moral corruption on the harsh streets of Kansas City, his mother conceded and sent him first to a Catholic orphanage in Kansas City and then in 1912 to the Jewish Orphan Asylum in Cleveland, where life turned from harsh to grim.

The school, depicted in *Because I Was Flesh* and the novels, could have been a model for the Little Orphan Annie comic strip or a Shirley Temple movie melodrama. The children were segregated, given numbers for names, regimented with scrubbings and boredom behind barred windows. Dahlberg later recalled how the children, with only one another as sources for affection, nevertheless developed patterns of brutality that further damaged his emotional stability: "They had no manual skills in affections and were sore afraid of touching another except to harm and punish." Though he came away in 1917 with memories of "Moses Mush Tate's" defiance, of "Doc's overalls, Christine's stale drawers, Benny Marble's bungers, Watermelonhead's ringworms, Mooty's dandruff," he survived through a certain resilience and humor that permanently colored his vision of life.

In 1917 and 1918 he worked as a messenger boy for Cleveland's Western Union and began his youthful, sexual questing. Then, he returned to his mother and to a Kansas City that had become "a hot, wanton town, that pallbearer's Sabbath had ruined a large portion of a coarse and good-humored populace." Here he worked briefly as a drover in the Kansas City stockyards, served for a short time as a private in the U.S. Army, and began a period of hoboing through the West, where he worked as a dishwasher, cook, and day laborer. He was also beginning to write movie scenarios, though unsuccessfully. Then in 1919 he stationed himself in a Los Angeles YMCA and began taking lessons on becoming a literary aesthete from the resident chief mentor, Max Lewis (also referred to in *Because I Was Flesh* as Lao Tsu Ben). Lewis was a self-educated dropout from the world of commerce who

The class of 1917 at the Jewish Orphan Asylum. Dahlberg is sixth from left in the last row.

enticed young Edward with such diverse readings as Nietzsche, Samuel Butler, Ralph Waldo Emerson, and the *Rig Veda.* Dahlberg later referred to himself then as "a crazy waif of the muses," and recalled his misguided enthusiasm for the life of the writer, "After I discovered that Goethe, Heine, Beethoven and Nietzsche had all had syphilis, I thought I could not be a genius unless I found a woman who would be lenient enough to share this disease with me." He followed his mentor down the road of sexual excess until one day Lewis announced he would become a hermit and did Dahlberg the favor of pointing him in the direction of higher education.

In 1921 he enrolled at the University of California at Berkeley majoring in philosophy and anthropology. He promptly shaved his head and sought to win feminine attention by his ascetic devotions. Between 1922 and 1923 he began to publish his writings. Two philosophical tales, "The Sick, the Pessimist, and the Philosopher" and "The March of the Newer Generation," appeared in the Berkeley literary magazine, the *Occident.* Disillusioned with school at Berkeley, he transferred to New York's Columbia University in 1923 to complete his degree, "For New York was to become a place of the skull for me." He was soon teaching at New York's James Madison and Thomas Jefferson high schools, and writing an early philosophic

and autobiographic novel, "Mimes," an apprentice work modeled after Beethoven's life, which he did not publish until 1976 when he included it—with other previously unpublished early works—in a collection of his writings.

In 1926 Lizzie Dahlberg came to live with her son in Astoria, New York, near the Calvary Cemetery described in *From Flushing to Calvary* (1932). But Dahlberg soon married Fanya Fass, daughter of a Cleveland industrialist, and moved to Paris, Monte Carlo, and Brussels, where they lived in self-imposed exile and were soon divorced. During these expatriate years Dahlberg was friends with writers Hart Crane, Robert McAlmon, and Richard Aldington. While living in Brussels in 1928 he completed his first and best-known novel, *Bottom Dogs.* Ethel Moorhead, friend and editor of *This Quarter,* published the opening section of the book, as "Beginnings and Continuations of Lorry Gilchrist," along with his story "Ariel in Caliban," an essay, and two poems in the Spring (1929) issue of *This Quarter.* The full novel appeared in England in 1929 and in the United States in 1930. Both editions included an introduction by D. H. Lawrence, acclaiming Dahlberg as a naturalist par excellence, much to Dahlberg's chagrin. The work garnered critical praise and controversy. While Edmund Wilson found it "a work not merely of personal texture and color, but even of distinction" (*New Republic,*

26 March 1930), it was derided for its sordid subject (Dahlberg's early life) by reviews in the *New York Times* (6 April 1930), *Saturday Review* (22 March 1930), and *New Statesman* (8 February 1930) and was quickly labeled a "proletarian novel," thus becoming a model for the many novels of poverty published during the 1930s in America. Though it is a bleak and despairing book, based on his experience in the Cleveland Jewish Orphan Asylum, it goes beyond any Marxist social theories or naturalistic views of life, and beyond class conflict to a deeper sense of human suffering. Impoverished characters battle their empty environments; yet Dahlberg's focus on individual sensibility is at the work's real center. As Horace Gregory pointed out in a review for *Books* (2 March 1930), "The people in the novel were beaten and smashed before the novel started. . . . It is a painful record, fascinating in its meticulous detail, slowly unrolling before our eyes."

Dahlberg's second novel, *From Flushing to Cal-*

Edward Dahlberg, July 1932 (photograph by Hagemeyer)

vary (1932), written in New England in the early 1930s, carries through the methods, themes, and subject of *Bottom Dogs*. Dahlberg had been making a name for himself by writing social and literary criticism for such diverse publications as *Poetry*, *Pagany*, *Nation*, the *New Masses*, and the *New Republic*. Chief influences on him during this time came from writers such as Dostoyevski and James Joyce, and Knut Hamsun. The final section of *From Flushing to Calvary*, published separately by Cleveland's White Horse Press as *Kentucky Blue Grass Henry Smith* (1932), is a fine example of Dahlberg's early poetic style, and he himself referred to it as a "prose poem." This sequence, in which the character Lizzie recalls her last lover, Henry Smith, demonstrates Dahlberg's ability to interject rhythmic and imagistic energy into his already rich metaphoric style: "Oh, Henry Smith, Kentucky Henry Smith, his sweet bluegrass eyes, oh how she thought of Henry Smith. And that night on the *Chester* up the Mississippi on their way to St. Louis. How they laughed. Their laughter just broke the springs of the bed in the cabin. Their kisses were long drinks of Missouri wellwater, and their chuckles fizzed over their lips, and rippled life." Here and in many other segments of this narrative collage, the power is often unharnessed as poetic elements seem to rise from within the material. The dream sequence of the main character, Lorry, is another example of poetry-charged prose, "He started up out of a bad dream, a dream stuffed with ratty secondhand furs, holey shoes, red-blooded suitcases lying in the showwindow of a 14th Street pawnshop. There were trapdrum moons, bassdrum streetlamps, gilded grapefruit pawnshop balls, all lit up by diamond electric lights." These expressionistic techniques found in all the early novels erase any misconceptions of them as being simple naturalism. As Harold Billings declared in his introduction to the 1976 collection, "It is on the achievement of a lyrical prose style . . . that his critical reputation as a masterful American writer has been made secure." In his prose Dahlberg thus developed a style for all his writings that included the methods of a natural storyteller. Frequently using classical and biblical cadences within protean forms, his method is aptly described by Billings, "All the prose he has written is distinguished by the devices of fiction—anecdote, character sketch, vivid sense of place, accurate and witty dialogue, and narrative that moves like an arrow." These storytelling devices are finely adapted to his essays, criticism, autobiography, stories, novels, as well as to his mythic poetry.

A later incident in Germany, where Dahlberg

was beaten in a Berlin bar by uniformed Nazis, triggered international attention and a new political novel, *Those Who Perish* (1934). Written in 1933 and 1934, the book is a bold Marxist view of the Nazi menace and a study of the American Jew. Dahlberg carried through on his passionate demand for a literature to treat the moral issues of the day by helping to organize the first American Writers' Congress which met in 1935 at the New School of Social Research in New York, where he delivered his paper on "Fascism and Writers." In this period, which Dahlberg called his "literary apprentice years," he became friends with Sherwood Anderson and Alfred Steiglitz, two lasting influences on his life. Together they organized the Friends of William Carlos Williams group to help promote an appreciation of Williams's writings. Dahlberg held a strong admiration for Williams's provocative historical essays in his *In the American Grain* (1925). In 1936 he wrote "Bitch Goddess," part of an uncompleted novel on the New York literary scene. This segment did, however, appear in a 1936 issue of *Signature*. The remainder of the decade found him traveling about from New York to Mexico City, Boston, San Antonio, Chicago, Washington, New Orleans, and Los Angeles while he worked on his first big compilation of criticism, *Do These Bones Live* (1941). It was a decade of intense literary and political activity, which brought him his share of personal and critical animosities and which ultimately left him ignored and frustrated with his own work.

The 1940s were a time of consolidation and evolution in vision for Dahlberg, who recounted his own mythic rite of passage in the preface to the 1976 collection: "I went towards a mirror and saw a stranger. He made some ambiguous gesture. As I bowed I noticed he was also inclining his head towards me. I said why are you standing in my way, and suddenly realized I was my own obstacle." What grew out of this awareness was a broader, more prophetic vision, one based on a classic and deeply mythological view of life that existed beyond any immediate historic reference. Dahlberg adopted as his literary peers thereafter, Shakespeare, Cervantes, the Bible; Americans Melville, Thoreau, Poe, Dickinson; and almost no writer from the machine-ridden rabble of the twentieth century. His shift is apparent in his studies of these figures in *Do These Bones Live* and in *The Flea of Sodom* (1950), an unclassifiable piece of allegorical fiction, profoundly mythic, highly unintelligible, and filled with his most poetic prose. In particular, Dahlberg embraced wholeheartedly Sherwood An-

derson's view that civilization was being sacrificed to mechanized "progress." His later themes carry through his early humanist leanings in espousing the Cain-and-Abel myth of man's self-alienation and need for affection. In depicting man's bestiality, the inevitability of human suffering, and man's basic isolation from one another, Dahlberg held forth the only possibility of renewal: a rediscovery of our mythological past. These recurring themes are most pronounced in his mythic poetry.

In his personal life he had also undergone change: a new marriage, to Winifred Sheehan Moore in 1942, and the birth of two sons, Geoffrey and Joel. Yet, perhaps the most critical event came in 1946, when his mother died. It is hard to overstate the profound effect her death had upon his life. Harold Billings suggested in 1976 that, for Dahlberg, "Reality was Lizzie Dahlberg. At least forty years before her death, and for thirty years since, the absence and death of his mother have been greater obsessions than his own death." His lasting affection for her led him to depict her tragic yet heroic life and her lonely death in several works, perhaps most poignantly in the conclusion of *Because I Was Flesh*. In a 1955 interview Dahlberg would make this declaration, "My greatest teachers were not Lao Tze, Heraclitus, Pliny or Sir Thomas Browne, whom I read with bacchic avidity, but my mother, Kansas City, and the Cleveland orphanage." His rich feeling for his past with all its suggested love and location has been the source of most of his finest writings.

In October 1950 Dahlberg met and married Rlene LaFleur Howell and began another series of moves from New York to Berkeley, Topanga, and Santa Monica. In addition to studying pre-Columbian American history and myths, he was writing essays for *Tomorrow* and the *Freeman*. He and his wife lived near Berkeley until 1956, when they traveled to Bornholm, Malaga, Ascona, Paris, and finally Majorca, where he completed *The Sorrows of Priapus* in 1957. It is a richly allusive and demanding book on the theme of man's basic carnal nature, which links man with beasts and keeps him from achieving a higher life. This conflict of the intellect and the sensuality of humankind is carried through in the sequel, *The Carnal Myth*, which appeared much later, in 1968. Both books are written in a poetic-prose form using the paragraph as a stanza. When *The Sorrows of Priapus* appeared with the handsome illustration by Ben Shahn, it brought a share of critical praise for Dahlberg. And yet, Dahlberg would write to publisher and friend Jonathan Williams in 1958, "I am absolutely nowhere in

*Charles, — I am mentally
wounded by silence; it is more
destructive than the tongue. —*
Edward Dahlberg

THE FLEA OF SODOM
"O my friends there is no friend."
Aristotle

Let us admit, going over the Atlantic
was a tragic mistake, and that he who drinks
the vile, oceanic froth of Cerberus
loses his memory, and goes mad. Hercules
took his cows no farther than Cadiz, beyond
which men haunt the pitchy fens of the
cormorant and the unclean ibis.

Homer's geography is purest Metaphysics; Cimmerians
occupy fetid, purblind Bosphorus, which is near Hades;
Tartarus almost touches the Pillars, more perfidious than
the Sirens. Hera went no farther than Europe's Oceanus
and Odysseus trod upon the marge of the sea at the
Gates, and retired. The lotus his companions ate yield
spicy, Afric sleep, not Atlantic's horrid Lethe.

Do not pass the Pillars, hankering after new places.
Shun hyperborean lands: impious Prometheus was banished
to the blizzards of Caucasus. Recall how soon Cadmus
forgot the Phoenician shores girt with shells whence
Helen's robes got their Tyrian purple, and sowed
dragon's teeth from which the gory Theban buckler,
spear and iron javelin were wrought. Unknown
countries are Sorcerer's regions of baleful ore. It
is better to be slain by a bow of cornel wood or
face a warrior in a helmet made of the rind torn from
the cork-tree than perish by metal. The weapons by
which man dies reveal whether he lived with the roe
and the hind close by the founts of Helicon, or in
Boreal, gloomy towns. The fleecy Ram of Colchis,
Jason's cargo of copper, iron and coal, is Caesar's Furnace.

Forsake the metal cities, brewing Chimera's noisome
breath, lest you disappear. Zeus' docks are in soft,
Lybian climes. The Bethlehem manger is not far from
Apollo's Ethiopic stables. Jerusalem, Sidon, Crete,
Egypt, Deneter's Basket, is the Kosmos. The dog-
parent, Atlantic, is the sea of oblivion: unhallowed
people, return to the tender fig where the **MUSES**
sing.

Dahlberg sent this section from his 1950 book to poet Charles Olson (by permission of Colburn Britton, the Estate of Edward Dahlberg; courtesy of the Literary Archives, University of Connecticut Library)

Edward and Rlene Dahlberg, 1956

America at the age of 58. I have been in exile in this land since I was a boy. But it is the only country I know, and homeless here I somehow or other touch the ground, a threshold, and a few people who are my kindred even if they don't recognize it."

From 1958 to 1964 Dahlberg was living, writing, and sometimes teaching in Majorca, New York, and Dublin. He completely revised the critical writings in *Do These Bones Live,* which he retitled *Can These Bones Live* (1960), and wrote an epistolary critical book, *Truth Is More Sacred* (1961), with friend Herbert Read. This book, however, fostered critical splits in theory and caused some lasting tensions in the relationship of the two writer-critics. Also in 1961 Dahlberg received a grant from the National Institute of Arts and Letters, which helped to supplement his minimal royalty payments. As Dahlberg explained, "I never wrote a book for lucre, though after it was published I petitioned the Elements, cold as a blizzard to Prometheus." Even his failure was mythic.

In 1964 Dahlberg accomplished an autobiographical retelling of his early life in *Because I Was Flesh,* generally regarded as his finest work. In it Dahlberg uses all the conventions of fictional narrative to mythologize both his life and that of his mother. The book is a synthesis of Dahlberg's pithy epigrams, his concise realistic detail, and his passages of philosophic reverie. It fuses myth and reality in a flowing style that encompasses emotion, thought, and humor. As Paul Carroll concluded, the book wins you with its intelligence and beauty of style: "What commends this style are the cadence and dignity of its sentences and the rich, queer erudition. What is most memorable is its treatment of myth." The writing embraces the poetic in its treatment of subject and form. Dahlberg had created an American classic and his essential stance as a poet of prose. Arno Karlen, reviewing the book for *Nation* (30 March 1964), concluded, "He has continued to risk failure by living at the inventive frontier of his art, and has won as his prize a rich, unique and expressive voice that spurns the conventions of genre."

A third collection of criticism, *Alms for Oblivion,* appeared in 1964 with key essays on Melville, the expatriates, Samuel Taylor Coleridge, and Edgar Allan Poe, and with personal portraits of his friends Alfred Steiglitz, Sherwood Anderson, and Theodore Dreiser. Though he attacks William Carlos Williams's *Paterson* (1946-1958) for its lack of "moral force," he praises highly his *In the American Grain,* a book which shaped his own critical stance.

In 1965 Dahlberg returned to his native ground in Kansas City, where he taught as a visiting professor of English literature at the University of Missouri. He also received a Rockefeller Foundation grant that year and completed a book of aphorisms, *Reasons of the Heart.* The book ranges in subjects from writing to sloth, myth and religion, lust and suffering. They are heavily didactic in answer to his own demand for a moralist writing. "What man's head would do is always defeated by his scrotum" indicates his sharp yet aged and moral wit.

Though Dahlberg had been writing poetry all along, it wasn't until 1966 that he published a volume of his poetry, *Cipango's Hinder Door,* with an introduction by Allen Tate. Other poems appeared the following year in the collection of his essays and poems, *The Leafless American* (1967).

Edward Dahlberg's poetry can be described as epigrammatic, lyric, densely mythical in reference (yet written outside any immediate historical frame), rhythmic, intense, and progressing in associative or lyrical leaps. The poems are written in a relaxed metric form or in prose-poem paragraphs (sometimes together, as in "Cipango's Hinder Door"). Their tone is a mixture of nostalgic, prophetic cry for a reawakening to ancient wisdom and a negative blast at the despair of the modern. Not easily compared with anything modern, they have been linked with Walt Whitman's visionary *Song of Myself* and with William Carlos Williams's immediacy in *In the American Grain* and his mythic fabric in *Paterson.* Allen Tate compared them with the Old Testament writings of the prophets, a point Harold Billings reinforced, in his introduction to *The Leafless American:* "Dahlberg's words are shaped in a matrix of winds from the four geographic corners of his sensibility: the Hellenic, the Hebraic, the American primitive-pastoral, and what he would perhaps term his own personal 'Pulse.' " The poems that evolve from this dense frame of reference seek proportion, moralism, a faith in the simple and natural, and present Dahlberg's own sense of human suffering. The cadences are classical and biblical, and as Billings observes, "every aphoristic line is black-letter verse." The central theme is the Cain-and-Abel story, with Cain representing the renegade civilization in his denying

the murder of Abel, our own slain past which we must reenter through Cipango's back door. While many reviewers lamented the diverse and heavily worn mythic allusions, Allen Tate celebrated the universal and timeless method of Dahlberg's making, finding it "a *style* of great eloquence and enormous range." What must be reckoned with in Dahlberg's poetry is his essential faith that the writing must be integral with the man, that Dahlberg's dense style grows out of the cohesiveness of his own complex nature.

There are thirty poems in *Cipango's Hinder Door* and two others, "The Leafless American" and "The Garment of Ra," in *The Leafless American.* The two finest poems, "Walt Whitman" and "The Leafless American," use the Whitmanesque techniques of cataloguing and the long line in tributes that are also essential refutations of Whitman's ungrounded optimism. Both poets sought to create the American myth and vision, to embrace and connect a tradition, and yet, as Tate concluded, "Where Whitman's 'universality' was asserted, Mr. Dahlberg's is experienced." Whitman is the greater poet, but Dahlberg's view contains the greater truth by experience. The lamenting conclusion of Dahlberg's "Walt Whitman" reinforces this view:

> The country is still more than half whole,
> For we go to water quicker than to fire or to blood,
> And we are a kinless people
> Still suffering for the flood sins.
> Whitman, our Adam, has died in our loins.

In "Cipango's Hinder Door" Dahlberg demonstrates his intuitive sense of form by intermixing passages of metric verse and passages of prose-poetry in paragraph units. It is an effective technique, at one with the broad theme and dense fabric of the poem's vision. This brave defiance of formal conventions is acclaimed and explained by Allen Tate as indicative of Dahlberg's poetic sense. Tate termed it "the tact of imagination" and "the timeless intuition of the poet." Dahlberg is both formally adept and intuitively open to poetic statement.

Frank McShane has asserted that Dahlberg's "short lyrics . . . are those to which the reader is most likely to return." The final fourteen short poems in *Cipango's Hinder Door* do issue from a stronger sense of experience and achieve an emotional intensity; yet they too are woven into the mythic fabric of Dahlberg's vision and nature. In one the reader is struck by the personal reflection, "I am sixty-three;/I go slow,/ The bitter waters of dotage in my veins," and, in another, one shares his love and guilt, depicted through telling images, "I have on my father's shirt/That I may wear the dew his body shed./The sweat of my father is my wafer and wine./I keep his ghost within my breast,/ For when he lived I wounded him." Other outstanding poems include "February Ground," in which he creates a vivid and rich sense of place out of the American landscape and myth; the declarative "Trust Is a Fool"; and the final four poems declaiming the moral waste of modern man. It is a mass "I" that Dahlberg proclaims in his verse, still a timeless and universal oneness that he writes toward. His poetry is a shrill and empassioned cry, as dense and evocative as the man.

The 1960s were, in a sense, the period of a Dahlberg renaissance, which culminated in the 1967 publication of his letters, *Epitaphs of Our Times*, and the collection of criticism, *The Edward Dahlberg Reader*. *The Carnal Myth*, the second half of the mythic allegory started in *The Sorrows of Priapus*, appeared in 1968. In 1967 he married Julia Lawlor. Though he never achieved a wide audience, he found a devoted body of readers in the counterculture of the 1960s. In the introduction to the *Edward Dahlberg Reader*, Paul Carroll provided a portrait of the older Dahlberg delivering one of his literary tirades at the Cliff Dwellers Club in Chicago in 1958: "Members of the local intellectual community sat over cocktails, many of us aghast as Dahlberg—tall, dressed in Harris Tweed and silk foulard ascot, handsome with white hair and trim, regimental moustache—fascinated and outraged by his high, bitter invective against most of the idols of contemporary American writing.... Only the cadence of his sentences and cultivated accent seemed to keep Dahlberg's words from becoming a scream." His years of poverty, his defiance of critical in-circles, his early proletarian novels, and his literary denunciations earned him the respect of young and impassioned intellectuals.

In 1970 Dahlberg's friend Jonathan Williams edited *A Festschrift for Edward Dahlberg*, a special Dahlberg issue of *Tri-Quarterly*. His autobiographical sequel to *Because I Was Flesh* appeared in 1971 as *The Confessions of Edward Dahlberg*. In 1972 he edited and wrote an essay for *The Gold of Ophir: Travels, Myths and Legends in the New World*, and his last novel, *The Olive of Minerva*, was published in 1976. Though none of these last books reached the clarity and stylistic virtuosity of his earlier works, it should be remembered that Dahlberg was in his seventies when he wrote them. He died on 27 February 1977, preeminently an American man of let-ters, having outlived and outwritten most of his critical detractors.

As Harold Billings pointed out shortly before Dahlberg's death, "For a half century this fierce old lion of letters has labored, 'bethump'd by words' and thumping us in turn.... As critic, he was harsh and true; as novelist, a realistic and expressionistic storyteller and mythmaker; as aphorist and poet, a passionate yet rational moralist of our times; as autobiographer, a master." Billings thus provided the truest summation: "Dahlberg is so much, so complex, he cannot be reduced to explication. He can only be read, reread, and accepted as a writer unique, and uniquely American.... How can the bones of American literature help but live fleshed with writing such as his."

Letters:
Epitaphs of Our Times: The Letters of Edward Dahlberg (New York: Braziller, 1967).

Bibliography:
Harold Billings, *A Bibliography of Edward Dahlberg* (Austin: University of Texas Press, 1971).

Biography:
Charles DeFanti, *The Wages of Expectation: A Biography of Edward Dahlberg* (New York: New York University, 1978).

References:
Harold Billings, Introduction to *The Leafless American* (Austin, Tex.: Roger Beacham, 1967), pp. vii-x;

Billings, ed., *Edward Dahlberg: American Ishmael of Letters* (Austin, Tex.: Roger Beacham, 1968);

Paul Carroll, Introduction to *The Edward Dahlberg Reader* (New York: New Directions, 1967), pp. xi-xxii;

Jules Chametsky, "Edward Dahlberg: Early and Late," in *Proletarian Writers of the Thirties*, edited by Donald Madden (Carbondale: Southern Illinois University Press, 1968);

Ihab Hassan, "The Sorrows of Edward Dahlberg," *Massachusetts Review*, 5 (Spring 1964): 457-461;

Josephine Herbst, "Edward Dahlberg's *Because I Was Flesh*," *Southern Review*, new series 1 (Spring 1965): 337-351;

D. H. Lawrence, Introduction to *Bottom Dogs* (London: Putnam's, 1929);

Fred Moramarco, "An Interview with Edward Dahlberg," *Western Humanities Review*, 20 (Summer 1966): 249-253;

Moramarco, *Edward Dahlberg* (New York: Twayne, 1972);

Allen Tate, "A Great Stylist: The Prophet as Critic," *Sewanee Review,* 76 (Spring 1961): 314-317;

John Wain, "Eating Fables," *New York Review of Books,* 11 (2 January 1969): 13-14;

Jonathan Williams, "Edward Dahlberg's Book of Lazarus," *Texas Quarterly,* 6 (Summer 1963): 35-49;

Williams, ed., *A Festschrift for Edward Dahlberg, Tri-Quarterly,* no. 19 (Fall 1970); republished as

Edward Dahlberg: A Tribute (New York: David Lewis, 1971);

Edmund Wilson, *The Shores of Light* (New York: Farrar, Straus & Young, 1952), pp. 442-450.

Papers:

The largest collection of Dahlberg's papers is in the Humanities Research Center at the University of Texas, Austin.

Richard Eberhart
(5 April 1904-   )

Joel Roache
University of Maryland, Eastern Shore

BOOKS: *A Bravery of Earth* (London: Cape, 1930; New York: Cape & Smith, 1930);

Reading the Spirit (London: Chatto & Windus, 1936; New York: Oxford University Press, 1937);

Song and Idea (London: Chatto & Windus, 1940; New York: Oxford University Press, 1942);

A World-View (Medford, Mass.: Tufts College Press, 1941);

Poems, New and Selected (Norfolk, Conn.: New Directions, 1945);

Burr Oaks (London: Chatto & Windus, 1947; New York: Oxford University Press, 1947);

Brotherhood of Men (Pawlet, Vt.: Banyan Press, 1949);

An Herb Basket (Cummington, Mass.: Cummington Press, 1950);

Selected Poems (London: Chatto & Windus, 1951; New York: Oxford University Press, 1951);

Poetry as a Creative Principle (Norton, Mass.: Wheaton College, 1952);

Undercliff: Poems 1946-1953 (London: Chatto & Windus, 1953; New York: Oxford University Press, 1953);

Great Praises (London: Chatto & Windus, 1957; New York: Oxford University Press, 1957);

The Oak: A Poem (Hanover, N.H.: Pine Tree Press, 1957);

Collected Poems: 1930-1960 (London: Chatto & Windus, 1960; New York: Oxford University Press, 1960);

Collected Verse Plays (Chapel Hill: University of North Carolina Press, 1962; London: Oxford University Press, 1963);

The Quarry: New Poems (New York: Oxford University Press, 1964; London: Chatto & Windus, 1964);

Selected Poems, 1930-1965 (New York: New Directions, 1965);

Thirty-One Sonnets (New York: Eakins Press, 1967);

Shifts of Being (New York: Oxford University Press, 1968; London: Chatto & Windus, 1968);

The Achievement of Richard Eberhart, edited, with an introduction, by Bernard Engel (Glenview, Ill.: Scott, Foresman, 1968);

Three Poems (Cambridge, Mass.: Pym-Randall, 1968);

Fields of Grace (New York: Oxford University Press, 1972; London: Chatto & Windus, 1972);

Two Poems (Westchester, Pa.: Aralia Press, 1975);

Poems to Poets (Lincoln, Mass.: Penmaen Press, 1976);

Collected Poems, 1930-1976 (New York: Oxford University Press, 1976; London: Chatto & Windus, 1976);

Hour, Gnats: New Poems (Davis, Cal.: Putah Creek Press, 1977);

Of Poetry and Poets (Urbana: University of Illinois Press, 1979);

Survivors (Northport, N.Y.: Boa Editions, 1979);

*Richard Eberhart, 1972 (photograph by
LaVerne Harrell Clark)*

Four Poems (Winston-Salem, N.C.: Palaemon Press,
1980);

New Hampshire: Nine Poems (Rosedale, Mass.: Pym-
Randall Press, 1980);

Ways of Light: Poems, 1972-1980 (New York: Oxford
University Press, 1980);

Chocorua (New York: Nadja Press, 1981);

Florida Poems (Gulfport, Fla.: Konglomerati Press,
1981);

*The Long Reach: New and Uncollected Poems, 1948-
1984* (New York: New Directions, 1984).

PLAY PRODUCTIONS: *The Visionary Farms,* Cambridge, Mass., Poets' Theatre, 1952; Seattle,
Wash., 1953;

Triptych, Chicago, 1955;

Devils and Angels, Cambridge, Mass., Poets' Theatre, 1956;

The Mad Musician and *Devils and Angels,* Cambridge,
Mass., 1962;

The Bride of Mantua, adapted by Eberhart, Hanover,

N.H., Dartmouth College, 1964.

OTHER: *The Arts Anthology: Dartmouth Verse 1925,*
includes poems by Eberhart (Portland,
Maine: Mosher Press, 1925);

Cambridge Poetry, 1929, includes poems by Eberhart
(London: Hogarth Press, 1929);

Michael Roberts, ed., *New Signatures,* includes
poems by Eberhart (London: Hogarth Press,
1932);

War and the Poet, edited by Eberhart and Selden
Rodman (New York: Devin-Adair, 1945);

Forty Dartmouth Poems, edited by Eberhart (Hanover, N.H.: Dartmouth Publications, 1962);

To Eberhart from Ginsberg: A Letter About Howl *1956,*
edited by Eberhart (Lincoln, Mass.: Penmaen
Press, 1976).

It is tempting to search in a poet's life for the
themes of his poetry. Such an exercise is both easy
and dangerous. It is easy because the most important themes are universal to both life and poetry.
It is dangerous because the examination of such
universals is rarely a promising method of discovering the unique, of revealing the special character
of either poet or poetry.

Richard Eberhart, however, is perhaps a special case, for the conflicts central to his verse, the
tensions between spirit and matter, order and
chaos, are mirrored in the vicissitudes of his life,
especially through its first four decades. First, an
almost idyllic childhood and early youth were shattered by sudden and inexorable tragedy. Then,
after a period of personal restructuring and ma-
turation, he faced years of struggle to maintain the
integrity of his talent and vision before achieving
substantial recognition of his work.

The son of Alpha LaRue and Lena Lowen-
stein Eberhart, Richard Ghormley Eberhart was
one of three children born to a prominent, close-
knit, and quite well-to-do Austin, Minnesota, family. His father was a self-made man who became a
vice-president at the Hormel Meat Packing Company; his mother was devoted to her children and
encouraged the literary inclinations that emerged
very early in her son's life, inclinations which produced volumes of high-school essays, short stories,
and poems, at least one of which, "Indian Pipe,"
made its way into his published work years later,
in *Undercliff: Poems 1946-1953* (1953). The poem
projects the reader from the present into the past,
into history, through a simple image, and shows
Eberhart's characteristic sharp eye for the concrete
image and his tendency to moralize upon it. Writ-

ing was not his only interest, however. As an adolescent he was also a five-letter athlete, served as an officer in his high-school fraternity, and participated in a variety of other activities.

It was an enviable life, a kind of American idyll, portrayed with considerable accuracy in Eberhart's verse play *The Visionary Farms* (in *Collected Verse Plays*, 1962). The play also chronicles the collapse of the idyll, beginning with the decline of the family's fortunes, in 1921. When Hormel lost $1.25 million to an embezzler, his father's stock plummeted in value, and in January 1922 he left the company after a disagreement. The company bought the stock at its then depressed value and the family, though never poor, were thereafter in somewhat straitened circumstances. In the summer of 1921, too, Mrs. Eberhart began to waste away in what was to be a long drawn-out and painful death from lung cancer, and Richard, just graduated from high school, watched, waited, and cared for her. Eighteen years later Eberhart would record something of the trauma of that experience in the rather melodramatic "Orchard," published in *Song and Idea* (1940). His mother died on 22 June 1922, when the young poet was eighteen. Eberhart himself has said that the death of his mother made him a poet, and some critics have suggested that this experience helps to account for what they consider his dominant preoccupation with death, but it is probably more important that his mother's death, coupled as it was with the decline in the family's income and standard of living, completed his traumatic separation from an environment which had constantly validated his identity, from a sense of belonging that he would not feel again for some time.

The separation was confirmed with his matriculation at the University of Minnesota in 1922 and then, in 1923, at Dartmouth College. He became less the assertive, all-round student he had been in high school, finding it necessary to devote a great deal of time just to keeping up his grades. His major extracurricular activities were literary, and he had by this time come to think of himself as a poet. He published poems in both of the college's undergraduate periodicals, and his work was included in *The Arts Anthology: Dartmouth Verse 1925*, which contained an introduction by Robert Frost, who was thus the first important literary figure to comment on his work.

Upon receiving his B.A. in 1926, he descended abruptly from this rarefied Ivy League atmosphere: following his father's wish that he go into business, he took a job as a basement floor-

Richard Eberhart at Dartmouth College (courtesy of the Richard Eberhart Collection, Baker Library, Dartmouth College)

walker (he also wrote a few advertisements for ladies' underwear) at Marshall Field and Company's department store in Chicago. He did some writing in his spare time and had a few poems accepted by Harriet Monroe (whom he met in Chicago) for *Poetry: A Magazine of Verse*, but after a few months, in May 1927, he left for San Francisco, en route the long way round for Cambridge University. He worked his way around the world on a succession of tramp steamers, with stops in Shanghai, Manila, Sumatra, Port Said, and many other lesser-known ports. It was not an easy journey, and on one leg of the trip, even though the captain of a German freighter, the *Etha Rickmers*, had agreed to carry him as a nonpaying passenger, he found himself set to work painting the ceiling of the engine room, at 120°F. He jumped ship at Port Said and finished his journey in comfort as a paying passenger on the S.S. *Rajputana*.

Finally, on 14 October 1927, a week late for the start of the term, he entered St. John's College, Cambridge, beginning what he would later call "a dream of life as it ought to be." It was a life permeated with intellect and with literary values, often of the highest order. He attended debates featuring George Bernard Shaw and G. K. Chesterton, and his teachers and tutors included Arthur Quiller-Couch, Gilbert Murray, F. L. Lucas, and F. R. Leavis. He also formed a lifelong friendship with I. A. Richards, who regularly and actively encouraged and criticized his poetry, and sometimes—as in *Cambridge Poetry, 1929* (1929)—helped get it published.

At Cambridge, the lines between curricular and extracurricular were easily blurred and at tea parties he met such people as C. P. Snow and William Empson. The cultural life of London and the Continent was in easy reach. On one tour of Ireland, Eberhart spent an evening with William Butler Yeats, AE (George Russell), and Oliver St. John Gogarty, and other vacation trips took him to the cathedrals of France and as far as Majorca.

Eberhart spent slightly less than two years at Cambridge, graduating in 1929 with his second B.A. (in due course, after the payment of the proper fee, he received his M.A. in 1933). His performance as a student was characteristically respectable, if not distinguished, and by the time he left his reputation as a poet was established. Harriet Monroe had already, in November 1927, published eight of his poems in *Poetry,* and several more were published in British periodicals such as the *London Mercury* and *Experiment,* which in November 1929 published "For a Lamb," a poem whose almost Whitmanesque sense of death as a fusion with life anticipates the later and much more celebrated "The Groundhog":

> I saw on a slant hill a putrid lamb,
> Propped with daisies. The sleep looked deep,
> The face nudged in the green pillow
> But the guts were out for crows to eat.
>
> Where's the lamb? whose tender plaint
> Said all for the mute breeze.
> Say he's in the wind somewhere,
> Say, there's a lamb in the daisies.

A similar and decidedly romantic impulse seems to leap from the opening lines of his first book, *A Bravery of Earth* (1930): "This fevers me, this sun on green,/On grass glowing, this young spring." It is a current that persists into the late work, too, as

in, say, "Ichetucknee," in *Ways of Light* (1980):

> It is the continuous welling up from the earth
> We must remember. Dawn comes, and the waters
> Spring fresh, clear, vital from the earth.
> Night comes, they well unabated from the dark.

Some of his poems were included in *Cambridge Poetry, 1929,* and he and Empson were the only poets there to be singled out for comment in a review by F. R. Leavis.

While at Cambridge he completed *A Bravery of Earth,* which he had begun during a vacation bicycle trip in the spring of 1928. A long, philosophical, and autobiographical narrative poem, it consumed much of his creative energy during 1929, as he completed it under the criticism of I. A. Richards. Another Cambridge don put him in touch with a publisher, and the book came out in both England and America in 1930.

A Bravery of Earth, now out of print for more than half a century, has been uniformly ignored by critics, and only a few passages have been included in Eberhart's collected works. Nonetheless, the book merits study, for it establishes the dialectic, pervasive in his later work, between a sensuous enthusiasm for life and a brooding consciousness of death. In *A Bravery of Earth* he begins his lifelong exploration of the parallel dichotomy between the human being's life-seeking, order-creating spirit, and the death-dealing chaos of the exterior, "objective" world, a dichotomy that finds its only, albeit temporary, resolution in art.

The years at Dartmouth and Cambridge, intellectually and socially rewarding, stimulating, and productive in terms of poetry, restored to Eberhart something of the idyllic quality of his earliest years by providing him with a sense of community, a community which on the one hand upheld the primacy of the imagination and the reality of the intellect, and on the other confirmed his own sense of himself as primarily a poet. Despite the collapse of his childhood idyll, he kept a certain but perhaps intermittent level of intuitive optimism intact, though it was tempered by a sense of tragedy. Optimism and tragedy were both responses to the material world, and his experiences at Dartmouth and Cambridge equipped him to attempt the reconciliation of that world, and the world of feeling, with the world of intellect. The need for such synthesis provided his major themes, and the locus of that synthesis became art, poetry itself, wherein Eberhart found an identity that he would maintain thereafter. It was, however, a decidedly abstract identity, and the 1930s were a period when it was in conflict with an irresistibly concrete world. The years at Dartmouth and Cambridge, perhaps, also left him ill-prepared to deal practically with the Great Depression; Eberhart would not, indeed, feel that he was in his true milieu as a poet until, at the age of forty-eight, he received his first academic appointment.

Upon his return to America in late August 1929 Eberhart worked for three months in a New York slaughterhouse, getting to work at 4:30 in the morning, at first making production tests on the killing floor in Manhattan and, later, checking hams in and out of cold storage in Brooklyn. He once called the slaughterhouse "a vision of hell actual." In his spare time he wrote book reviews for Edmund Wilson, associate editor at the *New Republic*, and evaluated manuscripts for Bobbs-Merrill. In December he got a job in Florida as tutor to two daughters of Mr. and Mrs. Rodney Procter (of Procter and Gamble), and in the fall of 1930 he took a job as tutor to the adopted son of the King of Siam. Eberhart recorded his distaste for the job in his comic-satiric poem "The Rape of the Cataract" (published in *Reading the Spirit*, 1936), in which, when "the veil" was "drawn off the ancient East," instead of reflecting Oriental wisdom, King Prajadhipok keeps the President of the United States waiting so that he can make "timid, deft essays with a model airplane/Its little rubber bands expanding./As with a gentle whirr it takes the air." With his savings from these jobs, Eberhart spent most of a year in Germany, returning in 1932 in time to enter graduate school at Harvard, where he studied under Irving Babbitt and G. L. Kittredge and met T. S. Eliot, who on several occasions consented to discuss his own poems with the young poet. Although his grades were uneven but quite creditable, he was uncomfortable with an academic system that was much more highly structured than England's, and early in 1933, short of funds, he began to look for a teaching position; he joined the staff at St. Mark's School, in Southboro, Massachusetts, where he remained for seven years.

He was a conscientious teacher and took an active part in the life of the school. The work itself, however, was scarcely what he had envisioned for himself, though it had its bright spots. Robert Lowell was among his students and began bringing Eberhart poems for comment and criticism in 1935, beginning an enduring friendship. A few years later in 1938, Eberhart was able to arrange with the headmaster that W. H. Auden, recently arrived from England, should teach at the school for a

month, a visit that considerably enlivened the intellectual and literary atmosphere of the school.

His position at St. Mark's kept him within range of New England social and cultural life. He met Ford Madox Ford and R. P. Blackmur, and attended lectures and readings by a number of poets and critics, including Wallace Stevens. If his situation was not ideal, it was often congenial, and he was at least protected from the ravages of the Depression that gripped the nation. Then, in December 1940, the Depression caught up with him. As a result of declining enrollments, St. Mark's had to let him go, and it was eighteen months before he found another position, this time at the Cambridge School, in Kendal Green, Massachusetts.

These eighteen months marked an important transitional moment in Eberhart's life. His long search for a new position, a livelihood, underscored the sharpness of his struggle throughout the 1930s to continue writing and to gain some degree of literary recognition. He had had his successes, to be sure. In 1932, some of his poems were included in a British anthology, *New Signatures*, whose editor, Michael Roberts, hoped to promote work less obscure and less remote from contemporary life than currently fashionable poetry. *New Signatures* also included work by Auden, Stephen Spender, and C. Day Lewis, whose names came to be associated (quite arbitrarily) with Eberhart's for many years. Then, on 22 August 1934, the BBC's weekly the *Listener* published "The Groundhog," which came to be his best-known poem. It made the first of its many anthology appearances in England in 1935 in a collection of pieces from the *Listener, Poems of Tomorrow*, edited by Janet Adam Smith, and it was collected in Eberhart's second book, *Reading the Spirit*, published in England in 1936. It later appeared in *A Book of Modern Verse* (published in England in 1940) and in the United States in 1941 in Oscar Williams's annual, *New Poems: 1940*. In later years Eberhart recalled a meeting of the poets' discussion group, at which he had "enjoyed the rigorous criticism" of "The Groundhog," which some members felt should end with the narrative part, deleting the last nine lines: "If I had left them off I am sure the poem would never have got into one anthology."

In the summer of 1930, between his two jobs as tutor, Eberhart had stayed by himself as guest of his friends the Fosters in Phoenixville, Pennsylvania, at a farmhouse called Walden. "I look out on the earth for the first time," he wrote. "Every cell seems fresh to act." And it was there that he "surveyed" the corpse of a shot groundhog, lying on a plank "flat to the open sun." The animal "had lost all its form," he wrote, "all that we call grace and trimness; it was a seething mass of maggots; the shock of the sea-like motion and swirl of these was at first so great as to give the illusion of the viscera pulsing and moving. One looks at one's face in the glass, and wonders on the eternal question of consciousness. . . . It takes calm reason to stave off revulsion at decay. I think we must come to love that reality of decay, symbol again of the very force of life. Life is the animating principle, and we are nothing but its nurslings."

In elaborating these reflections into his poem, Eberhart moved beyond the ideas he had enunciated in "For a Lamb," for the focus of the poem is not on the dead animal itself, but on the poet's reaction to it, on the intellect:

> In June, amid the golden fields,
> I saw a groundhog lying dead.
> Dead lay he; my senses shook,
> And mind outshot our naked frailty.

The mind takes its materials from the concrete and particular and seeks to transcend them; it turns to a dead groundhog, then back to itself; it conceives of death, then of life-in-death. Through reflection it creates a "wall of wisdom" that can "quell the passion of the blood" and allow the poet enough tranquillity to move, at the end of the poem, outward in time and space in a vision of the struggle of the human spirit with intractable reality, in a vision of time and humanity (represented by the soldier, the scholar, and the saint) controlled by the same forces that work in the decaying groundhog:

> I stood there in the whirling summer,
> My hand capped a withered heart,
> And thought of China and of Greece,
> Of Alexander in his tent;
> Of Montaigne in his tower,
> Of Saint Theresa in her wild lament.

The themes of the poem, life and death, man and nature, mortality and immortality, mind and body, concreteness and transcendence, recur throughout Eberhart's career, and they draw upon the central dilemma of his work, a dilemma summed up in "If I could only live at the Pitch that is near Madness" (*Poetry*, January 1938, collected in *Song and Idea*, 1940), which he wrote while he was, in his own words, "a struggling poet and had . . . no status," teaching at St. Mark's School. In this poem the sense of struggle between the natural and the spiritual is couched in terms of the contrast between the innocence of childhood, when every-

thing is "Violent, vivid, and of infinite possibility," and the adult world of experience, limitation, and disillusion:

> I gave the moral answer and I died
> And into a realm of complexity came
> Where nothing is possible but necessity
> And the truth wailing there like a red babe.

The grimness of these closing lines reflects the grim necessities that Eberhart saw surrounding him, for despite such occasional successes as "The Groundhog," the 1930s were for Eberhart-the-poet a bleak landscape. Although he made a fairly reasonable income (he managed to save $1600 in his first year teaching at St. Mark's), he was strangely depressed about money. "I would give much," he said, "for security, enough money, the possibility of family." Friends such as Frederick Prokosch rebuked him for his continual brooding, and Elizabeth Foster told him, "You think too much about money and relate too many things to it." What Eberhart wanted, of course, was recognition: recognition as a poet. But instead he met rejection. Harriet Monroe, for instance, declined to print his work in *Poetry* during this period, calling one group of poems (including "The Rape of the Cataract") "incredibly crude. I can't understand how you could pass such stumbling halting lines. You must know better." He fared better with *Poetry* after Monroe's death in September 1936, but most periodicals, including the *Criterion* and *Scrutiny*, refused his work. What poems he did publish each year attracted little or no attention: *Reading the Spirit* was rejected by several American publishers on economic grounds (thus perhaps reinforcing his obsession with money) before the American edition finally came out at the end of 1937 to mixed reviews. He was very much alone with his art throughout the decade, sustained almost exclusively by the conviction—nourished at Dartmouth, emphatically reinforced in his years at Cambridge, but hardly confirmed at all by his publishing record—that he was a poet by calling and that his poetry was important. What he saw as undue neglect reinforced his sense of desolation and perhaps of isolation.

But October 1940 brought radical change, for he then met Helen Elizabeth Butcher, a teacher at the Buckingham School in Cambridge. Shortly before he took up his position in the Cambridge School at Kendal Green, on 29 August 1941, Richard and Elizabeth were married, and the future looked reasonably bright. But the Japanese attack on Pearl Harbor in December changed that future, too, and by the end of the summer of 1942 Eberhart was a naval officer teaching aerial gunnery. During the next four years he served in various training and administrative capacities at naval stations in Hollywood, Florida (until May 1943); Dam Neck, Virginia (until November 1944); Wildwood, New Jersey (until August 1945); and Alameda, California, where he served as personnel officer, at the rank of Lieutenant Commander, until his discharge in the spring of 1946. In California the Eberharts met and became good friends with Kenneth and Marie Rexroth, and Richard Eberhart gave poetry readings at Mills College and (at the invitation of Josephine Miles) at the University of California, Berkeley. Despite their nomadic character, these years were apparently comfortable: "I have enjoyed my Navy Career to date," he wrote to W. H. Auden from New Jersey; "a complete refreshment from the stuffiness of literary people, literary attitudes." They were also productive

Eberhart with one of the kites he used in his work as an aerial-gunnery instructor (courtesy of the Richard Eberhart Collection, Baker Library, Dartmouth College)

years: he wrote some of his best-known poems, including "Dam Neck, Virginia" and "The Fury of Aerial Bombardment," both published in Oscar Williams's annual, *New Poems: 1944*, and collected in *Poems, New and Selected*, published in January 1945 by James Laughlin's New Directions, and he edited, with Selden Rodman, the anthology *War and the Poet* (1945). The period was also crowned, in October 1946, by the birth of a son, Richard.

By this time, Eberhart had accepted a position in his wife's family business, the Butcher Polish Company in Boston, and returned to the fertile cultural milieu of Cambridge and Boston, enjoying the company of such people as John Malcolm Brinnin, Howard Moss, Richard Wilbur, Wallace Stevens, T. S. Eliot, I. A. Richards, William Carlos Williams, Robert Frost, and many others. Eberhart stayed with the Butcher Polish Company until 1952. These years were remarkably energetic and productive: in addition to taking part in the general intellectual and social life around Harvard, he belonged to a group of poets who met, at John Ciardi's suggestion, irregularly from 1948 until 1950, for "reading and strict criticism of poems, no holds barred. And the pleasure of any consideration of poetry" (Ciardi's words). Members of the group included Ciardi, Eberhart, John Holmes, May Sarton, Richard Wilbur, Archibald MacLeish, and Robert Lowell. In June 1950 he joined William Lyon Phelps and Molly Howe in founding the Poets' Theatre in Cambridge, and the month he spent at Yaddo, the artists' colony near Saratoga Springs, New York, beginning on 5 July, was indeed fortunate. Working in a studio next to one occupied by William Carlos Williams, vitalized by the possibility of a poets' theater, in three weeks he wrote about a hundred pages of a verse drama. The enforced and uninterrupted eight-hour writing day gave Eberhart the encouragement and impetus he and the others needed to make the Poets' Theatre a success. By the spring of 1952, when Eberhart left Boston, the company had produced twenty plays, including Eberhart's *The Visionary Farms* on 21 May 1952 (the Poets' Theatre would produce another of his plays, *Devils and Angels*, in January 1956). At Yaddo, too, he began to put together the selection of poems that became *Undercliff* (1953).

Between 1946 and 1952, while he was working for the family business, Eberhart's poems were appearing regularly in various periodicals: he gave numerous public readings, and in addition to a few pamphlets published two books, *Burr Oaks* (1947), and *Selected Poems* (1951). The war had given Eberhart a strong sense of liberation: while the world was at its most coercive, he came to terms with the "necessity" he had struggled with in the 1930s. "Peace has come with war," he wrote in "An Airman Considers His Power" (*Furioso,* Fall 1946, collected in *Burr Oaks*). From 1946 on Eberhart published voluminously. Sustained in part by the emotional security of his new family and his unambiguously defined social role, he projected more clearly than ever before his role as poet, as in "The Horse Chestnut Tree" (collected in *Undercliff*), where he recollects chasing young boys away from the tree in his yard. "Still I moralize upon the day," the poem ends,

> And see that we, outlaws on God's property,
> Fling out imagination beyond the skies,
> Wishing a tangible good from the unknown.
>
> And likewise death will drive us from the scene
> With the great flowering world unbroken yet,
> Which we held in idea, a little handful.

Under different historical circumstances, he might have continued indefinitely after the war as a corporate executive, while seeking out his "little handful" (much as did his friend, insurance-executive Wallace Stevens), letting his life and his art run their parallel but separate courses. But postwar prosperity brought with it the lecture circuit, the visiting writer, and the writer-in-residence. In addition Eberhart had, while tenaciously pursuing his art throughout the previous two decades, built up a reputation among professional *literati,* and that reputation won him, finally, the kind of synthesis of the personal and the professional that had been his goal since Cambridge.

Autumn 1952 found Eberhart in Seattle—with his wife, son, and one-year-old daughter, Gretchen—on a one-year teaching appointment (as poet-in-residence) at the University of Washington. It was an active year which saw Eberhart teaching one course in modern poetry and another in creative writing, giving public readings, watching rehearsals (and then performances) of some of his verse plays, and—perhaps because he found life rather slow after Cambridge—developing a system of "trying to snatch everybody within range" (as Robert Heilman, chairman of the English department, put it): Eberhart arranged for visits and readings by Oscar Williams, Caroline Gordon, Richard Wilbur, Kenneth Rexroth, and others.

Though he did not know it at the time, he was finished with the polish business forever: the appointment at Seattle was the first of a series of visiting professorships, fellowships, and the like. Eberhart had at last reached the position where his writing was the reason for his employment. After his year at Washington he taught at the University of Connecticut at Storrs, replacing R. W. Stallman for 1953-1954, and then at Wheaton College (1954-1955). Awarded a fellowship from the National Institute of Arts and Letters in 1955, he delivered the Christian Gauss Lectures and served as resident fellow at Princeton University during 1955-1956, and in the fall of 1956 he was appointed professor and poet-in-residence at his alma mater Dartmouth College, beginning an association with that institution that lasted until 1980: in 1968 he became Class of 1925 Professor at Dartmouth, a position which he held until 1971 when, officially retired, he continued to teach as professor emeritus. But he also had duties elsewhere: in 1959-1961 he served as Consultant in Poetry at the Library of Congress; in 1967 and in 1972 he returned to Seattle as a visiting professor; in the spring of 1975 he was adjunct professor at Columbia University, following this appointment with a regents' professorship at the University of California, Davis, that fall. Since 1974 he has taught classes both as distinguished visiting professor at the University of Florida and as professor emeritus at Dartmouth, spending his summers at Undercliff, the family's vacation home near Cape Rosier, Maine.

His university positions have allowed Eberhart ample time to write, and his teaching life, primarily devoted to poetry, has enabled him, for a period of more than thirty years, to live for poetry as writer, teacher, and catalyst. The writing has been prolific, and it has brought Eberhart recognition and honor: besides the appointment to the Library of Congress, the most prestigious of the long list of awards and honors includes a 1962 Bollingen Prize, which he shared with John Hall Wheelock; a 1966 Pulitzer Prize for *Selected Poems 1930-1965* (1965); a 1977 National Book Award for *Collected Poems 1930-1976* (1976); and election to one of the fifty chairs of the American Academy of Arts and Letters (1982).

The years since his appointment at Seattle at the age of forty-eight may be seen as long, felicitous resolution to the complex and strenuous dialectic between self and world that has informed the whole of his poetic career, and although a certain serenity of tone is characteristic of much of his later work, which shows a greater clarity and a firmer mastery of his medium, the bulk of his work is more remarkable for its consistency in theme and approach

The Eberhart family in Washington, D.C., 1960 (courtesy of the Richard Eberhart Collection, Baker Library, Dartmouth College)

than for its developmental patterns. The sense of struggle between the natural and the spiritual, visible in "If I could only live at the Pitch that is near Madness" (1938), is equally present in the breathtaking moment of suicide in "On Returning to a Lake in Spring" (collected in *Shifts of Being*, 1968); the momentary epiphany, the imaginative interpenetration of abstract vision and observed reality, commonplace in the late poetry, is nevertheless nowhere more fully embodied than in the very early "The Groundhog" (1934).

The remarkable consistency and coherence of the work enables one to discuss the early work alongside late to advantage and thus see the persistence of Eberhart's characteristic themes, concerns, and techniques. His vision has always been rooted in the ancient confrontation between innocence and experience, between the drive for order and the awareness of reality, a confrontation that seems unresolvable in the actual world. On the side of order and innocence (a label frequently applied by earlier reviewers) are the images and motifs and tonalities that critics have called "romantic"—they are, like Emerson's, concerned with the true, the ideal, the transcendent. On the

other side, there is temporality, imperfection, the ephemeral, and the disorderly: the poet's much-remarked preoccupation with death. Thus, on the side of innocence, from "Incidence of Flight" (*Collected Poems 1930-1976*):

> I spring joy out of my rib cage
> Like a flash of pigeons flying North
> ....
> Joy uncages man to love.

and in "The Poem as Trajectory" (1976):

> I ask questions about the poem
> Because it deals with reality,
>
> An intractable substance, which, if hit,
> May favor timelessness.

Yet, as Emerson put it, "Nature, as we know her, is no saint." "A name may be glorious," Eberhart wrote in "I Walked over the Grave of Henry James" (*Burr Oaks*, 1947), "but death is death," and we find the almost identical thought in "Loss," pub-

Richard Eberhart, Philip Booth, Daniel Hoffman, and Robert Lowell in Maine, 1965 (courtesy of the Richard Eberhart Collection, Baker Library, Dartmouth College)

lished in 1960 (*Massachusetts Review,* collected in *The Quarry,* 1964):

> I do not know how to say no
> To time that goes on in any case.

The balance between innocence and experience, the tension between ideality and necessity, in which virtually all his work is firmly grounded, finds perhaps its clearest expression in "The Secret Heart" (*Fields of Grace,* 1972), which asserts that we are all "Gripped by nature as was the first man/ . . . /We are compelled in this great adversity."

There is a distinctly modernist ring, tempering the romantic view, in the poem's reflection that "Eventually all ideas go underground,/The only triumph is some elegance of style."

Whereas the inspiration of the original romantics was the discovery of an eternal, natural (and/or divine) order, the heightened awareness of the modernist allows merely the creation of an order that is temporary, artificial, an "elegance of style." Transcendence is a temporary achievement

at best, and is, as he writes in the first two stanzas of "Meditation Two" (*The Quarry*), a matter of style:

> Style is the perfection of a point of view,
> Nowise absolute, but held in a balance of opposites
>
> So that for a moment the passage of time is stopped
> And man is enhanced in a moment of harmony.

There are few intimations of immortality, whether in concrete reality or in abstract art. The "moment of harmony" after all lasts but "for a moment." Eberhart continues to struggle with death without ever falling into the illusion that he has won. More than the work of many of his contemporaries, his work is permeated with the realization that the best to be said of "the only triumph" is that it is the best that we can do.

Eberhart's, then, is a romantic sensibility enclosed within a modernist mentality. It is a sensibility that demands transcendence, that "cannot believe that man is here to die," that insists instinctively on a noumenal reality. And it is a mentality that insists with equal vigor upon a recognition of the finality of death, and the inevitability of the cruelty and chaos in life. He stands poised between a Whitmanesque affirmation of life-in-death and an aestheticist construction of an imaginative armor against death-in-life, awestruck by the irrevocable reality and the pathetic inadequacy of both, in wonderment at the irresolution, the mystery, the very absence of synthesis.

It is the achievement of his poetry to dwell at the still center of the mystery, and it is not a position accessible to strictly "rational" analysis. Instead, he tells in *Of Poetry and Poets* (1979), "the poet's mind is a filament informed with the irrational vitality" of what he calls "extraordinary states of being" that "come upon one unannounced" while "in an elevated state of mind. . . ." The immediacy which results from such a method is that the significance attributed to reality seems to have been discovered, not invented or created. The poet becomes something akin to Emerson's naked eyeball, unaided either by a limiting theory or a transcendent faith. And yet, the vision brings us as close to transcendence as the contemporary mind is likely to come. Watching (in *Collected Poems*, 1960),

> a half-blind, burly, old
> Man, half bent to earth
> Who once on the Princeton campus
> Spears stray papers with a nail-
> Ended stick. . . .

we claim the old man's burdens as our own

> As time bends us to earth
> And we pick up what gems and scraps
> There are from magnificence.

The thought is close to that concluding "The Groundhog" in its vision of space and time, in its view of the spirit locked in the temporal and struggling against it. In "Ospreys in Cry" (from the same book), watching an osprey catch a fish, the poet identifies with the duality, the whole process, of nature:

> I felt a staggering sense
> Of the victor and of the doomed,
> Of being the one and the other,
> Of being both at one time,
> I was the seer
> And I was revealed.

If critics have persisted in calling Eberhart romantic or religious, they have done so perhaps

because he rages, in Dylan Thomas's phrase, "against the dying of the light," against irresistible fatality; at the same time, his realization that consciousness is finite allows us to identify with such infinite continuities as the ongoing processes of nature, the essential presentness of all time, the stubborn persistence in our species of the demand for meaning, and even for justice, where none seems to exist. Eberhart's is finally a kind of innocence that finds essences in experience, and thus seeks to convey an essential wisdom of experience, that makes tragedy not remote but accessible.

In April 1986 he received the Poetry Society of America's Robert Frost Medal.

References:

R. P. Blackmur, Review of *Reading the Spirit, Partisan Review,* 5 (February 1938): 52-56;

Lousie Bogan, Philip Booth, and William Stafford, "On Richard Eberhart's 'Am I My Neighbor's Keeper?,' " in *The Contemporary Poet as Artist and Critic,* edited by Anthony Ostroff (Boston & Toronto: Little, Brown, 1964), pp. 143-157;

Philip Booth, "The Varieties of Poetic Experience," *Shenandoah,* 15 (Summer 1964): 62-69;

Denis Donoghue, *The Third Voice* (Princeton: Princeton University Press, 1964), pp. 194-195, 223-235;

Bernard F. Engel, *Richard Eberhart* (Boston: Twayne, 1972);

Engel, "Richard Eberhart—Reader of the Spirit," in *The Achievement of Richard Eberhart* (New York: Scott, Foresman, 1968), pp. 1-21;

Donald Hall, "Method in Poetic Composition," *Paris Review,* 1 (Autumn 1953): 113-119;

James Hall, "Richard Eberhart, the Sociable Naturalist," *Western Review,* 18 (Summer 1954): 315-321;

Daniel Hoffman, "Hunting the Master Image, the Poetry of Richard Eberhart," *Hollins Critic,* 1 (October 1964): 1-12;

Sydney Lea and Jay Parini, eds., *Richard Eberhart: A Celebration* (Hanover, N.H.: *New England Review* Festschrift, 1980);

Ralph J. Mills, Jr., "Richard Eberhart," in his *Contemporary American Poetry* (New York: Random House, 1965), pp. 9-31;

Mills, *Richard Eberhart* (Minneapolis: University of Minnesota Press, 1966);

John Crowe Ransom, "Lyrics Important, Sometimes Rude," *Furioso,* 1 (Summer 1941): 68-70;

Joel Roache, *Richard Eberhart: The Progress of an*

American Poet (New York: Oxford University Press, 1971);

Selden Rodman, "The Poetry of Richard Eberhart," *Perspectives USA,* 10 (Winter 1955): 32-42;

Peter Thorslev, "The Poetry of Richard Eberhart," *Northwestern Tri-Quarterly,* 2 (Winter 1960): 26-32; revised and republished in *Poets in Progress,* edited by Edward Hungerford (Evanston: Northwestern University Press, 1962), pp. 73-91;

Wade Van Dore, *Richard Eberhart: Poet of Life in Death* (Tampa, Fla.: American Studies Press, 1982);

Sue Walker, ed., *Negative Capability,* special Eberhart issue (forthcoming 1986).

Papers:

Eberhart's papers are in the Richard Eberhart Collection at the Baker Library, Dartmouth College.

Paul Engle

(12 October 1908-   )

Joseph Wilson
Anna Maria College

SELECTED BOOKS: *Worn Earth* (New Haven: Yale University Press/London: Oxford University Press, 1932);

American Song (Garden City: Doubleday, Doran, 1934; London: Cape, 1935);

Break the Heart's Anger (Garden City: Doubleday, Doran, 1936);

Corn: A Book of Poems (New York: Doubleday, Doran, 1939);

New Englanders (Muscatine: Privately printed at the Prairie Press, 1940);

West of Midnight and Other Poems (New York: Random House, 1941);

Always the Land (New York: Random House, 1941);

American Child: A Sonnet Sequence (New York: Random House, 1945); revised and enlarged as *American Child: Sonnets for My Daughters, with Thirty-Six New Poems* (New York: Dial, 1956);

The Word of Love: Poems (New York: Random House, 1951);

For the Iowa Dead (Iowa City: State University of Iowa, 1956);

Poems in Praise (New York: Random House, 1959);

Robert Frost (Iowa City: State University of Iowa Library, 1959);

Prairie Christmas (New York: Longmans, Green, 1960);

Old Fashioned Christmas (Des Moines: Register &

Tribune Syndicate, 1960); republished as *An Old-Fashioned Christmas* (New York: Dial Press, 1964);

Golden Child (Kansas City, Mo.: Hallmark Cards, 1960; New York: Dutton, 1962);

Who's Afraid? (New York: Crowell-Collier, 1963);

A Woman Unashamed, And Other Poems (New York: Random House, 1965);

Embrace: Selected Love Poems (New York: Random House, 1969);

Women in the American Revolution (Chicago: Follett, 1976);

Images of China: Poems Written in China, April-June, 1980 (Beijing: New World Press, 1981; New York: Sino Publishing, 1981).

TELEVISION: *Golden Child,* libretto by Engle, music by Philip Bezanson, *Hallmark Hall of Fame,* NBC-TV, 16 December 1960.

OTHER: *Prize Stories: The O. Henry Awards,* volumes 34-36, edited by Engle and Hansford Martin (Garden City: Doubleday, 1954-1956); volumes 37-39, edited by Engle (Garden City: Doubleday, 1957-1959);

Reading Modern Poetry: A Critical Anthology, edited by Engle and Warren Carrier (Chicago: Scott, Foresman, 1955; revised, 1968);

Paul Engle, early 1940s

Midland: Twenty-Five Years of Fiction and Poetry Selected from the Writing Workshops of the State University of Iowa, edited by Engle, with Henri Coulette and Donald Justice (New York: Random House, 1961);

Poet's Choice, edited by Engle and Joseph Langland (New York: Dial Press, 1962);

On Creative Writing, edited by Engle (New York: Dutton, 1964);

Poems of Mao Tse-Tung, translated by Engle and Hualing Nieh Engle (New York: Simon & Schuster, 1972); republished as *The Poetry of Mao Tse-Tung* (London: Wildwood House, 1973);

Writing From the World, edited by Engle and Hualing Nieh Engle (Iowa City: International Writing Program, 1976).

PERIODICAL PUBLICATIONS: "The American Search," *Poetry,* 63 (December 1943): 159-162;

"A Writer Is A Teacher Is A Writer," *New York Times Book Review,* 17 July 1955, p. 1.

Since the 1930s Paul Engle's influence on poetry and creative writing has continually increased.

His impact has been felt in three areas, any one of which would have been an entire career for someone less determined and energetic. In the 1930s and 1940s he was known as the poet from the heartland who was expected to revitalize a Whitmanesque vision of America. From 1942 to 1965, instead of continuing to focus on his own poetry his influence spread through his directorship of the Writers' Workshop at the University of Iowa in Iowa City. Under Engle this writing program developed a nationwide reputation because of his abilities to raise funds, to attract talented students and faculty members, and to justify the writer's place in the university to skeptics both in and out of academics. He is especially renowned for his ability to encourage talented students such as Flannery O'Connor and instructors such as Kurt Vonnegut. Since 1967 Engle has devoted his energies to the International Writing Program which he and his wife Nieh Hualing (she is also referred to as Hualing Nieh and has used the name Hualing Nieh Engle on her publications with Engle) founded at the University of Iowa. Because of the impact of these programs, in 1976 he and his wife were nominated for the Nobel Peace Prize. As one commentator observed, "The alumni—and teachers—of Engle's program read like a directory of contemporary letters; and no survey of Midwestern writers is ever compiled without him."

In addition to poetry, Engle has written textbooks, fiction, reminiscence, reviews, translations, and even history. While his potential as a poet has not been in serious doubt, the wide range and fast pace of his activities probably has detracted from the quality and craftsmanship of his verse. Furthermore, Engle's personality has sometimes provoked his students and faculty to divide into camps of supporters and detractors, just as reviewers have alternately celebrated and dismissed his poetry.

Both Engle's poetry and prose are unabashedly, enthusiastically American. Early critics observed that for Engle "the word America is almost the lifeblood of poetry." As a result, readers have been unusually emotional and sweeping in both their praise and condemnation, responses which often reflect the speaker's approval or condemnation of national policies as much as toward Engle's poetry. His technique is frequently oratorical. Engle provided a revealing insight to his views on prosody in an article he wrote for *Poetry* magazine (December 1943) in praise of Stephen Vincent Benét: "In a day of the concentrated line and compressed lyric, it is proper to have a fair quantity of poetry that is genial, expansive and narrative.

When so much verse is allusive (rightly and richly so) it is excellent to have some whose taste in the mouth is plain, concrete, unmistakable." A principal reason his poetry has never fulfilled the promise noted by many readers is that it is also painstakingly derivative. In the early volumes there are frequent echoes of Walt Whitman and occasional reminders of T. S. Eliot, Archibald MacLeish, and Robert Frost. Later, there are reflections of Roethke, the confessional poets, and others. Engle has learned from all of these voices, and has tried to adapt each, but usually he has imitated without developing his own talent or craft to its fullest. In effect, his voice and vision are muffled by techniques insufficiently mastered. Reflecting on his career for an entry in *Who's Who*, Engle wrote that: "A grindstone does its job by a perpetual turning in one place, wearing itself down slower than the steel." He was quoting lines he had written forty years earlier. Then, they had seemed like a promise, rather than a personal reflection, when he ended the title poem, "Corn," with the same words.

The son of Thomas Allen and Evelyn Reinheimer Engle, Paul Hamilton Engle was born to a Cedar Rapids, Iowa, farming family of German heritage, and he grew up tending the horses his father raised, trained, and sold. As a youth in the 1920s he earned money for books by delivering newspapers, working in a drugstore, and doing odd jobs for families in the local Jewish community. He lit fires on Sabbath as a "Shabas goy." A school librarian encouraged his interest in poetry by showing him an anthology of British and American verse, and Engle began writing verse in high school. While he was a student at Coe College, where he earned a B.A. in 1931, Engle considered studying for the Methodist ministry and tried preaching at the Stumptown church on the outskirts of Cedar Rapids, but "heard no call." Also during his years at Coe, his sonnet "The Second Coming" appeared in *Literary Digest;* it was his first publication in a national periodical.

Engle went on to the University of Iowa in 1931 and earned an M.A. in 1932, submitting for his thesis "One Slim Feather," a collection of poems that won the Yale Series of Younger Poets Prize and was published by the Yale University Press as *Worn Earth* (1932). The first University of Iowa poetry thesis to be published as a book, *Worn Earth* contains some poems, such as "These are the Things," that have remained favorites of Engle's; he has included them in later volumes. *Worn Earth* was republished by AMS Press in 1971. The volume is divided into four sections: "Elegies," "Men with Dirty Hands," "For a Girl," and "Wind-weathered." The book received cautious reviews, but William Rose Benét in the *Saturday Review* (24 December 1932) called it "a good beginning." Even critics who admired his poems were suspicious of content and language, with William Plomer for the *Spectator* (6 January 1933) expressing concern about Engle's use of "unhappy social conditions" and the *Times Literary Supplement* (8 December 1932) criticizing his "too violent and strident idiom."

Engle spent 1932-1933 at Columbia University doing graduate work in literature and anthropology, and in 1933 he became a Rhodes Scholar, studying at Merton College, Oxford, where he remained until 1936. He is proud that while he was at Oxford he played for his college cricket team and rowed in the college eights. The British poet, Edmund Blunden, was his tutor and friend, and he came to know several of the Oxford poets, including W. H. Auden, C. Day Lewis, and Stephen Spender, though they never became close friends. "I was out of line," he explained years later, because of his involvement in athletics which met with their disapproval.

While he was at Oxford, two new volumes of his poetry were published. *American Song* (1934) includes several longer poems, among them, "America Remembers," which had won the *Poetry* magazine prize in 1933 for "a poem to celebrate the achievements of a century." Howard Blake found the optimism of *American Song* "pompous" (*American Review*, October 1934) and Malcolm Cowley asserted in the *New Republic* (29 August 1934) that Engle was "not a poet at all" but an "orator." Nonetheless the book became a best-seller, and J. Donald Adams wrote an enthusiastic review that appeared on the front page of the *New York Times Book Review* (29 July 1934), thereby providing banner-headline credibility for Engle's stature as "A New Voice In American Poetry." "Mr. Engle may not fulfill the high expectations which are aroused by a reading of his book," Adams said, "but if *American Song* does not prove in the long run to become something of a literary landmark, this review may be set down as an unfortunate venture in prophecy." Most readers found Engle's Whitmanesque images in the longer poems to their liking and were quick to applaud his affirmative stance, exemplified in a "Complaint to Sad Poets": "Will you never be done with barking at the moon/ . . . /With baying from the low hills of your lives?" But Engle's ability to appreciate the craft of "sad poets" is also apparent when he imitates T. S. Eliot's rhythms and contrasting images of spring and old men in a "Reproof To Death." Engle's best work has been in his short poems. The strongest efforts in *American Song* are not the longer national celebrations but are short lyrics such as "Whittling" and "Mary," a love poem for Mary Nomine Nissen, the Cedar Rapids woman he would marry at the Oxford registry office on 3 July 1936.

Break the Heart's Anger was published the same year, and while the Engles traveled in Europe an almost unanimously negative reaction to the volume developed. *Break the Heart's Anger* attempts to voice disillusionment with Europe and America; Engle is trying to show the other side of his American song. Writing for the *Saturday Review* (11 April 1936), William Rose Benét, who had been an outspoken supporter of both Engle's earlier books, was reserved and seemingly confused at the latest one; *Poetry* (July 1936) offered outright condemnation; and Malcolm Cowley was even more certain than he had been earlier that Engle was "the orator rather than the poet—he delivers his orations on May Day now, instead of the Fourth of July" (*New Republic*, 1 April 1936). The bitterness in *Break the Heart's Anger* took readers by surprise, and a number found a new "Marxist attitude" in the young American studying and writing in Europe.

Having been granted an A.B. from Oxford University in 1936 (he was awarded an A.M. in 1939), Engle returned to America. He joined the faculty at the University of Iowa in 1937 and traveled throughout the Midwest. At a workshop he gave in Chicago, Gwendolyn Brooks was in his class, and he was able to provide her with early encouragement. The young black poet was one of the first talented authors Engle would recognize and support.

Corn (1939) announced Engle's return from the study of Europe to the heartland. The best of Engle's early volumes, the book reinstates the manner and vision of *American Song*, but each poem exercises greater control and has a sharper focus. Reviewers were once again pleased and applauded the book's "meditative spirit" (Kerker Quinn, *Books*, 4 June 1939) and "honesty" (Selden Rodman, *Saturday Review*, 3 June 1939). "It is a good book because it contains poetry by a poet writing about things he knows and understands," said the reviewer for the *Christian Science Monitor* (17 June 1939). As before, the strongest work is in the short poems. Engle still echoes Whitman and offers a global vision which has more grandeur than poetry to it, but in the poems of *Corn*, including the title poem, the imagery and rhythms are more controlled—

It is today we want
. . . .
It is the touchable, plain loaf on the table
Before us, in a definite room, the bright knife there.
It is a lived-in house we want, no steeple
Bare of a man's things, filled with bat's mutter.

Engle's direction is clear and personal, and, while the verses dealing with the contemporary horrors of 1939 are usually weakened by an excess of oratory, these topical poems are as controlled as they are impassioned, and poems such as "For 1939" are among his finest. One of the short poems, "Windy Night"—where the poet states "What moved against the window one long night/Whether a face or leaf, I could not tell"—received several approving comments and seems to succeed because of Engle's ability to imitate successfully another poet, this time Robert Frost:

I did not ask, watching it turn and swing,
Why it came to me in so cold a season.
For whether human or natural thing
It had its own good reason.

Engle returned to earlier themes, topics, and methods even more definitely in *West of Midnight* (1941), a volume which was seen as more praiseworthy than even *Corn*. Engle's American song of celebration, which was welcome in the depths of the Depression, was an even greater relief in the midst of World War II. While a few critics were again dissatisfied (with W. T. Scott for *Poetry*, May 1942, complaining that "one finishes the book largely unrewarded and disappointed" at Engle's failure to compose disciplined verse and create a conceptual framework to fulfill the promise of *American Song*), most were delighted. The *New York Times* claimed that "The emergence of an American poet is complete, arriving at his full maturity." In the same year, Engle published his only novel, *Always the Land*, concerning Iowa farmers who, like his father, were horse breeders and traders. The novel has little plot and, as a result, disturbed some readers. On the other hand, the incidents, images, and language in the novel are rich celebrations of nature and special moments in rural life. Reviewers were surprised and delighted by this evidence, as some took it, of Engle's ability to use poetic detail and observation. Following *Always the Land*, when Engle wrote prose he chose the essay or reminiscence form.

After he became acting director of the Iowa Writers' Workshop in 1942 and director in 1943,

Paul Engle (right) with Robert Frost at a reading for students and faculty in the Iowa Writers' Workshop

Engle's attention began to shift dramatically from his own poetry toward providing a supportive environment for other writers. In the 1940s and 1950s he devoted more and more of his time to developing the Writers' Workshop program into a national literary force. His workshop was so successful that it became the model for the many other university-based creative writing workshops which have proliferated into the 1980s. Engle taught in the Iowa workshop, secured funding from foundations and businesses, convinced the university to allot classroom space and student scholarships, and designed the experimental curricula which became one trademark of the program. Engle is noted for his ability to spot and nurture talent and for his passionate pursuit of capable people for his programs. He recruited students in whom he sensed talent, driving each night at midnight to the Iowa City railroad depot to give the conductor on the Rock Island railroad letters to potential students so they could be mailed the same night in Chicago. A determined administrator, he recruited faculty with similar commitment. Kurt Vonnegut, who went to Iowa City to write *Slaughterhouse-Five* (1969) and to teach in the workshop, has called Engle "an extremely important man culturally. I can't think

of any institution, except maybe the Guggenheim Foundation, that has encouraged as many writers as the Iowa Workshop." Flannery O'Connor was a student in 1945-1948. Engle later recalled his first meeting with her: "She walked into my office one day and spoke to me. I understood nothing, not one syllable" because of her heavy Georgia accent. When Engle spoke to her, she had to reply on a pad of paper; he wanted to see her writing. "She handed me this paper. I read four lines. You don't need to eat all of an egg to know if it's good or bad. I looked at her and said to myself, 'Christ, this is it. This is pure talent. What can I do? I can't teach her anything!' I taught her a little. She had a few isolated problems—with her society, her illness." O'Connor dedicated her M.F.A. thesis, "The Geranium: A Collection of Short Stories" (1947), to Engle.

Although the quantity of Engle's poetry diminished in the 1940s, his new verse met with considerable success. The author of an entry on Engle in *World Authors: 1950-1970* (1975) has observed that "For a time in the 1940s Engle's optimistic Whitmanesque verse made him one of the most popular and widely read American poets of his generation." In 1945 Engle published a sonnet sequence, *American Child*, which became one of his most widely admired books. Dedicated to Engle's daughter Mary, the sequence celebrates a father's love. Many reviewers agreed with Richard Sullivan that the majority of the poems were "almost completely fresh, sound, authentic work" (*New York Times*, 28 October 1945), although a good number once again felt, as did R. E. Spiller, that he was "less successful when he philosophizes" (*Saturday Review*, 13 October 1945). He was so popular that *Life* magazine ran an article about him with Engle family photos in 1946. In 1956, Engle republished the book with thirty-six new poems, for Mary and his younger daughter, Sara. Reviews for this edition were still more positive. In *Poetry* John Woods found "a poetry as clear as glass with a fire at its center" and John Frederick Nims lauded "the qualities of tolerance, courage, and gayety that live everywhere in these honest and supple poems" (*Chicago Sunday Tribune*, 10 June 1956).

The focus on love, which characterizes some of Engle's strongest and most successful writing, continued in *The Word of Love*, published in 1951. The poems in this volume, which deal with the need for love and love's power, continue his tendency,

Paul Engle in his home office where he spent his evenings keeping up with Writers' Workshop correspondence

evident as early as *Corn* in most of his best short poems, toward direct statement. Some critics felt the success of the poems was largely superficial, but the *U.S. Quarterly Book Review* (Summer 1951) called the book a "very real and attractive achievement." Nims waxed enthusiastic again, asserting that of all Engle's work "*Word of Love* is the strongest in intensity and honesty of passion, in appropriateness and control of form" (*Chicago Sunday Tribune*, 15 April 1951).

Because of Engle's intense involvement with the Iowa workshop, and an increase in his editorial activities, his output of poetry decreased even further in the 1950s. During those years the Iowa Writers' Workshop recruited students with exceptional literary talents, including poets W. D. Snodgrass, William Stafford, and Donald Justice. In 1954, on a trip to Hobe Sound, Florida, Engle met Averell Harriman, and developed a friendship which proved invaluable in pursuing workshop funds.

Through a curious and ominous irony of the period, Engle, a most American poet, was identified as a possible member of the Communist front, perhaps because someone remembered the so-called Marxist attitude of *Break the Heart's Anger*. At the height of the McCarthy scare in 1952 the *New York Times* (9 November 1952) reported that Engle and others had been dropped as speakers at a program planned by the American Legion on the basis of the allegations; ten days later, the *Times* reported, Engle and the other lecturers were approved "in spite of protests."

Throughout the 1950s Engle received public recognition for his work as a poet and writing teacher: Guggenheim Fellowships in 1953, 1957, and 1959; and positions as a judge for the National Book Award (1955, 1970) and as judge for the Lamont Award (1958-1961). From 1954-1959 Engle acted as editor for the annual O. Henry Award *Prize Stories*, a series which continued to receive praise under his direction. He and Warren Carrier edited *Reading Modern Poetry* (1955), a critical anthology that encouraged a more open and less formalist reading of poems than in other such textbooks.

During the years from 1959 to 1966 Engle was engaged in a large number of activities which added to his literary credibility and gained important publicity for the Iowa workshop. He published two volumes of seasonal reminiscence in poetry and prose (*Prairie Christmas*, 1960; *Old Fashioned Christmas*, 1960). In 1960 he wrote the libretto and narrative text for *Golden Child*, an opera televised on the *Hallmark Hall of Fame*. The next year he edited *Midland* (1961), a volume of work by present and former students and faculty in the Iowa writing programs. In 1962 he and Joseph Langland edited *Poet's Choice*, a valuable anthology of poems with comments by their authors, and he wrote *Who's Afraid?* (1963), a story for children. The textbook *On Creative Writing*, which he edited in 1964, has become a classic in the field. Engle became a Rockefeller Foundation Fellow in 1963, and in 1965 he was appointed by President Kennedy to a National Cultural Advisory Committee on the Arts; he was the only poet named to the National Council on the Arts. He also found time to write two volumes of poetry. Both *Poems in Praise* (1959) and *A Woman Unashamed* (1965) received disappointing reviews. It is likely that the uneven quality of the poetry is the result of the breathless pace of Engle's life during these years.

Poems in Praise covers a wide range of subjects—sometimes satirically—from children to an old Palestinian donkey. A few readers were unqualified in their enthusiasm, but most agreed with the *Kirkus* reviewer, who called the book "a rather disappointing and stylistically eclectic selection of 'poems.' . . . His language throughout is often fanciful, but seldom imaginative." *A Woman Unashamed* is a stronger, if imperfect, volume. It contains a series of reflections on Asia (which he visited for the first time in January-April 1963), a remembrance of his Oxford tutor, Edmund Blunden, and a section concerning his love for Christmas. While reviewers had reservations concerning the hurried and incomplete craftsmanship of some of the poems, they agreed that the volume had greater substance than *Poems in Praise*—although one often-quoted reader, Paul Fussell, felt the work was merely sentimental and that Engle "is apparently too nice a man to write very good poems." In *A Woman Unashamed*, Engle adopts a wider range, using a confessional stance in the "Poems Lived in Asia" section and clearly relying on Theodore Roethke for voice in poems such as "Lightning." The immediacy of observation which had been noteworthy in *The Word of Love* fourteen years earlier is sharpened here by his exposure to the Orient, and he appears to have learned from younger poets who had been imitating oriental tones and forms. The result is often striking, as in these lines from "Notes": "Butterfly trembles when the wind blows./ You walk near me."

Philip Roth, who was an instructor at the workshop in the 1960s, saw that "Iowa City is what a whole generation had, instead of Paris. And it wasn't so bad, either." Beginning in 1965 and for the next five years, Paul Engle's life was in turmoil. After more than twenty years as director of the Iowa Writers' Workshop and after raising more than $500,000 to sustain the program, Engle resigned his position. Further, his marriage to Mary Engle was drawing to a conclusion. In 1967 Engle began a new project. With the support of a Chinese novelist, Nieh Hualing, he founded the International Writing Program at the University of Iowa, the only such program in the world. Much like the Writers' Workshop, this program brings together writers to discuss and understand one another's work and ideas. This time writers come from foreign countries, not only to become better artists but to attempt international dialogue. Since the university does not provide funds for the foreign writers who take part in this program, Engle's time has been devoted to diligent fund raising. He claims to have raised more than $2 million with the help of Nieh Hualing, whom he married on 14 May 1971 following his 1970 divorce from Mary Engle.

In this period of turbulence Engle assembled a volume of what may be his best poetry, *Embrace* (1969). A collection of love poetry, the book contains many previously published poems, including some from *Worn Earth*. The poems he selected for *Embrace* represent his work at its very best—brief, tight, and controlled by emotion and imagery which is clearly focused, immediate, and authentic—demonstrating a newfound ability to judge his own work. Unfortunately, the book attracted little critical attention.

Engle has continued to be active in the 1970s and 1980s and has extended his range of writing still further, translating *Poems of Mao Tse-Tung* (1972) with Nieh Hualing, and completing *Women in the American Revolution* (1976) and a volume of poems written on a 1980 trip to China. *Images of China* (1981) is composed in English verse forms but with the haste and attempted spontaneity of journal entries, resulting in some brilliant images and juxtapositions. One poem on the Cultural Revolution has been much admired in China: "Walking, I kicked a stone/And heard a voice inside/ Crying: Leave me alone/I came down here to hide."

Engle and his wife were nominated by their friend Averell Harriman for the Nobel Peace Prize in 1976. In support of the nomination, Harriman wrote: "I have known the Engles and watched their dedicated efforts to bring peace and understanding to the world by bringing writers of every country, language and culture to their program in Iowa City. . . . They invented the idea and gave their

Paul Engle (photograph © The Washington Post, *27 March 1983)*

years to raising funds to finance it from many sources, most of them private individuals and corporations. This is unprecedented in the history of international relations, which are almost always governments talking to governments."

Also in 1976, at the age of sixty-eight, Engle relinquished the directorship of the International Writing Program to his wife, and he became a consultant. The Engles live in Iowa City, where he is working on two volumes: a prose reminiscence, "Engle Country: Memoirs," and a volume of verse, "Engle Country: Poems."

One of his former students, John Engels, has described Engle as "charming, difficult, cantankerous, demanding, generous, cold and reserved, warm and open, a man of so many contradictions it would be presumptuous of me to attempt to resolve them." Probably Paul Engle will not be re-

membered as much for his poetry as for the two writing programs which he founded at Iowa. Engle once wrote that his idea was "to run the future of American literature, and a great deal of European and Asian, through Iowa City." The Iowa Writers' Workshop grew under his direction from a nearly dormant program to one that boasts an enrollment of approximately 250 graduate students. Since 1967 the International Writing Program has accommodated more than 500 writers from all parts of the world.

References:

Malcolm Cowley, *Think Back On Us* (Carbondale, Ill.: Southern Illinois University Press, 1967), pp. 66-70;

Stephen Wilbers, *The Iowa Writers' Workshop* (Iowa City: Iowa University Press, 1980).

Vincent Ferrini
(24 June 1913-)

George F. Butterick
University of Connecticut

BOOKS: *No Smoke* (Portland, Maine: Falmouth Publishing House, 1941);

Injunction (Lynn, Mass.: Sand Piper Publishers, 1943);

Blood of the Tenement (Lynn, Mass.: Sand Piper Publishers, 1944);

The Plow in the Ruins (Prairie City, Ill.: James A. Decker, 1946);

Tidal Wave: Poems of the Great Strikes (New York: Great Concord Publishers, 1946);

Sea Sprung (Gloucester, Mass.: Cape Ann Press, 1949);

The Infinite People (New York: Great Concord Publishers, 1950);

The House of Time (London: Fortune Press, 1952);

In the Arriving (Gloucester, Mass.: Heron Press, 1954);

Timeo Hominem Unius Mulieris (Liverpool, U.K. & Gloucester, Mass.: Heron Press, 1954);

Mindscapes (Mount Vernon, N.Y.: Peter Pauper Press, 1955);

The Square Root Of In (Gloucester, Mass.: Heuretic Press, 1957);

The Garden (Gloucester, Mass.: Heuretic Press, 1958);

Five Plays (London: Fortune Press, 1959);

Book of One (Gloucester, Mass.: Heuretic Press, 1960);

Mirandum (Gloucester, Mass.: Heuretic Press, 1963);

I Have the World (London: Fortune Press, 1967);

The Hiding One (Brookline, Mass.: Me & Thee Press, 1973);

Ten Pound Light (Gloucester, Mass.: Church Press, 1975);

Selected Poems, edited by George F. Butterick (Storrs: University of Connecticut Library, 1976);

Know Fish (Storrs: University of Connecticut Library, 1979);

Know Fish, Book III: The Navigators (Storrs: University of Connecticut Library, 1984).

Vincent Ferrini, July 1982 (photograph by Janet Knott)

OTHER: *Four Winds,* edited by Ferrini and others, nos. 1-4 (1952-1953);

Ferrini & Others, edited by Ferrini (Gloucester, Mass.: Nessuno, 1953);

Innermost I Land, in *The Best Short Plays 1952-1953,* edited by Margaret Mayorga (New York: Dodd, Mead, 1953), pp. 1-56;

Telling of the North Star, in *The Best Short Plays 1953-1954,* edited by Mayorga (New York: Dodd, Mead, 1954).

PERIODICAL PUBLICATIONS:

POETRY

"Poem in Theme," as Vincent Ferrous, *Smoke*, 5 (Spring 1936): 7;

"Teachers," *Smoke*, 6 (May-August 1937): 16;

"Struggle," *Intermountain Review*, 2 (Fall 1937): 4;

"Everywhere," *New Anvil*, 1 (May-June 1940): 29;

"The Dream," *Moosehead Review*, 1, no. 2 (1978): 16-19.

DRAMA

The Man His Father Knew, Mutiny, 2 (Autumn 1959): 103-113.

NONFICTION

"From Massachusetts . . . ," *Pound Newsletter*, no. 8 (October 1955): 28-29;

"A Frame," *Maps*, no. 4 (1971): 47-60;

"G. E. Days, A Chapter in Autobiography," *Athanor*, no. 2 (Fall-Winter 1971): 26-40;

"Local Universe," *Review of Contemporary Fiction*, 1 (Summer 1981): 285-286.

Vincent Ferrini may be the only American poet to have participated in both the WPA program of the 1930s and the CETA program of the 1970s, the chief federally sponsored efforts to provide meaningful work for the nation's unemployed artists. This is of significance, because the relationships of work to life and life to poetry have been his most persistent themes. Through a long career, he moved from being a proletarian writer—one of the most authentic, if overlooked, examples of the worker-poet in this country—to his own independent visionary status. At each stage he embodied the ages he passed through, at the same time never giving up his earliest commitments. Walter Lowenfels called him "the last surviving Proletarian Poet"—which he certainly is, but he is much more besides.

He was born Venanzio, named after the patron saint of his father's hometown, in Saugus, Massachusetts, across the river from Lynn. His parents, Rena DeCarlo and Giovanni Ferrini, had arrived in the great wave of immigration of 1909; his father went to work in the shoe factories that gave Lynn its nickname of Shoe City. The young Ferrini grew up in the Brickyards section of the city against the Boston and Maine Railroad tracks, moving from tenement to tenement with his family. Early memories include "The terrible winters, snows six feet high. My mother heating the andiron, wrapping a towel around it and placing it under my feet, going to the Welfare office for foodstamps. I am dragging over ice and snow the 100 pound bags of coal from Lamper's Wharf. I am guarding my baby sister in her highchair by the stove when it explodes, kills her, gashes my arm and forehead, my brother Dante under the stove, escaping, and I am crying my heart out, 'What are we going to do about Yolanda, what are we to be without her,' the doctor stitching my arm up, and the corner of my eye."

There was no precedent known to him for a life of poetry, and no encouragement. In high school, he discovered Shelley and was inflamed with romanticism, although when he showed his poems to an English teacher she decreed, "You will never be a poet." His father, too, reminded him roughly, "You can't be a poet, you are born in the wrong class. You are the son of a shoemaker, you will work for a living like I do!" After high school, he found work in one of Lynn's many shoe factories, turning soles for a stitching machine, the next summer working in a tannery, pulling dried cow hides from stretchers. He continued his education at the public library. As the Depression lengthened, he obtained a job under the WPA working on ships' logs at the Peabody Museum in Salem, and, when the project came to an end, as an adult-education teacher under WPA sponsorship. In 1936 he published his first poem in the magazine *Smoke* under the nom de plume Vincent Ferrous, suggesting the iron of his resolve, and other poems in journals such as Jack Conroy's *New Anvil*. When he was twenty-seven, in January 1941, he married Margaret Duffy, a schoolteacher and summa cum laude graduate of Radcliffe, who shared his political beliefs. With the outbreak of World War II, he was hired as a bench hand in the General Electric plant, and taught briefly at the politically oriented Samuel Adams School in Boston. There were three children to heighten the tension between life and art. He remained at G. E. for nine years (described in his autobiographical narrative "G. E. Days"), during which time he joined the Communist party, exploring an uneasy relationship with dogmatism. In 1948, he moved up the coast to Gloucester, eventually quitting both G. E. and the "Church of Politics," opening up a new phase of his life.

Ferrini himself feels there are three distinct stages to his literary career. The first began in Lynn in the years of the Great Depression and continued until he left that city in 1948. His early poetry is a deeply felt articulation of the struggle of the urban working class for economic survival. Published in the *Daily Worker* and similar forums, these poems probably enjoyed a larger and more diverse audience than any of his work until the publication of his *Selected Poems* in 1976. It was, however, an audience without influence as far as literary reputa-

Vincent Ferrini and his father (seated fifth and sixth from left) with family and friends, circa 1923

tion went. As the poet has pointed out, "those who made up this audience were not schooled in the universities and drawing rooms of their day. They got their schooling in the factories and on the picket lines; and art, if it spoke to them, came out of that tension between living and creating, out of that resurgence of the little man, what he was and lived for." Ferrini thus continued little known to critics, literary historians, and editors; indeed, it was not until 1972 that his work was anthologized (as that of a "ghetto" writer, in Wayne Miller's *Gathering of Ghetto Writers*), with selections from his first collection, *No Smoke*.

Written in the late 1930s and published in 1941, *No Smoke* contains the carefully worded disclaimer—more familiar to prose than poetry—"any similarity in this book to the names of persons living and dead is coincidental." For good reason: the book is a series of frank and undisguised portraits of Lynn and its people, a *Spoon River Anthology* of the industrial Northeast; only, more than Edgar Lee Masters's portraits, Ferrini's are fired with rage and commitment. The book's title signifies one of the most essential and dreaded aspects of a factory town, a sight even more conspicuous by its absence: no smoke from the smoke-stacks of industry, no

production, and, most important for the wage earners, no work. Summarized in a single image is the enforced idleness of the Depression with all of its concomitant suffering. The poems were originally titled with actual peoples' names, but the poet was pressured into fictionalizing them, something he always regretted—especially when measuring himself against Charles Olson, who named names in his epic *Maximus Poems* series—so that when it came time to write his own Gloucester epic, Ferrini made a point to let the true names boldly stand. The volume begins with a portrait of the city itself, the starkly simple facts: "15 years ago this city was the shoe hub of the world./160 factories hummed a song of joy"; now, the people "Huddled in tenements/Starve in the shadows of dead factories." Following this introduction, the people step forward one by one and speak, or, for those less willing, the poet causes them to stand revealed. In all, seventy-seven personalities, including a defunct local railroad, speak. They speak, and they speak. There are the ragmen, strikebreakers, scabs, bag ladies, the institutionalized. There are newspapermen, disabled World War I veterans, WPA administrators, sweatshop bosses, abused wives, effete artists, arrogant bankers. There is the informer,

Youthful Bard Tells Bitter Story Of Lynn Characters in New Volume

Ferrini Depicts His View of City

By HERBERT L. SCHON

Literary bombshells fell on Lynn this week.

A thin, brown-covered book of poetry about Lynn, its factotums, functionaries and foibles is responsible for many a local residents turning to the Muse in the past few days. "No Smoke" is the volume's title and Vincent Ferrini of 297 Summer street is the author.

In "No Smoke" Ferrini has limned in bold relief practically every person in the city who has achieved notice either by his position or peculiarities. Without too much critical hedging, the book can be described accurately as poetry that does not pull its punches. In many instances it is painfully graphic and bitter.

It is one of the few books of poetry dealing entirely with Lynn since old Alonzo Lewis, Lynn's venerable historian, wrote of the charms of nearby woods and the beauties of King's Beach at sunset. Here the comparison ends. Ferrini does not sing of nature. His work deals with people that one meets every day in Central Square and along all the other streets which lead to that hub.

See FERRINI, Page 2, Col. 5

A BARD WHO SINGS OF LYNN and its characters is Vincent Ferrini of Summer street, whose new book, "No Smoke," has just been published.

Story in the Lynn Daily Evening Item *shortly after the publication of* No Smoke

Murray Quist, whose "ears write down decisions behind closed union doors./Lonely as a skunk,/He exhales a queer happiness." The range of names suggests the classic American melting pot: Martha Jefferson, Sarah Katsenclimer, George Alkaluvious, Enzo Hadd, Circe Mendoza. A clever system of headnotes—commentary by one townsperson about another—interrelates the citizens and binds the book. The volume ends as it began, with the factories themselves given voice: "O workers, we are yours for the taking./For what are you waiting?" The language is folk simple. There is the broken-down ward heeler whose "command of English is the sorrow of a cat." Each dramatic cameo or mug shot seeks to be a moral more than an aesthetic achievement. The poems are raw in power, unfinished in their ambition and insistence. Questions are raised none too politely. Often too angry to be poignant, the lines are direct addresses to issues not to be aestheticized away. The local public library, which in a sense had made the poems possible by allowing Ferrini to expand his trust in language, kept the book under lock and key for a number of years, available from the restricted shelf in the reference room only by special request, like certain comprehensive medical manuals.

His next two books reflect the years of World War II, the home front, defense work at the massive plant that took the place of the shoe factories in dominating Lynn. In *Injunction* (1943), he calls it the "Electric Asylum." The poems are narrated in a staccato of fact and image. Each line is a machine stroke, an implacable march of single images:

> Buttons on collars are identity.
> The boy pulls his loaded newspaper cart
>   as if it were a bad dream.
> Headlines drop depth bombs upon us.
> The guard at the gate is a sunflower
> Or a tower of ice.

The industrial images are served up with the same brutality as in life, while the regularity of rhyme rings in counterpoise to the metrically irregular lines:

At every minute
The hum is a front at the rear and we're in it
Signals exploding blood cells
Electric saws in aluminum splitting atoms of the air
Hornet buzz of coils and care
Heels and mallets pound foundry soot soft as moon-
    light
Coal smudges on bodies spoon bright
Blue pain of the acetylene torch tearing the flesh.

Ferrini is the authentic representative of the industrial worker, one of the most perfect examples of the proletarian poet possible. He writes both for the workers and, most important, as one of them. His gripes are their gripes, his wrath theirs. His feet are firmly planted among the grit and filings of the factory floor. The poems read true, down to their occasional infelicities. The themes are the perils of the working class, the draft which emptied cities, working conditions, the disabled, the poor (always the poor), protests against war profiteering and the "gas of anti-semitism," and pleas for racial justice. Pervading all is the war—or almost all, because transcending even the war is a more fundamental consciousness and precariousness, the proletarian consciousness of dependency and vulnerability. Despite the obvious common enemy abroad, there is still another, even more universal foe: the continued exploitation of labor. "Letter to My Brother"—which ends, "For the weapons we send you/And your bayonet/Will anneal the People's Revolutions/And you come back to a country where Ma and our kids won't ever go to the Welfare again"—was a bold poem to write in the midst of the war effort. He rallies and goads his fellow workers, after celebrating their prowess in "Forge Plant," by asking the pertinent question: "Energies paid by War/Why have you never worked like this in Peace time?" There is also the dignified "Skeleton in the Mind," a succinct history of the times that concludes:

These envelopes have the worms of the Depression
    in them
Food is rationed, shadows of no work and fear
Stick to our thoughts and we scrimp dollars
Against the time that will too soon be here.

But perhaps noblest of all, and the culminating poem of the book, is "Talking Tenements." The derelict, eyeless factories of *No Smoke* become these outspoken structures of *Injunction*, metaphoric of the nation. Built brick by brick of the people, they dare to propose a future of challenge, beginning with the simple plea for solidarity: "One man is an

atom of sand/37,000 are a brick." These are poems of plight, as if facing things squarely will relieve sufferings. "Cripples on the ground/Like hit and run victims . . . /Today they were roses/Tomorrow with dogs trailing." There is bitterness, perhaps, but no cynicism; just a fronting of the issues. Ferrini does not write soothingly, meltingly, devious with ingenious rhetorical distractions. Nor are the poems studiously simple. They are direct because they have to be, and as "simple" as survival. Some, such as "The Salt Is Paid Its Worth" and "The Idea Wheels the Carriage," verge on the surrealist in their stark disjointedness of image. "The Dead Hours are Tall Lampposts" might easily have been a painting by de Chirico:

The moonlight is an enamel table top
The house is an egg at the edge of it
And the hum of automobile tires on the pavement
The approaching bombers.

It is an inadvertent surrealism, perhaps, for in each the causal connections between images are too closely in reach to be most strictly surreal. Max Harris, Australian editor of *Angry Penguins*, where some of Ferrini's work appeared, in reviewing *Injunction* found the poems derive "from the short impressionistic line of Mayakovsky with the slick elision that is possible in the American language," but the most notable praise came from Mike Gold, author of the classic Depression novel *Jews Without Money* (1930), who wrote that the poems were as "genuine as a soldier's wound or a row of stamping machines."

Ferrini's third book, *Blood of the Tenement* (1944), begins with poems written in the late 1930s, including tributes to the victims of the bombed Spanish city of Guernica. There are also autobiographical love songs mixed with those of social responsibility: "Quarrel" ends with the timeless, appealing image, "I am the snow/With sparrow's footmarks/Wanting to be the sparrow." Metaphor remains his strength and chief device. The poems consist of a simple, progressive rhythm of images, each a line or breath long. There are few puns or other forms of rhetorical display and little effort at syntactical dexterity. The theme of the working man prevails, as seen in such poems as "After 20 Centuries" concerning the "slavery of hire and lay-off." The voice is firm and beats out:

No more hydra teeth of unemployment
No more whirlpool fists of food bills doctor bills rent
    bills

Vincent and Margaret Ferrini, 1944

Around our necks
No more jungles of worries
Or rat traps of misfortunes
No more days of vaults
Sinking into quicksand
Rewarding us with the ragbag of lost years[.]

It is a confrontational voice of deep feeling. Not all the poems are as polemical, however. There is the tender "Wine of the Heart," a testament to love and to the poet's ideals: "I looked for you in alleys/ In the moon's room on a wave." Its final lines give the book its dramatic title:

We shall be together so long
It will seem like yesterday
For the blood of the tenement stopped
And ours were the hands removing the knife.

The Plow in the Ruins (1946) celebrates a postwar world of possibilities in poems such as the rousing "Paean to the Red Armies," with the oppressed on the march, newly liberated, forming armies of "exact demonstration" sweeping away "quislings and the structural odor of death." The poems reflect the sweep of history and include laments for victims of the extermination camps and Hiroshima, hymns to revolutionary China and to the British workers upon electing a Labour government, and verses with the universal poignancy of "Photograph of Starved Child Dumped in a Burial Cart." The book concludes with "The Human Dawn," a celebration of "the genius locked in the common man." In all, Ferrini's sincerity is beyond challenge. The same basic, unadorned vocabulary employed in his previous books is forged into new images by his loving ferocity. Also appearing that year was *Tidal Wave*, with rough drawings throughout of massed workers, making it look like the labor-union tract it was. It contains tough-minded poems of the picket line and rallying cries uncompromisingly clear, such as the address "To the Legislators," demanding that the politicians obey the popular will or get kicked out "With the toe of our votes." They might be read as perennial watchdog poems, or an example of poetry as a tool, for hefting, raising, performing practical work—language as a crowbar or tire iron. The most refreshing aspect of Ferrini's early poetry is that it is without sentimental exaggeration of the working class. It is also without self-consciousness: he does not elect himself "voice" of the workers, and we are sufficiently aware of his own limitations. Further, by presenting specific individuals and episodes, he avoids flaccid generalizations, the instant death of political poetry; while his vision of essential human dignity and the effective dignity of language surpasses all bitter partisanship.

The second phase of Ferrini's life and work began after his move to Gloucester, when he sought, in his own words, to "integrate the enigmatic tensions between the need for personal and social evolution, and the conflicting desires for economic and artistic independence." A painter living in Gloucester had paid the poet a visit after reading Mike Gold's review of *Injunction;* returning the visit, Ferrini was enchanted with the city of fishermen and artists, and moved his family there in early 1948. For a year and a half he commuted to Lynn, and then, seizing an opportunity to hammer out an independent life, he set up as a frame maker in a small shop that in later years would also serve as a home. His range of literary contacts expanded. In 1949 some of his poems caught the attention of Charles Olson, who sought him out while on a visit to Gloucester, initiating a stormy but ultimately invincible friendship (described by Ferrini in his memoir, "A Frame"). It was Ferrini that introduced Olson to Robert Creeley, thus beginning that most important of literary relationships, and Olson's *Maximus Poems* was begun as letters to Ferrini.

Sea Sprung (1949) was written directly following the poet's removal to Gloucester and marks the beginning of his commitment to the city which has been his home (and stage) since. Rather than conceptualizing or socializing the local, the approach is through the senses, in a series of snapshots, without overt anger and no longer doctrinaire or combative. Man at his labors is praised, nature intermingles. There are poems to the fishermen, net menders, clam diggers, the seiners, the gulls, a lighthouse. The volume ends, as is appropriate, with "The Sea," its "clang of iron/on iron/against the stars." The forms continue to be attractively unfinished. Lines are short and loosely elastic, a spill of images, punctuated by spacing alone. In "Fishcutters," the lines almost stumble on beauty:

> the scales of the dawn
> stick to the skin
>
> of the cutters
> ankle deep in fisheyes
>
> white bony skeletons
> sleep with them
>
> and follow them
> back to these wharfs
>
> wet with the smell
> of old love that anchors
>
> them to the innumerable fish
> that come forth
>
> perpetually
> and is their breathing

This quality of authenticity, the natural grain, continues to be more important than polish in Ferrini's work.

The Infinite People (1950) continues the theme of "uncommon man" in the glory of his possibility. The same victims of the tenements from the early poems are there, and even a belated tribute to "Sacco & Vanzetti," but there is a new calmness, a relaxedness that approaches wisdom. Some of the verse has the quality of a fable; indeed, one is called "Folk Inscription" (changed in *Selected Poems* to "Folksong") and is a beatitude, deliberately paced

slowly: "If you ever/want to find/me/and know me/ leave behind/yourself/and enter/the caves/of other/people. . . ." Images are still of the sort practiced by Carl Sandburg, or, later, Lawrence Ferlinghetti ("the wind is homeless/and naked/ perpetually rubbing its back/against the sheet/for warmth")—populist images, basic, intimate with our needs.

With *The House of Time* (1952), Ferrini extends his exploration of identity. "Transmigration" is a splendid mobile of shifting states of being, written in couplets, appropriately enough, emphasizing the "double" or protean quality of man and nature, man and his "other." It is a fable, truly enough, stressing the interrelation of all of creation. A man and a gull emerge with exchanged identities after diving together into the elemental deep. The setting itself contributes to the interchange: just as the sky is "overburdened" and pressed upon the sea, the grey sea itself "was chopping/the air." Sea and sky are as actively intermingled as man and gull. The poem is a symbolic evocation with metaphysical implications. "A Little Autobiography," on the other hand, achieves its effect by combining the "false" simplicity of surrealism (or dream) with a narrative of fabulous simplicity. A dog has run "down the night/with my left hand." The poet pursues, asking a lamppost along the way for assistance, but the lamppost—in an exaggeration of the obviously true, characteristic of fables or a riddle— "hung its head/it had no tongue." The poet must persist unaided, hunting "the dogtrack/down the endless night" until revelation: "and on a hill/I saw the dog/burying the bone/of my left hand/in the moon." The discovery of the wonder of the event is reward enough.

There is an element of mystery to these poems. The poet is interchangeable with gulls and shadows, he is childlike and even elfen:

> the tiny room
> in the tree
> is where
> I live
>
> I leave
> with the dawn
> key
> and enter
> with the moon

The poems' special charm is Ferrini's ability to achieve mastery through mystery, and mystery through simplicity. The final section of *The House of Time* is given over to a verse drama called "The In (Out," concerning the effects of time on the life of a family and the dreams that challenge "the same corroding/grind" of work, stirred forth by the hovering spirit of the Poet, who is identified as "the conscience and consciousness of time." It was during these years that the poet began writing plays, some performed locally as well as in Boston and at the Judson Poets' Theatre in New York. Two were included in *The Best Short Plays* series, and all were later collected in *Five Plays* (1959). During this time also, Ferrini assembled a small anthology of poetry, intended to be an anonymous publication (none of the poems were signed and the publisher was given as "nessuno," Italian for "no one."). The German printer, however, mistakenly titled the volume *Ferrini & Others*, resulting in some embarrassment—the "others" being Olson, Creeley, and Cid Corman.

In 1952 and 1953, Ferrini also edited a little magazine, *Four Winds*, from Gloucester. It disappointed Olson, who attacked him harshly in *Maximus Poems*, both for what he felt was misrepresenting Gloucester and for getting himself "lost in an abstraction," mass man. Paradoxically, it was this attack that assured Ferrini a place in literary history and would lead to his discovery by another generation of poets and critics. More immediately, the attack prompted *In the Arriving* (1954), addressed to Olson, "whose drive, insight & perception are the mark of the/maker, the/Poet/ with a voice most original, provocative &/contagious." It is a long poem written projectively over the page, not in defiance or rebuttal of Olson, but seeking to engage him on the level of highest friendship and mutual faith. Loosely symbolic and philosophical, it drifts between states of "prebirth" and "postbirth," between specificity and an abstract "country of discovery." Ferrini gently rebukes Olson, who had swarmed upon him with perhaps unnecessary vehemence, and insists that each individual be respected "in his own/weight/& specific/value" and, above all, that "love does not/ judge/it/is/too busy/making/anew."

Ferrini's struggle for artistic definition continued through the decade and into the 1960s, and included experiments with minimalist syntax and an overall condensation of style. The poems grow gnomic, knowing is substituted for anger, and influences other than social welfare guide him, as seen in the haikus and koans of *Mindscapes* (1955) and *The Square Root Of In* (1957). Solidarity and the united fist of images give way to a gentler sense of

responsibility, as in "The Gold" in *I Have the World* (1967):

> The suddenness flowers have
> startle the air
> with their fire and ether
> as we do with what is ours
> because we are
> the gardeners of each other.

Dabney Stuart in praising *Mirandum* (1963) called this voice (which is also the ego of the title *I Have the World*) "an unassertive *I* authentic because of its value as an agent of timeless imagination, which it recognizes as larger than itself." During this time Ferrini lost a daughter to leukemia and his first marriage broke up. He subsequently married painter Mary Shore, but that also ended in divorce.

The third and present phase of Ferrini's career began following the death of Olson in 1970, which freed him to be the poet of Gloucester, the Dante of his city, and to create a new world of authority about himself. He summarized the three stages again in a 1976 conversation with his friend Peter Anastas: "First there was the social, then the personal, and now there's the social and personal together." In this most recent phase, his work has driven toward "achieving fuller artistic integrity, annihilating the longstanding and heartfelt schism between art and morality, and synthesizing life and literature in such a way that each has become a direct and complete expression of the other." This synthesis is readily exemplified by his activities in Gloucester—firing letters to the newspaper, spearheading neighborhood preservation groups, appearing before city-council meetings armed with poems in hand, enjoining the politicians to "return the city to its people, the sea to its fishes and fishing peoples," and generally fulfilling his role as conscience of the city. It is seen, too, in radio plays written on a 1976 Massachusetts Council of the Arts grant, activities under the CETA program during 1977-1978 that included workshops at the county jail, appearances at local colleges, where he has lectured repeatedly about the integration of art and life, and by his poems in *Know Fish* (1979). This is the Ferrini described in the *Boston Globe* (5 August 1974) as "a laser beam on horseback." In 1976 his *Selected Poems* was published, gaining him new recognition, especially among readers who might otherwise have thought that his sole significance was as a footnote to Olson's *Maximus Poems*, a model of how *not* to conduct a literary life.

In recent years Ferrini has continued to write

Vincent Ferrini "listening" to Homer, a mask by Mary Shore, his second wife, circa 1970 (photograph by Vincent Castagnalli)

and publish as much as ever. The poems have a fullness of being not possible earlier, reflecting the changed times as well as developments in the poet's life. If his earlier poems sprang from and confronted the great moral mystery—why many were poor and few were rich—these later poems give voice to more abstract intricacies. Heart cries give way to multiple mysteries aching for definition. "The Tides," for instance, published in 1971, is representative of the development of Ferrini from proletarian writer to psychic explorer. It is a perfectly poised poem with all requisite profundity. Life now is "a plant of functions/the leaves events, the branches thinking,/the loam in the clay pot/the flesh around this dreaming air/the plant loves in" (the reader notes the deliberate substitution of "loves" for "lives"). Lines are extended, rhythms more variable; the imagery is no longer as simple as in the early poems, where it advanced one image or metaphor every line or two until the necessary gravity was achieved. Now the poet freely mixes symbols and moods, as his approach to life is less constrained by economic and family preoccupations, his attitude more generally spontaneous. The poems are more adventuristic, more tolerant of in-

direction, more mystical and privately symbolic. "Tongue II" from *The Hiding One* (1973), for example, is not the voicing of a class consciousness but the cabbalistic murmur of things not yet fully embodied. The ultimate fusion of the elements of his career can be seen in the eleventh section of *Ten Pound Light* (1975), which is playfully yet significantly titled after a lighthouse on the island of that name in Gloucester Harbor. It begins autobiographically, the end of a day at the frame shop: "I pull the plug out at 5/and all the nightbirds start whistling in my ears/trade is arrested/my hands forget the table/I'm in the bell throated song. . . ." Daily labor, requiring controlled effort and a subdued will, is left for the relief of pure inspiration.

Ferrini's energies during this latest period have been concentrated into an epic series called *Know Fish*, his most ambitious effort since *No Smoke*, the title itself echoing that of the earlier book. It seeks to do for Gloucester what he had done forty years previous for Lynn, and, with more installments forthcoming, it no doubt seeks to rival Olson's *Maximus Poems* as well. The initial volume consists of two sections or "books," the first of which is called "The Lady of Misbegotten Voyages" (after

Ferrini, revisiting Lynn, in December 1976 (Lynn Daily Evening Item photograph by Bob Crosby)

Our Lady of Good Voyage, protectress of the city and "muse" of Olson's *Maximus Poems*). It is a series which chronicles the present life of Gloucester against an ideal view of the city projected in the elegiac opening poem, which begins: "Once there were so many ships in the harbor/you couldnt see the Ocean . . . ," and includes letters to the local newspaper and proclamations before the city council, naming names throughout as it twits and gibes, denounces and salutes. The second section, "Da Songs," is written entirely in a pidgin Italian-American dialect ("we r da bambini ov irritashuns/wit n witout suppa—/in da Rebel is da Noble/upsettin da setuppa"). As Boston reviewer Christina Robb says, Ferrini fights his battles "in the toughest foul-weather gear he can construct out of the English language."

A third "book," called "The Navigators," appeared in 1984. It incorporates the earlier *Ten Pound Light* sequence and includes a remarkable series of dream-poems subtitled "travelling with Maximus & some others," in which Ferrini's old friend and inspiration, Charles Olson, appears as vivid a visitant as he was in life. Other notable poems are included in the volume, such as "Hand's Breath," "A Good Harbor Tale," and "Beloved Country." Ferrini's familiar theme that there is no art or poem apart from life is summarized again in the final lines of "Hand's Breath"—the title itself uniting the forces of his life, the hand of the worker-craftsman, the breath of the poet: "when speaking of a plumb line's go/living's the Poem we all know!" The volume itself concludes with a one-act play, "Base-Ball," in which one generic Gloucester family tears itself apart while rapacious real-estate developers throw dice for the community's future.

With *Know Fish* comes a new injunction to his fellow citizens: to "know fish" is to recognize the economic and historical roots of Gloucester—once the fishing capital of the Atlantic the way that Lynn was shoe capital of the world. It is also to know the place of man in the evolutionary chain at a time when fishing is threatened by offshore drilling and indiscriminate harvesting, and there could conceivably be "no fish" as there once had been "no smoke." Ferrini explains in his introduction to volume one: "only when we connect with the interior

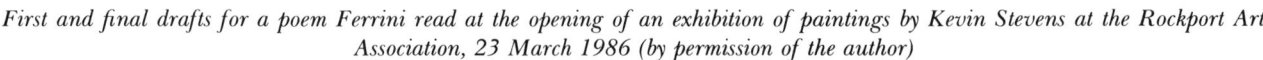

LIFE & THE ARTIFACT

Life is a mystique of zest & surrender
short as a wave coming upon another
singing water of the whole assignment-
as a facsimile or reflection is neither
& arrested in its track as a millstone
wanting the minute hand in the watch of the heart-

where am I, what am I for, who is mulling this
contest between three eternities-

or is there only one Art of these fleeting ties
that escapes the materials & the tricks of illusion-
the you between, the quicksilver hastening
to itself staying still!

        O the enlightening
soul's other eye without a surrogate
has overthrown Art, each is both at once,
& giving up the dead & artificial struggle
is the knowing self of no loses & no wins

        Vincent Ferrini

First and final drafts for a poem Ferrini read at the opening of an exhibition of paintings by Kevin Stevens at the Rockport Art Association, 23 March 1986 (by permission of the author)

fishes are we discovering and extending rules of the Earth, and thereby saving the self, the family, the city, and the planet." His vision is one grand ecology of being, in which the old fervor abides. The book is addressed once again to "the uncommon people enduring the decayings of a bankrupt order" and

> the same old shitty refrain of the sell out
> the Leaders, the fakers, don't you kick
> the hand who shoves you the minestrone,
> Jobs is all there is to go by

—which returns him full circle to the concerns of his earliest poems.

Ferrini has indefatigably lived the life of the poet for more than fifty years, a model of endurance. National reputation has eluded him, although appreciation for his accomplishments has begun to grow. Early discovery was deterred by his unfashionable commitment to Marxism in the late 1940s, by Olson's attack, by his isolation in Gloucester, and by the need to work by hand to earn a living. Largely self-taught, his mistakes are all his own, but so are his glories. He has changed as the world has changed, while remaining faithful to his roots. Despite—or because of—his romanticism, he has survived. He has written a perfect handful of honest and enduring poems. He never gave up his cherished role as social gadfly—denouncing, defending, uplifting. His career, in those terms, is one of the more remarkable.

Interviews:

Peter Anastas, "Ferrini: A Review & Dialogue," *North Shore Magazine,* 18 December 1976, pp. 6-9;

"Ferrini & McKim: A Dialog," *Stony Hills,* no. 4 (1979): 1, 13;

Mary R. Littlefield, "Ferrini: The Hometown Poet," *North Shore Magazine,* 3 February 1979, pp. 8-9.

References:

Peter Anastas, "I have the world," *North Shore '67,* 23 September 1967, p. 19;

Hugh Fox, Review of *Selected Poems, Stony Hills,* no. 1 (1977): 1;

Alan Golding, "Da Rebel n Da Noble," review of *Know Fish, Chicago Review,* 32 (Autumn 1980): 51-55;

Max Harris, Review of *Injunction, Angry Penguins* (Autumn 1944): 94;

Edward Kaplan, "Ferrini's Ordeal: Human Struggle," *Newsart,* no. 9 (August 1982): 66;

Kaplan, "Vincent Ferrini in Hell's Kitchen," in *Menu,* edited by George Myers, Jr. (Grosse Pointe Farms, Mich.: Lunchroom Press, 1985), pp. 19-21;

P. J. Laska, "The Dialectics of Poetry," review of *Know Fish, Minnesota Review,* new series 15 (Fall 1980): 128-130;

Lynn Voices Collaborative, "Know Fish: An Introduction," *Stony Hills,* no. 7 (Summer 1980): 3-4, 6; no. 9 (1981): 6;

Elizabeth McKim, Review of *Selected Poems, Stony Hills,* no. 1 (1977): 10;

Paul Metcalf, "Driving Through the Underbrush," *Parnassus,* 7 (Fall-Winter 1978): 224-251;

Wayne Charles Miller, Introduction to his *A Gathering of Ghetto Writers: Irish, Italian, Jewish, Black, and Puerto Rican* (New York: New York University Press, 1972), pp. 39-40;

Olga Peragallo, *Italian-American Authors and Their Contribution to American Literature,* edited by Anita Peragallo (New York: S. F. Vanni, 1949), pp. 99-100;

Christina Robb, "Songs from a fisher of words," review of *Know Fish, Boston Globe,* 11 April 1980, p. 37;

Dabney Stuart, "Seven Poets and a Playwright," review of *Mirandum, Poetry,* 104 (July 1964): 258-264;

Mona Van Duyn, "Conscience: Personal, Political, Philosophical," review of *Blood of the Tenement, Poetry,* 66 (August 1945): 284-289.

Papers:

Ferrini's papers are in the Literary Archives, University of Connecticut Library.

Hildegarde Flanner

(3 June 1899-   )

Karen L. Rood

BOOKS: *Young Girl and Other Poems* (San Francisco: Crocker, 1920);

Mansions: A Play in One Act (Cincinnati: Stewart & Kidd, 1920);

This Morning (New York: Shay, 1921);

A Tree in Bloom and Other Verses (San Francisco: Lantern Press, 1924);

Time's Profile (New York: Macmillan, 1929);

The White Bridge: A Play in One Act (New York & London: Appleton, Century, 1938);

If There is Time (Norfolk, Conn.: New Directions, 1942);

In Native Light (Calistoga, Cal.: Privately printed, 1970);

The Hearkening Eye, edited by A. Thomas Trusky (Boise, Idaho: Ahsahta Press/Boise State University, 1979);

A Vanishing Land (Portola Valley, Cal.: No Dead Lines, 1980);

Brief Cherishing: A Napa Valley Harvest (Santa Barbara: John Daniel, 1985).

Hildegarde Flanner, late 1920s

Hildegarde Flanner is a religious poet in an age when belief is most often coupled with doubt and a regional poet, a celebrator of the California landscape, at a time when her region as she knows it is "a vanishing land." Her poetry demonstrates the emergence of a modern sensibility: from its early romantic assurance it moves on to deal with modern doubt and disillusion. In 1979 Flanner described this evolution as a move from "romantic abstractions, possibly effective of their kind, but windy and regal" to "a smaller, stronger focus, perhaps on similar themes." She calls this focus "the worm's eye view, the pebble's eye view," yet she will not forget "God's eye view, you understand, for my earlier poetry contains religious writing which I miss now, since it was an ardent expression of my youth." While her religious sense has changed with time, it has not been lost. As she said recently, "Sophistication eventually takes the place of an early lack of questioning. Whenever one has been imbued with an early sense of religious feeling, the feeling remains even if it isn't expressed." As Flanner's faith evolved so did her concepts of nature. While her early poems treat natural objects abstractly as symbols of higher meanings, by midcareer her nature poems focus on the particularity of the thing itself, and still later her poems mourn the destruction of the land she has celebrated. As she says in *A Vanishing Land* (1980), an essay written in the late 1950s, "even the earth itself is altered. That which overtakes me now, threatens to become a memory."

Born in Indianapolis, June Hildegarde Flanner was the third daughter of Francis William and Mary-Ellen Hockett Flanner. Frank Flanner, a businessman who had some success with real estate, "would have been a philanthropist" if he had been wealthy, his youngest daughter suggests. Shortly after the turn of the century, concerned with the plight of Negroes in Indianapolis, he established Flanner House, a community center that offered tuberculosis and dental clinics, laundry facilities, and a day nursery. First located in a small house, the center still exists in new, much larger quarters. Mary-Ellen Flanner, who as a child had played Little Eva in a traveling-show production of *Uncle Tom's Cabin,* was one of the founders of little theater in Indianapolis, where she directed and acted in such roles as Deirdre and Kathleen ni Houlihan. She imparted to her daughters a love of the arts. The oldest, Mary Emma (called Marie) became a musician and composer. Janet Flanner became well known for her Paris letters published in the *New Yorker.* While primarily a poet, Hildegarde Flanner is also an essayist and the author of one-act plays, including *Mansions* (1920) and *The White Bridge* (1938).

As the youngest child, Hildegarde Flanner remembered later, "I was never an initiator, a rebel; I only followed and sat with decorum where I was set down, lamentably biddable, and a sweet, true comfort to my mother." She attended Tudor Hall, a private girls' school in Indianapolis, from kindergarten until 1909, when the family went abroad so that Marie Flanner could study piano in Berlin with Ossip Gabrilovitch, Samuel Clemens's son-in-law. Janet Flanner said later that she and her younger sister did not care for Berlin and that their mother "equipped [Hildegarde Flanner] with a large doll which she didn't love very much but which she dragged about." After spending the winter of 1909-1910 in Berlin, the Flanners went to Munich and traveled in England and Scotland before returning to Indianapolis.

Hildegarde Flanner continued at Tudor Hall until her father's death in 1912, when she transferred to Short Ridge High School. After her high-school graduation, she spent one year at Sweet Briar College in Sweet Briar, Virginia, and in 1919 she went on to the University of California at Berkeley, where she studied poetry writing with Witter Bynner. "Young Girl," a group of poems she wrote at Berkeley, was awarded the university's Emily Chamberlain Cook Prize for 1920 by judges Edgar Lee Masters, Harold L. Bruce, and Paul Shorey. Flanner and her mother spent summer 1920 in Norwalk, Connecticut, and winter 1920-

1921 in New York City to be near Janet Flanner. While Hildegarde Flanner was in New York, H. S. Crocker of San Francisco published for private distribution *Young Girl and Other Poems* (1920) in a limited edition, with an introduction and decorations by Porter Garnett. She had not known about arrangements for the publication of this book, poems from which had first appeared in the *University of California Chronicle,* the *Occident,* and the *New York Tribune.*

The poems in *Young Girl and Other Poems* are the autobiographical depictions of a young woman's search for self-knowledge and knowledge of God. The "Young Girl" section, composed of "This Morning," "Garden" (a sequence of seven flower poems), "Mood," and "Confession," begins with an expression of the poet's sense of God's mystery in nature, where "the studious earth,"

> Thinking what flowers to speak in next,
> Moves restlessly with small, wise birds
> Who read the tucks in the moss,
> The symbols on the beetle-wings,
> And the comedies on pink and yellow pebbles,
> Which I am too tall to see.

Other poems also seek meaning in nature, but more typically, as in the "Garden" poems, the speaker sees in nature not symbols of external meanings but reflections of her own feelings and perceptions. For example, in "Dianthus" she remembers that her grandmother, who "Did Vergil into French/And then had seven children" used to pick and wear dianthus, and she concludes, "I shall not pick you Dianthus." In "Confession," a love poem, the speaker chooses this world over heaven. She describes the bliss imparted by angels, but concludes, "I would rather live blessedly with you/Than go expectantly to heaven." The first of the other poems, "Discovery," also celebrates the physical—the speaker's discovery of her own beauty. Her aunts have always said, "She has a gentle soul/And mild," but, the poem concludes:

> And that is what came of listening
> To aunts who always lied.
> They never told me that I was
> White armed and amber-eyed.

While the poems in this volume are slight, they were recognized for their honesty. In his introduction Porter Garnett praised them for their "spontaneous and valid transcription of emotion" expressed in "naive but illuminating diction." The "Voices of Living Poets" column in the March 1921 issue of *Current Opinion* quoted four stanzas of "Discovery" and reprinted two of the "Garden" poems, "Nasturtium" and "Dianthus," in their entirety, commenting that "Few makers of contemporary verse have attained such perfection of concentrated expression in which temper and vision combine with such clarity and balance. . . ." Oscar Williams, reviewing a group of first books by young poets for the July 1921 issue of *Poetry*, found Flanner's the most promising, praising the "quaint simplicity" of the "delicate" poems. Yet he also said that "the book lacks music," preferring "Communion," Flanner's first poem to be published in *Poetry* (February 1921), in which he found "a hint of music and even strength."

"Communion" demonstrates the qualities that Williams detects in it and is far less autobiographical than earlier poems. While the poem is undoubtedly an expression of the young poet's strong religious faith, its report of a mystical experience that leads the speaker to assert, "I have spoken with the dead," is not based on any personal experience, says Flanner. The rhythm and piling up of images in such lines as the description of the voices of the dead are the beginning of a new development in Flanner's style, as she employs visual images to describe sound:

> Their voices are as white
> As altar candles. Their voices are as gold as wheat,
> And clustered in the dark their words are sweet,
> As ripened fruit. Their voices are the color of dim
>   rain
> Over grass where spring has lain.

Unlike the speakers of earlier poems, who seem complacent even in their assertions, this one demands that the reader believe her. She has heard the dead "sing until/The cup of silence fell in two and lay/Broken by beauty of what dead men say," and what she has learned gives her a special power:

> There is no loveliness I cannot see.
> There is no wall too stern for me.
> There is no doubt that can withstand
> The lifted symbol of my hand.
>
> I know an ancient shibboleth:
> I pass, for I have talked with Death!

While the poem's conclusion is not original, "Communion" represents in subject and technique a move away from Flanner's "delicate" apprentice work toward her more deeply felt later poems. She

Front cover by Frederick Monhoff for Hildegarde Flanner's 1921 pamphlet (courtesy of the University of Chicago Library)

recently described it as perhaps "a slight step forward."

"Communion" was first collected in *This Morning* (1921), the third pamphlet in Frank Shay's Salvo series, which also included a small collection of poems by Edna St. Vincent Millay. The cover for *This Morning* was designed by Frederick Monhoff, a 1921 graduate of Berkeley, whom Flanner married in 1926. This volume was the first of several Monhoff, an artist and architect, would illustrate for his future wife. In addition to "Communion" and twelve of the fourteen poems first collected in *Young Girl and Other Poems*, *This Morning* contains four other poems, none of which has the maturity of "Communion." Like Flanner's other early poems, they demonstrate her mastery of poetic conventions, but they are the work of a young poet who has yet to find her own voice.

In the September 1921 issue of *Poetry* Flanner made a discovery that was to affect significantly the direction her poetry would take: Edward Sapir's review of *Poems of Gerard Manley Hopkins*, edited by Robert Bridges. Although this first collection of Hopkins's poetry had been published in Great Britain in 1918, it had not found a publisher in the United States, and Hopkins was still relatively unknown in this country. Sapir's review was not entirely positive, but it sparked Flanner's interest, and she wrote to Humphrey Milford in London to order a copy of the book. The first fruit of her reading was a laudatory essay about Hopkins for the *Double Dealer* (August-September 1924). This essay was followed some years later by a review of the augmented edition of this volume for the *New Republic* (4 February 1931). Flanner is still proud to be one of Hopkins's earliest American supporters. While Flanner's poems are not imitative of Hopkins's, his poetry seems to have made her aware of new possibilities for poetic technique and to have led her to develop tendencies already apparent in her own work, such as the type of rhythm and imagery she had experimented with in "Communion." Her description in her 1924 essay of Hopkins's powers of observation might also be read as a statement of her aspirations for herself as a poet: "He was extravagantly alive to shades of sound, angles of light, and the passing of colours in the sky. He took pleasure in the quaint and lovable, the inconsequential and shy oddnesses which, like grass, are common and, like grass, unnoticed."

After their winter in New York Hildegarde Flanner and her mother returned to Indianapolis. In 1922 they decided to settle permanently in California. Mary-Ellen Flanner sold her house in Indianapolis and shipped its entire contents to Berkeley, where she bought a small house in the northern hilly section of the city. Hildegarde Flanner returned to her studies at Berkeley. She later wrote, in her introduction to *The Hearkening Eye* (1979), that her years at Berkeley were "a good time in which to begin to be conscious" and that she did not need to go to Paris to want to become a poet: "For me, at least, it was necessary only to be aware of visible things against which there was no rebellion. . . . Nor were, as yet, the most famous and coercive poetic influences of our time strong enough to shame the young poet out of his own shy sense of art. Our Father in Hopkins was not one to do that." In an atmosphere relatively free of the modernist influences of Pound and Eliot, she continued, working within traditional poetic forms, to refine her own poetic voice, but her second stay in Berkeley was to last only a year.

On 17 September 1923 the Flanners' house and all their belongings were destroyed in the great Berkeley fire, which in two hours destroyed sixty city blocks. The Flanners escaped in time and spent the winter of 1923-1924 in San Diego with Mary-Ellen Flanner's brother. Hildegarde Flanner's memoir of the fire, "Wildfire: Berkeley, 1923," was published in the 23 September 1974 issue of the *New Yorker*. A much earlier literary response to the fire was "To My Books Who Perished by Fire," an Elizabethan sonnet that first appeared in the September 1927 issue of *Poetry* and was later collected in *Time's Profile* (1929).

Late in 1924 appeared *A Tree in Bloom and Other Verses,* a small collection of poems that had first appeared in such periodicals as *Poetry,* the *Yale Review,* and the *Bookman,* as well as in "The Conning Tower," Franklin Pierce Adams's column in the *New York World.* The sixteen-page book, with a decoration by Frederick Monhoff, was published in a limited edition of 500 copies by the Lantern Press in San Francisco.

The first poems in the book are nine sonnets that demonstrate both her increased mastery of traditional poetic forms and her increased facility at developing and sustaining her own characteristic image patterns. "To a Tree in Bloom" gives images of whiteness and stillness, which characterize many of the poems in this book, a religious connotation. The Elizabethan sonnet begins with the assertion that "There is no silence lovelier than the one/That flowers upon a flowering tree at night." The sestet suggests that the Annunciation must have occurred under such a tree and concludes "It may be that a single petal fell,/Heavy with sorrow that it could not tell." Faith is not always so easy in the religious poems. The next sonnet is a prayer for an end to doubts, to the "burning wilderness in me," in which the speaker asks that "Tranquility alight upon my soul/Like a great bird upon a luminous bough!" The sonnets most frequently singled out for praise, when three appeared in this volume and later when all nine were published in *Time's Profile,* are Flanner's "Sonnets in Quaker Language." Genevieve Taggard, who praised Flanner's understanding of the form's demands in all nine sonnets, pointed out that "the quaint language of the Quaker sonnets covers all the stern architecture as a flowering vine might, with unconcerned loveliness" (*New York Herald Tribune Books,* 8 February 1925). The old-fashioned Quaker language of these Elizabethan love sonnets imparts a sense of restraint which suits the poems' subjects: not the ecstasy of the first moments of love but the conflicting demands of past and present, fears and desires, that the lovers must resolve. A far different nature poem from "To a Tree in Bloom" and other nature poems in the book is "Moment," in which the speaker says she saw a deer who suddenly ran away, "And his going was absolute,/Like the shattering of icicles/In the wind." Taggard found "An intensity somewhat like that in H. D. [Hilda Doolittle], only more splendid," in this poem, and "Moment" is more similar to an imagist or modernist poem than Flanner's other early work. The speaker describes what she saw, and, to use T. S. Eliot's term, she finds an "objective correlative" ("the shattering of icicles/In the wind") to describe the emotion that the deer's running away caused within her. There is no message for her in his action; she does not reach after a higher meaning. "Moment" is an early step away from what Flanner would later call her "windy and regal" abstractions and "those exhilarating, tempting runs of imagery and lyrical impulse in which the mind of a young poet was caught like a charmed fish in a stream."

Yet it was precisely the "runs of imagery and lyrical impulse" that contemporary reviewers found most praiseworthy in Flanner's poetry. In a review entitled "A True Poet" (*Saturday Review*, 25 April 1925) William Rose Benét called *A Tree in Bloom* "a slight, unobtrusive book" that has "more fundamental worth than in many more clamorous volumes," and he found in the poems numerous examples of "a delicate mastery of phrase, a beautiful precision of workmanship." While he suggested that Flanner's work may well prove "fugitive" and self-conscious, he concluded, "Yet there is also a concentrated emotion that partakes of the fine frenzy of true poetry, an energy of feeling that makes luminous the fitting word and the fitting phrase." While Taggard suggested that Flanner was too often "muffled by convention," she too found much to praise in the poem's imagery, and Sara Bard Field, who saw the faults in the poems to be those of "immaturity," devoted her entire review in the May 1925 issue of *Poetry* to a discussion of the poems' language. While the 1920s was a time of much poetic experiment, reviews such as these are reminders that traditional romantic and religious lyrics were still being written and admired. Flanner's lyrics of the 1920s were of that time, not anachronistic echoes of an earlier century.

After their winter in San Diego, Hildegarde and Mary-Ellen Flanner stayed briefly in Hollywood while a house was being built for them in nearby Pasadena. They stayed in this house for only a year, however, for in early 1926 Mary-Ellen Flanner bought a place she found more to her liking in Altadena, a suburb in the foothills above Pasadena. Their new home was an old mission-style garden of nearly half an acre surrounded by an eight-foot cypress hedge. Within the garden were three cottages, one of which Hildegarde Flanner and Frederick Monhoff took for their own home

after they were married on 29 June 1926. While Monhoff commuted to Los Angeles, where he taught design at the Otis Art Institute, a department of the Los Angeles County Museum, and worked for Los Angeles County as an architect (becoming principal architect in 1950), Hildegarde Flanner settled into the place that was to be her home for the next thirty-six years and wrote poetry that was to draw increasingly on the environment in which she found herself. (She describes her years in Altadena in "Roots and Hedges," a memoir published in the 4 December 1978 issue of the *New Yorker*.)

While Porter Garnett attempted to establish a case for calling Flanner a California poet in his introduction to *Young Girl,* the only justification for calling the poems in her first three books California poems is the fact that most of them were written there. The mainly generalized subjects of the early nature poems are not uniquely Californian. As Flanner says in *A Vanishing Land* (1980), "Romantic enthusiasm comes quickly, but insight into the unexpected delicacies and extremities of the dry western earth, a taste for its arid and cryptic literalness, and the excitement of its antiquity where the massive inner centuries have left their tracks in view, such familiarity comes only with living close enough to the earth and long enough, and under the touch of its very physical and poetic spirit of place."

Her deepening insight into her region is apparent in many of the new poems in *Time's Profile* (1929), her first large, commercially published collection, which, in addition to many poems written after 1925, includes poems from her first three books. Once again, the poems in *Time's Profile* are complemented by Monhoff's illustrations.

The new sonnets "Pacific Winter," "White Magnolia Blossom," "Quietly, Suddenly," "The Owl," and "The Snail" might well be set in Flanner's Altadena garden. While these poems focus on more specific objects in specific settings, they and other new nature poems in *Time's Profile* continue to exhibit characteristics of Flanner's earlier poems. The piling up of lyrical images, as in this description of the bee in "White Magnolia Blossom," is reminiscent not only of Flanner's early poems but, in its word order and internal off-rhymes, of Hopkins:

The rolling, staggering bee, the honey-fronted,
Shoves his gypsy face into the pollen,
Thrusts and wallows with delight unblunted
While over him the yellow snow has fallen
And under him the stamens deeply shaken
Tremble.

While in some of the earliest poems Flanner's lyrical runs of images seem to have been merely exhibitions of the poet's facility with language, these lines parallel in both visual and aural senses the movement of the bee. In poems such as this one, Flanner seems more in command of her craft than ever.

Some poems in *Time's Profile* follow earlier patterns of personifying nature or drawing higher, religious significance from it. Yet the new religious poems, like those in *A Tree in Bloom*, often depict longing for faith or faith well considered and hard-won, rather than easy, unquestioning belief. Louise Bogan, who had read only Flanner's first two books before coming to *Time's Profile*, remarked in her *New Republic* review (18 September 1929) that "speculation concerning time, space and a vanishing personal deity has been substituted for nebulous adolescent mysticism."

Among the most-successful poems in the book are, once again, the love poems. The "Sonnets in Quaker Language" sequence, now expanded from three poems to nine, was frequently mentioned by reviewers. "A Wreath for Ashes," a long love poem first published in the September 1927 issue of *Poetry* magazine, is also successful, as it creates a fresh approach to an old theme: the insignificance of human emotions and endeavors in the face of eternity. The poem begins with the poet's addressing the loved one who would separate from her, negating the love they have shared:

> Unsung, unsigned upon the dust of time
>   Shall we sink down, we two, and sift together,
> My song forgotten, and your lovely page
>   Blank in eternity's effacing weather?
>
> Will the rain waver, and the vacant snow
>   Replace the beauty of a path we trod,
> And the wind rustle and slip over us,
>   Lost between stars upon our way to God?
>
> How tragic anger, then, how futile hate,
>   When two dazed atoms, wafted out of sight,
> Vainly recall that such a thing as love
>   Existed this side of eternal night.

Given such a large perspective and facing the loss of the one she would have face an eternity with her, the poet is "bereft of any word to utter"; she is "widow to a word." Yet she forces herself to say "farewell," and the poem ends, not with reconciliation, but with a narrowing of focus that allows the poet to look away from the frightening vastness of eternity toward the comforting particulars of her own environment and to remind the loved one of what he has lost:

> When winter throws himself on summer's breast
>   And there begets dim snow and bitter hail,
> May you remember how the fields of home
>   Are sweet with lupin and the song of quail.
>
> ....
>
> When winter runs aloft his sombre column
>   To fly the tattered snow and ragged sleet,
> May you remember how another winter
>   Let up a host of freesias to your feet.

Not only has the lover left a warm climate for a colder one, but he has, by cutting himself off from the speaker's love, made himself one of the "dazed atoms" wandering "in eternity's effacing weather" described at the beginning of the poem. Such effective use of sustained metaphor is characteristic of many of the poems in *Time's Profile*.

Reviews for *Time's Profile* were somewhat mixed, depending in part on whether or not the reviewers were sympathetic to Flanner's experiments with language. The brief anonymous review in the *New York Times Book Review* (27 October 1929) dismissed her poems as "rococo" although it conceded that "Miss Flanner achieves many beautiful effects." Another brief review, in *New York Herald Tribune Books* (8 December 1929), praised Flanner's "direct forthright song," with "its thought ... clearly expressed, its language shaped for beauty and melody of phrase." Reviewing the volume for the *Nation* (13 November 1929), Eda Lou Walton asserted that it placed Flanner "among the recognized lyricists of America" and praised Flanner's ability to find "a poetic intensity in the religious search itself, and without denying her poet's heritage of doubt." While Walton sometimes heard echoes of Hopkins and Blake in Flanner's poems, she concluded that "Miss Flanner is not an imitator. Her moments of vision, like her techniques, are her own." Louise Bogan, in her review for the *New Republic* (18 September 1929), expressed admiration for a number of poems but suggested that "many poems in this book resolve into a collection of phrases." She judges the volume as perhaps too ambitious, too inclusive a collection of Flanner's work to date: "Were there fewer poems in the book, Miss Flanner's conspicuous successes would be more apparent." George Dillon's review for *Poetry* (December 1929) echoes Bogan's reservations in its assertion that some good lines "seem the merest idle acrobatics of fancy." Yet Dillon also finds much to praise in *Time's Profile* and concludes that the book's best poems make it "an interesting phase in Miss Flanner's still unpredictable career."

Throughout the 1920s and 1930s Flanner's poems appeared frequently in such periodicals as *Poetry*, the *Bookman*, the *Yale Review*, the *Nation*, *Saturday Review*, and the *New Republic* as well as in a number of smaller-circulation little magazines. Her reviews, essays, and travel articles about the Southwest also appeared in a number of periodicals. In November 1934 she was awarded *Poetry's* Guarantors Prize for "A Ballad and Lyrics," a group of six poems that had appeared in the January 1934 issue of *Poetry*. Two of these six poems, "Prayer for This Day" and "Driving Clock," were collected in *If There is Time* (1942), while "Ascent" had already appeared in *Time's Profile*. Flanner has not yet included the other three poems—"Orpha's Song," "Towers Like These," and "Ballad of Santa Monica"—in a collection of her poetry.

Despite her continued ability to place her poems in prestigious periodicals throughout the 1930s, Flanner did not have another collection of her poems published until 1942 when James Laughlin of New Directions included *If There is Time* in the Poet of the Month series. A brief pamphlet containing only twenty-four poems, *If There is Time*, by its very brevity, serves as a more effective showcase for Flanner's mature verse than *Time's Profile*, in which old and new poems are arranged thematically rather than chronologically. The poems in *If There is Time*, as the title suggests, were selected and arranged to suggest Flanner's preoccupation with time in its various aspects and implications, a preoccupation already apparent in *Time's Profile* (although the title of that volume seems intended more to indicate that the book is a profile of Flanner's career to date than to suggest a thematic unity in the poems).

The nature poems in *If There is Time* are still more firmly rooted in the actual. "Slow Boone" describes the long process by which the poet truly comes to own the land. It may have been "Got by our fathers' guns and Paiutes slain," but it will not be ours until we admit that "truth is deeper than the battlefield," and

Say all sure things that frenzy overtakes
Win to the greenest goal by their own powers
Say patience like the burning of a rock
Turns passion, then will the land be ours.

Then will the native heart be cleared for use,

The horny miles run inward to the mind
And the blood's visionary length at last
Be in the poet's actual vein refined.

Yet even as the poet possesses the land, it is changing, being destroyed by the very people who have been lured to California by its beauty. In "12 O'Clock Freight" the train tracks pass through "choking orange groves abandoned to/No rain and flaky pestilence of scale.//And then by palmy drives and boulevards/Where stucco gleams beside the carob-tree,/And Spanish patios in rain enclose/Lone hearts from Iowa and Kankakee." "Noon on Almeda Street" depicts an earthly hell created by man's materialism, where the only immortality resides in the sun, which "when it shines on traffic has a look/Of loaded radiance that might explode." The sound of horns creates a sense of foreboding, "For we have heard delirium in a claxon,/Seen revelation lit on chromium," and, the poet concludes:

For in this noon there is no light like light,
(Oh, tell us, dark on asphalt, of the sun)
But brightness spawning upon dirty glass,
But fever smoking at meridian,

But men and women riding in their graves
With hands upon a wheel they cannot keep
Clear in the rapt confusion of the crowd,
Crowd and the fate of motion and of sleep.

Other poems, written in the decade before World War II, reflect the fear that man will employ still more fearful means of destruction; yet nature, for all the consolation it may offer the poet, is not just a benign, innocent victim of man's carelessness and greed but, in poems such as "Hawk Is A Woman," "Flight," "Never Ask Why," and "Rattlesnake," a source of terror and seemingly senseless violence:

Never ask why, between dark hunger
And the last bloody sob of terror poured
On dust, never ask why this thing is so.
Always the fetid fury of the lion,
Always the lost, on-lilies-feeding doe.

Man's destructive impulses are part of a larger phenomenon. Yet, for all the imperfections of life on earth, "Let Us Believe" expresses the hope that "Flesh, that frail prophet that survives all fates,/Will, if it matters, make a more human race," and "Poem" (retitled "Sonnet: 1933" in *In Native Light*, 1970) asserts that in the face of natural and human disasters: "faint at intervals, benign and frail/A courage whispers, just this side of fate,/*Cling earth-*

ward, inward do not abdicate!" For, as the poet says in "Prayer for This Day," if perfect faith is now impossible, the poet may still discover faith in the mundane:

> If there is time to will
> Prayer from a heart too long by reason fondled,
> ....
> . . . We ask no vision, no heavenly light,
> But simple faith, like faith of grass, in earth,
> And seed's old dream against the night, the night.

Among the poems in *If There is Time* are two that Flanner singled out as personal favorites when they were republished in *The Hearkening Eye* (1979). In "Smith Brothers' Lumber Shed" the poet, finding a dead northern wild flower clinging to a tree cut down in Oregon, envisions the forest from which it came and meditates on the slow creative process of nature and the swiftness with which man may cut it short. Of "Letter to an Old Home," in which the poet remembers listening to a whip-poorwill when she was a child, Flanner commented in 1979, "It is close to the experience it deals with, it takes hold of it and does not let go, or so I believe." The poem succeeds early in creating an effective depiction of the child's complex feelings about the bird's song:

> That bird can sing a most devouring note,
> Can sing you clean without a pause for grace,
> Leave only your cold mortal marrow somehow
> And the white hark of a startled face
> Yes, and your dry throat gritty on your breath.

And the poem sustains the metaphor effortlessly:

> I never was so fed upon by music
> As when, a chilly child in the large night,
> That song sprang on me from a fence corner,
> And sucked my being out in hard delight.

Yet, as the poet realizes, this seemingly perfect metaphor is only an approximation of the feeling she experienced so long ago. With the passage of time the poet has paradoxically both lost and kept the moment she remembers, part of a larger paradox that links death and survival, beauty and fear:

> Time cannot resurrect nor would I wish
> Ever to lose the dying I took alive
> When hungry revelation ate me up
> But missed a morsel, panting to survive.

"Letter to an Old House" illustrates the relationship

to nature that is only advocated and hoped for in "Poem."

If There is Time was Flanner's finest collection to date, illustrating clearly her move to a simpler style in which metaphor is more controlled yet still capable of creating striking impressions and expressing her more limited, but still hopeful, beliefs. Yet, despite the book's strengths, reviews were less positive than those for Flanner's earlier books. Louis Untermeyer stated in the *Yale Review* (December 1942): "A lyric poet of our own time, Hildegarde Flanner, a 'conservative' who has never received just praise, is represented at her best in 'If There is Time.'" Brewster Ghiselin and Harvey Breit are more representative in praising Flanner's technical skills but finding something lacking, what Ghiselin called a "lack of care for the integration of the spirit in terms that meet at the same time the demands of its own nature and of the outer world." Breit sees the lack of "the notion of necessity which promotes a tension, a drama, an excitement, a bewilderment, a form."

A change in taste, begun before the start of Flanner's career as a poet but accomplished largely between the publications of *Time's Profile* and *If There is Time,* had influenced the way in which reviewers and academics looked at traditional poetry. All too often modernist poetry was judged good by definition while traditional poetry, even when it expressed a modern point of view, was viewed as old-fashioned and not worthy of serious consideration. Hildegarde Flanner's poetry, while it still had its admirers, seemed to be going out of style, and over the next three decades she devoted more attention to other interests, writing fewer poems and submitting still fewer for publication. On 15 March 1941 her son, Jan Flanner Monhoff (who later changed his name to John), was born, and later in the decade both her mother and her oldest sister died. In 1950 and 1955 she visited Janet Flanner in France, and notable exceptions to her poetic silence were the poems, some inspired by her visit and some set in the West, that appeared in issues of *Botteghe Oscure* in 1951-1953 and 1958.

By the late 1950s the concerns about the environment that Flanner had voiced in poems as early as the 1930s had grown larger and more insistent. As she says in *A Vanishing Land,* from her garden in the hills she used to be able to see the Los Angeles City Hall eleven miles away, mountains as far away as sixty miles, and Catalina Island in the Pacific, but now, more and more often, "all those remarkable harmonies and differences of texture fade and flatten, while a horizon of spectral

Janet and Hildegarde Flanner, Frederick and John Monhoff at the Hôtel Continental in Paris, 1955

murk advances and takes the valley from below and to the east, flows up arroyos, climbs the foothills, surrounds and fills my own garden, and goes on west along the mountains, obscuring them from sight behind a mobile, drifting wall." Disturbed not only by what urbanization and industrialization were doing to the native flora and fauna but also by its adverse effect on native arts and architecture, the Monhoffs moved north in 1962 to the Napa Valley, where they built a new house on an old ranch near Calistoga. Later they enlarged the original ranch house for John Monhoff and his family. Flanner describes the ranch and the experience of tending a strong-willed goat in "Jacinto" (*New Yorker,* 5 October 1981; collected in *Brief Cherishing,* 1985).

The new environment provided settings for new poems, but, when Flanner put together her first collection in twenty-eight years, she included mainly poems written in the 1930s and the early 1940s. The purpose of the privately printed *In Native Light* (1970) was not to bring Hildegarde Flanner's poems back before the public eye but to share with friends the engravings Frederick Monhoff had made to illustrate some of her poems. In her preface Flanner says that these engravings "are not illustrations only, but although based on the details of the poems, they are subtle miniatures of the landscape of another mind. The engravings are the real motive for this book; the poems are the remoter cause." John Monhoff helped in the production of the volume by doing the lithography.

Eight of the thirty poems in this volume were first collected in *If There is Time,* the only one of Flanner's books for which Monhoff provided no illustrations. Many of the other poems are collected in *In Native Light* for the first time, and some later poems (including "Traveller A-Maze" from *Botteghe Oscure*) are included without illustration. Yet, despite her decision to add these poems, Flanner makes clear in her preface that the book's contents were largely determined by the engravings, not by her "present feelings" about the poems: "Certain ones of them were once truly contemporary and are now lyrical keepsakes." She speaks with pride, however, of "Tin Cans at Keeler," written in 1932 but published here for the first time, a poem that she says "may well be the senior anti-litter poem of our scandalously littered century." "Traveller A-Maze *à bord le S.S. Flandre*" is a California poem

Engravings by Frederick Monhoff to illustrate (top) "To Be in Rain" and "A Way to Know"; (bottom) "High Stream's End" and "Valley Quail" by Hildegarde Flanner (by permission of the author)

disguised as a travel poem. The poet aboard ship looks at the sea and sees, in a mirage, California, the land she most possesses and about which she writes her best poems. "On a Hill," in which the speaker walks up a firebreak on Holly's Hill, concludes with a metaphoric definition of the poet's place in the California landscape: "A grain of sensibility in native light,/Barely lodged upon a granite hill." Despite her initial reservations about the contents of *In Native Light,* near the end of her preface Flanner states, "I discover, while being close to them after long reserve, that I have a grateful attachment. In them I can see again the fascination and difficult attractions of the earth I was looking at for the first time so many years ago with surprise, concentration and sheer lyrical greed."

In 1979 A. Thomas Trusky selected thirty-three of Flanner's poems to be published in Ahsahta Press's Modern Poetry of the West series. Nearly one-third of the poems in *The Hearkening Eye* (its title a reference to Flanner's career-long tendency to employ imagery relating to one sense to describe the impressions related by another) were originally collected in *If There is Time.* The collection also includes "Moment" from *A Tree in Bloom,* "Dictionary" from *Time's Profile,* two poems from *In Native Light,* and three of the western poems that had been published in *Botteghe Oscure* during the 1950s. In her introduction to the volume Flanner mentions "Moon Poem," a recent poem "which begins with the moon as I often see it, rising just beyond the woods very close to my home. In this poem something strange happened, something frightening, in fact, for the clear light of the moon turned into the light of dread that illuminates mankind in our time." In "Moon Poem" the speaker begins by stating natural facts but goes on to assume some sort of relationship between herself and the moon, half expecting the moon to acknowledge her existence and reflect her feelings:

> Naturally it was the naked moon
> That lay in naked trees in evening woods,
> Only the naked moon gives half her light
> And lets the rest seep downward to the roots
> While I am waiting. But she did not rise.

The speaker calls on the moon to rise, and when it fails to rise further, she feels "Bristles of animal fear stand on my scalp." In the second stanza she

Hildegarde Flanner, Frederick Monhoff, and a friend, 1970s

189

realizes that she has equated the moon with her grief, and that for her it is no longer a natural phenomenon but a symbol of something personal and spiritual:

> My error to call it the moon, my grief,
> Rather, some weary spiritual light
> That wastes from the lives of men away,
> A mortal light, a light of dread.
> Whatever it is it suffers for us,
> Let us give it a suffering name,
> Give it a holy suffering name
> As it goes down, as it goes out
> And the cold fire
>   relinquishes its flame.

Nature plays a similar role in "In Memory," an elegy in which the speaker calls up images from nature to express feelings she cannot put into other words:

> Joy is a season of short grass,
> And death must be believed,
> And here we stand, here we look up
> Into the eyes of a tall man we love, trying
> To say good-by, the word that has no mercy
> And will not be deceived.
> Speak for us earth, we cannot.

She concludes by asking "rough orchard bough and ever-lasting vine" to "speak truth to our friend/As to one we cannot do without,/And left the majesty of your buds/Against all dying."

Flanner's most-recent book, *Brief Cherishing: A Napa Valley Harvest* (1985), is a collection of four essays, once again illustrated with wood engravings by Frederick Monhoff. A poetic evocation of the Napa Valley landscape and a chronicle of the Monhoffs' efforts to preserve it, the volume is also a love story of a long and happy marriage and a memorial to Frederick Monhoff, who died recently. As May Sarton commented, "in the end what shines through it all is love." For Kay Boyle, the book confirmed Flanner's creation of "her own moving legend of the land, a legend in which plant and fern proclaim by their mere presence a gracious lineage, and trees are inherited nobility. . . ." Janet Lewis's foreword to *Brief Cherishing* contains what is perhaps the most cogent assessment of Hildegarde Flanner's strengths as both poet and prose writer: "She writes with wit and freshness, 'an unpretentious grace,' an ease of colloquialism and an extraordinary sense of language, of centuries of culture—oriental as well as western—behind her natural way of speaking. Tender, and never sentimental, very sharp, and wonderfully indignant at the foolish behavior of the human race, and greatly sad at the tragedy of some human choices—like war."

Hildegarde Flanner said recently that she has "never wanted to sound like anyone else"; yet, while she likes to write about "what's happening around me" and she now feels "pretty well rooted" in California, she realizes that "some of my poems are definitely of a twentieth-century woman." Her poetic voice is most often meditative and personal; her finest poems tend to be love poems or intimate perceptions of well-known landscapes. Yet, the strength of Flanner's best poetry lies in its ability to express the twentieth-century dilemma in original, and apt, phrases, in images that surprise and delight the mind with unexpected parallels and equations.

Charles Henri Ford
(10 February 1913-   )

Karen L. Rood

See also the Ford entry in *DLB 4, American Writers in Paris, 1920-1939*.

BOOKS: *The Young and Evil,* by Ford and Parker Tyler (Paris: Obelisk Press, 1933; New York: Arno Press, 1975);

A Pamphlet of Sonnets (Majorca: Caravel Press, 1936);

The Garden of Disorder and Other Poems (London: Europa Press, 1938; Norfolk, Conn.: New Directions, 1938);

ABC's (Prairie City, Ill.: James A. Decker, 1940);

Charles Henri Ford

The Overturned Lake (Cincinnati: Little Man Press, 1941);

Poems for Painters (New York: View Editions/Vanguard, 1945);

The Half-Thoughts, the Distances of Pain (New York: Prospero Pamphlets, 1947);

Sleep in a Nest of Flames (Norfolk, Conn.: New Directions, 1949);

Spare Parts (New York: Horizon Press, 1966);

Silver Flower Coo (New York: Kulchur Press, 1968);

Flag of Ecstasy: Selected Poems, edited by Edward B. Germain (Los Angeles: Black Sparrow Press, 1972);

7 Poems (Kathmandu, Nepal: Bardo Matrix, 1974);

Om Krishna I: Special Effects (Cherry Valley, N.Y.: Cherry Valley Editions, 1979);

Om Krishna II: From the Sickroom of the Walking Eagles (Cherry Valley, N.Y.: Cherry Valley Editions, 1981);

Om Krishna III: Secret Haiku (New York: Red Ozier Press, 1982);

Haiku & Imprints I (Kathmandu, Nepal: Operation Minotaur, 1984);

Handshakes from Heaven (Paris: Handshake Editions, 1985);

Haiku & Imprints II (Kathmandu, Nepal: Operation Minotaur, 1985);

Emblems of Arachne (New York: Catchword Papers, 1986).

OTHER: "Letter from the Provinces," in *Readies for Bob Brown's Machine,* edited by Bob Brown (Cagnes-sur-Mer: Roving Eye Press, 1931), pp. 132-133;

"Displeasure in an Orchard," "Color Cold on Your Lips," "Morning," and "Sonnet," in *Americans Abroad: An Anthology,* edited by Peter Neagoe (The Hague: Servire, 1932), pp. 158-161;

"April 12: Algeria—Frenchman Shoots Errant Wife in Algeria," "December 3: U.S.A.—Thanksgiving Bounty," and "December 11: U.S.A.—Local Strikes all over U.S.," in *365 Days,* edited by Kay Boyle, Laurence Vail, and Nina Conarain (London: Cape, 1936; New

York: Harcourt, Brace, 1936), pp. 134, 419, 427;

"Bed-Time Ballad," in *New Directions in Prose & Poetry*, no. 3, edited by James Laughlin (Norfolk, Conn.: New Directions, 1938), n. pag.;

"Diagriphos" and "An Afternoon with André Breton," in *New Directions in Prose & Poetry*, no. 4, edited by Laughlin (Norfolk, Conn.: New Directions, 1939), pp. 113-115;

"ABC's" and "How to Write a Chainpoem," by Ford; "Chainpoems," edited, with lines, by Ford; Louis Aragon, "Le Linertinage (Fragments)" and "Treatise on Style (Fragment)," translated by Ford, in *New Directions in Prose & Poetry*, no. 5, edited by Laughlin, Edgar Kauffman, Jr., and Nicolas Calas (Norfolk, Conn.: New Directions, 1940), pp. 315-322, 359-379, 463-465;

"From Poem in Three Times," in *New Directions in Prose and Poetry*, no. 6, edited by Laughlin (New York: New Directions, 1941), pp. 434-442;

The Mirror of Baudelaire, edited, with a poem, by Ford (Norfolk, Conn.: New Directions, 1942);

A Night with Jupiter and Other Fantastic Stories, edited by Ford (New York: View Editions, 1945; London: Dobson, 1947);

"Your Horoscope," in *New Directions in Prose & Poetry*, no. 13, edited by Laughlin (Norfolk, Conn.: New Directions, 1951), pp. 192-195;

"Plaint," "Baby's in jail . . . ," "The Living Corpse," and "The Overturned Lake," in *The American Genius: An Anthology of Poetry with Some Prose*, edited by Edith Sitwell (London: Lehmann, 1951), pp. 176-178;

"A Little Anthology of the Poem in Prose," edited by Ford, in *New Directions in Prose & Poetry*, no. 14, edited by Laughlin (Norfolk, Conn.: New Directions, 1953), pp. 329-408;

"This is a Prosaic Age," "Flag of Ecstasy [prose version]," and "Message to Rimbaud," in *New Directions in Prose & Poetry*, no. 15, edited by Laughlin (Norfolk, Conn.: New Directions, 1953), pp. 351-352, 374, 391;

"Plaint," in *The Atlantic Book of British and American Poetry*, edited by Sitwell (Boston & Toronto: Atlantic Monthly/Little, Brown, 1958), p. 936;

"Marcel Duchamp," *NY Talk*, 2 (July 1985): 41.

One of the first American poets to employ the techniques of the French surrealists, Charles Henri Ford has nonetheless, in the course of a long career, written poetry that is distinctly in the American grain—poems very much in the tradition of Walt Whitman and William Carlos Williams, poems whose images and cadences have evoked for their own purposes the popular American culture of their times.

Born in Brookhaven, Mississippi, to Charles Lloyd and Gertrude Cato Ford, Charles Henri Ford began his poetic career early, having a poem published in the *New Yorker* when he was only fourteen ("Interlude," 20 August 1927). The following year the *New Yorker* published another of his poems, "In the Park (For a Gold Digger)" (26 May 1928), and by 1929 he had also had poems published in such little magazines as *free verse, Contemporary Verse, Bozart,* and *Palo Verde.* During these years he was educating himself about the kind of avant-garde literature that was not taught in Mississippi high schools, and in 1929 he dropped out of high school to edit his own little magazine in Columbus, Mississippi, with two somewhat older poets, Parker Tyler and Kathleen Tankersley Young, as associate editors.

As its title suggests, *Blues: A Magazine of New Rhythms* was founded as an outlet for experimental writing, and the list of contributing editors—Herman Spector, Oliver Jenkins, William Carlos Williams, Jacques Le Clercq, Joseph Vogel, and Eugene Jolas, all contributors to or editors of other avant-garde magazines—is suggestive of Ford's literary interests as well as his broad self-education. Williams was especially enthusiastic about the magazine, hoping it would be an antidote to the tendency of post World War I writers to turn away from prewar literary advances "to dullness, to stupidity, to regimentation, to business." Writing for the second issue of *Blues* (March 1929), he warned, "the young writers of today must not be allowed to lose what those of 1914 and thereabouts won—even to be held as weakly as it is—with difficulty."

Ford had chosen another valuable ally in Eugene Jolas, editor of the influential Paris-based magazine *transition*, whose pages had included fragments of James Joyce's *Work in Progress* (*Finnegans Wake,* 1939) and the work of such American writers as Gertrude Stein, Kay Boyle, Harry Crosby, H. D. (Hilda Doolittle), Laura Riding, and Laurence Vail, all of whom contributed to *Blues.* During his magazine's brief life Ford also published the work of Americans such as Ezra Pound, Harold Rosenberg, Witter Bynner, Erskine Caldwell, James T. Farrell, Alfred Kreymborg, Kenneth Rexroth, Mark Van Doren, and Louis Zukofsky.

Ford and Jolas shared an enthusiasm for surrealism, from which Jolas had derived the conviction that the poet must create a new language to describe the visions that arose from his unconscious mind, the true source of all creativity. Ford's "Optional" and "To Be Pickled in Alcohol," both published in the March 1929 issue of *Blues* and collected in *Flag of Ecstasy* (1972), demonstrate the extent to which he was attempting to create such a new language by employing the surrealist technique of juxtaposing incongruous images, which, nonetheless have a sort of unconscious linkage not unlike the logic of dreams. In lines such as "an existence is nullified in the omega of a cracked hickorynut" ("Optional") or "i hold tightly to an ivy wreath and a shudder/with torn nails i build grandly the last madhouse for a burned dream" ("To Be Pickled in Alcohol") Ford practices the surrealist's craft, which for all its reliance on the unconscious is not automatic writing and, indeed, is syntactically and grammatically correct.

At the same time Ford's poems are distinctly American. In these and other early poems, including "Somewhat Monday" (published in the November 1929 issue of *transition* and collected in *Flag of Ecstasy*), "Digressive Announcement of Spring" (published in the June 1930 issue of *transition*), and "why ears," "n. b.," "denudation of tributes," and "poem" (all published in *Blues* in 1929 and, except for "why ears," collected in *Flag of Ecstasy*), the lack of punctuation and capital letters suggests the rather marginal influence of E. E. Cummings, one which he soon outgrew. More important, there is throughout Ford's poetry the American tendency to the epigrammatic and the frequent and conscious evocation of Walt Whitman in both technique and theme. Moreover, while he did not follow the French surrealists in eschewing traditional poetic forms, Ford, true to the name of his magazine, infused his poetry with the rhythms of American jazz.

In January 1930 Ford joined Parker Tyler in New York City, where they continued editing *Blues*, which folded after the publication of two more issues. For what would prove to be their last issue (Fall 1930) the editors asked Williams for "internal criticism," and Williams responded with "Caviar and Bread Again: A Warning for the New Writer," in which he stated that too many younger writers were following in the line of T. S. Eliot (whose work, for Williams, was taking modern poetry away from its "native grain") and that their preoccupation with technique led to neglect of substance. Yet, despite his general criticisms, Williams remained interested in Ford's poetry, and, when he wrote the foreword for Ford's *The Garden of Disorder and Other Poems* (1938), he found in Ford's poems (some dat-

ing from the *Blues* era) the kind of merger of form and substance he had called for eight years earlier.

While Williams's comments had been offered as constructive criticism, others had reacted to the magazine's contents with open hostility. The *New York Times*, the *Criterion*, and Edward Titus's conservative Paris-based little magazine, *This Quarter*, had all devoted considerable space to attacking the magazine. In "*Blues*: What Happens to a Radical Literary Magazine"(*Sewanee Review*, January-March 1931) Ford and Tyler implied that, if such established periodicals devoted so much effort to attacking a little magazine that "strayed in from Columbus, Mississippi," their "attempt at cultural renovation" in *Blues* must have achieved some measure of success. *Blues* had also received favorable notice, mainly from poets such as Williams, Jolas, Pound, Witter Bynner, Mark Van Doren, Kay Boyle, Alfred Kreymborg, Laura Riding, and Gertrude Stein. In *The Autobiography of Alice B. Toklas* (1933) Stein later wrote, "Of all the little magazines which . . . have died to make verse free, perhaps the youngest and freshest was the Blues." She went on to say of Ford "that he and Robert Coates alone among the young men have an individual sense of words."

"Out of his New York experience," Parker Tyler wrote, "Ford has evoked a naughty novel on which he has persuaded me to collaborate, *The Young and Evil*, so plainspoken that, for this still innocent era the only possibility of publication seems to lie in Paris." Basing the novel on their experiences in New York's Greenwich Village, Ford and Tyler had written alternating chapters, with Ford devising the narrative style. One of the characters, Karel, is for the most part Tyler, and Julian is largely Ford. While the novel would not be considered pornographic by 1970s or 1980s standards, its fairly frank depiction of homosexuality made impossible its publication in the United States during the 1930s. (It was finally published in New York by Arno Press in 1975, and a new edition, with eight previously unpublished illustrations by Pavel Tchelitchew, will be published by SeaHorse Press in 1986.) The manuscript had been rejected by Liveright, Cape, and Gollancz by the time Ford sailed in April 1931 for Paris to "present it for Gertrude Stein's approval." Stein not only admired the novel but sent Ford to literary agent William Aspenwall Bradley, who in turn sent the book to Jack Kahane of Obelisk Press. *The Young and Evil* was published in August 1933 in an edition of 2,500 copies, with dust-jacket blurbs by Bernard Faÿ, Djuna Barnes, and Gertrude Stein, who compared the novel to F. Scott Fitzgerald's *This Side of Paradise* (1920) as an authentic depiction of the new generation. Few if any copies of the novel made it into the United States or Great Britain. British customs officials burned 500 copies and American officials turned back large shipments. The reviews in Paris were mixed. Kay Boyle praised the novel, but Waverly Root, the reviewer for the *Paris Tribune* (the European edition of the *Chicago Tribune*), called it "very dull dirt." The only American review appeared in the *New Republic,* where Louis Kronenberg wrote, "The first gloves-off account of more or less professional young homosexuals . . . it is both authentic and alive."

Upon his arrival in Paris Ford called on not only Gertrude Stein but a number of other writers with whom he had corresponded as editor of *Blues,* including Djuna Barnes (whom he met first in New York in 1930). Ford and Barnes traveled to Vienna with another friend in late 1931, and in summer 1932 Ford went to Italy and then Tangier, where he saw Paul Bowles again and wrote to Barnes, inviting her to join him. While she was in Tangier with him, Ford typed part of her novel *Nightwood* (1936) and wrote to Tyler about their "positive attraction for each other." Barnes sent Tyler a short story she had written about Ford, in which she described his eyes as going "around the sides of his head like an animal's." In the 1960s Tyler expanded upon this description of Ford, calling him "an adult stamped with permanent boyishness," whose "blue eyes, shedding their confidingness remarkably like a child's, are set in his face like stones. When he was quite young (I knew him then), the whites of the eyes seemed to curve round his head and make a gesture of spacious looking."

After he returned to Paris in summer 1932 Ford became increasingly involved with Russian neoromantic painter Pavel Tchelitchew, to whom Barnes introduced him not long after his arrival in Paris. Tchelitchew's 1933 *Portrait of Charles Henri Ford in Blue* depicts the young poet much as Barnes had described him the previous year. The developing relationship between the poet and the painter met with opposition from friends, however. Not only had Tchelitchew been living with American pianist Allen Tanner since the early 1920s, but Edith Sitwell was in love with Tchelitchew and fond of Tanner. According to Tyler, she wrote to Tanner suggesting that if Ford became "tiresome," he should send him to England with some copies of *The Young and Evil.* She would make sure the authorities gave him "from three to six months board and lodging free, from the moment he lands!" At

Pavel Tchelitchew's Portrait of Charles Henri Ford in Blue *(1933) (collection of Charles Henri Ford)*

the same time Gertrude Stein, who had cut Tchelitchew from her circle in about 1928 but who took to Ford, warned him against the painter when Ford visited her at Bilignin in summer 1933. Ford and Tchelitchew spent some months in England and Spain in 1934 before settling in New York later that same year, and they continued to live together until Tchelitchew's death in 1957. Sitwell eventually accepted Ford's role in Tchelitchew's life and came to like Ford and admire his poetry, but the break with Gertrude Stein and Alice B. Toklas was permanent. Tchelitchew took a measure of revenge when in *Phenomena,* his major painting of 1936-1938, he depicted Stein as "Sitting Bull" and Toklas as "The Knitting Maniac." (In contrast Sitwell is flatteringly depicted as "The Sequestered One.")

In the midst of the uproar surrounding his personal life Ford never ceased writing and having his work published. An experimental prose piece, "Letter from the Provinces," appeared in *Readies for Bob Brown's Machine* (1931), whose editor intended to have his various contributors' works printed on reels of paper for use in a machine he had devised to streamline the process of reading.

In addition to poems published in the little magazines *transition, New Review, Front,* and *Tambour,* he had four poems published in *Americans Abroad* (1932), an anthology edited by Peter Neagoe that has become a sort of "who's who" of American expatriate writers in the 1920s and 1930s. Moreover, while in Spain with Tchelitchew in summer 1934, he began a series of sonnets, which were added to one of his poems from *Americans Abroad,* "The Jeweled Bat," and other sonnets to make up his first book of poetry. *A Pamphlet of Sonnets* (1936) contains sixteen sonnets addressed to Christopher Marlowe and Paris friend Marie Laure (Vicomtesse de Noailles) as well as to Tyler, Barnes, and Tchelitchew.

All the sonnets may be classified as Italian or Elizabethan, or as traditional variants on one or the other form, but frequently the rhymes are off-rhymes and in some cases only similar sounds. In fact, they come close to being parodies of the classical, predetermined form, examples of what happens when man's rational designs encounter the strange irrevocable logic of the world of dreams. In "The Jeweled Bat" (for Barnes) the sonnet form itself comes to represent the cavern in which the terrified bat is trapped, and the speaker's words imitate its frantic movements and cries.

According to the dreamlike logic that governs Ford's poem, subject may become object and object, subject; objects may be equated to their attributes or their opposites. The bat, a creature associated with darkness, is jewelled, and its jewels become associated with the sun. Thus "entan-/gled in a sun it cannot see," the bat itself becomes linked with light, an element alien to its nature. Through this unnatural linkage, it becomes the embodiment of its own terror. It can escape light not by immersion in darkness, but through "the love promised to man/by angels: madness; heaven overripe." Ironically, since madness is "heaven overripe" this escape is an immersion in even too much light.

In the sestet the bat's glory, associated with light, "reveals the hidden corpse of the mammal," but, in enabling the bat to perceive the death of the body in which it is trapped, glory is equated with terror. Having now created this seemingly illogical link, the sonnet moves toward resolution. The jeweled bat is immersed in tears, and this same "acrid obdurate salt" is what "the lovely black bat used to fly across/not knowing then the solitude that was." Before it was "jeweled," before it experienced extremes of emotion incompatible to its sanity and very being, the innocent, unperceiving bat—unaware of its lack of knowledge—was free from sorrow, the ocean of "obdurate salt." The bat is finally a metaphor for the poet, who gives up innocence in return for great knowledge and in so doing becomes imprisoned not only because of, but in, that knowledge. His perceptions give him a sense of power, of glory (like the bat's jewels)—but they also frighten him because he sees that total immersion in this hidden source of knowledge, his unconscious mind or the Jungian collective unconscious, is madness (itself both light and dark, escape and imprisonment). Seen in this way the sonnet form is itself paradoxical. It represents rational order, a creation of the rational mind. While rationality can be imprisoning, a deterrent to fuller understanding, the speaker's ability to create even a semblance of order in the face of madness is liberating. In the poem's final unspoken paradox rationality and irrationality are both freedom, both imprisonment. The poet does not, and cannot, resolve the paradox.

Ford's poet is not Emerson's, who "turns the world to glass and sees all things in their right progression," but he is part of the same romantic tradition. While Dada, the precursor of surrealism, was nihilistic, obsessed with the total subjectivity of

Ford standing in front of a 1933 portrait of him by Tchelitchew

the individual poet's perceptions, the surrealists set out to reconnect the poet and the world, or, as Eva Balakian explains in her study of the French surrealists, *Surrealism: The Road to the Absolute* (1959), "to revitalize matter, to re-situate the object in relation to themselves so that they would no longer be absorbed in their own subjectivity." The surrealist, like Emerson's transcendentalist, is a poet/seer who is also a seer, but Emerson's poet is a passive observer of Platonic unity in which *all* things are in their right order. The surrealist is an active creator; instead of seeing a concrete object as a symbol of an abstraction, he adds to its qualities, making something that has not existed before. Indeed, Paul Eluard, the French surrealist to whom Ford is most frequently compared, defined writing poetry as changing the world by turning objects away from their physical properties and usual roles, thus inventing new objects. The jeweled bat is such an object. Although some of the sixteen sonnets in *A Pamphlet of Sonnets* are more surrealist than others, as a whole they are notable for their striking imagery, their creation of objects that have not existed before. Indeed, when William Carlos Williams wrote the preface for Ford's first full-length collection of poetry, *The Garden of Disorder and Other Poems* (1938), he noted that, although he disliked the sonnet form in general, Ford's sonnets should be read for their "tenuous but concretely imagined word appositions."

In New York Ford became fascinated with the Freak Museum on Fourteenth Street. Seeing the freaks as surreal objects created not by the mind of the poet but by nature, he began work on "The Garden of Disorder," a poem that would employ this naturally surreal condition as the controlling metaphor. He also communicated his discovery to Tchelitchew, who became similarly fascinated, viewing such deformity, Tyler said, as "a natural portrait of the purely formal devices of modern painting: nature's, not Picasso's, way of mocking man's perfectionism," and employing it in the startling visual metaphors of his major painting *Phenomena*. According to Paul Mariani, Ford's discovery influenced William Carlos Williams as well. After reading Ford's poem in spring 1937 Williams's curiosity was piqued, and he visited Tchelitchew and Ford's New York penthouse to see the still-unfinished *Phenomena*. Later, Mariani says, when Williams began writing *Paterson*, he "peopled it as well with dwarfs and hydrocephalics . . . and himself, the monstrous poet dreaming the grotesque dream of the poem."

In "The Tortuous Straightness of Charles Henri Ford," his introduction to *The Garden of Disorder and Other Poems*, Williams explained and defended Ford's surrealist method: "The poems form a single, continuous, running accompaniment, well put together as to their words, to a life altogether unreal. By retaining a firmness of extraordinary word juxtapositions while dealing wholly with a world to which the usual mind is unfamiliar a counterfoil to the vague and excessively stupid juxtapositions commonly known as 'reality' is created. The effect is to revive the senses and force them to re-see, re-hear, re-taste, re-smell, and generally re-value all that it was believed had been seen, heard, smelled, and generally valued. By this means poetry has always in the past put a finger upon reality."

While deformity is the controlling metaphor, Ford's title poem is not exclusively peopled by the denizens of the Freak Museum. Rather it examines and equates all types of deformity, whether created by nature or by man. In this first attempt at a longer poem, Ford employs T. S. Eliot's method from *The Waste Land* (1922) of using fragments of the past to shore up the ruins of the present. "The Garden of Disorder" echoes and alludes to Shakespeare, *Beowulf*, and Negro spirituals, among others, but the dominant voice in the poem is Walt Whitman's, as Ford echoes *Song of Myself* at key points in his poem, unconsciously challenging the reader to compare the two poems, to see Whitman's vision of cosmic order twisted and deformed, as Ford's poem depicts a disordered world on the eve of war, dominated by chaos and revolution.

"The Garden of Disorder" begins with a catalogue, one of Whitman's characteristic techniques, but Ford's, which begins "To lodge your harvest in the lion's mouth,/to telescope the bugs that feed flowers," lists distortions of so-called reality. The poet eventually explains how to create such distortions. Yet after exhorting the reader "to despise, despise nothing/but the mote of shame in your eye," he breaks into his long list to explain that one must "reverence the monster/as well as the paragon blade of grass that God made" because:

> though He will make another
> freaks are not mothers, even to freaks:
> the vine that shrieks is normality's:
> banality's blister may be pricked after twilight;

the monster is as much a symbol of God's creation as Whitman's blade of grass. Nature's freaks are not the source of the world's disorder, rather one should look to the so-called normal and the banal

THE
GARDEN OF DISORDER
AND OTHER POEMS

BY
CHARLES HENRI FORD

WITH AN INTRODUCTION BY
WILLIAM CARLOS WILLIAMS

AND A FRONTISPIECE BY
PAVEL TCHELITCHEW

LONDON
EUROPA PRESS
7 Great Ormond Street, W.C.1

Frontispiece and title page for Ford's first full-length collection of poems that, according to William Carlos Williams, forced the reader "to re-see, re-hear, re-taste, re-smell, and generally re-value all that it was believed had been seen, heard, smelled, and generally valued"

for the root of evil. While Whitman too would accept the monster as part of God's creation, Ford's catalogue moves to a far different sort of resolution than Whitman's, explaining that to do the things the poet has listed earlier, "you may launch like five fishes/your five senses in aquatic regions/of the mind," and

> resolve to recapture the machinery
> of odors, the private rainbows, the leafless motors,
> nor dread the drums of drought,
> tear-gas of the sensational nor the
> reactionary apple in the garden of the irrational.

Whitman catalogues the inhabitants of the world that exists outside himself and says that they "tend inward to me, and I tend outward toward them"; that is, he accepts the world as it is and asserts his part in it. Ford suggests how to re-create the world, how to see it differently than it has been seen before, not by moving outward to embrace the world but by moving inward to mine the unconscious and the irrational.

The second section of the poem begins with "Let us try dividing the impersonal and the personal," a line that echoes Whitman's "It is time to explain myself—let us stand up" and goes on to imply that, like Whitman, one can look to the phenomenal world for meaning. Yet, unlike Whitman, who explained himself by explaining the universe and found evidence of God's purpose in all the world, this poet cannot find answers to his questions, cannot separate subjective impression from objective perception, and the section is composed of increasingly fear-filled questions about war and peace in a seemingly indifferent universe. Not only does he find no answers to his questions about conscious purpose in nature, but he finds no relationship between the punishment and the crime, no reasons for destruction. The last stanza of this section echoes Old English alliterative verse and ends: "Oh why are we afraid? For Beowulf bellows/across the centuries to bravery's bedfellows." The poet's quest for meaning is incomplete, but he learns one unsettling lesson: that the deformed, the truly monstrous, is not a modern invention.

At the beginning of the third section the poet attempts to counter his fear with a humorous and surreal evocation of the passage in *Song of Myself* that begins "Houses and rooms are full of perfumes, the shelves are crowded with perfumes," but the mood soon darkens:

> Perfume the clock and the cricket will take care of
>   Aunt Bess
> but the poet forgot to put on his odor-proof vest:
> how staunch the scent of words?
> Dilute the sadistic monopoly's
> whirlpool that twisted
> the artist out of all recognition:
> he will trail the secret brook
> that runs with the fragrance of perdition.

This poet does not follow Whitman out of the house, with all its perfumes of past association, to breathe the odorless atmosphere; he cannot escape from subjectivity to objectivity. The word *staunch* introduces ambiguity into the poet's question. When it is read as an adjective he is asking, how strong or enduring is the odor of words? But when the world is read as a verb, he is asking how to extinguish their scent. He answers both questions: even when the poet escapes the connotations imposed by others—by grammarians, admen, politicians . . .—he cannot escape his own. The surrealist transforms the world, but he does so not because he had access to Whitman's great, objective Truth, but because he reaches into the Jungian collective unconscious, where subject and object are one. Later in part three the poet returns to the metaphor of scent, addressing world events:

> You might deodorize the bat,
> yet aeroplanes are not aghast at the night:
> redolent are the boar and nettle,
> though naught reeks of war save the fetid battle.

Even if one were capable of removing all fearful connotations from it, war would have the same effects. Whitman may inhale the odorless atmosphere as he asserts his oneness with the cosmos and proclaim, "It is in for my mouth forever, I am in love with it," but who, this poet asks, has a taste for war:

> Inhale the constellations
> and you may find them appetizing,
> but mobilize the nation,
> and whose gastronomy is it?

The fourth and final section of "The Garden of Disorder" begins by addressing the chaotic politics of the late 1930s directly: "Lenin has withdrawn to a dialectic/paradise and counts with sociological eyes/the biffs of the nightsticks, the devil's police." He acknowledges similar hysteria in the past and its eventual end ("No witch flies out the window/in witchless New England"), and then he mourns all such events, asking the question:

> But how many roofs besides my own
> leak with remorse
> at liberty's affliction,
> be the rain fine or coarse?

The poem ends with a list of mutable oracles, all of whom finally are the oracles of any

>   wizard reason
> to convict you of subjective treason,
> a traitor to the snow-gardens and the equator,
> to the zodiac masses, the classless solution
> in May's revolving botany: boquets of terror
> from the garden of revolution.

Ford's poem is, finally, a reconciliation of his art and his politics. The surrealists were, for the most part, at least nominally Communists, with some more politically involved than others. Yet by the time "The Garden of Disorder" was written, the Soviet Union was calling for social realism in art and literature. There were other important political issues inherent in the Soviet Union's brand of communism, issues over which the surrealists would finally split. In rejecting Stalinism, Ford is also defending his position as a surrealist writer, as a neoromantic different from, but in the tradition of, Whitman. By imposing his mind on the world and forcing his readers to view its deformity in new ways, he made a bid to influence their politics as well as their aesthetics.

Two other poems in *The Garden of Disorder*, "Dicty Glide in Central Park Menagerie" and "Plaint: Before the Mob of 10,000 at Owensboro, Ky.," were singled out by Williams in his introduction. "Dicty Glide in Central Park Menagerie," beginning "Cowboy, where's your class-conscious horse?," draws together the clichés of modern culture to satirize that very culture. As such, the poem displays one of Ford's greatest talents: what Williams called "using the banal to escape the banal." "Plaint," in which Ford's social consciousness is overt, draws on more traditional associations to describe a lynching in Owensboro, Kentucky. In fact, it is shaped by a pattern of metaphors that is more metaphysical than surrealistic, though individual images in the poem are surreal. The poem is, as Williams points out in his introduction, a version of the Crucifixion; and the association of the cross and the tree goes a step further to a link with the tree in the cherry-tree legend. Yet the dying young black, as his blood runs "into the orchard that excluded me," questions whether there is a place for him in the white man's heaven. As he bleeds from his wounds, so do

> the minutes like black cherries
> drop from my shady side.
> Oh who is the forester must tend to such a tree, Lord?
> Do angels pick the cherry-blood of folk like me, Lord?

The tree is the tree of death, and the poem includes no promise of rebirth.

Reviews for *The Garden of Disorder and Other Poems* were mixed, though only George Barker was wholly negative, dismissing the book in *Life and Letters To-Day* (Summer 1938) as "an artificial chrysanthemum." The reviewer for the *Times Literary Supplement* (23 April 1938) admired Ford's "surprising word juxtapositions" but found a "fantastic meaninglessness" in many of the poems. Peter DeVries, reviewing the book for *Poetry: A Magazine of Verse* (July 1938), also greeted the book with incomprehension: "It is regrettable to have to report of Ford's splendid virtuosity that it does nothing so well as seal him hermetically in Ford." Yet he admired some poems, including "The Jeweled Bat" and "Plaint," and he concluded, "Ford's further development will be interesting to note. In this collection he has grown better as he has broadened." In a comment written for the New Directions edition of the book Herbert Read stated, "There are few poets writing today whose work is so personal and so prophetic." R. P. Blackmur, reviewing the book for *Partisan Review* (Winter 1939), found in it "a flair for the commonplace seen as gusty because slightly twisted and distrait"; yet he also found fault with Ford's archness, claiming that in the fifteen-line "Plaint" (while it is "quite the best poem in the book") the first six "magnificently direct" lines are followed by "seven lines of arch fill-

ing which obfuscate precisely as the dictate the distich of ending." In her introduction to *Sleep in a Nest of Flames* (1949) Edith Sitwell answered charges of Ford's obscurity by explicating this poem, concentrating particularly on the lines Blackmur criticized. She later included it in two anthologies, *The American Genius: An Anthology of Poetry with Some Prose* (1951), where she called it "one of the most beautiful, true, and felt poems written by one of the younger poets in our time," and *The Atlantic Book of British and American Poetry* (1958).

As Sitwell's comments suggest, her attitude toward Ford had warmed considerably since 1934. The first public evidence of her change of heart is her review of Ford's 1940 pamphlet, *ABC's*. Writing for *Life and Letters To-Day* (October 1940), Sitwell called the twenty-six quatrains "an alphabetical history of the spiritual existence of our time," and praised their "individuality" and "integrity," explaining that Ford "has really something to say, and he has found the right medium. Indeed, medium and meaning are so fused as to be one body." Thomas Howells, reviewing *ABC's* for *Poetry* (September 1940), also noted the poem's relevance to the times and admired the blend of surrealism and pointed comment.

The pamphlet, with a front cover by Joseph Cornell, bears on its back cover a dedication drawn from Ford's poem "Comedy of Belief"—"for the child of no one, who grows up to look like everyone's son"—suggesting the universality of the threat Ford perceives, in a world where the victim may as easily prove victimizer.

The quatrain for *K*, which Sitwell in a personal letter to Ford labeled her favorite, focuses on the danger inherent in words:

> Kinky as blood, the gutter feeds
> on words that look like waste;
> garbage on which the mind may bleed
> dwells flagrantly chaste.

In the quatrain for *N*, where he drops his surrealist stance for the kind of direct commentary Howells admired, Ford states what may be the central concern of the whole poem:

> Nothing, nothing is so valuable
> as freedom, Dante said.
> Nothing, nothing is less haveable:
> ask anyone. Dante's dead.

Henry Treece, a poet of the British New Apoca-

Parker Tyler, Charles Henri Ford, and Pavel Tchelitchew in Weston, Connecticut, circa 1938

lypse movement, compared *ABC's* to the works of Donne and Herbert and concluded that it was "a metaphysical rather then surrealist work." For all his affinities with the surrealists, Ford has always been willing to turn to other sources of inspiration as well and to differ from the surrealists. Commenting on the surrealists' iconoclasm in a conversation with surrealist poet Nicolas Calas (*View*, November 1940), Ford said that surrealism's refusal to find any value in the art of the past was "surrealism's strength . . . but also its weakness." He went on to explain that "real strength consists in greatly affirming as well as greatly negating. I do not see how Surrealism deals with equity towards all that the past leaves us of man's inspiration, i. e., great works of art."

As *The Garden of Disorder* and *ABC's* suggest,

Ford was politically active during the late 1930s and into the 1940s. Until the outbreak of World War II, he and Tchelitchew spent part of each year in Europe, and in Paris in 1938 he had become involved in FIARI, a loosely constructed international federation of revolutionary and independent artists, which took a Communist position but did not support the Soviet Union. (While the founding manifesto was signed by André Breton and Diego Rivera, it is believed to have been written by Breton and Leon Trotsky; at this point Paul Eluard and Louis Aragon broke with other surrealists to express their support for the Soviet Union.)

During World War II, Ford and Tchelitchew divided their time between New York City, Weston, Connecticut, and Derby Hill, near Pawlet, Vermont. In September 1940 Ford founded the little magazine *View* to publish the work of the surrealists and poets of related movements. Yet Tyler reported later, the magazine's "critical distinctions" were intentionally "short on delicate definitions and nuances of taste."

Beginning as a "newspaper for poets" in tabloid form, *View* in April 1942 went to a coated-paper format permitting reproductions of artworks. While its contents reflect Ford's flair for the avant-garde in literature and art, *View*'s editorial policy was never doctrinaire. William Carlos Williams called *View* "the impossible magazine of the arts that no one could have dreamed," and added, "It's not a party organ and has no more relation to SURREALISM than that has to the moment, and no less. . . ." Indeed, the magazine is notable for the breadth as well as the quality of its contents, publishing works by elder statesmen of experimental writing such as Wallace Stevens, William Carlos Williams, André Breton, André Masson, Edith Sitwell, E. E. Cummings, Henry Miller, and Lawrence Durrell, as well as then-lesser-known writers such as Paul Bowles, Thomas Merton, Tom Scott, Norman MacCaig, Randall Jarrell, Bryon Gysin, Robert Duncan, Louis Zukofsky, Philip Lamantia, Richard Eberhart, and Jorge Luis Borges. *View* also featured the works of artists, including Joseph Cornell, Max Ernst, Yves Tanguy, Pavel Tchelitchew, André Masson, Georgia O'Keeffe, Marcel Duchamp, Isamu Noguchi, and photographer Man Ray, to name only a few; and it published articles on art, music, and literature by critics such as Meyer Schapiro, James Thrall Soby, Lincoln Kirstein, Kenneth Burke, Wallace Fowlie, Lionel Abel, and Denis de Rougement. An expensively produced, sophisticated magazine of the arts, *View* continued to occupy much of Ford's time through the publication of its final issue in fall 1947, when it folded due to ever-increasing printing costs that could not be matched with revenues from circulation and advertising.

At the same time he continued with his poetry, poetry that from some quarters at least, continued to face charges of obscurity. John Crowe Ransom turned down the title poem of Ford's next collection, *The Overturned Lake* (1941), for the publication in the *Kenyon Review* because, he said, "Where you are clear, you don't seem distinguished. But when you sound distinguished, you are not (to me) clear. . . . You are the logical end to which modern tendencies come, I am sure of that." The editors of *Poetry*, however, found sufficient merit in "The Overturned Lake" to include it in their April 1940 issue. Ford's supporters have

continually found themselves forced to defend him against charges that his poems are collections of subjective images intelligible only to himself (for Ransom, that "logical end to which modern tendencies come"). In his introduction to *Flag of Ecstasy: Selected Poems* (1972), Edward B. Germain answers Ransom's charges directly, explaining that, while "The Overturned Lake" is indeed a poem about the poet's unconscious mind, it is not obscure.

Ford's aesthetic, quoted in a publisher's advertisement for *The Overturned Lake*, is a description of the method employed in the book's title poem: "To arouse the image to apocalyptic flow, to throw the opal shadows of its blood with the disquieting rhythm on the marvelous and melancholy sound-screen of the heart's desire. . . ." The images in the poems shift wildly, as the poet asserts his power over them, metaphors wrenched from the unconscious mind. The lake is a tongue that speaks the thoughts of a mountain/brain: "Blue unsolid tongue, if you could talk, the mountain would supply the brain," but he says *if* because he knows that nature has no message for him; "mountains are mummies," their silence disturbed only by the noise of trucks and buses ("manmade worms") passing through its tunnels. Thus the lake is the "Tongue of a deafmute, . . . inarticulate."

This conclusion leads to a new pattern of imagery:

You are like the mind of a man, too:
surface reflecting the blue day,
the life about you seemingly organized, revolving
   about you,
you as center.

The surface of the lake projects an image of order. Because it reflects its surroundings, it seems to interact with them as well and, like the conscious mind, create a rational picture of that world. But beneath the lake's surface are things that are more difficult to fathom. The revolutionary poet, who must overturn the order of the mind, get past the sentries of reason, the logic of the metaphor. This, the poet tells the lake:

   I am concerned in your overthrow:
I should like to pick you up, as if you were a woman
   of water,
hold you against the light and see your veins flow
with fishes, reveal the animal-flowers that rise
nightlike beneath your eyes.

He explains not what the lake is but how he will transform it:

I shall equip you with the strength of a dream,
rout you from your blue unconscious bed,
overturn your unconcern,
as the mind is overturned by memory, the heart by
dread.

If there is to be meaning in the objects of the external world, the poet must create it by reaching down to the great collective unconscious of mankind and using what he learns there to remake those objects according to his own definitions. The lake is a symbol of the unconscious mind because the poet "overturns" it and recreates it as such.

Ford does not make order, so much as disorder; yet, because it is disorder of his own creation, he has a measure of control over it, often through the distancing device of humor. As Wallace Stevens noted, "to be the master of disorder required so very much more than to be the master of order—and among other things the hilarity that Mr. Ford appears to possess." One poem in *The Overturned Lake*, which begins "Baby's in jail; the animal day plays alone,/tame as the animal baby behind bars of the crib," intersperses serious predictions on baby's future with lines typical of Ford's absurdist humor. In the first stanza, after commenting on baby's lack of experience, the speaker concludes, "Baby will come to grief and love," but he adds, "Visitors to the family zoo/do not go to see a vegetarian tiger." In the second stanza he repeats superstitions about good and bad luck, as if to say that very little can be predicted about anyone's life, and the second stanza ends on an ominous note. His pronouncement is preceded rather than followed by "humour noir," and there is a reversal of word order in the final line: "Baby will come to love and grief."

But there are times when humor triumphs. "What grouchy wartanks intend to shred/or crouch the road's middle to stop my copy?," the poet asks in "He Cut His Finger on Eternity: A Poem for Walt Whitman." Imagining Whitman as a modern-day hitchhiker, he takes him on an exuberant journey, flaunting the poetic magic that allows them to transform the world's evils:

Like libertines we'll plunge frontiers
romantic as a journey, unromantic as a slum,
wrap up in a river for a spy's disguise,
and wig you with time, the waterfall.

This poet acknowledges that his world differs from the one Whitman perceived: "here every object turns into its opposite,/and there every sound contains your haw and hem." Yet, while "The haze on the hill is there to take you from me,/I pluck you back on the sting of a stem." They end up at Whitman's "hovel, two tough customers/cocky as gobs with bullet-proof bibs." Refusing to give up Whitman as irrelevant to the modern world, Ford has adapted Whitman's voice to fit his surrealist aesthetic and metaphysics.

The Overturned Lake met with the usual charges of obscurity, with Howard Blake asserting that the poems are "arty" occasional verses comprehensible only to the poet's inner circle (*Poetry*, April 1942). Peter Monro Jack, however, compared Ford to Parker Tyler and concluded, "There is no heaven, of course in the theocracy, nor any hell: there is only a curious twisted humanity, extraordinarily equipped, as both Tyler and Ford are, in showing how different they are from ordinary responses. Tyler and Ford are the anarchists of poetry. The trouble is, they write of their destruction so well . . . and so hopelessly" (*New York Times Book Review*, 14 December 1941). Henry McBride of the *New York Sun* commented that if "the great mass of American citizenry had a hunger for poetry and instinctively recognized it wherever it appeared and in whatever form it appeared," then "Charles Henri Ford's new book of remarkable poems, ought to be a best-seller. . . ." Edith Sitwell included three poems from *The Overturned Lake*, "Baby's in jail . . . ," "The Living Corpse," and "The Overturned Lake," in *The American Genius* along with "Plaint."

From *The Garden of Disorder* onward Ford's poems had expressed his concern with the poet's role in society, a concern that quite naturally intensified during World War II. The result was not a change of direction but a further refinement of his surrealist position. In an editorial for the April 1943 issue of *View* (and in a response to a letter from Philip Lamantia in the next issue) he and assistant editor Tyler assert that the artist of their time could afford neither to devote himself solely to "giving form to his own dreams" nor to see his mission as voicing "the deeper feelings of the masses." When, they say, "the behavior of men has led to a devaluation of human life, the problem is not what inspires us but what values should determine our conduct." The solution is not escape into the self, nor is abrogation of self in favor of "social realism." Rather, in approaching the problem of what to do with his devalued world, the poet must reach into himself and project his ideas and emotions outward, realizing that "Artists should have the courage to follow their ideas and emotions to the utmost limits." They call for the artist to be the "contemporary magician," but they categorically reject the notion that the artist should create "new myths," new systems of belief by which humanity can order its chaotic existence, pointing to the pernicious consequences of one such created myth, Hitler's theory of the master race. Rather the artist/magician must oppose "imagination and insight" to "escapism through myths": "Insofar as artists can decide by their own volition what shall affect them, they regulate their conduct according to methods that help perpetually to renew our deepest emotional contact with the world. Seers, we are for the magic view of life."

The first poem in Ford's next book, *Poems for Painters* (1945), demonstrates such magic through its evocation of Marcel Duchamp. "Flag of Ecstasy" celebrates Duchamp's creation of his own magic views, which allow him to triumph

> Over the towers of autoerotic honey
> Over the dungeons of homicidal drives
>
> ....
>
> Over the saints of debauchery
> Over the criminals of gold
>
> Over the princes of delirium
> Over the paupers of peace
>
> Over signs foretelling the end of the world
> Over signs foretelling the beginning,

indeed over all that is deformed or wrong in his world. Thus, Ford applauds the Dadaist (which Duchamp always remained) as a "flag of ecstasy":

> Like one of those tender strips of flesh
> On either side of the vertebral column
>
> Marcel, wave!

One of the View Editions series produced by the publishers of *View* magazine, *Poems for Painters* also includes poems addressed to Leonor Fini, Esteban Francès, Yves Tanguy, and Pavel Tchelitchew, and it is illustrated with black-and-white photographs of works by these avant-garde artists. Reviewers by now appeared better versed in surrealism. The reviewer for the *New Yorker*, for example, compared Ford to Paul Eluard (7 July 1943), while Brewster Gheselin noted that Ford, like the painters he addressed, "is continually mov-

ing into tracts of consciousness little cultivated in our time or wholly neglected" (*Rocky Mountain Review*, Summer 1945). Francis C. Golffing, reviewing the book for *Poetry* (September 1945), noted Ford's "orthodox surrealist technique of joining the incongruous and reconciling the disparate" and "the manner in which Ford has adapted the iconography of Chirico, Tchelitchew, and Dali to his verbal phantasies." But, acknowledging his passion and perception, she asserted that "his poems fall apart for lack of a center."

Beginning in 1938 and continuing into the early 1950s, Ford's work frequently appeared in James Laughlin's *New Directions* anthologies. New Directions also published the first American edition of *The Garden of Disorder,* and in 1942 the New Directions Poet-of-the-Month series included *The Mirror of Baudelaire,* a bilingual edition of three poems by Baudelaire, selected by Ford, with translations by William Candlewood. The book also has a preface in prose by Paul Eluard and a prefatory poem, "Ballad for Baudelaire," by Ford. In 1949 Laughlin published a volume of selected poems by Ford, *Sleep in a Nest of Flames,* which includes thirteen poems from *The Overturned Lake,* "Plaint" from *The Garden of Disorder,* "There's No Place to Sleep in this Bed, Tanguy" from *Poems for Painters,* and five new poems. The book also includes a laudatory preface by Edith Sitwell, whose 1948 lecture and reading tour of the United States Ford had been instrumental in organizing. Finding in Ford's poems "a strange and real originality" and "a great vitality," Sitwell noted his surrealist affinities, but she saw his poetry as "a strange, raw poetry, the poetry of a new race of Living from which nearly all exteriors have been stripped."

The five previously uncollected poems in *Sleep in a Nest of Flames* tend toward the epigrammatic. Yet while the form seemed in *ABC's* to suit Ford's brilliant gift for the extraordinary image, these poems seem to substitute his genuine, and justifiable, concern over the events of the time for surrealist magic. Yet, as a whole, the collection contains many of Ford's best poems. While the reviewer for the *New Yorker* felt that, because of Ford's affinity with the surrealists, Sitwell overstated his originality, he also noted that Ford "has a distinctive sense of humor, . . . and at his best he can react with more than Surrealist directness to a concrete event. . . ." The *Times Literary Supplement* reviewer reacted against Ford's surrealism, while praising some of the poems. Dudley Fitts, reviewing the book for *Saturday Review* (14 January 1950), felt that Sitwell gave exaggerated praise to Ford, though he found

Sitwell "right in finding the authentic strangeness here, the virtuosity which does not exist for its own sake, but which is an ordered and meaningful organic part of the whole." Howard Nemerov in a review for *Poetry* (July 1950) found no such unity, suggesting that the longer poems, "though they contain many brilliant things suffer from deliberate eccentricity and inconsequence, so that the better part is often more than the whole." He concluded that "through all the violence, eccentricity and 'modernism' Mr. Ford may be seen as a romantic poet, putting off as much as establishing the seriousness of his dissatisfactions by parody, self-mockery and play. . . ." While this comment was intended at least in part as criticism, it is in effect a definition of the surrealist poet, a definition which suggests the dilemma that seems to have become increasingly acute for Ford in the 1940s: how to reconcile his politics and his poetic.

One poem that several of these reviewers praised, "Plaint," is an example of how Ford successfully employs original, surrealistic images to heighten and intensify his political message. He also has some success in "The Garden of Disorder" (which was not included in *Sleep in a Nest of Flames,* perhaps because it is a poem of successful parts rather than a unified whole), and in *ABC's.* Yet in many of the poems written after the publication of *The Overturned Lake,* he seems to be choosing between brilliant images and overt political message, as though the press of events often made it impossible for the poet to work the magic that Ford and Tyler called for in their April 1943 editorial.

A symptom of Ford's dissatisfaction with so much rhymed poetry may be his editing of a section of the 1953 New Directions annual. Devoted to prose poems, it includes a piece by Ford called "This is a prosaic age" and "Flag of Ecstasy" rewritten as prose. By the time *Sleep in a Nest of Flames* was published, the first phase of his poetic career was at an end. He had been working at play writing for some time, and in 1952 he and Tchelitchew moved to Italy, away from his American literary connections. In Europe Ford became more and more immersed in painting and photography, and by 1954 he had virtually abandoned written poetry. Despite his absence, his influence continued to be felt, especially on poets of the New York School—such as Frank O'Hara and Kenneth Koch—and San Francisco poet Robert Duncan. Parker Tyler has also noted echoes of Ford in the poetry of Theodore Roethke.

Flag of Ecstasy (1972), which includes many of Ford's poems from the 1930s and 1940s (some of which had been published in little magazines but had not been collected in any of his books), gives a good overview of the first half of Ford's poetic career. The introduction by Edward B. Germain is an insightful discussion of Ford as a surrealist.

While they were in Europe Ford and Tchelitchew designed the sets for William Faulkner's *Requiem for a Nun,* adapted for the stage by Ford's sister, Ruth Ford, which premiered in London at the Royal Court Theatre in 1958, with Ruth Ford in the leading role. Ford's photographs were exhibited in London in 1955, and the following year he had his first one-man show of paintings and drawings in Paris; the foreword to the catalogue was written by Jean Cocteau.

After Tchelitchew's death in Rome in July 1957 Ford continued to live in Europe and to have his work exhibited in Paris. In 1962 he returned to New York and began an association with the pop artists and underground filmmakers. At the same time he started to combine his artistic and literary interests, first for an exhibition, "Poem Posters," in a New York gallery. The film Ford made of this show was chosen for the Fourth International Avant-Garde Film Festival in Belgium.

The second result of the new impetus he found in New York is *Spare Parts* (1966), what Ford calls an "artist's book, produced in colorphoto-litho" in which words, parts of words, and phrases cut from newspapers and magazines are pasted over montages, wash drawings, and photographs by Ford. The handsome, large-format book was printed by hand in Athens, Greece, in a limited edition of 950 copies.

For a poet who in the late 1920s had infused his poetry with jazz rhythms, street slang, and advertising clichés; who in the 1930s had seen the deformed beings in a freak museum as nature's own surrealist images; and in 1953 could write in "This Is a Prosaic Age," "Our tribal chants are advertising slogans. A runic melody is almost unheard of "; *Spare Parts* is the logical result of his method. It is, in a sense, found poetry, tapping the collective consciousness of an entire society by a method not unlike the way in which automatic writing taps the depths of the individual mind. The poet's choice of words is determined not by the imagination but by what he finds. Yet at the same time he shapes and rearranges. Like the true surrealist, he creates the strange from the familiar, causing the reader to see everyday phenomena in new ways.

For all the strangeness of *Spare Parts,* for all the pages on which words and pictures merge and seem to be neither one nor the other, the many "spare parts" do merge into one coherent whole, made up of a multitude of interrelated themes.

Not surprisingly, for a poet who has spent ten years away from his native country, the poem begins with a suggestion of how much popular culture and its language has changed (slashes indicate blocks of cut-out type): "STARTS HERE/H/ow brutally/The/LEGEND/is changing:/any soup and sandwich/ELECTRA/KEEPS MAKING IT/GAY MODERN POP'S IN/And suddenly the /FREE SWEDISH TOOTHPASTE/AMAZES!" Like these lines, with their open allusions to homosexuality, incest, and so-called Scandinavian free love, the rest of Ford's book implies much more than it says, though sometimes its social and sexual messages are humorously and blatantly apparent. (To Bill Katz's favorable review of the book in *Library Journal* is appended an editor's note suggesting that "libraries in sensitive areas should examine before purchase.")

Throughout the poem Ford turns the language of the advertising world and American pop culture—both obsessed with youth and sex— against itself, making the reader see it anew and question its message, its value to the individual. Throughout are references to the lost individual, unwilling or unable to keep up with the images projected by popular culture. At one point the poet identifies with the lost child: "There's a/little kid alone/'Come on, I'm not scared.'/it's my own unspoiled/creative force/inching through life." Yet if the poet is to speak to this society, to perform a necessary critical role at a time when such a role seems urgent ("Poems Wanted *NOW!*"), he must use society's language. As he noted at the beginning of the book, "The/*LEGEND*/is changing." The old legends, the bases upon which Western civilization was built, are forgotten, and the new legends have been created by advertising.

At one point Ford refers to pop artist Andy Warhol: "How Important is Andy?/Everybody's/ Taken in/That's the wrong reason." The criticism is less directed at Warhol than at those who fail to see the satire implicit in his paintings. Indeed, Ford goes on to say, employing the traditional symbol for the psyche, "NO ONE EVER NOTICES/ groggy butterflies beneath the snow." Old symbols are meaningless to new audiences, he implies, and

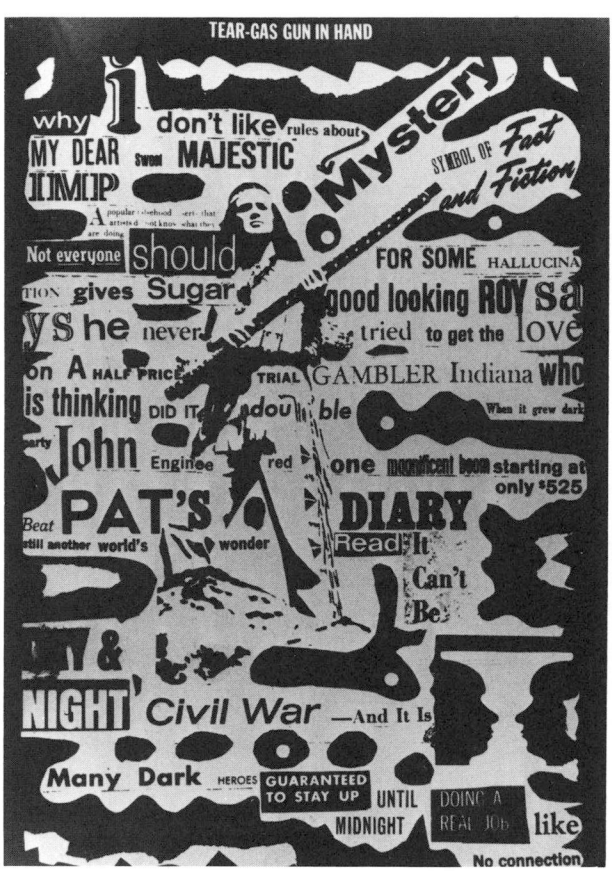

Pages from Spare Parts

no one seems interested in traditional poetry and the image of the poet associated with it.

Thus he embraces the language of the culture he criticizes, celebrating its possibilities at the same time he points out its limitations. The book ends with an exclamation/warning that captures the contradictions of his position in perilous equilibrium: "It's/the/bus/you'll never miss/with all the nutty joy of total/Turn on,/COUNT DRACULA'S/getting ready/for those black lace moods."

Spare Parts was largely ignored by mainstream reviewers. No one seemed sure what it was. (*Library Journal* put Katz's review under "Drawing & Graphic Arts.") As Katz pointed out, the book was confusing to those "who are accustomed to separate compartments for art, poetry, bookmaking, dirty pictures, and the like." Yet Katz also noted that anyone familiar with the work of John Furnival, Ian Hamilton Finlay, and other concrete poets would recognize Ford's method. He went on to assert that in Ford's rearrangement of their words "the gods of the market slit their own throats, and Ford proclaims himself a first-rate artist and social muse." Though Katz's prognosis for the book's impact was overly optimistic, Robert D. Spector of the *Saturday Review* did refer to it in passing as "a beautiful volume."

Silver Flower Coo, Ford's 1968 book, is similar to *Spare Parts* but visually less elaborate (and thus less expensive to produce). Designed and priced to reach a larger audience, the book has fewer pictures and all the pages are printed in black on white or white on black. The word cut-outs themselves are visually interesting, and the book's appearance is arresting.

While *Silver Flower Coo* is once again constructed from cut-outs of found words and phrases, it also contains some words written in by hand. Sometimes the words are so-called obscenities, but at other times they are simply references to obscenities (such as "talking dirty") or totally innocuous ("daisy chain," for example). Since Ford could presumably put together any words he wants from pieces of other words (as he does in the line below "daisy chain" with a reference to homosexual gang rape) these written-in words seem a device to call attention to the idea of censorship and to satirize the logic behind what is considered obscene.

The book as a whole is more linear and accessible than *Spare Parts* and has an air of Whitmanesque epic, as in Ford's earlier long poems. Whitman is mentioned a few times, in lines such as "Whitman's/Barefoot Trade/Always stays in/Explodes/at no extra cost," and "to know about/Whit-

man/famous for friendship/and/*Underground*/freedom/brush up on/his '*Wonder Years.*'"

For all his admiration of Whitman's freedom Ford is determined to go still further. In a section that aptly begins in a Whitmanesque manner with the words "CH/SPEAKS UP" Ford sets out to explain: "The new artists for the new era are now appearing/Balanced/6 times longer/How/did/TERRIFIC/St. Charles/'open up'/his fellow men/he carved with/ideas./NOT/everyone can have a mother . . ./without feeling its bite. . . ./*Everyone's MOVING UP to*/dream rooms./THE DAYLIGHT, PLEASE. and Now—/WINNERS OF THE MOSCOW CRAFTSMEN AWARD/dual-purpose/PESTS/will provide/A little/sleek/revolution./so many/feast on the beauty of/A LIFETIME NAIL DRESSER . . ./What should you expect from/your own two hands?" The new poet is more explicit than Whitman ("in/an/AGE of/killer/TRENDS/To hell with/WINGFOOT/sublimation"), and he is far less optimistic about the future of his world, in which the dreams created by admen create a thin veneer over the reality of revolution and the arms race.

This poem ends more positively than *Spare Parts*, in an affirmation of love that is qualified, yet—for all that has gone before—Whitmanesque. In the final section of *Silver Flower Coo* the poet explains, "These/Pages/finish/with/19.7 cubic feet of 1 belief/Because/THIS SYMBOL/comes in continuous lengths for uninterrupted beauty," and the book ends on a Whitmanesque note: "Love/broke/me/Isn't it time you enjoyed it?/Yes ☑."

After the publication of *Silver Flower Coo*, which Richard Kostelanetz described as "like no other book ever published in America," Ford did not have another volume published until 1979. During the preceding years he conceived, directed, and filmed in Crete a feature film titled *Johnny Minotaur*, which was produced in 1969 and premiered in New York in 1971. "The Kathmandu Experience," an exhibition of wood carvings, wall hangings, and prints designed by Ford and made by Nepalese craftsmen, appeared in 1974 in New York, where the following year "Thirty Images from Italy," photographs earlier displayed in London, were also shown. Another exhibition of photographs, "Layouts & Camouflages," was held in 1980 at the Robert Samuel Gallery in New York.

"The Kathmandu Experience" grew out of Ford's stay in Nepal, where he went for the first time in 1972 and where he maintains a home, The Hermitage, in Kathmandu and spends much of his time. Another result of his life in Nepal is *Om*

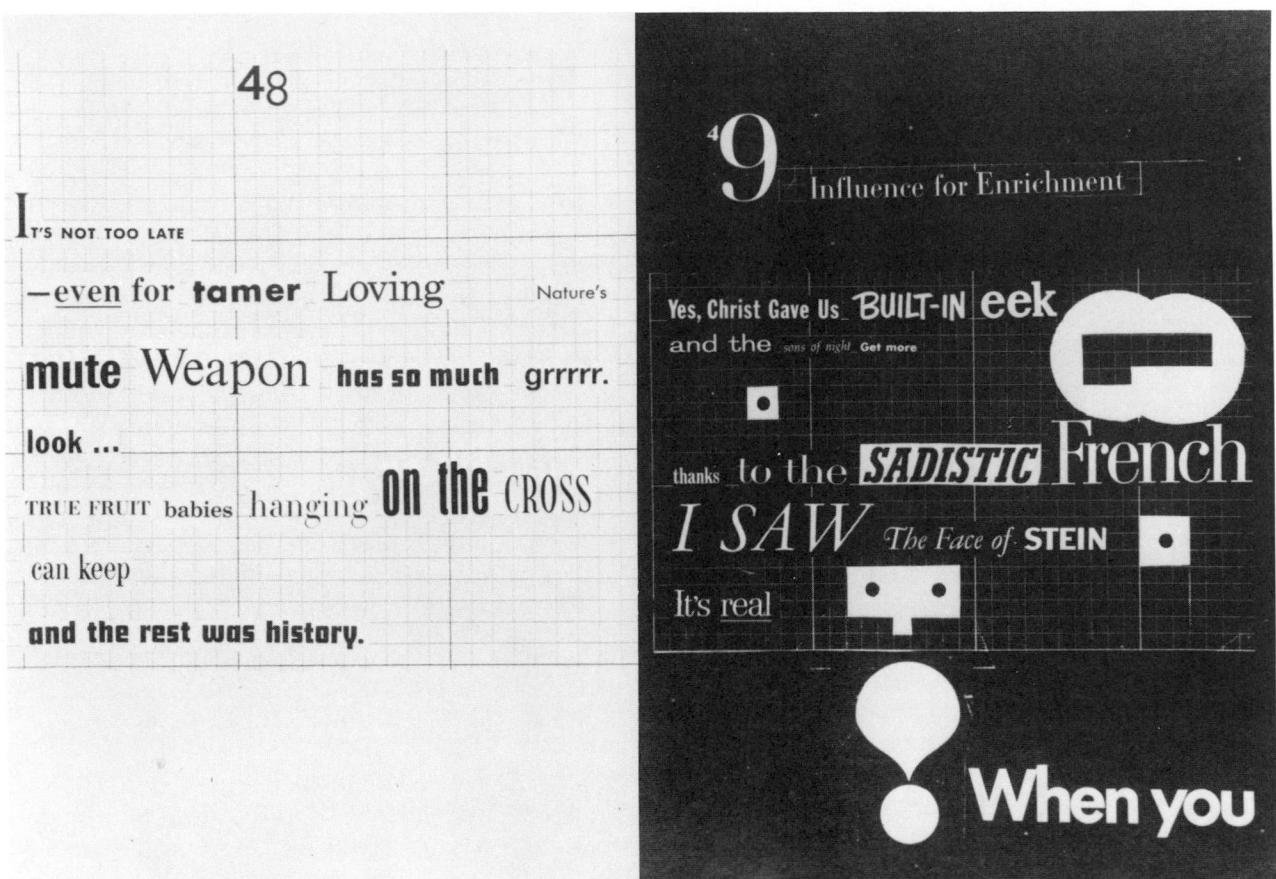

Pages from Silver Flower Coo

Krishna, a long four-part poem of which three parts have been published so far, in 1979, 1981, and 1982. Although *Om Krishna I: Special Effects, Om Krishna II: From the Sickroom of the Walking Eagles,* and *Om Krishna III: Secret Haiku* reflect Ford's immersion in Indian and Buddhist mythology, he continues to employ surrealistic juxtaposition of images and to be aware of and allude to the epic tradition of Whitman.

Om Krishna is, as its name says, a mantra. Traditional mantras, many written after prolonged meditation on the mysteries and powers of sound, may appear meaningless to ordinary humanity but are in fact possessed of a hidden, sacred significance beyond man's powers of comprehension—including even that of its composer. Invoking Krishna, the most popular god in the Hindu pantheon and the most important avatar of Vishnu the preserver, Ford's mantra seeks to aid its speaker to rise above *maya,* the temporal and deceptive veil of the phenomenal world, and to approach Brahma (or Brahman, the supreme existence, awareness,

and truth that exists above *sansara,* the endless cycle of meaningless existence).

The first section of *Om Krishna I* begins with a reminder of the lack of connection between modern art and any living tradition (a likeness "executed in furnace slag/.../... may con correspondents at the next Biennale/and be offered to Peggy Guggenheim") and goes on to evoke the chief divine attention of Shiva, Nandi, who "Raises his head in adoration of the lingam," a phallic emblem of Shiva, who is both the god of destruction, a personification of the disintegrative forces of the cosmos, and the god of regeneration and sexuality. At the same time,

> A portuguese commands in the ante-chamber wipes
>   brick-dust from his eyebrows
> The mystery is no mystery. Whatever you suppose
>   him to be feeling he is feeling whatever reality
>   you imagine is the reality.

If all beings in the phenomenal world are illusions, the result of *maya,* one vision of temporal existence

Front cover for the first section of Ford's four-part poem

molecules will do. . . .

. . . .

. . . Inaudible as the interlacing roots of
an artesan well, cyclonic as the absurd rhetoric
of epic poetry, we rise . . . and dissect.

Even as he satirizes Whitman's concept of progress, juxtaposing images of the absurd that represent Western civilization with images from the symbology and mythologies of the East, he continues his homage to Whitman, paying tribute to his vision even as he denies his optimism. The poet has no more access to the myth than anyone else, and worldly actions are all based on deceptions:

Put your trust in me I shall be inspired by
    falsehood
My awkwardness only makes you more graceful
To deny is to embrace without possessiveness
If tomorrow you are the same I shall await the
    day after

. . . .

What would we do without our deceptions
We are the childless children of ourselves.

For all life's deceptions, the poet asserts, "The validity of sensuality is beyond dispute," and he defends the writing of poetry for its value on this level alone, declaring:

The process of continuing to write poems
    may be equated
With bones shedding their crustacean armor in
    an opalescent vacuum
Though at times analogous to an extravaganza in
    a re-entry vehicle;

and asserting, "My love may not be pure but it is complete/And poetry is a lyric wisdom or it doesn't last." Despite such affirmation, *Om Krishna I* ends on a note of ambivalence, with the knowledge that the soul goes on after the death of individual being and—while its *karma* will determine in what form the soul is reborn—that fate is unknown to the dying individual:

All mistakes have at last been made and there
    are none left to make
But the unvanquished sun whips the blood
Engendering giants of the incalculable
Leaving in their wake an aftersense of spasms of
    awareness.

Just as the first part of Ford's epic is set in the realm of Shiva, *Om Krishna II* takes place in the realm of Krishna, mixing allusions and references

is as real as any other. Yet, the section ends with the assertion that poetry still has a role: "To transform the dreadful into the lyrical—what else is poetry, Rainer Maria," says the poet, addressing Rilke.

Yet even a poem of epic proportions must be an anti-epic; gone is the surety of evolution to higher and higher stages of perfection in this world that forms the basis for Whitman's epic. In Ford's poem there is no linear progression, but rather *sansara* the ceaseless transmigration of the soul, a nightmarish cycle of birth, death, and rebirth that is not ended in this world, where even "To be reborn human is not easy." If Whitman can marvel "every atom belonging to me as good as belongs to you," picturing a great meaningful whole of which he is part, the source of meaning for Ford is entirely apart from the phenomenal world, and he contradicts and trivializes Whitman even as he echoes him:

From the arsenal of incongruity any kind of

Covers for the second section of Ford's surrealistic mantra

to Krishna's exploits on behalf of his people with images from the fragmented modern world. He is more than the subject of the poem; he is the means by which the poem is written: "Krishna is the air itself without him music would not be possible." Marianne Moore maintained that the poet must seek to create real toads in imaginary gardens; Ford presents his own seemingly fragmented but all-inclusive method: "Signs and portents come in plain wrappers/Beginning with toads and climaxing with sadhana." *Sadhana,* the method by which one may gain supernatural powers or knowledge and release oneself from *sansara,* leads to a reality beyond Moore's toads. His poem is now moving toward a giant synthesis and he prays "not to move not even with the mind/Until the masterpiece has been mas-

tered." The final section begins with an assertion, "What seems like fragmentation is making all in one," and he goes on to praise Tchelitchew, "Excelsior of sensory disturbances," a prophet whose "enchanter's hand//Grounded planets in process of formation" and who went beyond his uncomprehending subjects:

> He left them as he found them unconverted
> Ginseng roots wrenched from their circuits
> Mix with the dregs of a dreamless sleep.

Evoking the last lines of *Song of Myself,* in which Whitman assures those readers who have failed to understand his poem that "I stop somewhere waiting for you," Ford asserts that his work (and Tchelitchew's) will, like Whitman's be understood. Also like Whitman, he now has a system of belief upon which to base a true epic. The anti-epic of part one has been transformed to epic. Whether or not Ford, in the last volume of his poem, will create the great cosmic synthesis that such a poem required remains to be seen.

"Om Krishna IV: Distilled Birthmarks" is complete but not yet published. Ford is now in the process of ordering and composing what he considers one of his major works, "The Minotaur Sutra: A Haiku Testament," a manuscript of more than two hundred pages to which he has devoted thirteen years of work in Nepal. He is also preparing another exhibition, "The Kathmandu Experience II."

Charles Henri Ford suffered the obscurity of many original poets during the 1930s and 1940s, and during the 1950s, when a new generation was rediscovering poets such as Williams and Louis Zukofsky, he had largely removed himself from the poetry scene. Though his poetry can be uneven and some of it seems intentionally private, his best poems reward the sensitive reader with insights into the workings of an innovative mind.

References:

Andrew Field, *Djuna: The Life and Times of Djuna Barnes* (New York: Putnam's, 1983);

Hugh Ford, *Published in Paris: American and British Writers, Printers, and Publishers in Paris, 1920-1939* (New York: Macmillan, 1975);

Edward B. Germain, Introduction to *Flag of Ecstasy: Selected Poems*, edited by Germain (Los Angeles: Black Sparrow Press, 1972);

Paul Mariani, *William Carlos Williams: A New World Naked* (New York, St. Louis, San Francisco, Toronto, Sydney, London, Mexico & Hamburg: McGraw-Hill, 1981), pp. 289-292, 402-404;

John Bernard Myers, *Tracking the Marvelous: A Life in the New York Art World* (New York: Random House, 1983);

Parker Tyler, *The Divine Comedy of Pavel Tchelitchew* (New York: Fleet, 1967).

Papers:

The Humanities Research Center, University of Texas at Austin, has a collection of Ford's papers.

Horace Gregory

(10 April 1898-11 March 1982)

David Zucker
Quinnipiac College

BOOKS: *Chelsea Rooming House* (New York: Covici-Friede, 1930); republished as *Rooming House* (London: Faber & Faber, 1932);

Pilgrim of the Apocalypse: A Critical Study of D. H. Lawrence (New York: Viking, 1933; London: Secker, 1934);

No Retreat, Poems (New York: Harcourt, Brace, 1933);

A Wreath for Margery (New York: Modern Editions Press, 1933?);

Chorus for Survival (New York: Covici-Friede, 1935);

Poems, 1930-1940 (New York: Harcourt, Brace, 1941);

The Shield of Achilles: Essays on Beliefs in Poetry (New York: Harcourt, Brace, 1944);

A History of American Poetry, 1900-1940, by Gregory and Marya Zaturenska (New York: Harcourt, Brace, 1946);

Selected Poems (New York: Viking, 1951);

Poet of the People: An Evaluation of James Whitcomb Riley, by Gregory, Jeanette Covert Nolan, and James T. Farrell (Bloomington: Indiana University Press, 1951);

Robert Graves: A Parable for Writers, Partisan Review, 20 (January-February 1953);

Amy Lowell: Portrait of the Poet in Her Time (Edinburgh & New York: Nelson, 1958);

The World of James McNeill Whistler (New York: Nelson, 1959; London: Hutchinson, 1961);

The Dying Gladiators, and Other Essays (New York: Grove Press, 1961);

Medusa in Gramercy Park (New York: Macmillan, 1961);

Alphabet for Joanna, A Poem (New York: Holt, Rinehart & Winston, 1963);

Collected Poems (New York: Holt, Rinehart & Winston, 1964);

Dorothy Richardson: An Adventure in Self-Discovery (New York: Holt, Rinehart & Winston, 1967);

The House on Jefferson Street: A Cycle of Memories (New York: Holt, Rinehart & Winston, 1971);

Spirit of Time and Place: Collected Essays (New York: Norton, 1973);

Another Look: Poems (New York: Holt, Rinehart & Winston, 1976).

OTHER: *The Triumph of Life: Poems of Consolation for the English-Speaking World*, edited, with an introduction, by Gregory (New York: Viking, 1943);

The Portable Sherwood Anderson, edited, with an introduction, by Gregory (New York: Viking, 1949);

Vernon Lee (Violet Paget), *The Snake Lady & Other Stories*, edited, with an introduction, by Gregory (New York: Grove Press, 1954);

Robert Browning, *Selected Poetry*, introduction by Gregory (New York: Rinehart, 1956);

The Mentor Book of Religious Verse, edited by Gregory and Marya Zaturenska (New York: New American Library, 1957);

The Crystal Cabinet, an Invitation to Poetry, edited by Gregory and Zaturenska (New York: Holt, Rinehart & Winston, 1962);

The Silver Swan: Poems of Romance and Mystery, edited by Gregory and Zaturenska (New York: Holt, Rinehart & Winston, 1966).

TRANSLATIONS: *The Poems of Catullus* (New York: Covici-Friede, 1931);

Ovid, *The Metamorphoses* (New York: Viking, 1958);

Ovid, *Love Poems: Amores, The Art of Love, The Cures for Love* (New York: New American Library, 1964).

Although Horace Gregory's *Collected Poems* (1964) received the Bollingen Prize in Poetry in 1965 and he was a member of the National Institute of Arts and Letters, these prestigious recognitions of his excellence did little to alter the politely appreciative but muted response to Gregory's work during his long and productive life. As poet, translator, biographer, editor, critic, and teacher, he was the essential man of letters. Everything about him was intensely literary. Reading his graceful, honest, vivid (and, again, somewhat neglected) autobiography, *The House on Jefferson Street* (1971), one becomes saturated in Gregory's reading life. A man who was happily married to another poet and who experienced life richly, Gregory always gave the impression that he filtered all experience, though finely, through his passion for poetry and through his passion for the life of the writer. Partly, this intense literariness, sometimes bordering on belletrisme, owed much to his childhood illness. Barely surviving birth and infancy, afflicted by tuberculosis of the spine that left him for the rest of his life with a tremor and partial paralysis, he was nursed in the family house in Milwaukee and read to by his mother and aunt. Thus encouraged to devour books, he became obsessed with words and the rhythms of language. Gregory's poetry is notable for its masterly balance between colloquial and formal in rhythm and diction and its brilliant dra-

Horace Gregory (photograph by Nancy Rosenfeld)

matic intelligence, no mean companion at its best to the monologues of Robert Browning, T. S. Eliot, and John Berryman. Indeed anthologists and literary historians ought to be more aware of such poems as "Dempsey," sections of "Chorus for Survival," "Four Monologues from *The Passion of M'Phail*," "Police Sergeant Malone and the Six Dead Drinkers," "The Beggar on the Beach," and "Opera! Opera!" as masterpieces of portraiture. Yet, except for a few poems, Gregory's work is seldom anthologized. Although he developed his own voice and outlook, his work frequently has a derivative quality—too Eliotic, too steadily classical-humanist-Anglo-Irish-Emersonian, too consciously literary with a philosophically vague cast. In spite of the recognition he has received, he has never had the following of those post-World War II poets such as Randall Jarrell, Delmore Schwartz, and John Berryman, who also had solid academic and critical rootedness. His best work was published in the 1930s, after the deluge of Ezra Pound and T. S. Eliot and just before the innovative vigor of the postwar explosion of new voices. He assimilated into his steady style the limpid classicism, imagism, and allusiveness of Pound, Eliot, and H. D. (Hilda Doolittle); the Anglo-Irish eloquence and symbolic range of William Butler Yeats; the freewheeling, sardonic proletarianism of Kenneth Fearing. Yet the very similarity of his work to that of such better-known poets prevented him from gaining a major reputation.

Of Irish and German stock, Horace Victor Gregory was born in Milwaukee, Wisconsin, to Anna Catherine Henckel Gregory and Henry Bolton Gregory. At the time of his birth his parents lived over one of the two drugstores Henry Gregory owned, but by the end of Horace's childhood he had set up his own general supply company, dealing mainly in chemical and bakery supplies and machinery. The family was highly literate and somewhat eccentric; with only two years of formal schooling as a child, Henry Gregory had taught himself Latin and mathematics from books at home, and his brother John (Horace's uncle), editor-in-chief of the *Evening Wisconsin* and one of the founders of the first printers' unions in Milwaukee, spent most of his waking hours reading and writing verse, best enjoyed himself regaling dinner guests with poetry recitations late into the night, and was often thought drunk when in fact he was simply elated with literary ardor. The young Horace regularly spent Saturday afternoons and evenings at his uncle's house, where he would read the *New York Evening Sun* and the *Boston Evening*

Transcript as well as books by Charles Darwin, Walter Scott, Shakespeare, Samuel Johnson, George Eliot, and others. His Aunt Victoria regularly took him to poetry recitals in his teens, and by the time he was sixteen he had attended readings by James Whitcomb Riley, Carl Sandburg, and Robert Frost. He met both Sherwood Anderson and Emanuel Carnevali while in his teens.

When he was about ten years old Gregory was in the hospital for six months and then convalescent at home for the same length of time, and he became an avid though eclectic reader. In 1918, after a year of private tuition at home, he entered the German English Academy (renamed the Milwaukee University School during World War I); while there he went to the theater once a week, seeing works by Shaw, Synge, Verhaeren, Chekhov, and others, and avidly read modern poetry (notably Edward Marsh's *Georgian Poetry* annuals). In 1918 he visited New York and Long Island for six weeks, witnessing the briefly notorious "Slacker Raid" (in which able-bodied men not in military uniforms were arrested and imprisoned), and returned disaffectedly to a Wisconsin which he now thought was provincial. His parents, however, refused to send him east for his schooling, and in the summer of 1919 he enrolled at the University of Wisconsin at Madison, graduating with a B.A. in 1923. "Madison was far less provincial than I feared," Gregory recorded in his autobiography *The House on Jefferson Street* (1971): "its faculty had been recruited from the faculties at Yale, Harvard, and Columbia." Gregory spent the summer of 1919 learning to loaf, he later recalled; he wrote at least one exercise in verse a day and read voraciously. When in October 1919 the returning veterans from World War I, disillusioned from their battlefield experience and filled with youthful excess, arrived on campus, the tone of life on the campus intensified; and Gregory found himself stimulated in particular by William Ellery Leonard, professor of Anglo-Saxon, who took him under his wing after reading a sonnet the student had submitted to the literary magazine. The "youthful Epicureanism" fed both by Leonard's personal magnetism and his translation of Lucretius had a profound effect on Gregory, and it was because of Leonard's insistence that Gregory resumed his earlier Latin studies and began to translate Catullus.

Another source of stimulation for Gregory was the proximity of Chicago, which included Madison in its cultural orbit. Not only was Chicago the home of Harriet Monroe's *Poetry*, but it had been the starting place for Margaret Anderson's *Little*

Review; Sherwood Anderson had had an impact there, championing young writers such as Ernest Hemingway, William Faulkner, and Hart Crane; the Chicago press reprinted James Gibbons Huneker's weekly *New York Sun* columns on European arts, and the city was source not only for copies of the *Little Review* but also for *Vanity Fair* and the *Dial.* "Without knowing it," Gregory recalled, he and his friends "were preparing themselves for the writings of the late 1920s, for a renewed appreciation of Gide, for Joyce and Proust, and that strange something that Eugene Jolas in his magazine, *transition,* was to call the 'Revolution of the word.' " Gregory was open not only to modernism and the search for a new aesthetic but also for a new politics: he fell briefly under the spell of Wisconsin Senator Robert Lafollette's Centrist Progressivism and flirted with leftist politics. But Gregory always held radicalism at arm's length: it was another experience, intensely felt, earnestly examined, but never made his raison d'être. In the early 1930s he refused in New York to join the Communist party, essentially because, "unimpressed by writers who talked incessantly of their political beliefs," he was appalled by its intellectual rigidity, and specifically, by a refusal to discuss T. S. Eliot, whose *The Waste Land* (1922) had been, in the *Dial,* "an explosion even more devastating than the magazine's revelation of the work of Thomas Mann," Gregory said.

In addition to Leonard, another Madison influence was Margery Latimer (for whom he wrote a fine elegy in 1932), who avoided all fads and even all literature courses. In 1925 or 1926 in New York she re-introduced him to Kenneth Fearing (Fearing had entered the University of Wisconsin while Gregory was there). Gregory later called Fearing one of the literary ancestors of the New York-Black Mountain-San Francisco schools of poets of the 1980s; his wit, colloquial power, and genuine proletarian passions were important shaping forces in Gregory's poetry.

Gregory's receptivity to such strongly individualist personalities, combined with the mixed blessing of a confined childhood surrounded by highly literate eccentricity, kept him away from the narrowing herd instincts that reduced to mediocrity so many of his contemporaries. Although one hears constant echoes of Yeats and Eliot (his chief literary masters, both of whom he met and whose personalities affected him), by and large he assimilated them into his humble yet passionate style.

When he arrived in New York in February 1923 with fifty dollars in his pocket, he had already had some poems accepted by Harriet Monroe's *Poetry,* and he was determined to survive as a writer. When he ran out of funds (he stubbornly refused to cash the occasional checks his mother sent him), he found a job reading manuscripts for Horace Liveright for roughly twenty dollars a week, an income he supplemented by writing movie reviews (for the *Amalgamated Garment Makers Union Weekly*) and reports on scenarios for Paramount Pictures' New York office. He walked the streets of Hell's Kitchen and Chelsea (where he had a room on 23rd Street), seeing both the city's wretched and its literary types as potential dramatis personae. He soon broke with the genteel literary models that he followed for a time. He commented in *Twentieth Century Authors* in 1942 that he "contributed formal verse to *Vanity Fair, The Nation* . . . but I soon found the facile 'charm' of these verses lacking in everything I wanted to say." He had taken his New York experience and Fearing's poetry to heart. Gregory's books, beginning with *Chelsea Rooming House* (1930), include none of these facile poems.

Gregory left Chelsea early in 1924 and took a room in Greenwich Village at six dollars a week and in November contracted a severe case of jaundice; he was hospitalized until his mother arrived from Milwaukee and moved him into the Brevoort Hotel. The crisis of that illness crystallized his New York experience and influenced his work and life. His observations in the hospital had some of the visionary intensity he had felt as a sickly child: "I went into silent rages against the injustice of the world, its brutalities, its terror." After recuperation he began to see into the heart of "life's dramatic action" and realized that a good poem "should stand as a metaphor of human destiny. My hope was to accomplish this end in the poetry I wrote. And I also thought that the best proof of my convictions was to write the poems, rather than to theorize too much about them—that a poem's meaning was implicit, composed of the right (often the fewest) words in the best order." The resulting poems, in *Chelsea Rooming House,* combine romantic grandeur with classical and imagist purity.

Recovered from his jaundice, Gregory convalesced in Milwaukee for two weeks and then returned to New York, getting a job writing real estate advertisements and renting a room in the west seventies. He spent most of his free time in the New York Public Library, reading widely in American history, fiction (especially German: he read Thomas Mann's *Buddenbrooks*), and Latin and was inspired to continue his English versions of Catullus. Kenneth Fearing introduced him to the

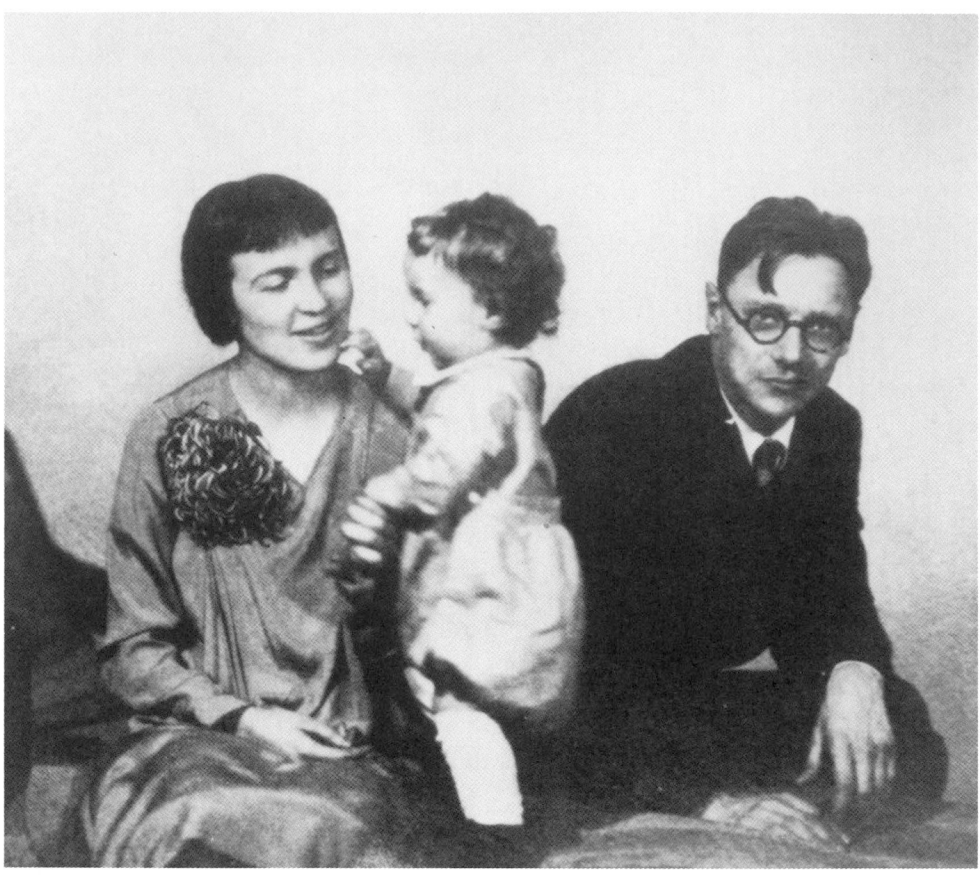

Marya Zaturenska, Joanna Gregory, and Horace Gregory, 1928

poet Marya Zaturenska, who had just returned to New York after two years at the library school at Madison, and had heard about Gregory from William Ellery Leonard; they married on 21 August 1925. (They had two children, Joanna, born in 1926 and Patrick, born in 1931.) Living on Washington Square, Gregory lost his copy-writing job after a brief illness and started to make a living as a book reviewer until the summer of 1926, when the couple moved to an apartment on President Street in Brooklyn and Gregory took a job as production manager publishing engineering books. The job did not last long, for in March 1927 Gregory contracted scarlet fever (with a two-month-old baby in the apartment), and when he got back to work he discovered the book publishing division of the company was closing down. Gregory had by this time published poetry in the *New Yorker* (pseudonymously) and elsewhere, and after an ill-fated attempt to write promotional articles for *Women's Wear* (he lasted a month) he tried to live off book reviews for the *Nation* and the *New Republic* and in order to survive found himself forced to accept

twenty-five dollars a week support from his father.

In the summer of 1927, with the help of Horace's father, the Gregorys moved to the experimental Sunnyside housing development on the edge of Long Island City (Lewis Mumford was a neighbor), and with the crash of 1929, like many literary people who had little to lose, the Gregorys managed to get by. Deeply affected by the despair of those around them, they began to drift politically to the left. Gregory joined the John Reed Club briefly (1930-1931) and attended a few Communist meetings, contributing to *New Masses* as well as to little magazines such as *Pagany, Blues,* and *Hound and Horn.* The bleakness of the years 1929 to 1932 was relieved in part by holiday trips to Milwaukee, with stopovers in Chicago to stay with Harriet Monroe; in part by meeting such people as James T. Farrell, Van Wyck Brooks, Morton D. Zabel, and Norbert Wiener; and in part by the publication in 1930 of *Chelsea Rooming House,* by Covici-Friede, then a new and avant-garde publishing house, publishing Richard Aldington, Wyndham Lewis, and Ezra Pound's magazine the *Exile.* At this time Covici-Friede also agreed to bring out Gregory's *The Poems of Catullus* (1931).

The years of hard work, illness, and loneliness gave rise to the keen observations of the varied life of the city that inform the poems in *Chelsea Rooming House*, one of the most impressive first books by any modern American poet. Fifty years after its publication, the book does not, stylistically, appear especially adventurous, and certainly free verse had long been established as the dominant form for avant-garde poetry; but Gregory's free verse is open, remarkably well controlled, and dramatically paced, employing the vigorous and flexible rhythms that he was to perfect for the rest of his life. In *Chelsea Rooming House* Gregory mastered the genre which became his trademark: the elegiac monologue. At the same time that he observed so accurately the human types surrounding him, he was finishing his masterly translations of Catullus, and his attempts to control the colloquial vigor of that poet stood him in good stead for his own poems. In *Chelsea Rooming House* he grasped both the smallness and the sadness of his time. Often close in tone to Sherwood Anderson's *Winesburg, Ohio* (1919), the poems are rendered by a romantically and even religiously informed power of allusion. The tone which controls much of the book is well illustrated by "No Cock Crows at Morning," which begins:

> There is no cock crowing in our bedroom,
> waking good morning startled by his cries:
> the great bird has vanished in a fiery dream,
> his clamorous wings are shut
> and his rolling golden eye
> has gone blind. . . .
> and his radiant comb is a laurel of ashes.

Terrifying, lucidly elegant in cadence, the poem is not confessional, but it is nevertheless a deeply observed and personally anguished response to external and internal realities. Proletarian poems can date badly; yet most of Gregory's, such as "Dempsey," have a reach beyond the topical moment. Gregory was lucky to have the support of a literary house like Covici-Friede to publish both *Chelsea Rooming House* and his Catullus translations.

A major relief from the poverty of life at Sunnyside came in 1932 when, partly on the strength of good reviews for his first book of poetry, and partly as a result of intervention by Malcolm Cowley, the Gregorys were invited to stay at Yaddo for three months. With day-care provided for the Gregorys' two small children (Joanna was now six,

Patrick was one), both parents were free to write, and Gregory completed his next book, *No Retreat* (1933). The book draws on Gregory's interest in occult experience, heightened both by his rereading of work by Yeats in 1931 and 1932 and by his own experience with heightened consciousness in his illnesses as a child and in New York: like *Chelsea Rooming House, No Retreat* is characteristically surrealistic in imagery and dreamlike in atmosphere. The book also contains Gregory's elegy for Margery Latimer, "A Wreath for Margery"; the poem provoked a correspondence with Bryher (Winifred Ellerman), who admired Latimer's fiction, and in 1934, when visiting New York, Bryher invited the Gregorys to stay with her for the summer in England, giving them a check for their passage. It was early in 1934, too, that Gregory, having moved further away from the left as a result of his rereading of Yeats and reading of Eliot's *For Lancelot Andrewes*, met Eliot at a dinner given by Horace Kallen. With the critical success of his first two books of verse, Gregory was beginning to achieve recognition, and on their return from England, Gregory (who had in 1933 published his study of D. H. Lawrence, *Pilgrim of the Apocalypse*) took a faculty position at Sarah Lawrence College, where he taught until his retirement in 1960. The trip to England confirmed much in his developing imagination. There he met H. D. (Hilda Doolittle) and Dorothy Richardson, strengthened his acquaintance with Eliot, and visited Yeats in Dublin (who told him he had a vision of Gregory's grandfather—who, unknown to Yeats, had claimed to be related to the Gregorys of Coole). Gregory loved Dublin and loved the extension of the city in Yeats's "wonderful 18th-century eloquence." His reading during the journey intensified his interests in spiritualist phenomena. Visions, ghosts, visitations in his work are not simply literary devices but border on convictions that the mind can transcend, as well as be rooted in, time and place. In England he finished his next book of poems, *Chorus for Survival* (1935), in which the elegiac grew increasingly philosophic. In one sequence, Emerson emerges as the representation of Gregory's, and all America's, consciousness. In *No Retreat* and *Chorus for Survival*, Gregory developed into an excellent philosophical lyric poet. His characterization of Robinson Jeffers, expressed in an essay written in 1951, identifies his own best qualities: "a master of style without nervous reference to recent fashions in literary criticism. . . . He is well removed from the kind of company where poetry is 'taught' so as to be understood, where critics and reviewers are known to be instructors of literature in colleges and universities." The landscapes and characters of *Chorus for Survival* are shadowy yet intensely imagined; at the same time, they are reflections of the spiritual sources of American history—and all history—especially as it is colored by classical humanism. (Gregory felt from his Madison days the necessity of seeking his European, as well as American, roots.)

His autobiography, *The House on Jefferson Street*, with its many illuminations of the spirit of time and place and with its keen assessments of literary movements as well as individual writers, ends in the 1930s. For the rest of his life he developed quietly and firmly his remarkably intense intellectual and political vision.

By the age of thirty-five, Gregory had found his voice. His wife, Marya Zaturenska, continued to refine her poetic talents, and she won the Pulitzer Prize for *Cold Morning Sky* (1937) in 1938. In 1937 Gregory began a literary journal, *New Letters*, with Eleanor Clark, but it was discontinued after a year.

The title character in "Fortune for Mirabel," a suite collected in *Poems, 1930-1940* (1941), illustrates Gregory's sense of the poet's visionary role, sometimes playfully conceived, which was developing in *Chorus for Survival*. The poet-prophet continues to take stock of history and legend in noble, sometimes monotonously dignified and melancholy appraisals of the emptiness of history, as in these lines from "The Wakeful Hour," a section of "Fortunes for Mirabel":

> a vision of life within motion,
> Volition within life
> That has no beginning and no end
> And is always near.

Thematically and stylistically effective though these lines are in their echo of Eliot, there are in the whole book too many echoes of *Burnt Norton* (1936), the first of Eliot's *Four Quartets* (1936-1942), for the writing to be wholly satisfactory. Far more successful is "Four Monologues from *The Passion of M'Phail*," the imaginative triumph of *Poems, 1930-1940* and probably the most powerful sequence Gregory ever wrote. A masterpiece of ironic portraiture, the monologues climax the mode of elegiac meditation which elsewhere in the book is rather too abstract. In "Four Monologues from *The Passion of M'Phail*," Gregory characterizes a supersalesman, whose self-consciously brilliant and tormented confessions have a magnificent sardonic edge:

> If you are strong as I am, you can hear
> yourself talking to yourself at night
> until your hair turns gray:
> "I am God's white-haired boy,
> I almost love the way I sell
> my lips, my blood, my heart. . . . "

Gregory never lost touch with this frighteningly (and charmingly) hubristic American character; M'Phail is a familiar spirit of his work, as much a part of him as Emerson. M'Phail can say: "I am not the same as other men;/. . ./Everything I live for is not quite lost." In such passages, Gregory shows a genuinely democratic love, a sharing of the American landscape from top to bottom, a direct development of his social consciousness that he never sentimentalized, institutionalized, or abandoned.

"The Door in the Desert," a section in *Selected Poems* (1951), demonstrates Gregory's continuing progression away from the immediately local concrete particular: he cultivated a more pure philosophical tone, divorced from time and space; the verse is frequently circular and undramatic, and the melancholy strain in his own temperament became increasingly choral, detached. Odysseus, in one poem, symbolizes the artist himself, and in "Venus and the Lute Player," Gregory comments on the Odysseus-artist figure by pointing to the sheer inadequacy of art to capture or move the eternal spirit: Venus's disembodied voice says, "I am eternal/Even beyond the sight of artful men," and concludes:

> I, the world's Mistress, remain indifferent
> To strings that tremble, to reads that blow.
>   I am what you seek,
> And all you need to know.

The world of art is utterly detached from the physical world in its disembodiment, and it is the mystery of eternal forces—his fascination with Yeats's occultism making a strong appearance from this point on in his poems—that moves him most deeply in fine poems such as "The Ladder and the Vine," in which his religious imagination and the poet's vatic inheritance are most clearly felt.

Ten years later, in *Medusa in Gramercy Park* (1961), Gregory was as accomplished as ever with monologue; but there are fewer poems that have the energy of the earlier books. A distanced, lyrically attenuated voice dominates; themes repeat themselves too predictably, even mechanically; and the intense spiritualism of "The Door in the Desert" appears forced. One of his stage-Irishmen and witty commentators, MacMurry O'Keefe, hovers between clever light versifier and bore, and often reflects an excessive archness. "If It Offend Thee. . . ," however, stands out as vividly convincing, the dramatic occasion of a guilt-ridden man releases its full power, almost as if the poet is absent. It is one of Gregory's best monologues.

In old age, Gregory published his last book, *Another Look* (1976), which has the same cool, beautifully modulated meditative tone that Gregory spent his life perfecting. It shows his continued fascination for the sources of the imagination, but aesthetically and spiritually it is in the same vein as *Medusa in Gramercy Park*—a few high moments but otherwise a sometimes deadly sameness. But those high moments have rare insight and beauty, as they combine unearthliness and colloquial sardonic power, as in "The Muse Behind the Laurel," in which Gregory came as close as he ever did to rendering a dramatically vital moment of the Imagination's struggle against banality and the implacability of history (alluding, however, to Eliot at a key moment):

> "Make me imperishable and violent, all wings,
> a Muse of History: blood, hail, and fire
> still falling from the skies—
>   see, I am broken,
> a thankless prophetess, held in a bulletproof cage
> for fools to stare at."
>   Was that her fate?
> And was she fit for sanatorium or museum?
> Not quite.
> . . . .
> She will not threaten you, nor sing, nor weep.
> And should you question her, she may not hear you,
> and if you gaze at her, she will not turn,
> and if you touch her, she is as stern as iron—
> an effigy of peace, and painted white.

Gregory continued to teach modern poetry and classics in translation at Sarah Lawrence until his retirement in 1960, living for many years in an eighteenth-century house in Palisades, in Rockland County, New York. His translations from Catullus and Ovid are superb and will endure, triumphs of his often magic ability to combine colloquial and grand power in English. In those translations, his language perfectly mirrors the transforming powers of both Latin poets.

Considering that most of it was occasional, Gregory's criticism shows a remarkable range of erudition and solidity of judgment: in his autobiography he somewhat ruefully recalls pacing back and forth in search of the exact word, for a review that would be forgotten the day after it was printed, and his gradual hatred of book reviewing in the years before 1934 reinforced his hatred of mediocrity. Once he was secure in his faculty position at Sarah Lawrence he reviewed only those books he found worthwhile. Collections of his essays—*The Shield of Achilles* (1944), *The Dying Gladiators* (1961), and *Spirit of Time and Place* (1973)—show a steadiness of critical integrity. Sometimes his judgments appear pedestrian, but only because they are juxtaposed, in the various collections, with his keener judgments, for instance, on tone in Lawrence's fiction or on the combination of religious and common imagery in Beckett's plays. His essays are consistently informed by beauty and force of style. Most of all, one always senses that Gregory the critic, like the poet, was his own man: his themes have his visionary fervor tempered by shrewd common sense.

Gregory's wife, Marya Zaturenska, often his collaborator on anthologies and on *A History of American Poetry, 1900-1940* (1946), died on 19 January 1982. Not quite two months later, a month before his eighty-fourth birthday, Horace Gregory died in a nursing home in Shelburne Falls, Massachusetts.

Reference:

Modern Poetry Studies, special Gregory issue, 4 (Spring 1973).

Papers:

Most of Gregory's papers are at the Syracuse University Library.

Langston Hughes

R. Baxter Miller
University of Tennessee

See also the Hughes entry in *DLB 7: Twentieth-Century American Dramatists.*

BIRTH: Joplin, Missouri, 1 February 1902, to James Nathaniel and Carrie Mercer Langston Hughes.

EDUCATION: Columbia University, 1921-1922; B.A., Lincoln University (Pennsylvania), 1929.

AWARDS AND HONORS: *Opportunity* magazine poetry prize, 1925; Amy Spingarn Contest (*Crisis* magazine) poetry and essay prizes, 1925; Harmon Gold Medal for *Not Without Laughter*, 1931; Rosenwald Fellowships, 1931, 1941; Guggenheim Fellowship, 1935; Litt.D., Lincoln University (Pennsylvania), 1943; National Institute and American Academy of Arts and Letters Award in Literature, 1946; Anisfield-Wolf Award, 1953; Spingarn Medal, 1960; Litt.D., Howard University, 1963; Litt.D., Western Reserve University, 1964.

DEATH: New York, New York, 22 May 1967.

BOOKS: *The Weary Blues* (New York: Knopf, 1926; London: Knopf, 1926);
Fine Clothes to the Jew (New York: Knopf, 1927; London: Knopf, 1927);
Not Without Laughter (New York & London: Knopf, 1930; London: Allen & Unwin, 1930);
Dear Lovely Death (Amenia, N.Y.: Privately printed at the Troutbeck Press, 1931);
The Negro Mother and Other Dramatic Recitations (New York: Golden Stair Press, 1931);
The Dream Keeper and Other Poems (New York: Knopf, 1932);
Scottsboro Limited: Four Poems and a Play in Verse (New York: Golden Stair Press, 1932);
Popo and Fifina: Children of Haiti, by Hughes and Arna Bontemps (New York: Macmillan, 1932);
A Negro Looks at Soviet Central Asia (Moscow & Leningrad: Co-operative Publishing Society of Foreign Workers in the U.S.S.R., 1934);
The Ways of White Folks (New York: Knopf, 1934;

Langston Hughes (photograph by Carl Van Vechten; by permission of Joseph Solomon, the Estate of Carl Van Vechten)

London: Allen & Unwin, 1934);
A New Song (New York: International Workers Order, 1938);
The Big Sea: An Autobiography (New York & London: Knopf, 1940; London: Hutchinson, 1940);
Shakespeare in Harlem (New York: Knopf, 1942);
Freedom's Plow (New York: Musette Publishers, 1943);
Jim Crow's Last Stand (Atlanta: Negro Publication Society of America, 1943);
Lament for Dark Peoples and Other Poems (N.p., 1944);
Fields of Wonder (New York: Knopf, 1947);
One-Way Ticket (New York: Knopf, 1949);

Troubled Island [opera], libretto by Hughes, music by William Grant Still (New York: Leeds Music, 1949);

Simple Speaks His Mind (New York: Simon & Schuster, 1950; London: Gollancz, 1951);

Montage of a Dream Deferred (New York: Holt, 1951);

Laughing to Keep from Crying (New York: Holt, 1952);

The First Book of Negroes (New York: Franklin Watts, 1952; London: Bailey & Swinfen, 1956);

Simple Takes a Wife (New York: Simon & Schuster, 1953; London: Gollancz, 1954);

The Glory Round His Head, libretto by Hughes, music by Jan Meyerowitz (New York: Broude Brothers, 1953);

Famous American Negroes (New York: Dodd, Mead, 1954);

The First Book of Rhythms (New York: Franklin Watts, 1954; London: Bailey & Swinfen, 1956);

The First Book of Jazz (New York: Franklin Watts, 1955; London: Bailey & Swinfen, 1957);

Famous Negro Music Makers (New York: Dodd, Mead, 1955);

The Sweet Flypaper of Life, text by Hughes and photographs by Roy DeCarava (New York: Simon & Schuster, 1955);

The First Book of the West Indies (New York: Franklin Watts, 1956; London: Bailey & Swinfen, 1956); republished as *The First Book of the Caribbean* (London: Edmund Ward, 1965);

I Wonder As I Wander: An Autobiographical Journey (New York & Toronto: Rinehart, 1956);

A Pictorial History of the Negro in America, by Hughes and Milton Meltzer (New York: Crown, 1956; revised, 1963; revised again, 1968); revised again as *A Pictorial History of Black Americans,* by Hughes, Meltzer, and C. Eric Lincoln (New York: Crown, 1973);

Simple Stakes a Claim (New York & Toronto: Rinehart, 1957; London: Gollancz, 1958);

The Langston Hughes Reader (New York: Braziller, 1958);

Famous Negro Heroes of America (New York: Dodd, Mead, 1958);

Tamborines to Glory (New York: John Day, 1958; London: Gollancz, 1959);

Selected Poems of Langston Hughes (New York: Knopf, 1959);

Simply Heavenly, book and lyrics by Hughes, music by David Martin (New York: Dramatists Play Service, 1959);

The First Book of Africa (New York: Franklin Watts, 1960; London: Mayflower, 1961; revised edition, New York: Franklin Watts, 1964);

The Best of Simple (New York: Hill & Wang, 1961);

Ask Your Mama: 12 Moods for Jazz (New York: Knopf, 1961);

The Ballad of the Brown King, libretto by Hughes, music by Margaret Bonds (New York: Sam Fox, 1961);

Fight for Freedom: The Story of the NAACP (New York: Norton, 1962);

Something in Common and Other Stories (New York: Hill & Wang, 1963);

Five Plays by Langston Hughes, edited by Webster Smalley (Bloomington: Indiana University Press, 1963);

Simple's Uncle Sam (New York: Hill & Wang, 1965);

The Panther & The Lash (New York: Knopf, 1967);

Black Magic: A Pictorial History of the Negro in American Entertainment, by Hughes and Meltzer (Englewood Cliffs, N.J.: Prentice-Hall, 1967);

Black Misery (New York: Knopf, 1969);

Good Morning Revolution: Uncollected Social Protest Writings by Langston Hughes, edited by Faith Berry (New York & Westport: Lawrence Hill, 1973).

PLAY PRODUCTIONS: *Mulatto,* New York, Vanderbilt Theatre, 24 October 1935;

Little Ham, Cleveland, Karamu House, March 1936;

When the Jack Hollers, by Hughes and Arna Bontemps, Cleveland, Karamu House, April 1936;

Troubled Island, Cleveland, Karamu House, December 1936; opera version, libretto by Hughes, music by William Grant Still, New York, New York City Center, 31 March 1949;

Joy to My Soul, Cleveland, Karamu House, March 1937;

Soul Gone Home, Cleveland, Cleveland Federal Theatre, 1937;

Don't You Want to Be Free?, New York, Harlem Suitcase Theatre, 21 April 1938;

Front Porch, Cleveland, Karamu House, November 1938;

The Organizer, libretto by Hughes, music by James P. Johnson, New York, Harlem Suitcase Theatre, March 1939;

The Sun Do Move, Chicago, Good Shepherd Community House, Spring 1942;

Street Scene, by Elmer Rice, music by Kurt Weill, lyrics by Hughes, New York, Adelphi Theatre, 9 January 1947;

The Barrier, libretto by Hughes, music by Jan Meyerowitz, New York, Columbia University, January 1950; New York, Broadhurst Theatre, 2 November 1950;

Just Around the Corner, by Amy Mann and Bernard Drew, lyrics by Hughes, Ogunguit, Maine, Ogunguit Playhouse, Summer 1951;

Esther, libretto by Hughes, music by Jan Meyerowitz, Urbana, University of Illinois, March 1957;

Simply Heavenly, New York, Eighty-fifth Street Playhouse, 20 October 1957;

The Ballad of the Brown King, libretto by Hughes, music by Margaret Bonds, New York, Clark Auditorium, New York City YMCA, 11 December 1960;

Black Nativity, New York, Forty-first Street Theatre, 11 December 1961;

Gospel Glow, Brooklyn, New York, Washington Temple, October 1962;

Tambourines to Glory, New York, Little Theatre, 2 November 1963;

Let Us Remember Him, libretto by Hughes, music by David Amram, San Francisco, War Memorial Opera House, 15 November 1963;

Jerico-Jim Crow, New York, Village Presbyterian Church and Brotherhood Synagogue, 28 December 1964;

The Prodigal Son, New York, Greenwich Mews Theatre, 20 May 1965.

OTHER: Alain Locke, ed., *The New Negro,* includes nine poems by Hughes (New York: A. & C. Boni, 1925);

Four Negro Poets, includes twenty-one poems by Hughes (New York: Simon & Schuster, 1927);

Four Lincoln University Poets, includes six poems by Hughes (Lincoln University, Pa.: Lincoln University Herald, 1930);

Elmer Rice and Kurt Weill, *Street Scene,* lyrics by Hughes (New York: Chappell, 1948);

The Poetry of the Negro, 1746-1949, edited by Hughes and Arna Bontemps (Garden City: Doubleday, 1949);

Lincoln University Poets, edited by Hughes, Waring Cuney, and Bruce McM. Wright (New York: Fine Editions Press, 1954);

The Book of Negro Folklore, edited by Hughes and Bontemps (New York: Dodd, Mead, 1958);

An African Treasury: Articles/Essays/Stories/Poems by Black Americans, selected, with an introduction, by Hughes (New York: Crown, 1960; London: Gollancz, 1961);

Poems from Black Africa, edited by Hughes (Bloomington: Indiana University Press, 1963);

New Negro Poets: U. S. A., edited by Hughes (Bloom-

ington: Indiana University Press, 1964);

The Book of Negro Humor, edited by Hughes (New York: Dodd, Mead, 1966);

The Best Short Stories by Negro Writers, edited, with an introduction, by Hughes (Boston & Toronto: Little, Brown, 1967).

TRANSLATIONS: Federico García Lorca, *San Gabriel* (N.p., 1938);

Jacques Roumain, "When the Tom-Tom Bears" and "Guinea"; Refino Pedroso, "Opinions of the New Chinese Student," in *Anthology of Contemporary Latin-American Poetry,* edited by Dudley Fitts (Norfolk, Conn.: New Directions, 1942), pp. 191-193, 247-249;

Roumain, *Masters of the Dew,* translated by Hughes and Mercer Cook (New York: Reynal & Hitchcock, 1947);

Nicolas Guillén, *Cuba Libre,* translated by Hughes and Ben Frederic Carruthers (Los Angeles: Ward Richie Press, 1948);

Leon Damas, "Really I Know," "Trite Without Doubt," and "She Left Herself One Evening," in *The Poetry of the Negro, 1746-1949,* edited by Hughes and Arna Bontemps (Garden City: Doubleday, 1949), pp. 371-372;

García Lorca, *Gypsy Ballads,* Beloit Poetry Chapbook, no. 1 (Beloit, Wis.: Beloit Poetry Journal, 1951);

Gabriela Mistral (Lucila Godoy Alcayaga), *Selected Poems* (Bloomington: Indiana University Press, 1957);

Jean-Joseph Rabearivelo, "Flute Players"; David Diop, "Those Who Lost Everything" and "Suffer, Poor Negro," in *Poems from Black Africa,* edited by Hughes (Bloomington: Indiana University Press, 1963), pp. 131-132, 143-145.

Possibly the most influential black American writer of the twentieth century, Langston Hughes set an example of self-determination and artistic integrity. Beginning in the Harlem Renaissance during the early 1920s, his career extended to the Black Arts Movement of the late 1960s. In his early twenties Hughes mingled with such different writers and artists as Countee Cullen, Zora Neale Hurston, Aaron Douglass, and Josephine Baker; during his forties he helped to inspire the young writers Margaret Walker and Gwendolyn Brooks. Finally, he encouraged writers of a third generation, including Ted Joans, Alice Walker, and Mari Evans.

During the forty-six years between 1921 and

1967, Hughes became well known and loved. Even before he helped to open the doors of the major periodicals and publishing houses to young black writers, he worked to free American literature from the plantation tradition, infusing his technically accomplished writings with self-assurance and racial pride and earning acclaim for his innovations in literary blues and jazz.

James Mercer Langston Hughes was born to Carrie Mercer Langston Hughes and James Nathaniel Hughes on 1 February 1902 in Joplin, Missouri. On his mother's side the family had a fairly prominent place in the history of emancipation. His grandfather, Charles Howard Langston, married in 1869 the poet's grandmother Mary Leary, widow of one of the casualties of John Brown's 1859 raid on Harpers Ferry, and in 1870 he moved with her to the abolitionist stronghold of Lawrence, Kansas. Charles Langston was, like his brother John Mercer Langston (1829-1897), an active abolitionist and the first Afro-American representative to Congress from Virginia. Carrie Langston, the poet's mother, had had a year of college and had literary inclinations which included writing poetry but which more frequently manifested themselves in the recitation of dramatic monologues in costume. James Nathaniel Hughes, the poet's father, was an ambitious man, who, after the frustration of studying law by correspondence course from Chicago and then being denied permission by the all-white examining board to take the Oklahoma Territory bar examination, moved to Joplin in 1899 with his wife. There, after four years of marriage and the death of his first child (in 1900), angered by unremitting poverty and faced with supporting an eighteen-month-old child, the hard-working James Hughes, driven by ambitions and hungers that racial prejudice denied, left the United States in October 1903 for Mexico, where he eventually prospered and thus was able to contribute to the support of his son. Carrie Hughes refused to accompany him, and unable to get even menial jobs in Joplin, she constantly moved from city to city (Topeka, Kansas; Colorado Springs) looking for work, occasionally taking the young Langston with her. For most of the next nine years, however, the young Langston Hughes lived by and large in Lawrence with his grandmother (who died in 1912). The son, however, repeated the mother's peripatetic and rootless life. He visited her briefly in Topeka, stayed with her in Colorado, and traveled with her to Mexico in 1908 to see his father. As he sardonically put it to Richard Wright some years later, "Six months

in one place is long enough to make one's life complicated."

Grandmother Langston, unlike most black women in Lawrence, refused to take menial work and managed by renting rooms to students from the University of Kansas. These were poverty-ridden years, but they were not uneventful. In 1907, while the five-year-old Langston lived with his mother in Topeka, she not only introduced him to the resources of the town library ("even before I was six," recalled the poet, "books began to happen to me, so that after a while there came a time when I believed in books more than in people which, of course, was wrong") but also to the delights of poetical and dramatic recitation. On one occasion he made faces behind her back while she performed and reduced the audience to outrageous laughter. From the subsequent whipping, he learned to respect other people's art. When he was six-and-a-half, his mother enrolled him in the white Harrison Street School—an experience which on the one hand made him feel something of an outcast among his school fellows, and on the other—amid the clamor that arose because of his attendance at the school and the support he got from teachers and from children—taught him "not to hate *all* white people."

His grandmother took him to hear speeches by Booker T. Washington, and in 1910 to Osawatomie, where as the last surviving widow of John Brown's raid, she sat on the speaker's platform with Theodore Roosevelt. When his grandmother died and her house was repossessed for lack of mortgage payments, Hughes went to live with family friends Uncle and Auntie Reed. Here for the first time, he later recalled, he got not only enough to eat but also a sense of belonging to a family. Their settled way of life included regular attendance at Sunday school and church. On one occasion, sent to a revival meeting, Hughes feigned conversion because it was expected of him and then spent the night alone in bed in tears, feeling lost and deceitful, let down by a Jesus who had not appeared. The proselytism of the Reed household, by negative example, gave the young Hughes a capacity for intellectual tolerance and helped shape his social and literary imagination. Religion as an expression of piety did not impress him; yet in later life his verse would echo black spirituals and would express by turns the anger and the doubts of the man who wanted to believe yet could not.

In 1914 his mother remarried and Hughes joined her in Lincoln, Illinois. When he graduated from grammar school in the spring of 1916 his classmates elected him class poet, though he had never written a poem before, presumably because they thought blacks had rhythm. He was an avid and indiscriminate reader, but the only poets he knew were Paul Laurence Dunbar and Henry Wadsworth Longfellow. He enjoyed fiction because in novels the mortgage always got paid and people had enough to eat. He had no thought of becoming a writer.

In the summer of 1916 his stepfather, Homer Clark, moved the family to Cleveland, where he had found work in a steel mill and where Hughes entered Central High School in the fall. The years he spent there, from 1916 to 1920, were stimulating and fruitful, despite his stepfather's inability to stand the heat in the steel mill and subsequent shifting from job to job, and despite financial insecurity and erratic poverty. Like most urban blacks in those years, the Clarks spent most of their income on rent and lived in a succession of attic or basement quarters. But at Central High, and at the Neighborhood Association (later known as Karamu House), Hughes discovered his major interests. Through his teacher Clara Dieke he developed a talent for the graphic arts. Studying painting with her, he learned much about order and stamina, that "the only way to get a thing done is to start to do it, then keep on doing it, and finally you'll finish it, even if in the beginning you think you can't do it at all." In his sophomore English class Ethel Weimer told the students that "there are ways of saying or doing things, which may not be the currently approved ways, yet that can be very true and beautiful ways that people will come to recognize in due time." She read them work from the Chicago school of poets: Edgar Lee Masters, Vachel Lindsay, and—especially influential on Hughes's work—Carl Sandburg, about whom he wrote a poem. Sandburg's poems, he wrote at fifteen, "Fall on the white pages of his books/Like blood-clots of song/From the wounds of humanity." With Sandburg as his "guiding light," Hughes regularly published poems in the school literary magazine, the *Belfry Owl.*

At Central High Hughes discovered the pleasures of gregariousness. He went to his first symphony concert; he mixed with the children of foreign-born parents, who were friendlier than native-born whites; he read *The Gadfly* (Ethel Boole Voynich's 1891 novel about the reunification of Italy), *Jean Christophe* (Romane Rolland's 1904 novel about a musician's struggle as an artist in an alien world), the *Liberator,* and the *Socialist Call,* all lent him by fellow students who took him to hear a

speech by Socialist leader Eugene V. Debs. He was secretary of the French club; he was a good student with a place on the honor roll; he was active in student affairs and even in athletics. As Faith Berry puts it in her biography of Hughes, *Langston Hughes: Before and Beyond Harlem* (1983), "It was in part from this school . . . , from the war years and their aftermath, and from what he saw and learned of the plight of blacks during the Great Migration, that young Langston Hughes received his first education in radical politics. That education would begin to show in some of his poems as early as 1925, five years after his graduation from high school, and during the depression of the 1930s it would reach its peak." Though Hughes never became a self-avowed and unquestioning leftist, these years entrenched his commitment to the poor.

He spent the summer of 1918 in Chicago, and that of 1919 in Mexico, visiting his father. It was a wretched trip, in which he became disillusioned with his father's focus on money, in which—knowing little or no Spanish and cut off from the life of the small village of Toluca—he was depressed and intensely lonely. His father insisted he learn bookkeeping, but he took long rides alone on horseback through the surrounding countryside. One day he took a pistol from his father's desk drawer, and held it to his head, loaded, for a long time. Yet, he thought, "I might miss something. I haven't been to the ranch yet, nor to the top of a volcano, nor to the bullfights in Mexico, nor graduated from high school, nor got married. So I put the pistol down and went back to my bookkeeping."

On his return to Cleveland he concentrated on his schooling, encouraged by his father, who assumed he would go on to college, and battling with his mother, who expected that after graduation from high school, he would get a job and help support her. Continuing to write verse, he edited the school yearbook, was on the monthly honor roll, and on the track team. He decided to go back to Mexico for the summer of 1920, a decision which his mother greeted angrily, cruelly, and disconsolately. The misery of his parting from her not only persisted but generated some of his early published work. "I felt pretty bad when I got on the train," he wrote about this episode. "I felt bad for the next three or four years, to tell the truth, and those were the years when I wrote most of my poetry." On the way to Mexico, as the train crossed the Mississippi River to St. Louis, he jotted down on the back of an envelope one of his best-known poems, "The Negro Speaks of Rivers." Through the images of water and pyramid, the verse suggests the endurance of human spirituality from ancient Egypt to the nineteenth and twentieth centuries. From the train window he saw the muddy water flow toward the South and began to think about the past, remembering that the slaves were once sold down such rivers and that Abraham Lincoln once took a raft down the Mississippi to New Orleans. Finally he thought about the roles of other rivers in the human past—the Euphrates, the Congo, and the Nile.

That summer he wrote several poems, prose sketches, and a one-act play, mainly because he was unhappy. Though his father wanted him to attend a German university, he wanted to attend Columbia in New York. Meanwhile he went to bullfights in Mexico City almost every weekend, attempting ambitiously and futilely to write prose about them, but discovering, he said, that it was like trying to describe ballet. He wrote instead an article about Toluca and another about the Virgin of Guadalupe. Later, he mailed *The Gold Piece*, his one-act play, to the *Brownie's Book*, a young people's magazine just begun by W. E. B. Du Bois and the staff at the *Crisis*. The play was accepted and when Jessie Fauset, literary editor for the *Crisis*, encouraged Hughes, he sent her "The Negro Speaks of Rivers." It appeared in the June 1921 issue of *Crisis*.

Finally, with his father's financial support, Hughes registered at Columbia University by mail, and in the fall of 1921, when the nineteen-year-old arrived to claim his dormitory room, he discovered that Columbia's unstated policy was not to house Negro students. The university authorities reluctantly gave him his room, but it was an unsatisfactory start to an unsatisfying academic year. The winter of 1921 was depressing for the young poet. School bored him, and he abandoned lectures at Columbia for popular shows, books, and lectures by Norman Thomas, Scott Nearing, and Ludwig Lewisohn at the Rand School, which became an important part of his radical education.

By this time his mother, separated from her husband, was living in Harlem, a place which provided more and more inspiration for his poetry. In the spring he missed an important exam to attend the funeral of the famous black performer Bert Williams, and he wrote his father, who never replied, that he was quitting Columbia and would need no more support. With great difficulty he got a job for the summer on a truck farm on Staten Island, and in the fall he found himself unemployed and depressed in Manhattan: to assuage his feelings he wrote poetry. In 1922 he published thirteen poems in the *Crisis*, including "Negro," "My

People," "The South," and "Mother to Son." After a brief stint as a delivery boy for a florist, he found a job at Jones Point, opposite Peekskill on the Hudson River, as a mess boy on the S. S. *West Hassayampa*, master ship and quarters for a crew of Swedes and Spaniards maintaining a fleet of mothballed freighters.

In January 1923, while Hughes was there writing poetry and improving his Spanish conversation, Alain Locke, a well-known scholar, teacher at Howard University, and the first black Rhodes Scholar, started to write to him and in February proposed they meet. Locke was gathering material for his anthology *The New Negro* (1925), seminal to the Harlem Renaissance, and he wanted to include Hughes's work. Once again, Hughes's shyness got in the way, and he declined to meet Locke (they would meet in Paris, in 1924). That winter, Hughes worked on, but did not complete, "The Weary Blues," later the title poem to his first volume of poetry. About a piano player Hughes heard in Harlem, the poem depicts a black musician who plays his song ironically on the piano's white keys, creating a heightened moment that purges him, as well as the listener and reader, from human suffering.

In the spring of 1923, his imagination fired by the tales he heard from the crew at Jones Point, Hughes took a job as cabin boy on a freighter. From June to November he voyaged to West Africa and back and, as the ship sailed past Sandy Point, New Jersey, en route for Africa, he threw a box of books into the sea in a symbolic repudiation of his attic-and-basement life in Cleveland. His first sight of Africa was an emotional experience that he would refer to again and again: "My Africa," he wrote in *The Big Sea* (1940), "Motherland of the Negro peoples! And me a Negro! Africa! The real thing." At the same time, though he did not feel its force until later in life, Africa provided the young Hughes with a sharp object lesson in white colonialism and black subjugation; it was an Africa of "white men with guns in their belts" which taught him that "civilization" survives only through exploitation. It was also, ironically, an Africa which rejected him as a black: in spite of his protestations, Africans insisted he was white.

When he got back to New York in November he planned a short visit with his mother, reconciled with Homer Clark and living in McKeesport, near Pittsburgh, but he delayed his visit by ten days (and thus spent the money he had saved to give to his mother) in order to see the great Italian actress Eleonora Duse in Henrik Ibsen's *The Lady from the Sea* (1888). Duse, seriously ill, was "just a tiny little old woman, on an enormous stage, speaking in a foreign language, before an audience that didn't understand," and he naively saw in her performance the artist's failure to be great and to impart to others her sympathy and sensitivity.

In December he took a job on a ship (coincidentally named the *McKeesport*) sailing to Holland, and spent ten memorable days in Rotterdam over Christmas, getting back to the United States early in January. In February 1924, after a brief visit with Countee Cullen in New York City, he rejoined the ship on its next voyage, resigning his job when they reached Rotterdam. He reached Paris with seven dollars in his pocket. There he shared a room in Montmartre with Sonya, a penniless danseuse whose ballet troupe had disbanded for lack of funds; she got a job in a night club and more than a month later Hughes found work as doorman (and, to his dismay, as bouncer) at a night club for fifteen francs a night (roughly twenty-five cents) plus breakfast. But he heard many of the leading black musicians who were then in Paris, and in the spring he met and fell in love with Anne Coussey (whom he called Mary in *The Big Sea*), the mulatto daughter of a wealthy Nigerian. She wanted to elope with Hughes to Florence, but her father quickly sent a black doctor from London to fetch her home. That spring, too, Alain Locke visited Hughes in Paris to ask for some more poems for the special Harlem issue of *Survey Graphic*, which became the nucleus for *The New Negro*.

In July the night club where Hughes worked closed for the summer, and he went with two coworkers to their villages in Italy, joining up with Alain Locke in Venice. Hughes rapidly tired of palaces, churches, and famous paintings (and English tourists), noting that Venice too had its back alleys and its poor. He arranged to visit Claude McKay in Toulon on the French Riviera, but was robbed of his wallet and passport on the train. Fearing he could not enter France without his passport he got off the train at Genoa and lived in a flophouse, hustling with a band of beachcombers. Finally, he managed to get passage on a ship to New York, working without pay in exchange for the journey, and in November, on his arrival, he visited Countee Cullen to show him his new poems. Cullen took him to a benefit dance for the NAACP, where he met Walter White, Mary White Ovington, James Weldon Johnson, and Carl Van Vechten.

Hughes almost immediately joined his mother (once again separated from her husband) in Washington, D.C., and spent most of that winter working in a variety of ill-paid jobs, living with his mother and brother in an unheated two-room apartment. The cold and hunger of that winter motivated him to write more than had the life of Paris, and the winter of 1925 was fruitful for his poetry. He published work in the *Buccaneer* as well as in his customary outlets the *Crisis* and *Opportunity*. Some of his first political poems appeared in the *Workers Monthly*. In March 1925 he worked briefly for the black historian Carter G. Woodson at the Association of Negro Life and History, but the paperwork hurt his eyes. Thereafter he worked as a busboy at the Wardman Park Hotel. On 1 May 1925 he was back in New York City to attend the presentation banquet for *Opportunity*'s literary prizes, having won first prize for poetry, and it was at this banquet that, renewing his acquaintance with Hughes, Van Vechten asked the poet for some of his poems: Van Vechten sent the manuscript to his publisher, Alfred A. Knopf, who agreed within three weeks of receiving the poems to publish them. They appeared in February 1926 as *The Weary Blues*.

In August 1925 Hughes was back in New York City, this time to receive the second prize for essays and the third prize for poetry in the first Amy Spingarn Contest in Literature and Art, announced in the November 1924 issue of the *Crisis*. Here he met such painters as Miguel Covarrubias, Aaron Douglas, and Winold Reiss, whose pastel drawing of Hughes would appear on the March 1927 cover of *Opportunity*. In December 1925 Hughes got a breakthrough. He had begun writing poems in the idioms of blues and spirituals, and had already sold some poems to *Vanity Fair* (his first actual sales of verse). Vachel Lindsay (then one of the best-known poets in America) was a guest at the Wardman Park, where he was to read his poems. Hughes, too timid to approach the poet directly, placed three of his previously published poems—"Jazzonia," "Negro Dancers," and "The Weary Blues"—beside Lindsay's dinner plate, and, in his own words, "went away, afraid to say anything to so famous a poet, except to tell him that I liked his poems and that these were poems of mine." That night, Lindsay announced he had discovered a "Negro busboy poet" and read Hughes's poems to his audience. On the way to work the next day, Hughes read the story in the headlines, but the subsequent publicity and hounding by newspaper reporters and curiosity seekers drove Hughes to resign his job and return to New York.

There, at a party given by Van Vechten in his honor, Hughes met Arthur Spingarn, a prominent lawyer. Earlier that day, he had accepted a long-standing invitation to tea from Spingarn's sister-in-law, Amy Spingarn. In Faith Berry's words: "emotional ties were formed between Hughes and the Spingarn family that lasted for the rest of their lives. As Hughes's attorney and personal friend for more than forty years, Arthur Spingarn made the poet's personal concerns his own and was unstinting in his public praise and admiration of Hughes." Amy Spingarn, a woman of considerable personal wealth, became a secret benefactor of the poet and provided him continual encouragement. It was she who offered, during the Christmas season of 1925, to finance his education. In February 1926 Hughes enrolled as a student at Lincoln University, a black, all-male college in Pennsylvania. He was twenty-four years old, and his first book of poetry was about to appear.

Critical response to *The Weary Blues* was mixed. Reviews in the *New York Times, Washington Post, Boston Transcript, New Orleans Picayune, New Republic,* and elsewhere were laudatory; the only derogatory review in a white publication was in the *Times Literary Supplement,* which called him a "cabaret poet." Reviewing the book in the February 1926 issue of *Opportunity,* however, Cullen found some of the poems "scornful in subject matter, in photography and rhythmical treatment of whatever obstructions time and tradition . . . placed before him" and called Hughes one of those "racial artists instead of artists pure and simple." Jessie Fauset in the *Crisis,* praised Hughes's liberation from established literary forms. No other poet, she said, would ever write "as tenderly, understandingly, and humorously about life in Harlem." Admiring the book for the cleanness and simplicity, Alain Locke viewed Hughes, in *Palms,* as the spokesman for the black masses.

In the summer of 1926 Hughes stayed in a rooming house on 137th Street in Harlem, and with Wallace Thurman, Zora Neale Hurston, Gwendolyn Brooks Bennett, and others founded a short-lived black quarterly of the arts, *Fire!,* a liberal and innovative periodical. The only issue came out in November, and was generally condemned. Rean Graves, in the influential *Baltimore Afro-American,* began his scornful notice, "I have just tossed the first issue of *Fire* into the fire." Of Hughes's two poems in the issue he said, "Langston Hughes displays his usual ability to say nothing in many words." But the venture was not wasted, and Hughes's friendship with Hurston would lead, in the summer of 1927, to his accompanying her in her car from New Orleans to New York, occasionally stopping to collect folklore (Hughes had, ear-

lier that summer, been on a poetry-reading tour of the South and a boat trip to Cuba), and to their later ill-fated collaboration on "Mule Bone."

Hughes paid his own way through the summer of 1926 by writing lyrics for a projected revue, "O Blues!," but the production plans fell through. He learned much about music and about the theater, however, and wrote "lots of poems about house-rent parties." He also wrote "Mulatto" (published in the *Saturday Review of Literature,* 29 January 1927), his second poem on a theme that would recur throughout his work. "I worked harder on that poem than on any other I have ever written," he recalled in *The Big Sea.* When he read the poem one evening in August 1926 at James Weldon Johnson's, the well-known lawyer Clarence Darrow called it the most moving poem he had heard. According to Hughes, "Mulatto" is about "white fathers and Negro mothers in the South," but the craft transcends this paraphrase. A victim of miscegenation, one son suffers the white father's contemptuous indifference and later the rejection of his legitimate white half brother. More symbolically the poem illustrates the callousness of white America in particular—and humanity in general—and signifies the inner collapse racism brings upon the human family. The verse reinforces the theme and techniques used in the ballad "Cross," published a year earlier. The theme of the tragic mulatto would engage Hughes again, as he enlarged the basic inequality among blacks themselves into social and symbolic meaning: the "problem of mixed blood . . . one parent in the pale of the black ghetto and the other able to take advantage of all the opportunities of American democracy." Both "Cross" and "Mulatto" appeared in *Fine Clothes to the Jew,* which was published in February 1927. Most black critics objected to the book ideologically, disliking the book's proletarianism. Their philosophical differences with Hughes went back to 1924-1925, when Hughes had decided to serve the black masses and to avoid middle-class affectation. Black academicians, however, still insisted that black writers who depicted the black "lower" classes hurt the cause of racial integration. A headline in the *Pittsburgh Courier* read "Langston Hughes's Book of Trash"; another headline, in New York's *Amsterdam News,* appeared as "Langston Hughes, the Sewer Dweller." Such impassioned reviewers were too preoccupied to notice Hughes's experimentations with the ballad form, and his vivid re-creations of the sorrow songs.

During his years at Lincoln University the young Hughes met Charlotte Mason on a weekend trip to New York in spring 1927. Locke had introduced him to the elderly white lady, who lived in a well-appointed large apartment on Park Avenue, and she became patron ("Godmother," as she preferred to be called) to both Hughes and Zora Neale Hurston. She provided him with an income and a suburban cottage while he worked on his first novel, *Not Without Laughter.*

In the winter of 1929, his senior year at Lincoln, he worked at revising the novel, and for a senior project in sociology he undertook a survey of upperclassmen at Lincoln which demonstrated that sixty-three percent of Lincoln's predominantly black student body preferred to be taught by white professors. The survey caused a sensation. Letters from several southern black colleges vowed that they would not hire Lincoln graduates if they believed blacks incapable of teaching blacks. A former Lincoln graduate, who cautioned the young writer to be more deferential and conservative, made Hughes wonder: "I had never thought much before about the nature of compromise. For bread how much of the spirit must one give away?"

Following graduation in June 1929, he stayed by himself in a large dormitory on campus, working on *Not Without Laughter.* Confident that the book was finished at last, he went to Canada for the end of the summer, but when he returned to the United States and went to live in a boardinghouse in Westfield, New Jersey, the novel "seemed so bad," he said, "it made me sick." Mrs. Mason pressed Hughes to complete it and hired a stenographer, Louise Thompson, to help. Once the novel was finished, Thompson worked for Hughes and Hurston in their collaboration, "Mule Bone," the first black folk comedy written by blacks.

In the winter of 1930 Hughes broke irreparably with Mrs. Mason. Their relationship had been complex, familial, and paradoxical. He had loved her kindness and generosity, including her sincere support for black advancement and liberal causes. Yet they had disagreed profoundly on political philosophy as well as on matters of race. Mason believed that the expression of political opinions should be left to white people like herself and that black artists should foster a cultural exoticism in America, linking whites to the primitive life. But Hughes saw the economic aspect of the oppression of blacks, and wrote a leftist poem, "Advertisement for the Waldorf Astoria," attacking the luxury hotel "where no Negroes worked and none were admitted as guests." The poem appeared in 1931.

Following the break with Mrs. Mason, Hughes moved in December to Cleveland where his mother was now living with Homer Clark. While there, he broke, too, with Zora Neale Hurston. The agreement with Hurston had been that Hughes would construct the plot and develop the characters for "Mule Bone," while she would do the dialogue, working on an authentic southern tone and nuance. By May 1930, with Louise Thompson as typist, the collaborators had completed the first and third acts and a part of the second, and Hurston took the draft south with her for the summer. She stayed in the South until November, while Hughes worked on his own play, *Mulatto,* and was preoccupied by the publication (and mixed reception) of *Not Without Laughter,* which appeared in July 1930.

Unable to afford surgery for the severe tonsillitis that kept him in bed over Christmas and unable to get a job in depression Cleveland, Hughes learned in January 1931 from his old friends the Jelliffes, directors of Karamu House, that they had been offered, for their Gilpin Players (America's oldest black theater group) an excellent black comedy by Hurston, "Mule Bone." The ensuing conflict, with its agreements and recantations, reads like a rather grim farce, Hurston finally saying that she called the play exclusively hers because Hughes had wanted to share the royalties with Louise Thompson, whom she disliked. The play, at one point titled "A Bone of Contention," was not produced. Part of act three was published in *Drama Critique* in Spring 1964.

The trauma of this fiasco for the seriously ill Hughes (his badly infected tonsils were not removed until mid-March) was palliated by the welcome news, received a few days before the final quarrel, that for *Not Without Laughter* he had been awarded the Harmon Gold Medal and $400 cash. By the end of March he had finished *Mulatto* and prepared the volume of poems *Dear Lovely Death* for private publication by Amy Spingarn. He met Zell Ingram, a student of the Cleveland School of Art, and the two young men, borrowing Ingram's mother's car, set off on a tour of the South, 22 March 1931, with $300 apiece. On the road to Florida they read of the Scottsboro case (on 25 March 1931 nine black youths were accused of raping two white women on a freight train passing through Alabama). Within a few months the Scottsboro case would be an international cause célèbre, and Hughes would write a number of poems about it. But at Bethune-Cookman College in Daytona Beach, where he stayed for two days, Hughes was more concerned about how he could make a living as a writer. Mary McLeod Bethune suggested that Hughes make a living reading his poems and inspiring black youth. She envisioned him as a symbol of black achievement, despite the prevailing racial prejudice.

Hughes and Ingram sailed to Cuba and then spent the summer in Haiti, mostly in the revolutionary fortress town of Cap Haitien. In August they returned to New York via Daytona, taking Bethune in the car with them. In late September the Rosenwald Fund gave Hughes a $1000 grant to undertake a reading tour of the South. Without a driver's license, he purchased a Ford and then struck a deal with Radcliffe Lewis, a fellow alumnus of Lincoln, to share the proceeds of the tour if he would drive and manage accounts while Hughes read his poetry. Both would share the profits. Hughes would not return to Harlem until 1935.

The trip deepened Hughes's commitment to racial justice. He observed unhappily that black colleges were silent about the Scottsboro case, which continued to concern him as he spent nearly all of that November giving poetry readings in North

Tony Buttitta and Langston Hughes in Chapel Hill, North Carolina, fall 1931 (courtesy of Tony Buttitta)

Carolina. Two students, Anthony Buttitta and Milton Abernathy, learning of the possibilities of Hughes's arrival at the all-white University of North Carolina, had asked for some work for their magazine, *Contempo*: "White Shadows" appeared in the 15 September issue. The 1 December issue featured one of his most indignant Scottsboro essays on its front page, and "Christ in Alabama" inside. The two young men invited Hughes to share their room and later challenged racial segregation by eating with him in a southern restaurant. Hughes's visit was extremely tense—his reading at the campus theater especially so—but this visit helped to set a new tone for race relations in Chapel Hill. At various stops in other towns, the poet's audiences overflowed, and he crisscrossed some states two or three times before Christmas. At Huntsville, Alabama, he was the guest of Arna Bontemps and left Alabama in January for Miami. He was bitterly disappointed in February by his visit to Tuskegee Institute and asked, "If the Communists don't awaken the Negroes of the South, who will?" Most depressing of all was his visit to the Scottsboro boys in Kilby Prison in Montgomery. He ended up, early in 1932, in San Francisco, as guest of Noel Sullivan, to whom he brought a letter of introduction from mutual friends. With a car at his disposal, he took in the sights of San Francisco. For his convenience, a secretary recorded his letters, and two gardeners placed vases of flowers in his bedroom. His trip reaffirmed his opposition to prostitution and poverty, encouraged the literary relationships which shaped his imaginative life, and made him speculate on both the nature and the obligation of art. Such affluence and peace would frame his journey to Russia that year and his return.

In May Louise Thompson invited Hughes to join her and twenty other blacks on a trip to the Soviet Union, where they were to make a film about exploited black American workers titled "Black and White" and directed by the German filmmaker Karl Younghans. The film's English dialogue was to be written by Hughes, but the script, written by a Russian who had never been to America, was appallingly inept. The group left Moscow for Odessa in August to begin filming, but on 12 August the film was cancelled and the group, its members in acrimonious disagreement, returned to Moscow and split up. Hughes elected to take an offered tour of Soviet Central Asia and stayed in Russia for six months. In Ashkabad, the regional capital of Turkmenistan, at the edge of the Kara Kum Desert, Hughes met Arthur Koestler, and the two explored Soviet Asia together, separating in Tashkent where—convalescing from illness—Hughes learned Uzbek. When he left, returning to Moscow in January 1933, he had been paid sixty thousand rubles for the Uzbek translation of *The Weary Blues*, and was writing regularly for *Izvestia*. He stayed in Moscow for five months, making a fairly comfortable living writing for *Izvestia*, *Krasnaya Nov* (Red Virgin Soil), and *International Literature*. During his stay that winter he had a romantic alliance with Si-lan Chen, an Oriental ballerina at the Bolshoi theater, but the relationship could not be deep or lasting. Hughes was struggling with the problems of his sexual identity and was ambivalent about his relationships with women; his tolerance of those who demanded affectionate attention was low.

But his stay in Moscow was fruitful for his writing: he translated Boris Pasternak and, after reading D. H. Lawrence's short stories, was inspired to write his own, which he sent to New York for publication. He produced a great deal of proletarian and revolutionary verse, and published both *The Dream Keeper and Other Poems* (1932) and *Scottsboro Limited: Four Poems and a Play in Verse* (1932). On 7 June he left Moscow for Vladivostok via the trans-Siberian Express, then went to Tokyo by ship. In Tokyo he was welcomed by the left-wing Tsukiji Theater and was something of a celebrity. His poetry had been translated into Japanese, and he was well known there. He was also politically suspect, and the Tokyo police not only shadowed him when he sailed for China on the *Empress of Canada* on 1 July but also warned the Japanese consulate to keep track of him in Shanghai. On his return to Tokyo the police detained him as a Communist spy and then asked him to leave the country and never come back.

On 25 July he sailed for San Francisco, where he got a royal welcome from Noel Sullivan, who gave him rent-free accommodation at his cottage in Carmel. Hughes stayed there a year and worked ten to twelve hours a day, completing at least one article or story a week. He finished his book of short stories, *The Ways of White Folks*, in time to give the completed manuscript to Noel Sullivan, to whom the book is dedicated, for Christmas. It was published by Knopf in June 1934. Hughes sold ten of the book's fourteen stories to good markets—including *Scribner's Magazine*, *Esquire*, the *New Yorker*, and *Harper's*—much of his earnings going to his sick mother, once more separated from her husband. He joined radical protest movements on the West Coast, participated in fund-raising activities for the defense of the Scottsboro boys and for the relief of migrant farm workers. His cottage was visited by a steady stream of intellectuals, artists, and entertainers, and he was also a target for a group of self-styled vigilantes, whose self-appointed task was to break all strikes and all protests, and to destroy the John Reed Club Hughes had joined. In early September 1934 he left California, downhearted, with, in Faith Berry's words, "the draft of an article he had started more than once and been unable to finish. . . . 'The Vigilantes Knock at My Door.' "

Hughes fled to Reno, announcing that he was tucked away at a resort in the Sierras writing his book on Soviet Central Asia (although *A Negro Looks at Soviet Central Asia* had already been published in Moscow), and spent eight weeks there writing prolifically but selling very little. He finished the vigilante article, but it was never published. One story, "Mailbox for the Dead," was written one evening at the end of November, triggered by his walk that afternoon which ended up, on the side of a parched hill in sight of "a forlorn little mountain cemetery. . . . I was startled to see on the cemetery gate—with no house or living person about—what looked to be a mailbox." Writing the story he kept thinking about his father—and the next afternoon he got word that his father had died that night. A few days later, in early December, Hughes left Reno for Mexico City—he arrived after being delayed a week at Nogales, Arizona, by American immigration officials who denied him entry into Mexico for lack of an entrance permit stating he was "colored." His father had left all his money to the elderly Patinos sisters who had cared for him in his last years after he had suffered a stroke; Hughes was not even mentioned in the will. When Louise Thompson visited James Hughes in the summer of 1931, the only question he had asked about his son was "Is he making any money?" When Thompson told him that his son had earned a worldwide reputation as a poet, James Hughes said he should not count on that: "The *golden eagle*," he said, "is your only friend." What the poet thought of his father's response—and his father's will—is difficult to determine: a private man who kept his inner life to himself, he was characteristically silent. The three women offered to share the estate with him, but he refused, eventually accepting a portion of his father's savings in order to pay back what he had borrowed to get to Mexico. But he spent six months in Mexico, writing popular fiction to raise cash, and writing only the truth as he gauged it for leftist publications. Early in 1935 he was one of the first to sign the "Call for an American Writers Congress" to establish a League of American Writers, and he was invited to deliver a speech at its first session in New York City on 26 April 1935. His speech, "To Negro Writers," was one of his most revolutionary writings of the decade, but it was delivered by a substitute because he could not afford the fare from Mexico. He spent the winter of 1934-1935 translating Mexican and Cuban "stories of the people" and traveling with the photographer Henri-Cartier Bresson (whom he met in Mexico City). He read Cervantes' *Don Quixote* for the first time; later he would credit Cervantes with influencing his conception of his character Jesse B. Simple. He eventually made enough money from his writing and from tutoring to get back to the United States. In March he was awarded a Guggenheim Fellowship of $1,500 for nine months (most of it went to his mother in Cleveland), and in June 1935 he went to Los Angeles to collaborate with Arna Bontemps on another children's book. He would not return to Mexico until the decade he died.

That August, the collaboration with Bontemps complete ("Bon Bon Buddy" was not to find a publisher), Hughes headed east, visiting his sick mother in Oberlin, Ohio. He applied for work with the WPA but was rejected because his income was "too high," and in the fall he went to New York to sell his stories. There, to his surprise, he found *Mulatto*, his play, in rehearsal. Much revised, it ran successfully on Broadway for a year (a record for black plays), and then went on the road for two seasons. Hughes had difficulties collecting royalties, and in December he moved to Cleveland, where the Gilpin Players, in March, performed his three-act comedy *Little Ham*, paying him ten dollars a night for each performance in a two-week run. Meanwhile his one-act play *Angelo Herndon Jones* won first prize (fifty dollars) in the *New Theater* competition, and the Gilpin Players, in 1936-1938, performed five of his plays in all. Hughes, however, needed money to pay for his mother's treatment (she had breast cancer) and spent the winter of 1936 in Chicago reading, writing, and lecturing. There he met Richard Wright and ran afoul (not for the first time) of the FBI because of his radicalism and Communist sympathies.

His awareness of white exploitation of blacks

Arna Bontemps and Langston Hughes (courtesy of the James Weldon Johnson Collection, Beinecke Library, Yale University)

was heightened in the summer of 1936 by the Italian annexation of Ethiopia, which he expressed in the fiery poem "White Man":

> I hear you name ain't really White Man
> ....
> Is your name spelled
> C-A-P-I-T-A-L-I-S-T?
> Are you always a White Man?
> Huh?

He wrote other poems about Ethiopia (notably "Broadcast on Ethiopia"), and the newspapers were filled with news of Adolf Hitler's sweeping election in June, and the July rebellion in Spain of the troops under Generalissimo Francisco Franco against the elected Republican government. Hughes moved to New York to work on "Cock O' the World," which Columbia Pictures had expressed interest in, but by December 1936 he had heard nothing definite about either his script or the score by Duke Ellington, and he spent the next few months traveling through the United States, concentrating on the theater and on lectures to scrape a living. In June the *Baltimore Afro-American* asked him to be a war correspondent covering black Americans in the International Brigades on the front lines of the Spanish civil war. Hughes had already written his long militant poem "Song of Spain" (it was read at a mass rally that summer), exhorting workers to "make no bombs again . . . lift no hand again/To build up profits for the rape of Spain," and for ideological as well as financial reasons he welcomed the opportunity to go. He sailed on 30 June.

En route for Spain, Hughes attended the Second International Writers Congress, in July 1937 at Paris. Having been denied Spanish visas and press credentials by the U.S. State Department, on 17 July at the closing session, he voiced his anger at the state department, at the British (who had seized Raj Anand's passport), and at the Fascists in no uncertain terms; he got a standing ovation. He eventually got to Spain, and wangled his press credentials indirectly. In Spain he met Ernest Hemingway, and teamed up with the Cuban poet Nicholas Guillén to investigate the war. In addition to journalism, he wrote a number of poems in the heat of events: "Air Raid: Barcelona," "Moonlight in Valencia: Civil War," and "Madrid—1937" among them, and in a series of twenty-two articles took up the banner of the International Brigade; he also began translating—among other things— García Lorca's *Gypsy Ballads* and *Blood Wedding*. Per-

haps the greatest effect on him was the well-known flamenco singer La Niña de los Peines, Pastora Pavón, whose blueslike art resisted both war and death. When Hughes heard that she had refused to leave the besieged Madrid, he prepared himself for the front. He saw her there at eleven o'clock one morning. Now an old woman, sitting straight in a chair among guitarists she slowly began to dominate the performance, as she half-spoke and half-sang a *solea*. As the guitars played in accompaniment, he listened only to her voice. It was wild, hard, harsh, lonely, and bittersweet: her flamenco was like black southern blues implying heartbreak but signifying the endurance of a people. Beyond the detachment of Duse, the realism of De Maupassant, and the narrative consciousness of Lawrence, her spiritual intensity captivated the black poet because it reminded him that great art subsumes and transcends great pain.

In Madrid Hughes stayed on the top floor of the Alianza de Intelectuales Antifascistas, his room facing the Fascist guns. He met more white American writers than ever before. Hemingway and Martha Gelhorn were already in Madrid; playwright Lillian Hellman and critic Malcolm Cowley would join them; sometimes correspondent Nancy Cunard and poet-critic Stephen Spender turned up. So did French novelist Andre Malraux and the leftist poet from Chile, Pablo Neruda. Hughes returned to Paris with Guillén by train, getting there in time for Christmas and for talk of war. It was a grim new year: Russian intellectuals told Hughes that Spain was only a training ground for Hitler and Mussolini, providing bombing practice by Fascist pilots, and a world war was impending. When Jacques Roumain (an old friend from the Haiti days) claimed the world would end, however, Hughes quipped, "I doubt it . . . and if it does, I intend to live to see what happens." "You Americans," Roumain said, shaking his head. Hughes still drew upon the optimism of his dead grandmother: "What's wrong with you boy?," she had asked; "you can't expect every apple to be a perfect apple. Just because it's got a speck on it, you want to throw it away. Bite that speck out and eat that apple, son. It's still a good apple." The writer contemplated, "That's the way the world is . . . take the specks out . . . still a good apple." On New Year's Eve in Paris Hughes saw a slightly limping figure. Familiar with the crippled walk from his days in Moscow, he turned to greet Seki Sano, the Japanese director he had met once at a Meyerhold rehearsal. Pleasantly surprised to meet each other, the two went into a sidewalk café enclosed by glass, where they ordered drinks. At a second table (all others were empty), a pretty woman sat alone.

While midnight approached, Sano said that he had read about Hughes's expulsion from Japan in 1933, and that he himself had been expelled. He philosophized about the many people wandering around the world, especially those who could not go home. The list included expatriated Germans, South Americans, Chinese, and Japanese. Though Americans in the states were exceptions, Sano prophesied gloomily such a day might come for them too. Hughes doubted him: "That's one nice thing about America . . . I can always go home—even when I don't want to." As the two writers parted in the New Year, Sano walked toward the left bank; Hughes headed to Montmartre. Hughes and Sano would literally take different roads. Hughes's life became a tale of friendship, optimistic will despite infirmity, and artistic order; it reaffirmed his determination, "But that is what I want to be, a writer, recording what I see, commenting upon it and distilling from my own emotions a personal interpretation." From 1938 to his death in 1967 he succeeded admirably.

Invited to spend the whole of the winter in Paris, Hughes declined (his mother was still ailing with cancer) and he returned home on the S. S. *Berengaria*. He reached New York on 17 January 1938, penniless as usual; he could not afford to go to Cleveland and did not know what he would do when he got there. So he stayed, for the nonce, in Harlem with his old friends Toy and Emerson Harper, to plan a lecture tour. The Harlem stay was crucial and marks the beginning of an extraordinary, productive period for Hughes. At the Harpers' suggestion he moved his mother (now terminally ill) to New York, and he rented a Harlem studio apartment at 66 St. Nicholas Avenue, where he could write without disturbance. Here his mother could stay when he was away. He booked himself a lecture tour taking in Chicago, Milwaukee, Cincinnati, Cleveland, Buffalo, Durham, Richmond, and Washington, D.C., but reserved the bulk of his energies for the theater project he began in February: the Harlem Suitcase Theater, a community-based radical theater group experimenting with theater-in-the-round. His play *Don't You Want to be Free?*, staged in April 1938, ran for 135 weekend performances. The theater was housed in the International Workers Order Community Center, and soon the branch in Chicago asked for Hughes to put the play on there. Hughes was by now overcommitted, and the Chicago branch had to work without him. His radical poetry celebrating the international workers' movements was published in *A New Song* (1938). On 3 June his mother died—and Hughes paid for the funeral by borrowing from Mrs. Spingarn. In July he accompanied Theodore Dreiser to Paris to represent the United States at the International Congress of Writers for the Defense of Culture.

By May 1938 Hughes had more requests for lectures than he could meet, and he needed help. He hired a part-time secretary, Frances Wills, who worked for him for nearly two years—and through her assistance and management Hughes managed to stabilize his income. From this time on he would be busy indeed, and he would never again be destitute. Not content with founding the Harlem Suitcase Theater, traveling and lecturing, Hughes wrote social verse, lyrics, drama, history, comedy, autobiography, and film scripts. In 1939 he founded the New Negro Theater in Los Angeles (while there he also worked on the script for a Hollywood film, *Way Down South*, 1939). From May to September, in Chicago, he wrote his autobiography *The Big Sea* (1940). The publication of that book brought him a Rosenwald Fellowship to write historical plays, and he moved to Noel Sullivan's farm near Monterey, California, to work. For 1941 Hughes was back in Chicago, where he founded the Skyloft Players—who produced his musical, *The Sun Do Move* (1942).

In 1942 he moved back to Harlem and lived with the Harpers. He wrote verses and slogans to help sell U.S. Defense Bonds and published *Shakespeare in Harlem*, a well-crafted book which had a mixed reception. In the blues monologue, "Southern Mammy Sings," a poor black narrator opposes a white socialite. In biblical overtones the speaker criticizes present and past war as well as the failure of interracial democracy. "Ballad of the Fortune Teller" presents humorously and colloquially the ironic story of a woman who supposedly foretells the future for others but fails to prophesy her lover's desertion of her. In the deceptively simple "Black Maria," an enthusiastic urbanite chooses life, represented by the music playing in a tenement, over death—symbolized by a hearse passing in the street below.

Such meanings escaped most of the critics. Saying that *Shakespeare in Harlem* was a "careless surface job" and that Hughes was "backing into the future looking at the past," Owen Dodson was unduly harsh. Alfred Kreymborg was reminded of such "master singers of Vaudeville as Bert Williams and Eddie Leonard . . . a subtle blending of tragedy and comedy, which is a rare, difficult, and exquisite

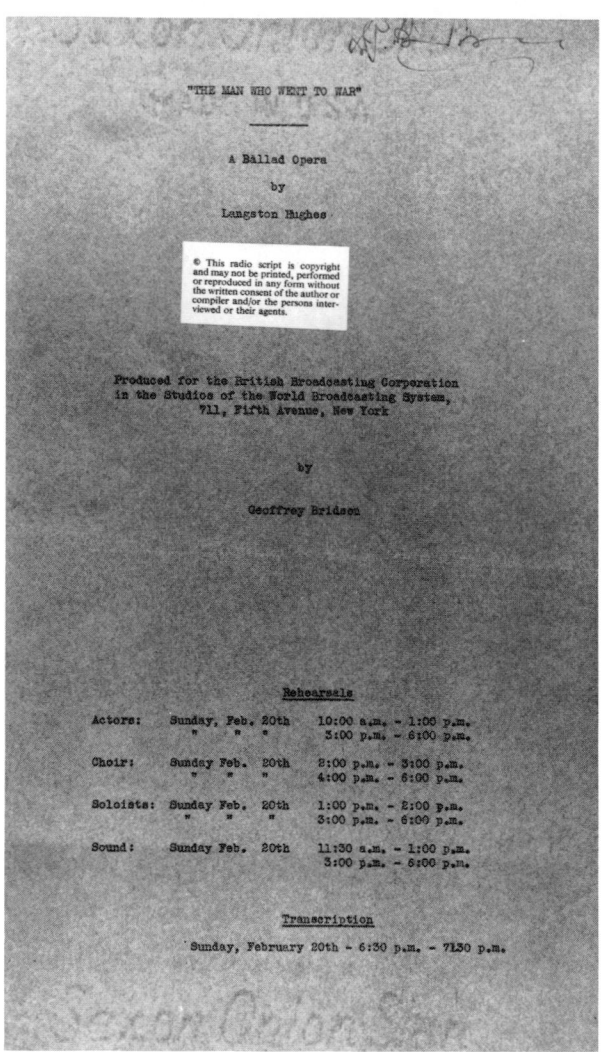

"THE MAN WHO WENT TO WAR"

A Ballad Opera

by

Langston Hughes

© This radio script is copyright and may not be printed, performed or reproduced in any form without the written consent of the author or compiler and/or the persons interviewed or their agents.

Produced for the British Broadcasting Corporation in the Studios of the World Broadcasting System, 711, Fifth Avenue, New York

by

Geoffrey Bridson

Rehearsals

Actors:	Sunday, Feb. 20th	10:00 a.m. - 1:00 p.m.
	" " "	3:00 p.m. - 6:00 p.m.
Choir:	Sunday Feb. 20th	2:00 p.m. - 3:00 p.m.
	" " "	4:00 p.m. - 6:00 p.m.
Soloists:	Sunday Feb. 20th	1:00 p.m. - 2:00 p.m.
	" " "	3:00 p.m. - 6:00 p.m.
Sound:	Sunday Feb. 20th	11:30 a.m. - 1:00 p.m.
		3:00 p.m. - 6:00 p.m.

Transcription

Sunday, February 20th - 6:30 p.m. - 7:30 p.m.

Front cover for a radio script Hughes wrote in 1943 (courtesy of the Lilly Library, Indiana University)

art." Overlooking the poet's new growth in complexity and symbolic depth, Edna Lou Walton wrote: "Hughes only writes as he always has. His poems, close to folk songs, indicate no awareness of the changed war world. . . . Easily listened to, they do not invoke sufficient thought."

By 1943 Hughes was regularly hearing his name on the radio; his poems were set to music (and sung by Paul Robeson), and they were recited by Paul Muni; he took part in panel discussions. In London the BBC broadcast his script *Ballad of the Man Who Went to War*. And on 13 February 1943 he introduced—in his regular column in the *Chicago Defender* (which he had been writing since November 1942)—his folk character Jesse B. Simple in a "conversation" which would run for twenty-three years. In 1943 he received an honorary Doc-

tor of Letters from Lincoln University; by 1946 he had been elected to the National Institute of Arts and Letters. In 1947 he was visiting professor of creative writing for a semester at Atlanta University, and two years later, in 1949-1950, he was poet-in-residence at the Laboratory School of the University of Chicago. The year 1949 saw the publication of *One-Way Ticket*, in which Alberta K. Johnson is the hilarious counterpart to the comic Jesse B. Simple. Here the folk environment both exonerates and elevates the alertly humorous and tough black woman, ironic, bitter, rueful, victim of white brutality, comic but transcendent, reciter of the blues. The poems reminded G. Louis Chandler of Walt Whitman, and he praised Hughes's ability to extend the racial into universal experience. Rolfe Humphries praised the language but wanted more complexity, less blues, more imagistic writing. But Hughes could not abandon black folk life for a more consciously literary tradition, and his *Montage of a Dream Deferred* (1951), his first book-length poem, played dramatic and colloquial effects against the underlying lyricism.

Over the next few years engagement with history and fiction as well as editing (*The First Book of Negroes*, 1952; *Laughing to Keep from Crying*, 1952; *Simple Takes a Wife*, 1953) drained his poetic energy, and his style became more direct and cryptic. In 1953 he won the *Saturday Review*'s Anisfield-Wolf Award for the best book of the year on race relations (*The First Book of Negroes*), but in March he was interrogated by Joseph McCarthy's anti-Communist House Un-American Activities Committee—one effect of which, probably, was to reduce the number of public readings Hughes would give over the next eight or so years.

By 1960 Hughes was the "Dean of Negro Writers." To young writers such as Gwendolyn Brooks or Julian Mayfield he was a revered example and friend; Lorraine Hansberry's *Raisin in the Sun* took its title from his poem "Harlem." In 1960 he visited Paris for the first time in twenty-two years, and he would from then on make many trips on cultural grants from the state department—an irony indeed, since until 1959 he was on the "security index" of the FBI's New York office. He would visit Africa a number of times, and revisit Europe. The year 1961 saw the publication of Hughes's crowning achievement. *Ask Your Mama* is as much Juvenalian as Horatian in its satiric response to the rising anger of the 1960s. Fusing poetry with jazz, he interweaves myth and history. He moves now into the child's mind and then into the man's; he reverses himself and begins afresh.

HORN OF PLENTY - 2

FROM LESSER STARS IN ORBIT $ $ $ $ $ $
TO MOVE OUT TO ST. ALBANS $ $ $ $ $ $
WHERE THE GRASS IS GREENER $ $ $ $ $ $
SCHOOLS ARE BETTER FOR THEIR CHILDREN $
AND OTHER KIDS LESS MEANER THAN ¢ ¢ ¢ ¢
IN THE QUARTER OF THE NEGROES ¢ ¢ ¢ ¢ ¢
WHERE WINTER'S NAME IS HAWKINS ¢ ¢ ¢ ¢
AND NIAGARA FALLS IS FROZEN ¢ ¢ ¢ ¢ ¢
IF SHOW FARE'S MORE THAN 30¢ ¢ ¢ ¢ ¢ ¢

"Hesitation
Blues" 8 bars

I MOVED OUT TO LONG ISLAND
EVEN FARTHER THAN ST. ALBANS
(WHICH LATELY IS STONE NOWHERE)
I MOVED OUT EVEN FARTHER FURTHER FARTHER
ON THE SOUND WAY OFF THE TURNPIKE--
AND I'M THE ONLY COLORED.

GOT THERE! YES, I MADE IT!
NAME IN THE PAPERS EVERYDAY!
FAMOUS--THE HARD WAY...
FROM NOBODY AND NOTHING TO WHERE I AM
THEY KNOW ME, TOO, DOWNTOWN,
ALL ACROSS THE COUNTRY, EUROPE--
ME WHO USED TO BE NOBODY,
NOTHING BUT ANOTHER SHADOW
IN THE QUARTER OF THE NEGROES,
NOW A NAME! MY **NAME** -- A NAME!

HORN OF PLENTY
by
Langston Hughes

From: "ASK YOUR MAMA:
12 Moods For Jazz" to
be published by Alfred
A. Knopf, Autumn, 1961

SINGERS
SINGERS LIKE O-
SINGERS LIKE ODETTA--AND THAT STATUE
ON BEDLOE'S ISLAND MANAGED BY SOL HUROK
DANCERS BOJANGLES LATE LAMENTED $ $ $ $
KATHERINE DUNHAM AL AND LEON $ $ $ $ $
ARTHUR CARMEN ALVIN MARY $ $ $ $ $ $ $
JAZZERS DUKE AND DIZZY **ERIC DOLPHY** $ $
MILES AND ELLA AND MISS NINA $ $ $ $ $
STRAYHORN HID BACKSTAGE WITH LUTHER $ $
DO YOU READ MUSIC? AND LOUIS SAYING $
NOT ENOUGH TO HURT MY PLAYING $ $ $ $ $
GOSPEL SINGERS WHO PANT TO PACK $ $ $ $
GOLDEN CROSSES TO A CADILLAC $ $ $ $ $
BONDS AND STILL AND MARGARET STILL $ $
GLOBAL TROTTERS BASEBALL **BATTERS** $ $ $
JACKIE WILLIE CAMPANELLA $ $ $ $ $ $ $
FOOTBALL PLAYERS LEATHER PUNCHERS $ $ $
UNFORGOTTEN JOES AND SUGAR RAYS $ $ $ $
WHO BREAK **AWAY LIKE** COMETS $ $ $ $ $ $

Typescript (by permission of George H. Bass, the Estate of Langston Hughes; courtesy of the Lilly Library, Indiana University)

Through fantasy, travesty, allusion, and irony, he depicts singers, actors, writers, politicians, and musicians. With a deepened imagination, he draws upon the rich themes of his entire career, such as humanism, free speech, transitoriness, and assimilation; nationalism, racism, integration, and poverty. He speculates about Pan-Africanism and personal integrity. Praising Hughes's commitment to universal freedom, Rudi Blesh called *Ask Your Mama* "a half angry and half derisive retort to the bigoted, smug, stupid, selfish, and blind." Dudley Fitts, who compared it to Vachel Lindsay's *Congo* (1914), drew parallels between Hughes and the Cuban poet Guillén, as well as between Hughes and the Puerto Rican Luis Matos.

Though many white Americans believed blacks had moved too fast, Hughes complained about slowness and regression. The last poem he is said to have submitted for publication before his death in New York City's Polyclinic Hospital on 22 May 1967 was "Backlash Blues." Yet other poems are more optimistic. In "Frederick Douglass" his narrator anticipates the return of good, despite a period of regression, like that which began in 1895, the year of Douglass's death, with Booker T. Washington's Atlanta Compromise speech in which he spoke of the races as being "separate as the five fingers." Douglass is one of the many complex heroes which Hughes had portrayed, including such memorable figures as Roy Williams, Oceola Jones, or Bert Norwood (all in *The Ways of White Folks*). Creative and good people reinforce one another in human history, and they come again.

Following Hughes's death critical commentary was respectful. Reviewing *The Panther & The Lash* (1967), Bill Katz praised the writer's commitment to diverge from both liberal and reactionary views of race. Lamine Diakhaté called Hughes a "pilgrim who affirmed the identity of man in the face of the absurd . . . showed the problems of blacks in a democratic society, restored the rhythmical language of Africa introduced by jazz in America, and demonstrated inextinguishable hope." Francois Dodat noted Hughes's humanistic faith. Most celebrators mention the writer's great generosity.

While Hughes's reputation today is even more secure, his life and times still merit serious scholarship. Early on he engaged the serious interest of scholars such as Arthur Davis, Darwin Turner, and James Emanuel. More recently the writings have received the scrutiny of Charles H. Nichols, Faith Berry, Richard K. Barksdale, and Arnold Rompersad. Indeed, Hughes's creative work has in-

Langston Hughes at the time he wrote Fight for Freedom: The Story of the NAACP

spired significant studies in imagery, structure, and myth. His technical and spiritual contributions to black American literature will endure.

Letters:

Arna Bontemps-Langston Hughes Letters, 1925-1967, edited by Charles H. Nichols (New York: Dodd, Mead, 1980).

Bibliographies:

Donald C. Dickinson, *A Bio-Bibliography of Langston Hughes, 1902-1967* (Hamden, Conn.: Shoe String Press, 1967);

R. Baxter Miller, *Langston Hughes and Gwendolyn Brooks: A Reference Guide* (Boston: G. K. Hall, 1978).

Biography:

Faith Berry, *Langston Hughes: Before and Beyond Harlem* (Westport, Conn.: Lawrence Hill, 1983).

References:

Richard K. Bardsdale, "Langston Hughes: His Times and His Humanistic Techniques," in *Black American Literature and Humanism*, edited by R. Baxter Miller (Lexington: University Press of Kentucky, 1981), pp. 11-26;

Bardsdale, *Langston Hughes: The Poet and His Critics* (Chicago: American Library Association, 1977);

Black American Literature Forum, special Hughes issue, edited by R. Baxter Miller, 15 (Fall 1981);

Lloyd W. Brown, "The Portrait of the Artist as a Black American in the Poetry of Langston Hughes," *Studies in Black Literature,* 5 (Winter 1974): 24-27;

Arthur P. Davis, "Langston Hughes: Cool Poet," *CLA Journal,* 11 (June 1968): 280-296;

Davis, "The Tragic Mulatto Theme in Six Works by Langston Hughes," *Phylon,* 16 (Fourth Quarter): 195-204; republished in *Five Black Writers,* edited by Donald B. Gibson (New York: New York University Press, 1970), pp. 167-177;

W. E. B. Du Bois and Alain Locke, "The Younger Literary Movement," *Crisis,* 27 (February 1924): 161-163;

James Emanuel, *Langston Hughes* (New York: Twayne, 1967);

Emanuel, "The Literary Experiments of Langston Hughes," *CLA Journal,* 11 (June 1967): 335-344;

Theodore Hudson, "Langston Hughes' Last Volume of Verse," *CLA Journal,* 11 (June 1968): 345-348;

Nathan Huggins, *Harlem Renaissance* (New York: Oxford University Press, 1971);

Blyden Jackson, "A Word About Simple," *CLA Journal,* 11 (June 1968): 310-318;

David Levering Lewis, *When Harlem Was in Vogue* (New York: Knopf, 1981);

Peter Mandelik and Stanley Schatt, *Concordance to Langston Hughes* (Detroit: Gale Research, 1975);

R. Baxter Miller, " 'Even After I Was Dead': THE BIG SEA—Paradox, Preservation, and Holistic Time," *Black American Literature Forum,* 11 (Summer 1977): 39-45;

Therman B. O'Daniel, ed., *Langston Hughes: Black Genius* (New York: Morrow, 1971);

Stanley Schatt, "Langston Hughes: The Minstrel as Artificer," *Journal of Modern Literature,* 4 (September 1974): 115-120;

Darwin T. Turner, "Langston Hughes as Playwright," *CLA Journal,* 11 (June 1968): 297-309;

Jean Wagner, "Langston Hughes," in *Black Poets of the United States,* translated by Kenneth Douglas (Urbana: University of Illinois Press, 1973), pp. 385-474.

Papers:

The James Weldon Johnson Memorial Collection, Beinecke Library, Yale University includes letters, manuscripts and typescripts of published and unpublished work, lecture notes, and various magazine and newspaper clippings and pamphlets. Additional materials are in the Schomburg Collection of the New York Public Library, the library of Lincoln University in Pennsylvania, and the Fisk University library.

Laura Riding Jackson

(16 January 1901-   )

Joyce Wexler
Loyola University

BOOKS: *The Close Chaplet,* as Laura Riding Gottschalk (London: Hogarth Press, 1926; New
York: Adelphi, 1926);

Voltaire: A Biographical Fantasy, as Gottschalk (London: Hogarth Press, 1927);

A Survey of Modernist Poetry, as Laura Riding, with
Robert Graves (London: Heinemann, 1927;
Garden City: Doubleday, Doran, 1928);

Contemporaries and Snobs, as Riding (London: Cape,
1928; Garden City: Doubleday, Doran, 1928);

Anarchism Is Not Enough, as Riding (London: Cape,
1928; Garden City: Doubleday, Doran, 1928);

A Pamphlet Against Anthologies, as Riding, with
Graves (London: Cape, 1928; Garden City:
Doubleday, Doran, 1928);

Love As Love, Death As Death, as Riding (London:
Seizin Press, 1928):

Poems: A Joking Word, as Riding (London: Cape,
1930);

Four Unposted Letters to Catherine, as Riding (Paris:
Hours Press, 1930);

Experts Are Puzzled, as Riding (London: Cape,
1930);

Though Gently, as Riding (Deyá, Majorca: Seizin
Press, 1930);

Twenty Poems Less, as Riding (Paris: Hours Press,
1930);

Laura and Francisca, as Riding (Deyá, Majorca: Seizin Press, 1931);

No Decency Left, as Barbara Rich, with Graves (London: Cape, 1932);

The First Leaf, as Riding (Deyá, Majorca: Seizin
Press, 1933);

The Life of the Dead, as Riding (London: Barker,
1933);

Poet: A Lying Word, as Riding (London: Barker,
1933);

Pictures, as Riding (London, 1933);

14A, as Riding, with George Ellidge (London: Barker, 1934);

Americans, as Riding (Los Angeles: Primavera,
1934);

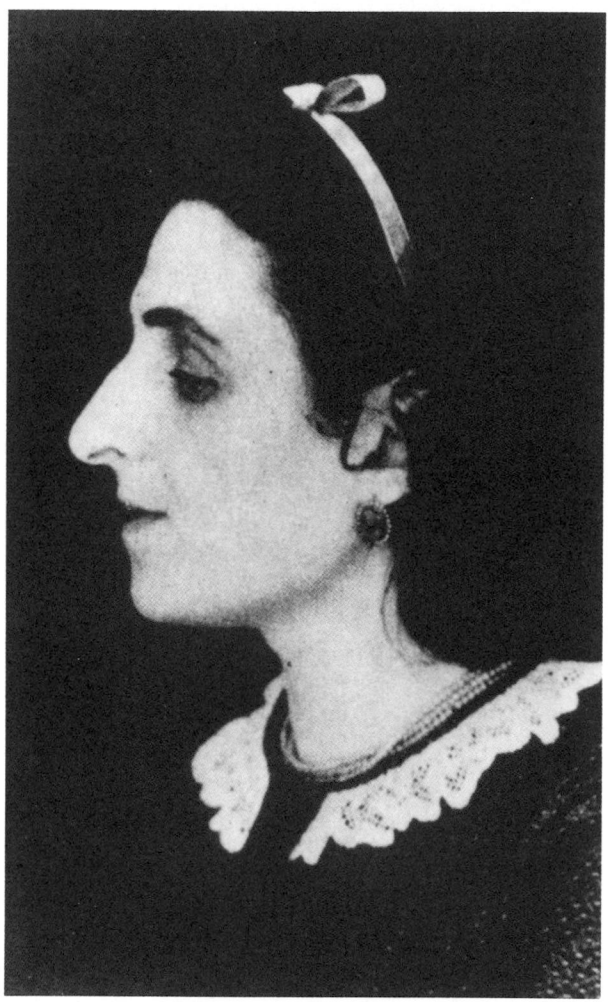

Laura Riding Jackson

The Second Leaf, as Riding (Deyá, Majorca: Seizin
Press, 1935);

Progress of Stories, as Riding (Deyá, Majorca: Seizin
Press/London: Constable, 1935; enlarged edition, New York: Dial Press, 1982);

Convalescent Conversations, as Madeleine Vara
(Deyá, Majorca: Seizin Press/London: Constable, 1936);

A Trojan Ending, as Riding (Deyá, Majorca: Seizin

Press/London: Constable, 1937; New York: Random House, 1937);

Collected Poems, as Riding (London: Cassell, 1938; New York: Random House, 1938); republished as *The Poems of Laura Riding: A New Edition of the 1938 Collection,* as Laura (Riding) Jackson (Manchester: Carcanet New Press, 1980; New York: Persea Books, 1980);

The World and Ourselves, as Riding (London: Chatto & Windus, 1938);

Len Lye and the Problem of Popular Films, as Riding (London: Seizin Press, 1938);

The Covenant of Literal Morality, as Riding (London: Seizin Press, 1938);

The Left Heresy in Literature and Life, as Riding, with Harry Kemp and others (London: Methuen, 1939);

Lives of Wives, as Riding (London: Cassell, 1939; New York: Random House, 1939);

Selected Poems: In Five Sets, as Riding (London: Faber & Faber, 1970; New York: Norton, 1973);

The Telling, as Laura (Riding) Jackson (London: Athlone Press, 1972; New York: Harper & Row, 1973);

From the Chapter "Truth" in "Rational Meaning: A New Foundation for the Definition of Words" (Not Yet Published), as Jackson (Berkhamsted, U.K.: Priapus Press, 1975);

It Has Taken Long, as Jackson (New York: Chelsea Associates, 1976);

How a Poem Comes To Be, as Jackson (Northridge, Cal.: Lord John Press, 1980);

Description of Life, as Jackson (New York: Targ Editions, 1980);

Some Communications of Broad Reference (Northridge, Cal.: Lord John Press, 1983).

OTHER: *Everybody's Letters,* edited, as Laura Riding (London: Barker, 1933);

Epilogue, 1-3, edited, with contributions, as Riding (Deyá, Majorca: Seizin Press/London: Constable, 1935-1937).

TRANSLATIONS: Marcel Le Goff, *Anatole France at Home,* as Laura Riding Gottschalk (New York: Adelphi, 1926);

Georg Schwarz, *Almost Forgotten Germany,* as Laura Riding, with Robert Graves (Deyá, Majorca: Seizin Press/London: Constable, 1936; New York: Random House, 1936).

In the late 1920s Laura Riding's poems and essays catapulted her to the front line of modernism. Like other poets beginning their careers after World War I, Riding distrusted the rhetoric and rules of traditional literature and refused to follow discredited models in her writing. Fighting for new aesthetic standards, she saw poetry as the repository of truth. Turning inward to discover both her subject and an appropriate form, she was confident that introspection would reveal a universal essence. She found a voice within herself that reached back to Percy Bysshe Shelley and anticipated the postmodernists' verbal self-consciousness.

Early in her career, she wrote Donald Davidson that she found solace for her loneliness and sense of homelessness in her writing. Providing a way to unify and intensify experience, her poetry writing was less a retreat to a private world than a way of creating an alternative world, not only for herself but for everyone. She discovered the universal within herself and called on others to recognize it in themselves too.

After the publication of her *Collected Poems* in 1938, Riding's search for perfect unity of thought and words culminated in a renunciation of poetry in favor of linguistic study. Having grappled with the recalcitrance of language as a poet, she came to feel that any concern for formal patterns was a luxury her moral purpose would no longer permit.

Born in 1901 in New York City to Nathaniel S. and Sarah Edersheim Reichenthal—"Jewish (but not religiously so) parents," she called them in 1942—Laura Reichenthal grew up with domestic disruptions caused by her father's frequent job changes and her mother's invalidism. Riding later blamed her father's unsuccessful business career on his socialism, but his political activities also brought intellectual vitality to his relationship with his daughter. Intelligent, well-informed, and eager to propound his views, he encouraged her to defend her opinions. Although he hoped she would become an American Rosa Luxemburg, she began to disentangle her values from his by repudiating his leftist sympathies. Instead she turned to poetry to find the stability her family life lacked.

Winning several scholarships to Cornell University, she began college in 1918 but left in 1921 before graduating. In 1920 she had married Louis Gottschalk, then a history instructor at Cornell. In a feminist gesture, she asked him to take her name. Thus he became Louis Reichenthal Gottschalk, partly in respect for her father. Yet around 1927 she altered her maiden name to become Laura Riding Gottschalk because she felt Reichenthal Gottschalk would be too unwieldy.

As Gottschalk's academic career took the couple to Urbana, Illinois, and then to Louisville, Kentucky, in 1923, Riding enrolled in courses that interested her but never completed a degree. She preferred to write poems. After submitting her work to the *Fugitive* in 1923, she was invited to become a member of the group that published the magazine. The Fugitive Group, which included John Crowe Ransom, Donald Davidson, Allen Tate, and Robert Penn Warren, announced it was rebelling against the "high-caste Brahmins of the Old South." As unlikely as it might seem for a Jewish girl from New York to become an ally, literary or otherwise, of these southern gentlemen, they shared her conviction that new forms were necessary to express a new sensibility. The Fugitives praised Riding's originality, intellectuality, and irony—qualities now familiar to readers of modernist poetry but rare then. Allen Tate welcomed Riding as the female poet who would save America from the Edna St. Vincent Millays.

The Fugitives' support encouraged Riding to pursue a career as a poet, but her commitment to her vocation took her husband by surprise, and they were divorced in 1925. She moved back to New York, while continuing to help with the *Fugitive*, which ceased publication after the December 1925 issue. She became, in Hart Crane's words, the "engrossing female" of New York literary circles. Crane dubbed her "Rideshalk-Godding," presumably in tribute to her intense personality and outspoken way of expressing herself, until he later replaced this epithet with the disenchanted "Laura Riding Roughshod." Riding's exuberance faded as she saw the destructive effects of powerful critics on young poets, particularly on Crane. Glad to leave New York after less than a year, she accepted in 1926 an invitation from Robert Graves and his wife Nancy Nicholson to join them in England. Their friendship began when Graves, also an early contributor to the *Fugitive*, had written to Riding to express his admiration for her poetry. Marking a pivotal year, Riding's first book of poems, *The Close Chaplet*, took its title from one of Graves's poems and was dedicated to Riding's sister and Graves's wife.

Published in 1926, when she was twenty-five, *The Close Chaplet* introduced themes that continued to interest Riding throughout her career, but the form of these early poems was more ornate than that of her mature work. Although she employed classical allusions, stylized diction, and dramatic narratives to distance the content from herself, she later considered these poems too personal to have lasting value.

Many of the poems portray the difficulty of being a woman with a mind. Like many women poets, Riding wrote about a sense of fragmentation, often expressed as a separation between body and mind. "Samuel's Elegy for Amalthea of the Legends" creates a male persona who discovers unity underlying woman's multiplicity:

> I have come with Amalthea in my veins
> Into a fifth season. Time drops slow.
> For winter is over, yet I see no summer,
> Now it is always snow.
> What woman was Amalthea? She was many once
> Before I found her one. . . .

Like other early poems, this one uses an assumed persona and the apparatus of myth as distancing devices; like Riding's later poems, however, it abandons metaphor in favor of an interlocking verbal network based on seasons and numbers and an intensely literal use of words. The period between winter and summer is not *like* a fifth season; it *is* a fifth season—too much snow to be spring, too late to be winter.

Related to the theme of the separation between body and mind in *The Close Chaplet* is the conflict between sensory experience and thought, one that persisted in Riding's work; ultimately, she resolved the opposition by renouncing poetry. In "Truth and Time" beauty was still a temptation even though the poet realizes that "too much loveliness is Lethe" and that "The succession of fair things/Delights, does not enlighten." Since sensory experience is transitory, Riding felt it revealed nothing about permanent, eternal verities. Only when thought transcends the "succession of fair things" can it "enlighten."

Renouncing beauty, Riding knew she was denying life. Her poems present death, not life, as the apotheosis of truth. "The Simple Line" traces the path from verse to truth to death by contrasting the beauty and variety of nature with the unity of truth:

> And the voice opening to cry: I know,
> Closes around the entire declaration
> With this evidence of immortality—
> The total silence to say:
> I am dead.

According to the poem's inexorable logic, life brings change; only death gives permanence. To be permanent, immutable, immortal—like truth—is to be dead. Death

seems a simple verse
And, of all ways to know,
Dead or alive, easiest.

The finality of poetry, of truth, and of death connects all three. In Riding's poetry death becomes desirable, a logical necessity.

While writing poems, Riding also promulgated her aesthetic beliefs in critical essays and books, as well as in her work for the Seizin Press, which she and Graves founded in 1928. In the earliest statement of her creed, an essay titled "A Prophecy or a Plea" published in the *Reviewer* (April 1925), she defined poetry as a way of using words to give life meaning. The poet's ability to separate the meaningful from the insignificant, she said, endowed poetry with truth. At this time she believed the poet's meaning was "inevitably rhythmical." The formal patterns of poetry galvanized the common ore of language to make it a durable medium for truth. In *A Survey of Modernist Poetry* (1927), written with Robert Graves, and *Contemporaries and Snobs* (1928), Riding elaborated her conception of poetry. The poet said something previously unknown about human identity that nonetheless elicited recognition from the attentive reader. The success of this human circuit depended on articulating thought. Superior to sensory perception, only thought could uncover transcendent meaning and be communicated completely. To emphasize the distance between truth and the natural world, Riding referred to permanent values as "unreal," "final," "nothing," and "dead" because they were beyond physical existence. Eschewing details of time or place or personality, Riding attempted to render the process of thought as precisely as other poets portrayed the world. Let the scientists observe, the philosophers generalize; the poets were to articulate the mind's consciousness of itself. Riding's strongest argument for a poetry of thought was her poems.

In *Love As Love, Death As Death* (1928) Riding implemented the critical principles of her essays. The title emphasizes the literalness of her purpose: she wanted to know love as love, death as death, each thing as itself. She tried to define the essence these familiar but ineffable words signified. In her effort to isolate the essence or "self" of her subject, she avoided using analogy, allusion, or sensory imagery, and she used metaphor sparingly because she sought to demonstrate that things cannot be known by their resemblance to other things. Relying on strict control of diction and syntax, often departing from conventional usage, she forced the reader to dwell on the precise meaning of each word.

Three of the best poems in *Love As Love, Death As Death* present death in the form of suicide. No longer a word for the immutable, death had begun to signify an escape from life into knowledge. "The Tiger" represents the speaker's passion as a beast hunted by men. The symbol of the tiger distances passion from the speaker; yet its fierce beauty expresses her wish to experience passion in all its violence. Contemptuously, she describes her pursuers' fear of the tiger in her:

Ah me, ah me, says every lady in the end,
Putting the tiger in its cage
Inside her lofty head.

She accuses men of preventing her from knowing lust by failing to conceive of a woman who can be proud and wise as well as sensual. By crashing through glass, her essential self escapes both from her own lust and from those whose lust she fears.

"In Nineteen Twenty-Seven" voices once again the temptation to crash through glass to escape the complications of love. Although the poem is neither autobiographical nor confessional, in its willingness to cite a specific time and place it is one of Riding's most personal. The speaker attempts to find some correspondence between her subjective sense of herself and her objective awareness of the city where she lives: "City air was pastoral/With teeming newspapers and streets." The difficulty of integrating subjectivity and objectivity leads to thoughts of suicide:

Then, where was I, of this time and my own
A double ripeness, a twice-dated festival?
Fresh year of time, my youth,
Late year of my age, renounced desire—
Ill-mated pair, this gaudy vantage
Looks on death, it is a window
Not worth leaping out of.

Because her emotional state is ineffable, she can only name the points on its perimeter:

And this is both love and not love,
And what I pledge both true and not true,
Since I am moved to speak by the season,
Happy and unhappy speed and recession,
Climax and suspension.

Other poems, including "All Nothing, Nothing" and "Footfalling," also evoke the disorienting malaise brought on by the need to define what seems undefinable. Riding not only chose to render what was most difficult to express, but she often detected difficulty and complexity where others did not. Refusing to accept common polarities as the boundaries of her experience, she transformed opposites into paradoxes. To avoid being strung between binary concepts, she joined poles to neutralize them. Thus her attitude is "both love and not love," "both true and not true," "happy and unhappy," a state of "speed and recession," "climax and suspension."

The problem of definition is also associated with suicide in "Death as Death." In this attempt to know the ultimate unknown, the speaker resorts to similes that link dissimilar images:

> To conceive death as death
> Is difficulty come by easily.
> A dullness fallen among
> Images of understanding,
> Death like a quick cold hand
> On the hot slow head of suicide.

Death seems to reveal itself to the suicide, but only for "one instant." The poem concludes by accepting death as itself; it is "like nothing else," a "similarity/ Without resemblance." Impervious to description through metaphor, Death became Riding's subject. Striving for a poetry of definition, she stripped poems of ornamentation but infused them with the force of her effort to press the full literal meaning from every word.

The verbal rigor of Riding's work was the product of her idea of the poet's vocation: she wanted every word to be not merely effective but also true. Such scrupulous attention to every element of a poem, demonstrated at length in *A Survey of Modernist Poetry*, is at the base of the New Criticism. Internal consistency and the intricate network of verbal relationships within the poem were the only authorities modernists accepted.

The positive connotations of death in Riding's early poems assumed a biographical importance when she attempted suicide in 1929. Too literally, she stepped out the window she had been writing about for years. While such a drastic act can never be explained, it was precipitated by a challenge to the personal commitments she had made soon after coming to England in 1926. She lived with Robert Graves, Nancy Nicholson, and their children in an irregular but compatible household until Irish poet Geoffrey Phibbs (who later changed his surname to Taylor) entered their lives. He urged Riding to leave the Graves family with him. She refused and to end what seemed to her an impasse, she jumped

from a second-story window. She did not expect to die, she said later, but she saw no other way to end the paralysis she felt. She could not anticipate the events that followed. Instead of nursing Riding, who spent three months in the hospital with a compound spinal fracture, Phibbs became involved with Nancy Nicholson. As soon as Riding could travel, she left London with Graves. At Gertrude Stein's suggestion, they settled in Majorca. They moved the Seizin Press to the village of Deyá and began to rebuild their lives.

For Riding rebuilding her life required relearning how to speak. Feeling betrayed by words, she tried to purify language of its ambiguity, to make words incapable of lying. What she later called "the stuttering slow grammaring of self" in "Memories of Mortalities" (written in 1938) proceeded slowly. Bearing the scars of 1929, her poems of the early 1930s are almost incomprehensible without some knowledge of the events behind them. With some idea of what is left unsaid, however, the reader can respect her determination to repress turbulent feelings. Riding seemed to be

Laura Riding in Deyá, Majorca, circa 1930

writing in restraints. Poets had betrayed her; poetry had betrayed her; her own poems lied. In *Poet: A Lying Word* (1933), the volume that collects the poems of this period, she unleashed her fury at the inadequacy of language.

Riding's fall broke her connection with the past. Having sought physical pain to extinguish emotional pain, she emerged from her stern, self-imposed cure determined to eliminate the risks of change from her life. Treating her fall as a purposeful act that had allowed her to shed her personal identity and to achieve a universal state of being, she described herself as one who was dead, who had arrived at a permanent prospect from which she could address everyone else. In a phrase from "The Last Covenant," her transformation was a "suicidal resurrection."

The poems of the early 1930s are halting first steps in Riding's exploration of death. Finding the language of her past tainted and unreliable, she attempted to purify words by experimenting with repetition in ways that fostered comparisons to Gertrude Stein. Riding also invented words to express her new perceptions. She made nouns of adverbs—as in the phrase "An onlywhere of everywhere"—and formed her own antonyms by adding the prefixes "un," "no," or "non"—as in "no-sense." Words such as "nowhere," "nothing," and "dead" assumed positive connotations. In "There Are As Many Questions As Answers" Riding presented a catechism of fundamental propositions she could rely on:

What is to start?
It is to have feet to start with.
What is to end?
It is to have nothing to start again with.

Starting again, Riding defined herself as a poet in "Then Follows"; she was a creature between God and man. Like God, she was "a creature of mind," like man, "a creature of mouth." Her sui-

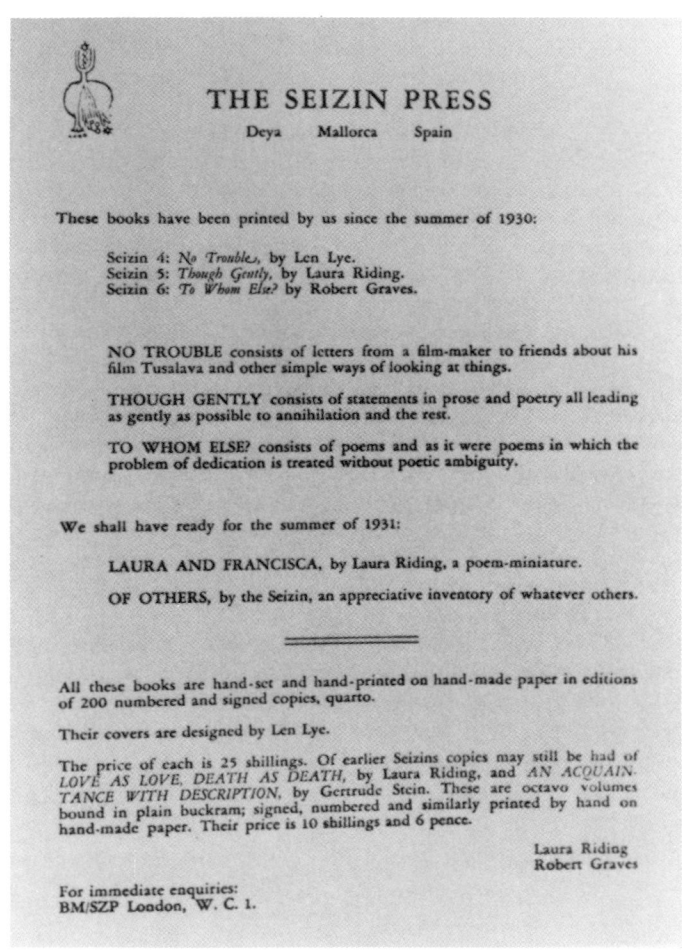

THE SEIZIN PRESS
Deyà   Mallorca   Spain

These books have been printed by us since the summer of 1930:

Seizin 4: *No Trouble*, by Len Lye.
Seizin 5: *Though Gently*, by Laura Riding.
Seizin 6: *To Whom Else?* by Robert Graves.

NO TROUBLE consists of letters from a film-maker to friends about his film Tusalava and other simple ways of looking at things.

THOUGH GENTLY consists of statements in prose and poetry all leading as gently as possible to annihilation and the rest.

TO WHOM ELSE? consists of poems and as it were poems in which the problem of dedication is treated without poetic ambiguity.

We shall have ready for the summer of 1931:

LAURA AND FRANCISCA, by Laura Riding, a poem-miniature.

OF OTHERS, by the Seizin, an appreciative inventory of whatever others.

All these books are hand-set and hand-printed on hand-made paper in editions of 200 numbered and signed copies, quarto.

Their covers are designed by Len Lye.

The price of each is 25 shillings. Of earlier Seizins copies may still be had of *LOVE AS LOVE, DEATH AS DEATH*, by Laura Riding, and *AN ACQUAINTANCE WITH DESCRIPTION*, by Gertrude Stein. These are octavo volumes bound in plain buckram; signed, numbered and similarly printed by hand on hand-made paper. Their price is 10 shillings and 6 pence.

Laura Riding
Robert Graves

For immediate enquiries:
BM/SZP London, W. C. 1.

Publishers' announcement, 1931

cide attempt represented the death of her individuality and the birth of her universal human selfhood. While her first accounts of this universal self were fragmentary, her ability to describe it expanded steadily. Once she worked out the meanings of basic words, her next step was to examine the relationship between herself and other people. Focusing on the differences between men and women, she accused men of being preoccupied with action rather than thought. Although men tried to impose their preoccupation on women, she would resist them by asserting her superior unity of action and thought.

Dreading the duplicity of words, Riding came to value silence. Because words were too "flesh-seeming" to be worthy of truth, she exhorted them in "Come, Words, Away" to join "the silent half of language," where speech would not "blaspheme" thought. Words were to follow her example and extinguish themselves to achieve transcendence. The "miracle" of truth occurred only if words originated in "the soundless telling" which guaranteed a perfect identity of thought and language. As truth teller, the poet was to say what she knew with certainty and then fall silent.

After the fury of *Poet: A Lying Word,* Riding accepted her dependence on language, for a time choosing poetry over silence. Not only was language the locus of her being, but it was the only means of overcoming the isolation of subjectivity: the universal had to be stated so others could recognize it. Believing the only durable bond between people was the common effort to uncover truth, Riding felt morally compelled to foster a community of truth seekers. She gathered a group of disciples in Deyá by nourishing their ambition to be better poets and better people. Typically a young man would write her a letter admiring her poems and enclosing some of his own for her comments. Flattered by more criticism than he had expected, the novice would sustain a bulky correspondence. Riding usually found too much to say to continue the relationship by mail and often invited him to join her and Graves in their work.

Sooner or later most of these friendships, including those with Norman Cameron and Thomas Matthews, ended because Riding failed to respond to others as unique individuals. She thought of herself as a trusting person and generously devoted time and attention to her disciples' poems or lives or both, but eventually they felt they were being required to believe in her rather than in truth. A moment would arrive when their self-respect prevented them from agreeing with her, but she regarded dissent not merely as a difference of opinion but as a willful rejection of revealed truth. She wrote James Reeves that he might be shocked or disgusted, but those who left her left truth. That so many recognized her authority was testimony to her personal magnetism, composed of intelligence, energy, and charm. In 1933 she provided an accurate and forbidding description of herself: "I am tidy, quick, hard-working, good-humoured, and let absolutely nothing go by." Thomas Matthews, once a devoted disciple, conveyed the effect of her presence in terms of her costume: "When *she* was in full regalia her dignity matched and enhanced her costume, and I can't remember anyone thinking it laughable or even eccentric that on these occasions she was crowned by a tiara of gold wire that spelled LAURA." Another account of Riding's compound reported the rumor that her bedroom wall bore the inscription "God is a Woman."

Riding enlisted the members of her enclave in various projects designed to expand the number of truth tellers. The most ambitious of these undertakings was the founding of the hardbound periodical *Epilogue* with an editorial policy of refusing to publish anything that did not demonstrate consciousness of a "final degree: which has not an aftertime quality, which is not a fitting epilogue of its kind." Riding's belief that men and women became human through the ability to discover and articulate truth engendered a moral need to allow nonpoets to call themselves human too. True poets, rare as they were, remained her model. Through *Epilogue* Riding tried to teach the public how to be like poets.

In contrast to the politically committed poets of the left, who wanted poets to be more like the people, Riding aligned her personal quest for permanent values with the contemporary search for new certainties that characterized the political right. Riding was even able to link the widespread fear of a "Next Great War" to her own appreciation, after her suicide attempt, of the value of death as the end of a limited point of view. As Europe faced World War II, Riding regarded the collective suicide of a culture as an opportunity to awaken to truth. She felt none of the nostalgia for the past that some of her male contemporaries, such as William Butler Yeats, T. S. Eliot, and Ezra Pound, expressed.

Riding wanted to protect the validity of individual experience, which she saw as endangered both by the mass movement of the left and by the state control of the right. In the polarized political climate of the late 1930s, however, her defense of private values, especially since it included personal attacks on leftist writers, notably W. H. Auden, was inevitably interpreted as pro-Fascist. Her actual remoteness from political reality was evident in *The World and Ourselves* (1938). Valuing letters above all other forms of social action, she argued that only letter writing could change the world. Confident that international relations would improve if everyone could speak English, she proposed that English-speaking peoples "honor" the rest of the world by writing personal letters to private citizens in foreign countries. Aware her scheme would be considered impractical, Riding nevertheless advanced it because it met her standards of truth: each letter writer would articulate the portion of truth he or she discovered. Accordingly, half the volume contained letters from sixty-five contributors, many of whom had spent time with Riding in Deyá.

Riding's confidence that she had mastered language was evident in her last poems. No longer searching, no longer denouncing error, these poems resonate with celebration. They express a serene understanding of the relationships between men and women, the individual and humanity, language and thought. Though these poems are difficult, their message rather than their form makes them demanding. Their subject is the unfamiliar and unappealing realm of death, but the ellipses, distorted syntax, and private symbols which made the poems of the early 1930s so obscure have disappeared. These poems elucidate Riding's discoveries in benevolent tones.

Reviewing her past from an impersonal perspective, Riding examined old emotional wounds, probing for a universal essence. Once she separated this "self" from surrounding circumstances, she was able to confront the pain that the actual experience had caused. She came to value the disappointments of childhood and love because they had led to poetry. She triumphantly transformed pain into knowledge.

In "Memories of Mortalities" she describes the process of becoming "unreal." Death is clarified as the state of mental readiness for truth, the point where the universal overwhelms the personal. The associations of death with her suicide attempt are submerged. Unlike the poems of the early 1930s that labored to escape isolating, flesh-bound life, this poem reconciles body and mind as a progression. The speaker inherits both physical and spiritual being from her mother. The spiritual self is grounded in nature because, though self is made linguistically, life is given biologically:

> Therefore such quickness as makes life,
> The stuttering slow grammaring of self
> That death with memories seeming crowns.

Compressing the themes of much of Riding's work, these lines assert that the death of personal identity "crowns" the ascent from individual life to universal selfhood. Language makes this procession possible. The spirit sloughs off flesh as it grows.

The progression from physical to spiritual love between people is charted in "When Love Becomes Words." Ordinarily such a title would suggest a diminution of love, but Riding's values reverse the expected pattern. Applying terms appropriate to the body to the superior functions of the mind, Riding shows the similarities between the claims of the body and mind as well as their different values:

> To be loving is to lift the pen
> And use it both, and the advance
> From dumb resolve to the delight
> Of finding ourselves not merely fluent
> But ligatured in the embracing words
> Is by the metaphor of love,
> And still a cause of kiss among us,
> Though kiss we do not—or so knowingly,
> The taste is lost in the taste of the thought.

Returning to metaphor, Riding makes the spiritual as concrete as the physical. The vocabulary of bodies illuminates the function of minds: words such as "ligatured," "embracing," "kiss," "taste" lend emphasis to the value of thought. Drawing her metaphors from lovemaking, Riding portrays love itself as the exchange of thoughts, people confiding in one another.

Riding also used metaphor in a late poem about change. While earlier poems about modulation or movement between identifiable poles express the motion sickness of someone thrown off balance, "After So Much Loss" presents the rhythm of transition as a harmony. Comparing a life to the seasons, something Riding was unable to do in "In Nineteen Twenty-Seven," the poem describes the balance of the year:

> After so much loss—
> Seeming of gain,
> Seeming of loss—
> Subsides the swell of indignation
> To the usual rhythm of the year.

The seasons are a reminder that temporal things

come to an end. The only way to avoid loss is through the uniquely human capacity to transcend time through thought. Dance illustrates an escape from time because it is an arbitrary but purposefully designed pattern. To "release our legs from the year's music," we "Dance—grinding from primroses the tears/They never of themselves would have shed[.]" Subject to its own cycles, nature knows neither tears nor joy. But we, who are both victims of chance and masters of time, can invest nature with our feelings and thus defy the indifference of the natural world. The complex attitude of the poem is that it would be easy to succumb to the rhythm of nature and easy to resist it, but the difficult task is to endure the effects of natural cycles while knowing they are both inexorable and accidental. Hatred for what we cannot control inspires us to dance:

> It is easy as spring to yield to the year,
> And easy as dance to break with the year.
> But to go with the year in partition
> Between seeming loss, seeming gain,
> That is the difficult decorum.
> Nor are the primroses unwelcome.

This poem is more convincing than many of Riding's bare assertions. The measured form tempers the extremity of her positions and forestalls her insistent tone. The formal harmony reflects a balanced view rare in her writing. When Riding discovered that readers were able to admire her poems yet disregard her meaning, she concluded that the formal aspects of poetry interfered with the moral purpose of language.

As the Spanish Civil War intruded on the enclave of truth seekers in Majorca in 1936, Riding, Graves, and a few of their friends were forced to look for a new home. After several temporary addresses in France and England, they went to New Hope, Pennsylvania, in 1939 to accept the hospitality of Schuyler B. Jackson, a friend of Thomas Matthews, who brought Jackson and Riding together because he considered them the two most brilliant people he knew. Jackson was the author of a *Time* review (26 December 1938) that hailed Riding as the only living poet who could perform the poet's true function, "making words make sense" and using language so that "every word carries its fullest literate meaning." The consequences of this meeting resembled the turmoil of 1929. Jackson divorced his wife and married Riding on 20 June 1941. Alan and Beryl Hodge, members of the Deyá group, were also divorced, and Robert

Graves married Beryl Hodge in 1950. In 1943 the Jacksons moved to Wabasso, Florida, and Riding stopped writing poems.

Since Riding withdrew from the literary world and Graves became increasingly prominent, Riding's silence was sometimes attributed to Graves's departure. After her extravagant claims for poetry in the 1938 preface to her *Collected Poems,* the rumored explanation for her sudden reversal was that she rejected poetry because Graves had rejected her. But the quality of their relationship throughout the 1930s, as documented in *Epilogue,* the books he dedicated to her, and the testimony of witnesses such as Matthews, all portray Graves as a humble and grateful acolyte attending his revered instructress. Once she refused to help Graves with his poems, he had no reason to remain with her. His subsequent acknowledgments of Riding's "influence" rankled her because she never believed he understood the core of her insights.

By 1970 Riding was spurred to stifle rumors by discussing her reasons for renouncing poetry. After publishing no book for thirty-one years, she republished some of her work in *Selected Poems.* In a preface written for this volume, she stressed that she still considered her poems as truthful as any poems could be, but that she perceived an error in assuming truth would be "inevitably rhythmical." Formal and aural harmonies did not necessarily accompany the harmony of word and thought she sought as truth. Through its capacity to create the illusion of possessing moral value, poetry deceived her, she said, by implying more than it actually stated. Because poetry could evoke a mood beyond its literal content—a property she called the "poetic oblique"—Riding felt there was a basic contradiction in poetry: its creed, at least as she had understood it, promised truth, but its craft appealed only to the senses. Even her ascetic poetry seemed overly concerned with aesthetic effects rather than meaning.

The dichotomy of body and mind that tormented her in her earliest poems finally encompassed the elements of poetry itself. No longer able to see the formal unity of a poem as the verbal equivalent of truth, she veered to the opposite pole and held that sensory effects could have no relationship whatsoever to thought. Renouncing poetry, she purged one more element of sensory experience from her life.

Riding's break with poetry also had a moral impulse behind it. As long as she tied truth to poetry, nonpoets could not be considered fully human. Riding now perceived a disparity between the talent to create aural patterns and the ability to utter truth. Since poets cultivated original voices rather than a universal one, they contributed nothing to the general ability to articulate inner knowledge. Poets worked in isolation, and their poems existed in a social vacuum. Without moral virtue, linguistic virtuosity served the poet's personal ambitions rather than humanity's needs. In *The Telling* (1972) Riding decided to dedicate herself to teaching humanity how to achieve a "oneness" with the "whole."

Riding's use of such words, sometimes capitalized, became increasingly specific for her, if increasingly vague for her readers. Without the concrete details and forms of poetry to link her perception of the ultimate to the reader's knowledge of the immediate, her world began to seem more private as she tried to make it more general. Despite her desire to communicate, her writing became opaque again. Like the riddling poems she wrote after her suicide attempt, the pieces of the early 1970s redefine her sense of herself. Both times she brought her new self to fruition in extraordinary literary forms, first in her puzzling poems and essays of the 1930s, later in *The Telling*, which she described as "a personal evangel." Her intelligence pervades her writings of both periods, but after she renounced poetry, her distrust of aesthetic factors led her to make her writing "homely," a word she used with approval in *The Telling*. Although she wanted to be more direct, her deliberate disregard for rhetorical effect resulted in a prolix style full of clichés.

When Riding dethroned poets from their rank as truth tellers, she installed women in their place. She would lead humanity to truth as a woman if not as a poet. Expatiating on the differences between the dualism of men in separating thought and action and the integrity of women that she had pointed out earlier in her career, Riding noted a bias in the English language, which referred to men and women generically as "man." Opposed to the feminist movement for equal rights, Riding claimed women were the ideal men should emulate because domesticity through the ages nurtured women's spiritual superiority.

Riding's poetry justified her faith in words as the ground of her being, but the poet's wisdom lost its compelling force when uprooted from her poems. Her preoccupation with definitions and literal meaning was responsible for the precision of her poems. When she transferred her principles to general speech, however, they became an obstacle to her ability to communicate and failed to generate a practical example for others to follow.

Riding's pursuit of constants to believe in, her need for certainties beyond time and place, her distrust of established disciplines reflected her own insecurities and ambitions, yet they were also characteristic of her generation. Becoming a poet in a decade when poetry seemed the last value to believe in, Riding tried to make it serve others as it had helped her. Poetry infused language with meaning and distilled the permanent from the rest of life. Without resorting to religious accounts of the soul, she managed to express a spiritual dimension of human nature rooted in words. Trying to wrench both cosmic and aural harmonies from language, she made her poems vibrate with the intensity of her effort to pursue thought to its source.

While a single moral purpose motivated Riding throughout her career, her work also reveals personal reasons that the search for the universal and the immutable was the center of her life. Since the pursuit of truth, as she conceived it, ministered to her deepest spiritual needs, it became a sacrosanct creed. She willingly explained it to others, but she could not alter any part of it without yielding her authority and control. Her inner need for certainty determined both her conception of truth and the tenacity with which she upheld it. Her work is unique in its single focus on language as the source of meaning and in the quality of poetry that singleness produced.

Bibliography:

Joyce Piell Wexler, *Laura Riding: A Bibliography* (New York: Garland, 1981).

References:

T. S. Matthews, *Jacks or Better, A Narrative* (New York: Harper & Row, 1977);

Joyce Piell Wexler, *Laura Riding's Pursuit of Truth* (Athens: Ohio University Press, 1979).

Papers:

Cornell University has the authorized Laura and Schuyler B. Jackson Collection; Joint University Libraries in Nashville, Tennessee, holds letters from the Fugitive period; the State University of New York at Buffalo holds letters from the 1930s; the Northwestern University Library holds galleys, page proofs, and letters from the 1960s.

Randall Jarrell

Suzanne Ferguson
Wayne State University

BIRTH: Nashville, Tennessee, 6 May 1914, to Owen and Anna Campbell Jarrell.

EDUCATION: B.A., 1936; M.A., 1939; Vanderbilt University.

MARRIAGES: 1 June 1940 to Mackie Langham (divorced). 8 November 1952 to Mary von Schrader.

AWARDS AND HONORS: *Southern Review* Poetry Contest prize, 1936; Jeannette Sewell Davis Prize, 1943; John Peale Bishop Memorial Prize for "The Märchen," 1946; Guggenheim Fellowships, 1946, 1963; Levinson Prize (*Poetry* magazine), 1948; National Institute and American Academy of Arts and Letters Award, 1951; Oscar Blumenthal Prize (*Poetry* magazine), 1951; National Book Award for *The Woman at the Washington Zoo*, 1961; elected to the National Institute of Arts and Letters, 1961; O. Max Gardner Award, 1962; D.H.L., Bard College, 1962; Ingram Merrill Literary Award, 1965.

DEATH: Chapel Hill, North Carolina, 14 October 1965.

SELECTED BOOKS: *Blood for a Stranger* (New York: Harcourt, Brace, 1942);

Little Friend, Little Friend (New York: Dial Press, 1945);

Losses (New York: Harcourt, Brace, 1948);

Randall Jarrell at the University of North Carolina at Greensboro, 1961 (courtesy of Mary Jarrell)

The Seven-League Crutches (New York: Harcourt, Brace, 1951);

Poetry and the Age (New York: Knopf, 1953; London: Faber & Faber, 1955);

Pictures from an Institution (New York: Knopf, 1954; London: Faber & Faber, 1954);

Selected Poems (New York: Knopf, 1955; London: Faber & Faber, 1956);

The Woman at the Washington Zoo: Poems & Translations (New York: Atheneum, 1960);

A Sad Heart at the Supermarket: Essays and Fables (New York: Atheneum, 1962; London: Eyre & Spottiswoode, 1965);

The Bat-Poet (New York: Macmillan/London: Collier-Macmillan, 1964);

Selected Poems, including The Woman at the Washington Zoo (New York: Atheneum, 1964);

The Gingerbread Rabbit (New York: Macmillan/London: Collier-Macmillan, 1964);

The Animal Family (New York: Pantheon, 1965; London: Hart-Davis, 1967);

The Lost World (New York: Macmillan/London: Collier-Macmillan, 1965; London: Eyre & Spottiswoode, 1966);

The Complete Poems (New York: Farrar, Straus & Giroux, 1969; London: Faber & Faber, 1971);

The Third Book of Criticism (New York: Farrar, Straus & Giroux, 1969);

Jerome: The Biography of a Poem, edited by Mary von Schrader Jarrell (New York: Grossman, 1971);

Fly by Night (New York: Farrar, Straus & Giroux, 1976);

Kipling, Auden & Co.: Essays and Reviews, 1935-1964 (New York: Farrar, Straus & Giroux, 1980);

Randell Jarrell's Letters (Boston: Houghton Mifflin, 1985).

RECORDINGS: *Randall Jarrell Reads and Discusses His Poems Against War* (Caedmon, TC 1363, 1972);

The Gingerbread Rabbit (Caedmon, TC 1381, 1972);

The Bat-Poet (Caedmon, TC 1364, 1972).

OTHER: "The Rage for the Lost Penny," in *Five Young American Poets*, edited by James Laughlin (Norfolk, Conn.: New Directions, 1940), pp. 81-123.

TRANSLATIONS: Brothers Grimm, *The Golden Bird and Other Fairy Tales* (New York & London: Macmillan, 1962);

Ludwig Bechstein, *The Rabbit Catcher and Other Fairy Tales* (New York & London: Macmillan, 1962);

Anton Chekhov, *The Three Sisters* (New York: Macmillan/London: Collier-Macmillan, 1969);

Brothers Grimm, *Snow White and the Seven Dwarfs* (New York: Farrar, Straus & Giroux, 1972; Harmondsworth, U.K.: Kestrel, 1974);

Brothers Grimm, *The Juniper Tree and Other Tales*, 2 volumes, translated by Lore Segal, with four translations by Jarrell (New York: Farrar, Straus & Giroux, 1973; London: Bodley Head, 1974);

Goethe's Faust: Part I (New York: Farrar, Straus & Giroux, 1976);

The Fisherman and His Wife (New York: Farrar, Straus & Giroux, 1980).

Best known for his poetry of World War II and his incisive, memorably witty criticism, Randall Jarrell belonged to the second generation of American modernist poets. Like Robert Lowell and John Berryman—contemporaries and personal friends—he worked in his early years in the shadow of T. S. Eliot and W. H. Auden, gradually freeing his poetry from their influence in order to write his own characteristic work. Although educated in the South and a student in the early 1930s of Fugitive poets John Crowe Ransom, Donald Davidson, and Robert Penn Warren at Vanderbilt University—where he also associated with Allen Tate—Jarrell was a poet of midcentury American urban and suburban life, a confirmed Freudian in his view of personality and creativity, a Marxist in his interpretation of history, a liberal in politics. Though interested in modern theology, he was not religious; he wrote to Allen Tate in 1939, "I never had any certainties, religious or metaphysical, to lose, so I don't feel their lack. . . . I raised myself on Russell and Hume." An avid amateur tennis player, he was also an aficionado of sports cars, professional football, and opera (especially Richard Strauss).

A professor of creative writing and literature for virtually all his adult life, except for a stint in the U.S. Army Air Force during World War II and two years as Poetry Consultant at the Library of Congress in 1956-1958, Jarrell was a genuine man of letters, writing not only poetry but reviews and critical essays, introductions to anthologies, translations of poetry and plays, an unorthodox novel, and several children's books. In addition to creating the most poignant poetic representations of the ordinary American soldier or flyer of World War II (in such poems as "2nd Air Force," "A Pilot from the Carrier," "Siegfried," "Eighth Air Force," "Lines," "Absent with Official Leave," and "The Death of the Ball-Turret Gunner"), Jarrell also wrote striking poetic reworkings of traditional stories to show their underlying psychological significance (in "Cinderella," "A Quilt Pattern," "In the Ward: The Sacred Wood," "Sleeping Beauty: Variation of the Prince," "Jamestown," "The House in the Wood"); a superb evocation of childhood in early 1920s Hollywood—his own *Remembrance of Things Past*—(in "The Lost World" and "Thinking of the Lost World"); sympathetic dramatic monologues and narrative poems of middle-class loners, often women ("Burning the Letters," "Seele im Raum," "The Woman at the Washington Zoo," the 1961 poem titled "Hope," "Next Day," "Jerome"); and a number of poems engaging with works of visual art or sculpture ("The Knight, Death, and the Devil," "The Bronze David of Donatello," "The Old and the New Masters"). His shrewd and admiring assessments of Robert Frost, William Carlos Williams, Walt Whitman, and W. H. Auden set the tone for much subsequent criticism, and his critical witticisms are often quoted in present-day reviews and articles. Sensitive to and appreciative of the verbal gifts of other poets, he was more concerned in his own poems with moral understanding and feeling than virtuosic verbal display or sophisticated formal experimentation. "It is better to have the child in the chimney corner moved by what happens in the poem," Jarrell wrote, "in spite of his ignorance of its real meaning, than to have the poem a puzzle to which that meaning is the only key."

Randall Jarrell was the first of two sons born to Owen and Anna Campbell Jarrell. A daughter had died in infancy before he was born, and the motif of the lost sibling, particularly the sister, surfaced in Jarrell's work throughout his life (for example, "Orestes at Tauris," "The Black Swan," *The Animal Family*). On the other hand, the younger brother who lived is rarely an important figure. The working-class Jarrells came from rural Shelbyville, Tennessee, while Anna Campbell Jarrell was from a well-to-do Nashville business family. She was, according to her second daughter-in-law, "an immaculate person" and "a costly wife . . . [but] a devoted mother." Her frequent spells of fainting are recorded in the 1961 poem called "Hope," and she seems to have had health problems most of her life. From 1915 to 1925 the family lived in California, mostly in Long Beach, where Owen Jarrell worked for a photographer. Other members of the Owen Jarrell family had also settled in southern

California. In 1925 Anna separated from her husband, taking her sons with her back to Nashville, where they were provided for by her candy-manufacturer brother, Howell Campbell.

During the spring of 1926, while his mother was in the hospital, Randall posed for the figure of Ganymede on the pediment of the concrete replica of the Parthenon in Nashville's Centennial Park. The sculptors, Belle Kinney and Leopold Scholz, were "enchanted with this child who told them myths of the gods while he posed," wrote Jarrell's widow in 1966. "Long afterwards his mother said the sculptors had asked to adopt him, but knowing how attached to them he was she hadn't dared tell him. 'She was right,' Randall said bitterly. 'I'd have gone with them like *that*.' "

In 1926 Randall went back to Hollywood to spend the summer and fall with his paternal grandparents, the couple called Mama and Pop in "The Lost World." The mingled happiness and pain of this time remained with Jarrell all his life, and he was able to write about it directly only in 1962, when his mother's returning to him of the letters he wrote her in 1926 stimulated a flood of magical memories. His affection for his grandparents (in addition to the great-grandmother, "Dandeen," and the Aunt Bettie who owned the M-G-M lion) was dashed when they let him go back to Nashville and his mother's family, and he never wrote to them or saw them again. His distress and feeling of guilt over this rupture is recorded in "A Story" (1939) and "The Lost World" (1962).

Although he was expected to help his mother—in straitened circumstances after the divorce—by delivering newspapers and doing odd jobs, he was active in writing, music, and dramatics during his school years. When he could not be persuaded to take an interest in his uncle Howell Campbell's candy business, Campbell generously sent him to Vanderbilt, where he completed work for a B.A. in 1935 (receiving the degree in 1936) and earned an M.A. in 1939. Although majoring in psychology, Jarrell studied with Ransom, Davidson, and Warren and edited an undergraduate humor magazine, the *Masquerader*. Ransom—Mr. Ransom, Jarrell called him all his life—became his mentor. Tate, who lived in nearby Clarksville, helped and encouraged him with his poetry. Warren not only taught Jarrell at Vanderbilt but later published many of Jarrell's early poems and reviews after he went to teach at Louisiana State University and became an editor of the *Southern Review* in 1935 (Jarrell won the *Southern Review*'s poetry contest in 1936). Davidson directed Jarrell's master's thesis, "Implicit Generalization in Housman," after Ransom left Vanderbilt. Jarrell had wanted to write his thesis on Auden, who was then thirty— too "new" a poet for the conservative Vanderbilt English department. In 1937, when Ransom was offered a job at Kenyon College, Jarrell organized student efforts to get the Vanderbilt administration to make Ransom a counter offer, but Ransom left and Jarrell followed him to Kenyon, in Gambier, Ohio, where he held a part-time instructorship (and coached several sports, including tennis) until 1939. In later years Ransom was to recall Jarrell swooping down the Gambier hillsides on skis, arms outflung, calling "I feel just like an angel!" (to the disapproval of the Episcopal administration of the college). His first year there, Jarrell roomed in Ransom's house with an undergraduate student, Robert Lowell, who had transferred to Kenyon from Harvard to study with Ransom. During 1938-1939 the young men moved into college housing with Peter Taylor, who had followed Ransom to Kenyon from Vanderbilt that year. Taylor and Lowell became Jarrell's lifelong closest friends.

During his Vanderbilt years, Jarrell had

Randall Jarrell at twenty-four (courtesy of Mary Jarrell)

formed an attachment to Amy Breyer, a medical student several years older than he and one of several children of a friendly Jewish family who welcomed Jarrell into their Nashville home. The relationship was deep but, in the end, troubled: Breyer felt unable to live up to Jarrell's intellectual and emotional expectations. While he was at Kenyon she broke off with him and soon married a young surgeon in Boston. A number of poems record the painful end of the relationship: "Che Faro Senza Euridice?," "The Christmas Roses" (whose medical imagery may have come from Breyer), "On the Railway Platform," "In Those Days," "The Bad Music" (which substitutes—no doubt significantly—Jarrell's mother's name, Anna, for that of the lost beloved), and "A Story" (which also closely parallels the loss of his father's family in his childhood).

In 1939 Jarrell took a teaching post at the University of Texas at Austin, where he met his first wife, Mackie Langham, who had just received her M.A. from that university. They were married on 1 June 1940, and Jarrell's first collection (of twenty poems), "The Rage for the Lost Penny," appeared in *Five Young American Poets* (1940). The other contributors were John Berryman, W. R. Moses, Mary Barnard, and George Marion O'Donnell. Ransom reviewed the volume for the *Kenyon Review* (1941), praising Jarrell's "angel's velocity and range with language, and . . . dazzling textures of meaning," but reproving the "phonetic raggedness so consistent that we know he must be nursing some infection of puritan principle." Jarrell excluded all but two of these poems, which were strongly influenced by Auden and Tate, from *Selected Poems* (1955). In most of these poems he takes a sociological approach to the human condition, generalizing in imagery that is concrete but not specific, as in "The Automaton," with its

> great shape . . .
> The slave and remnant of the slain,
> . . . .
> Unconquered, inexhaustible,
> The genius of a world's desire,
> And cast at that world's judgment
> Into the world-consuming fire—

The subject of many of the poems is the imminent and inevitable self-destruction of human civilization, the result of greed, lust for power, and solipsistic indifference.

Jarrell's first independent volume, *Blood for a Stranger* (1942), contained all twenty poems from

"The Rage for the Lost Penny" and two dozen others, including the more characteristic "90 North," with its theme of the child's confrontation with nothingness; "Children Selecting Books in a Library," the first of several "library" poems explaining the power of literature to "cure that short disease, myself " by allowing the child to live other lives by vicariously "trading another's sorrow for our own"; and "The Memoirs of Glückel of Hameln," in which the poet speaks to a historical figure, an eighteenth-century Jewish woman who, after she was widowed, ran the family business and wrote her memoirs for her children. Reviewing the volume for the *New York Herald-Tribune Book Review* (29 November 1942), Ruth Lechlitner criticized the impersonal international-modernist style of the poems (and was the first to point out the resemblance of "90 North" to Stephen Spender's "Polar Exploration"), but she identified Jarrell's "recurrent theme . . . that humanity walks in an inescapable maze of guilt."

The poems of *Blood for a Stranger* are not war poems (most were written before World War II) though many address the deteriorating international situation caused by the tendency of "States" to seek infinite power and of individuals to lose themselves in egotism. Besides poems in which the poet speaks directly to the reader, there are quasi-narrative or dramatic poems whose protagonists are often children, or adults looking back into childhood. The style of the poems, like that in *Five Young American Poets*, seems adapted from Tate (to whom the volume is dedicated) and Auden, with echoes of Thomas Hardy, A. E. Housman, and Ransom (especially in "The Blind Sheep"). However, in the speaker who addresses his characters, urging them to "change" their lives, and in the imagery drawn from fairy tale and traditional fantasy, a number of the poems foreshadow Jarrell's mature writing.

By 1941 Jarrell was already embroiled in literary controversy because of his mordant reviewing. Malcolm Cowley wrote to the *New Republic*, whose associate editor, Edmund Wilson, had hired Jarrell in 1940, complaining of "the technical skill and the attitude—the *dandysme*—of the reviewer" which become "more important than the subject matter" in Jarrell's negative review of Conrad Aiken's *And in the Human Heart* (1940). (Jarrell had, among other things, likened Aiken's rhetorical skills to "Merlin's pulling a quarter from a schoolboy's nose," and his poems to "finger exercises by Liszt.") Jarrell's response insisted that he praised

poetry he admired and unrepentantly extended his objections to Aiken's book.

Early in 1942 Jarrell enlisted in the U.S. Army Air Force and was sent for aviation training to Sheppard Field in Wichita Falls, Texas. "Washing out" as a pilot, he was sent to Chanute Field, in Rantoul, Illinois, for training as a flight instructor and, eventually, celestial-navigation instructor. During the training period he was separated from his wife (and his beloved black Persian cat, Kitten) and wrote her many detailed letters describing the minutiae of life at the base. He turned some of this material into poems: "Lines," "Absent with Official Leave," "The Soldier," and "Soldier, T. P." An assignment in the mail room led to "Mail Call," and his hospitalization for an illness produced "The Sick Nought." In a letter to one editor from this time, Jarrell said he wrote more about "the Army" than "the War"; the boredom, senselessness, and uncertainty of army life characterize these poems. At Chanute, too, he wrote a second "library" poem: "Carnegie Library, Juvenile Division," a considerably darker poem than "Children Selecting Books in a Library." Though the children go to books for vicarious experience, they can learn only "to understand but not to change."

From late 1943 until his discharge in 1946, Jarrell taught flight navigation in a celestial-navigation tower (a training dome similar to a planetarium) at Davis-Monthan Field near Tucson, Arizona. Reunited with his wife, who got a job with the Red Cross (and Kitten, who appears in several poems and remained his adored pet until struck by a car in 1956), he wrote the rest of the poems of *Little Friend, Little Friend* (1945)—and some of those published in *Losses* (1948)—drawing upon his experiences with the flyers and planes and upon news dispatches by Ernie Pyle and others. The book was reviewed enthusiastically by Delmore Schwartz in the *Nation* (1 December 1945) for its advances over the earlier collections in theme and technique. The war gave the theme, but Jarrell's stance toward it was his own. He took "the particular part of the dead" who seek to understand the reasons for their deaths. Schwartz praised Jarrell's "justified repetition, hurried anapests, and a caesura fixed by alliteration" which give a "wonderfully expressive syncopation of movement" that enhances the obsessive questioning of the characters. Some of Jarrell's best-known poems appear in *Little Friend, Little Friend:* "2nd Air Force," "A Pilot from the Carrier," "Losses," "The Dream of Waking," "Siegfried," "The Metamorphoses," "The Wide Prospect," and "The Death of the Ball-Turret Gunner." The motif

Pfc. Randall Jarrell at Chanute Field, June 1943 (courtesy of Mary Jarrell)

of the soldier as a child who barely learns the meaning of his life before he loses it, who lives and dies in a dream, estranged, anonymous, unable to see himself either as murderer or victim, is developed in one striking poem after another, as in these lines from "Siegfried":

> Under the leather and fur and wire, in the gunner's
>   skull,
> It is a dream: and he, the watcher, guiltily
> Watches him, the actor, who is innocent.
> *It happens as it does because it does.*

Also in the volume is the haunting poem "The Snow-Leopard," that "heart of heartlessness" who looks indifferently at the caravan of humans suffering and dying in its mountain environment as they struggle to bring trade across the Himalayas: the leopard is for Jarrell a symbol of Spinozan Necessity, the working out of "Natural Law."

As a result of the reception of *Little Friend,*

Little Friend, Jarrell was given his first Guggenheim Fellowship after his discharge in 1946. He had recently taken over the "Verse Chronicle" reviewing column for the *Nation,* and while its literary editor Margaret Marshall took a sabbatical he went to New York to assume her job as well from April 1946 to April 1947. The statement of interests that he thought qualified him for her job is instructive: "Gestalt psychology, ethnology and 'folk' literature, economics (especially Marxist), symbolic logic and modern epistemology and its origins." These interests lie behind the attitudes and subjects of many of Jarrell's poems from this period, though not obtrusively, for by this time Jarrell was careful to embody his ideas in characters and situations. Also in 1946-1947 he held a part-time teaching position at Sarah Lawrence College in Bronxville, New York, where he gathered much of the material for his long prose fiction *Pictures from an Institution* (1954). The then-president of Sarah Lawrence,

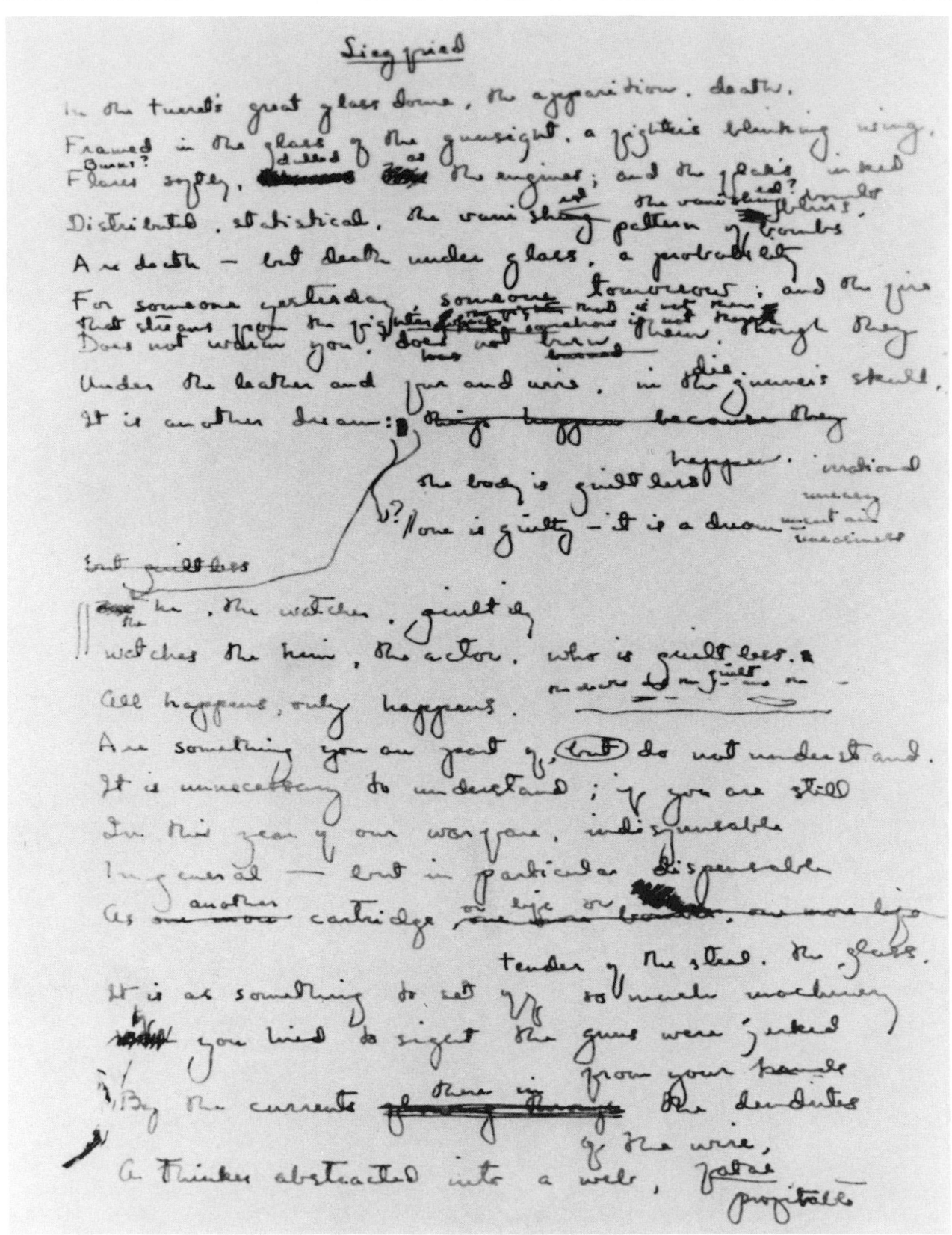

Two drafts for a poem collected in Little Friend, Little Friend *(by permission of Mary Jarrell; courtesy of the Special Collections Division, Walter Clinton Jackson Library, University of North Carolina at Greensboro)*

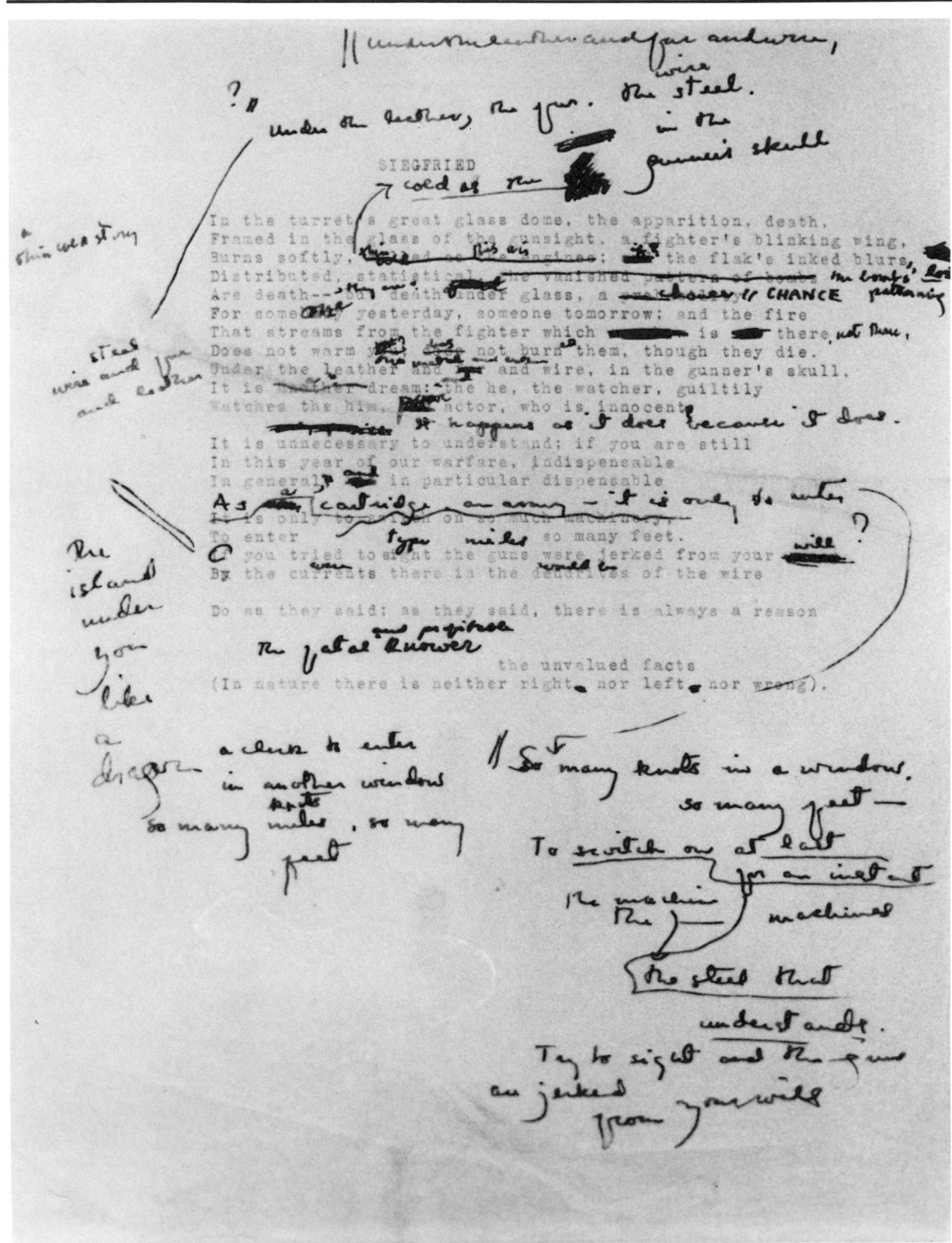

Randall and Mackie Jarrell with Kitten, 1949 (courtesy of Mary Jarrell)

Henry Taylor; his wife; and New York friends Jean Stafford, Hannah Arendt and her husband, Heinrich Bluecher, were among those who served as models for characters in the novel (as did Sara Starr, the daughter of long-time Jarrell friends from Nashville, Monroe and Zaro Starr; Mary McCarthy; and other "Lady Writers"). The idyllic campus of Sarah Lawrence, its well-to-do, pretty girls, and its progressive educational philosophy also took their place in the book, although it was more than half a decade before Jarrell would finish the work.

Jarrell came to dislike New York, and in the fall of 1947, encouraged by Peter Taylor, who was already teaching there, Jarrell went to Woman's College, later the University of North Carolina at Greensboro, as an associate professor. His wife, Mackie, had an instructorship. The couple bought a duplex with the Taylors and settled in.

Losses appeared in 1948. About two-thirds of its poems are related to the war and its aftermath. Jarrell's interest in modern theology (spurred by

his attraction to Auden) emerges in several poems, such as "The Place of Death," a meditation in a cemetery; "Eighth Air Force," in which he examines the question of the guilt of bomber pilots; and "Burning the Letters," in which the widow of a flyer tries to come to terms with his death and her continuing life, unable to use the religion that once promised eternal life. A number of the poems in *Losses* deal with the war dead: victims of the concentration camps in "A Camp in the Prussian Forest" and "In the Camp There Was One Alive"; dead soldiers or flyers in "The Dead in Melanesia," "New Georgia," "The Subway from New Britain to the Bronx," "The Dead Wingman," and "The Range in the Desert"; the death of the old civilization in "1945: The Death of the Gods" and "The Rising Sun"—whose protagonist is a Japanese child left, like the widow of "Burning the Letters," to understand the death of a loved one and of a whole tradition. Prisoners are the subject of "Stalag Luft," "O My Name It Is Sam Hall," and "Jews at Haifa"; the sick and wounded of "A Field Hospital," "In

Randall Jarrell in Greensboro, North Carolina, 1948 (courtesy of Mary Jarrell)

the Ward: the Sacred Wood," and "A Ward in the States." The volume also contains Jarrell's "elegy" for the (presumably imaginary) little black girl, "Lady Bates"; his most extended, obscure poem about fairy tales and their significance, "The Märchen"; and a much earlier poem, very long and several times revised, "Orestes at Tauris."

This poem, first published in the *Kenyon Review* in 1943, had been among the poems with which Jarrell won the *Southern Review* poetry contest in 1936, but it was not published in the *Southern Review* at that time because it was so long. Like many Jarrell poems it is deeply personal but hides its intimacy beneath the surface of retold myth. Jarrell's own sense of loss and estrangement from his family seems to inform the feelings of the protagonist, who moves as if in a dream to his reunion with Iphigenia—now a priestess of the fierce Taurian Artemis—which becomes his death. Orestes' resignation to being beheaded by his lost sister seems a projection of Jarrell's own complex attitude toward women (which would take a comic/ironic form in several later poems). "Orestes at Tauris" displays fear, love, desire for recognition and for union: emotions growing out of Jarrell's relations with his paternal grandmother—who beheaded

chickens for her little grandson to eat—with his mother, and with Amy Breyer. Helen Hagenbüchle connects the threatening female figures of "Orestes at Tauris" and other poems with Jarrell's relationship not only to his mother but to his muse, explaining, "Orestes' quest in fact symbolizes the poet's quest, for, as Jungian psychology maintains, the artist's dependence on the Great Mother as a wellspring of inspiration is so strong that he is never capable of the matricide necessary for the liberation of the anima and its differentiation from the mother archetype." It is perhaps not coincidental that Jarrell's estrangement from his first wife coincides with periods in which he felt unable to write poems, periods brought to an end by new romantic attachments.

The dark strain of Jarrell's poetry has been pointed out by some critics as evidence that the poet had a terribly unhappy life. Jarrell's comment on the themes of "horror, loathing, morbidness, final evil" in the work of Robert Penn Warren (in a 1944 letter to Amy Breyer di Blasio) can apply very well to Jarrell's own: "to somebody who knows Red it's plain he manages his life by pushing all the evil in it out into the poems and novels. . . . All his theory says is that the world is nothing but evil, whereas the practice he lives by says exactly the opposite. . . . his poetry is a therapeutic device, the most wonderful one you could want. . . ." Jarrell shows his awareness of the problem with the therapeutic use of poetry when he continues, "the best poetry there is isn't that. There's a dialectical contradictory relationship between Red's life and his poetry, and either is to an extent falsified by the mere existence of the other." Jarrell's poetry is not, however, unrelievedly bleak; even in treating painful subjects Jarrell can find humor and beauty in human experience.

Losses was generally less favorably reviewed than *Little Friend, Little Friend*, with W. S. Graham attacking it in the September 1948 issue of *Poetry* (which nonetheless awarded the volume its Levinson Prize that year) as "a collection of poems which are mostly spun from what should be the involuntary incidentals of a poem, rather than the poem's being made first for the poetic action . . . little conversational phrases trailing off to dots which, as a device, have a loosening effect upon a poetic line which is, in the first place, conceived at too low-grade a tension. . . . the timbre of the prosodic voice is old-fashioned and laboriously clichéd." Many of these accusations were to return in other forms in criticism of later volumes; but the traits to which they attach were essential to Jarrell's poetic aims, announced as early as 1940 in a letter to Allen Tate: "I'd rather seem limp and prosaic than false or rhetorical, I want rather to be like speech." This is not to say, as some critics have, that Jarrell was indifferent or lazy about the aural qualities of his verse. The many pages of manuscript held by the University of North Carolina at Greensboro and by the Berg Collection of the New York Public Library (those to "Jerome" were published in 1971) show how Jarrell worked with his poetic lines, frequently scanning them to check out his metrical patterns, and keeping lists of words and images in his quest for the exact diction that would best convey his vision. He wrote, for John Ciardi's anthology *Mid-Century American Poets* (1950), "Rhyme . . . is attractive to me, but I like it best irregular, live, and heard." He delighted in the coincidental concinnities of the signifier and the signified, even when the effects, for others, proved crude ("the burlaps/lapping and lapping each stunned universe" of "The Snow Leopard," for example, offended James Dickey). Jarrell repeatedly championed both poetry and prose that took seriously as its subject "reality"—which to him meant daily life as experienced by people—in Walt Whitman, Robert Frost, William Carlos Williams, Marianne Moore, Christina Stead, Rudyard Kipling, and Anton Chekhov. To Moore he wrote, in 1954, "I'm particularly fond of poetry that doesn't remove itself from speech and prose and Life in Particular." The transformation of the commonplace into art was his ideal (hence his adoration of Rainer Maria Rilke), but it was a difficult quest, in which a misstep in one direction meant pretentiousness, in another, triviality.

It was "between books" and apparently somewhat disaffected from his wife that Jarrell went to teach at the Salzburg Seminar in American Civilization in the summer of 1948. Here he fell in love with Germanic Romantic civilization (to which he had already been attracted, though he was also repelled by its culmination in the two World Wars and the atrocities against the Jews) and formed a romantic attachment with one of its representatives, an Austrian woman named Elisabeth Eisler, herself a victim of Naziism and a creative person, a ceramist. The stimulation provided by the experience resulted in such poems as "Hohensalzburg: Variations on a Theme of Romantic Character," "A Soul," "Orient Express," "A Game at Salzburg," and "An English Garden in Austria." A number of letters from Jarrell to Eisler, annotated and published by Mary Jarrell in *American Poetry Review* in 1977, show Jarrell's characteristic way of working with phrases, images, or ideas drawn from his reading, his experiences, or his correspondence. The germs—even occasional phrases—of several of these poems in fact come from Eisler's letters to him.

The Seven-League Crutches (1951) contains the Salzburg poems and a number of poems based on fairy tales and literary works. It also includes some of Jarrell's first translations, from Tristan Corbière and Rilke, and his first extended treatment of a work of visual art, his "translation," as he liked to call it, of Albrecht Dürer's *The Knight, Death, and the Devil*. Several interesting longer poems also appear in the volume: "A Conversation with the Devil," in which the poet makes a mock-Faustian deal with Mephistopheles; "The Night Before the Night Before Christmas," which, despite its adolescent female protagonist, Mary Jarrell has called "semi-autobiographical"; and "A Girl in a Library." This poem is Jarrell's contemplation of the archetypal American college girl, so different from the fictional romantic heroine who is her foil in the poem, Pushkin's Tatyana Larina, but elementally human, and, in her own way, mythic:

> Don't cry, little peasant. Sit and dream.
> One comes, a finger's width beneath your skin,
> To the braided maidens singing as they spin;
> ....
> The firelight of a long, blind, dreaming story
> Lingers upon your lips; and I have seen
> Firm, fixed forever in your closing eyes,
> The Corn King beckoning to his Spring Queen.

This poem was placed first in the 1955 *Selected Poems*. Its emotional opposite, the painful, memorable dramatic monologue "Seele im Raum," ends *The Seven-League Crutches*. The portrait of an individual who, amid her "normal" family life, nonetheless experiences a secret existence—symbolized by the imaginary eland which sits at her table and is a personification of her misery, her *elend*—"Seele im Raum" suggests Jarrell's projection of himself into his protagonist. *The Seven-League Crutches* received some strongly favorable reviews, including an ecstatic one from Robert Lowell in the *New York Times Book Review* (7 October 1951), and inspired the first substantial criticism of Jarrell's themes and techniques, Parker Tyler's long review essay in *Poetry* (March 1952), "The Dramatic Lyrism of Randall Jarrell."

In the summer of 1951 Jarrell taught at the University of Colorado School for Writers, where he met and encouraged a promising young poet,

Mary von Schrader and her daughter Beatrice, 1951 (courtesy of Mary Jarrell)

W. D. Snodgrass, and an aspiring novelist, the newly divorced, Germanic-named Mary von Schrader, who helped him read proof on *The Seven-League Crutches* and get over the feeling that it might be his last book of poetry. She was never to finish her novel, but Jarrell began writing some new poems. At the end of the summer, Jarrell arranged a formal separation from Mackie, who returned to the University of Texas for a Ph.D. in English and a career as a professor at Connecticut College. Jarrell went off to Princeton to teach creative writing and lecture in the Princeton Seminars in Literary Criticism. Here he associated with Berryman and Philip Rahv, wrote "The Lonely Man," and sent frequent, voluminous letters to Mary, who was back in California with her two daughters.

Not least among Mary's attractions was the fact that, born only days before him, she too had been brought up in Long Beach at exactly the same time, even patronizing the photographer for whom Jarrell's father worked and visiting her physician-father's office perhaps at the same time as Jarrell might have been waiting there for his mother, whose doctor shared the office. Mary von Schrader was, in a sense, the "sister" he had never had, as

well as a new love. She shared his passion for sports cars (and owned, when they met, the same model and color Oldsmobile that he had), and when they were able to marry, on 8 November 1952, they spent part of their honeymoon at sports-car races at Madera, California. She was to write, "To be married to Randall was to be encapsulated with him. He wanted, and we had, a round-the-clock inseparability." His long poem "Woman," finished in the fall of 1952, suggests both his new happiness and his habitual wry self-consciousness about women.

In 1952 Jarrell had taught in a hot but convivial summer session as a fellow of the Indiana School of Letters, consolidating a long-lasting friendship with Robert Fitzgerald and coming to admire Leslie Fiedler (whom he had not expected to like). Fitzgerald later recalled days of swimming in a nearby quarry, where, "hanging on a floating log in the quarry pool, [Jarrell] began one day to quote aloud the poem, 'Provide, Provide,' and to his growing astonishment and delight succeeded in going straight through it from memory. 'Why, *I* didn't know I had memorized *that*!' Randall is one of the few men I have known who chortled. He really did. 'Baby doll' he would cry, and his voice simply rose and broke with joy." In his long, important essay on Frost, "To the Laodiceans," which appeared that autumn in the *Kenyon Review*, Jarrell praised "Provide, Provide" as "an immortal masterpiece . . . full of the deepest, and most touching moral wisdom—and it is full, too, of the life we have to try to be wise about and moral in. . . ."

His first book of criticism, *Poetry and the Age*, was published in the summer of 1953. In addition to two significant general essays on the state of poetry and criticism, "The Obscurity of the Poet" and "The Age of Criticism," the volume contained a number of Jarrell's most influential essays elevating or revaluating the work of important American poets: "Some Lines from Whitman," "Reflections on Wallace Stevens," two essays on Frost, two on Marianne Moore, his introduction to the *Selected Poems of William Carlos Williams* (1949), and a powerful review-essay on Lowell's *Lord Weary's Castle* (1948). The volume was well received, with rave reviews from Delmore Schwartz and John Berryman. Reviewing the book for the *New Republic* (11 February 1953), Berryman called it "the most original and best book on its subject since *The Double Agent* by R. P. Blackmur and *Primitivism and Decadence* by Yvor Winters." Jarrell was always somewhat resentful that he was able to place virtually any of his prose pieces, while it was difficult to get

Mary and Randall Jarrell with her daughters, Alleyne and Beatrice, 1953 (courtesy of Mary Jarrell)

his poems published. "The Obscurity of the Poet" and others of his more general essays both reflect this resentment and confirm it by being just the kind of witty, readable critiques of the writer's situation and public that editors loved to print.

Having taught for the spring semester of 1953 at the University of Illinois, Jarrell brought Mary and her daughters, Beatrice and Alleyne, to Greensboro in the fall. During this time, Jarrell was revising *Pictures from an Institution* and preparing his *Selected Poems* for publication. The novel, or "comedy," as he called it, is a collection of "portraits" juxtaposed to one another in a dialectical or "musical" arrangement, as the title, with its reference to Modest Musorgski, suggests. The pictures of faculty, students, and administration in a progressive women's college after World War II express Jarrell's frustration with and affection for such "education." Academic personality types are satirized, some gently—the pompous sociology professor, the accommodating but null "head" of a midwestern university English department, the

sincere but dopey creative-writing student, the maiden-lady creative-writing teacher—and some more acerbically—the vapid, charming, young college president and his artificial, unpleasant wife, the waspish novelist who "smokes heads" for the novel she is writing about the college, and a pretentious teacher of painting whose students all imitate his work. Motifs of adoption by the ideal parents and of the quest for *good* art in a consumer-oriented culture are subsidiary themes, and many of Jarrell's enthusiasms and bêtes noires surface in allusions. His own zest for life and art, as well as his at times superior, even ingenuously cruel, disdain for the shoddy or mediocre, are distributed among several of the book's characters and judged with both sympathy and severity. Robert Lowell called *Pictures from an Institution* "a unique and serious jokebook," and Eric Bentley wrote, "At the root of his writing is enjoyment and love; not misanthropy, envy or spiritual anemia. Jarrell is gay, defiant, and good for the soul." Other critics found the book fragmented and destructively funny at the expense of its characters and the people they presumably caricatured.

Though he enjoyed writing the novel and was apparently happy with his new wife's devotion (she even attended his classes), Jarrell was increasingly writing prose rather than poetry, and this situation worried him: "A bad fairy has turned me into a prose writer," he would sometimes complain. He was also doing more translating. A lover of Rilke's poetry from his first acquaintance with it in the 1940s, Jarrell translated more Rilke and undertook a translation of Goethe's *Faust*. Later he also translated several Grimms tales, some Eduard Mörike, Henrikas Radauskas, and Chekhov's *The Three Sisters*.

In the fall of 1956 Jarrell began a two-year appointment as Poetry Consultant at the Library of Congress. He found Washington living agreeable and made himself useful at the library, soliciting manuscripts from poets and arranging tapings of poets' reading. Two of his most touching later poems came from the Washington milieu: "The Woman at the Washington Zoo" (thought by some to be his best poem), and "Jerome." The es-

sential loneliness of the middle and upper-middle classes in contemporary American society is mirrored in these poems, as in other poems of the 1950s that went into *The Woman at the Washington Zoo* (1960): "Nestus Gurley," "Over the Rainbow" (a long, "California" poem drawn partly on one of Mary's aunts), "Windows," and "The Lonely Man." The woman at the zoo speaks for all: "so/To my bed, so to my grave, with no/Complaints, no comment. . . ./The world goes by my cage and never sees me."

A summer trip to Italy in 1958 with Mary gave Jarrell the material for several poems on works of art, including the stunning sculpture poem, "The Bronze David of Donatello," with its sympathy for the defeated, bearded-like-Jarrell Goliath and its mixed attraction/repulsion for the androgynous, young, triumphant David. The poems and translations of *The Woman at the Washington Zoo* won Jarrell a National Book Award in 1961, and reviews were generally appreciative, though some found the number of translations—almost a third of the book—disquieting.

Jarrell kept up a full schedule of poetry read-

Alastair Reid, Robert Graves, and Randall Jarrell in Washington, D.C., 1957 (Library of Congress photograph, courtesy of Mary Jarrell)

ings, appearances at literary festivals, and academic assignments from the time of his return to Greensboro in 1958. There were frequent trips to New York to work with editors, visit the Arendts, and attend opera with and without friend and music critic B. H. Haggin. The Jarrells usually stayed at the Plaza Hotel, where Mary overheard the conversation that became "Three Bills" in *The Lost World*. Sometimes they took side trips to see the Warrens in Connecticut or other friends in the Northeast.

The *Faust* translation was taking most of Jarrell's creative energy in 1959, he wrote to his editor at Random House and later Atheneum, Hiram Haydn. He continued to work on *Faust*, but only part one and fragments of the second part were complete at the time of his death. During the summer of 1959 the Jarrells finally moved into a house of their own, built to their specifications in a wooded area on the edge of Greensboro near Guilford College.

In the summer of 1960 the family traveled in the western United States, staying for a time in Montecito, California, a suburb of Santa Barbara. There Jarrell completed the poem "In Montecito," with its expressionistic image of a death: "there visited me one night at midnight/A scream with breasts. As it hung there in the sweet air/That was always the right temperature, the contractors/Who had undertaken to dismantle it, stripped off/The lips, let the air out of the breasts." Its uncharacteristic violence jars against a more typical late Jarrell milieu: "Greenie has left her Bentley./They have thrown away her electric toothbrush, someone else slips/The key into the lock of her safety-deposit box/at the Crocker-Anglo Bank...." In spring 1961 Jarrell was elected to the National Institute of Arts and Letters.

In that year Jarrell was able to complete several more poems for *The Lost World*, "Washing," "Well Water," and "The One Who Was Different," as he continued teaching and working on various translating and editing projects, notably the preparation of *A Sad Heart at the Supermarket*, essays mostly from the 1950s, which was to be published in 1962 by Atheneum. The volume enhanced Jarrell's reputation as a critic of modern culture with such pieces as "The Intellectual in America," "The Taste of the Age," "The Schools of Yesteryear," and the title essay. Also included were his introductions to the selection of Kipling short stories he had made for Doubleday (1961) and to *The Anchor Book of Stories* (1958), and the essay he wrote for the 1960 revision of Brooks and Warren's textbook,

Understanding Poetry, explaining the genesis of "The Woman at the Washington Zoo." It is his most revealing public statement about his composing process.

In 1962 several significant events occurred: first, Jarrell contracted hepatitis, which put him in the hospital and left him with intestinal and neuralgic disorders that were to plague him the rest of his life. While he was in the hospital, Michael di Capua, who was then children's book editor for Macmillan and later Jarrell's editor there and at Farrar, Straus and Giroux, proposed that Jarrell contribute a translation of several Grimms Brothers' fairy tales to an illustrated edition in a series including other well-known writers' translations and introductions. Di Capua was so pleased with Jarrell's work on "Snow-White" and "The Fisherman's Wife" that he invited the poet to write his first children's book. By the end of the year, not only *The Gingerbread Rabbit* but *The Bat-Poet* (both published in 1964) was finished.

Also in 1962 Jarrell's mother returned to him the letters he had written her from California during the summer and fall of 1926. These letters unlocked a torrent of memories, and like one of his favorite writers, Marcel Proust, he began to recover the past. He was encouraged in this effort by his wife, who had similar memories. In a burst of creativity, he wrote many of the poems that would appear in *The Lost World* (1965), reading some of them in September at the YMHA in New York. The book was essentially complete by April 1963. In the same creative period he had also written *Fly by Night* (1976), like *The Bat-Poet* a quasi-autobiographical children's story. During this time he formed his friendship with Maurice Sendak, who illustrated all but the first of the children's books.

When it first appeared in the spring of 1965, *The Lost World* was greeted with mixed reviews, some very negative indeed, but in retrospect it appears to be a significant volume. In it Jarrell continued to use the style and approach of the poems in *The Woman at the Washington Zoo* to write about aging middle-class women, in "Next Day" and "A Well-to-Do Invalid"; about the dead, in "The One Who Was Different" and "In Montecito"; and about a baffled man's attempt to escape and/or embrace the "mothers" in his life, in "Hope" and "Woman." In "Woman," written in 1952 but not included in *The Woman at the Washington Zoo*, Jarrell had used more hexameter lines among his staple pentameters than in earlier poems, and many of the later poems maintain that freedom and sense of spaciousness. Several of the poems in *The Lost*

World come from *The Bat-Poet* (the intrusion of so-called juvenile verse into an adult book was objectionable to some critics) and there are other brief, observation-based pieces such as "Well-Water" and "The X-Ray Waiting Room in the Hospital." The nightmarish folktalelike poems "A Hunt in the Black Forest"—a revision of a 1948 poem—and "The House in the Wood" recall earlier themes, while "In Galleries" and "The Old and the New Masters" belong to the group of responses to art works, again stimulated by a summer trip to Europe (in 1963). In "The Old and the New Masters" Jarrell disputes Auden's contention, in "Musée des Beaux Arts," that paintings by "the Old Masters" show humans' indifference to suffering and miracles, citing to the contrary Hugo van der Goes's *Nativity* (the *Portinari Altarpiece*) and Georges de la Tour's *St. Sebastian Mourned by St. Irene*. In a turn that reflects his attack on modernist painting in "The Age of the Chimpanzee" (a 1957 essay for *Art News*), Jarrell concludes in "The Old and the New Masters" that the indifference to spiritual values which characterizes modern art accurately foreshadows the end of civilization:

> in abstract
> Understanding, without adoration, the last master
>   puts
> Colors on canvas, a picture of the universe
> In which a bright spot somewhere in the corner
> Is the small radioactive planet men called Earth.

Besides "Woman," "Next Day," and "The Lost Children," a poem based on Mary Jarrell's account of her dream about her then-grown daughter and a girl who died, the important poems of *The Lost World* are the title poem and its companion-piece, "Thinking of the Lost World." Especially in the title poem, autobiography is presented as an American child's myth. In the myth, problems are solved by wishes and by the daily miracles of life—visits to the aunt who owned the M-G-M lion, drives to the library in an electric car with "yellow roses/In the bud vases" and a friendly, decorous "Half wolf, half police-dog" on the back seat; the world is just as the child would have it if he could invent it himself. Fears of the radio "mad scientist" are soothed by the grandfather. The world portrayed is clearly artificial, made to conform to fantasies: on the way home from school the boy sees "dinosaur/And pterodactyl, with their immense pale/Papier mâché smiles" looking out over Melrose Avenue, and "a star/Stumbl[ing] to her igloo through the howling gale/Of the wind machines." The verse form of

"The Lost World" is terza rima, though the tercets are run together, and the language is so colloquial that the rhymes become unobtrusive (like the couplets of Robert Browning's "My Last Duchess," a poem Jarrell particularly admired, alluding to it in "Hope").

While the memories Jarrell summoned up for the poem are presented nonchronologically, its psychological plot takes off from the boy's impressions of his weekend: playing, listening to his grandfather tell stories of *his* boyhood, eating dinner, driving to the library with Mrs. Mercer, "Floating by on Vine, on Sunset" in the electric car. This first section is titled "Children's Arms": the fantastic and real experiences arm the child for life. The second and third sections, "A Night with Lions" and "A Street off Sunset," are spoken by the man looking backward, imposing the perspective of later years upon the child's view. Now he can admit the sexual attractiveness of the aunt who kept the lion and who talked to him "Of *Jurgen* and Rupert Hughes, till in the end/I think as a child thinks: 'You're my real friend.'" Even now, "my breath comes fast/Whenever I see someone with [her] skin,/Hear someone with [her] voice." Only now can he confront the pain of having left these loving relatives. He feels "real remorse . . . : the little girl is crying/Because I didn't write. Because—/of course,/I *was* a child, I missed them so. . . ." He lives again through the horror of his grandmother's killing a chicken for dinner and his realization that the same thing could happen to a rabbit, his pet rabbit:

> The farm woman tries to persuade
> The little boy, her grandson, that she'd never
> Kill the boy's rabbit, never even think of it.
> He would like to believe her . . . And whenever
> I see her, there in that dark infinite,
> Standing like Judith, with the hen's head in her hand,
> I explain it away, in vain—a hypocrite,
> Like all who love.

After years of guilt and confusion, he can now look back with happiness, recovering the memories, which he calls, at the end of "Thinking of the Lost World," "the nothing for which there's no reward." Of this line John Crowe Ransom wrote, "I felt at first that this was a tragic ending. But I have studied it till I give up that notion. The NOTHING is the fiction, the transformation; to which both boy and man are given. That World is not Lost because it never existed; but it is as precious now as ever." Denis Donoghue compared Jarrell's position here to that of Wallace Stevens, who created a world out of nothingness through imagination. "Stevens thinks of it as a wonderful resilience of perception. It is what Jarrell comes to, at the end: winter, and then, 'in happiness,' the mind of winter. In his case I think of it as a resilience, equally wonderful, of love."

The children's books written during this period also tend to illuminate the mature Jarrell's reconciliation with the pangs of estrangement he felt as a gifted child in an ordinary environment. *The Bat-Poet* is a parable about the poet's development, as the young bat tries to look carefully at experience and translate it into language. Imitating his models (mockingbird, bluejay, chipmunk, owl), performing for his devoted fan, the chipmunk, and his mentor and critic, the mockingbird, the bat achieves several elegant poems about things he admires or fears by projecting himself into them. The task of knowing and writing about himself is harder, but in the end his poem about bats is his best. After writing it he goes back simply to being a bat, not with the anxiety that plagued Jarrell when he was "between" poems or books of poems, but peacefully.

Fly by Night is a more obviously Freudian portrayal of a child's dream life. Only in dreams has David, the protagonist, the power of flight; in sleep he floats out away from his dreaming family, his pets, and the farm animals into the wild world, where the animals seem to speak to him in verse. Meeting a mother owl—who like Mama in "The Lost World" kills to be a good mother—he goes home with her and hears her bedtime story to her children. In mother owl's verse story, a lonely baby owl finds an orphaned owlet who becomes his sister. The motifs of quest, adoption, and transcendence reverberate in *Fly by Night* as in the last children's story Jarrell wrote, *The Animal Family* (1965). Writing a review of *Fly by Night* for the *New York Times Book Review* (14 November 1976), John Updike remarked upon "the tact of his language and the depth at which his imagery seeks to touch . . . the forbidden actual. All of Jarrell's children's tales have a sinister stir about them, the breath of true forlornness felt by children."

The idea for *The Animal Family*, of the man who brings home a mermaid and makes her his wife, had occurred to Jarrell in 1951 (soon after he met Mary von Schrader). The essential differentness of women from men and their more "elemental" quality is embedded in the mermaid image, as it is in other images of the poetry and *Pictures from an Institution*. Many objects the Jarrells had collected for the house they built on the wooded outskirts of Greensboro turn up in the book: a hunting horn, a window-seat, and a ship's figurehead, described as "a woman with bare breasts and fair hair, who clasped her hands behind her head; she wore a necklace of tiny blue flowers, and had a garland of big flowers around her thighs. But her legs and feet weren't a woman's at all, but the furry, delicate, sharp-hooved legs of a deer or goat—and they were crossed at the ankles. . . ." Since the man and the mermaid have no children of their own, they adopt animals—a bear and a lynx, like the one the Jarrells fed at the Washington Zoo—then find a shipwrecked, orphaned boy to bring up as their own. As the boy grows, he refuses to believe he is a foundling, and in the end it seems to the man and mermaid that they have had him "always."

While Jarrell was writing this wish-fulfilling story, he was going through a difficult period. Depressed in the spring and early summer of 1964, and still troubled by intestinal problems (see "The X-Ray Waiting Room in the Hospital"), Jarrell visited a psychiatrist he had met socially in Cincinnati when he taught there for six weeks in 1958. The psychiatrist increased the dosage of a new mood-elevating drug (Elavil) earlier prescribed by Jarrell's internist and sent him to a gastroenterologist who put him on a new diet. For a while he seemed to get better, but the drug unbalanced him in the opposite direction, so that he became continually elated and hyperactive. He slept little, felt inspired, wrote many poems and fragments—including his last finished poem, "The Player Piano"—harangued his classes and colleagues, and quarreled with his wife and friends. When, in February 1965, he was taken against his will to North Carolina Memorial Hospital in Chapel Hill, he was diagnosed as a manic-depressive. In the hospital, taken off Elavil and put on Thorazine, he became despondent, wrote to his agent of impending divorce from his wife, and in April cut his left wrist and arm in a suicide attempt. Afterward, off the Thorazine, he began a recovery that reconciled him with Mary by late spring and brought him home on the first of July. Although he wrote Robert Penn Warren in September that he was not yet writing any poems, he was happy to be at home and back to teaching. He was also planning trips (including one to Russia) and making notes for an essay on Emily Dickinson. In October, bothered by pain and impaired mobility and control in the wrist he had injured, he went back to Chapel Hill, to Memorial's Hand Rehabilitation Center, for physical therapy and possible corrective surgery. A few evenings

THE BLIND MAN'S SONG
(Rainer Maria Rilke)

I am blind, you out there. That is a curse,

An abomination, a contradiction,

A daily weight.

I lay my hand on my wife's arm,

My gray hand on her gray gray,

And she leads me through empty space.

You move and shove and think that you

Sound different from stone on stone.

You are mistaken: I alone

Am, am in torment, and bawl.

Inside me something interminably

Howls, and I can't tell what's howling,

My heart or my bowels.

You recognize the songs? You haven't sung them

Not in this key, quite.

To you, at morning, the new light

Comes warm in your open house.

And you've a sense of seeing eye to eye,

And that tempts one to show mercy.

Typescript for one of Jarrell's Rilke translations (by permission of Mary Jarrell; courtesy of the Lilly Library, Indiana University)

later, while walking about a mile from the hospital along a country highway, he was struck by a car and killed. Although the circumstances were suspicious—the couple in the car said he "appeared to lunge" into the side of their vehicle—they were inconclusive and the death was ruled accidental.

After the poet's death, his literary executor, Mary Jarrell, and his editor, Michael di Capua, put together *The Complete Poems* (1969), which included, along with all the poems from his other volumes, drafts and fragments and early uncollected poems; and *The Third Book of Criticism* (1969), which contained, among other pieces, Jarrell's long essay on Christina Stead's *The Man Who Loved Children*—a novel he had long recommended to friends and students; two essays on Auden; long review essays on Stevens and Robert Graves (especially interesting for Jarrell's comments on the "Mother-Mistress-Muse" of *The White Goddess,* 1948, an archetype that appeared often in his own work); an extended explication of Frost's "Home Burial"; and his 1962 National Poetry Festival address, "Fifty Years of American Poetry." This lecture had not been especially well received at the time, Jarrell had felt, because it slighted many of the poets in the audience. Its ranking of the modern American poets of the first part of the twentieth century now seems remarkably just, with only a few eccentricities. *Fly by Night* and Jarrell's translation of *Goethe's Faust, Part I* were published in 1976, followed in 1980 by another volume of criticism, *Kipling, Auden & Co.,* which contains previously uncollected reviews, introductions, and some essays from the out-of-print *A Sad Heart at the Supermarket.* In 1973 Mary Jarrell began assembling, transcribing, and annotating Jarrell's letters. From a total of about 2,500 she selected about 400 for publication in *Randall Jarrell's Letters* (1985). The letters do not so much add a new dimension to the personality revealed in the poems and public prose as they confirm and deepen what was already known. In addition to letters to his two wives and other family members and "official" letters written as an editor (mostly for the *Nation*) and as Library of Congress poetry consultant, there are interesting letters to his poet friends and to editors announcing his own principles, and, to Lowell and Adrienne Rich, long letters giving frank and detailed criticism of individual poems and entire volumes sent him for comment.

A memorial service was held for Jarrell at Yale in 1966, organized by Cleanth Brooks, Robert Penn Warren, Robert Lowell, and Peter Taylor. The memoirs and tributes read there, with others and

with republished reviews of several of Jarrell's books, were collected in *Randall Jarrell, 1914-1965* (1967). Jarrell was lucky in always having had a few sympathetic, perceptive reviews for each volume, and the serious criticism of Jarrell began in reviews by such writers as Lowell, Karl Shapiro, Schwartz, Berryman, William Meredith, Updike, John Logan, Philip Booth, and such critics as Helen Vendler and John Lucas. The first extended essays about Jarrell were Parker Tyler's review-essay on *The Seven-League Crutches* (1952) and Sister M. Bernetta Quinn's "Randall Jarrell: His Metamorphoses," in her book *The Metamorphic Tradition in Modern Poetry* (1955). Walter Rideout's substantial essay " 'To Change, to Change!' The Poetry of Randall Jarrell" in *Poets in Progress* (1962) stimulated interest in Jarrell, and later surveys by M. L. Rosenthal (1972), Jerome Mazzaro (1980), and Frederick J. Hoffman (1970) helped place Jarrell in his generation. The first book-length study was *The Poetry of Randall Jarrell* (1971) by Suzanne Ferguson.

Assessments of Jarrell's significance vary. To his admirers—Lowell, Schwartz, Quinn, Rideout, Hoffman, and, more reservedly, Vendler, Mazzaro, and Rosenthal—his poetry does what he intended it should: it records distinctively the life of midcentury America. Jarrell's sense of what was missing from Theodore Roethke's poetry suggests what he thought was important to put in his own: "hydrogen bombs, world wars, Christianity, money, ordinary social observation, . . . everyday moral doubts." It is this sense of "life" which continually draws him readers. William Pritchard has written that "even though the number of fully achieved poems is small, and the amount of dross in the *[Complete] Poems* is substantial, he is, along with Lowell, the American poet from the later part of this century I return to most often, and with continuing rewards, new discoveries. . . . [Other poets] can be admired as creators of more finished, concentrated, even verbally distinctive poems; yet Jarrell has something more, and to be as embarrassing as possible I will claim that what he has more of in his poetry is life." James Dickey, who found the *Selected Poems* on the one hand "the most untalentedly sentimental, self-indulgent, and insensitive writings that I can remember" (see his amusing "dialogue" review in *Sewanee Review* in Spring 1956), and thought that Jarrell had not "the power, or the genius, or the talent, or the inclination, or whatever, to make experience rise to its own most intense, concentrated, and meaningful level" in language, turned back upon these strictures to argue that "the poems give you the feel of a time, our time, as no other poetry of our century does, or could, even. They put on your face . . . the uncomprehending stare of the individual caught in the State's machinery: in an impersonal, invisible, man-made, and uncontrollable Force. They show in front of you a child's slow, horrified, magnificently un-understanding and growing loss of innocence in which we all share and can't help . . . : He gives you, as all great or good writers do, a foothold in a realm where literature itself is inessential, where your own world is more yours than you could ever have thought, or even felt, but is one you have always known."

Jarrell's intellect was far-ranging, inquisitive, and continually testing, and his poems reveal his strong perception of the ironic incongruity between people's ideals and the way they live, as well as a sure feeling for the moral and psychological crises people have in common and a messianic vocation to show others what he learned and saw in the contemporary world. Consciously limiting himself to a poetry of everyday life (and its corollary dream or nightmare) recorded in a language at times too much like that of everyday life, accepting perhaps too uncritically the Freudian model of motivation and behavior, Jarrell reserved for himself a place not among the great poets of the century, but among the very good, very representative ones.

Jarrell's criticism is less controversial, in retrospect, than his poetry because so many of Jarrell's judgments have turned out to be premonitory of the reputations now held by the various poets on whom he wrote. Reviewing *Kipling, Auden & Co.* (1980) for the *Times Literary Supplement* (19 June 1981), John Lucas commented: "his critical judgments feel unerring and final. . . . It is almost impossible to catch him out." Jarrell's praise of Lowell and of Elizabeth Bishop, his criticism of Cummings, Spender, Williams, and the later Auden are remarkably telling. It is not only the judgments but the metaphoric and witty style that distinguish the criticism, as Pritchard, Vendler, and Lucas (among others) have noted. Indeed, it is difficult to resist the reviewer who wrote, for example, of the Auden of *The Age of Anxiety*, "The man who, during the thirties, was one of the five or six best poets in the world has gradually turned into a rhetoric mill grinding away at the bottom of Limbo, into an automaton that keeps making little jokes, little plays on words, little rhetorical engines, as compulsively and unendingly and uneasily as a neurotic washes his hands."

Perhaps Vendler is right: Jarrell put his talent into his poetry and his genius into criticism. Al-though his work is not at present much taught in universities, Jarrell's poetry continues to find readers in the literate public—a situation that on the whole would have pleased him.

Letters:

Randall Jarrell's Letters: An Autobiographical and Literary Selection, edited by Mary von S. Jarrell (Boston: Houghton Mifflin, 1985).

Bibliographies:

Charles Adams, *Randall Jarrell: A Bibliography* (Chapel Hill: University of North Carolina Press, 1958);

Adams, "A Supplement to Randall Jarrell: A Bibliography," *Analects*, 1 (1961): 49-56;

Karl Shapiro, *Randall Jarrell* (Washington, D.C.: Library of Congress, 1967), pp. 25-47;

Stuart Wright, *Randall Jarrell: A Descriptive Bibliography, 1929-1983* (Charlottesville: University of Virginia, 1985).

References:

Analects, special Jarrell issue, 1 (1961);

Suzanne Ferguson, *The Poetry of Randall Jarrell* (Baton Rouge: Louisiana State University Press, 1971);

Ferguson, ed., *Critical Essays on Randall Jarrell* (Boston: G. K. Hall, 1983);

Helen Hagenbüchle, *The Black Goddess: A Study of the Archetypal Feminine in the Poetry of Randall Jarrell*, Schweitzer Anglistische Arbeiten, volume 79 (Bern: Francke, 1975);

Frederick J. Hoffman, Introduction to *The Achievement of Randall Jarrell*, edited by Hoffman (Glenview, Ill.: Scott, Foresman, 1970);

Robert Humphrey, "Randall Jarrell's Poetry," in *Themes and Directions in American Literature*, edited by Ray B. Browne and Donald Pizer (Lafayette: Purdue University Press, 1969), pp. 220-233;

Mary von S. Jarrell, "The Group of Two," in *Randall Jarrell, 1914-1965*, edited by Robert Lowell, Peter Taylor, and Robert Penn Warren (New York: Farrar, Straus & Giroux, 1967), pp. 274-298;

Jarrell, "Ideas and Poems," *Parnassus*, 5 (Fall-Winter 1976): 213-230;

Jarrell, "Letters to Vienna," *American Poetry Review* (July/August, 1977): 11-17;

Jarrell, "Peter and Randall," *Shenandoah*, 28 (Winter 1977): 28-34;

Jarrell, "Randall Jarrell at Work," *Columbia Forum*, 2 (Summer 1973): 24-30;

Jarrell, "Reflections on Jerome," in *Jerome: The Biography of a Poem* (New York: Grossman, 1971), pp. 11-18;

Robert Lowell, Peter Taylor, and Robert Penn Warren, eds., *Randall Jarrell, 1914-1965* (New York: Farrar, Straus & Giroux, 1967);

Jerome Mazzaro, "Between Two Worlds: The Postmodernism of Randall Jarrell," in his *Postmodern American Poetry* (Champaign: University of Illinois Press, 1980), pp. 32-58;

Sister M. Bernetta Quinn, *Randall Jarrell* (Boston: Twayne, 1981);

Quinn, "Randall Jarrell: His Metamorphoses," in her *The Metamorphic Tradition in Modern Poetry* (New Brunswick: Rutgers University Press, 1955), pp. 168-206;

Walter Rideout, " 'To Change, to Change!' the Poetry of Randall Jarrell," in *Poets in Progress:*

Critical Prefaces to Ten Contemporary Americans, edited by Edward B. Hungerford (Evanston: Northwestern University Press, 1962), pp. 156-178;

M. L. Rosenthal, *Randall Jarrell* (Minneapolis: University of Minnesota Press, 1972);

South Carolina Review, special Jarrell issue, 17 (Fall 1984): 50-95;

Parker Tyler, "The Dramatic Lyrism of Randall Jarrell," review of *The Seven-League Crutches, Poetry,* 79 (March 1952): 335-346.

Papers:

The major collections of Jarrell's papers are at the library of the University of North Carolina at Greensboro and in the Berg Collection at the New York Public Library.

Stanley Kunitz

(29 July 1905-   )

Marie Hénault
Saint Michael's College

BOOKS: *Intellectual Things* (Garden City: Doubleday, Doran, 1930);

Passport to the War: A Selection of Poems (New York: Holt, 1944);

Selected Poems, 1928-1958 (Boston: Atlantic Monthly/Little, Brown, 1958; London: Dent, 1959);

The Testing-Tree: Poems (Boston: Atlantic Monthly/Little, Brown, 1971);

The Terrible Threshold: Selected Poems, 1940-1970 (London: Secker & Warburg, 1974);

A Kind of Order, A Kind of Folly: Essays and Conversations (Boston: Atlantic Monthly/Little, Brown, 1975);

The Poems of Stanley Kunitz, 1928-1978 (Boston: Atlantic Monthly/Little, Brown, 1979);

The Wellfleet Whale and Companion Poems (Riverdale-on-Hudson, N.Y.: Sheep Meadow Press, 1983);

Next-to-Last Things: New Poems and Essays (Boston: Atlantic Monthly Press, 1985).

OTHER: *Living Authors: A Book of Biographies,* edited by Kunitz as Dilly Tante (New York: Wilson, 1931);

Authors Today and Yesterday, edited by Kunitz, with Howard Haycraft and Wilbur C. Hadden (New York: Wilson, 1933);

The Junior Book of Authors, edited by Kunitz and Haycraft, with Hadden and Julia E. Johnson (New York: Wilson, 1934); revised edition, edited by Kunitz and Haycraft (New York: Wilson, 1951);

British Authors of the Nineteenth Century, edited by Kunitz and Haycraft (New York: Wilson, 1936);

American Authors, 1600-1900, edited by Kunitz and Haycraft (New York: Wilson, 1938);

Twentieth Century Authors, edited by Kunitz and Haycraft (New York: Wilson, 1942);

British Authors before 1800, edited by Kunitz and Haycraft (New York: Wilson, 1952);

Twentieth Century Authors, First Supplement, edited by

Stanley Kunitz (photograph © Renate Ponsold)

Kunitz and Vineta Colby (New York: Wilson, 1955);

Poems of John Keats, selected, with an introduction, by Kunitz (New York: Crowell, 1964);

European Authors, 1000-1900, edited by Kunitz and Colby (New York: Wilson, 1967).

TRANSLATIONS: *Poems of Akhmatova*, translated, with an introduction, by Kunitz with Max Hayward (Boston & Toronto: Atlantic Monthly/Little, Brown, 1973);

Andrei Voznesensky, *Story Under Full Sail*, translated by Kunitz, with Vera Reck, Maureen Sager, and Catherine Leach (Garden City: Doubleday, 1974);

Ivan Drach, *Orchard Lamps*, edited by Kunitz, translated by Kunitz and others (Riverdale-on-Hudson, N.Y.: Sheep Meadow Press, 1978).

Since the late 1920s Stanley Kunitz has consistently gone his own way. Meticulous in the craft of poetry, he has published his writings sparingly and seems to have been unaffected by the work of other poets. Though, as T. S. Eliot observed, "art never improves," an individual artist can improve and often does, and Kunitz's poems of the 1970s and 1980s are possibly better than, and certainly as good as, those of earlier decades. Most of his poems are exquisitely finished in both diction and form and are often profound in probing life's pain. He has a few nearly perfect poems—intense, passionate, and universal—and a further body of good poems to ensure his reputation. His one prose book and his translations from Russian round out a long, busy life that has been single-mindedly dedicated to poetry.

Though Kunitz's poetry is distinguished and has been recognized as such by his peers, for a great part of his career it has not received the recognition that it merits. This oversight was somewhat corrected after he was appointed as Consultant in Poetry to the Library of Congress for 1974-1975. In 1974 two important literary journals published interviews with him, and in 1975 the *New York Times Magazine* featured an article about his gardens and their relationship to his poetry. Later, in 1980, *Antaeus* devoted an issue to his work, and a book about his work was published, while in 1982 an interview with him appeared in *Paris Review*. In 1984 he was given $25,000 as one of four distinguished American writers granted Senior Fellowships by the National Endowment for the Arts. A second critical study of his writing came out 1985. His eightieth birthday in 1985 was celebrated in Provincetown, Worcester, and New York. Worcester honored him with a five-day Stanley Kunitz Poetry Festival in October 1985, and the September-October 1985 issue of the *American Poetry Review* included a special eight-page Kunitz supplement. Speaking of the festival Kunitz said, "It was such a rare phenomenon to have the sense of a whole community participating in welcoming someone for writing poems. I have to count it as one of the miracles of the age."

Born in Worcester, Massachusetts, Stanley Jasspon Kunitz was the third and last child of his Russian-Jewish parents. His father, Solomon Z. Kunitz, was a dress manufacturer who killed himself before Kunitz's birth. Kunitz's mother, Yetta Helen Jasspon Kunitz, carried on the business and, when Kunitz was eight, married Mark Dine, who died half a dozen years later. In Kunitz's poems the father is an obsessive, ghostly image.

In 1922, the year of the publication of the two landmark works of modernism, *The Waste Land* and

Ulysses, Kunitz was seventeen and valedictorian of his class at Worcester Classical High School. He won a scholarship to Harvard, from which he earned an A.B. (summa cum laude) in English in 1926 and an A.M. in English in 1927. "At Harvard," he has said, he "pronounced myself an advocate of the Moderns, from Hopkins down to Joyce and Eliot and Cummings." While in college, Kunitz spent his summers as an apprentice with the *Worcester Telegram,* and he continued to do so for a short while after earning his A.M. In 1928 he went to work for the H. W. Wilson Company in New York City, a publishing house with which he remained associated until the 1970s, though working largely from his home in Mansfield Center, Connecticut, and later Bucks County, Pennsylvania. He edited Wilson's house journal, the *Wilson Bulletin for Librarians* (which became the *Wilson Library Bulletin* in 1939) and contributed a monthly column to it. He also edited nine biographical dictionaries, beginning with *Living Authors: A Book of Biographies* (1931), which he edited under the pseudonym Dilly Tante, and continuing with eight other volumes, including *Twentieth Century Authors* (1942), one of several he edited with Howard Haycraft, and *European Authors, 1000-1900* (1967), edited with Vineta Colby. For the 1975 Wilson volume *World Authors, 1950-1970,* edited by John Wakeman, Kunitz served as editorial consultant.

These works made Kunitz's name widely known among librarians and scholars; they are pioneer reference works still useful for information about their subjects. As Kunitz has said, he did this editing because he "had to earn a living," and so, unlike his poetry, these thousands of pages are his journey work only.

Though Harvard was, in Kunitz's later sardonic estimate, "a great place" for discouraging poets, a visiting professor of composition there, Robert Gay, told Kunitz, "You are a poet—be one." At Harvard he won the coveted Lloyd McKim Garrison Medal for Poetry in 1926, and after college he began publishing his poems in *Poetry, Commonweal,* the *New Republic,* the *Nation,* and the *Dial.* Kunitz has noted that the "biggest thrill" of this time was an acceptance letter from the *Dial* written in editor Marianne Moore's "spidery hand."

These poems, collected in Kunitz's first book, *Intellectual Things* (1930), date, Kunitz has said, "from 1927, when I was 22," an age when he "had developed intellectually more than I had emotionally or experientially." The poems betray a lack of technical development as well, for the difficulties

in a good many of the poems, most of them never republished, are due not to the inadequacy of theme or content but to questions of form and control. Lacking any marked internal divisions, the fifty poems in the book rest heavily on the book's epigraph from William Blake: "The tear is an intellectual thing." Kunitz has written that he "meant to demonstrate . . . not that the poem was a cerebral exercise, but the contrary, that the intellect and the passions were inseparable. . . ."

Within this unifying theme, the poems appear to move from the universal to the particular. Thus the first half of the book includes relatively general, gloomy visions of man, the poet, and destiny, poems that attempt to bring together "mind" and "heart," which, along with "blood," "Time," and "thought," are among the most frequently used words in the book. Love, including the suffering and pain it causes, is the source of not only poetry but also the unity of the mind and the passions. A representative example of the more specific poems of the second half of the book is "Vita Nuova," a self-portrait, a summary, and a prayer. It is highly personal, and, though it is not "confessional," there is little distinction between the poet and the "I" of the poem. Further, the content, theme, imagery, tone, and form of the poem are all characteristic of Kunitz's poetry through the publication of *Selected Poems* in 1958.

In "Vita Nuova," as in most of his poems, Kunitz speaks in something very like his own voice, avoiding the masks and personae preferred by many poets of the first-generation modernists. "Now one of the marks of the lyric poet," Kunitz has said, "is a compulsion . . . to show his mask." Kunitz's "I," then, is the traditional lyric "I"—like Wordsworth's or Coleridge's, for example—and it displays a good portion of the "real" Kunitz. Yet it is a mistake, as Paul Valéry warned, to suppose that the man whom the poetry presents is the man who wrote the poetry. Thus some of the routine, trivial, more sordid activities of everyday life and thought that some contemporary poets unhesitatingly include in their poems are not in Kunitz's. His poetry deals rather with moments of heightened sensitivity and awareness, of self-revelation. "Formal verse is a highly selective medium," he has said. "A high style wants to be fed exclusively on high sentiments." Until the 1960s most of Kunitz's poems were formal in versification and lofty in theme.

The "I" of "Vita Nuova" announces a Dantean "new life" of single-minded concentration. He vows to "peel" from his brain the vision of the many conflicting selves of his past and to "go, unburdened." In the final stanza he invokes the "Moon of the soul" to

> accompany me now.
> Shine on the colosseums of my sense.
> Be in the tabernacles of my brow.
> My dark will make, reflecting from your stones,
> The single beam of all my life intense.

It is a fierce, solemn poem of self-examination and revelation, typically introspective and hard on the self in its asserting a new determination to be dedicated to a singleness one rarely achieves.

"Vita Nuova" is also dense with Kunitz's exact diction and consistent imagery—verbs such as "abdicate," "gnawed," and "peel," nouns such as "apocalypse," "visor," "colosseums," and "tabernacles." Like most of Kunitz's poems until the late 1950s, this one is careful in form: four five-line stanzas rhyming *ababb*, each line with ten syllables. Kunitz also makes frequent use of a quatrain stanza rhyming *abab* with lines ranging in length from six to eight syllables. Still, the truly Kunitzian poems are later ones with long stanzas of varying lengths or verse paragraphs written in a loosened blank verse or free verse—poems such as "The Science of the Night," "Father and Son," "Foreign Affairs," or "Reflection by a Mailbox," the meditative "war" poem that led off his second book of poems, *Passport to the War* (1944).

By this time Kunitz was almost forty and going off to war. In 1937 he had been divorced from his first wife, Helen Pearce, whom he had married in 1930, and on 21 November 1939 he married Eleanor Evans, with whom he later had a daughter, Gretchen. In 1943-1945 he served in the U.S. Army, Air Transport Command, rising to the rank of staff sergeant.

Passport to the War collected many of Kunitz's recent poems with an almost equal number from the out-of-print *Intellectual Things*. *Passport to the War* includes "Father and Son," the most written about of Kunitz's works, a poem of primordial power. Some of the effect of this dream-narrative surely comes from the universality of its theme, based as it is on the aching, unassuageable grief at the loss of a father.

Overtly "Father and Son" is in the tradition of the quest of the lost father: the son journeying down a "sandy road," through "fields" and "years," following his father to "tell him my fable," the whole sequence of his life since his father's departure. The speaker overtakes his father at last, "At the water's edge, where the smothering ferns lifted/

Their arms . . . ," symbolically at the last possible moment before his father's disappearance. "Father!" the son cries,

> Return! You know
> The way. I'll wipe the mudstains from your clothes;
> No trace, I promise, will remain. Instruct
> Your son, whirling between two wars,
> In the Gemara of your gentleness,
> For I would be a child to those who mourn
> And brother to the foundlings of the field
> And friend of innocence and all bright eyes.
> O teach me how to work and keep me kind.

The son's narrative of the years since his father's death and his promise and final request take up seventeen of the poem's thirty-four lines. The father, in contrast, says nothing, and even his face at the end is a mere "white ignorant hollow": "ignorant," it has no knowledge to impart did it speak.

For Kunitz, as for many men of his generation and the one just younger, World War II was his "darkest time," when the rest of his life had to be held in hiatus. After his war service he held a Guggenheim Fellowship in 1945-1946, living in Santa Fe, and then in autumn 1946, at the prompting and insistence of his friend and fellow poet Theodore Roethke, he went to teach at Bennington College in Vermont.

After he had completed his A.M. at Harvard in 1927, he had expected to be offered a teaching appointment there, "not because I was already a poet but because of my scholarship record." Yet, as was not uncommon in American universities at that time, he "was told indirectly through the head of the English department that Anglo-Saxons would resent being taught English by a Jew, even a Jew with a *summa cum laude*. That shook my world," Kunitz said later. "It seemed to me such a cruel and wanton rejection that I turned away from the academic world completely."

Finally back in academic life after nearly twenty years, Kunitz remained at Bennington until 1949 and later taught at other colleges and universities "on a year-to-year basis, without tenure." He spent 1949-1950 at Potsdam State Teachers College (now the State University of New York at Potsdam) and directed seminars at their summer creative workshops until 1953. In 1950 he became a lecturer at the New School for Social Research in New York, and in 1955-1956 he was visiting poet-in-residence at the University of Washington, Seattle. The following academic year he was a poet-in-residence at Queens College (now part of the

City University of New York), and in 1958-1959 he taught at Brandeis University. After a stint as poetry-workshop director at the Poetry Center of the YMHA in New York and an appointment as Danforth Lecturer at various colleges and universities, he began what became his longtime association with Columbia University in 1963. Yet he maintained his "freedom" by signing only a one-year contract and did not accept tenure. An "adjunct professor, attached to the graduate school of writing," he taught, he said, for the students, not for the institution. In 1968 he also helped to organize and became a member of the staff at the Fine Arts Work Center in Provincetown, Massachusetts. In 1970 he was a visiting professor at Yale, and in 1974 he was at Rutgers University. In 1985 Kunitz resigned from his regular teaching post at Columbia. He continues, however, with seminars, lectures, and readings at a number of colleges, including Columbia.

When asked by young poets if they should become teachers, Kunitz tries to discourage them. "On the whole I think it's stultifying for young poets to leap immediately into the academic life," he has explained. "They would be better off testing the rigors of a less regulated existence."

For himself, coming to teaching "late" he "found it second nature." How did he teach the writing of poetry? "Thoroughly," he said. "Passionately. Long ago," he added, "I discarded theories. The danger of the poet-as-teacher lies in his imposing his *persona* on his students. I welcome any kind of poet; I don't care if he is my kind or not. Some of the best students I've worked with have turned out to be my own opposites."

The importance of Kunitz's teaching is apparent in the number of poets who name study with him as an essential part of their training. Some of his students as well as some other younger poets whose work he had edited or whom he had encouraged gathered together at the University of Virginia in a four-day festival to honor Kunitz in March 1980. Among them were Olga Broumas, Carolyn Forché, Tess Gallagher, Daniel Halpern, Louise Glück, Robert Hass, Gregory Orr, and Michael Ryan. The last four, along with David Ignatow, have essays on Kunitz's poetry in the Spring 1980 issue of *Antaeus*. Gregory Orr published a book on Kunitz in 1985. Along with Glück, Halpern, Ignatow, Gallagher, Ryan, and others, Orr took part in the 1985 Worcester Stanley Kunitz Poetry Festival. In 1986 a Festschrift in Kunitz's honor, edited by Stanley Moss, is to be published by Sheep Meadow Press.

In 1958 when *Selected Poems* was published, Kunitz was firmly established in teaching; he was in his fifties, married for the third time (to Elise Asher, whom he married on 21 June 1958, after his divorce from his second wife). *Selected Poems* contains eighty-five poems, including all fifty from *Passport to the War* and two poems from *Intellectual Things* that had been excluded from *Passport to the War*. Since nearly one-half the poems in *Passport to the War* are also in *Intellectual Things*, *Selected Poems* is a collection of all the poems written up to 1958 that Kunitz wanted to keep. The book was awarded a Pulitzer Prize in 1959.

Because, as Kunitz has said, he tends "to think of a book as a composition, a joining of parts into an architectural whole, not just a throwing-together of the poems as written," each of Kunitz's books is carefully crafted, having what he calls "an interior logic." Each of his first two books contains fifty related poems and each begins and ends with thematically significant poems. *Selected Poems* opens with "The Science of the Night," a reflective love poem, and ends with "A Spark of Laurel," a poem about poetry, two of the thematic poles in the book.

Before putting together this third book Kunitz reexamined the relationships among the poems

Stanley Kunitz (photograph © 1974 by Layle Silbert)

and arranged them, he says in an author's note, "in groups that bear some relevance to the themes, the arguments, that preoccupied me since I began to write." In these groups new poems are mixed in with old, and all are arranged in a new order.

These groupings are titled with phrases taken from poems, each highly figurative and suggestive. The second of these section titles, "The Terrible Threshold" (the title also of Kunitz's 1974 book), is from "Open the Gates," a short Blakean lyric typical of the poems in the section. The three tetrameter quatrains, the same stanza form employed in Tennyson's "In Memoriam," present a strange action in which the naked "I" prowls through "the city of the burning cloud" dragging his life behind him in a sack. He knocks at a door; the door opens, and he stands "on the terrible threshold" and sees "The end and the beginning in each other's arms."

In 1971 Kunitz published *The Testing-Tree*, revealing a new, freer poetry, looser forms, shorter lines, lowercase line beginnings. With seven translations and twenty-three original poems, this slim volume is enlarged by the quality and depth of the poems. Overall the Kunitz of this book is a "new" Kunitz, one who has grown and changed in the thirteen years since *Selected Poems*.

In April 1971, when Kunitz read at the Worcester Poetry Festival at the Worcester Library, he "mentioned how, for many years after leaving the city [of his birth], he drove miles out of the way to avoid it." He doubted, he said, that he would ever "forget Worcester" because it had "scarred" him so. Once back there, he has written, he "looked for the old house at the city's edge and those Indian woods" that he had roamed in as a boy nearly sixty years before: "The place had turned into a technological nightmare . . . an express highway running through my childhood. On the site of my nettled field stood a housing development ugly enough for tears." This "depressing adventure" was "one reason why I had to write 'The Testing-Tree,' " the title poem of this volume.

A sense of loss, regret, waste, and misunderstanding, present in many poems in this book, is explicit in "The Illumination," a lyric of mystical insight and paradox in which a Dante-Christ figure appears to the persona. This stark thirty-line poem, written in short lines that are nearly free of adjectives, is compact with meaning and emotion beyond its brevity. The scene is a hotel room, where "my life/rolled in its socket/twisting my strings" and all his "mistakes" from his "earliest/bedtimes," rise against him: "the parent I denied,/the friends I failed,/the hearts I spoiled/including at least/my

own left ventricle—/a history of shame." In a shattering dream moment, an apparition of Dante appears and says, "I know neither the time/nor the way/nor the number on the door . . ./but this must be my room,/I was here before." The emotion mounts up the twenty-ninth and next-to-the-last line in which the crosslike key seems literally held up on the page:

> Dante holds
> up in his hand
> the key
> which blinded me.

The result is an unembellished, terrifying poem reflecting on a lifetime's shames and inadequacies.

Kunitz's visit to Russia in 1967 as part of a cultural exchange program resulted in his becoming "deeply involved," he has said, "in the lives and fates of her poets." Of these poets Anna Akhmatova was the most important to him. His translation of a selection of her poems, published in 1973, occupied Kunitz for years. Coming close after *The Testing-Tree* and around the same time as three other books—*The Terrible Threshold*, a selection of his poems for British readers; *Story Under Full Sail* (1974), a translation of a dramatic poem by his friend Andrei Voznesensky; and *A Kind of Order, A Kind of Folly* (1975), a prose volume—*Poems of Akhmatova* gave him four books in three years, a change from his previously slim output, so much so that he was, he said, "suddenly threatening to become prolific—for me, that is." As Kunitz has noted, "most of the big reputations in modern American poetry have been made on the basis of a large body of work." However, he added, "that doesn't happen to be my style. Over a lifetime I've written poems only when I felt I had poems to write. . . ."

The Poems of Stanley Kunitz, 1928-1978, published in 1979, won the Lenore Marshall Prize for the best book of poetry published in the United States in 1979. Some of the sixteen new poems in this book, about a sixth of the whole, are quite long, and some—including a seven-part "Garland": "Words for the Unknown Makers"—are quite different from Kunitz's earlier poetry. The rest of the book contains 146 poems from each of his four earlier books, arranged in reversed chronological order. The last of the new poems, "The Layers," written in a single stanza of forty-four short lines, seems a recollection of a long life and a valedictory. The first-person persona is "directed" by "a nimbus-clouded voice" to "Live in the layers,/not on the litter." Both "layers" and "litter" resonate with meaning. "Though I lack the art," the persona concludes,

> to decipher it,
> no doubt the next chapter
> in my book of transformations
> is already written.
> I am not done with my changes.

Like "The Layers," Kunitz's recent poems are unsparingly honest, most often with short lines, precise images, and simple language, the whole brought to an exalted height of meaning. The title poem for his 1983 book, "The Wellfleet Whale," a 143-line poem in five sections (first published in November 1981), is an austere and ambitious philosophic poem about the beaching and death of a whale at Wellfleet on Cape Cod. Its first-person-plural speaker gives the poem an elevated tone that allows the whale to become "like a god in exile/. . . delivered to the mercy of time":

> Master of the whale-roads,
> let the white wings of the gulls
> spread out their cover.
> You have become like us,
> disgraced and mortal.

With some of the grandeur and elevation of his early high style but in the simple, almost bare, stripped-down syntax of his later work, this poem shows that Kunitz is indeed "not done with [his] changes."

Interviews:

David Lupher, "Stanley Kunitz on Poetry: A Yale Lit Interview," *Yale Literary Magazine*, 136 (May 1968): 6-13;

"Craft Interview with Stanley Kunitz," *New York Quarterly*, 1 (Fall 1970): 9-22;

Michael Ryan, "An Interview with Stanley Kunitz," *Iowa Review* (Spring 1974): 76-85;

Cynthia Davis, "An Interview with Stanley Kunitz," *Contemporary Literature*, 15 (Winter 1974): 1-14;

Selden Rodman, *Tongues of Fallen Angels* (New York: New Directions, 1974);

Chris Busa, "The Art of Poetry XXIX. Stanley Kunitz," *Paris Review*, 24 (Spring 1982): 204-246;

Caroline Sutton, "PW Interviews: Stanley Kunitz," *Publishers Weekly*, 228 (20 December 1985): 67-68.

References:

Antaeus, special Kunitz issue, 37 (Spring 1980);

Robin Brantley, "A Touch of the Poet," *New York Times Magazine*, 7 September 1975, pp. 80-83;

Jean H. Hagstrum, "The Poetry of Stanley Kunitz: An Introductory Essay," in *Poets in Progress*, edited by Edward Hungerford (Evanston: Northwestern University Press, 1967), pp. 38-58;

Marie Hénault, *Stanley Kunitz* (Boston: Twayne, 1980);

Robert Lowell, "On Stanley Kunitz's 'Father and Son,'" in *The Contemporary Poet as Artist and Critic*, edited by Anthony Ostroff (Boston: Little, Brown, 1964), pp. 71-75;

Ralph J. Mills, Jr., *Contemporary American Poetry* (New York: Random House, 1966), pp. 32-47;

Gregory Orr, *Stanley Kunitz: An Introduction to the Poetry* (New York: Columbia University Press, 1985);

"A Special Supplement: Stanley Kunitz," *American Poetry Review*, 14 (September-October 1985): 23-30.

James Laughlin

(30 October 1914-   )

John A. Harrison
University of Arkansas
and
Donald W. Faulkner
Yale University

See also the New Directions entry in *DLB 46, American Literary Publishing Houses, 1900-1980: Trade and Paperback.*

BOOKS: *The River* (Norfolk, Conn.: New Directions, 1938);
Some Natural Things (New York: New Directions, 1945);
Skiing East and West, text by Laughlin, photographs by Helen Fischer in collaboration with Emita Herran (New York: Hastings House, 1946);
Report on a Visit to Germany (Lausanne: Henri Held, 1948);
A Small Book of Poems (Milan & New York: Vanni Scheiwiller & New Directions, 1948);
The Wild Anemone & Other Poems (Norfolk: New Directions, 1957);
Confidential Report, and Other Poems (London: Gaberboccus, 1959); republished as *Selected Poems* (Norfolk: New Directions, 1959);
The Pig (Mt. Horeb, Wis.: Perishable Press, 1970);
In Another Country: Poems 1935-1975, edited by Robert Fitzgerald (San Francisco: City Lights Books, 1978);
Gists & Piths: A Memoir of Ezra Pound (Iowa City: Windhover Press, 1982);
Stolen & Contaminated Poems (Isla Vista, Cal.: Turkey Press, 1985);
The Deconstructed Man (Iowa City: Windhover Press, 1985);
Selected Poems 1935-1985 (San Francisco: City Lights Books, 1986);
The House of Light (New York: Grenfell Press, 1986).

OTHER: *New Directions in Prose and Poetry,* nos. 1-   , edited by Laughlin (Cambridge, Mass./ Norfolk, Conn./New York: New Directions, 1936-   );
Samuel Bernard Greenberg, *Poems from the Green-*

James Laughlin (photograph by Andrew Chase)

berg Manuscripts: A Selection from the Work of Samuel B. Greenberg, edited, with a commentary, by Laughlin (Norfolk, Conn.: New Directions, 1939);
The Fourth Eclogue of Virgil, translated by Laughlin (Windham, Conn.: Printed for J. Laughlin by Edmond Thompson, 1939);
A Wreath of Christmas Poems by Virgil, Dante, Chaucer

and Others, edited by Laughlin and Alfred M. Hayes (Norfolk, Conn.: New Directions, 1942);

Alvin Lustig, *Bookjackets by Alvin Lustig for New Directions Books*, includes a statement by Laughlin and Lustig (New York: Gotham Book Mart, 1947);

Spearhead: Ten Years' Experimental Writing in America, edited by Laughlin (New York: New Directions, 1947);

Perspective of Burma, edited by Laughlin and U Myat Kyaw (New York: Intercultural Publications, 1958);

A New Directions Reader, edited by Laughlin and Hayden Carruth (New York: New Directions, 1964);

The Asian Journal of Thomas Merton, edited by Laughlin, Naomi Burton, and Patrick Hart (New York: New Directions, 1975).

James Laughlin is most often acknowledged by the public as a publisher and seldom as a poet. Since he founded the publishing house New Directions in 1936, he has chosen to remain in the background of an effort which has placed before the public more than 1000 volumes of some of the best experimental and avant-garde writing of the last fifty years. When Yale University awarded him an honorary doctorate in 1982, the citation praised him as an "Editor, poet, book collector, loyal friend of literature and the other arts," who had "created and sustained a publishing house of unique importance to contemporary letters." It went on to praise Laughlin's discernment of talent and his unflagging support of "literary endeavor."

Laughlin is perceived as a minor poet, in part because he has chosen to publish so little. *In Another Country* (1978), his collected poems, contains only fifty-eight pages of poems, a fact that Hayden Carruth attributes to "Laughlin's reticence in all personal matters." That Laughlin continues to apologize for his poetry is unfortunate, for it has been recognized as fresh, concise, full of wit, of impeccable quality, lucid, ironic, and often intense.

James Laughlin IV, a descendant of the founder of Jones & Laughlin Steel Corporation, was born in Pittsburgh to Henry Hughart and Marjory Rea Laughlin. He grew up in the Squirrel Hill section of Pittsburgh in an enclave of relatives and went to school in Switzerland before enrolling at Choate. While he has reported that he did not read much until he reached Choate, two of his teachers there, Carey Briggs and Dudley Fitts, found him a willing pupil, and Fitts introduced him to the writings of such modernists as Gertrude Stein, James Joyce, T. S. Eliot, Ezra Pound, and William Carlos Williams. When he entered Harvard in 1933, he was disappointed to find that the curriculum lacked courses on these literary figures and during his sophomore year he took a leave of absence from Harvard and went to Europe.

With an introduction from Bernard Faÿ, he was able to obtain a position as handyman and student with Gertrude Stein. As he described them later, his services as a "chauffeur" for Stein included not only changing the tires on her car but also helping her to prepare articles for the American press in preparation for her autumn 1934 visit to the United States. Then, with a letter of introduction from Dudley Fitts, Laughlin went to see Ezra Pound in Rapallo, where he spent six months studying with Pound at his so-called Ezuversity.

Laughlin often relates how Pound slashed words from poems by his aspiring students, Laughlin among them. Finally in despair Pound told him to go home and become a publisher. The time he spent with Pound was undoubtedly a turning point for Laughlin. He realized that he would never be a great writer, but he learned many of the hallmarks of modernist writing.

On leaving Pound at Ezuversity, he went skiing on the slopes of Austria. Though an early skiing accident seriously injured him, skiing became a regular and important part of his life, sometimes taking precedence over publishing. Once, to William Carlos Williams's distress, *White Mule* (1937) went out of print while Laughlin was skiing. Another time, he let the unsolicited manuscript for Thomas Merton's *The Seven Storey Mountain* (1948) languish on his desk while he went on a ski vacation. Without apology for such incidents, he has continued to ski to this day, and for many years he has spent the ski season in Alta, Utah, at a ski resort in which he invested.

When he returned to Harvard in 1935 Laughlin served as a guest literary editor for Gorham Munson's Cambridge-based social-credit magazine *New Democracy*, gathering contributions for a section called "New Directions in Prose & Poetry" from writers such as Pound, Eliot, Marianne Moore, Kay Boyle, E. E. Cummings, and William Carlos Williams. In 1936, when Laughlin published his first *New Directions* anthology, they were all included along with works by Wallace Stevens, Gertrude Stein, Henry Miller, Louis Zukofsky, Jean Cocteau, Dudley Fitts, and many others. This *New Directions* anthology for 1936 was the first of a series that continues to be published today. Though

James Laughlin and Ezra Pound in the Dolomites on a drive from Venice to Salzburg, 1935 (photograph by Olga Rudge)

Laughlin originally intended to publish it annually, intervals of as many as three years separated issues during World War II. Now an issue appears each year.

Laughlin was later to publish books by many of the writers represented in this remarkable 1936 collection with a loyalty and thoroughness that is unmatched in the history of American literature. He saw himself as having a responsibility to publish works of literary merit even when there appeared to be no commercial market for them, and he remained loyal to his writers. Because he felt strongly about his ideals, it was twenty-five years before the company began to show a profit.

Laughlin's father had given him $100,000 when he started college. He invested this money, and the income from it supported him and his publishing venture until he inherited more in the 1950s. By the 1960s his efforts began to have some impact. A number of his books were adopted for

use in college classrooms, and the company began to pay its own way.

By the time he earned an A.B. from Harvard in 1939, Laughlin had published more than a dozen books, including *Pianos of Sympathy* (1936) by Montagu O'Reilly (Wayne Andrews), the first New Directions publication; Williams's *White Mule* (1937) and *Complete Collected Poems, 1906-1938* (1938); Pound's *Guide to Kulchur* (1938); and Delmore Schwartz's first book, *In Dreams Begin Responsibilities* (1938). In 1942 Laughlin married Margaret Keyser, with whom he had two children, Paul and Leila. They were divorced in 1952, the year Laughlin became president of Intercultural Publications, a subsidiary of the Ford Foundation, which published a literary-cultural magazine, *Perspectives USA* (1952-1956), designed to teach Europeans about American culture. Among his other duties, Laughlin edited some issues of the magazine as well as some special "Perspectives" sections on the cultures

James Laughlin in the original New Directions office in a stable in Norfolk, Connecticut, 1939

of India, Burma, Indonesia, Japan, the Arab World, and Greece, which appeared in the *Atlantic Monthly*. (His affiliation with Intercultural Publications ended in 1969.) On 19 May 1957 Laughlin married Ann Clark Resor. They had two children, Robert and Henry. Laughlin has lectured at some thirty colleges and universities. Recently he has held a visiting lectureship at the University of Iowa (1981-1982) and an adjunct professorship at Brown University (1983).

Despite Pound's advice, Laughlin never entirely gave up writing poetry, and his contributions of poems to little magazines as well as the occasional publication of short books continues to this day. Hayden Carruth has described Laughlin's work as "a kind of poetry composed on a typewriter in which each succeeding line could vary from the typewritten length of the first line by no more than two spaces either way, or in rare emergencies three spaces"—a practice Laughlin described in the 1930s and has continued since that time. Laughlin himself has remarked, "I 'play' an arbitrary visual pattern against the sound pattern of a colloquial cadence to get tension and surprise." While others have even tried it, he notes, without much success,

a reading of the poems shows that it has worked well for him. The short lines, unhindered by punctuation, seem to have an impact that makes his work more memorable.

This technique, combined with his seemingly simplistic subject matter, creates poems that are, as Denise Levertov has noted, "free of bombast and of any pretentiousness." She has also said, "Emotion is disciplined in the precision of his diction and the strictness of his idiosyncratic form. . . ."

Laughlin says of his own work, "It's very light; it's sentimental, it deals with no great subjects, no great thoughts . . ." but Donald Hall responds, "perhaps, if the poet pretends that he does not take his work seriously, he is free to continue it."

Each of his books of poetry is already an expression of mature form; yet in the last three years he has been experimenting with long-line poems, macaronics (mixing languages such as English and Provençal), and poems in "American" French. In almost every case the subject of the poem is carried forth by its own novelty, as in these lines from "Old Doctor God":

Sure everybody laughs at

Old Doctor God and his medi-

cine sometimes it kills
you sometimes it cures

you sometimes it leaves
you just like you were[.]

The striking sensuality of many of the poems is especially noticeable in the long poem "In Another Country" (*In Another Country,* 1978) where Italian and English are combined effectively in a dialogue that conveys the love between an American boy and an Italian girl. The "Giacomino" section of the poem begins

she called vieni qua splashing her
arms in the clear green water vieni
subito and so I followed her swimming around a point of rock to the

next cove vieni qua non hai paura
and she slipped like an eel beneath
the surface down through the sunken
entrance to a hidden grotto where

the light was soft and green on fine-
grained sand e bello no? here we can
be together by ourselves and nobody else
has ever been here with me it's my se-

cret place here . . .[.]

Shorter poems such as "The Cave" (*Selected Poems,* 1959), where "her hair/makes a cave around her/ face," are equally evocative in their sensuality, but they are too brief to be as well realized as "In Another Country."

In "Technical Notes" (*In Another Country*) Laughlin propounds his poetic theories, rejecting so-called poetic diction in favor of "plain brown bricks/of common talk American talk" and assert- ing "love/is my subject & the lack of love." Describ- ing his technique, he writes:

I roll the
words around my mouth & count the
letters in each

line thus eye and ear contend inside the poem and draw its movement tight Milton

thought rhyme was vulgar I agree
yet sometimes if it's hidden in
the line a rhyme

will richen tone. . . [.]

He says that while he agrees with Catullus, who "knew a poem is like a blow/an impact strik-//ing where you least expect," he believes that "a poem is finally just/a natural thing." The influence of Wil- liam Carlos Williams's early poems is evident in "Technical Notes," and it continues still. In a more- recent poem, "The Person" (*Poetry,* June 1980), Laughlin explains the subconscious nature of crea- tivity by saying that his poems are written by some- one else, whom "I wonder about/. . . but will never know," a person who "lives in some other/sphere" and "when he feels like it" sends him poems "through space":

they arrive complete

from beginning to end
and all I have to do

is type them out. . . [.]

Perhaps Robert Fitzgerald's short foreword to *In Another Country: Poems 1935-1975* (1978) cap- tures the essence of Laughlin's total output best in noting the ability of his "cool and simple" poems to "secrete bitter knowledge" as well as "lyrical joy," to convey humor as well as to "fix historical mo- ments" with precision. The poems are "utterly clear, stained by no muddiness," and, most impor- tant, "They are unique: no one but James Laughlin could have written them."

Laughlin still writes poems occasionally and he continues to give readings of his own work, but quite often such readings are combined with read- ings of letters from Pound or William Carlos Wil- liams and are well salted with anecdotes. Unless questions are directed to his own writing, he dwells on the early days of the great literary effort he directed, with such modesty that the audience is likely to come away almost forgetting that it was James Laughlin who made it possible.

Although his few poems are of high quality, his most profound influence on American poetry is certainly in what he chose to publish. In the first twenty-seven years of New Directions, nearly 200 of the 500 titles he published were poetry. In an article for *Poetry* magazine (January 1982) he dis- cussed in his most modest manner how he pub- lished about twenty-five books (in thirty-four editions) for Pound and nineteen for Williams (in twenty-eight editions in 1963). Not only did New Directions publish the work of Pound, Williams,

Manuscript (by permission of the author; courtesy of the Poetry Collection, State University of New York at Buffalo)

Gary Snyder and James Laughlin at Kitkitdizzie, Synder's home in the Sierras, circa 1970 (photograph by Ann Laughlin)

and many other authors, with few exceptions their work has been kept in print.

As a poet, Laughlin has chosen the poetics of the Pound-Williams heritage. As a publisher, through his support of Williams and those that followed Williams's "idiom" (among them, Robert Creeley, Gregory Corso, Denise Levertov and Gary Snyder), Laughlin established a family tree of modernist American poetry with its roots in Pound and Williams.

Beyond the fostering of this American heritage, Laughlin introduced to generations of American writers the budding traditions of French modernism, Eastern European realism, and the Latin American lyric that have served to make American poetry more truly cosmopolitan. In recent years he has worked on and appeared in documentary films about Thomas Merton, Ezra Pound, William Carlos Williams, and Romain Gary.

Always effective in combining classical tradition (from an awareness of Latin and Greek poetry doubtless won from Pound, Fitts, and Fitzgerald) with a sense of the modernist lyric, Laughlin has shown how his standards as a publisher are enhanced by his standards as a poet.

Interviews:

Susan Howe, "New Directions: An Interview with James Laughlin," in *The Art of Literary Publishing: Editors on Their Craft,* edited by Bill Henderson (Yonkers, N. Y.: Pushcart Press, 1980), pp. 13-48;

Robert Dana, "James Laughlin: An Interview," *American Poetry Review,* 10 (November/December 1981): supplement, pp. 19-32.

Bibliography:

John A. Harrison, "A Checklist of the Publications of James Laughlin," *Conjunctions,* 1 (Winter 1981-1982): 284-286.

References:

Miriam Berkley, "The Way It Was: James Laughlin and New Directions," *Publishers Weekly,* 228 (22 November 1985): 24-29;

Hayden Carruth, "Notes about Laughlin's Typewriter," *Conjunctions,* 1 (Winter 1981-1982): 87-96;

Robert Coles, "A Struggle for Humility," *Conjunctions,* 1 (Winter 1981-1982): 244-246;

Richard Eberhart, "Homage to James Laughlin," *Conjunctions,* 1 (Winter 1981-1982): 141;

I saw her first
on an amphora in the
museum at Delphi and

knew she was Heliodora
The girl in Meleager's

poem and she with her hair
in a fillet and her tiny

feet and her breasts like   pray to the Gods that
little pears and thirty years   my Heliodora will
                                    return.

later we were together in
a faded room in that

small
little hotel in the rue
de la Harpere she spoke

French of course and first
                     but
she was shy ~~and~~ then she
              tenderly
was ^passionate she was
                        even
Heliodora will she ~~return~~

~~again~~ ~~will~~ she come back
to me I make my

I SAW HER FIRST

on the red-on-black amphora
in the museum at Delphi and

knew at once she was Heliodora the girl in Meleager's

poem with her hair in a fillet and her tiny feet and her

breasts like little pears then
thirty years later we were to-

gether in a faded room in that
small hotel in the rue de la

Harpe she spoke French of
course and at first she was

shy but then she was tenderly
passionate yes it was Helio-

dora will she ever come back
to me will she even come to

stay I make my prayer to the
Gods that Heliodora return.

Two drafts for a recent poem (by permission of the author; courtesy of the Poetry Collection, State University of New York at Buffalo)

D. W. Faulkner, "James Laughlin—Poet and Publisher, A Profile of the Founder and Editor of New Directions Books," *Connecticut Artists*, 3 (Spring/Summer 1980): 6-15;

Donald Hall, "Ezra Pound Said to Be A Publisher," *New York Times Book Review*, 23 August 1981, pp. 13, 22-23;

Walter Hamady, "A Letter to the Editor, and A Poem," *Conjunctions*, 1 (Winter 1981-1982): 227-231;

Denise Levertov, "About James Laughlin," *Conjunctions*, 1 (Winter 1981-1982): 68-69;

Bradford Morrow, "An Interview with Kenneth Rexroth [about James Laughlin and New Directions]," *Conjunctions*, 1 (Winter 1981-1982): 48-67;

Miriam Patchen, "Kenneth and Miriam Patchen's Early Days at New Directions," *Conjunctions*, 1 (Winter 1981-1982): 253-257.

Papers:
Laughlin's papers will be deposited in the Houghton Library at Harvard University, which now has correspondence between Laughlin and William Carlos Williams. Laughlin's correspondence with Ezra Pound and other papers are in the Beinecke Library at Yale University.

Ruth Lechlitner
(27 March 1901-)

Paula L. Hart
University of British Columbia

BOOKS: *Tomorrow's Phoenix* (New York: Alcestis Press, 1937);

Only the Years (Prairie City, Ill.: Press of J. A. Decker, 1944);

The Shadow on the Hour (Iowa City: Prairie Press, 1956);

A Changing Season: Selected and New Poems, 1962-1972 (Boston: Branden Press, 1973).

OTHER: "To the Wild Rose," in *The Poets of the Future: A College Anthology for 1920-1921*, edited by Henry T. Schnittkind (Boston: Stratford, 1921), pp. 46-47;

"Corn," in *Anthology of Magazine Verse for 1926 and Yearbook of American Poetry*, edited by William Stanley Braithwaite (Boston: Brimmer, 1926), pp. 249-250;

"Of What Superb Mechanics," in *Biographical Dictionary of Contemporary Poets* (New York: Avon House, 1938), p. 289.

PERIODICAL PUBLICATIONS: "The Radical," *Nation*, 127 (25 July 1928): 90;

"Come Let Us Praise," *New Republic*, 75 (14 June 1933): 123;

"A Winter's Tale," *Poetry*, 56 (September 1940): 298-299;

"Night in August," *Poetry*, 68 (August 1946): 258-259;

"Lines for the Year's End," *Poetry*, 73 (November 1948): 72-73;

"He Who Rides a Tiger" and "Matinee," *Literary Review*, 10 (Autumn 1966): 44-46;

"Drawing by Ronnie C., Grade One," *Saturday Review*, 50 (15 July 1967): 39;

"The Voice of the Dolphin," *Saturday Review*, 52 (8 March 1969): 23;

"Persimmon," *Literary Review*, 16 (Fall 1972): 103.

Ruth Lechlitner has been writing poetry for more than half a century. Her collections span the period from 1937 to 1973, but one of her first poems appeared in *The Poets of the Future: A College Anthology for 1920-1921* (1921), and one of her latest was published in the *Southwest Review* in 1983. Appearing in such diverse periodicals as *Ladies Home Journal* and *Poetry*, her poems have reached a wide audience.

Lechlitner has let her poetry speak for her almost exclusively, and little is known of her personal life. Born in Elkhart, Indiana (near South Bend), to Jessie Wier James and Martin Lechlitner, Ruth Naomi Lechlitner received a B.A. from the University of Michigan in 1923 and an M.A. from the University of Iowa in 1926. She married Paul F. Corey and lived in Cold-Spring-on-Hudson, New York, in the 1930s before settling in Sonoma, California, in the late 1940s. Although she has also written radio verse plays, prose word-portraits of literary figures such as children's author and illustrator Marguerite de Angeli, book reviews, and thoughtful appraisals of poets such as W. H. Auden and William Carlos Williams, her chief work has been poetry.

Her poem "To the Wild Rose," which was included in *The Poets of the Future* when she was only nineteen, displays a prairie girl's love of nature, and it is nature, as subject and setting, that has been a consistent and successful theme in her poetry. The poem is clearly juvenilia, showing an openness to experience and an easy sentimentality caught in sweeping generalizations:

> Poets have sung to you beautiful songs,
> Little pink-dressed wanderer,—
> But you are so small, and life is so big, and
>   words are so few[.]

By the time "Corn" was published in William Stanley Braithwaite's *Anthology of Magazine Verse for 1926*, Lechlitner was more sophisticated, economical, and detailed in her pictures of nature. As the opening stanza shows, the setting is enhanced by an undulating rhythm and by the fresh and happy phrasing of the last two lines:

> Here at our side
> Corn flows, row upon row
> Beneath the white light of the moon.
> Ribbons of supple silver and green shadow
> Ripple with soft, warm rhythm
> Under a wind
> Flesh-sweet with summer.

The rolling cornfield curves around a neglected burial site, and at twilight the lovers in the poem are struck by the astonishing harmony of nature's cycle: life comes from death. The lovers themselves hold no interest beyond their recording of this impression; setting is everything. The great and equally vital contrasting images in this poem—the seed and the snow—have retained a fascination for Lechlitner throughout her poetic career.

Yet Lechlitner has done more than explore the nuances of favorite bucolic themes. She has been very much aware of life around her: of the rediscovery of the metaphysical poets in the literary world and of the turmoil and change in the political and social world. At times her conceits remained disturbingly obscure, as in the following lament from "The Radical" (*Nation*, 25 July 1928), which addresses an individual who discovered too late the need for breaking old patterns:

> Fall, Sword: this weight is not your own,
> But the blood-heavy, vital chain
> You carved in circles that I must
> Count link by link—and break again.

Some of her surest handling of the need for social change comes through her use of familiar nature images, as in "Come Let Us Praise" (*New Republic*, 14 June 1933), that sees life only in process: life in the seed and life in the flower, giving the lie to traditional mythic stress on an afterworld:

> Come let us praise the good
> Brief-budded flower, and a moment after
> Gather the ripe fruit; . . .
> . . . .
> Praise bread, desire, meat, sin—all things that sever
> Life from eternal life, ever and forever.

When *Tomorrow's Phoenix*, the first collection of Lechlitner's verse, appeared in 1937, it presented the work of a seasoned and varied poet. Reviewing the volume for *Poetry* (December 1937), Samuel French Morse found some works too doctrinal, yet he also found much to praise. He noted her experimentation with form but thought her most successful poems were those adhering to formal verse patterns. The best works in the collection, he believed, made an outstanding contribution to American revolutionary poetry: "In these poems is found the welding of the natural and human worlds; Miss Lechlitner has made order from disorder so that the expanded image becomes an event." In one of the poems Morse liked, "Of What Superb Mechanics," the poet chides her fellow humans for a too-narrow concern with self and material comforts. Her own questing for the generating life spark, however, shows an extension to the cosmic level:

> Of what superb mechanics are
> The wheels of change, the cycle driven;
> And what equation for a star
> Set us in motion? . . .

A few years later the global havoc of World War II, with its added threat of widespread devastation gave rise to a haunting science-fiction poem: "A Winter's Tale" (*Poetry*, September 1940). The setting is an underground settlement some seventy years after worldwide destruction by a devastating warhead. A small child asks about snow and is told to ask his great-grandfather, who delivers a tormented recollection that fuses the sensation of falling snow crystals with "shattered building-walls and blood/And flesh in jagged glass. . . ." This ironic employment of the snow image seems most suitable for the futuristic theme, which is actually an extension of Lechlitner's sense of nature's cycle, as seen in the concluding stanza:

> We came into night, the stars lost from our shoulders,
> Into these obscene roots for maggot-living—
> We sewer neighbors, rat to crawling rat,
> To save ourselves from snow . . . Snow was white I
>   tell you
> Not the tombed light in this design for dying!
> I remember the cold air, the smell of frozen apples,
> Snow seeding white birth, Christmas snow,
>   December . . .[.]

In *Only the Years* (1944), a selection of poems written between 1938 and 1944, reviewers noted further reflections of the unsettled times and Lechlitner's anti-fascist spirit. Yet Jessica Nelson North, who titled her review "The Split Tongue" (*Poetry*, July 1946), found Lechlitner's traditional forms inadequate for treating such modern concerns, labeling her "a poet of the 1930's." Though, like other reviewers, she fully credited Lechlitner's power in describing nature and in creating "the extremely satisfying music in which she specializes," she pointed out an inability to show emotional depth in portraying personal relationships.

Lechlitner's third collection, *The Shadow on the Hour*, did not appear until 1956, but some of the poems had been published earlier in journals and echoed concerns of the previous decade. One such piece was "Night in August," in which Lechlitner again uses ironic juxtaposition as a powerful device to explore her theme. In a homey pastoral setting, a woman sits on her green lawn awaiting the summer stars, when her lazy summer thoughts are pierced by the metallic crackling of a neighbor's radio carrying the report of a bombing (a veiled reference to the bombing of Hiroshima on 6 August 1945): "And I in this August night, hear now one bird that calls/From the black hemlock bough. And one star falls." In his review for the *New York Times Book Review* (20 October 1957), Kenneth Rexroth referred to this poem as evidence that, though the collection was "woman poetry, about home and husband and children," its domesticity was "the nexus of a web of unending implications."

The middle-American mother "And the child asleep upstairs in her small bed" were not remote from the destruction in Japan.

Leonard Nathan, writing in *Poetry* (August 1957), found it more difficult to accommodate Lechlitner's contrasts, declaring that the poems often tore themselves apart in an effort to house incompatible elements: shifts from regular meter to free verse, from reflection to "deliberately obscure" philosophy. One of the poems he singled out for criticism was "Lines for the Year's End" (first published in the November 1948 issue of *Poetry*). Its beginning has a familiar sound:

> The dropped fruit lies beneath its tree,
> And this that was our future, now
> Becomes a seed for history.

Nathan objected to the jarring change in tone, which becomes mock-heroic in the beginning of a later stanza: "Or, shelving Freud with Marx, invite/ Faith by salvation redefined."

More striking, however, is the poet's radical shift in thought and subject. Here, what characteristically has been the source of optimism—the seed in wintertime—is now viewed pessimistically:

> Our atom-dwelling God will spare
> From all mankind a chosen few
> To build a deathless future. Where,
> Lacking that grace, go I, go you?

It is not surprising that commentators once again preferred the poems in *The Shadow on the Hour* that best showed the poet's talents for the sharply drawn picture, as in the lyric "Two Into Spring."

Ruth Lechlitner continued to capture the world around her in magazine verse during the 1960s and 1970s. Yet some vital images are marred by philosophizing that creates more freight than the themes can bear, as in "He Who Rides a Tiger" (*Literary Review*, Autumn 1966). The rider, who begins riding a "treacherous Beast, earth-pugged and heaven-winged," becomes enslaved, "Chained to the Beast-spoored jungle carrousel/That circles an ego-centred rod. . . ." She could still seem unable or reluctant to get any closer to personal emotions than in the icy vignette, "Matinee" (*Literary Review*, Autumn 1966). Two lovers, becoming reconciled over cocktails in a lounge, are cheated out of the shared excitement that might have cemented their relationship when the fire emergency across the street turns out to be a false alarm.

Other responses, nevertheless, remained as

true as ever. In one of her freer forms, "Drawing By Ronnie C., Grade One" (*Saturday Review*, 15 July 1967), she captured both the actions and the mood of a small boy at work. The young artist is searching his crayon box for the right sky color:

> Gray won't do, either:
> gray is for rain that you make with
> dark slanting lines down-paper.
>   Try orange!

Her perspective has changed, but her view of life and youth, offered in precise detail, make each sensation fresh, as in the delightful poem "The Voice of the Dolphin" (*Saturday Review*, 8 March 1969):

> In earliest years we know
> Rarities of hearing—wind's crisscross
> Sigh like a snow of moths above
> Blazing August wheat; the slack
> Bubble breath of caught lake perch
> Plopped into pail-shallow water[.]

Lechlitner's most-recent collection, *A Changing Season: Selected and New Poems, 1962-1972* (1973), did not receive as much critical attention as *The Shadow on the Hour*. Perhaps it had been too long between collections. But, again, there were ready words of praise for her nature poetry. One poem in the collection, "Persimmon," provides an interesting contrast to her earliest published poem, "To the Wild Rose." In "Persimmon" her subject is more in keeping with the "changing season" of her matured perspective. Yet, if the end turn of the life cycle is stressed in the closing line, the black seeds of new life are as prominent in Lechlitner's outlook as they are in the fruit itself:

> But not for a child, this ripeness;
> Only lovers, learning delight
> in the succulent, lip-luscious pulp,
> find (if not careful) around
> black seeds new-celled with life,
> the acrid taste of death.

References:

Samuel French Morse, Review of *Tomorrow's Phoenix, Poetry*, 51 (December 1937): 157-159;

Leonard Nathan, "Three American Poets," review of *The Shadow on the Hour, Poetry*, 90 (August 1957): 329-330;

Jessica Nelson North, "The Split Tongue," review of *Only the Years, Poetry*, 68 (July 1946): 224-227;

Kenneth Rexroth, "Shape and Substance," review of *The Shadow on the Hour, New York Times Book Review*, 20 October 1957, p. 47.

Phyllis McGinley

(21 March 1905-22 February 1978)

Michael Hennessy
Southwest Texas State University

See also the McGinley entry in *DLB 11, American Humorists, 1800-1950*.

BOOKS: *On the Contrary* (Garden City: Doubleday, Doran, 1934);

One More Manhattan (New York: Harcourt, Brace, 1937);

A Pocketful of Wry (New York: Duell, Sloan & Pearce, 1940; revised edition, New York: Grosset & Dunlap, 1959);

Husbands Are Difficult; or, The Book of Oliver Ames (New York: Duell, Sloan & Pearce, 1941);

The Horse Who Lived Upstairs (Philadelphia: Lippincott, 1944);

The Plain Princess (Philadelphia & New York: Lippincott, 1945);

Phyllis McGinley (Gale International Portrait Gallery)

Stones from a Glass House (New York: Viking, 1946);

A Name for Kitty (New York: Simon & Schuster, 1948; London: Muller, 1950);

All Around the Town (Philadelphia: Lippincott, 1948);

The Most Wonderful Doll in the World (Philadelphia: Lippincott, 1950);

Blunderbus (Philadelphia: Lippincott, 1951);

The Horse Who Had His Picture in the Paper (Philadelphia: Lippincott, 1951);

A Short Walk from the Station (New York: Viking, 1951);

The Make-Believe Twins (Philadelphia: Lippincott, 1953);

Love Letters (New York: Viking, 1954; London: Dent, 1955);

The Year Without Santa Claus (Philadelphia: Lippincott, 1957; Leicester, U.K.: Brockhampton Press, 1960);

Merry Christmas, Happy New Year (New York: Viking, 1958; London: Secker & Warburg, 1959);

Lucy McLockett (Philadelphia: Lippincott, 1959; Leicester, U.K.: Brockhampton Press, 1961);

The Province of the Heart (New York: Viking, 1959; London: Catholic Book Club, 1963);

Times Three: Selected Verse from Three Decades, with Seventy New Poems (New York: Viking, 1960; London: Secker & Warburg, 1961);

Sugar and Spice: The ABC of Being a Girl (New York: Watts, 1960);

Mince Pie and Mistletoe (Philadelphia: Lippincott, 1961);

Boys Are Awful (New York: Watts, 1962);

The B Book (New York: Crowell-Collier, 1962; London: Collier-Macmillan, 1968);

A Girl and Her Room (New York: Watts, 1963);

How Mrs. Santa Claus Saved Christmas (Philadelphia: Lippincott, 1963; Kingswood, U.K.: World's Work, 1964);

Sixpence in Her Shoe (New York: Macmillan, 1964; London: Dent, 1966);

Wonderful Time (Philadelphia: Lippincott, 1966);

A Wreath of Christmas Legends (New York: Macmillan, 1967);

Saint-Watching (New York: Viking, 1969; London: Collins, 1970);

Christmas con and pro (Berkeley: Hart Press, 1971);

Confessions of a Reluctant Optimist, edited by Barbara Wells Price (Kansas City, Mo.: Hallmark Editions, 1973).

PLAY PRODUCTION: *Small Wonder,* lyrics by McGinley; sketches by Charles Spalding, Max Wilk, George Axelrod, and Louis Laun; score by Baldwin Bergersen and Albert Selden; New York, Coronet Theatre, 15 September 1948.

SCREENPLAY: *The Emperor's Nightingale,* narration by McGinley, Jiri Trnka (Czechoslovakia), 1951.

OTHER: *Wonders and Surprises: A Collection of Poems,* selected by McGinley (Philadelphia: Lippincott, 1968).

PERIODICAL PUBLICATIONS: "Woman's Place Is . . . ?," by McGinley and Sidney Callahan, *Sign,* 44 (July 1965): 22-26;

"The Light Side of the Moon," *American Scholar,* 34 (Autumn 1965): 555-568;

"New American Family," *Saturday Evening Post,* 241 (13 July 1968): 26-32.

Though she was also a prolific essayist and writer of children's books, Phyllis McGinley is known chiefly for her light verse. From 1934 to 1958 she published eight collections of her poems, and in 1960 she gathered many of them in *Times Three: Selected Verse from Three Decades, with Seventy New Poems,* a book that earned her a Pulitzer Prize in 1961. The recipient of various other honors (including election in 1955 to the National Institute of Arts and Letters), McGinley enjoyed a wide readership in her lifetime, publishing her work in newspapers and women's magazines as well as in literary periodicals, including the *New Yorker,* the *Saturday Review* and the *Atlantic.* Besides her popular reputation, she earned the admiration of a number of critics and poets, including W. H. Auden, who praised her imagination and technical skill in his foreword for *Times Three.* As a commentator on the passing social scene and a champion of midcentury American suburban life, McGinley achieved in her best work a high degree of wit and polish, and managed, especially in her later writing, to narrow the division between light and serious verse.

Phyllis Louise McGinley was born in Ontario, Oregon, the daughter of Daniel and Julia Keisel McGinley. When she was still an infant, her father, a land speculator, moved the family to a ranch that he had been unable to sell near the northeastern Colorado town of Iliff. In a 1965 interview for *Time* McGinley remembered the ranch as looking "like a stage set for *High Noon.*" There she and her brother spent a lonely childhood (the nearest neighbors were miles away), attending a remote country school when a teacher was available and learning at home from their mother when one was not. McGinley remembered her early years as unsettled, filled with reading from the family's many books. She recalled writing her first poetry at the age of six. In 1917, when she was twelve, McGinley's father died and the family moved to Ogden, Utah, to live with relatives, leaving her again with a sense of having no "real home."

After attending Sacred Heart Academy and Ogden High School, McGinley spent her college years at the University of Southern California and the University of Utah, where she masked her brightness and her inclination for learning. "Brainy women," she said in the *Time* interview, "were not appreciated. I made myself over into a giddy prom trotter." But while there she wrote poetry and fiction, entering her work in school competitions under an assumed name. She repeatedly won these competitions and decided during her college years to become a poet.

Following her graduation in 1927, McGinley taught school for a year in Ogden and continued to write poetry, some of which she had sold by 1929. Inspired by her initial success, she decided to leave Utah and move to New York. While making her living as a junior-high-school teacher in New Rochelle, seventeen miles north of New York City, McGinley placed some of her work with the *New Yorker*—"serious, sad Swinburne-ish" poetry, she called it. But a letter of acceptance from *New Yorker* fiction editor Katherine White—who wrote, "We are buying your poem, but why do you sing the same sad songs all lady poets sing?"—sparked a sudden change of style and launched McGinley's career as a writer of light verse. Having found a style that suited her talent and appealed to editors, McGinley was soon publishing regularly, most often in the *New Yorker.* A short time later, she quit her teaching post and moved to New York City, where she worked as a free-lance writer; for the next several years, except for a brief job with an advertising agency and an even briefer one for two months in 1937 as poetry editor of *Town and Country*, McGinley devoted herself full-time to writing.

During her years in Manhattan, McGinley developed and redefined her skills, experimenting with various verse forms and searching for a subject matter that suited her. She wrote a good deal of what she later described as "*really* light verse," topical poems commenting on news items, fads, personalities of the times, and the trivia of day-to-day living. Many of these poems were gathered in her first book, *On the Contrary*, which was published in 1934, the year she met her future husband, Charles L. Hayden, a Bell Telephone Company employee. By the time she and Hayden married on 25 June 1937, McGinley had completed and published a second book, *One More Manhattan* (1937), which, like its predecessor, centered on urban themes. This collection, however, has less of the "*really* light" quality of the earlier volume and offers glimpses of the poet who gradually emerges in later collections. Most of the poems are playful lyrics, such as "Song to Be Sung After Labor Day," in which McGinley celebrates a welcome end to summer weekends:

> No more, with luggage laden down,
> I'll leave the snug, the tranquil town,
> For windy hills or tossing breakers
> Or someone's poison-ivied acres.

Some of the best poems in *One More Manhattan* turn to biting social satire, commenting on the economic misery of the 1930s ("Trinity Place") or the shadow of war and militarism that clouded the decade ("Carol with Variations, 1936"). The volume as a whole earned praise from reviewers, including John Holmes who wrote in the *Boston Transcript* of McGinley's "faultless ear" and "natural inventiveness."

McGinley's third book, *A Pocketful of Wry*, appeared in 1940, a year after the birth of her first daughter, Julia Elizabeth (Julie). By this time, she and her husband had left New York City and settled in Larchmont, New York, which McGinley described in her *Time* interview as "an adorable town full of old Victorian houses." There the family began the suburban life that she was to celebrate and defend in much of her subsequent poetry. *A Pocketful of Wry*, however, is still largely a product of her urban years. A few poems of social criticism appear, including the skillful "Ballad of Fine Days," in which McGinley comments ironically on a BBC news broadcaster's observation that warm weather made conditions ideal for World War II bombing raids. Poems such as this one illustrate McGinley's characteristic ability to give point to her verse, to narrow the gap between light and serious poetry. Most of the verse in *A Pocketful of Wry*, however, is more frivolous and personal than in these poems, including two of her best-known pieces, "Apology for Husbands" and "Why, Some of My Best Friends are Women."

Both these poems were also included in *Husbands Are Difficult*, published in 1941, the year her second daughter, Phyllis Louise (Patsy), was born. Combining new poems with several from earlier collections, the book records with good humor the bumbling folly of men and the sensible competence of their female companions. Underlying the poems is a sense of McGinley's having settled comfortably into her role as a suburban wife and mother, a role she celebrated and defended in the poetry she wrote during the next several years. As her daughters grew up she also began to write children's books, publishing seventeen of them from 1944 to 1966.

The suburban sentiments of *Husbands Are Difficult* surface again in *Stones from a Glass House* (1946), which balances light, topical poems such as "P.T.A. Tea Party" and "Surcease at the Hairdressers" against several poems about the war. Many of these topical poems are fully serious ("Soldier Asleep"), though some, such as "Fiesta in the Reich," adopt a satiric tone. Perhaps the best-known poems in the volume are "The 5:32" and "Confessions of a Reluctant Optimist," both of which record the poet's contentment with suburban living, a theme that, to an even greater degree, dominates her next volume, *A Short Walk from the Station* (1951). At times McGinley's "suburban poems" seem trivial and complacent, losing the satiric edge found in her earlier work. But at her best, and often in her briefest poems, she can give commonplace observations point and charm, as she does in "Honest Confession," where she notes that as she grows older, it is harder to discern not only the line between wrong and right but also:

> Whereto we hie
>   From where we've been to;
> The needle's eye
>   A thread goes into.

McGinley's 1954 volume, *Love Letters*, moves away from the suburban preoccupations of earlier work and is, with the exception of *Times Three*, her most varied and impressive book. In the ten years following its publication, *Love Letters* sold nearly

My heart is on feyer
Fr Untermeyer
I can aspeyer,
I think, no heyer
(when I string my leyer)
than a fervid deseyer
* to count him friend
and hope that he's
Kinder than all anthologies.
　　　　　　　　appreciatively,
　　　　　　　　Phyllis McGinley

This is what I do when I
write verse without a scratchpad.
　　　　　　　　P. McG.

Poem written for Louis Untermeyer (by permission of the Estate of Phyllis McGinley; courtesy of the Lilly Library, Indiana University)

80,000 copies in hardback and paperback, establishing McGinley as one of America's most widely read poets. Reviewing the volume for the *New York Times,* Charles Jackson praised McGinley for restoring "delight" to poetry and for achieving a "magical sense of communication and intimacy between herself and the reader."

Love Letters contains many topical, domestic poems in McGinley's characteristic style, and there are a number of light, satirical pieces, notably the short poems in the section called "A Gallery of Elders" and those about television in "The Jaundiced Viewer." But the book's most noteworthy poems are in its opening section, "A Little Praise." Several of these rely less on the predictable rhythms and stanzaic patterns found in most light verse; some are fully "serious," illustrating McGinley's growing ability to handle sophisticated themes and techniques without losing her light touch. Among the most widely admired poems are two inspired by her daughters, "Ballade of Lost Objects" and "The Doll House." In "The Doll House" McGinley uses a catalogue of domestic details to describe the toy house and to evoke a melancholy sense of loss at the passage of time:

> There stood the dinner table,
> Invincible agleam
> With the undisheveled candles, the flowers that
>   bloomed
> Forever and forever,
> The wine that never
> Spilled on the cloth or sickened or was consumed.

Lines like these, placed alongside the more typically light poems in *Love Letters,* suggest the range of styles in McGinley's later work.

That range is even more apparent in *Times Three,* the Pulitzer Prize-winning selection of her poetry that McGinley published in 1960. Omitting more than half of her published poems (including all but a handful from her first book), McGinley provided an overview of her work, arranged by decade. The book combines seventy previously uncollected poems with more than 200 from earlier books, giving the reader a clear retrospective of McGinley's development—her topical, light pieces from the 1930s; her social satires; her gentle and amusing poems about 1940s suburban life; and her varied, mature work of the 1950s, which often defies easy classification as light verse. The popular and critical reception of *Times Three* testified again to McGinley's wide readership: the book sold more than 50,000 copies during its first five years in print

and was well received by reviewers. David McCord, for example, writing in *Saturday Review,* praised McGinley's "eloquent moments, her compassion." And a reviewer in *Library Journal* placed McGinley among the "most gifted writers of light verse of our time."

Except for *A Wreath of Christmas Legends,* a group of fifteen seasonal poems published in 1967, McGinley wrote no new books of poetry after *Times Three.* She turned instead toward prose. Even before *Times Three* she had published a first collection of essays, *The Province of the Heart* (1959), a spirited defense of suburban values. *Sixpence in Her Shoe,* a best-selling collection with similar themes, followed in 1964, and *Saint-Watching,* fourteen essays designed to "rescue [Christian saints] from their pious niches," appeared in 1969. During the 1960s, McGinley also wrote seven books for children and edited *Wonders and Surprises,* a collection of poems for children. From 1972, the year of her husband's death, until her own death in 1978, she published little. She spent her final years in New York City.

Although her contemporary reputation does not match the popular status she achieved in her own lifetime, McGinley is regarded today as one of America's foremost writers of light verse. Critics have placed her alongside other practitioners of the genre—Dorothy Parker, Ogden Nash, and A. P. Herbert, for example. But such comparisons fail to suggest the individual character of her poetry, her ability to combine the traditional techniques of the genre—the use of conventional forms, the reliance on wit and wordplay—with a subject matter and sensibility distinctly her own. "The views from my own terrace," she wrote in the *American Scholar,* "are the ones I describe, small, personal, domestic." And while she was able, as David McCord put it, "to pare the world's wormy apple with a razor blade," she also managed to temper her satire with compassion and common sense. It is for this combination of qualities that she is likely to remain a significant figure in the development of American light verse.

References:

L. F. Doyle, "Poems of Phyllis McGinley," *America,* 92 (18 December 1954): 320-322;

"The Lady in Larchmont," *Newsweek,* 56 (26 September 1960): 120-122;

David McCord, "She Speaks a Language of Delight," *Saturday Review,* 43 (10 December 1960): 32;

Gerard Previn Meyer, "Urbane Suburbanite," *Saturday Review,* 37 (18 September 1954): 11-12;

Bette Richart, "The Light Touch," *Commonweal*, 73 (9 December 1960): 277-279;

K. Sullivan, "Phyllis McGinley," *Catholic World*, 185 (September 1957): 420-425;

"The Telltale Hearth," *Time*, 85 (18 June 1965): 74-78;

Linda Welshimer Wagner, *Phyllis McGinley* (New York: Twayne, 1971).

Papers:
The Syracuse University library has a collection of McGinley's papers.

Thomas Merton
(31 January 1915-10 December 1968)

Ross Labrie
University of British Columbia

See also the Merton entry in *DLB Yearbook: 1981.*

SELECTED BOOKS: *Thirty Poems* (Norfolk, Conn.: New Directions, 1944);

A Man in the Divided Sea (Norfolk, Conn.: New Directions, 1946);

Figures for an Apocalypse (Norfolk, Conn.: New Directions, 1948);

Exile Ends in Glory: The Life of a Trappistine, Mother M. Berchmans, O. C. S. O. (Milwaukee: Bruce, 1948; Dublin: Clonmore & Reynolds, 1951);

Thomas Merton (photograph by Ralph Eugene Meatyard)

The Seven Storey Mountain (New York: Harcourt, Brace, 1948); abridged as *Elected Silence: the Autobiography of Thomas Merton* (London: Hollis & Carter, 1949);

What Is Contemplation? (Holy Cross, Ind.: St. Mary's College, 1948; London: Burns, Oates & Washbourne, 1950);

Seeds of Contemplation (Norfolk, Conn.: New Directions, 1949; London: Burns & Oates, 1960);

The Waters of Siloe (New York: Harcourt, Brace, 1949); republished as *The Waters of Silence* (London: Hollis & Carter, 1950);

The Tears of the Blind Lions (New York: New Directions, 1949);

What Are These Wounds? The Life of a Cistercian Mystic, Saint Lutgarde of Aywières (Dublin: Clonmore & Reynolds, 1949; Milwaukee: Bruce, 1950);

Selected Poems (London: Hollis & Carter, 1950);

A Balanced Life of Prayer (Trappist, Ky.: Abbey of Gethsemani, 1951);

The Ascent to Truth (New York: Harcourt, Brace, 1951; London: Hollis & Carter, 1951);

The Sign of Jonas (New York: Harcourt, Brace, 1953; London: Hollis & Carter, 1953);

Bread in the Wilderness (New York: New Directions, 1953; London: Hollis & Carter, 1954);

The Last of the Fathers: Saint Bernard of Clairvaux and the Encyclical Letter, Doctor Mellifluus (New York: Harcourt, Brace, 1954; London: Hollis & Carter, 1954);

No Man Is an Island (New York: Harcourt, Brace, 1955; London: Hollis & Carter, 1955);

The Living Bread (New York: Farrar, Straus & Cudahy, 1956; London: Burns & Oates, 1956);

Praying the Psalms (Collegeville, Minn.: Liturgical Press, 1956); republished as *Thomas Merton on the Psalms* (London: Sheldon, 1970);

The Silent Life (New York: Farrar, Straus & Cudahy, 1957; London: Burns & Oates, 1957);

The Strange Islands (New York: New Directions, 1957; London: Hollis & Carter, 1957);

The Tower of Babel (New York: New Directions, 1958);

Thoughts in Solitude (New York: Farrar, Straus & Cudahy, 1958; London: Burns & Oates, 1958);

Nativity Kerygma (Trappist, Ky.: Abbey of Gethsemani, 1958);

Secular Journal (New York: Farrar, Straus & Cudahy, 1959; London: Hollis, 1959);

Selected Poems (New York: New Directions, 1959; enlarged, 1967);

Spiritual Direction and Meditation (Collegeville, Minn.: Liturgical Press, 1960; London: Burns & Oates, 1961);

Disputed Questions (New York: Farrar, Straus & Cudahy, 1960; London: Hollis & Carter, 1961);

The Behavior of Titans (New York: New Directions, 1961);

The New Man (New York: Farrar, Straus & Cudahy, 1961; London: Burns & Oates, 1962);

New Seeds of Contemplation (New York: New Directions, 1962; London: Burns & Oates, 1962);

Original Child Bomb: Points for Meditation to be Scratched on the Walls of a Cave (New York: New Directions, 1962);

A Thomas Merton Reader, edited by Thomas P. McDonnell (New York: Harcourt, Brace & World, 1962; revised edition, Garden City: Image Books, 1974);

Clement of Alexandria (New York: New Directions, 1962);

Life and Holiness (New York: Herder & Herder, 1963; London: Chapman, 1963);

Emblems of a Season of Fury (Norfolk, Conn.: New Directions, 1963);

Seeds of Destruction (New York: Farrar, Straus & Giroux, 1964); abridged as *Redeeming the Time* (London: Burns & Oates, 1966);

The Way of Chuang Tzu (New York: New Directions, 1965); republished as *Meditations on Liturgy* (London: Mobray, 1976);

Seasons of Celebration (New York: Farrar, Straus & Giroux, 1965);

Raids on the Unspeakable (New York: New Directions, 1966; London: Burns & Oates, 1966);

Conjectures of a Guilty Bystander (Garden City: Doubleday, 1966; London: Burns & Oates, 1968);

Mystics and Zen Masters (New York: Farrar, Straus & Giroux, 1967; London: Burns & Oates, 1968);

Cables to the Ace (New York: New Directions, 1968);

Faith and Violence: Christian Teaching and Christian Practice (Notre Dame: University of Notre Dame Press, 1968);

Zen and the Birds of Appetite (New York: New Directions, 1968);

My Argument with the Gestapo (Garden City: Doubleday, 1969);

The Climate of Monastic Prayer (Spencer, Mass.: Cistercian, 1969; London: Irish University Press, 1969); also published as *Contemplative Prayer* (New York: Herder & Herder, 1969; London: Darnton, Longman & Todd, 1973);

The Geography of Lograire (New York: New Directions, 1969);

Opening the Bible (Collegeville, Minn.: Liturgical Press, 1970; London: Allen & Unwin, 1972);

Thomas Merton: Early Poems/1940-1942 (Lexington, Ky.: Anvil Press, 1971);

Contemplation in a World of Action (Garden City: Doubleday, 1971; London: Allen & Unwin, 1972);

Thomas Merton on Peace (New York: McCall, 1971; London: Mobray, 1976); revised as *The Nonviolent Alternative,* edited by Gordon C. Zahn (New York: Farrar, Straus & Giroux, 1980);

The Asian Journal of Thomas Merton, edited by Naomi Burton, Patrick Hart, and James Laughlin (New York: New Directions, 1973; London: Sheldon, 1974);

Ishi Means Man (Greensboro, N.C.: Unicorn Press, 1976);

The Monastic Journey, edited by Patrick Hart (Mission, Kans.: Sheed, Andrews, McMeel, 1977; London: Sheldon, 1977);

The Collected Poems of Thomas Merton (New York: New Directions, 1977; London: Sheldon, 1979);

Love and Living (New York: Farrar, Straus & Giroux, 1979; London: Sheldon, 1979);

Thomas Merton on St. Bernard (Kalamazoo, Mich.: Cistercian Publications, 1980; London: Mowbray, 1980);

The Literary Essays of Thomas Merton, edited by Patrick Hart (New York: New Directions, 1981);

Introductions East & West: The Foreign Prefaces of Thomas Merton, edited by Robert E. Daggy (Greensboro, N.C.: Unicorn Press, 1981);

Woods, Shore, Desert: A Notebook, May, 1968 (Santa Fe: Museum of New Mexico Press, 1982).

OTHER: Nicanor Parra, *Poems and Antipoems,* edited by Miller Williams, translated by Merton and others (New York: New Directions, 1967).

In the light of Thomas Merton's primary allegiance to the monastic life, one feels somewhat perplexed by his prodigious publication record. Merton was born in Prades, France, 31 January 1915, the son of two artists, Owen Heathcote Merton, a New Zealander, and Ruth Jenkins Merton, an American. His mother died when he was six, and he spent his youth as something of a nomad, living alternately with his father in various Transatlantic settings, and with his mother's family on Long Island, New York. His father died in England when Thomas was fifteen. He was educated at the Lycée de Montauban in France (1926-1928) and the Oakham School in England (1929-1932) and spent a year at Clare College, Cambridge, before entering Columbia University, where he obtained a B.A. in 1938 and an M.A. in 1939, having written his thesis on William Blake. At Columbia he began a lifelong friendship with the distinguished critic, Mark Van Doren. There as well he met the poets John Berryman and Robert Lax; Lax was to remain a friend throughout Merton's life, whereas the relationship with Berryman did not continue past Columbia. From 1939 to 1941 he taught English at St. Bonaventure University in Upstate New York, and at the same time contributed reviews to the *New York Times Book Review* and other journals.

Outwardly he seemed destined for a successful career as a university teacher and scholar. Van Doren, for one, thought highly of his prospects, noting in retrospect that he had "never known a mind more brilliant, more beautiful, more serious, more playful." However, on 10 December 1941, Merton entered the Abbey of Gethsemani south of Louisville, Kentucky, and immersed himself in the life of a Trappist monk until his accidental death in Thailand in 1968 while attending a meeting of contemplatives.

Merton's vocation involved isolation from the world, silence, austerity, and obedience to his superiors. The contemplative in him had need of a deep and lasting silence, whereas the artist felt the need to celebrate his solidarity with mankind, with those very people whom he had left behind upon entering the monastery. This ambivalence was to remain with him all of his life, and, while it was a source of some anxiety to Merton himself, it is one of the strongest centers of excitement in approaching his work as well as being one of the clearest ways in which to see his role in twentieth-century letters.

The conditions under which Merton wrote were remarkable. In the 1940s life at Gethsemani was physically demanding and the diet poor. The monks slept on straw and boards in long dormitories. The monastery was marginally heated in the bitter Kentucky winters, and there was no relief in the torrid summers, when the monks worked in the fields in mid-July wearing heavy robes; they were eventually given permission to wear lighter clothes in the heat. From 1955-1965 Merton was in charge of the training of novices, a position second only to that of the abbot.

Of his more than 50 books and 300 articles, the greater part involve expository writing even though Merton felt most comfortable in writing poetry and keeping his journal. He seems to have had few people to talk to about literary matters even when the rule of silence was somewhat relaxed in the 1950s and 1960s. He made up for this lack in being an energetic if somewhat eclectic reader and notetaker, and by the 1960s he had developed relationships with a number of writers and artists outside the monastery. In addition, he corresponded with a number of distinguished authors, including some, such as Boris Pasternak, of international stature.

Merton mentioned shortly before his death that he had had trouble with censors within his order. This censorship infuriated Merton, and he complained in a letter to Naomi Burton that it concentrated not on faith and morals but on a vague category called "opportunité," that is to say whether it was opportune for a particular book to be published. Anything at all, "with or without reasons given," he concluded, could cause a book to be suppressed.

His superiors left him relatively free after the mid-1950s to write whatever he pleased, and various journals sought contributions from him throughout his later years. He often generously complied, even frequently sending work to rather obscure publications. This sort of pressure to produce always brought about the same reaction in him, a desire for solitude, which in turn was followed by a flurry of writing activity and renewed contacts with the world around him.

There were occasions when the monastic life seemed ideal for the sort of writing that he did. The interval between night and dawn, a very active time for monks, was especially fruitful, as Merton noted in his best-selling autobiography, *The Seven Storey Mountain* (1948): "After two or three hours of prayer your mind is saturated in peace and the richness of the liturgy. The dawn is breaking outside the cold windows. If it is warm, the birds are already beginning to sing. Whole blocks of imagery seem to crystallize out as if it were naturally in the silence and the peace, and the lines almost write themselves."

New Directions published his poetry faithfully from his first book of poems in 1944 until his death, and his publisher James Laughlin was helpful in putting him in touch with other important New Directions poets. In this way he began to correspond with Lawrence Ferlinghetti, Kenneth Patchen, and William Everson (Brother Antoninus) and from there was led to an acquaintance with other poets. He wrote to and met with Denise Levertov and Wendell Berry, and he came into contact with some young Louisville poets in the 1960s. In one of his taped lectures Merton said that he believed he lived in an age of good poetry, and he did his best, finally, to catch up with what was going on. He became especially attracted to the Beat poets—Allen Ginsberg, Jack Kerouac, Ferlinghetti, and Gregory Corso. He liked both the egalitarian spirit of the Beats and their style, a spontaneous outpouring from the unconscious. He found the Beats a relief from what seemed to him to be the stifling academicism that had overtaken recent American verse.

Poetry was for Merton a free, associational medium that carried the tide of his creative ideas and that became his principal arena for experimenting with language. Merton's ideas about contemporary man focus on the value of solitude. Setting himself against the grain of a culture in which solitude was viewed as a sign of neurosis and alienation, he reversed this conventional picture by showing that these effects were more likely to be observed in group man.

Thirty Poems (1944), part of the New Directions Poets of the Year series, marked the beginning of Merton's career as a poet. The thirty poems were part of a group of poems that had been entrusted to Mark Van Doren when Merton entered the monastery. Van Doren thus made the selection. The poems had been composed in Greenwich Village, at St. Bonaventure University in Olean, New York, and at the Abbey of Gethsemani. In *The Seven Storey Mountain* Merton recalled vividly the circumstances surrounding the composition of some of the Greenwich Village poems: "I would get an idea, and walk around the streets, among the warehouses, towards the poultry market at the foot of Twelfth Street, and I would go out on the chicken dock trying to work out four lines of verse in my head, and sit in the sun. And after I had looked at the fireboats and the old empty barges and the other loafers and the Stevens Institute on its bluff across the river in Hoboken, I would write the poem down on a piece of scrap paper and go home and type it out."

Merton's memory of his time at St. Bonaventure is equally evocative. Out of his window he would look beyond the chapel to the garden, the fields, and the woods. "My eyes often wandered out there," he recalled, "and rested in that peaceful scene," and as the months went on "I began to drink poems out of those hills." Merton's poetic fertility at this time coincided with the excitement that preceded his decision in 1941 to enter the Abbey of Gethsemani. He would not be such a prolific writer of poetry again until the later 1960s, when he decided to wind down his involvement in other kinds of writing and duties.

All copies of the small edition of *Thirty Poems* were sold. Yet Robert Lowell noted that Merton's poetry had "attracted almost no attentive criticism" and concluded that the "poet would appear to be more phenomenal than the poetry." Merton liked many of his poems of the 1940s, and included a number of them in his 1959 *Selected Poems*. Their range is limited; there is little sign of the presence of the larger society, except perhaps for faint echoes of the war in "Lent in a Time of War" and in "The Dark Morning." It was an enclosed world on the whole. As far as religious verse was concerned, Merton had hopes for himself as a renovator of this sort of poetry, writing to the Catholic Poetry Society *Bulletin* in 1941 that he was tired of "well-intentioned, fairly commonplace, half-sentimental" religious poetry and calling for an authentic poetry that was "profoundly mystical."

The title of *A Man in the Divided Sea* (1946) is drawn from the Israelites' miraculous crossing of the Red Sea, and acknowledged Merton's gratitude at having escaped the grasp of a meretricious culture. It also expressed the dualism underlying the book's themes, which are both secular and religious. Many of the poems deal with Greek themes. Ever since his father had read him stories from Greek mythology, Merton had used these stories as the basis of a religion and of a philosophy that he later recognized as contributing to his intellectual formation. The Greek poems balance the Christian poems as twin pillars in his thought and outlook. As opposed to the austerity of the Christian lyrics, however, the Greek poems tend to be ripe and sensual.

Merton's handling of the contemporary scene in *A Man in the Divided Sea* is pointed and graphic. The influence of Hart Crane is perceptible in "Aubade—The City" in the description of Brooklyn Bridge with its "choiring cables." For Merton, as for Crane, New York was *the* city, the archetype of the modern city, for better or for worse. Both saw it as a Dantean inferno inhabited by repressed inhabitants who moved about like captive wolves. In "Aubade—The City" the buildings have faces and the elevator doors "clash like swords." Even the organic world, twisted out of shape by urbanization, is intimidating.

Figures for an Apocalypse (1948) does not measure up to *A Man in the Divided Sea,* but it does offer some interesting innovations in technique. The book's principal problem is its declamatory style. The long title poem sets the tone for the collection, and Merton appears to have hoped that the power implicit in his apocalyptic vision would rub off on the poetry. *The Tears of the Blind Lions* (1949) is a slimmer volume than its predecessors, containing only seventeen poems. This paucity was a reflection of Merton's increased workload and of his scruples about the usefulness of poetry to the life of contemplation. There are few innovations in theme, but there is an increased attention to structuring. A good example is "Dry Places," in which Merton daringly paints a picture of an abandoned mining town overlaid on the biblical desert of austerity, madness, and demonic temptation:

> the dusk
> Is full of lighted beasts
> And the mad stars preach wars without end:
> Whose bushes and grasses live without water,
> There the skinny father of hate rolls in his dust
> And if the wind should shift one leaf
> The dead jump up and bark for their ghosts.

The Tears of the Blind Lions exhibits an accomplished blending of Merton's religious sensibility and poetic craft. Poems such as "The Reader" effectively convey both the hard surface and inner vitality of his monastic experience. He had simpli-

Thomas Merton at the Abbey of Gethsemani (photograph by Ralph Eugene Meatyard)

fied his poems and made them more direct, not only by concentrating on the details of his own experience but also by stripping from his writing the layers of similes which had cluttered earlier volumes.

Eight years elapsed before the appearance of his next volume of poetry, *The Strange Islands* (1957)—a gap that again reflected Merton's increased workload (by then he had been put in charge of the training of new monks) and his concentration on prose writing. The collection shows Merton moving toward a freer colloquialism, bringing him more into line with contemporary verse. He also experimented with different line lengths in order to build into the poems what he considered essential hollows of silence in which the reader was compelled to stop, be silent, and absorb the hidden meanings.

In place of the earlier bliss he included poems that focused wryly on the religious life, as in "To a Severe Nun," "Whether There is Enjoyment in Bitterness," and "Birdcage Walk." There are positive poems, however, and a few of these, like "Elegy for the Monastery Barn" and "Elias—Variations on a Theme," are exceptionally fine. "Elegy for the Monastery Barn" was written following an interrupted evening meditation in August 1953 when the old monastery cow barn burned down. The poem's success derives in part from its complex tone, which is sympathetic yet satiric, warm yet urbane, tender yet witty. The wit of the poem lies in the vision of the ancient, flaming barn as a grand old dowager overtaken suddenly by a completely uninhibited mood.

Merton's next volume of poetry, *Emblems of a Season of Fury* (1963), appeared in the midst of his strenuous social-prose writing, much of which was directed against conventional and nuclear war. The shift to social protest was stimulated by Merton's sense that civilized values had declined. In "Elegy for James Thurber" he wrote bluntly: "Business and generals survive you." The poems seethe with urgency and discontent. Even the Greek myths, which Merton generally used as symbols of order in a chaotic world, seem hard-pressed to contain their volatile subjects, as in "Gloss on the Sin of Ixion." The matter of Merton, a contemplative monk, writing poems of social protest was paradoxical to say the least. He read voraciously and eclectically, making notes on everything. He received books and magazines from friends when these were not available in the monastery's library, and he was especially interested in receiving liberal

periodicals such as the *Nation* and *I. F. Stone's Weekly*.

The flow of information to him became more reliable as the monastery's system of censorship relaxed in the 1960s. In addition, he wrote to James Laughlin, on his trips to town he would usually drop in at the University of Louisville in order to catch up with what was going on. He complained to friends on occasion that he frequently had to depend on secondhand news. At other times he came to value his remoteness. If it was true that news had become stale by the time it reached him, the delay could be an advantage. Through this delayed perspective, he felt that he was better able to distinguish the real happening from the pseudo event.

The mid-1960s brought about a revolution in Merton's style and themes as well as in his situation. In 1963 Merton moved out of the abbey into a hermitage that had been built on land owned by Gethsemani. He called *Cables to the Ace* (1968), a major experimental poetic sequence of the 1960s, an "antipoem" and indicated in his prologue that it was a poem without emphasis on imagery, sound, and rhythm. The stimulus to write antipoetry came principally from Merton's contact with the Chilean poet Nicanor Parra, some of whose poetry he translated in 1967. Parra's style was flat, understated, and relaxed, eschewing any hint of lyricism or symbolism. Merton was fascinated by Parra's dry, disconcerting voice, and he took to heart Parra's liberating advice to the poets of the world in his *Poems and Antipoems:* "In poetry everything is permitted."

In writing *Cables to the Ace* Merton was also influenced by folksinger Bob Dylan, whose iconoclastic songs seemed to him to have the sort of saltiness he wanted. Herbert Marcuse also affected him at this time, having demonstrated that mass culture tended to be "anticulture," stifling creative work by the "sheer volume of what is 'produced,' or reproduced." Given this situation, Merton noted in *The Asian Journal of Thomas Merton* (1973), the poet no longer had to parody; it was enough to quote.

Cables to the Ace is a mosaic of prose and poetry. The effect of this structure, Merton explained in a letter to his friend and fellow poet Robert Lax, was to create an atmosphere in which the parts of the poem were suspended in "mid air between true and false, between the Island of Staten and the Island of Coney, an everlasting pons asinorum." He had thus brought his work into line with the montage technique used by a number of his contemporaries, although his tonelessness and anti-poetic approach are unusual. With an eye on Ezra Pound's practice he referred to the sections of *Cables to the Ace* as cantos and tried to create the impression of a poem that could be read either forward or backward.

Cables to the Ace focuses on a world that strives toward hedonism but that finds natural and spontaneous physical pleasure no longer possible. Merton was appalled by the antiseptic format that advertising gave to love: even lust was no longer animal; it was chemical and electric. Following the lead of the advertisements, his poeticized lovers assure themselves: "We are not overheated, we smell good and we remain smooth. No skin needs to be absolutely private for all are quiet, clean, and cool." Privacy has been stripped away, and men and women are manipulated through the scenarios of love suggested by the media into a synthetic, dissonant sexuality. Poets are portrayed as able to counteract the debasement of language, but theirs is an underground existence. Poetic cables to the world are therefore coded, as indeed is Merton's sequence of poems, gibberish to conventional minds, but meaningful to those who are alert and pure of heart.

A looming thematic world in *Cables to the Ace* is that of nature and God—the "Ace" of Merton's title. Technology is polarized, with God and nature as a burlesque of the life force. The movement of *Cables to the Ace* shifts toward the end from being unfocused and ironic to the concentrated lyrical pursuit of the destination of all cables—"Infinite Zero," the "ace of freedoms."

The Geography of Lograire (1969) was greeted with respectful nods by critics, Jascha Kessler in the *Saturday Review* calling it the "year's most important book of poems." Merton had begun the work in 1967, writing to Laughlin that he had started on yet another long poem that would again be "far out." He wrote to W. H. Ferry in the same year that he thought the new poetic sequence would develop into something quite lively and complex, calling it his "summa of offbeat anthropology."

In a prefatory note Merton wrote that he regarded *The Geography of Lograire* as a "purely tentative first draft of a longer work in progress," what he called the "first opening up of the dream." Sister Thérèse Lentfoehr in a note appended to *The Geography of Lograire* has written that the name "Lograire" was derived from the real name of François Villon (François de Loges) as well as a type of log cabin used by French foresters, an obvious connection with Merton's wooded hermitage. What-

ever the exact referents of Merton's title, he launched himself ambitiously with *The Geography of Lograire* as a poet of psychogeography.

He arranged his sequence into a loose alternation of prose and poetry, encompassing the experience of both man's history and his own. Among the passages of prose and poetry Merton included quotations from his readings in history and anthropology. His method of mixing cultural anomalies, such as the Sioux ghost dances and the cargo cults of the South Pacific, with his own experience as a contemporary man had the effect of integrating these anomalies into the stream of contemporary thought so that their relevance could be appreciated. For Merton the secrets of healthy civilization had been lost beneath the withering impact of industrialism, and, while some of his examples of culture were bizarre and obscure, he tried to demonstrate that all could yield insights into the human condition with examples of cultural shock that overtook not only primitive but modern man.

The poem begins with "South" because that is where Merton was, and he is the center of the geography of Lograire. The American South is dramatized against the background of Kentucky and Florida, and the dominant motif of the Civil War is narrowed to fit the Kentucky landscape. "South" is followed by "North." This polarizing allows the qualities of the two geographical, cultural, and psychic worlds to appear in sharp relief. In terms of Merton's personal geography "North" is where he came from. Thus, this section deals initially with New York and London, the scenes of his childhood and adolescence, which although sometimes dimly remembered were always a deep part of him—"Forgotten world/All along/Dream places/Words in my feet." Following the general pattern of placing civilized societies next to primitive ones, Merton included in "North" a section on the Arctic wilderness.

The civilized world is represented in "East" by the anthropologist Bronislaw Malinowski, whose *Diary in the Strict Sense of the Term* (1967) Merton used as a symbol of the white man's experience of cultural shock. Malinowski's experience serves as a foil to sections that portray the shock to primitive societies brought about by the encroachment of the white man. Merton's portrayal of Malinowski suggests that the modern anthropologist continued the colonial attitudes of an earlier period.

"West" brings the book full circle, completing Merton's circumnavigation of the world. With his bent toward science Western man liked to deny, Merton believed, that he was guided by any sort of myth-dream. Merton's geographical and historical cycles point repeatedly to the same truth: Man's deepest needs have not been met by his experiments in culture, and this failure has been especially evident in the West—where the material world has been most successfully brought under control.

The Geography of Lograire, a major poem in recent American writing, was Merton's way of coming to terms with developments in American poetry. Earlier, he had avoided the forms used by contemporary poets because he associated these with sterile experimentation. By the 1960s he had convinced himself that the use of open forms with their idiosyncratic variations in line, image, and rhythm could be harnessed to carry the weight of his teeming social and spiritual themes. *Cables to the Ace* represented his first attempt to bring all of these elements together in a lyric/epic format that was to reach consummate expression in *The Geography of Lograire.*

Although he lived much of his life in contemplative isolation, Merton managed to touch the lives of millions of readers whose lifestyles were markedly different from his own. Black activist Eldridge Cleaver, for example, read *The Seven Storey Mountain* while serving a term in Folsom Prison and recorded his reaction in his best-selling autobiography, *Soul on Ice* (1968). In spite of his rejection of Merton's theism, Cleaver found that he "could not keep him out of the room." At first sight Merton's writings could appear to be an anomaly in terms of the social and intellectual temper of his time. However, as is reflected in the breadth of his reading audience, he seemed to reach those hidden springs in all people, whose existence he felt it vital to affirm.

Letters:

Pasternak/Merton: Six Letters (Lexington: King Library/University of Kentucky, 1973);

A Catch of Anti-Letters, by Merton and Robert Lax (Mission, Kans.: Sheed, Andrews & McMeel, 1978);

The Hidden Ground of Love: The Letters of Thomas Merton on Religious Experience and Social Concerns, edited by William Shannon (New York: Farrar, Straus & Giroux, 1985).

Bibliographies:

Marquita Breit, *Thomas Merton: A Bibliography* (Metuchen, N.J.: Scarecrow, 1974);

Frank Dell Isola, *Thomas Merton, A Bibliography,* re-

vised edition (Kent: Kent State University Press, 1975).

Biographies:

Edward Rice, *The Man in the Sycamore Tree: The Good Times and Hard Life of Thomas Merton, An Entertainment* (Garden City: Doubleday, 1970);

James Forest, *Thomas Merton: A Pictorial Biography* (New York: Paulist, 1980);

Monica Furlong, *Merton: A Biography* (New York & San Francisco: Harper & Row, 1980; London: Collins, 1980);

Michael Mott, *The Seven Mountains of Thomas Merton* (Boston: Houghton Mifflin, 1984).

References:

Daniel J. Adams, *Thomas Merton's Shared Contemplation: A Protestant Perspective,* edited by Teresa A. Doyle (Kalamazoo, Mich.: Cistercian Studies, 1979);

Raymond Bailey, *Thomas Merton on Mysticism* (Garden City: Doubleday, 1975);

James Baker, *Thomas Merton—Social Critic* (Lexington: University of Kentucky, 1971);

James Finley, *Merton's Palace of Nowhere* (Notre Dame, Ind.: Ave Maria, 1978);

Donald Grayston and Michael W. Higgins, eds., *Thomas Merton: Pilgrim in Process* (Toronto: Griffin House, 1983);

Patrick Hart, ed., *The Message of Thomas Merton* (Kalamazoo, Mich.: Cistercian Studies, 1981);

Hart, ed., *Thomas Merton/Monk: A Monastic Tribute* (New York: Sheed & Ward, 1974; enlarged edition, Kalamazoo, Mich.: Cistercian Studies, 1983);

John J. Higgins, S.J., *Merton's Theology of Prayer* (Kalamazoo, Mich.: Cistercian Studies, 1971);

Frederic J. Kelly, *Man Before God: Thomas Merton on Social Responsibility* (Garden City: Doubleday, 1974);

Victor Kramer, *Thomas Merton* (Boston: Twayne, 1984);

Ross Labrie, *The Art of Thomas Merton* (Fort Worth: Texas Christian University Press, 1979);

Thérèse Lentfoehr, *Words and Silence: On the Poetry of Thomas Merton* (New York: New Directions, 1979);

Elena Malits, *The Solitary Explorer: Thomas Merton's Transforming Journey* (New York: Harper & Row, 1980);

Dennis Q. McInery, *Thomas Merton, The Man and His Work* (Kalamazoo, Mich.: Cistercian Studies, 1974);

William H. Shannon, *Thomas Merton's Dark Path:*

The Inner Experience of a Contemplative (New York: Farrar, Straus & Giroux, 1981);
Gerald Twomey, ed., *Thomas Merton: Prophet in the Belly of a Paradox* (New York: Paulist, 1978);
Paul Wilkes, ed., *Merton By Those Who Knew Him Best* (New York & San Francisco: Harper & Row, 1984);
George Woodcock, *Thomas Merton: Monk and Poet*

(New York: Farrar, Straus & Giroux, 1978; London: Canongate, 1979).

Papers:
The largest collection of Merton's manuscripts is at the Thomas Merton Studies Center, Bellarmine College, Louisville, Kentucky.

Josephine Miles
(11 June 1911-12 May 1985)
Vernon H. Liang

SELECTED BOOKS: *Lines at Intersection* (New York: Macmillan, 1939);
Poems on Several Occasions (Norfolk, Conn.: New Directions, 1941);
Wordsworth and the Vocabulary of Emotion, University of California Publications in English, volume 12, number 1 (Berkeley & Los Angeles: University of California Press, 1942); republished in *The Vocabulary of Poetry: Three Studies* (Berkeley & Los Angeles: University of California Press, 1946);
Pathetic Fallacy in the Nineteenth Century: A Study of a Changing Relation Between Object and Emotion, University of California Publications in English, volume 12, number 2 (Berkeley & Los Angeles: University of California Press, 1942); republished in *The Vocabulary of Poetry: Three Studies*;
Major Adjectives in English Poetry from Wyatt to Auden, University of California Publications in English, volume 12, number 3 (Berkeley & Los Angeles: University of California Press, 1946); republished in *The Vocabulary of Poetry: Three Studies*;
Local Measures (New York: Reynal & Hitchcock, 1946);
The Primary Language of Poetry in the 1640's, University of California Publications in English, volume 19, number 1 (Berkeley: University of California Press, 1948); republished in *The Continuity of Poetic Language: Studies in English*

Poetry from the 1540's to the 1940's (Berkeley: University of California Press, 1951);
The Primary Language of Poetry in the 1740's and 1840's, University of California Publications in English, volume 19, number 2 (Berkeley: University of California Press, 1950); republished in *The Continuity of Poetic Language: Studies in English Poetry from the 1540's to the 1940's*;
The Primary Language of Poetry in the 1940's, University of California Publications in English, volume 19, number 3 (Berkeley: University of California Press, 1951); republished in *The Continuity of Poetic Language: Studies in English Poetry from the 1540's to the 1940's*;
Prefabrications, Indiana University Poetry Series, number 9 (Bloomington: Indiana University Press, 1955);
Eras & Modes in English Poetry (Berkeley: University of California Press, 1957; revised and enlarged, 1964);
Poems, 1930-1960, Indiana University Poetry Series, number 18 (Bloomington: Indiana University Press, 1960);
Renaissance, Eighteenth-Century, and Modern Language in English Poetry: A Tabular View (Berkeley: University of California Press, 1960);
Kinds of Affection (Middletown, Conn.: Wesleyan University Press, 1962);
Ralph Waldo Emerson (Minneapolis: University of Minnesota Press, 1964);

Josephine Miles at eighteen (courtesy of John O. Miles)

Civil Poems (Berkeley: Oyez Press, 1966);

Style and Proportion: The Language of Prose and Poetry (Boston: Little, Brown, 1967);

Saving the Bay (San Francisco: Open Space, 1967);

Fields of Learning (Berkeley: Oyez Press, 1968);

American Poems (Berkeley: Cloud Marauder Press, 1970);

Poetry and Change: Donne, Milton, Wordsworth, and the Equilibrium of the Present (Berkeley: University of California Press, 1974);

To All Appearances: Poems New and Selected (Urbana: University of Illinois Press, 1974);

Coming to Terms: Poems (Urbana: University of Illinois Press, 1979);

Working out Ideas: Predication and Other Uses of Language (Berkeley: University of California, Berkeley Bay Area Writing Project, 1979);

Collected Poems, 1930-83 (Urbana: University of Illinois Press, 1983).

PLAY PRODUCTION: *House and Home*, Berkeley, 1960.

OTHER: Ann Winslow (Verna Elizabeth Grubbs), ed., *Trial Balances,* includes poems by Miles (New York: Macmillan, 1935);

The Poem: A Critical Anthology, edited by Miles (Englewood Cliffs, N.J.: Prentice-Hall, 1959); revised and abridged as *The Ways of the Poem* (Englewood Cliffs, N.J.: Prentice-Hall, 1961);

"A Factor Analysis of the Vocabulary of Poetry in the Seventeenth Century," by Miles and Hanan Charles Selvin, in *The Computer and Literary Style: Introductory Essays and Studies,* edited by Jacob Leed (Kent: Kent State University Press, 1966), pp. 116-127;

"Robinson's Inner Fire," in *Edwin Arlington Robinson: A Collection of Critical Essays,* edited by Francis E. X. Murphy (Englewood Cliffs, N.J.: Prentice-Hall, 1970);

"Blake's Frame of Language," in *William Blake: Essays in Honour of Sir Geoffrey Keynes,* edited by Morton D. Paley and Michael Phillips (Oxford: Oxford University Press, 1973).

PERIODICAL PUBLICATIONS: "Wordsworth and Glitter," *Studies in Philology,* 40 (July 1943): 552-559;

"Some Major Poetic Words," *Essays and Studies by Members of the English Association,* 14 (1943): 233-239;

"From 'Good' to 'Bright': A Note in Poetic History," *PMLA,* 60 (September 1945): 766-774;

"The Language of the Donne Tradition," *Kenyon Review,* 13 (Winter 1951): 137-149;

"Emerson's Wise Universe," *Minnesota Review,* 2 (Spring 1962): 305-313;

"What We Compose," *College Composition and Communication,* 14 (October 1963): 146-154;

"Reading Poems," *English Journal,* 52 (March 1963): 157-164, 243-246;

House and Home, First Stage, 4 (1965): 196-202;

"A Poet Looks at Graphs," *Michigan Quarterly Review,* 4 (Summer 1965): 185-188;

"American Poetry in 1965," *Massachusetts Review,* 7 (Spring 1966): 321-335;

"Styles in Lyric," *Style,* 5 (Fall 1971): 226-230;

"Values in Language; or, Where Have *Goodness, Truth,* and *Beauty* Gone?," *Critical Inquiry,* 3 (Autumn 1976): 1-3;

"A Comment in Retrospect," *Style,* 11 (1977): 303-305.

Josephine Miles's major interest was always poetry. In the course of a long career as poet and academic she wrote volumes of poetry and critical books about poetry in roughly equal numbers, examining and practicing the poet's craft with the same sense of commitment.

The daughter of Reginald Odber and Josephine Lackner Miles, Josephine Louise Miles was born in Chicago, but she spent most of her life in California. Living there sporadically during her early years, the family went to southern California when she was one because of her father's insurance business, and they returned when she was five hoping that the aridity of the nearby desert would ease her arthritis. In the desert, where the family, which also included two brothers, often went camping, Miles came to love the open bareness of Andreas Canyon. Back in Evanston, Illinois, when she was eight, Miles wrote her first poem, already a political one, about the Armistice. Her first published poems appeared in *St. Nicholas,* a children's periodical her parents bought for her. (From this early experience with publishers, Miles learned the value of submitting material ahead of the deadline.) Aside from providing her an early opportunity for publication, Miles's family was not particularly interested in literature, but schoolteachers encouraged her writing by helping the ten-year-old Miles to stage her own plays. Her arthritis, she explained, gave her more time to write. After acquiring a solid background in the Greek and Roman classics in Los Angeles High School, Miles attended the University of California, Los Angeles, earning a B.A. in 1932. She went on to graduate school in English at the University of California, where her major field of study was the philosophy of language. Having received an M.A. in 1934 and a Ph.D. in 1938, Miles was appointed an instructor at Berkeley in 1940. She continued to teach there, becoming a full professor in 1952, and in 1978 she retired as a Distinguished Professor Emerita.

Her first commercially published adult poems appeared in *Trial Balances* (1935), an anthology of work by new poets. Her early work as a poet earned her a Shelley Memorial Award in 1936 and the following year she received the Phelan Memorial Award. In 1939, the year her first book was published, she was granted a fellowship by the American Association of University Women.

The fifty poems in Miles's first book, *Lines at Intersection* (1939), are arranged in a progression from dawn through morning, midday, afternoon, evening, to morning again. Dealing with the intersection of everyday circumstances with significance, the poems tend to be formal in structure. Hopkins's sprung rhythm, the Anglo-Saxon four-beat line, frequent internal and line-end rhyme are employed frequently, although a more colloquial voice enters toward the end of the book. The reviews of *Lines at Intersection* were generally favorable. Writing for *Poetry* (February 1940), Jessica Nelson North especially admired the more colloquial poems in which she found "a world made vivid by the elimination of detail, a world of small pictures brightly illuminated."

Miles's second book, *Poems on Several Occasions* (1941), was published as part of the New Directions Poet of the Month series. The "Several Occasions" are those parts of the human cycle of birth, possible marriage, and death that, for Samuel Johnson, provided the poet a scope too narrow for much interest. Intending to show how the conception of poetry has changed since Johnson's time, Miles set out to demonstrate that these so-called too-familiar "occasions" may have supreme importance.

Varying from occasionally strict to more frequently relaxed meters and rhymes, the poems deal with daily occasions no more exceptional than a visit to a museum, waiting for an appointment in a doctor's office, or leaving a movie theater. To reflect the daily round of human activities, the twenty-five poems are arranged roughly in a sequence beginning with the business of the day, through the afternoon slowdown, to evening. As in *Lines at Intersection* there is a movement from intricate poems, when rhyme and meter twist the tongue, at the beginning of the book, to more relaxed poems, written in easy, conversational tones, toward the end.

A comparison between stanzas from earlier and later poems in *Poems on Several Occasions* shows the shift from acrobatics to choreography. "Modern Dance Program: American Document" begins,

> God how we gallop, the youth of the land,
> Every shoulder atlas Atlastic,
> Sleuthing slowly and of sudden hurray, enthus-
> Iastic.

The poem progresses in a similar manner through two more stanzas, each ending on an increasingly precarious balance in the third and fourth lines, as the speaker goes through linguistic contortions to maintain the regular rhyme scheme. The lines of "Moonrise in City Park" are looser, as in this stanza, where a spectator receives instruction on viewing a cityscape which includes a hairdresser's shop:

> From this park bench look up and say divine,

To the dark levels speak and say divine,
To the moon whisper also and say divine,
And the sigh will join you, saying Beauty
Culture, saying the sign.

The repeated sounds in these lines are more subtle, without the regular line-end rhyme, without the self-consciously regular hemistichs. The repetition lends a hypnotic effect to the declaration that all this human endeavor is beauty and culture. More significant, a human voice declares the scene divine, the voice's whispering reinforced by the, usually banal, hairdresser's Beauty Culture sign.

Miles's poetry often reflects what she discovered in her extensive scholarship. She began her dissertation on Wordsworth (published separately in 1942 and as part of her *The Vocabulary of Poetry* in 1946) by stating that what critics consider "essentially poetic" changes according to the taste of the times. The purpose of her study "is rather the description of some poetry than prescription for it," a purpose that remained the goal of all her criticism, whether she wrote of prose or of poetry.

When *Local Measures,* a sizeable collection of sixty-two poems, appeared in 1946, most critics reviewed it well, often mentioning its continuation of the interest in small, everyday matters from Miles's two previous collections and praising the poems' clear, competent, and, as Dudley Fitts wrote for the *Nation* (31 August 1946), "virtuoso" style. The tone is conversational; the poems and stanzas short; the meter simplified.

New for Miles in this collection is a pronounced tendency to dramatize her ideas about poetry. "Dancer," for instance, uses bodily and architectural terms to show how a performer blends form with function. The performer seeks, through foot and knee, to suit his motion to his "doubting heart" and his body to "the room he is in." The toe's purpose is

To tell to the cord of the dancer
What footing and follow is
On every fleeting platform,
And what platform his.

The "cord," with a slight pun (through French *corps*) on "body," is not simply the dancer's tendon (connecting the muscles) but also a flexible line— the *form* of the dance, the form for which the heart provides function. The poem, as her colleague Robert Beloof wrote in *Prairie Schooner* (Winter 1958-1959), "celebrates the knee, the foot, and the toe as synecdoches of man's essential adjustment to the material world." At the same time it examines Miles's own search for form to fit poetic statement.

In her major three-part study, *The Primary Language of Poetry* (1948-1951; the three parts were published together as *The Continuity of Poetic Language* in 1951), Miles explained that her "interest has been in the similarities, rather than the differences, of poetic practice, . . . to repeat, over and over, the main lines of agreements in the various forms they take. . . ." She found that literature has followed a cyclical pattern from the fifteenth century to the present. Thus, she predicted that, while the epithet *good,* with its humane and metaphysical connotations, no longer has prominence in literary vocabulary, this sense of the good or its equivalent should return to prominence in the late twentieth century.

Miles's poetry attempts to return to this notion of goodness. By writing of what is essentially good in humanity, she sought to demonstrate how this quality constitutes a main line of agreement between individuals and generations.

The sixty poems in *Prefabrications* (1955), her fourth book of poetry, are carefully organized into three parts that demonstrate her sense of continuity in the human community, despite man-made obfuscations, both concrete and abstract, that create barriers between one person and another or between people and their surroundings.

"Two Kinds of Trouble," the long poem that begins part two, is dedicated to Michelangelo and argues that, while Michelangelo's artistic practice was subject to the vicissitudes of religious strictures and Medician rule (one kind of trouble), modern art is based on a jerry-built culture too featureless and meretricious for transformation into creations which endure.

In part three Miles set out to show that while a good man is not so hard to find, interest in what constitutes goodness has declined. The first poem of part three, "The Plastic Glass," establishes where the goodness lies. Seeing "Shattuck Avenue and the Safeway Stores" reflected "In Herndon's globe of friendly credit" and discovering in that plastic globe "the whole trash/Flats of Berkeley floated in suspense/Gold to the Gate and bellied to the redwood/ Cottages," she finds not merely goodness but grace and realizes:

in this dear and christian world the blessing
Falls not from above; the grace
Goldens from everyman, his singular credit
In the beatitude of place.

The good man is everyman: man in his commonality issues grace from within, "not from above."

After receiving the Oscar Blumenthal Prize in 1959, Miles published *Poems, 1930-1960* in 1960. The book includes seven poems from *Trial Balances* (1935) as well as selections from all her previous books of poetry, and fifty-five new poems in a section titled "Neighbors and Constellations." The general subject of the neighbor poems is familiar: the commonality that binds people to one another. Commonality is indeed "singular credit."

But the new poems concern a loss of faith whose immediate origin lies in the fracturing of relationship between one human being and another. Then comes the deeper fissure between human and universe as manifested in the physical bonds of body and place and in the metaphysical ones of time and being. From the small scale of individual to the grand scale of universe, much remains as remote as the constellations. Rather than fostering continuity between neighbor and constellation in these poems, Miles doubts, and then re-establishes that connection. Among these poems are Miles's most agitated, swinging between belief and disbelief, as if the loss of an old touchstone were itself unbelievable. Miles later explained that these poems were partly a response to the dark era of McCarthyism in the 1950s in America.

"Generation," the final poem in "Neighbors and Constellations," returns to belief, bespeaking a sense of continuity from father—the biblical Joseph—to son, faith in the individual ability to create perfection, and thus, give to all humanity the probability of divinity.

Starting with *Kinds of Affection* (1962) Miles began to work out in her poetry a theory of metaphor consistent with her belief in the commonality of human experience—a theory which she developed over the next five years and published in *Style and Proportion: The Language of Prose and Poetry* (1967). The book suggests that, since prose often draws upon those latencies in syntax, vocabulary, and sound which, exploited to the full, distinguish verse from prose, then both verse and (written) prose can and should be viewed as variations of a verbal norm: there is, then, a commonality between them. Miles's notion of metaphor rejects conventional divisions of metaphor into tenor and vehicle, and descriptions of it in terms of paradox or tension. She suggests instead that metaphors work by breaking down customary lexical boundaries, so that nonessential attributes are seen as essential, and so-called "necessary" or "essential" attributes are understood to be arbitrary—hence, "The dove

is a cabbage." Such a metaphor undermines or destroys identities; in doing so, it asserts—or brings toward recognition—new identities. Thus the poem beginning "As difference blurs into identity" is a discussion of metaphor, or more accurately a perception of it. If difference can "blend into identity" on the one hand, or blur "into obliteration" on the other, then we must "withdraw our belief and baggage" and recognize that nothing we *know* can be certain. Language is uncertain; "our position at the center" of belief, form, structure, is "zero":

As barriers between us melt, I may treat you
Unkindly as myself, I may forget
Your name as my own. . . .
. . . .
As assonance by impulse burgeons
And that quaver shakes us by which we are spent
We may move to consume another with us,
Stir into parity another's cyphers.

Hence the necessity for affection—where the abstractness of theory must and can be translated into daily terms, the *norm:* the balance is indeed between identity and difference, and the function of metaphor is to keep that balance vital. *Kinds of Affection* (and the puns and echoes in the title are important) extends Miles's notion of commonality.

Miles's only published play, *House and Home,* was produced in Berkeley in 1960 and published in a 1965 issue of *First Stage.* Written in free verse, it centers on family upheaval and its theme is similar to that of "Neighbors and Constellations." In the same year *House and Home* was published, Miles was awarded an American Council of Learned Societies fellowship.

In the revised edition of *Eras & Modes in English Poetry* (1964) Miles predicted that American poetry will turn to praise and "a strong sense of ceremony and of public concern." In an article expressing the need for "Public Poetry" she called on the poet to relate the identity he has found through past art to the present world, accepting his accountability for the new things he has made and the technological things surrounding him. Her own poetry became significantly political.

Civil Poems (1966) investigates the ironies of the Vietnam War and the turbulent emotions that spread from Berkeley to other campuses and communities. Several poems engendered by the events of the 1960s rigorously criticize America; yet as a poet Miles accepted her share of its guilt in disobedience to human values. In 1967 she received a National Endowment for the Arts grant.

Fields of Learning (1968), a chapbook of twelve

poems written "In debt to Berkeley," reflects her theory that every three generations poets renew vocabulary and even subject matter, tailoring each to the time in which the individual talent lives. Despite such change there is a continuity in poetry and in other fields, even though in our time the culture of the past is distilled by technology:

> When we go out into the fields of learning
> We go by a rough route
> Marked by colossal statues. Frankenstein's
> Monsters, AMPAC and the 704
> AARDVARK, and deoxyribonucleic acid.

The icons of the past "guard the way" and influence what is written in the future:

> For they figure us, they figure
> Our next turning.
> They are reading the book to be written.

This sense of history looking both forward and backward continues in *To All Appearances: Poems New and Selected* (1974), as Miles sought a view of history that could draw a response from the present. The thirty new poems move from Gettysburg to space travel, carefully incorporating

Josephine Miles, 1974 (courtesy of John O. Miles)

new-age objects into the credo of her poetry. For her, technology is part of the mundane and intellectual forces which, as students of our times, we must use in the search for peace through understanding of human commonality.

The sixty poems of *Coming to Terms* (1979) are a kind of summing up of the poet's professional life and work and an assessment and adjustment (she retired from the University of California in 1978). Structurally the poems in *Coming to Terms* lie a considerable distance from the strict formality of Miles's earliest work. In "Island," for instance, she used metric deviation to correspond to meaning, as in the anapestic ease of "By the waves of its waters," which echoes the lapping waves, and in the closing three stresses of the pronouncement: "I am land."

Miles placed the most important poem, "Center," last, preceding it by "Makers," a poem from which "Center" derives its title. The sequence explores and extends the poet's notions of commonality and interconnectedness, and of historical cycles. If the poetry movement at Berkeley (the subject of "Makers") is in its continuity and individuality a microcosm of the movement of world poetry, then "Center," in its investigation of the universal and the individual in American poetry, in its concern for Miles's own poetry, in its belief that the universal is to be found in the local, suggests that the poem "Center" is *itself* microcosmic, and of Miles's own work, of the Berkeley poetry movement, and of world poetry: the work is representative. And so is the artist.

She declares that makers—or artists—are here in this center to take risks so as to create "substance and grace." The risks a maker must assume recall the social, political, and technological awareness of Miles's "public poetry." She prays for what is human ("Give us to err/Grandly as possible . . ."), then elevates that quality to divinity. From error and risk-taking comes creation, a possibility that goldens from everyman.

Collected Poems 1930-83 (1983) gathers, in addition to work from all of Miles's previous books, twenty-one new poems. Many of the recent poems, as *Library Journal* observed, "deal with scenes in California and with her life as a professor at Berkeley"; the book as a whole forcefully illustrates Miles's concern through her career with public issues as with domestic life: war, politics, the bomb, ecology: the issues are public issues. But they are also seen as domestic, for Miles did not compartmentalize the world into mutually exclusive areas, and the life of the family is as important—indeed more important—as the life of the State. Reviewing the book for *Library Journal* (August 1983) Daniel L. Guillory called Miles a poet of the first rank whose work "might well be compared with that of William Carlos Williams and Marianne Moore." *Choice* (March 1984) commented that, despite the adversity in Miles's own life, the poems are notable for their consistent focus on happiness rather than on disappointment. The *Choice* reviewer pointed to Miles's versatility, a note also sounded in K. Chase's review in *World Literature Today* (Summer 1984), which summed up her career as "impressive."

Until her death in May 1985 Miles continued to live in Berkeley, taking part in the local poetry group which had grown to a steady hundred weekly participants, including a number of active faculty members. As Miles predicted in both her poetry and criticism, the group's poetry is political and accessible, addressing itself not only to auto-biography but to issues such as American intervention in Central America. There is a lack of critical attention to her work, although its importance is unquestionable. No one has executed such detailed structuralist studies of literature in English nor applied those findings so systematically to the writing of poetry. Miles felt no contradiction in being a scholar-poet, equally at home in more than one field of endeavor: "Everybody," she explained, "is like that at Berkeley."

References:
Robert Beloof, "Distances and Surfaces," *Prairie Schooner*, 32 (Winter 1958-1959): 276-284;

Lawrence R. Smith, "Josephine Miles: Metaphysician of the Irrational," *Pebble*, no. 18-19-20 (1979): 22-35.

Lorine Niedecker

Lisa Pater Faranda
Pennsylvania State University, Berks Campus

BIRTH: Fort Atkinson, Wisconsin, 12 May 1903, to Henry E. and Theresa Daisy Kunz Niedecker.

EDUCATION: Beloit College, 1922-1924.

MARRIAGES: 29 November 1928 to Frank Hartwig (divorced). 26 May 1963 to Albert Millen.

AWARD: Notable Wisconsin Writers Award, 1978.

DEATH: Fort Atkinson, Wisconsin, 31 December 1970.

BOOKS: *New Goose* (Prairie City, Ill.: Press of James A. Decker, 1946);

My Friend Tree (Edinburgh: Wild Hawthorn Press, 1961);

North Central (London: Fulcrum Press, 1968);

T & G: The Collected Poems (1936-1966) (Penland, N.C.: Jargon Society, 1969); enlarged as *My Life by Water: Collected Poems, 1936-1968* (London: Fulcrum Press, 1970);

Blue Chicory (New Rochelle, N.Y.: Elizabeth Press, 1976);

The Granite Pail: The Selected Poems of Lorine Niedecker, edited by Cid Corman (San Francisco: North Point Press, 1985);

From This Condensery: The Complete Writing of Lorine Niedecker, edited by Robert J. Bertholf (East Haven, Conn.: Jargon Society/Inland Book Company, 1985).

OTHER: "The President of the Holding Company," "Fancy Another Day Gone," and "Mother Geese," in *New Directions in Prose and Poetry*, no. 1, edited by James Laughlin (Cambridge, Mass.: New Directions, 1936), pp. 101-112;

"Uncle," in *New Directions in Prose and Poetry*, no. 2, edited by Laughlin (Cambridge, Mass.: New Directions, 1937), pp. 81-107;

"For Paul," in *New Directions in Prose and Poetry*, no. 12, edited by Laughlin (Norfolk, Conn.: New Directions, 1950), pp. 181-185;

"Switchboard Girl," in *New Directions in Prose and*

Lorine Niedecker (photograph by Gail H. Roub)

Poetry, no. 13, edited by Laughlin (Norfolk, Conn.: New Directions, 1951), pp. 87-89.

PERIODICAL PUBLICATIONS: "The Poetry of Louis Zukofsky," *Quarterly Review of Literature,* 8 (Spring 1956): 198-210;
"The Poetry of Cid Corman," *Arts in Society,* 3 (Summer 1966): 558-560;
"Featuring Lorine Niedecker," *Origin,* third series no. 2 (July 1966): 1-37;
"Featuring Lorine Niedecker," *Origin,* fourth series no. 16 (July 1981): 1-48.

Though Basil Bunting once called her "the best living poetess," Lorine Niedecker's death went virtually unnoticed. To readers familiar with her work she is an enigmatic, nearly legendary, figure; and even to those who actually knew her, she remains something of a mystery. But the mystery is not difficult to solve—Lorine Niedecker Millen simply had "more trees for friends than people," as she wrote to Cid Corman in 1965, and chose to live most of her sixty-seven years in a cabin on a small island near a small town in Wisconsin. Her death certificate records her "Usual Occupation" as "author and poet" and her "Kind of Business or Industry" as "housewife." For a time in the late 1950s and early 1960s she also scrubbed floors and cleaned the kitchens in the local hospital while she wrote poetry that "sweetened by the way/she saw the good/imaginable America."

These lines are from Charles Middleton's memorial poem included in *Epitaphs for Lorine* (1973), a memorial volume edited and published by Jonathan Williams in order, he says in the introduction, "to register a sense of what the poems— and her devotional life—have meant to a number of poets." Among the thirty-one poets who celebrated Niedecker and her poetry were Allen Ginsberg, who called her a "lonely poet/far from cities/ one in the world," and Edward Dorn, who admired her "strict eye" and her poetry, like "the line of a simply exquisite rope."

Her reputation has crossed the Atlantic, and her career spanned three generations of poets, with her work taking its place among the poems of their most prominent representatives. When the *New York Times* failed to print an obituary for Niedecker, Jonathan Williams wrote the editor: "During the forty years that Ms. Niedecker wrote her savory, laconic, superbly crafted poems, she commanded the admiration of William Carlos Williams, Louis Zukofsky, [Basil] Bunting, Edward Dahlberg, Kenneth Rexroth, Herbert Read, James Laughlin, Robert Duncan, Cid Corman . . . and a small audience capable of telling real peony bushes from plastic hydrangea plants."

The roster of her admirers continues to grow, but Lorine Niedecker has remained a relatively obscure poet, primarily because she refused to follow the rules established by the publishing and marketing establishment. "Had she chosen," James Laughlin wrote in his contribution to *Epitaphs for Lorine,* "to play the games of poetry politics, she could probably have ended up as well known as the ladies who are now wearing the establishment's official 'laurels,' but that just wasn't her way, so it will be up to time to prove her merits, and I have no doubt what the judgment will be." In the years since her death, growing numbers of readers concur with Jonathan Williams that Lorine Niedecker was the "most absolute poetess since Emily Dickinson."

Her own estimates of her work and worth are characteristically modest. In a 1970 letter to Williams, Niedecker wrote: "I probably show a folk base . . . and that so far as I see it it might actually be my only claim to any difference between most poets and meself." This distinction is unpretentious, but her poetry is no mean accomplishment. When Louis Zukofsky included one of her poems in his anthology *A Test of Poetry* (1948), he placed it in a section titled "Recurrence" and called it folk poetry, saying "the less poetry is concerned with the everyday existence and the rhythmic talents of a people, the less readable that poetry is likely to be."

Endeavoring to discover value in modern life, she emerged in the 1930s as an avant-garde poet experimenting with language and techniques that would break open the shackles of habitual meaning. Her strongest affinities are to nominalist and objectivist poets. Only by careful and painstaking examination of particulars, kaleidoscopic and diverse as they appeared to modern eyes, could Niedecker reaffirm her sense of value in human life.

The trust in language as a means of communicating that faith links Niedecker not only to the literati of her time but, like many of her peers, to Emersonian tradition and the generative principles of American literature. With unblinking attention to even the smallest detail, Niedecker rediscovered what Emerson called "the meter-making argument that makes a poem." She is the poet "who re-attaches things to nature and the Whole—." Her task was rooted in the traditions of the American Renaissance, but she knew, as her contemporaries had too, that any rebirth could be achieved only by attention to and action in the present. Theirs became a search for what Charles Olson called "an actual earth of value," and in that search Niedecker's art was able to reassert the value and possibility of wonder in human life.

Her life was characterized by an intrinsic irony. Her extreme urge to privacy and her refusal to engage in the business of poetry were matched by the extremely personal base for her poetry and her strong desire to have her work made public. Also, while Blackhawk Island was her "beloved" home, she was in many ways an outsider to its community. She kept her writing secret, knowing distrust and disapproval would follow if her neighbors discovered that she spent "two months on six lines/ of poetry." Yet, she knew too that she must be "right down among 'em" and that it was the "folk from whom all poetry flows." Niedecker opted for a life apart from the mainstream of social, professional, intellectual, and community life, but she did so in order to write.

Poetry was her connection to the world and her means of participating in it. In his introduction to her second book, *My Friend Tree* (1961), Edward Dorn calls Niedecker's poems "notations of an inner world." "What is in," he writes, "will come out, it does not always work the other way." It did for Niedecker, Dorn tells us, for her "notations" register not a private world but one which is recognizable and shared. The poems are neither biographical nor confessional although Niedecker shared Zukofsky's belief that "the work says all there needs to be said of one's life." In her poems are the figures, images, and instances of her personal history and those of a context larger, but no less real or important to her. Mr. Van Ess and Aeneas McAllister share the field with Adlai Stevenson and Thomas Jefferson. To whomever or whatever Niedecker turned her attention, she brought herself, open and alert. Niedecker's poetry is ultimately one woman's experience in a world where what can be known of it is fundamentally communal yet always individually felt. Not merely personal, Niedecker's "notations," according to Michael Heller, display "a capacity to make of the representations of one's memory, the clean outlines of a myth."

She refused to clutter her vision with abstractions, and she insisted on condensation as a principle of form and content, stripping her language of cliché, conceit, and decoration. Hers was an economy of speech, of life, and of being, which proved the means of "re-attaching things to nature...." Unmediated experience, if it is to be shared, must be expressed as directly, as simply, and as precisely as possible. Niedecker accepted Zukofsky's well-known tenet that "Condensation is more than half of composition"; however, for Niedecker, such economy of language was a moral necessity and guiding principle of being, a morality she had developed as she "rose from marsh mud/ algae, equisetum, willows...."

Lorine Faith Niedecker was born on 12 May 1903 to Henry and Theresa (Daisy) Kunz Niedecker of Fort Atkinson, Wisconsin. Her family lived on Blackhawk Island, just outside town; they were long-standing residents in the community, owned land, and participated in the island's chief industry, carp fishing. Niedecker's early life on Blackhawk Island had a significant impact on her poetry; this place and its people informed not only her sense of the way the world works but her place within it. She later wrote to a friend: "Early in life I looked back of our buildings to the lake and said, 'I am what I am because all of this—I am what is around me—those woods made me.'"

The woods, marshes, river, and lake constitute a landscape from which Niedecker drew her life and her poetry. Blackhawk Island is a small island at the mouth of the Rock River which empties into Lake Koshkonong at The Point, the tip of the island. It is not a spectacular place, just a place where things grow wild. From her cabin Niedecker could take a snapshot of a friend's house and obtain what she called a "kind of pristine, first morning of creation picture. . . ."

When she came of age, Niedecker began a series of moves away from and back to Blackhawk Island, but at no time did she ever live far from water. She retained the lessons learned in childhood, and her measure of experience was how one lived by water.

From her parents she learned two incompatible approaches to life by water. Theirs was a marriage of silent battles between her "mother/tall, tormented/darkinfested" and her "sometimes/happy fatherphospher." As a carp seiner, Lorine's father drew their livelihood from the water, but he had "leaky boats" because his drinking and philandering kept him from properly tending to his business. As her "absent father's distrait wife," Lorine's mother was "moored to this low shore by deafness" and encroaching blindness. She turned inward and away from her husband and the world. Henry Niedecker's world was boisterous, unreflective, and often cruel; his wife's was silent, thoughtful, and often painful. Finding a way to float between them was a psychological necessity for the child and an artistic one for the poet she became. "Floating" and "flying" became the metaphors she used for managing the balance needed to survive by the "soft/ and serious—/water." In "As praiseworthy" she wrote:

> As praiseworthy
> The power of breathing (Epictetus)
> while we sleep. Add:
> to move the parts of the body
> without sound
> and to float
> on a smooth green stream
> in a silent boat.

That balance, like the movement of a boat or the flight of a bird skimming the water, Niedecker achieved in the act of writing. She saw herself in terms of such images when she wrote: "I was the solitary plover/a pencil/for a wingbone."

Niedecker remembered her childhood as a sensory experience of the environment: "I spent my childhood outdoors—redwinged blackbirds,

willows, maples, boats, fishing (the smell of tarred nets), twittering and squawking noises from the marsh." Her senses grew sharp on Blackhawk Island, where marshland hosts hundreds of species of migrating birds and myriad indigenous flora and fauna. She learned to care for the smallest creatures; necessity joined inclination to teach her to attend, to notice "the little/thin things." She learned nature's harsh lessons too, for life on the island was a constant negotiation with the elements. They taught her the cruelties of nature, as she heard "the wild/wet rat muskrat/grinding his frogs and mice," and the certainties:

> Springtime's wide
> water—
>   yield
> but the field
> will return[.]

Niedecker's sense of place included the sights and sounds of people living in it. The people she heard talking were no less fascinating than the birds she could identify by call. Her grandfather, she remembered, "somehow, somewhere got hold of nursery and folk rhymes to entrance me" and her mother "spoke whole chunks of down-to-earth magic." Her father, quite unintentionally, gave her "a source/to sustain her—/a weedy speech,/a marshy retainer." The folk are not only the subject of Niedecker's poetry; their talk determines the sound of it. The cadences, the pronunciation, and "rhythmic talents of the people" reflect their treaty with the environment, their pact with the world in which they live. Niedecker had a keen ear for their talk and was adept at translating its sound into insight.

She graduated Fort Atkinson High School in 1922, and her class yearbook contains her first published poem, "Wasted Energy." Naive in its adherence to strict patterns of rhyme and meter, it clearly has her wit and reveals her finely tuned ear. She gently mocks, though precisely records, "this modernized method of talk." Her ear was also well tuned to music, and her voice was good. A schoolteacher predicted she would become a famous singer, but by the time she was eighteen Niedecker had chosen poetry. She recalled in a 1964 letter to Cid Corman: "When I was 18 I bought a Wordsworth and took the book with me down here [to the river] toward evening. I didn't quite know, yet I think I was vaguely aware that the poetry current (1921) was beginning to change." Niedecker left home for the first time in 1922, to study literature at Beloit College, but she stayed only two years. She returned to Blackhawk Island to care for her ailing mother and never completed her degree, choosing instead to live a settled life on the island. On Thanksgiving Day, 29 November 1928, she married Frank Hartwig, and they moved into Fort Atkinson, where she went to work as a librarian's assistant at the local public library. In the same year she published the poem "Transition" in the little magazine *Will-o-the-Wisp*. In 1930, after Hartwig defaulted on a loan and the couple lost their house, they separated, and Niedecker returned to her parents' home. She and Hartwig were finally divorced in 1942.

In 1931 Niedecker discovered Louis Zukofsky and Objectivist poetry when she read the so-called Objectivist issue of *Poetry* magazine (February 1931), of which Zukofsky was guest editor. This issue introduced the Objectivists, who included William Carlos Williams, Carl Rakosi, Charles Reznikoff, and George Oppen, as well as Zukofsky. At the insistence of *Poetry*'s regular editor Harriet Monroe, Zukofsky had reluctantly supplied the term "Objectivist" as the label for a poetry motivated by "sincerity and objectification," the two principles of the poem which Zukofsky explained in the issue's "Program: 'Objectivists' 1931" and "Sincerity and Objectification." Niedecker appreciated Zukofsky's notion of the poem and always thought of these essays as seminal pieces in the development of her own work. Her sensitivity to details drew her naturally to Zukofsky's idea that "Writing occurs which is the detail, not mirage, of seeing, of thinking with things as they exist, and of directing them along a line of melody." The implications for form greatly appealed to her. She believed that details were not enough, that condensation was an act upon particulars that made form emerge and provided a sense of completeness—a belief that approximated Zukofsky's "objectification."

Niedecker was so delighted by this issue of *Poetry* that she initiated a correspondence with Zukofsky that lasted the rest of her life. Her letter launched her career, for it was a declaration of her dedication to poetry, and it introduced her to a community of poets whose work would affect the course of American literature. Niedecker greatly admired Zukofsky's poetry. The first of her only two ventures into critical writing was a glowing appraisal of Zukofsky's poetry, an essay that remains one of the important appreciations of his technique. From Zukofsky she learned much. Zukofsky often made critical suggestions and changes in the

poetry she sent him; thirty years later Niedecker told Corman, "He has been generous. O very generous." For the first fifteen years their correspondence was quite frequent; it was a testing ground for their poetry. A letter in which she discussed her poem "February almost March" is characteristic: "Now lessee—I have lots to say about Feb. almost March but we're both fed up on talking about it. Her a goddess? Because I mention Eden (God)? You see, this thing of changing a poem means a different thing, different rhythm and pretty soon the whole original idea and movement in the mind of the writer is gone and the whole thing would have to be done over. However, I'll keep your suggestions. Copy of it enclosed. . . ."

Contact with Zukofsky introduced her to a world of literary journals and brought her directly within the current of contemporary poetry. Like many other young intellectuals of the time, Niedecker's interest in politics and social reform was keen. Like many others, she believed writing was intimately related to everyday existence. Her poetry of the early 1930s transformed the lessons of necessity and austerity learned in childhood into ideologies which seemed to have a counterpart in the politics of the Social Credit party. She found human society wasteful and seriously and unnaturally inequitable.

She published poetry in journals such as *New Democracy* and *Bozart—Westminster* and took her place in the literary avant-garde. Her poetry was surrealistic in its juxtaposition of sense and nonsense and in its often startling mixture of incongruous images. Her first major publication was a small selection of poems (as well as two short plays) in the first issue of the *New Directions* anthology (1936), which James Laughlin extrapolated from the "New Directions" section he had edited for *New Democracy*. Laughlin's aim was to print the best examples of experimental writing because he was convinced that such writing was the vanguard of social reform.

While the selection of Niedecker's poems, "Mother Geese," has as its "folk base" the irresistible tune of the nursery rhyme, she speaks of serious aberrations in modern life. The group of poems opens with, "O let's glee glow as we go/there must be things in the world—/Jesus pay for the working soul,/fearful lives by what right hopeful." While she employs the compelling rhythms of the rhymes most readers recite almost without thinking, the effect becomes unsettling as the reader, innocently enough, realizes the situation:

The land of four o'clocks is here
the five of us together
    looking for our supper
Half past endive, quarter to beets,
seven milks, ten cents cheese,
    lost, our land, forever.

Between 1938 and 1942 Niedecker worked in Madison, Wisconsin, for the W.P.A., first as a writer, then as a research editor in the Federal Writers' Project which produced the *Wisconsin Guide*, which, like the guides for the other forty-seven states, canvassed the state's geography, history, and culture. Her letters to Zukofsky from this time talk of research into Wisconsin's early history, particularly that of her own Blackhawk Island. For a short time in 1942 Niedecker worked as a script writer for WHA, a Madison radio station. There are no records of her tenure there but the Humanities Research Center at the University of Texas at Austin has a typescript for her radio adaptation of William Faulkner's *As I Lay Dying*. Letters to Zukofsky expressed her disenchantment with city life, and in 1942 Niedecker returned to Blackhawk Island, this time to remain for twenty years.

When she returned, Niedecker filed for divorce from Hartwig, and in 1944 she went to work, as a stenographer and proofreader, at Hoard's, the local printer of the regionally well-known journal *Hoard's Dairyman*. Her poem beginning "In the great snowfall before the bomb" alludes to her work at Hoard's and her position within the community. She returned at age thirty-nine with no illusions about the innocence of the folk, to whom she attributed both the inspiration for poetry and the power to make bombs.

When her first book, *New Goose,* was published in 1946, Niedecker kept it a secret from her community. She gave out only three copies to very close friends and requested each of them not to tell anyone in Fort Atkinson about it. She knew the questions her "scribblin" would raise, as she wrote her friend Frances Dollase: "I have to ask that it be kept mum—folks might put up a wall if they knew ('she writes poetry, queer bird, etc. . . .') and I have to be among 'em to hear 'em talk so I can write some more!"

The practical and mundane matters of the world provide the content for most of the poems in *New Goose*: moving in, visiting neighbors, a "lawnmower," "spitbox," or "wall thermometer." However, it is not a world cloistered from the larger realities of "Bombings" or "red Russia." Amidst

daily frustrations and failures when there are "laws for fishing thru the ice—," the gift of a "bluebottle gentian" or a "first-hand country shake" is important "enough to carry one through." What is essential and what is waste, what is natural and what is not are primary concerns for Niedecker. Not dependent upon ideologies or platitudes, she looks to specific instances that may enlighten.

She is still concerned with the distance that grows between an individual and society and the attenuation of human qualities over that distance, but in *New Goose* the questions are solid, inviting, sometimes bitter, but always honest, answers. In the poem "Du Bay" John Du Bay "shot a man for claiming his land" and "Witnesses judged him as good as the average/for humanity, honesty, peace./ The court sent him home to his children. . . ." There is still sharp criticism of an economy of "gain." Poems such as "Hop Press," "My coat threadbare," "A lawnmower's one of the babies I'd have," and "I doubt I'll get silk stockings out" deal directly with the inequities that emerge in a world hoping for "miracles of profit."

Most of the poems in *New Goose* do not startle; they rely on Niedecker's keen eye and what objectivist poets called "sincerity," "thinking with things as they exist." "A monster owl" predates but approximates Williams's famous prescription "no ideas but in things." The "monster owl" is there, "out on the fence," and when he flies away, it is a "sign of" no more but certainly no less than "an owl." Ending the poem with a line composed only of "an owl" gives importance to the thing itself. It does not obscure the owl with thoughts about it.

Niedecker turns her attention to human beings as sincerely as she does to things in the world. In *New Goose* what may be said of human nature is evident through the actions, thoughts, and words of particular people. The figures in the poems are real, though many, like Chief Black Hawk or John James Audubon, Niedecker never met, and many, like the "sharecropper," never actually existed. The poems are after more than realism; they present characters who are archetypal figures and speak to us of ourselves while remaining utterly unique.

Her portraits are kinetic and more like landscapes than figures. Often speaking for themselves, the people move among others. The short tight poems frame single instants without freezing them into still lifes. The moments of the poems are whole occasions yet not detached from the unceasing process of life. "Don't shoot the rail," for instance, opens in medias res, focusing on a moment of rest for "grandfather." Even in his "falling" asleep there is motion. The child's "wild eyes" energize the scene, and all three figures move in and out of the reader's consciousness as the child has the speaker's attention and seeks the grandfather's.

New Goose demonstrates Niedecker's interest in the world of ordinary people. Everyone, even Audubon and Chief Black Hawk, is ordinary in the sense that everyone faces failure, must endure the dangers and difficulties of nature, and has to weather the storms man creates and for which he is accountable. In one sense it is a dark book, but the poems do not simply condemn; they attest to the difficulties of life, yet despite error, one feels a warmth.

Shortly after the publication of *New Goose*, Niedecker built a cabin on the riverbank, on her father's property near her parents' home. By the summer of 1947, she was at home in a one-and-a-half-room cabin which had a view of the river and built-in bookshelves she called her immortal cupboard. On these shelves she kept her favorite writers, among them: Bashō, Cid Corman, Emily Dickinson, D. H. Lawrence, Henry David Thoreau,

William Carlos Williams, and Louis Zukofsky. In many respects the cabin was primitive; water came from an outside pump, and there was no indoor plumbing for the fifteen years she lived there.

Niedecker continued to work at Hoard's until 1950, leaving when her already impaired eyesight had so deteriorated that she could no longer read without the aid of a magnifying glass. During the 1950s Niedecker lived quietly. As Emerson said of Thoreau, Niedecker "chose to be rich by making [her] wants few." She had copied this quotation onto a slip of paper and left it in her copy of *Walden* (1854).

In 1951 Theresa Niedecker died, leaving Lorine to care for her father. Her mother's last words were "wash the floors, Lorine, wash clothes! Weed!" Haunted by them, Niedecker used these words in the poem beginning "Old Mother turns blue and from us." In this poem as in many others, Niedecker expressed compassion for her mother's isolation and bitterness; she understood the need to fill the emptiness and keep chaos at bay as well as the claustrophobia of a life lived with "the heart, a thimble in her purse." Soon after, in 1954, Henry

A 1980 photograph of the house Niedecker built on Blackhawk Island in 1947 (photograph by Thomas Faranda)

Niedecker died, leaving Niedecker virtually alone in the world. She had inherited two cottages and a few thousand dollars, and she withdrew to her cabin, where she was to live for a few years without working. She leased the cottages but found herself burdened by the cares of proprietorship. Tenants were unreliable and irresponsible, leaving her massive cleaning jobs and unlooked-for expenses. In more than one poem she vented her anger at what she called "the dirty business of property." She eventually sold the land and the cabins.

In 1957 Niedecker ventured out once more and began working again, this time in the local hospital cleaning the kitchen and scrubbing floors. Though the past ten years had been reclusive, they were not years away from poetry. Throughout the 1950s, Niedecker had published poetry in literary journals. In 1960 she began a correspondence with Cid Corman, editor of *Origin,* a magazine vitally important to the poets pushing beyond modernism. *Origin,* begun in 1951, was a source of postmodern art and itself an important development in the structure and format of literary magazines. Niedecker's friendship with Corman was her link with the poets of a younger generation. In his "With Lorine" Corman wrote, "she never sent me work that I wasn't grateful to print." Niedecker admired his talent and applauded his service to literature. While her first piece of literary criticism had been devoted to Zukofsky's art, her second, and last, examined and lauded Corman's. They shared a concern for clarity and sparseness that infuses their poetry with an urgent need to communicate and do it plainly.

My Friend Tree, Niedecker's second book, was published in 1961 in Scotland, by Ian Hamilton Finlay, a poet and publisher Niedecker had learned of through Corman. It is a small book of sixteen poems, half of which had already been published in *New Goose,* fifteen years earlier. For many readers, however, the intervening years made the poems seem new while the arrangement of the poems added another dimension to her work.

Edward Dorn, an American poet whose work of that period also turned upon the precision and solidity of each word, wrote the introduction to *My Friend Tree.* He admired the poems because "they attach an undistractable clarity to the word, and then because they are unabashed enough to weld that word to a freely sought, beautifully random instance—the instance being the only thing place and its context can be; the catch in the seine."

The poems of *My Friend Tree* fasten the themes of earlier work to nature. The title and title poem place the poet in relation to the natural world, making nature the ground from which the questions she raises regarding human need, endeavor, and failure arise and return for answers. In *My Friend Tree* there is confidence in the universe and its natural processes that supports her frank examination of daily life, making one at home in the world. "Along the river" expresses this confidence:

> Along the river
>> wild sunflowers
> over my head
>> the dead
> who gave me life
>> give me this
> our relative the air
>> floods
> our rich friend
>> silt

The influence of Zukofsky and Williams is evident as the lines move out and back following the cadence of human speech. The activity of establishing relationships actually occurs within the poem. The prepositional relations are transformed into "our rich friend" through a series of elements that turns on the verbal phrase "Give me this." The relative pronoun "who" is the point of coincidence between the two sides of the poem, and the echo of "who gave me life" in "give me this" brings all together—life is "this," these relationships.

Niedecker was a nature poet, but her setting was not pastoral or ideal. Despite Niedecker's reverence for nature, history and experience taught her that in any landscape the human presence brings the possibility of failure and disappointment as well as the capacity for endurance and friendship. The failures can be collective as in "Black Hawk held: In reason" or personal as in "Well, spring overflows the land." It is important that in *My Friend Tree* even those poems originally published in *New Goose* have a scale by which to measure the loss.

Nature, cruel as it may sometimes be, also offers models for survival, alternatives to "miracles of profit," and friendships with "nothing in it but my hand." Attention to nature teaches a way of being in the world that is generative and productive, economical and sustaining. And we can learn because the ability to think, while it may dislocate us, permits us to see as well.

My Friend Tree introduced Niedecker abroad and reintroduced her to American readers. Although by 1961 she had been a poet for more than thirty years, the arrangement of poems in *My Friend Tree* makes it a book of emergence, a brief statement of confidence, made in full awareness of the less-than-perfect human world as well as its potential for renewal.

By 1961 "the clothesline post is set./Yet no totem carvings distinguish the Niedecker tribe." She speaks clearly and honestly of her own anonymous place in an ordinary world. In this poem, the play on traditional rituals which have devolved into seemingly meaningless conventions is characteristic self-deprecation. The underlying jest playing on "all"—in the line "by the whiteness of their all"—adds humor to brighten and lighten the washload, but it is also a harsh confrontation with reality. Niedecker had no grand hopes or eloquent ideals; after all, what kind of life is promised if the choices are to "hang" or "fall"? Still, the pun on "all" adds more than humor; it adds dignity because in the routine of raising "hands from ground to sky" there is tenacity, and the effort is honorable.

The final decade of Niedecker's life opened with the publication of her second book and brought her modest but increasing recognition. A frequent contributor to *Origin*, she was its featured poet in the July 1966 issue. By then she had attained a modicum of acceptance among editors and critics as well as among fellow poets, and she could tell Corman that "Some of the mag. editors write me now for poems and in almost every case they keep what I send. . . ."

On 26 May 1963, to the surprise even of herself, Niedecker remarried. Her husband, Albert Millen, a housepainter from Milwaukee, had wanted to buy one of her cottages. Some have said their marriage was an unhappy one, and the images of marriage, of the irreconcilable differences between people, in Niedecker's poetry are bitter. No doubt she recalls her own experience as well as her parents' in "I married/and lived unburied." Niedecker and Millen were quite different; yet even if troubled, their marriage meant that for Niedecker there would be "At the close—/someone."

Al Millen also opened the way for Niedecker to strike out once again. The couple moved to Milwaukee in 1963 and returned the sixty miles to Blackhawk Island only for weekends, holidays, and summer vacations. In Milwaukee they lived in a small apartment in a rundown part of the city, filled with churches, taverns, trucks, sidewalks, shops, and people. In Milwaukee she also found the University of Wisconsin campus, the art center, the large library, and Kosciusko Park with its statue of

Robert Burns. All figure in her poetry. Having retired from her hospital job in 1963, she devoted much more of her time to writing, and these years were some of Niedecker's most prolific years. Unfortunately, her eyesight continued to deteriorate, and her health grew precarious, a heart condition making it necessary that she not overexert herself.

The Millens permanently retired to Blackhawk Island in 1969. They built a modest cabin in front of the one Niedecker had built for herself in 1947. It was close to the river bank, built high on cement blocks to keep out floodwaters, had indoor plumbing, two-and-a-half rooms. There was a lovely garden and a clear view of the Rock River.

North Central, Niedecker's third book, is based on the automobile trips the Millens took through the north-central region of the country. It was published in 1968, in London. Niedecker was sixty-five and still waiting for the publication of *T & G* (1969), the first collected edition of her poems. *My Friend Tree* had been applauded by important critics and poets such as Gilbert Sorrentino, Jonathan Williams, and Robert Creeley, but American publishers were still reluctant to take on her work because she was virtually unknown. Few readers had followed her writing over forty years, scattered as it was in the literary journals. In 1968 Niedecker was fast approaching the end of a lifetime devoted to poetry, having been heard as a persistent, honest, but minor voice.

When the collected editions of her poems were later published, however, they made clear that *North Central* represents a major development in Niedecker's art and is an important example of postmodern poetics. Still attentive to details the poems of *North Central* are forays into fields of experience. Familiar with the work of Charles Olson and Robert Duncan, Niedecker had herself felt the need to move beyond the nominalism of Imagism and Objectivism. She rarely discussed her own work theoretically but in a 1967 letter to her friend Gail Roub, she explained the new shape her work had begun to take: "Much taken up with how to define a way of writing poetry which is not Imagist nor Objectivist fundamentally nor Surrealism alone. . . . I loosely called it 'reflections' or as I think it over now, reflective, maybe. The basis is direct and clear—what has been seen or heard etc. . . .— but something gets in, overlays all that to make a state of consciousness. . . . The visual form is there in the background and the words convey what the visual form gives off after it's felt in the mind. A heat that is generated and takes in the whole world of the poem. A light, a motion, inherent in the

Gail —
I took this one early-morning hour
a couple of years ago, looking down
your way. Kind of pristine —, first
morning of creation picture — ??

No use trying to get the Kodak
studio to do the pictures non-gloss,
they won't —

Lorine

Niedecker took this photograph of the area of the Rock River where Gail Roub lives and sent it to him with this note (by permission of Cid Corman, the Estate of Lorine Niedecker; courtesy of Gail H. Roub)

whole. Not surprising since modern poetry and old poetry if it's good, proceeds not from one point to the next linearly but in a circle. The *tone* of the thing. And awareness of everything influencing everything. . . . I used to feel that I was goofing off unless I held only to the hard, clear image, the thing you could put your hand on but now I dare do this reflection."

The poems of *North Central* are "reflective," sustained acts of attention. Niedecker has allowed herself—as the responding center of the whole—into the poem to create the "whole world of the poem." She does not become subjective or impressionistic, but her own mind enters where "everything is influencing everything." The book opens with a declaration of coherence and continuity in a universe of particulars:

In every part of every living thing
is stuff that once was rock

in blood the minerals
of the rock[.]

There is a confidence here not only in nature but in man's place in it. It is a bold statement of cosmic proportions based entirely on physical actuality, on precise and verifiable data.

The form of "Lake Superior" grows out of this declaration, enabling the speaker to change a new and unfamiliar space into a familiar place. The geologic relationship frees the speaker to move around in time and space and bring more than the "thing you put your hand on" into the poem. Because of the geology of the situation, however, she can roam without leaving the realm of concrete reality, without losing touch with the earth. She brings others' experience, history, research, and personal sensation to bear on the placemaking activity of the moment, thus opening the present, extending it. By making herself the locus of experience, she makes the poem the place in which experience can be shared. There is nothing "supra-rock" or abstract in this method because the rock itself connects the speaker to the place historically, intellectually, emotionally, and ultimately physically. Being there at that moment is an immediate experience of all time:

> Greek named
> Exodus-antique
> kicked up in America's
> Northwest
> you have been in my mind
> between my toes
> agate[.]

North Central takes Niedecker beyond the single, "beautifully random instance" to areas of activity. The poem is no longer a single object, but space into which the reader may enter and reenact the movement of the poet. The open poem is one which does not develop linearly or with consistent velocity; sometimes attention is concentrated, sometimes diffuse, because the poet is a complex of responses. In *North Central* the poet is at the center looking about, moving backward and forward. The motive force is not the experience, but the human need to speak. The utterance itself generates the form.

Evolution and geology opened the world to Niedecker. She could find "Traces of Living Things" in a "Museum" or on "TV" and write poems with a "strange feeling of sequence."

Through her powers of observation, Niedecker discovered a way out of Blackhawk Island without losing ground, without disconnecting herself from nature and without sacrificing that sense of being at home in the world which she had nurtured on Blackhawk Island. At the close of "Lake Superior" she asks with ease, "Why should we hurry home?"

Human being remained Niedecker's ultimate concern, but evolution and geological time provided a perspective in which to re-examine the "human bean." Part marvel, man is also "part coral/ and mud/clam." "We are what the seas/have made us," and knowing this Niedecker could laugh at us and chide us. In terms of geologic time we are babies, unexpected ones at that:

> Human bean
> and love-over-the-fence
>
> just up
> from swamp trouble[.]

The immensity of eons and the magnitude of universal procreation shrink man to more fitting proportions. While this perspective may make his achievements seem inconsequential, it soothes the sting of his failures. We are "just up/from swamp trouble" and soon to "sink to water Death." In between is the space of a lifetime, time enough to "Smile/to see the lake" and to glory, as Walt Whitman did, in the "procreant urge" of even the dragonfly "out for an easy/make." Because we can participate, smile, and share the knowledge, we are human; in "that hard/contact—" is something durable as "Stone."

The final poem of the volume, "Wintergreen Ridge," is one of Niedecker's finest. It is a long poem informed by her rediscovery of the ever-changing but ever creative universe:

> Life is natural
>   in the evolution
>   of matter[.]

Coming into life is a natural movement within an unceasing process of change. Change implies death but ultimately means "continuous life." The poem, a climb to the "flowering ridge," confronts the problem of art such a realization suggests:

> Man
>   lives hard
>   on this stone perch
>
> by sea

imagines
    durable works[.]

The climb itself structures the poem; when the speaker reaches the ridge, she can announce: "and here it is." Following the "signs," the poet weaves a place out of landscape, memory, and present reality for her own "creation/here as in the center of the world." Reaching "Wintergreen Ridge," the poet discovers "the grass of parnassus" grows there.

Shortly after the publication of *North Central,* Niedecker welcomed the publication of *T & G: The Collected Poems (1936-1966)* (1969). It had indeed taken "a lifetime/to weep/a deep/trickle." She borrowed the title for *T & G* from Lawrence Durrell's "Tenderness and Gristle," and her publisher, Jonathan Williams, added "Tongue and Groove (if you're a carpenter)." Both gloss the accomplishment of this collection of moments of tenderness and irreducible pain. In it a world is examined with a tough compassion. The joinery makes for solid construction, the kind of stance that keeps one standing, overwhelmed by neither sentiment nor pain.

T & G exhibits the wit and clarity that typifies Niedecker's vision. Her exacting eye and ear can perceive "spring-marsh frog-clatter peace" as it "breaks out." However, *T & G* is more than a collection of discreet acts of attention; the "beautifully random instances" combine to create a record of thirty years of attention.

The poems are not arranged chronologically, but the first of the six sections in the volume includes poems from her first two books. Section two addresses Louis Zukofsky's son Paul, then a child and a musical prodigy for whom Niedecker had great affection. She speaks from experience, knowing "Not all that's heard is music," and offers the wisdom earned from seeing "the little/thin things." As the third section opens with a nod to Henry James in "HJ," Niedecker knows that the examined life is the only consolation for growing up. "Consciousness is illimitable/too good to forsake/tho what we feel be misery/and we know will break." Consciousness is the mark of being adult, and it is inescapable. Trusting her own powers of observation and the communality of language, she used herself as the measure of being alive and believed her experience could be shared.

She was able to share it by speaking precisely and concisely. Under compression, her words have power. In just ten words, for instance, she images the ecological process of nature, transforms its hor-

ror into splendor, and establishes the necessity of both:

Something in the water
like a flower
will devour

water

flower[.]

Not all the poems are short, but all are tightly made. Rhyme and cadence depend upon the sight, sound, sense, and even absence of words, and the poems create a sphere of meaning in which the words, each of consequence, reflect each other and reverberate. As the poems proceed from beginning to end, the word particles dance within like rays from a Drummond light. Sounds create aural and intellectual echoes, as for example, "brotherhood/ Resolved . . ." becomes "dissolved enmity." Punning creates humor and unsettles habitual associations to extend meaning. Word play, such as "you cross your Leggs/while sitting," adds scope as, in this example, it brings the present into a poem containing a message from John Adams to his future wife, Abigail Smith. Niedecker's ability to make the sound of the word tell the meaning makes the poems a sensory experience, and the use of spaces between words and lines adds meaning without adding words.

Such condensation demands unshakable honesty. Sadly, that honesty is sometimes the only comfort in the face of personal failure and tragedy. Clarity often reveals loneliness as in "his clear No marriage/no marriage/friend," missed opportunities, and "vacancy." But Niedecker does not become, as Michael Heller says, the "poet-victim of her condition . . ." because such clarity of expression has value.

In the twentieth century many writers have feared that language can no longer operate humanely. Yet Niedecker knew that it was not the language that had betrayed us but people who divert it from its role as communication. It is "the folk from whom all poetry flows/and dreadfully much else." In the section "In Exchange for Haiku" Niedecker responded to the haiku she cherished with her own compressed forms. In these poems, so precisely made, her faith in language matches Emerson's. In "Hear/where her snow-grave is/the *You/ah You*/of mourning doves" Niedecker's language is immaculate. We are asked to listen. If we do, the sound we will "Hear," in this place of

Three drafts for "Bird Singing" that Niedecker sent to Gail Roub (by permission of Cid Corman, the Estate of Lorine Niedecker; courtesy of Gail H. Roub) "mourning," lets morning break into the site of death. Death and rebirth are facts of nature revealed in the language. Niedecker makes words, as Emerson says in "Nature," the "sign of natural facts."

However, unlike Emerson, Niedecker had no faith that such facts lead heavenward or to spiritual knowledge. For Niedecker the correspondence between words and things rested on the solidity of both. The "hard clear image" was difficult enough because the world keeps moving. Words had to stay concrete, for she had only language "to get a load/ of April's fabulous/frog rattle" as it moves off the page and nearly out of sight "like freight cars/in the night." Only by concision could such realities be shared. It is difficult, unremitting work, but despite the loneliness of it, Niedecker knew it was secure:

> No layoff
>   from this
>   condensery.

My Life by Water (1970) is Niedecker's second collected poems; she died shortly after it was published. The fact of it pleased her; after forty years of virtual obscurity, she had three books published in two years. Originally planned as a London edition of *T & G*, *My Life by Water* added the poems in *North Central* and a few previously uncollected poems. The title poem, originally published in *North Central*, as well as a new, long poem, "Paean to Place," form a preface to the whole. *My Life by Water* is not a complete collection of Niedecker's poems, but it does include the poetry written between 1936 and 1968 which she most prized. The title poem reminds readers that her life was attuned to the occasions when "silence/. . . if intense/makes sound." The poem invites the reader to "hear" for himself a life of "wild green/arts and letters." The cascading rhythm of the poem moves the reader "to [her] shore" on lines that move like "birdstart/ wingdrip/weed-drift/of the soft/and serious— Water."

"Paean to Place" is a poem hard won "From the secret notes/I must tilt/upon the pressure/execute and adjust." With birdlike alertness, this "solitary plover" has spent a lifetime dedicated to condensery, of having to "Throw *things* to the flood." Alone, she immerses herself in the "stream/ [of] moonnight memory/washed of hardships." Of this poem she wrote a friend that it's a "longish poem which is kind of In Memoriam of my father and mother and the place I've never seemed to really get away from." She moves through a stream of memories beginning at the source of all life: "And the place/was water." It is a personal poem, in which the present is flooded with memories of the past. She recalls her parents, their unhappy lives, her own childhood, choices and necessities. She "maneuvers barges/through the mouth" as she "rides the sloughs and sluices/of [her] mind" finally to emerge "with the persons/on the edge." It is a precarious, difficult, but perfect balance.

Niedecker was preparing the still-unpublished "Harpsichord & Salt Fish" when she died on the last day of 1970. It was months before most of her literary friends heard of her death. Her neighbors in Fort Atkinson were surprised to learn she had been a poet. Few even knew who she was. Thanks to the efforts of Cid Corman, *Blue Chicory* was published in 1976. It contains the final poems that Niedecker had intended for publication as well as some poems the poet abandoned but which, to Corman, seemed "to warrant safer keeping here." Interest in Niedecker's work had been increasing; *Epitaphs for Lorine* and the *Truck* magazine's memorial issue in 1975 kept her name and her work current. Coming six years after her death, *Blue Chicory* reminded readers of Niedecker's perennial gift.

She had written Corman early in 1970 that for the first time in her life she had felt "an undercurrent of hurry"; her letters grew more and more concerned with publishing her work. While not necessarily intentional, the voice and atmosphere of *Blue Chicory* seem infused with a premonition of death. Certainly many of the poems confront the possibility. There is a tone of quiet wondering, not in anxious doubt but nonetheless uncertainty:

> You see here
> the inference
> of influence
>
> Moon on rippled
> stream
>
> "Except as
> and unless"[.]

What "inference" may be made at the close of a life devoted to "the hard clear image" is finally drawn from what is seen of beginnings: "And when an old boat rots ashore/itself once living plant/it sprouts." Placed on the page so the last line "sprouts," the poem invites questions about one's own death: What does one leave or leaf into? Despite talk of obliteration, however, "fruit flies rise/ from the rind. . . ." Ready to confront images of rot and decay, finding renewed life in even these, Niedecker is searching for the "oak leaves' law."

The sequences "His Carpets Flowered/William Morris," "Darwin," and "Thomas Jefferson" have the organic form she sought. They cull moments from the life and letters of these men to make them stand forth. It was not their public lives she cared about but the language that revealed them to others and herself in unexpected ways. Of William Morris she wrote Corman, "I can't read his poetry. I'd probably weary of his flowery designs in carpets, wall papers, chintzes . . . but as a man, as a poet, speaking to his daughter and his wife— o lovely." Somewhat like herself, Charles Darwin was a man "wholly, slowly," tracking man, finding him "in the same predicament/with other animals." Thomas Jefferson was the man "waiting for a quorum," the man who "rode horse . . ./to an enchanting philosophy," and faced, as Niedecker herself did, "the drift and suck/and die-down of life."

These sequences are Niedecker's most complex forms, but they operate much as the short poems do. Each of the poems within a sequence, like the particular words within a single poem, influences the others; together the poems manifest the whole. Each of the poems in a sequence is itself a complete poem, in which the same organic principles of form operate. Form grows out of "oak leaves' law" to express what the poet needs to say; with no predetermined line of development, what is said shapes itself in the saying.

Nonlinear forms have discernible movements, however. The sequence grows as one poem contains the germ of another. In "Darwin," for instance, the second poem is a demonstration of the first while it is also a move beyond it. The line break in "I'm ravenous for/the sound of the pianoforte" focuses on the appetite which places Darwin "in the same predicament/with other animals" and in doing so, reflects the previous poem. But the space between the lines also creates a space between man and other animals because his hunger is for music, civilization.

A continuous alternation between open and closed, between beginnings and endings, is implicit in the sequential poem, and the form thus answers questions of "inference" underlying many of the poems in Blue Chicory. Jefferson "imagined durable works," but in the natural course of things "soon must Monticello be lost/to debt/and Jefferson/to death." The final poem of the sequence opens with

"Mind leaving body, let body leave," but the single poem, the sequence and Jefferson's life close with the possibility of new growth, "and the seeds of the senega root." Remaining open, poetry, like human life, "is natural/in the evolution of matter."

Since the publication of Blue Chicory, Niedecker's work has continued to reach readers largely through the efforts of Cid Corman. The July 1981 issue of Origin featured Niedecker, presenting a few previously unpublished poems as well as some poems long out of print. On the other side of the Atlantic, interest in Niedecker's work also continues; Interim Press published "The Full Note" (1983), a volume of essays devoted to Niedecker's work. Her poetry continues to resist the anonymity and isolation of the poet's own life. In 1985 North Point Press published The Granite Pail: The Selected Poems of Lorine Niedecker and the Jargon Society published From This Condensery: The Complete Writing of Lorine Niedecker. Thomas Meyer says of Niedecker that "in a lifetime she exercised little direct influence upon her generation, or the next, making almost no disciples, yet producing work which, it is already clear, exerts a masterly influence."

Lorine Niedecker did not cut a large figure in American letters, but her place is secure. In 1970 she was nominated for the annual Council for Wisconsin Writers Award, and in 1978 she won the Notable Wisconsin Writers Award. She was far enough from literary fashions to write independently and well-read enough to learn from Bashō, Pound, Williams, and Zukofsky. Her talent and her example as a dedicated poet make her as important to American literature as Emily Dickinson. Just as it was for Dickinson, poetry was Niedecker's "letter to the World/That never wrote to [her]." From her isolation, each sent "The simple news that Nature told—," and both gave back to language the force of our human need to broach the silence. Niedecker labored to make the American language speak plainly and powerfully, to register "this modernized method of talk" and have it tell timeless truths. As long as her poetry remains available, it will draw readers, for ultimately, Niedecker's achievement rests on the clarity and precision with which she could communicate what it was like to be alive. Readers may come to her poems knowing little of the poet; they will leave them knowing more about themselves.

Letters:
"Selected Letters of Lorine Niedecker to Cid Corman," edited by Lisa Pater Faranda, *Conjunctions,* no. 5 (Fall 1983);

Between Your House and Mine: The Letters of Lorine Niedecker to Cid Corman, 1960-1970, edited by Faranda (Durham: Duke University Press, 1986).

References:

Jane Augustine, "A Woman Poet, Specifically," *Truck,* no. 16 (Summer 1975): 116-119;

Robert J. Bertholf, "The Solitary Plover," *Truck,* no. 16 (Summer 1975): 101-109;

Laura Chester, "Wash," *Truck,* no. 16 (Summer 1975): 154-157;

William Corbett, "For L. N.," *Truck,* no. 16 (Summer 1975): 153;

Corbett, "12 February," *Truck,* no. 16 (Summer 1975): 152;

Cid Corman, "With Lorine," *Truck,* no. 16 (Summer 1975): 57-90;

Kenneth Cox, "The Poems of Lorine Niedecker," *Truck,* no. 16 (Summer 1975): 94-100;

Donald Davie, "Lyric Minimum and Epic Scope," *PN Review,* no. 25 (Winter 1981): 31-33;

Alan Davies, "A Pencil for a Wing Bone," *Truck,* no. 16 (Summer 1975): 128-130;

Peter Dent, ed., *The Full Note: Lorine Niedecker* (Devon, U.K.: Interim Press, 1983);

Frederick Eckman, "Lorine Niedecker's Local," *Truck,* no. 16 (Summer 1975): 110-115;

Morgan Gibson, "Lorine Niedecker, Alive and Well," *Truck,* no. 16 (Summer 1975): 120-124;

Norman Granlund, "Birdwatcher," *Truck,* no. 16 (Summer 1975): 148;

Granlund, "Her Indifference to Our Words," *Truck,* no. 16 (Summer 1975): 147;

Michael Heller, "I've Seen It There," *Truck,* no. 16 (Summer 1975): 131-135;

Jane Knox, "Lorine," *Origin,* fourth series no. 16 (July 1981): 3-23;

Daphne Marlatt, "My Life By Water," *Truck,* no. 16 (Summer 1975): 125-127;

Thomas Meyer, "Chapter's Partner," *Parnassus,* 5 (Spring/Summer 1977): 84-91;

Bob Nero, "Remembering Lorine," *Truck,* no. 16 (Summer 1975): 136-140;

Jenny Penberthy, "Poems from Letters: The Lorine Niedecker-Louis Zukofsky Correspondence," *Line,* no. 6 (Fall 1985): 3-20;

Juanita H. Schreiner, "Lorine Niedecker: Reminiscences by a friend and former classmate," *Origin,* fourth series no. 16 (July 1981): 24-25;

Gilbert Sorrentino, Review of *Blue Chicory, New York Times Book Review,* 13 February 1977, p. 27;

James Stephens, "Progression," *Truck,* no. 16 (Summer 1975): 149-150;

Charles Tomlinson, "A Rich Sitter: The Poetry of Lorine Niedecker," *Agenda,* 7 (Spring 1969): 65-67;

David Wilk, "A/Round for Lorine," *Truck,* no. 16 (Summer 1975): 164-169;

Jonathan Williams, "An Epitaph for Lorine," *Truck,* no. 16 (Summer 1975): back cover;

Williams, "Letter to The New York Times," *Truck,* no. 16 (Summer 1975): 141;

Williams, "Think What's Got Away in My Life," *Truck,* no. 16 (Summer 1975): 91-93;

Williams, ed., *Epitaphs For Lorine* (Penland, N.C.: Jargon Society, 1973);

Geoff Young, "Seven Up," *Truck,* no. 16 (Summer 1975): 159-163.

Papers:

Niedecker's letters to Cid Corman are in the Berg Collection at the New York Public Library; the manuscripts for the unpublished collection "Harpsichord & Salt Fish" are in the Mugar Memorial Library at Boston University; the correspondence between Niedecker and Zukofsky and miscellaneous materials are at the Humanities Research Center of the University of Texas at Austin.

Elder Olson
(9 March 1909-   )

Thomas E. Lucas
Seton Hall University

BOOKS: *Thing of Sorrow* (New York: Macmillan, 1934);

The Cock of Heaven (New York: Macmillan, 1940);

The Poetry of Dylan Thomas (Chicago: University of Chicago Press, 1954);

The Scarecrow Christ and Other Poems (New York: Noonday Press, 1954);

Plays & Poems, 1948-58 (Chicago: University of Chicago Press, 1958);

Tragedy and the Theory of Drama (Detroit: Wayne State University Press, 1961);

Collected Poems (Chicago: University of Chicago Press, 1963);

The Theory of Comedy (Bloomington: Indiana University Press, 1968);

Olson's Penny Arcade (Chicago: University of Chicago Press, 1975);

On Value Judgments in the Arts, and Other Essays (Chicago: University of Chicago Press, 1976);

Last Poems (Chicago: University of Chicago Press, 1984).

Elder Olson

OTHER: "The Poetic Method of Aristotle: Its Powers and Limitations," in *English Institute Essays* (New York: Columbia University Press, 1951), pp. 70-94;

R. S. Crane, ed., *Critics and Criticism, Ancient and Modern*, includes contributions by Olson (Chicago: University of Chicago Press, 1952);

Aristotle's Poetics and English Literature: A Collection of Critical Essays, edited by Olson (Chicago: University of Chicago Press, 1965).

PERIODICAL PUBLICATIONS: "Rhetoric and the Appreciation of Pope," *Modern Philology*, 37 (August 1939): 13-35;

"Sailing to Byzantium: Prologomena to a Poetics of the Lyric," *University Review*, 8 (Spring 1942): 209-219;

"Recent Literary Criticism," *Modern Philology*, 40 (February 1943): 275-283;

"Is Theory Possible?," *Poetry*, 71 (February 1948): 257-259;

"A Symbolic Reading of the 'Ancient Mariner,'" *Modern Philology*, 45 (November 1948): 275-283;

"Education and the Humanities," *Pedagogia*, 1 (1953): 85-95;

"Louise Bogan and Léonie Adams," *Chicago Review*, 8 (Fall 1954): 70-87;

"The Poetry of Wallace Stevens," *College English*, 16 (April 1955): 395-402;

"The Poetry of Marianne Moore," *Chicago Review*, 11 (Spring 1957): 100-104;

"The Dialectical Foundations of Critical Pluralism," *Texas Quarterly*, 9 (Spring 1966): 202-230.

Elder Olson has been a published and widely recognized poet from his nineteenth year. He continues, after more than fifty years, to publish poems regularly in the *New Yorker, Virginia Quarterly Review, Chicago Review, Poetry: A Magazine of Verse*, and elsewhere. The senior member of the Chicago Critics, Olson has, from the beginning, been one of its leading apologists and practitioners; his theories inform his poetry and control it.

Elder Olson and the other Chicagoans—who include R. S. Crane, W. R. Keast, Richard McKeon, Norman Maclean, Bernard Weinberg, and Wayne Booth—are pluralists; they believe that all validly argued philosophies are complementary, and that literary theory is a branch of philosophy, which is, either explicitly or implicitly, part of a whole system of thought. Yet the major thrust of Olson's theorizing has been Aristotelian, with its emphasis on plot (or on its analogues in works too short for full plots), character, and thought, and on the ways in which these elements combine (through words) with form. Olson's work on Aristotle is impressive, but most important is his clarification of the idea that *plot* (in Aristotle's terms, "the human activity *imitated* in the poem") is not only central to *form* and therefore controlling, but that it is of a recognizable *moral* quality, degree of *seriousness*. Aristotle thought that human happiness depends on our ability to develop and use our *essential* capacity for rational activity; he identified happiness with the highest kind of virtuous actions. Hence, in poetry (as in life) actions (action implies choice and choice makes character possible) which conduce to happiness or to its loss are the most moving and serious. These principles are embodied in Olson's poems, among which are some of the most beautiful and serious traditional and formal lyrics of this century.

The son of Elder James and Hilda Schroeder Olson, Elder James Olson was born on 9 March 1909 in Chicago, Illinois. In 1927, when he was eighteen years old, he received the Witter Bynner Award, and in 1928 he published for the first time in Harriet Monroe's *Poetry: A Magazine of Verse*. He continued his association with *Poetry* over the next few years, receiving the magazine's Guarantor's Award in 1931. At some time during these years he had the ambition to be a concert pianist—an experience which played no small part in his grasp of metrics and his ear for poetic quantity. Yet his early poems are notable more for the promise they offer for his later work than for their actual accomplishment. In 1934, the year he received his B.A. from the University of Chicago, he published his first collection of poems, *Thing of Sorrow*. It was both a critical and an artistic success. The reviews were positive. William Rose Benét remarked on "the distinguished beauty of its writing" and said that Olson "awakens new hope for American poetry."

In these poems there are two distinct voices. One of them belongs to a young man, who, like most young men, has experienced the sweet despair of losing an early love, which, he realizes, was

an ideal incompatible with reality. The speaker in poems such as "The Strange Summer" is admirable not only for his ability to convey "the way love was" but also to refrain from becoming maudlin:

> He who is loved no longer
>
> And loves still beyond reason
> Is like one who would constrain summer
> Past summer's season.
> . . . .
> He goes distraught through the stark wood.
> It is summer, he cries. No cry avails him.
> In frenzy he puts back dead leaves to their branches
> Till the cold fells him.

The second voice, also clearly that of a young man because of its intensity, is philosophical. This young man speaks of such concepts as pantheism ("Essay on Deity"), idealism ("To Man"), the relationship of body and soul ("MS. Unearthed at Delos"), the nature of time ("Calendar"), and other such concerns. The second speaker earns esteem because he treats ideas of universal interest and importance and because he provides the right images in his treatment to convey them with vividness and power. In a 20 May 1982 letter Olson said of himself, "If I am any sort of poet—enough of one, at least, to be classified—I am a dramatic lyrist." Indeed, from this first book on, Olson has continued to use, as masks for his soon-mature young man, a number of voices and personalities who convey their feelings and ideas with increasing power and clarity in more and more brilliant images and innovative metrical patterns. "Calendar," which might be called an imagistic lyric of ideas, chronicles the changing seasons through a series of descriptions, ending as it begins in winter:

> At year's end, winter: the burning emblems
> Beyond the wind, bright snow in the lit
> Branches, the dumb sightless
> Moon wandering above the rim of the dead planet;
> They knew they would wake one day and the year be
>   gone.

As in "The Tale"—where "We pursued/Down immaterial/Autumn and ghostly spring/Time's wraith, the phantom year . . ."—the speaker in "Calendar," who reserves his comments on what he has observed until the last line, makes it clear that however evanescent the seasons and however partial one's observation of them, they are what create man's awareness of time's passage. The poignancy and nostalgia of the poem result equally from the concepts it treats, and from the beauty of the seasons, which revolve so rapidly and so few times in an individual life.

Thing of Sorrow won the Friends of Literature Award for 1935, the year in which Olson received his M.A. from Chicago and became an instructor in English at the Armour Institute of Technology in Chicago, where he stayed until 1942. During the next three years he worked toward his Ph.D., writing his dissertation "General Prosody, Rhythmic, Metric, Harmonic." He received his doctorate in 1938. On 13 February 1937 he married Ann Elizabeth Jones; the couple would have a daughter, Ann, and a son, Elder, before their divorce in 1948. In 1940 he published a long poem, *The Cock of Heaven*, which received generally negative reviews, especially in *Time* magazine. The poem's faults include the grandness of its concepts which are too elaborate and too ambitious. Olson prefaced the poem with this note: "*The Cock of Heaven* is a poem in the form of a commentary on a text. The text itself might be called an epitome of human history; consequently the commentary has the character of an historical summation." The text referred to identifies the cock which crowed when Peter denied Christ with the one which announced the birth of Christ from the dish of Herod and both of them with the angel Gabriel, who sat in the forbidden tree in Eden to warn Adam and Eve and who will announce the end of the world. Furthermore, says the text, the cock will crow in a time of great persecution of the Jews and of internecine wars (World War II and the Nazi persecution of the Jews were both realities when the poem was published) when the Devil becomes so sickened with the world's filth that he surrenders and when Judas, through complete repentance, has become as sanctified as Christ.

At that time too Ahasuerus, the wandering Jew, will return home; and the Magi, whose presence in the world saved it from the wrath of God, will die. For neither the seven Messiahs, who were sent into the world to combat the seven deadly sins, nor Christ, who was said to have cast out all seven, have been successful. The seven deadly sins still dominate the world. Man, consequently, is clearly damned. The sign of his damnation is the fact that the tree of Eden was cut down and made into the cross of Christ, and that the site of Eden became Calvary. Furthermore, all man's sins spring from his mortality; and the eating of the forbidden fruit is only a parable of "some question concerning death that could not be asked of God which man yet asked, and all our anguish is the answer." Finally, the only salvation lies in God's being born into the world, but even that event will make it only worthy of destruction.

Olson still considers the poem an artistic success; yet, while many of the individual lyrics which make up the long poem are beautiful, its premises, in William James's phrase, do not seem to create "a living hypothesis."

As Olson observed in his prefatory note to *Last Poems* (1984), he is a slow writer, and his next book of poetry, *The Scarecrow Christ*, would not appear until 1954. In 1942 he was appointed assistant professor of English at the University of Chicago, where he would stay until his retirement in 1977, becoming an associate professor in 1948, when he was Rockefeller professor at the University of Frankfurt, Germany. The year 1948, too, saw his divorce from Ann and his marriage, on 17 September, to Geraldine Hays (they would have two daughters, Inez Olivia and Shelley). During these years Olson was, in addition to producing poetry, steadily building his reputation as a scholar and critic, with essays on Pope, Yeats, Coleridge, and critical and literary theory. In 1952 he was a contributor to R. S. Crane's important anthology *Critics and Criticism*, and in 1953, the year he won the Eunice Tietjens Memorial Award, he became a full professor at Chicago, a position he would hold until 1971, when he became distinguished service professor. His book *The Poetry of Dylan Thomas* (1954) won the Poetry Society of America Chap-Book Award for a notable work dealing with poetry in 1955—the second edition of the book appearing in 1961.

Louise Bogan remarked of *The Scarecrow Christ* (1954) that Olson's "skill with strict and formal lyrics is marked and his diction and imagery are often startlingly precise." Separated from *The Cock of Heaven* by fourteen years, this—Olson's third book of poetry—contains twenty-three new poems, each an imagistic lyric of ideas, each notable for its powerful imagery. As Bogan observed in her *New Yorker* review, Olson has avoided many of the current literary trends in favor of traditional poetic concerns. The voices in this volume are more mature versions of those in *Thing of Sorrow*. While in some poems the emphasis is on the mood to be evoked and in others on the concepts which inform it, there are others, such as "Crucifix," in which the emphasis is almost equally divided between mood and concept.

"Crucifix" re-creates the horrors of the actual crucifixion to illustrate how mortals can have no idea of what it meant for an Infinite God to die as a human being. The poem's speaker, reminded of the actual crucifixion by the sight of a silver crucifix, asks the reader to

> think of the actual scene
> Friday, Friday the thirteenth, as some think
> Hot and bright at first, but gradually darkening
>   and chilling;

he describes through graphic images the nailing of Christ to the cross and

> The head, turning slowly from side to side,
> As always with the pinned or the empaled.
> The eyes already rapt with suffering,
> The hands nailed like frogs to the rough cross-timber,
> The feet spiked to the foot-block, amid cries and
>   murmurs
> The cross raised[.]

The line breaks to intensify the emotion. After a moving tale of the solitude of the cross and of the slowness and pain of Christ's death, the speaker tells the reader to consider the unguessable quality of Christ's suffering, for

> it is not
> Preeminence in pain that makes the Christ
> (For the thieves as well were crucified)
> No, but the Godhead; the untouchable unguessable
>   unsuffering
> Immortality beyond mortality,
> Which feigns our mortality as this silver feigns it,
> And of which we are ignorant as that multitude;
> For the pain comes from the humanity; the pain we
>   know;
> The agony we comprehend; of the rest, know
>   nothing.

Olson's next book, *Plays & Poems, 1948-58* (1958), includes his macabre play *The Carnival of Animals*, which in 1957 had won a joint award of the Academy of American Poets and Columbia Broadcasting System. Olson was, when the book appeared, visiting professor of literary criticism at Indiana University; that year, too, he gave the series of lectures at Wayne State University in Detroit that would be published, in 1961, as *Tragedy and the Theory of Drama*. During these years Olson began the pattern of traveling which would continue through the rest of his career, visiting Puerto Rico during the 1950s and 1960s, serving as Mahlon Powell Professor of Philosophy at Indiana University in 1955, and taking up a Rockefeller visiting professorship at the University of the Philippines in 1966-1967—a stay which ended with a Univer-

sity of the Philippines distinguished service award in 1967.

Plays & Poems, 1948-58 contains nineteen new lyrics which, along with the plays, were well received. James Dickey wondered why Olson's poetry "is not better known" and concluded that he "must leave Olson's relative neglect a mystery, trusting I have done what I could to rectify what seems to me a really shameful situation and hoping to enlist the aid of Time." The poems blend thought and feeling, as well as, or better than, ever before. One of his best poems, "The Last Entries in the Journal," in keeping with its title, is not a continuous argument; however, it is unified by a thread of hope, albeit a tenuous one, spun by a mind which knows the worst. The tone of the individual "entries" ranges from reasoned, to passionate, to wonderstruck. The optimism of these calm and rich lines is hard-earned:

> Problem: to hear the battering storm as music,
> But never, drunk with harmony, be deaf
> To all the dissonances compounding harmony.
> ....
>   Discord is meaningless
> Except as establishing the principle
> Of harmonies to be. Pain too, is meaningless
> ....
> Save as preluding peace, and suffering
> Itself ennobles no one; it degrades,
> Unless it is resolved at last to joy.

At other moments the thought and feeling are much more intense, some "entries" forming a progression from self-reproach to a bitter resolution, or from tormented disillusion to almost sardonic resignation. One such sequence runs from "Am I for this, then? To count the seasons out?," bitterly recognizing "that history of torment" and "Soul's-rape of birth,/Agony and shame of growth," culminating, with the sense of shipwreck, that we must take life as we find it:

> Peace, poor soul, peace, peace, for God's sake, peace;
> This is your world, and you were made for it;
> Why should the dung-beetle quarrel with the dung?

The final "entry" is one of the most perfect of Olson's lyrics, its remarkable insight conveyed with a brilliance of images compounded of starlight on snow. A grand and essentially abstract idea, evoking both surprise and wonder, is precisely rendered:

> Arise and look, the dream said; it is there.

And dreaming still, he rose and went outdoors.
All the air glistened with stars and snow.

The farthest star shot down a ray and struck
The nearest snow-flake, that itself a star.
And at its center kindled a new star
That lived just long enough to flash one ray
Back to the farthest star. There you have it.
Things with no connection, the immense, the minute,
The most perduring, the most transitory,
Somehow connected, across unimaginable gulfs.

Collected Poems (1963) includes nineteen new poems. These poems are more various and more experimental than the earlier ones; and, while none is so powerful as some of the more intense pieces in *The Scarecrow Christ*, or in *Plays & Poems*, they have a freshness which is exciting. It is not so much, in many cases, that the situations are fresh, but that the treatment brings them to life. In "Plaza Mexico" and "Taxco" for example, Olson has achieved better than anywhere else a goal he set for himself in the prologue to his first book of poems:

To speak, to say
With speech. This way,
See, see. It was this way.

The two poems are successful in conveying the sights, sounds, smells, and texture of Mexico, the tastes of its foods—and, as always with Olson, the transformation of rich sensory experience into insight. The authenticity of the imagery is startling.

"Taxco" details so many particulars in which essential aspects of Mexico are implicit that it has the vitality of a live experience, capturing as it does the contrasts and strange juxtapositions which characterize Mexico. Similarly, "Plaza Mexico" recreates the bull fight and penetrates to its central attraction. The poem moves from the antiquity, grace, and whimsicality of the spectacle, its gaudy fancy dress and ritual, to a portrait of the bull and its death:

The bull
Broods in his raying spears;
Tail up, charges; charges once again;
Ponders, at last in doubt;
Then, the sword-hilt plain
Amid the barbs, the blood,
Turns away, moves to the barriers;
There
Beds down; at the knife-blow rolls
Over, legs in air.
The mules jingle in and jingle out
And the crowd stirs, suddenly

Relieved that, after all,
It has not seen what it half hoped to see.

Collected Poems is a diverse and varied book both in matter and manner, and its publication led to a number of assessments of Olson's career to date. M. L. Rosenthal suggested, in the *New York Times Book Review*, that the poems range from "exquisitely sculptured, intense" work to the "robust." Olson's poems, he concluded, taken together, "are not quite a continuum, not quite in concentrated focus." Taken one at a time, however, they "yield not only hard gems but plain human revelations." Gilbert Sorrentino, in *Book Week*, found some poems "hopelessly marred by archaic syntax and verbiage," but confessed that he found Olson's "moods and interests . . . varied and rich, and his intelligence is remarkable." George Garnett of the *Virginia Quarterly Review* called the body of work a "considerable achievement" and Olson "a true poet." The poems in the book range from lyric to dialogue and drama; from satire to comedy; from portrayals of man as surpassing nature in his indifference and brutality, to meditations on the continuity of grief from age to age; from wry self-assessment to the unreality of dream.

The years following 1963 saw Olson visiting other universities in the United States and overseas. The year 1964 saw the publication of his anthology *American Lyric Poems: from Colonial Times to the Present*, in the preface to which he considered the relationship between the poet's own life and the poem itself. "The lyric voices the poet's innermost feelings?," he asked. "Precisely how do we know that? This is a historical proposition which in many thousands of instances—such as those of anonymous poems—we cannot possibly verify; what is more, it is frequently controverted in cases where we do not know the feelings of the poet. We can and do enjoy lyrics, moreover, without knowing anything about the poet."

This view accounts, in part, for the dramatic quality of Olson's poems, and for their apparent impersonality. As he himself said in the preface to his next book of verse, *Olson's Penny Arcade* (1975), "If these poems range from jocosity to fury and near-suicidal despair, that is because they reflect the kind of person I happen to be and the world we live in." The book contains a verse play and poems, including seventeen lyrics never before collected; like the earlier work they are notable for their virtuosity of imagery and versification and for the depth of their insights and feelings. *Olson's Penny Arcade* was well received, James Dickey praising it warmly. Paul Ramsey in the *Sewanee Review* called it "a fine book, not with the fineness of gossamer, or sighs, but of irony, of steel, of the true scholar's eyes focussing on the page. It is a privilege to be in the presence of so much intelligence, integrity, and fully controlled poetic skill." Like the earlier poems, these exhibit a considerable range of skill, feeling, insight, and form, as well as subject matter, from the evocation of place (as in "On Re-Reading H. M. Tomlinson's *The Sea and the Jungle*") to a sense of the fragility of man's hold on the world (in "A Restaurant in South East Asia") to a meditation (in "Reflections on Mirrors") on the mind which makes mirrors possible and perhaps shares its qualities. Characteristically, this is a slim but varied and accomplished book.

In 1975 when *Olson's Penny Arcade* appeared, its publisher, the University of Chicago Press, reprinted Olson's *Plays & Poems 1948-58*. In 1976 Olson received the Society of Midland Authors Award and the next year, aged sixty-eight, he retired from Chicago as distinguished service professor and became professor emeritus. He continued to write and to teach, spending 1978-1979 as M. D. Anderson Distinguished Professor

at the University of Houston, and in 1982 becoming visiting professor at the University of New Mexico. In 1984 he published *Last Poems,* explaining that "I have called this volume *Last Poems,* not because I think I shall write no more, but because—considering my rate of production—I think it unlikely that I shall make another collection." The poems are the fruit of nine years' work, and are, as before, notable for their formal versatility: lyric, meditation, aphorism, epigram.

Olson is a careful, scrupulous, and perhaps unfashionably meticulous poet whose work seems largely underestimated. His reputation as a scholar and teacher, certainly, overshadows his reputation as poet, perhaps because he refuses to advertise his own work. As Nicholas Joost wrote in the *Chicago Tribune,* "Olson is one of those American poets who never receives publicity and the adulation awarded to flashier talents among us. But his kind of poet keeps doggedly on, developing what he has to say until we recognize it immediately as the expression of a real person and not a literary fashion." The estimate is just, as is its conviction that Olson is a true—and neglected—poet.

Kenneth Patchen
(13 December 1911-8 January 1972)

Larry R. Smith
Firelands College, Bowling Green State University

See also the Patchen entry in *DLB 16, The Beats: Literary Bohemians in Postwar America.*

BOOKS: *Before the Brave* (New York: Random House, 1936);
First Will & Testament (Norfolk, Conn.: New Directions, 1939);
The Journal of Albion Moonlight (Mount Vernon, N.Y.: Kenneth Patchen, 1941);
The Dark Kingdom (New York: Harriss & Givens, 1942);
The Teeth of the Lion (Norfolk, Conn.: New Directions, 1942);
Cloth of the Tempest (New York: Harper, 1943; enlarged edition, New York: Padell, 1948);
The Memoirs of a Shy Pornographer (New York: New

Directions, 1945; London: Grey Walls, 1948);
An Astonished Eye Looks Out of the Air (Waldport, Oreg.: Untide Press, 1945);
Outlaw of the Lowest Planet, selected by David Gascoyne (London: Grey Walls, 1946);
Panels for the Walls of Heaven (Berkeley, Cal.: B. Porter, 1946);
The Selected Poems of Kenneth Patchen (Norfolk, Conn.: New Directions, 1946; enlarged, 1958);
Sleepers Awake (New York: Padell, 1946);
Pictures of Life and Death (New York: Padell, 1947);
They Keep Riding Down All the Time (New York: Padell, 1947);
See You in the Morning (New York: Padell, 1948; London: Grey Walls, 1949);

Kenneth Patchen, San Francisco, 1957 (photograph by Arthur Knight)

CCCLXXIV Poems (New York: Padell, 1948);

To Say If You Love Someone and Other Selected Love Poems (Prairie City, Ill.: Press of J. Decker, 1948);

Red Wine and Yellow Hair (New York: New Directions, 1949);

Orchards, Thrones & Caravans (San Francisco: Print Workshop, 1952);

Fables and Other Little Tales (Karlsruhe/Baden: Jonathan Williams, 1953); enlarged as *Aflame and Afun' of Walking Faces* (New York: New Directions, 1970);

The Famous Boating Party, and Other Poems in Prose (New York: New Directions, 1954);

Poems of Humor & Protest (San Francisco: City Lights Books, 1954);

Glory Never Guesses (Palo Alto: Kenneth Patchen, 1955);

The Moment (Alhambra, Cal., 1955);

A Surprise for the Bagpipe Player (Palo Alto: Kenneth Patchen, 1956);

When We Were Here Together (New York: New Directions, 1957);

Hurrah for Anything (Highlands, N.C.: Jonathan Williams, 1957); republished in *Doubleheader* (New York: New Directions, 1966);

Poemscapes (Highlands, N.C.: Jonathan Williams, 1958); enlarged as *Poemscapes and A Letter to God* (New York: New Directions, 1958); republished in *Doubleheader* (New York: New Directions, 1966);

Because It Is (New York: New Directions, 1960);

The Love Poems of Kenneth Patchen (San Francisco: City Lights Books, 1960; Northwood, U.K.: Scorpio Press, 1961);

Hallelujah Anyway (New York: New Directions, 1966);

The Collected Poems of Kenneth Patchen (New York: New Directions, 1968);

But Even So (New York: New Directions, 1968);

Selected Poems (London: Cape, 1968);

Love & War Poems, Whisper and Shout, no. 1 (1968);

Kenneth Patchen: Painter of Poems (Baltimore: Printed by Garamond/Pridemark Press, 1969);

Wonderings (New York: New Directions, 1971);

In Quest of Candlelighters (New York: New Directions, 1972);

The Argument of Innocence: A Selection from the Arts of Kenneth Patchen, edited by Peter Veres (San Francisco: Scrimshaw Press, 1976);

Patchen's Lost Plays (Santa Barbara: Capra Press, 1977);

Still Another Pelican in the Breadbox (Youngstown: Pig Iron, 1980);

What Shall We Do Without Us? (San Francisco: Sierra Club Books, 1984).

RECORDINGS: *Kenneth Patchen Reads His Poetry with the Chamber Jazz Sextet* (Cadence Records, 1958);

Kenneth Patchen Reads with Jazz in Canada (Folkways Records, 1959);

Selected Poems of Kenneth Patchen (Folkways Records, 1960);

Kenneth Patchen Reads His Love Poems (Folkways Records, 1961);

Patchen Reads from Albion Moonlight (Folkways Records, 1972);

Fables (GreenTree Records, 1974).

From the publication of his passionately proletarian volume of poetry *Before the Brave* in 1936 until his death in 1972, Kenneth Patchen produced roughly a book a year—all of them daringly bold in form and fiercely uncompromising in values and vision. Though deeply and broadly read and fundamentally romantic in his vision, Patchen followed no models other than William Blake, who knew no restraints. He joined no groups, accepted no schools, sought no academic or commercial acceptance, and remained at the forefront of rebellion in subject and form. He pioneered experiments in the antinovel, concrete poetry, the prose poem, poetry-and-jazz, irrational tales and verse, as well as a progressive synthesis of painting and poetry—"painted books," "poems and drawings," and finally "picture-poems." He accepted no boundaries between people or art forms, no false barriers between life and art, and thus managed to keep head and heart together with uncompromising character. Bridging the modern and the contemporary, Patchen, as a man and artist, has served succeeding generations of writers as a model of freedom and dedication. Poet William Everson best declared the archetypal image of rebellion which Patchen holds: "I best see Patchen as one who cocks a terrible right arm against the glass jaw of New York, stunning it with all the contradiction of its values he can summon against it. And if it seems impervious to his passion and his power that is only the deceptiveness of time, for he will survive it, as the power of the poet always survives the metropolis that hates and ignores him in the moment of his accusation. Bless him in his pain and passion, for his cry is heard." David Meltzer described the place Patchen holds for many younger poets: "Patchen's work is a Bible torn out of America's heart. It is the prophet's urgent warning. . . . Patchen's intense and humane visions have inspired new generations of poets and writers. Like Blake and Whitman, his spiritual forefathers, Patchen's work lays the vital groundwork of man's future." Fundamental to any consideration of Patchen's career is this recognition of his formative impact and his unrelenting drive toward an expansive synthesis—of life and art, of conscience and consciousness, of passion and form, of the heads and hearts of humankind. Forged in the proletarian furnaces of his youth, molded by his wife, Miriam, and by the rebellious avant-garde of Greenwich Village and Connecticut, recast in the anarchist and pacifist atmosphere of San Francisco, and finally tempered and formed in his Palo Alto years of crippling pain yet creative beauty, Patchen's life and art stands as a huge, exposed girder in the structure of American character and art.

Descendant from a proletarian family of coal miners and steel workers in the industrial Mahoning River Valley towns of Niles and Warren (in northeastern Ohio) Kenneth Patchen was born 13 December 1911, the third of five children to Wayne and Eva McQuade Patchen. In light of his own affirmation of love and peace, one can understand Patchen's pride in claiming as one of his forebears Sir Aaron Drake, a general who deserted the British army during the Revolutionary period to marry a Pennsylvania farm girl. Of English, Scotch, Irish, and French descent, the Patchens were part of the early industrial revolution sweeping over Ohio. His father worked for more than twenty-five years in the steel mills of the Niles-Warren area until he was injured there, and both Kenneth and his brother worked for a time in the mills. To supplement the family income, his father worked at building new and renovating old houses, causing the family to move frequently as the houses were built and sold. In 1916 they moved to Warren, where Kenneth entered primary school. The Mahoning Valley area cradled the early iron and steel industry, returning to the immigrant families subsistence incomes and a blanket of smoke and dirt upon their lives. President William McKinley was the town's hero, the son of a blast furnace operator. The Patchens were of the lower-middle socioeconomic class, due largely to the father's construction work, which crashed with the Great Depression of 1929. Eva McQuade Patchen was a caring mother yet severely religious in her rearing the children as Roman Catholics.

Images of his childhood ambivalence provide some concrete realizations of Patchen's later verse. He recalled the humble, hardworking father in "Family Portrait," where "Gray tarry wings splatter grayly up out of the blinding glare of the open-hearth furnaces," and, as his father arrives home, "washing at the kitchen sink. The grimy water runs into the matted hair of his belly. The smell of scorched cloth and sweat adds its seasoning to the ham and cabbage. The muscles of his back ripple like great ropes of greased steel. An awesome thing to see! Yet he never raised his hand in anger against any man." While Patchen learned from his father that suffering could be ennobling, he refused to maintain such a stoic silence against the human violation of industry. He did, however, follow his father's path of love and peace. He treated his mother with equal ambivalence, recalling how "My mother had the thought and hope that I would become a priest." Though he rejected her Catholic orthodoxy, he did become a poet-priest, a visionary and prophetic artist whose essential message is one of universal and personal compassion, further characterized by a belief in humankind's godhood and salvation. "Career for a Child of Five" presents an explanation for both the flamboyance of his art and his ultimate rejection of a fearful religion:

> My mother got the palms from the hands
> Of the priest himself; and being double blessed
> As they were, she would put them on the bureau
> Near candles, where their shadow reeled
> A devil's walk through my childhood.

In terror and intimidation the child is compelled to cry out at this pious threat:

> I started to say all the foul words
> That boys had taught me; beginning
> Softly . . . then louder, louder,
> Until Mother came and put soap
> In my mouth to rub them away.

Denying parental models of submissiveness, Patchen accepted a "Career" of cursing at the tactics of terror and waste which he found in the world. He acknowledged this psychological insight to himself and his art in the poem's close:

> And now, when I can't sleep,
> When the shadows bring the boy back,
> It's always he who is able to cry;
> The foul words remain to me.

The priestly mission behind Patchen's art of protest is this very cursing, turned into a passionate and prophetic preaching and celebration. From his parents he learned love and strength; from their lives he gained a sense of violation and outrage. This sense was heightened when Kathleen, his nine-year-old sister, was run over and killed by a car as she walked to church. Patchen was fourteen at the time and had already begun to write.

In his early proletarian verse his protest is registered in telling concreteness as he recalls his young life in "May I Ask You a Question, Mr. Youngstown Sheet & Tube?" In searing simplicity and terse irony he presents some of the aimless profanation of human potential he witnessed:

> Mean grimy houses, shades drawn
> Against the yellow-brown smoke
> That blows in
> Every minute of every day. And
> Every minute of every night. To bake a cake or have
> a baby,

> With the taste of tar in your mouth. To wash clothes
> or fix supper,
> With the taste of tar in your mouth.

Life's choices are held to the daily drudgery of labor and procreation amid the self-distortion of blind acceptance which he captures in daily imagery:

> Rain dripping down from a rusty eavespout
> Into the gray-fat cinders of the millyard
> . . . .
> The dayshift goes on in four minutes.

In this proletarian protest, one of his lifelong themes, Patchen does more than wave socialist banners and declaim against the cruelty of capitalist greed. He manages to reveal from the inside, and for the people themselves, the need to rebel. His stance as rebel-victim, coupled with his populist motive, becomes a permanent feature of his art.

During Patchen's years at Warren G. Harding High School (1926-1929) he earned respect from the student body for his achievements in track and football, as well as in scholarship and debate. He enjoyed watching Marx Brothers films, walking in the woods, and driving the old car his father bought for him. He had begun keeping a journal at twelve and published his first poems in the high school newspaper, beginning with his pacifist "The Christ of the Andes" in 1928. In an environment that did not pay ready homage to academics, he won respect yet was regarded as serious and quiet with women. In 1929 his sonnet "Permanence" was accepted by the *New York Times,* and appeared there in 1932. The poem is remarkable for its maturity of style and indicates his broad reading and romantic leanings:

> Oblivious, the stars—in dying—wave
> A threat of dust; and graves are deep
> and wide.
> For time and death are twins, of this be
> sure;
> And only dreams and things unsaid
> endure.

Striking for its clarity of image and formal exactness, Patchen's poem suggests his early readings of Shakespeare, Dante, Goethe, and Whitman—poets he favored his whole life.

The Patchen family was made destitute by the Depression of 1929, and Kenneth joined his father in the steel mill that summer in order to earn money for college. This experience provided a further initiation to the hard realities of industrial life. An early prose-poem recalls

> the time a friend of mine was picked off
> by a steel fan in the mills back home; it cut him
>   all to
> hell but the rolls didn't stop and nobody missed
>   eating
> at the proper time. I was seventeen and the
>   nightshift
> was pretty hard to take. Not much later I got
>   in on my
> first strike.

The young Kenneth had enjoyed talking with his father about unions, and for a time organized resistance became his answer to the travesty of life. In his "The Orange Bears: Childhood in an Ohio Steelmill Town," the poet stands with the people, the metaphoric "orange bears" covered with the orange-red smoke of industrial pollution, in resistance:

> Christ, before I left home they'd had
> Their paws smashed in the rolls, their backs
> Seared by hog slag, their soft trusting
> Bellies kicked in, their tongues ripped
> Out. . . .

His innocence devoured early by the mill's harsh realities, the youth then tracks through the woods with a volume of Whitman, and by a polluted stream he reflects:

> And I just sat there worrying my thumbnail
> Into the cover—What did he know about
> Orange bears with their coats all stunk up with
>   soft coal
> And the National Guard coming over
> From Wheeling to stand in front of the millgates
> With drawn bayonets jeering at the strikers!

These seminal works and experiences indicate his bonding of romanticism with realism, his synthesis of vision and protest into the role of poet-prophet. It also makes clear the necessity for his leaving that life if he was to do anything about it. The poem's passion overrules his sense of artistry—a characteristic of all his work—yet the hidden artistry of the broken-line timing, the metaphoric complexity blended with historic detail, and the natural and open form reveal the poet's fierce sincerity, his bold drive for a new unity of life and art. At eighteen he left the Niles-Warren areas of his childhood, but he never forgot the people and their struggle for meaningful lives.

In 1929 Patchen attended the University of Wisconsin, where he ran track and played football and took part in Alexander Meiklejohn's Experimental College. He followed Meiklejohn to Commonwealth College in Mena, Arkansas, for another semester; then he ended his formal education and took to the road. From 1930 to 1933 he wandered throughout the United States and Canada writing, reading, and working odd jobs as a migrant field worker, janitor, and caretaker for a hikers' shelter. In Georgia he was beaten and thrown in jail. These years of youthful rambling helped to shape his rebel views and prompted an outpour of writings, many lost in small towns. In 1932 he was working in a rubber factory in Boston when he was befriended by poets Conrad Aiken, John Wheelwright, and Malcolm Cowley. Some of his poems and short stories appeared that year in *Rebel Poet*, including his tribute "Lenin": "In the ashes of his tomb the sturdy feet of a nation/are stirring in their shackles./From the nostrils of his faith is blowing the fire/that shall melt the chains of man." Patchen had become the "proletarian poet" laboring with the masses and voicing a socialist promise.

On Christmas Eve 1933 this hungry and despairing rebel poet met a young coed from Massachusetts State College at a Boston party. Miriam Oikemus was the child of Finnish immigrants, who had brought her up with an intense awareness of social injustice and a sympathy for the Communist party. She had already organized an antiwar protest at her college and was equally disillusioned with academic life. Thus began one of the legendary love relationships of modern writing, one responsible for the "Miriam Edifice"—the countless love poems and a lifetime of shared dedication symbolized in the simple "For Miriam" dedication of all his works. In May of 1934 Patchen and Miriam Oikemus lived in New York City, and then traveled to his Ohio home. She was only seventeen, and her parents and college were searching for her. One day an FBI agent knocked at his father's front door and told them Kenneth was wanted under the Mann Act for transporting an underaged woman across a state border. He warned them that they must be married or face arrest. On 28 June 1934 Kenneth and Miriam eloped to nearby Sharon, Pennsylvania, where a justice of the peace agreed to ignore the lack of a parental-consent signature for their last ten dollars. They made it back to New York, where they moved into a one-room apartment above the Dutch Reformist Church in Greenwich Village.

In this avant-garde and leftist atmosphere

Manuscript facsimile and photograph of Miriam Patchen from a booklet that accompanied the Folkways recording Kenneth Patchen Reads His Love Poems *(by permission of Miriam Patchen)*

Patchen began reviewing books for the *New Republic* and writing on a New York guide series for the Federal Writers' Project of the Work Projects Administration (WPA). Miriam Patchen recalls how the 1930s was a period when socialism was discussed at all gatherings, yet she makes it clear that during Patchen's entire life he never joined any organization, a testament to his anarchist commitment. In 1935 he received a contract from Random House for his first book of poems, and he and Miriam Patchen moved to Rhinebeck, New York, where he completed his proletarian and revolutionary *Before the Brave*.

In many ways Patchen's artistic identity was already firmly grounded in the tripartite union of his artistic vision: a projection of the world's madness, an assertion of the necessity for artistic engagement in the struggles of humankind, and a visionary and romantic testament to the full wonder of life which humankind was profaning. Patchen never deviated from this basic vision; yet broadened the scope and intensity of each part as he matured. *Before the Brave* opens with a declaration of madness: "Let us have madness openly, O men/Of my generation. Let us follow/The footsteps of this slaughtered age." The madness of war

and heartless capitalism calls for expression, and he urges the "Class of 1934" to engagement: "Say something man, say something before the nations and the people;/tell them your story tell them the earth is a bitch gone crazy." His call to revolution is founded on basic faith in what we are, "The mountain is man," and "Power is in brotherhood." The poems are filled with realistic yet nightmarish images of waste, set against his principle of potential wonder: "Power is in living clean before our love/has written what we are/on every distant corner of Tomorrow's sky." Patchen clearly praises the laborer's cause as he pays tribute to unionist Joe Hill, the "wobblies" of the Industrial Workers of the World (IWW), and the "blood of pickets." He stares down both system and fear with "We are not cool: our hate has made us wise, not clever./. . . The heart breaks with the groan and the grind of a lever/Which lifts a world whose very sun retreats before the brave." Though the main emphasis is on the madness and the call to engagement, Patchen the poet-prophet found his voice and stance in his first book. The book won him strong reviews from poets such as Babette Deutsch (*New York Herald Tribune Books*, 15 March 1936), a testament to the intellectual leftist atmosphere of the times and to his mature vision and form. Amos N. Wilder compared him to W. H. Auden and Stephen Spender. Patchen was awarded a Guggenheim Fellowship in 1936, and the Patchens spent the year in Phoenix, Arizona, and Santa Fe, New Mexico.

By 1937 the Patchens were living in Los Angeles where he worked on a California guide for the WPA and began working on movie scripts. One day, while dislodging two cars which had locked bumpers, Patchen sustained a back injury which was to affect him the rest of his life. When he returned to the East in 1939, it was to work with Miriam Patchen, as the accounting and shipping staff for James Laughlin's budding New Directions publishing house. They lived at Laughlin's Norfolk, Connecticut, home while he traveled the United States setting up markets. Laughlin, whose family ironically owned the steel mills where Patchen's father worked, became Patchen's lifelong friend and publisher, bringing out his *First Will & Testament* in 1939. Miriam recalls the deep affection and admiration Laughlin held for Patchen's work despite other writers and "a kind of pseudo-intellectual crowd telling him how Kenneth was a nothing . . . nothing. Many of them worked under the table and around the corner to try to get Kenneth 'unpublished' by New Directions, but it never worked." Though the Patchens did no editing, they were in part responsible for Laughlin's choice to publish such writers as Dylan Thomas and Henry Miller. This alliance with New Directions has only strengthened through the years, as almost all of Patchen's books are now in print through New Directions. Laughlin recalls, "The Patchens' devotion, when the going was very rough, was remarkable. . . . He, along with Henry Miller, are the writers of his generation whom the alienated young of the underground sub-culture still 'dig' the most."

First Will & Testament and the short story "Bury Them in God," which Laughlin published the same year in his *New Directions* anthology for 1939, reveal a broadening in Patchen's political outlook. Refusing to glorify the poor, he recognizes instead the depth of their bondage: "Look, you bastard," says the narrator-artist of "Bury Them in God," "go out in the street and listen to your working class champing at the bit to sink its teeth into the Japanese and German working class." Disillusioned with proletarian mass reform and with any form of political organization, Patchen moved to his most defiant and universal stand as a dedicated anarchist and pacifist. The poems of *First Will & Testament* are fierce in their contempt for war and

profound in their deep personal testament to universal love. In "EARLY IN THE MORNING" he declares his role as poet-prophet, "I am the world-crier, and this is my dangerous career/. . ./I am the one to call your bluff, and this is my climate." For Patchen the life-corrupting lie of the world must be confronted, often with strong irony, and so he declares in the long "The Hunted City," this unrecognized message of political wars, "Humanity is a good thing. Perhaps we can arrange the murder/ of a sizable number of people to save it." The intense irony of his titles make his message clear: "I DON'T WANT TO STARTLE YOU but they are going to kill most of us," "Hymn to a Trench Gun," "Eve of St. Agony, or the Middle Class Was Sitting on Its Fat," "Elegy for the Silent Voices and the Joiners of Everything," "Do the Dead Know What Time It Is?," "Nice Day for a Lynching." It is a deadly serious humor, as he declares in "Nice Day for a Lynching," stating his deep engagement in the cause of social justice against human persecution, "Until it changes,/I shall be forever killing; and be killed." His stance and themes having grown into the broadest and deepest sense of universal humanity, Patchen's art became a shrill cry of moral conscience rising through his poetic being. His images became characteristically hard and nightmarishly real: "Our faces hunched over our brains like tight pods," "And a battle crackles through the fat, blue air above us," "Their calm faces,/Posed in rapid-glare of slick machine guns," "with a diamond/of thunderous sound, splitting the sky up like a fat fish's belly/(People hurry along like pictures taken through milk)." Along with his heavy irony and his nightmarish images, Patchen developed a personal and immediate directness of voice:

> Don't fight their war!
> Tell them to go to hell!
>
> This isn't a poem. This is a sob and a death rattle.
> Who will listen? who will care?
> A black wind blows in over the graves.

Patchen's answer to those who challenged his poetic boldness was simple, "My face is what it sees." In the midst of social injustice and the destruction of World War II, the poet could not afford to isolate himself in art for art's sake. "I sing for the flame and against the ever-grinning darkness," he declares, and reminds the reader that it all must be felt personally, for "All of the deaths are at your door." A counter-balancing voice to the terror in all his work speaks in Patchen's songs of love. In personal and universal love all sanity is restored, he declares in "As Frothing Wounds of Roses":

> As the cry of the bird-torn wind
> Hastens the heart beyond its usual need,
> So shalt thy dear loveliness,
> Upon the forlorn unrest of my cold will
> Be as that snowy stain the roses bleed.

Woven throughout *First Will & Testament* are these romantic songs of love as refuge and assurance. Particularly beautiful and revealing is "SHE HAD CONCEALED HIM IN A DEEP DARK CAVE":

> Warm houses stand within us
> Sleepy angels smile in doorways
> Little jewelled horses jolt by without sound
> Everyone is rich and no one has money
> I can love you Thank God I can love you
> . . . .
> But the way our bodies were wings
> Flying in and out of each other. . . .

This sense of underlying love and wonder is quite Blakean in its origins, and it becomes one of Patch-

en's lasting themes, an antidote to the world's madness. As is clear in this volume that closed the 1930s, Patchen's world view (including his poetic stance and forms) was already deeply rooted.

By 1940 the Patchens were back in Greenwich Village, where he became friends with other artists and writers, such as E. E. Cummings, Maxwell Bodenheim, and Henry Miller. Whether living in the Village, in Mount Pleasant, New York, or later in Old Lyme, Connecticut, the Patchens remained a presence in the avant-garde scene throughout the 1940s, an environment which nourished him as he nourished others. Harold Norse recalls his first meeting, as a young writer at a Village party, with Kenneth Patchen: "He possessed great warmth and something else, very rare, that seemed to emanate from his personality like a physical substance: compassion. I thought he looked like an Italian Renaissance master or ancient Welsh bard, maybe. Or even a Hebrew prophet. He was very gentle. With his walking stick (anachronistic, tho necessary), his imposing bulk, massive head and slow movements, he definitely stood out in the Village landscape." Another young writer attracted to the Patchens was

Kenneth Patchen in Greenwich Village, early 1940s

poet Robert Duncan, then a part of the Henry Miller and Anäis Nin circle. Miller became a close friend and published *Patchen: Man of Anger and Light,* the first important critical study of Patchen, in 1946; Nin offended the Patchens with her egotism and sexual aggressiveness, but Duncan became almost a disciple and, in fact, typed most of Patchen's *The Journal of Albion Moonlight* from Patchen's handwritten notebooks in 1940. A crucial split with Nin occurred when she encouraged Duncan to enlist in 1941, and the Patchens helped him to get a medical discharge only two months later.

Patchen's output during the 1940s was phenomenal: he produced more than fifteen books in that decade. First came his powerful antiwar novel, *The Journal of Albion Moonlight* (1941); then his mystical poems of *The Dark Kingdom* (1942); two more books of poems, *The Teeth of the Lion* (1942) and *Cloth of the Tempest* (1943); a second experimental and ironic novel, *The Memoirs of a Shy Pornographer* (1945); a collection of his pacifist poems, *An Astonished Eye Looks Out of the Air* (1945); a selection of poems published in England, *Outlaw of the Lowest Planet* (1946); experimental poems and prose in *Panels for the Walls of Heaven* (1946); *The Selected Poems of Kenneth Patchen* (1946); the radically experimental prose and poetry of *Sleepers Awake* (1946); and two further experimental mixtures of prose, poetry, and drawings in *They Keep Riding Down All the Time* and *Pictures of Life and Death* both in 1947. In 1948 he produced a conventional romantic potboiler novel, *See You in the Morning.* The year before he had written, "I have no children because I couldn't feed them. My wife never has a new coat and I may have to write novels." His production broke ground even in avant-garde New York; yet it never produced a financial success, and at times, despite Patchen's protests, Miriam Patchen had to go to work. Two other collections of poetry appeared in 1948, *To Say If You Love Someone and Other Selected Love Poems* and *CCCLXXIV Poems.* Patchen's work was also the staple of a loose network of anarcho-pacifist publications in the mid- to late 1940s. His provocative poems and solid stance lead off such magazines as George Woodcock's British *Now,* New York's *Retort: An Anarchist Review* and Robert Duncan's the *Experimental Review,* Berkeley's *Circle* and *Contour,* and San Francisco's *Ark.* This excerpt from *Sleepers Awake* prefaces *Ark,* no. 1, as a type of collective manifesto in its engaged declaration:

> O pray God that human beings may not forever be hunted down like blind beasts in a ditch; that they may not forever die of starvation in lands of unbelievable bounty, that they may not forever be driven to kill and be killed in furtherance of this brutal, cynical plan to keep madmen in the seats of power.

> ART IS NOT TO THROW LIGHT BUT BE LIGHT. OPEN THE DOOR
> FOR CHRIST'S SAKE OPEN THE DOOR! IF YOU CAN'T PRAISE
> THEN GODDAMMIT SHUT UP!

Patchen was then at the forefront of a long line of writers of commitment, including Kenneth Rexroth, Richard Eberhart, Thomas Parkinson, Paul Goodman, William Carlos Williams, E. E. Cummings, Sanders Russell, Woodcock, and Duncan, all of whom had work published in this issue of *Ark.* Another writer whose work was included was William Everson, who was then heading the fine printing at Untide Press at the conscientious objectors' camp in Walpole, Oregon. Everson brought out Patchen's pacifist poems, *An Astonished Eye Looks Out of the Air,* in 1945 and later declared of that time, "That's where we identified with Kenneth Patchen . . . in his undeviating stance of rebuke to the system." Patchen's impact on postwar life and writing was immediate and profound. One young poet and soon to be publisher who then worked closely with the Patchens at their cottage in Old Lyme, Connecticut (1947-1950), was Jonathan Williams. He recalls how "Kenneth and Miriam Patchen lived in a tiny red cottage up on a little hill . . . past a pond of turtles. . . . The cabin sat in Connecticut less than it did in the context of Kenneth's love poems. All the neighborhood animals sat on the lawn like hieratic beasts." Here, in 1950, Patchen dictated to Williams his fabulous creature fables, published as *Fables and Other Little Tales* in 1953 by Williams's Jargon Press.

Patchen's back injury had worsened during the 1940s, when it was misdiagnosed as arthritis. Only in 1950 did he receive some relief after a spinal fusion was performed on his slipped disc. Money for the corrective surgery was earned by readings done by a Writer's Committee which consisted of such fellow modernists as T. S. Eliot, W. H. Auden, Archibald MacLeish, Thornton Wilder, E. E. Cummings, Edith Sitwell, Marianne Moore, and William Carlos Williams. The Patchens left the East Coast for good in December 1950 for the new horizons of the West Coast, but his influence on the avant-garde of the East was deeply etched and has not diminished. Lafe Young recalls the per-

THE JOURNAL OF ALBION MOONLIGHT

May 2

The angel lay in a little thicket. It had no need of love; there was nothing anywhere in the world could startle it — ~~we can find peace too~~ ~~we~~ can lie here with the angel if we like; it couldn't have hurt much when they slit open its throat.

The evening slowly turns to black stone, and the hammer of god chips at the sky, making stars. A child stands on the road watching us; upon her forehead is the yellow brand of the plague-summer. She weaves to us and her hand, like a withered, white claw, falls to the ground; the fingers unclench once, then relax — I stuff the hand into my pocket, and we hurry on.

Very well. We knew we had no other course but to get away with all attainable speed. A light rain had fallen in the night, and morning brought the drizzle to storm proportions. Our coats were wet through as we sogged out of New York on the first leg of our trip. That a great distance seperated us from our goal we knew; that we were in danger of destruction at any hour of the day and night we knew; what we did not know was how near madness we would be; how alone; how defenseless; how beset we were with what we had heard; with what we had been taught — this, especially, we did not know.

My idea was to travel along rivers whenever it was feasable to do so. notwithstanding this intention, we saw no water today. We camped for the night in a little clearing about fifty yards from the highway, near a filling-station. About three in the morning, Jetter, who is my friend more than any of the others, complained of a pain in the back of his head. I managed to transfer the revolver from his pack to my own.

I would like to bring my armies to your city. We have several effective ways of putting down the trouble you have.

May 4

Yesterday we were set upon by great, ugly-tempered dogs. Two we shot, scattering the rest. In the evening, we held conference on the best manner by which to defend ourselves against these surly brutes for the forest we were entering was known to abound with them. Shooting seemed the only practical method of defense, yet we knew it unwise to have guns in our hands. We decided, at last, to arm ourselves

Page from the manuscript for The Journal of Albion Moonlight *(by permission of Miriam Patchen; courtesy of the Kenneth Patchen Archive, Special Collection, University of California, Santa Cruz)*

*Kenneth and Miriam Patchen, 1946 (photograph by
Robin Carson)*

sonal and symbolic stature which Patchen projected onto the Village landscape: "Near the wall of one of the rooms was a very large brass gong. Kenneth was magnetized by this beautiful gong and before long he was wailing away, whamming into it with a long padded drumstick. A few of us watched him—this vital, handsome poet pounding out and in tune with a wild and wonderful music."

Patchen's work was always admired most by fellow poets, especially by the young, for it gave them courage to go beyond the conventions of form and of academic or publishing circles. However, in the 1940s some critics, however haltingly, also began to appraise his impact. Harvey Breit's initial insight in "Kenneth Patchen and the Critical Blind Alley" (*Fantasy*, 1940) was important, for it pointed out the need for new critical approaches to his engaged poetics. Amos N. Wilder compared him with Muriel Rukeyser in a composite image of "the American proletarian poet," and Charles I. Glicksberg followed this ambiguous lead, calling Patchen "a fullfledged proletarian poet for whom revolt is a spiritual necessity." It was William Carlos Williams, however, who offered the clearest insight into Patchen's experimental method of madness and engagement. In his 1942 review of *The Journal of Albion Moonlight*, he declared, "What virtues are to be found here may be taken for madness. Could

we interpret them we should know the cure. That is, I think, Patchen's intention, so, in reverse, to make the cure not only apparent, but, by the horror of the picture imperative." Finally, it was Miller's 1946 study, *Patchen: Man of Anger and Light*, which recognized the dualistic character of Patchen's art, showing him as capable of great tenderness as well as blistering social indictment. Patchen was derided by many who could not accept his vision or his radically redirected art along the lines of Blake and Whitman. It would be years before his most experimental work would receive due appreciation, let alone artistic assimilation.

The Patchens moved on to the decade of the 1950s, a period of new frontiers and friendships, protean creativity and profound influence. Taking advantage of his new mobility they headed west to the expanded view of San Francisco's bohemian North Beach. For a brief time they stayed with friends—poet Holly Beye, who was heavily influenced by Patchen, and her husband David Ruff, whose fine press produced Patchen's *Orchards, Thrones & Caravans* in 1952. The Patchens moved into a small apartment at the top of Green Street on Telegraph Hill. Here they could readily view Coit Tower whose 1930s murals stood as a proletarian reminder of revolt, and they could easily walk to the bohemian centers of North Beach. Miriam recalls the environment as warm and open, "almost the kind that New York had in the late 30's and 40's. It was left wing, liberal . . . everyone knew everyone. . . . It was small and warm and the different political groups did not dislike each other. . . . There was not that 'at the throat,' 'behind the back' sneaky feeling that did exist, I'm sorry to say, pretty much elsewhere." Right-wing paranoia was already spreading across the United States as Sen. Joseph McCarthy launched his anti-Communist attacks; yet they were met with open and collective resistance in anarchist and libertarian San Francisco. It was a close, small area of fellow artists, yet the Patchens did little socializing. Chiefly Patchen wrote and kept their home open to old friends such as Kenneth Rexroth and Robert Duncan. In 1954 Patchen befriended a fellow migrant to the West, Lawrence Ferlinghetti. When Ferlinghetti's City Lights Books launched its important Pocket Poets series in 1954, the first books were Ferlinghetti's *Pictures of the Gone World*, Rexroth's *30 Spanish Poems of Love and Exile*, and Patchen's selected *Poems of Humor & Protest*. The next book in that series was by a young poet who had migrated west in part to meet Patchen. Allen Ginsberg, whose *Howl* appeared in 1955, recalls the stature

Patchen had as an independent force affecting the culture and artistic climate of the place: "Patchen was a senior survivor of the poetry spiritual wars who'd kept his verse-line open, spontaneous, and his heart in human body." When Ferlinghetti first introduced Ginsberg to Patchen at City Lights Bookstore, Ginsberg was struck, "He looked like a mild longshoreman, with a hat, slight painful smile, perhaps even low voice. . . . I was surprised to find him living so near the center of literary S.F., so available and friendly." Though Patchen defied any regionalist label, he was a central element in the emerging San Francisco Poetry Renaissance. He had done readings for the Spanish Loyalists and at the San Francisco Museum of Art. When the Beat Movement became part of the San Francisco Renaissance in the great cultural revolt of 1955, Patchen had been writing for twenty years and had already produced a sizeable body of the most avant-garde poetry, which had just been recognized with the 1954 Shelley Memorial Award. Along with Blake and Whitman, he served the Beats as an example of originality and independence, of uncompromising authenticity. His proletarian-anarchist-pacifist stand and his apocalyptic verse had seared the righteous wings of American conformity and given character to the poetry of revolt. Ginsberg praised his role as poet-prophet and his open form and reflexive line, acclaiming, "A new consciousness flowers in youthful U.S. that Whitman, Cendrars, and Patchen helped transmit."

Though Patchen gave encouragement and friendship to other young West Coast poets—David Meltzer, Michael McClure, Philip Lamantia, Philip Whalen—he maintained a sharp independence from the Beat Movement. Viewing their acceptance of drugs and loveless sex as immoral and objecting to their later publicity seeking, Patchen (and later Rexroth, Ferlinghetti, and Gary Snyder) declared his independence. His antagonism grew until he struck out at the hypocrisy that had crept into the movement, calling them "A Freakshow worth every Madison Ave. penny of the three-dollar-bill admission."

Patchen's *The Journal of Albion Moonlight* served the Beats and succeeding generations as a manifesto of engaged revolt, becoming a bible of commitment where art and life are one in their search for regeneration. His poem "Artist's Duty" in that anti-novel clarifies the image of the artist in the world:

So it is the duty of the artist to discourage all traces of shame
To extend all boundaries
. . . .
To establish problems
To ignore solutions
To listen to no one
To omit nothing
To contradict everything
To generate the free brain
. . . .
To tinkle a warning when mankind strays
To explode upon all parties
To wound deeper than the soldier
To heal his poor monkey once and for all.

The artist moves from acts of individualism to generating, exploding, wounding, and finally metaphorical healing. Patchen requires the artist:

To *happen*
. . . .
It is the artist's duty to be alive
To drag people into glittering occupations
. . . .
To blush perpetually in gaping innocence
To drift happily through the ruined race intelligence
To burrow beneath the subconscious
To defend the unreal at the cost of his reason
To obey each outrageous impulse
To commit his company to all enchantments.

This declaration and stance is Patchen's creative core and his chief legacy to contemporary poets, the wholeness of his vision of life and art and the authenticity of his creativity and protean forms.

Kenneth Rexroth's important study "Kenneth Patchen, Naturalist of the Public Nightmare" offered a 1956 perspective on Patchen's underlying methods and vision: "*Albion Moonlight* and *Sleepers Awake* . . . are realistic portrayals of the modern world. . . . The nightmares of Patchen's narratives are the daily vision of millions." Declaiming against the critical ignorance and fear of Patchen's work, Rexroth stated, "Against the conspiracy of silence of the whole of literary America, Patchen has become the laureate of the doomed youth of the Third World War." He rightly assessed Patchen's role (and his own) as committed: "His voice is the voice of a conscience which is forgotten. He speaks from the moral viewpoint of the new century, the century of assured hope." While most critics were ignoring or mistaking his work as surrealistic, Patchen set out on one of his most provocative and successful experiments, the poetry-and-jazz work of 1957, written in the midst of the Beat Movement.

In 1956 the Patchens had moved near Stanford University in Palo Alto on the southern end of the San Francisco Bay, so that Patchen could be closer to the Palo Alto Clinic, where he underwent a second spinal fusion. His peaceful Palo Alto home became the artistic center for the rest of his life. His *The Famous Boating Party, and Other Poems in Prose* had appeared in 1954, and his silkscreen portfolio of poems and drawings, *Glory Never Guesses*, was published the following year. Like Rexroth and Ferlinghetti, Patchen had been experimenting with a synthesis of brother art forms—contemporary poetry and jazz. As early as his *First Will & Testament* in 1939 Patchen had made allusions to jazz music, including his incorporating a list of "the disks you'll have to get if you want a basic jazz library" in his 1945 *Memoirs of a Shy Pornographer*. His jazz roots went deep, and the natural connections between rebel poet and jazzman as cultural outsider were clear. Both contemporary jazz and open-form poetry had evolved forms based on intuitive improvisation and emotional flow (whether "hot" or "cool"); both created a spontaneous art that fostered free expression of angry social protest as well as mocking humor and tender love. Jazzman and poet sought to offer the world a reflection of itself; and both were moved by a mystical kind of spirit and faith. Their feet firmly on the streets, both sing boldly of what is and is not there. Jonathan Williams further documents Patchen's early experiments with the synthesis of the two forms in the 1941 private tapings he did of the fables to the accompaniment of "the Bunk Johnson and George Lewis records that Bill Russell was sending from Chicago. . . . They were, to my knowledge, the first instances of the later poetry/jazz experiment." Miriam Patchen recalls even earlier tapings of Patchen's work to jazz records around 1948 in Connecticut.

The poetry-and-jazz movement went public when tapes of Patchen reading to jazz records were first broadcast on the Canadian Broadcast Corporation radio network, and in the spring of 1957 when Kenneth Rexroth and Lawrence Ferlinghetti began performing their own versions of poetry-and-jazz at San Francisco's jazz club, The Cellar. Their performances were taped by the Berkeley-based Fantasy Records as *Poetry Readings in "The Cellar"* with the Cellar Jazz Quintet. San Francisco was already a jazz center, and this new development created much national attention. A mutual friend, Richard Bowman, had introduced Patchen to Allyn Ferguson, who was director of the Chamber Jazz Sextet, and together they began performing at San Francisco's the Blackhawk. In 1958 they released *Kenneth Patchen Reads His Poetry with the Chamber Jazz Sextet* on the Cadence label and launched a highly successful tour of the West Coast and Canada. In his scarlet blazer, Patchen toured such universities as British Columbia, California at Los Angeles, Washington at Seattle, and did a two-month record-breaking performance at the Los Angeles Jazz Concert Hall. In 1959 he carried his poetry-and-jazz to New York's celebrated Five Spot Café. While his jazz play *Don't Look Now* was to appear at off-Broadway's Living Theatre, Patchen was working with jazz great Charlie Mingus. Vancouver, Canada, was the scene of a 1959 radio performance by Patchen and the Alan Neil Quartet and another recording with the Alan Neil Quartet—*Kenneth Patchen Reads with Jazz in Canada.*

In three years poetry-and-jazz had progressed from a strange new phenomenon to an exciting aspect of music and writing, and in the process it attracted a new and broader audience for contemporary jazz and poetry. It strengthened the oral tradition and the public nature of poetry. Among jazzmen and poets there were skeptics, but also strong supporters such as Mingus, Dave Brubeck, Lennie Tristano, Sonny Wayne, and Brue Moore. Jack Kerouac released *Blues and Haikus* with Al Cohn and Zoot Sims and appeared on television and record with Steve Allen, as Patchen did on Bobby Troup's televised "Stars of Jazz." There was very little cross influence by the poetry-and-jazz performers, but much mutual support. Patchen's work was clearly the best and most dedicated to a true synthesis of poetry-and-jazz into a new poetry-jazz. As John Ciardi observed at the time, "Patchen's poetry is in many ways a natural for jazz accompaniment. Its subject and its tone are close to those of jazz. And most of it is written not metrically, but in phrase groups that adapt naturally to jazz rhythms." In fact, Patchen used his voice as an instrument, blending with the music without competing with it. He achieved commanding yet intricate effects with timing, the kind of rhythmic suspensions characteristic of jazz. James Boyer May, editor of *Trace*, concluded, "Beyond mere harmonies and antiphonies, these performances are remarkable fusions." One of Patchen's most dedicated fans was the great jazz saxophonist Charlie Parker, who shared Patchen's searing and tender vision of life and art and who often recited lines of Patchen's poems between riffs.

Two things killed the movement—a proliferation of cheap imitations in coffee houses and clubs everywhere, which earned ridicule, and

Poster for the 1959 production of a jazz play by Patchen

Patchen's removal from the picture due to a "surgical mishap" in 1959 during exploratory surgery following his third spinal-fusion operation. Somehow Patchen was allowed to slip from the operating cart to the floor, severely damaging his spine and condemning him to a bedridden life of pain. Heightening the tragedy, Miriam Patchen had developed multiple sclerosis and could not work. In 1960 and 1961 fellow poets came to the rescue as William Packard organized a series of fund-raising tributes in coffee houses and clubs, and on campuses around the country. It climaxed in the reading at San Francisco's Marine Memorial Auditorium in January 1961 when Kenneth Rexroth served as master of ceremonies for tribute readings by Jonathan Williams, Philip Whalen, Michael McClure, and Lawrence Ferlinghetti. Despite this support from San Francisco Poetry Renaissance figures, Patchen drifted further and further from his earlier literary friends into a world of private pain, thus cutting off a life he could not share.

In addition to his direct work in poetry-and-jazz, he had written a group of jazzlike poems, *Hurrah for Anything* (1957), each poem following a jazz riff form and illustrated with a zany Patchen drawing. That same year he did an enlarged edition of *The Selected Poems of Kenneth Patchen* and *When We Were Here Together. Poemscapes,* brief numbered prose poems, evolved in 1958, and 1960 brought *The Love Poems of Kenneth Patchen* and the imaginative verse and drawings of *Because It Is.* All these works mark Patchen's transition to his final "Wonder Period" of intuitive and irrational celebrations of the world and human imagination. In *Hurrah for Anything* he refers to these works as "painful rejoicings," works that refuse to accept the borders of society or art and thus explode with a romantic's

Kenneth Patchen (far right) reading at a "Stars of Jazz" performance broadcast on KABC-TV (Los Angeles), 11 June 1958

celebration of language and love. Patchen had, in a sense, worked from the madness, through engagement, to wonder.

Thrown into a bedridden state and facing the death of a book he had planned ("The Human Winter"), Patchen fell into a depression which was happily broken by the happenstance presentation of some ancient Chinese paper by Stanford biologist Norman Thomas. The paper had been used in the botany labs as packing for stored specimens and was about to be discarded when Thomas thought of presenting it to Patchen, who immediately began working it into his celebrated picture-poems, the final synthesis of his arts. In his small bedroom Patchen managed to extend his world through his dynamic colors and caring creatures. Thomas described Patchen at work: "If you visit Patchen at midmorning . . . the sun will be spreading out, diffused, across tables bright with opened pots of paint and tufted with fists of paint brushes, over piles of books and sheets of painted poems, coming to rest as stripes on a tousled yellow and orange bedspread." As Patchen progressed from concrete poetry to painted books (each cover individually painted) to poems-and-drawings to picture-poems, his words and visual images became more and more one. As Milton Klonsky described it, "The poems cum pictures by Kenneth Patchen . . . are not 'illustrated' poetry, but rather the poems themselves extended into the modality of the visi-

ble." The creatures who inhabit the Patchen wonderland are reminiscent of the imaginative work of Ben Shahn, Joan Miro, and perhaps most tellingly, of the imaginative innocence of Paul Klee's world. They seem to move and speak the brief poems in a truly visual-aural experience. Patchen used conventional carbon inks, mortar-ground watercolors, casein, cloth dyes, and the highly favored Japanese earth colors. However, added to this list of unconventional materials were egg dye, cornstarch, and Japanese sumi sticks and glue. Besides brushes, Patchen used such unlikely instruments for application as tree sprigs, kitchen utensils, sponges, "and a whole range of household and garden utensils." The results are strikingly original and spontaneous.

In 1969 Patchen's artwork was collected from across the country for a one-man show at the Corcoran Gallery in Washington, D.C. The picture-poems were initially reproduced in book form without their brilliant colors, as in *Hallelujah Anyway* (1966), *But Even So* (1968), and *Wonderings* (1971). To be truly appreciated, however, they should be seen in full color, as in the three published collections *The Argument of Innocence: A Selection from the Arts of Kenneth Patchen* (1976), which includes photographs of his miniature sculptures, *Kenneth Patchen: Painter of Poems* (1969), and the Sierra Club book *What Shall We Do Without Us?* (1984). In 1967 Patchen was awarded a ten-thousand-dollar grant for a lifelong contribution to American letters by

I AM TIMOTHY THE LION

I live in an old sour maple tree
With Happy Jake, who is
A small goldfish;
There is also a short-necked swan,
Two very base players, a bull still wrapped
In pink tissue paper, and a policeman
Shaped like a watering can;
But they're all afraid of sunstroke,
So me and Jake just sit out on our limb here
And shout *Bon Dieu! Bon Dieu!*
Every time the phone rings up in one of those clouds.

Page from Hurrah for Anything *(by permission of Miriam Patchen and Jonathan Williams)*

the National Endowment for the Arts, and the following year New Directions published *The Collected Poems of Kenneth Patchen*, containing about two-thirds of his published poems. The book was reviewed with high praise, as the collected assemblage offered new insights and inner connections. Reviewing the book for the *New York Times Book Review* (20 October 1968), William Packard called it "A remarkable volume, although it is difficult to describe. One could say that it contains the animal honesty of Whitman, and the desperate exaltation of Hart Crane, and the simple delight in sense perception of D. H. Lawrence. One could also say that it contains the wrath of the Old Testament prophets, as well as the Christlike simplicity and sweetness of St. Francis. But one would be missing the really important point—that the book is many voices, all of them Patchen's, all of them sounding together in a curious orchestration."

In another important way Patchen kept his poetic voice and the oral tradition of poetry alive through a series of recordings for Folkways Records: *Selected Poems of Kenneth Patchen* (1960), *Kenneth Patchen Reads His Love Poems* (1961), and selections from *The Journal of Albion Moonlight* (recorded in 1959, though not released until 1972). His last recording was the witty celebrations of *Fables* (GreenTree, 1974). As in the poetry-jazz recordings, Patchen's voice ranges from mellow and tender in the love lyrics, to intense and robust in his tirades of life violation, to joyful and playful with the verbal ironies of the fables. John Ciardi found Patchen's voice "casual, almost matter of fact, yet sensitive, resonant, and immediately engaging. A gentle and easy voice, always deeply concerned for the natural rhythms of speech, yet kept exciting by small modulations and by a superb sense of timing." All made in Patchen's Palo Alto

"Everyman is me, I am his brother. No man is my enemy. I am Everyman and he is in and of me. This is my faith, my strength, my deepest hope and my only belief."

Last page from Wonderings *(by permission of Miriam Patchen and New Directions)*

home, the recordings were truly painful rejoicings of the world and the word that went beyond his bedroom walls.

Two close friends intimate with Patchen's Palo Alto world recall those final years of his creating beauty despite the daily round of pain. Norman Thomas remembered the bedroom studio, with its ready mix of painting and writing tools, and how "at midmorning his face is grey and the lines at the side of his mouth are deep, his eyes sunken and dark with miserable night memories. When he moves it is with so much care and with such apprehension." Despite this anguish, James Boyer May revealed that "Patchen's restraint is finally seen to be a shield, a cloak for a sensitive inner self. . . . The central key to his character lies in his love for all that lives: plants, animals, man . . . and stars. . . . He is a teacher, too. . . . For he teaches by his chosen *ways* of being." Miriam Patchen recalls how one day Kenneth was troubled that a tiny field mouse

might be destroyed by one of their many yard cats. When she returned from shopping and found Kenneth gone, she grew frantic, only to discover Kenneth standing in the doorway in a cold sweat, returned from a painful rescue journey to a nearby field. In loving simplicity Patchen's last work was a picture-poem that declared finally, "EVERYMAN IS ME, I AM HIS BROTHER. NO MAN IS MY ENEMY. I AM EVERYMAN AND HE IS IN AND OF ME. THIS IS MY FAITH, MY STRENGTH, MY DEEPEST HOPE, AND MY ONLY BELIEF." This love and identification extended to every creature and every thing in a true union in wonder.

On 8 January 1972 Kenneth Patchen died of a heart attack at his home. As one obituary pointed out, while one much celebrated American poet sought to escape life that month by jumping from a Chicago bridge, Kenneth Patchen had endured bravely with a fierce love of life and art. As Patchen modestly confessed in one of his last interviews,

"I've never stopped writing since I was 12. . . . It's just not occurred to me not to be sustained." On 22 February 1972 poets gathered at City Lights Poets Theatre to offer a memorial reading. Robert Duncan, Gary Snyder, Charles Lipton, Al Young, Ishmael Reed, Robert Creeley, and Morton Marcus, among others, offered testimony to Patchen's achievement and example. Miriam Patchen had instructed Al Young to announce that Patchen, in a final affirmation of union with existence, had asked to have his cremated ashes spread on the Pacific Ocean. His lasting friend Lawrence Ferlinghetti offered a final tribute, echoing Patchen's own directness and clarity:

> A poet is born
> A poet dies
> And all that lies between
> is us
> and the world.

Ferlinghetti squarely located the lasting qualities of the artist and man:

> he spoke much of love
> and never lived by "silence exile & cunning"
> and was a loud conscientious objector to
> the deaths we daily give each other.

Patchen is truly a poet's poet, who never asked for loyalty yet who has been given love by succeeding generations of those who care about poetry and life. As Jess Ritter has explained, "Cummings, Williams, and Patchen were the three between-the-wars poets who most fully explored the possibilities of American poetic language and form." His achievement is measured today both in terms of his dynamic output and his reestablishing the profound role of the modern poet. As Harold Norse has concluded, Kenneth Patchen is "probably the most independent poet of his generation, independent in every sense—pioneer in style, in subject, in sound, in language, in his special climate of compassionate awareness, in his poetic attitude."

Patchen's art is characterized by its abundance, its social relevance, its extreme individuality, and its formal innovations, as it moves from proletarian naturalism and Blakean vision through experiments toward synthesis in a universal oneness of art and life. The last decade has seen the publication of the early uncollected prose of *In Quest of Candlelighters* (1972), *Patchen's Lost Plays* (1977)—including the radio play *The City Wears a Slouch Hat* and the jazz play *Don't Look Now*—and the earliest poems and stories in *Still Another Pelican in the Breadbox* (1980). His visual works have been exhibited at Stanford University, the San Francisco Art Institute, the University of North Dakota, and San Francisco's Mandrake Gallery as part of the "Rolling Renaissance" celebration of 1968. Miriam Patchen has spread the Patchen word through readings, a theater production of his work with Richard King, entitled *Hallelujah Anyway!*, and a San Francisco Public Broadcasting program entitled "Kenneth Patchen: Hurrah for Anything." His manuscripts and paintings are now collected at the University of California at Santa Cruz.

As critics and poets have followed the pathways he forged, his work has received the broad attention and recognition it deserves. William Corrington has written of the necessity of viewing the entire Patchen canon to appreciate his vision and relevance: "We need Patchen. We need his strength and his genius; we need to have his poetry read and re-read, bought and digested by thousands of punks and graybeards who have never experienced this man, have missed a portion of exciting verbal champagne that should be counted among their cultural inheritance." As a visionary artist of the twentieth century, as a poet-prophet to the contemporary world, Patchen created an art dedicated to no less than the salvation and expansion of our world. His achievement within these magnificent life goals makes his work of permanent value to us all.

Interviews:

Doublas Dibble, "Rare Interview with the Poet," *Weekender, Alameda* [Cal.] *Times-Star*, 26 September 1967, p. 6;

Gene Detro, *Patchen: The Last Interview* (Santa Barbara: Capra Press, 1976).

Bibliography:

Richard Morgan, *Kenneth Patchen: A Comprehensive Bibliography* (New York: Paul Appel, 1978).

References:

Harvey Breit, "Kenneth Patchen and the Critical Blind Alley," *Fantasy*, 6 (1940): 21-25;

John Ciardi, "Kenneth Patchen: Poetry, and Poetry with Jazz," *Saturday Review*, 43 (14 May 1960): 57;

Frederick Eckman, "The Comic Apocalypse of Kenneth Patchen," *Poetry*, 92 (September 1958): 389-392;

Lawrence Ferlinghetti and Nancy Joyce Peters, "Kenneth Patchen," in *Literary San Francisco:*

A Pictorial History (San Francisco: City Lights Books/Harper & Row, 1980), p. 172;

Richard Hack, "Memorial Reading for Kenneth Patchen at City Lights Poets Theater, San Francisco: 2 February 1972," *Chicago Review*, 24, no. 2 (1972): 65-80;

Kenneth Patchen: Painter of Poems (Washington, D.C.: Corcoran Gallery of Art, 1969);

David Meltzer, ed., *The San Francisco Poets* (New York: Ballantine Books, 1971); republished as *Golden Gate* (Berkeley: Wingbow, 1976);

Henry Miller, *Patchen: Man of Anger and Light* (New York: Padell, 1946); republished in Miller's *Stand Still Like a Hummingbird: Collected Essays* (New York: New Directions, 1967), pp. 27-37;

Richard Morgan, ed., *Kenneth Patchen: A Collection of Essays* (New York: AMS Press, 1977);

Alan Neil, "Alan Neil's Account of the Session," cover notes to *Kenneth Patchen Reads with Jazz in Canada* (Folkways Records, 1959);

Miriam Patchen, Foreword to *The Argument of Innocence: A Selection from the Arts of Kenneth Patchen*, edited by Peter Veres (Oakland: Scrimshaw Press, 1976), pp. 5-6;

Kenneth Rexroth, "Kenneth Patchen, Naturalist of the Public Nightmare," in his *Bird in the Bush: Obvious Essays* (New York: New Directions, 1959), pp. 94-105;

Rexroth, "Some Thoughts on Jazz as Music, as Revolt, as Mystique," in *Bird in the Bush*, pp. 19-41;

James Schevill, "Kenneth Patchen: The Search for Wonder and Joy," *American Poetry Review*, 5 (January-February 1976): 32-36;

Carolyn See, "The Jazz Musician as Patchen's Hero," *Arizona Quarterly*, 17 (1961): 136-146;

Larry Smith, *Kenneth Patchen* (Boston: Twayne, 1978);

Smith, "The Poetry-and-Jazz Movement of the United States," *Itinerary*, no. 7 (Fall 1977): 89-104;

Tribute to Kenneth Patchen (London: Enitharmon, 1977);

Amos N. Wilder, "Revolutionary and Proletarian Poetry," in his *The Spiritual Aspects of the New Poetry* (New York: Harper, 1940), pp. 178-195;

William Carlos Williams, "A Counsel of Madness," *Fantasy*, 10 (1942): 102-107;

Peter Yates, "Poetry and Jazz," *Arts and Architecture*, 75 (May 1958): 30-33.

Papers:

The largest collection of Patchen's manuscripts and paintings is at the University of California, Santa Cruz.

Frederic Prokosch
(17 May 1906-   )

Robert H. O'Connor
North Dakota State University

SELECTED BOOKS: *The Asiatics* (New York & London: Harper, 1935);

The Assassins (New York & London: Harper, 1936; London: Chatto & Windus, 1936);

The Seven Who Fled (New York & London: Harper, 1937; London: Chatto & Windus, 1937);

The Carnival (New York & London: Harper, 1938; London: Chatto & Windus, 1938);

Night of the Poor (New York & London: Harper, 1939);

Death at Sea (London: Chatto & Windus, 1940; New York & London: Harper, 1940);

The Skies of Europe (New York & London: Harper, 1941; London: Chatto & Windus, 1942);

The Conspirators (New York & London: Harper, 1943; London: Chatto & Windus, 1943);

Chosen Poems (London: Chatto & Windus, 1944; Garden City: Doubleday, 1947);

Age of Thunder (New York & London: Harper, 1945; London: Chatto & Windus, 1945);

The Idols of the Cave (Garden City: Doubleday, 1946; London: Chatto & Windus, 1947);

Storm and Echo (Garden City: Doubleday, 1948; London: Faber & Faber, 1949);

Nine Days to Mukalla (New York: Viking, 1953);

A Tale for Midnight (Boston: Little, Brown, 1955; London: Secker & Warburg, 1956);

A Ballad of Love (New York: Farrar, Straus & Cudahy, 1960; London: Secker & Warburg, 1961);

The Seven Sisters (New York: Farrar, Straus & Cudahy, 1962);

The Dark Dancer (New York: Farrar, Straus, 1964; London: W. H. Allen, 1965);

The Wreck of the Cassandra (New York: Farrar, Straus & Giroux, 1966; London: W. H. Allen, 1966);

The Missolonghi Manuscript (New York: Farrar, Straus & Giroux, 1968; London: W. H. Allen, 1968);

America, My Wilderness (New York: Farrar, Straus & Giroux, 1972);

Voices: A Memoir (New York: Farrar, Straus & Giroux, 1983).

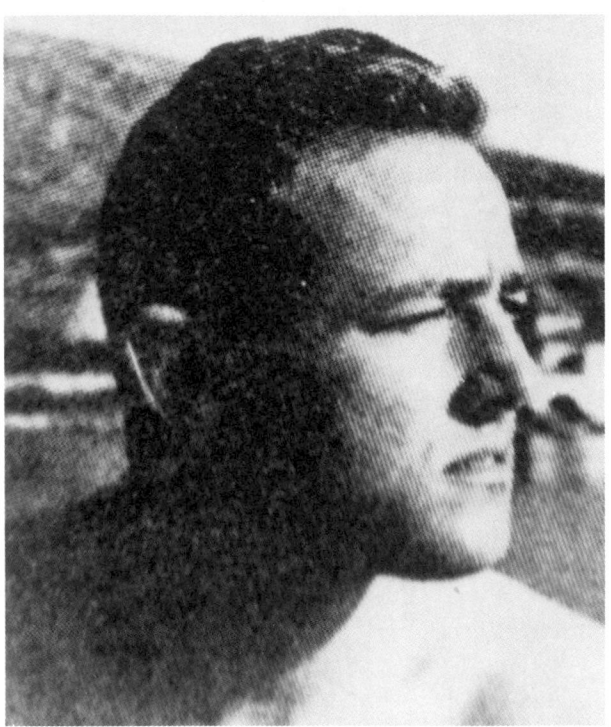

Frederic Prokosch

OTHER: *The Zephyr Book of American Verse*, introduction by Prokosch (London: Continental Book Company, 1945).

TRANSLATIONS: *Some Poems of Friedrich Hölderlin* (Norfolk, Conn.: New Directions, 1943; London: Grey Walls, 1947);

Love Sonnets of Louise Labé (New York: New Directions, 1947; London: Grey Walls, 1948).

Although Frederic Prokosch is best known as a novelist, having published sixteen novels between 1935 and 1972, he also produced, from the late 1920s to the mid-1940s, a distinctive body of poetry that drew favorable comments from, among others, T. S. Eliot, William Butler Yeats, and Edwin Muir. His poems appeared frequently in the literary journals and anthologies of this period, and during the 1930s and 1940s, he published four volumes of poetry. Despite considerable recognition of his skills as a poet, including his reception of the Harriet Monroe Memorial Prize for lyric poetry in 1941, his poetic output waned following World War II, and he directed his literary energies more and more single-mindedly to the production of novels.

Frederic Prokosch was born in Madison, Wisconsin, into a family whose members distinguished themselves through their professional activities. His father, Eduard, was one of this century's finest linguists, serving for several years as chairman of the German department at New York University before becoming Sterling Professor of Germanic Languages at Yale. He was elected to the presidencies of both the Linguistic Society of America and the Modern Language Association. His mother, Mathilde Dapprich Prokosch, was a brilliant pianist who performed before European royalty. His elder sister, Gertrude, was an outstanding teacher of dance, and his younger brother, Walther, was a prominent architect especially noted for his work on airport design. The future writer was raised among unusually talented people and manifested his own exceptional abilities at a relatively early age.

Prokosch began his education in, of all unlikely places for a non-Catholic male, a Catholic girls school in Madison. After his family moved to Austin, Texas, in 1913 so that his father could accept a position at the University of Texas, Frederic was sent to Europe to visit his grandfather in Eger, Austria, and to continue his education. In Austria and in Munich, he experienced the rigors of a Germanic schooling and became at least as fluent in German as he was in English. His schoolmates, however, taunted him as "the little Indian," and despite his quiet shyness, he was frequently caned. These experiences left him with a lasting impression of the sometimes incomprehensible injustices of life, an impression that was strengthened when he returned to Austin in 1915 and found himself, because of the anti-German feelings inspired by World War I, being taunted again, this time as "the little Kaiser." This period of anti-German prejudice cost his father his job, but after a sojourn in Chicago, during which his father published his *Elementary Russian Grammar* (1919), the family moved to Bryn Mawr, Pennsylvania, where Eduard be-

came a respected member of the faculty at Bryn Mawr College. Frederic attended high school in Bryn Mawr, spent another year studying and traveling in Europe, and then enrolled, in 1922, at Haverford College.

The years preceding Haverford were ones of introspective loneliness during which Frederic indulged his fascination with the family garden, with butterflies (a lifelong interest), with the dance (under the influence of Gertrude), and with puppet shows of his own creation. At Haverford he became more outgoing and distinguished himself both as a scholar and as an athlete. In addition to being valedictorian of the Haverford class of 1926, he began displaying the talent for tennis and squash that was eventually to earn him tournament victories in America and Europe. Besides his tennis triumphs in several American competitions and in Baden-Baden and Majorca, he was squash champion of Connecticut in 1933, of France in 1939, and of Sweden in 1944.

Prokosch's career as a published poet began at age twenty-one with the appearance of his work in the July 1927 issue of the *Virginia Quarterly Review*. His poetry and Allen Tate's were presented side by side as instances of the poetic "avant-garde." During the ensuing twenty years, Prokosch's verse was to appear in the *Bookman*, the *Adelphi*, the *American Mercury*, the *Criterion*, *Harper's Magazine*, the *London Mercury*, the *New Republic*, *New Verse*, *Poetry*, the *Spectator*, and *Century*, and, before the publication of his critically acclaimed novel *The Asiatics* in 1935, his literary reputation was based primarily on public awareness of the poetry published in these periodicals.

During these early years of his career, Prokosch was seriously considering the life of the scholar and teacher as an alternative to the life of the creative writer. In 1928 he was granted an M.A. degree from Haverford; in 1929 he served as a University of Pennsylvania research fellow; and in 1930 he was again a research fellow, this time at King's College, Cambridge, from which he received a second master's degree. He then studied and taught at Yale, where, in 1932, he received his doctorate. His research on the M.A. level concerned the playwright William Congreve; for his doctoral dissertation, he wrote on "The Chaucerian Apocrypha," a topic that he intermittently explored for the next several years. But after the resounding success of *The Asiatics* and the encouraging reception of his first full-length volume of poetry, *The Assassins* (1936), and his second novel, *The Seven Who Fled* (1937), Prokosch abandoned the life of academe. He had not been enthusiastic about much of the incidental drudgery associated with being an English instructor at Yale and later at New York University, and when, in 1937, he received a Guggenheim Fellowship and the Harper Prize for *The Seven Who Fled,* he turned wholeheartedly to his career as novelist and poet.

With the publication of *The Asiatics,* a picaresque novel with overtones of spiritual quest set in a series of exotic locations, Prokosch achieved sudden prominence. With the appearance of *The Assassins,* his reputation as one of America's rising literary lights increased. William Butler Yeats, for one, had high praise for the volume: "Mr. Prokosch's poetic gift is one which strikes me as, considering the time and place, astonishing. It is rich and immediate, musical always; the talent of a real visionary, and often magical." The anonymous commentator for the September 1941 issue of the *Reader* (a newsletter for the members of the Readers Club) also saw this verbal richness and suggested a parallel between *The Assassins* and *The Asiatics:* "The poems are notable for their exotic color, daring imagery and sharp, clear beauty of expression. As in *The Asiatics* the rich and varied tapestry of the East is the inspiration and the background for the comment of a true poet."

When Prokosch was putting together *The Asiatics,* he drew extensively on his reading of travel literature and on his personal knowledge of the travel experience, and that double influence also explains, at least partially, the exotic, magical qualities of *The Assassins.* "Port Said," for example, was written about a city that, according to a handwritten note in a copy of Prokosch's privately printed poem "The Red Sea" (1935), the poet had recently visited. The opening lines of "Port Said" are charged with a vivid sense of place:

> Do you feel, shivering, the touch of the world's knife?
> Look, cross the city, listen to the metal street,
> Cross the black bridge and behold the water-haired women
> 　　Grieving on the pebbles below, beating
> 　　Their spotted linen. . . .

Establishing this sense of place serves the purpose not of making a particular spot of ground real but of creating a context evocative of the human passions. Prokosch's places, whether he had seen them himself or only read about them, tend, like Yeats's Lake Isle or his Byzantium, to reflect states of mind, frequently dark states. The inhabitants of his Port Said are troubled and remind the poet

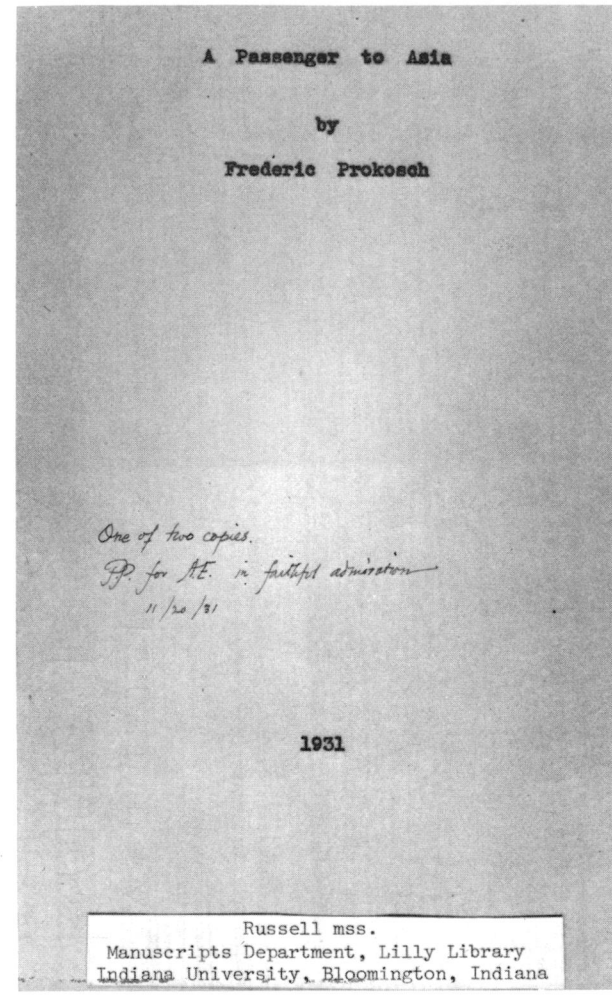

Mimeographed poem inscribed to AE (George Russell) (courtesy of the Lilly Library, Indiana University)

> of those other cities; the dead ones;
> The priests in their stained robes passing the urns, and the silken
> Virgins bearing the frozen nectarines,
> 　　Those led to the sacrifice, the
> 　　Sufferers, the girls with the curling
> 　　Tresses and eyes like pearls,
> Sick of a dead world . . .

Prokosch has often been called a neoromantic, and the melancholy of "Port Said" and of the other poems in *The Assassins* supports that view of him. This melancholy appears to be the direct product of what Prokosch interpreted as man's spiritual state during the prewar years, a condition in which the longing for love and beauty exists in tension with the sometimes greater powers of terror and destructive hatred. His trip to Port Said was part of a larger journey to the Old World that occurred during the hiatus in 1935 between his stays at Yale and New York University. The troubled political situation in the areas through which he traveled could only have darkened his view of life during the months in which he was completing *The Assassins* and may have helped to infuse what John Peale Bishop called a " 'Spenglerian' tone" into the volume's poems, poems that, according to John Crowe Ransom, contain "lines that express more truth about contemporary history than many whole volumes of recent political comment."

Music, visionary magic, and exotic lushness coexist, then, with the book's nightmarish moments of despair. The title poem, "The Assassins," speaks "Of our passionate and forever/Unregenerate spirit" and of "the consummate brow" within which "Such cruelties dwell/As into eternity/Flushed the subservient blood,/Flattened our silver cities/And covered them with wood." The "image/Of terrestrial beauty/More exalted than the eagle" is in opposition to "planetary distress/That allows to move/Beneath such loveliness/Such hostility to love,/Such horror and hate." "The Dolls" (containing suggestions of Prokosch's earlier interest in puppets) begins with music and magic. The dolls are described as "sweet shapes, pearl-lipped and crescent-eyed." The poem then moves on to horror:

> They reach into my secret night
> With pale and terrifying arms
> And offer in a dark delight
> Their subtle suicidal charms[.]

In "Empty Provinces" the "tapestry of the East" is evident, but the poem's mood is again dark and foreboding. The narrator and his companions "scaled the sacred hills in seventy days," carrying "the wounded with us" until they "Reached the dark land, the province of the lost." There, "one cried out in terrible tones how this/The Age of Passion now had killed the spirit." Others "wept at how the nations/Had fallen like whores and spread their false allures/In hideous postures." Still another "cried out at twilight/How dark as iron in our age comes love/And none are safe." A yearning for the regenerative power of love and beauty in a world declining into brutality pervades much of *The Assassins*.

Many of the poems in *The Carnival* (1938), Prokosch's second full-length book of poetry, exhibit this same dark tone. As Prokosch's biographer, Radcliffe Squires, puts it, they show a concern "with the environments of impending war." The "emotions of current history" touch "his lyricism and his landscapes" throughout the volume. Slightly different in focus are the remarks of the commentator for the *Reader*, who sees evidence in *The Carnival* of "the increasing maturity of the author" and notes with approval the poems' emphasis on "things closer to every-day knowledge without leaning on the rich and vari-colored background of the East." This same writer speaks of "the music of his lines" and his "profound understanding of the tragic and futile struggle to preserve the integrity of the individual in a chaotic world." In their *A History of American Poetry, 1900-1940* (1946) Horace Gregory and Marya Zaturenska also expressed pleasure with the volume's music and its concern with significant poetic themes, noting that "readers of contemporary verse are likely to find in it passages of relief from the tone-deaf, small-minded, ugly-tempered, sarcastic rather than satiric improvisations of those Americans who followed MacNeice with scant wisdom and thoroughly docile admiration."

The sense of impending doom that imbues much of *The Carnival* is perhaps most apparent in the following lines from "The Castle," lines that contain an echo of Yeats's "The Second Coming":

> all are swept into a land of warnings.
> The avalanche hovers: and the Föhn comes: only
>   For him whom love chains to the
>   Living, can there be hope!
>
> Nor is it wrong, but merely horrible
> That victory should fall to the beast's intensity,
>   The brooding, equalizing
>   Loins drawn through the desert.

Also illustrative of the volume's gloomy tone are these lines from "Eclogue," a poem whose despair goes far beyond the elegiac sadness of the tradition from which it derives its inspiration:

> All, all of us rot away.
> In broken barges drift
> The warm and cinnamon-skinned
> And in black Europe's wind
> The ice-edged lanterns sway.
> The carousels are silent,
> The towns are torn by sea
> And in their coiling streets
> The dragon snares his prey
> Till all of us rot away!

Two other elements of *The Carnival* are the touches of what Squires refers to as "Audenesque song" and the volume's moments of direct auto-biography. "Eclogue" itself shows the influence of Auden, as does "Evening," the book's opening poem, but as Squires suggests, the clearest echoes of Auden occur in "Nocturne." The first stanza of "Nocturne" was obviously written with Auden's "Lay your sleeping head human on my faithless arm" in mind:

> Close my darling both your eyes,
> Let your arms lie still at last.
> Calm the lake of falsehood lies
> And the wind of lust has passed[.]

Autobiography occurs most prominently in the long, concluding "Ode," a poem referred to by at least one critic as "extraordinarily beautiful" and "the poet's best work." The "Ode" traces the progress of a single day and weaves into that pattern the vicissitudes of human history and of the author's own life. History has reached a moment when

> What has faded away from the world is the candid
>   silence,
>   The faith in the eye and the wish to linger;
> And what has come is the victory by shock. Our nerves
>   are
> The vessels of speed and destruction.

His life, too, especially his life as a perceptive artist, has reached a turning point:

>   what I lovingly sought was some link or music's
> Conducting phrases: the pure and immediate channel
> From this small room, these papers, this catastrophe
>   To the eternal: the lucid: the song. But

> More sharply of late I have glimpsed how in visible
>   shapes
> The actual terrors and victories transpire; and slowly
> The meaning, the quiet, the power, out of the torrents
>   Of night.

These lines conclude the second section of the poem, a section which suggests a Wordsworthian "growth of the poet's mind." The imaginative fascination with the family garden among "hollyhocks with faces" gives way to the first period of travel among the "spires and maxims of towering Europe." Then comes the advent of the athletic years, "the discovery of the body; of Athens/And the gymnasium," followed by the dawning interest in scholarship and literature. The "charm of manuscripts found in the attic" precedes the days when "Asia

. . . held me," an obvious reference to the writing of *The Asiatics*. And during this time of developing artistic sensibility, he listens to

> those who saw the worm incessantly coiled in
> The ageing heart, and the limits of love and sorrow,
> Walkers in cities, invalids, Hölderlin and the
>   Sublime Racine.

Between the publication of *The Carnival* in 1938 and of *Death at Sea* in 1940, Prokosch continued his foreign travels, travels that were eventually to evolve into the life of the expatriate. In the meantime, his third novel, *Night of the Poor* (1939), appeared to a mixed critical reception. Although some reviewers treated it with great respect, others, including Mark Schorer and Clifton Fadiman, were less enthusiastic. This small crack in Prokosch's literary reputation widened when a number of critics attacked *Death at Sea*. Although the book drew some praise for its use of "symbolism with unerring precision" and its "images of exotic sensuousness," the majority of critical comment ranged from lukewarm to icy. Poet Kathleen Raine conceded that "His are verses that any editor could publish without embarrassment, and any critic read without pain," but Randall Jarrell and Louise Bogan were less charitable. Jarrell described Prokosch as "a sort of decerebrate Auden," and Bogan declared that the "real hunger, rage, analysis, terror, observation and tragic pathos which mark a poet of first and obvious rank are not in him."

This is not to say, however, that none of Prokosch's better work appears in *Death at Sea*. Although many of the poems, as Squires expresses it, "suffer from petulance" and give "the feeling that war interferes with Prokosch's lovemaking," a number of them are quite impressive. "Elegy," "The Athletes," and "The Victims" were published in the November 1940 issue of *Poetry* and won the Harriet Monroe Memorial Prize for the following year, while "The Sand" and "The Sunburned Ulysses" are among his most-admired poems. "The Sunburned Ulysses," one of Prokosch's most frequently anthologized works, centers on Ulysses' adventure with the Sirens and attempts to define the poet's own artistic yearnings. The song of the Sirens is the cry of human suffering, a sort of Wordsworthian "still, sad music of humanity" altered by a Shakespearean "sea change":

> He heard, rising from graves of sand, sea-pitted and
>   sea-pillared graves,
> The sobbing and interminable voices of the drowned.

Scarcely to be grasped as anything other than music,
Being almost wholly woven into the sound of waves,
    he heard
Emerging from the crested, sun-dipped lethargy of
    the afternoon,
Distinct and terrifying words.

But the poet has also approached the Siren and
been changed by the experience:

Some of us have glimpsed that rock, that goddess
    rising from the sea,
And as we labor to find for what we were intended,
Slowly, as the spirit is sharpened, the senses are vili-
    fied.

He, too, loves "the unattainable and forbidden"
while simultaneously possessing "Flesh fanned easily into fire." And he, too, recognizes "the frightful
necessity in the song of the sirens," the necessity of
death that makes the artistic task of drawing together the painfully temporary and the eternally
beautiful so important and alluring, and so difficult.

Although the publication of *Night of the Poor*
and *Death at Sea* had been less than triumphant,
Prokosch was still a lionized literary figure during
the early 1940s. When *The Asiatics* became the September 1941 selection of The Readers Club, Roger
Kafka described the month's author as something
of a wandering Colossus, "a young man with a lamentable disregard for tradition on at least three
scores. He is a youthful prodigy who made good.
He is a poet with the physique of an athlete and
the jaw of a dictator. And he is a scholar who writes
of far places, physical hardships, and queer people,
with fervor and understanding." The places he has
visited, Kafka says, include "Greece, Russia, Iceland, the Baltic countries, Bokhara, Samarkand,
France, Germany, Austria, and Portugal."

Lisbon, Portugal, in fact, became Prokosch's
home for a year or so, after which, in 1942, he
came back to the United States to accept a position
in the Office of War Information. In 1943 he went
to Stockholm, Sweden, as a member of the American Legation, and most of his life since then has
been spent abroad. The war years produced three
novels, *The Skies of Europe* (1941), *The Conspirators*
(1943), and *Age of Thunder* (1945), but very little
additional poetry. *Chosen Poems* was published in
England in 1944 but did not appear in America
until 1947, probably because of the hostile American reception of *Death at Sea*. It contains forty-eight
poems, all but six of which had appeared in previous volumes, and it seems to have been intended

as a farewell to poetry rather than as an attempt
by Prokosch to reestablish his poetic reputation.
After the appearance of *Chosen Poems*, Prokosch
continued a practice he had begun in 1932 of privately printing individual poems and small groups
of poems in miniature chapbooks, but these exquisite examples of the printer's art were published
in such limited numbers, generally forty-four or
fewer copies, that the poems they contain, except
those Prokosch chose to publish elsewhere, remain
private rather than public utterances. The definitive collection of these chapbooks is housed at the
Humanities Research Center of the University of
Texas at Austin.

Because of Prokosch's nearly total poetic silence since World War II and because of his neglect
by academic critics, a confident statement about the
significance of his poetry is difficult. Those who
have attempted an overview of his accomplishment
have tended to emphasize the musical qualities of
his verse and the high seriousness of his poetic
themes. They have praised or deplored his attention to structural detail and his pervasive romanticism, and, almost without exception, they have
noted the lushness of his language and the richness
of his imagery. As might be expected in the case
of a poet with Prokosch's brilliant academic background, an impressive diversity of poets have been
pointed to as influences on his work. Yeats, Auden,
Spender, Millay, MacLeish, Rimbaud, Rilke, Labé,
and Hölderlin all helped to shape Prokosch's poetic
sensibility, and Prokosch has himself translated
works by Labé and Hölderlin. Although Prokosch's
influence on his contemporaries has not been
nearly so extensive, at least one major poet, Dylan
Thomas, has admitted an indebtedness to Prokosch's verse. A Prokosch poem or two was often
included in Thomas's readings, and he mentioned
in his letters to Vernon Watkins "unconsciously"
using bits of Prokosch's poetry in his own.

Further light can be shed on Prokosch's poetic
career by examining what he himself has to say
about poetry and poets. In his introduction to *The
Zephyr Book of American Verse* (1945), he describes
America as "a land of inner tensions and inner
contradictions." The best of American art and literature "reflects these inner tensions" and manifests "at the center of it, . . . a single dominant
attitude: uneasiness." These "inner tensions" and
this "uneasiness" are certainly found in Prokosch's
own work. One deficiency of American poetry that
Prokosch seems to have been ambitious to correct
is the "almost complete absence," except in Eliot,
"of concentrated passion or analysis of passion."

The admirations he expresses in the introduction are also telling. He praises Poe's "The City in the Sea" and "To Helen," Whitman's "When Lilacs Last in the Dooryard Bloomed" and "Passage to India," and Wallace Stevens's "Sunday Morning," especially admiring the "magnificent and unfailing internal harmony" of "Sunday Morning." He considers Eliot's "The Waste Land" to be "The most important and much the most brilliant poem America has produced," but "Ash Wednesday" is "the more moving, and far the purer of the two poems." He finds Pound's "Ode pour L'Election de son Sépulchre" to be "a miraculous, witty, and acid performance," but he is "more attracted by the loose, aqueous imagery of his magical second canto." In general, he is drawn to richly musical poetry, serious in tone, which often centers on the elegiac, on human love, and on the soul's quest for salvation in a decadent world. Furthermore, as he stated elsewhere in 1974, these qualities are attractive only in poetry that avoids narcissism and propaganda. It is a mistake "To use a poem as a 'confessional,' a 'protest,' or a manifesto, a self-analysis or in any way as a self-indulgence"; instead, it "should aim for the perfection, the timeless impersonal stillness of a Chinese vase." Unfortunately, the present is not an age for poetry," but an age in which "The timeless impersonal stillness is drowned in an orgy of howls and moans, not to mention vituperations, indignations, and masturbations."

Prokosch's poetic silence since World War II is certainly consistent with this attitude. He has, nevertheless, remained a productive writer, with nearly a dozen novels to his credit since 1946. During the past three and a half decades, he has continued his expatriate existence, with only an occasional sojourn in America. Among other places, he has lived in Italy, Hong Kong, and France, which has been his home in recent years.

Reference:
Radcliffe Squires, *Frederic Prokosch* (New York: Twayne, 1964).

Papers:
The Humanities Research Center, University of Texas at Austin, has a collection primarily consisting of privately printed chapbooks.

Kenneth Rexroth
(22 December 1905-6 June 1982)

Larry R. Smith
Firelands College, Bowling Green State University

See also the Rexroth entries in *DLB 16, The Beats: Literary Bohemians in Postwar America,* and *DLB Yearbook: 1982.*

BOOKS: *In What Hour* (New York: Macmillan, 1940);
The Phoenix and the Tortoise (Norfolk, Conn.: New Directions, 1944);
The Art of Worldly Wisdom (Prairie City, Ill.: Decker Press, 1949);
The Signature of All Things (New York: New Directions, 1950);
Beyond the Mountains (New York: New Directions, 1951; London: Routledge, 1951);
The Dragon and the Unicorn (Norfolk, Conn.: New Directions, 1952);
In Defense of the Earth (New York: New Directions, 1956; London: Hutchison, 1959);
Bird in the Bush: Obvious Essays (New York: New Directions, 1959);
Assays (Norfolk, Conn.: New Directions, 1961);
The Homestead Called Damascus (New York: New Directions, 1963);
Natural Numbers: New and Selected Poems (Norfolk, Conn.: New Directions, 1963);
An Autobiographical Novel (Garden City: Doubleday, 1963; Weybridge, U.K.: Whitter Books, 1977);
The Collected Shorter Poems (New York: New Directions, 1967);
The Heart's Garden/The Garden's Heart (Cambridge, Mass.: Pym-Randall Press, 1968);
The Spark in the Tinder on Knowing (Cambridge,

Kenneth Rexroth (Gale International Portrait Gallery)

Mass.: Pym-Randall Press, 1968);

Classics Revisited (Chicago: Quadrangle Books, 1968);

The Collected Longer Poems (New York: New Directions, 1968);

The Alternative Society: Essays from the Other World (New York: Herder & Herder, 1970);

With Eye and Ear (New York: Herder & Herder, 1970);

American Poetry in the Twentieth Century (New York: Herder & Herder, 1971);

Sky Sea Birds Trees Earth House Beasts Flowers (Santa Barbara, Cal.: Unicorn Press, 1971);

The Rexroth Reader, edited by Eric Mottram (London: Cape, 1972);

The Elastic Retort: Essays in Literature and Ideas (New York: Seabury Press, 1973);

New Poems (New York: New Directions, 1974);

Communalism from Its Origins to the Twentieth Century (New York: Seabury Press, 1974; London: Owen, 1975);

On Flower Wreath Hill (Burnaby, B.C.: Blackfish Press, 1976);

The Silver Swan: Poems Written in Kyoto, 1974-75 (Port Townsend, Wash.: Copper Canyon Press, 1976);

The Morning Star (New York: New Directions, 1979);

Excerpts from a Life, edited by Ekbert Fass (Santa Barbara: Conjunctions Books, 1981);

Between Two Wars (Athens, Ohio: Labyrinth Editions/San Francisco: Iris Press, 1982);

Selected Poems (New York: New Directions, 1984).

RECORDINGS: *Poetry Readings in "The Cellar"* (Fantasy Records, 7002, 1957);

Kenneth Rexroth at the Black Hawk (Fantasy Records, 7008, 1960).

OTHER: *Selected Poems of D. H. Lawrence*, edited, with an introduction, by Rexroth (New York: New Directions, 1948);

The New British Poets: An Anthology, edited, with an introduction, by Rexroth (Norfolk, Conn.: New Directions, 1949);

The Buddhist Writings of Lafcadio Hearn, edited by Rexroth (Santa Barbara: Ross-Erikson, 1977);

Kazuko Shiraishi, *Seasons of Sacred Lust*, edited, with an introduction, by Rexroth, translated by Ikuto Atsumi (New York: New Directions, 1977).

TRANSLATIONS: *Fourteen Poems by O. V. de L. Milosz* (San Francisco: Peregrine Press, 1952);

One Hundred Poems from the Japanese (New York: New Directions, 1955);

One Hundred French Poems (Highlands, N.C.: Jargon, 1955);

Thirty Spanish Poems of Love and Exile (San Francisco: City Lights, 1955);

One Hundred Poems from the Chinese (New York: New Directions, 1956);

Poems from the Greek Anthology (Ann Arbor: University of Michigan Press, 1962);

Pierre Reverdy, Selected Poems (New York: New Directions, 1969);

Love in the Turning Year: One Hundred More Poems from the Chinese (New York: New Directions, 1970);

One Hundred Poems from the French (Cambridge, Mass.: Pym-Randall Press, 1971);

The Orchid Boat: The Women Poets of China, translated by Rexroth and Ling Chung (New York: McGraw-Hill, 1972);

One Hundred More Poems from the Japanese (New York: New Directions, 1975);

The Burning Heart, The Women Poets of Japan, translated by Rexroth and Ikuto Atsumi (New York: New Directions, 1976);

The Complete Poems of Li Ch'ing-Chao (New York: New Directions, 1979).

As American as Mark Twain yet more international than Ezra Pound, Kenneth Rexroth, for nearly half a century, was a cultural force as an intrepid artist and poet, an adept editor and translator, an outspoken critic and cultural personality. His fourteen volumes of poetry (and an equal number of translated volumes from the French, Spanish, Greek, Chinese, and Japanese), the exhibits of his geometric expressionistic paintings, his cultural soirée for Chicago and then San Francisco anarchists, pacifists, poets, and artists, his maverick criticism of politics, history, literature, art, and popular culture—all combine to make him one of the most forceful and persistent influences on American culture in the twentieth century. Rexroth wrote out of an engaged stance toward social, political, and natural environments with a consciousness firmly grounded in Eastern and Western philosophies. His work maintains a fidelity and clarity that is classical in its sensitive directness. The strong subjective base of his truth-saying results in the virtues of his poetry and the limits of his criticism. Poet-critic David Ray suggests of Rexroth's impact as a cultural model, "His own career has argued forcefully and by example for the importance of the poet in all his concerns, public and private." Dudley Fitts personified the composite Rexroth character in this telling analogy: "It is as though in Rexroth we had a Mark Twain who had grown up; who, without yielding an iota of his sense of the absurd and the pitiful, had discarded the clown's motley for the darker dress of the comic philosopher; and who had miraculously been endowed with the power of making poetry."

From mild Midwestern origins in South Bend, Indiana, to a rebellious adolescence in Toledo, Ohio, to a precocious creativity and leftist consciousness in bohemian Chicago, to a role as political organizer and literary midwife to the San Francisco Renaissance and Beat Movement, to his classical and cosmic position as international poet and translator, Kenneth Rexroth followed a clear and steady path toward his own deepest goal of a full and authentic self. His poetry is an intimate, revealing, and rewarding record of that growth.

Though he professed, "I have an intense dislike of all things German," Rexroth was quick to claim the abolitionist, socialist, and anarchist free thinkers in his strong German heritage. "I was born in South Bend, Indiana. Father, Charles Marion Rexroth, the son of a plumber, George Rexroth,

and a schoolteacher, Mary Moore. Mother, Delia Reed, daughter of Charles Reed, a horse trader, and Mary Newman, a foster child and servant. All these grandparents were of very old American stock, predominantly Pennsylvania Dutch in origin." In his profuse chronicle of his early years, *An Autobiographical Novel* (1963), Rexroth lavished detail, anecdote, and importance on his family background. His father's parents were early socialists and anarchists in Toledo, Ohio; and their parents worked on the abolitionists' underground railroad in the Sandusky Bay area smuggling runaway slaves over to Canada. He proudly claimed the strain of American Indian blood in his paternal grandmother, Mary Moore. His mother's family, which was distantly related to the Rexroth family, offered the example of Charles Reed, Rexroth's grandfather, who was a fellow drinker and friend of Eugene Debs, chief spokesman for the American Labor Movement. Reed's mother, Lucy Stoner, was an early socialist and feminist leader. His maternal grandmother, Mary Newman Reed, was a strong Irish woman whose courage and wit also affected Kenneth's early days.

When Kenneth's father, Charles, met his mother in Elkhart, Indiana, they had each spent a term at Oberlin College, dropped out, and taken the reins of their own progressive education. Delia (or Della as she was called) had gone to a finishing school run by nuns, played piano, read extensively, painted, and was an active suffragette. Charles had tried medical school at Northwestern, shifted to pharmacy, and spent a workaday summer in Europe. They eloped and settled into a comfortable Midwestern life in Elkhart, Indiana, where they maintained a remarkably culturally advanced home.

Soon after Kenneth was born 22 December 1905, in South Bend, Indiana, the family returned to nearby Elkhart where his father worked as a pharmaceutical salesman. The progressive atmosphere of Rexroth's youth helps to explain the precocious nature of his development and the multiplicity of his talents and interests. By the age of four, he had been taught by his mother to read fairy tales, science, the history of Livy, Francis Parkman, and William Hickling Prescott, as well as a healthy dose of mythology, stories of foreign life, and American folklore and fact. Rexroth remembered his mother's "great capacity for joy" and the graceful and loving atmosphere she provided. He spent time with his father on sales and fishing trips. At five, his chief companion was an eighty-five-year-old Indian herb doctor, Old Billy, who taught him how to enter into and value the natural world around him. His chief inheritance from his parents, besides their emphasis on art and learning, was a sincere social conscience akin to noblesse oblige without the taints of social status, something he translates as "magnanimity." As he commented in *An Autobiographical Novel,* "This play world of mine I know now was organized by my parents in terms of self-sufficiency and autonomy, and then of hospitality. I realize that I learned then while playing that only the autonomous can be hospitable, and that these two virtues add up to magnanimity." This thrust for an authentic caring about the mass of society Rexroth translated clearly as, "I learned this early: that the only effective action of a moral man takes place within his actual reach, on persons he sees in front of him, and inside himself." This belief is a cornerstone of his moral world view and the foundation of his motivation in art and life.

At age nine, Kenneth toured Europe with his parents, then returned to the United States, where the family settled in Battle Creek, Michigan, and encountered their first serious troubles. Kenneth's father, whom he fondly describes as "a good-time Charlie at poker, drinking, and wenching parties" went bankrupt from bad investments, and the family was dispossessed and forced to move into a tenement apartment. The marriage soon cracked under the strain, though they refused to part. His mother, he recalled, became "chronically mildly hysterical," and his parents thereafter maintained an early "open marriage." In 1915 they moved to Chicago, where his father worked in a wholesale drug house and drifted deeper into alcoholism. When his mother was told she would die in two months from tuberculosis, she returned with Kenneth to Elkhart. At age ten, he recalled, he went with her to choose a coffin; and soon after he watched her demise; he later stated, "The painful experiences of my childhood seem only to have given me a cast-iron psychological constitution." Things did not soon improve.

In 1917 he moved to Toledo, Ohio, where his father was working as a factory worker and where his progressively senile grandmother cared for and abused him. Despite his attaining the eagle rank in a local left-wing Boy Scout troop, his chief learning experience was from a Toledo street gang, where he was nicknamed "Duke" and became streetwise. World War I was going on, and at the homefront Kenneth gained his initial experience in the labor movement by participating in the huge Willys-Overland strike: "This was my first strike and . . . certainly my most enjoyable. . . . I started off in the

labor movement as a pie-card artist." In a later autobiographical poem, "Portrait of the Author as a Young Anarchist," he recalled the Toledo years of 1917-1919, when "I lived in Toledo, Ohio,/On Delaware Avenue, the line/Between the rich and poor neighborhoods." It was a symbolic position; he continued to hover between the haves and the have-nots throughout his youth. Later in the poem he described the area golf course with "rich kids/Who worked as caddies, and the poor kids/Who snitched golf balls." Characteristically Rexroth saw himself as a rebellious outsider "Who, after dark, and on rainy days,/Stole out and shat in the golf holes."

When he was thirteen his father died, and he began a series of homes with relatives until he arrived at his Aunt Minnie's Chicago home on 55th Street in the tough neighborhood where James Farrell later set his *Studs Lonigan* novels (1932-1935). By this time he had become an Anglo-Catholic without the orthodoxy, had discovered all the books of H. G. Wells, and had read deeply into socialist and naturalist writings. His poem "The Bad Old Days" depicts vividly his arrival in Chicago, where, having read Upton Sinclair's *The Jungle* (1906), he confronted the life:

> The first thing I did was to take
> A streetcar to the stockyards.
> In the winter afternoon,
> Gritty and fetid, I walked
> Through the filthy snow, through the
> Squalid streets, looking shyly
> Into the people's faces . . .

A survey of the "debauched and exhausted faces" conveys a sense of human misery out of which, "I felt rising/A terrible anger and out/Of the anger, an absolute vow." Rexroth remained an outspoken advocate of the working man. He also began writing poetry and studying music and art at Chicago's New School and its Art Institute. For a time he attended Englewood High School but was dismissed for his progressive talk and radical behavior. Though he continued to attend the Chicago Art Institute and to audit classes at the University of Chicago, from this time on his education was very much his own, and it is remarkably inclusive.

Rexroth's main activities were directed toward Chicago's 1920s bohemia, where he discussed literature, Lenin, bolshevism, and the Socialist Labor party at the home of Jacob Loeb in 1921. This salon of free thinkers, which attracted such figures as Clarence Darrow, Sherwood Anderson, Frank

Lloyd Wright, and Carl Sandburg suggested a model for Rexroth's own later soirée. He also could be found reading proletarian poetry on the soapbox street circuit for the Industrial Workers of the World (IWW). He recalls, "The lunatic fringe of radical Chicago in those days—the Hobo College, the Bug Club, the Dill Pickle, Bughouse Square— taught me one thing, that the orthodox view of the universe, although acceptable and empirically satisfactory, was probably so only because millions of men had devoted their work and their attention and their consent to see the universe in that way." His reading from this period was equally nonconformist—Jean Cocteau, Max Jacob, Louis Aragon, Ezra Pound, and Gertrude Stein. He was also working with the Chicago painters of early abstract expressionism. By 1921 he had read the classical writings of Plato and Augustine and later declared how he never lost "that sense of exaltation, that feeling of being on the brink of discovery of the Absolute" which so affects his writing. This exploration of the classics in the midst of the avant-garde, which is so characteristic of Rexroth, was expanded when he taught himself Greek and began translating Sappho, and with the aid of Arthur Waley's *Japanese Poetry* and its elementary grammar and vocabulary, began translating Oriental poetry. Of these earliest fragmentary translations from Sappho and the Orient he later exclaimed, "They are wonderful, those first kisses of the muse, and the memory remains, brilliant and poignant for the rest of life. . . . More than my own poems those two translations were the first intimation I had of what it meant to be a creative artist." So began the career of one of America's foremost translators.

The center of Chicago bohemia in the early 1920s was the Green Mask Club, a tearoom and center for artists and writers, which Rexroth co-owned. Here Clarence Darrow, Ben Hecht, and Sherwood Anderson spoke; Edgar Lee Masters, Carl Sandburg, Countee Cullen, and Langston Hughes read; and jazz musicians and poets experimented together. The group around the Green Mask also brought Rexroth in contact with small-time underworld figures, and one night when radical talk and marijuana were being passed out too freely he was arrested and served time in Chicago's notorious Bandhouse jail.

Out of jail Rexroth soon fell in love with his social worker, Lesley Smith, whom he refers to as Shirley Johnson in *An Autobiographical Novel*. It was his first long love affair and the inspiration for his celebrated long philosophical reverie, *The Homestead Called Damascus*. An aspiring story writer and

ten years his elder, Lesley Smith had a profound effect on young Rexroth prompting the development of his latent emotional life. Around 1925 he followed her to Smith College, where he could be near her for loving walks in the woods and where he could work on his writing. He followed her to Greenwich Village for a time where he attended the New York Art Students League and met with East Coast radical intellectuals. He had also been working as a journalist for various leftist publications and had managed an interview in 1926 with Sacco and Vanzetti, a meeting that affected him profoundly.

When he returned to Chicago he received court-appointed social and psychological help and befriended the Green Bay poet Olaf Olsen. Of his early verse (published later in *The Art of Worldly Wisdom*, 1949) he later admitted, "Although I was not writing it, I was trying to feel my way intellectually toward a hard, rugged, and anti-mellifluous verse." He developed friendships with students from the University of Chicago and the University of Illinois, and finished *The Homestead Called Damascus* around 1925, though it did not appear until 1957 in the *Quarterly Review of Literature* (when it appeared in book form in 1963 it was greeted with critical applause). It is a striking mixture of mythical allusion, philosophical dialectic, transcendent experience, and dense literary influences, and yet Rexroth's distinctive voice carries through its deep search for perfect love. It demonstrates the influence of T. S. Eliot's *The Waste Land* (1922), which Rexroth recalled reading then in the *Dial* (5 November 1922) while walking dazed through a Chicago park. Moved by what he viewed as the basic revolutionary nature of Eliot's statement, he shared Eliot's rich experience with French models, yet he was not a disciple of Eliot. As he remembers of *The Waste Land*, it became "a serious disease of young writers in my time."

Rexroth became embroiled again in Chicago's radical bohemia centered around The Gray Cottage tearoom and the Little Theatre company at the Radical Bookshop, where he did staging and acted as a clown. He had also begun taking trips to the West, where he worked in Seattle and the Pacific Northwest among the Wobblie towns of Red bohemia and worked in a Forest Service ranger station at Marblemount, Washington, along Lake Chelan.

He had begun his summer visits West as far back as 1921 when he was sixteen: "I worked the harvest out of Spokane, picked fruit near Wenatchee, got a job as a cook's helper on a ranch near

Pendelton. . . . Mostly I worked for the Forest Service as a patrolman, or as a cook and horse wrangler for trail crews and pack outfits in the spring drive or fall gathering." One summer he traveled to the Southwest to visit D. H. Lawrence's mecca at Taos, New Mexico, and to tote on horseback and pack mule "pamphlets on healthful diet, razor-strop ointment, miracle can openers, mend-all glue and vegetable graters, high pitching by kerosene flares on windy corners in faraway cow towns." It was a heady experience for a young man, one which brought him out of the city into a natural wilderness, challenged his rebellious violence in a daily struggle for survival, and became a comforting constant in his life. In many ways the western wilderness served as a mythic second parent in place of his own parents, who had died before he was fourteen.

Rexroth documents his early realization of self through Nature in another poem, "Gic to Har." Here he focuses on himself as a boy of twelve, who walks out of the noisy clutter of his Toledo boyhood into the connection and revelation which Nature held for him:

> a sycamore in the front of a ruined house,
> And instantly and clearly the revelation
> Of a song of incredible purity and joy,
> My first rose-breasted grosbeak,
> Facing the low sun, his body
> Suffused with light.
> I was motionless and cold in the hot evening
> Until he flew away, and I went on knowing
> In my twelfth year one of the great things
> Of my life had happened.

The pathway to Nature was clearly established by 1922, yet the migration west would come only after those troubled, searching years in Chicago's 1920s.

Another formative experience of paramount importance occurred on his early trip to the Southwest to visit the D. H. Lawrence group at Taos, New Mexico. Here he befriended poet and Chinese translator Witter Bynner, who revealed to him the excellence of Tu Fu. This Chinese poet of the eighth century was to become a profound influence on Rexroth's writing and life. Rexroth felt at one with Tu Fu's clear and concrete imagery and with his integrated acceptance of life's deeper currents, as is apparent in his excellent translations, including these lines of Tu Fu's "Jade Flower Palace":

> The stream swirls. The wind moans in
> the pines. Grey rats scurry over
> Broken tiles. . . .

> . . . .
> I sit on the grass and
> Start a poem, but the pathos of
> It overcomes me. The future
> Slips imperceptibly away.
> Who can say what the years will bring?

The carefully modulated tone and the directness of experience unite in the full human voice. Rexroth openly stated of Tu Fu, "I have saturated myself with his poetry for thirty years. I am sure he has made me a better man, as a moral agent and as a perceiving organism." In a review of Rexroth's *One Hundred Poems from the Chinese* (1956) for *Poetry* magazine (June 1957), William Carlos Williams pointed out, "As a translator of the Chinese lyrics of Tu Fu, his ear is finer than anyone I have ever encountered." The Oriental influence offered Rexroth a sane and unified way of viewing the world, one that could unite his rich natural imagery and his classical call to clarity. One would look far for a truer source of Rexroth's vision and work.

After a tour as a mess steward on a freighter to England and Buenos Aires in 1926, he returned to Chicago and to a chance meeting with a young commercial artist and cubist painter, Andrée Dutcher. She was a free spirit, an idealist, and, despite her epilepsy, an active outdoorsman. As Rexroth exclaims, "Most of our time was spent in uninterrupted, enraptured conversation. We agreed about everything." They married in 1927 and in the spring headed across country to San Francisco, where "It was pretty apparent that we had found the ideal environment for ourselves, at least in America. . . . We decided to stay and grow up with the town." At twenty-two Rexroth thus closed one important chapter of his life to begin another.

Kenneth Rexroth and his new wife arrived on sunny San Francisco streets in late August of 1927 after a summer-long sojourn through the western wilderness. They had hitchhiked through Wisconsin, Minnesota, and the Dakotas, to Montana, where they jumped a freight train north across the Rockies and around to Glacier National Park. There they began hiking again and literally slid down the Cascade Mountains into Washington, where they spent two secluded weeks living in a miner's cabin, two more working as sheepherders and then bar painters, and they finally wandered into Seattle "for a week of parties with the last remnants of the Wobbly intelligentsia and the university Reds." They moved on to Portland, then hiked down the wilderness coast of the Pacific into the open hostility of the "malignant native sons of far northern California." From there they hitched a ride through Mendocino County and ferried across the bay into San Francisco, where they hiked up Market Street and Mission Street with packs on their backs and only lists of names and letters of introduction in their pockets. As a fortuitous welcome they immediately found jobs painting pseudo-French furniture and were soon accepted into the San Francisco bohemia, which Rexroth recalled as "a tiny enclave in Italian North Beach in those days: a cooperative gallery that soon failed; a speakeasy; Isadore Gomec's (the old one down across the firehouse); a restaurant, the Casa Beguine; the Montgomery block; a row of studios in the next block on Montgomery Street; and a few shacks scattered among the dirt roads and goats on Telegraph Hill." Here, amid the large Italian population with its anarchist tradition, the French and Chinese theaters and restaurants, and the strong maritime unions, the Rexroths found their cultural nexus. Rexroth captured the town's attractive spirit in *An Autobiographical Novel:* "San Francisco was not just a wide-open town. It is the only city in the United States which was not settled overland by the westward-spreading puritan tradition, or by the Walter Scott, face-cavalier tradition of the South. It had been settled mostly . . . by gamblers, prostitutes, rascals, and fortune seekers who came across the Isthmus and around the Horn. . . . It was truly a Mediterranean city, and yet it had none of the horrors of poverty. . . . It was like an untouched Mediterranean village . . . and yet it was a great city, and in its own way not a provincial one but the capital of its own somewhat dated culture." The symbolic values and experiences implied in Rexroth's deliberate migration to a bold and natural West, from his precocious career as a Chicago socialist, poet, and cultural provocateur, provide the characteristic focus for his best writing and his most profound influence. His bond to the West was a sound and lasting marriage bringing a bounty of reward for both.

It all began much earlier, as Rexroth nostalgically recalls in "A Living Pearl":

At sixteen I came West, riding
Freights on the Chicago, Milwaukee
And St. Paul, the Great Northern,
The Northern Pacific. I got
A job as helper to a man
Who gathered wild horses in the
Mass drives in the Okanogan

And Horse Heaven country.
. . . .
. . . We took thirty head
Up the Methow, up the Twisp,
Across the headwaters of Lake
Chelan, down the Skagit to
The Puget Sound country.

In this poem Rexroth is back in the Washington wilderness in his fifties with his young daughters acknowledging his own mythic identification with the West:

Half my life has
Been passed in the West, much of it
On the ground beside lonely fires
Under the summer stars, and in
Cabins where the snow drifted through
The pines and over the roof.

More than his fading marriages and his international sense of culture, politics, and art, the West provides the cohering sense of place and self to Rexroth's life. Initiated early, it is the center of his own mythic sense of self as time, space, and relationships are measured against its natural geography.

Politically Rexroth discovered in the Pacific Northwest, the only real West for Western writers, an atmosphere of prolabor socialism and nonviolent anarchism, with Seattle and San Francisco as their centers. He joined forces with the Agricultural Worker's Industrial Union, the Industrial Workers of the World, and began writing and distributing the tabloid *Waterfront Worker* on San Francisco's docks. Later he added to this radical, independent political environment by organizing the first West Coast John Reed Club in the 1930s, followed by Libertarian and Anarchist Circles after World War II. Poet Gary Snyder remembers how for writers of the Beat 1950s, "anarchism as a credible and viable position was one of Rexroth's greatest contributions for us, intellectually." It was a Western political stance apart from party lines. Morgan Gibson describes the climate in which Rexroth's "nonviolent, communitarian anarchism set an independent line in opposition to totalitarian communism and fascism as well as to the injustices of capitalistic democracy." This position was and continues to be the radical political outlook of the Northwest, and it was one which Rexroth accepted and fostered.

As Morgan Gibson points out, Rexroth's "poems may be understood as rites of passage from one spiritual state to another, easing him and his

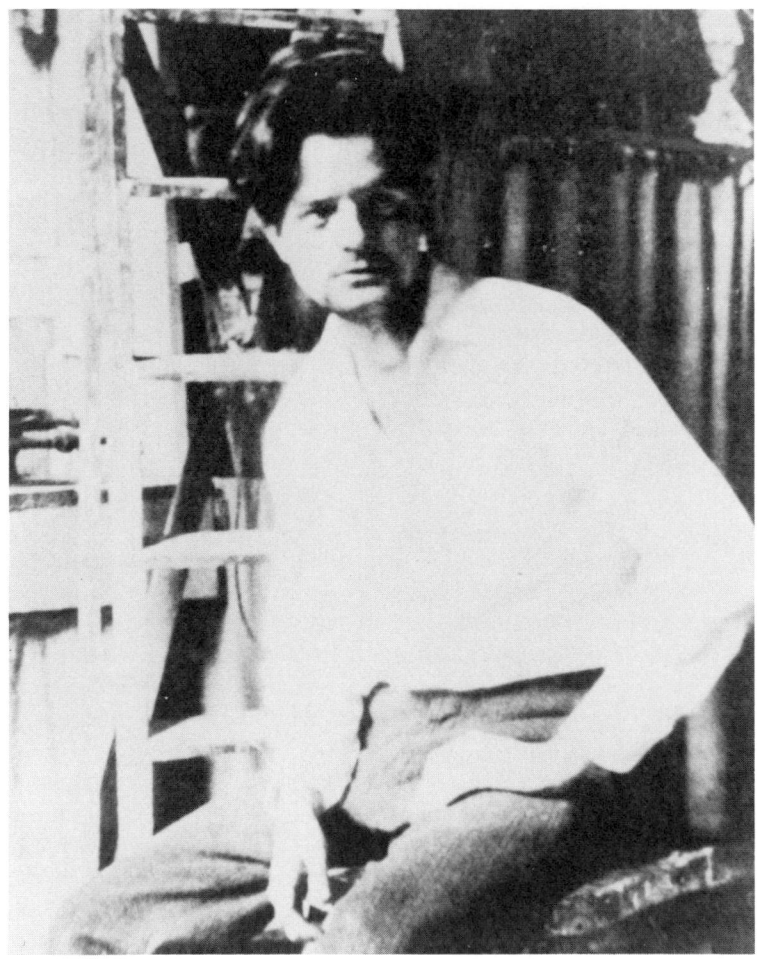

Kenneth Rexroth in San Francisco, 1935 (photograph by John Ferren)

readers through the traumas of change, from despair to love to loss to a larger love, and revealing the mysteries of the universal creative process." One such passage perceived by Rexroth as both personally and culturally symbolic was the execution of accused murderers and anarchists Nicola Sacco and Bartolomeo Vanzetti on August 1927. Rexroth's arrival in San Francisco was made even more emblematic by the news of their death, "A great cleaver cut through all the intellectual life of America. The world in which Andrée and I had grown up came forever to an end." It was an event which he treated later in his elegiac "Climbing Milestone Mountain, August, 1937," which dramatizes the wrong of execution by placing it in the tranquil natural setting of the Sierra Mountains:

> I kicked steps up the last snow bank and came
> To the indescribably blue and fragrant
> Polemonium and the dead sky and the sterile

Crystalline granite and final monolith of the summit.
These are the things that will last a long time, Vanzetti,
I am glad that once on your day I have stood among
   them.
Some day mountains will be named after you and
   Sacco.

Later from the even higher perspective of his 1963 collection, *Natural Numbers*, Rexroth charted the symbolic change in America since their deaths, "Something invisible was gone," and even his 1937 wish meets the final reality of the 1960s, where "No fourteen thousand foot peaks/Are named Sacco and Vanzetti./Not yet" and where "America grows rich on the threat of death." Poems such as these, from Rexroth's wiser personal perspective, make him most valuable as a poet chronicler of America's spiritual conscience.

What was the Western literary scene which the Rexroths encountered in 1927? In *An Autobio-*

graphical Novel he recalled how, "San Francisco was still in the grip of the Jack London, Frank Norris, George Sterling tradition. Everybody we met considered George Sterling the greatest poet since Dante." In particular, he described how in 1927 Robertson's Book Shop on Union Square celebrated the anniversary of Sterling's death (suicide by cyanide) with "its window, draped in black, and, in the center, put the poems of George Sterling, with Homer on one side, and Dante on the other." Clearly from the mock tone of his description the Rexroths were initially taken aback by this native provincialism. Rexroth's critical appraisal was typically sharp, if not curt. He found Sterling, "a most atrocious writer," writer Harry Lafler was "a wealthy bohemian and literary fellow traveller," and poet Joaquin Miller, "a kind of Wild West clown." With equal alacrity he dispensed with his closer peer Robinson Jeffers by objecting to the violent naturalism of his stance, which Rexroth viewed as a pose. However, as William Everson points out in his *Archetype West: The Pacific Coast as a Literary Region* (1976), it is this rich and radical tradition of the Western myth which most clearly connects and reveals Rexroth's best work. Everson concludes, "Of the Western poets who closely follow the moment of apotheosis and devolve from its implications, the chief is Kenneth Rexroth. Although not a native he found his voice in San Francisco, for the ingredients of an illimitable pantheism and an incipient violence provide the determinants of what he writes. Although he repudiates Jeffers, the stance, the point of view of the isolated consciousness subsumed in the Western landscape is Jeffers's own." Rexroth clearly found a ground for his poetry and his life in the free spirit of the West.

By the early 1930s the Rexroths had become active members of the Unemployment Council for the Filmore district and the League of Struggle for Negro Rights. He organized a "workers' theatre" with a mixture of black and white cast members performing Louis Aragon's *The Red Front* (1931), a Paris Commune play, some poetry recited to jazz, and some socialist one acts: "We organized a Blue Blouse Troop which performed regularly on a flatbed truck parked in the 'free speech area' at the corner of Ellis and Filmore Streets."

By then the Rexroths had developed literary friendships with such diverse writers as Gertrude Atherton and Elsa Gidlow, and with Rexroth's old friend from Chicago, Yvor Winters, then at Stanford University. In 1933, precisely at the repeal of prohibition, a young writer and scholar, Dorothy

Van Ghent, joined the Rexroths at their Montgomery Block apartment. She had just completed a thesis on Rexroth, Gertrude Stein, and Laura Riding. Soon she and her husband, Roger, became intimate with the Rexroths, in a four-way love relationship, until some years later she became a faculty member at the University of California at Berkeley, and they drifted apart.

Rexroth, who was active in organizing a West Coast Artists' and Writers' Union in the 1930s, became instrumental in heading up the WPA's Federal Arts Theatre, and Writers Projects begun in the mid-1930s on the West Coast. He edited natural history writings, and both he and Andrée did mural paintings for the Alemany Health Center. He and Andrée had separated as she became increasingly neurotic. It was as a labor organizer, working then for a Nurses' Union, that Marie Kass, the woman who was to be his second wife, came into his life. At the end of the 1930s Rexroth quit his job with the WPA and went to work as an orderly in the psychiatric ward of the San Francisco County Hospital. The early poetry seminars which he, Andrée, and Dorothy Van Ghent had organized in the mid-1930s now continued in his Potrero Hill home with Marie, whom he had married in 1940.

Nineteen-forty was a passage year, bringing the publication of his first book of poems, *In What Hour,* the death of Andrée, and his marriage later that year to Marie, both of whom he immortalized in a series of poems throughout his collections.

In What Hour is a seminal work in Rexroth's life, art, and influence. Its rich variety of styles and central themes of Nature, war, love, death are all brought together in his careful contemplative sensibility. In poems such as "Motto in the Sundial" or "August 22, 1939" his developed poetic voice records the times through the perspective of memory and the eternal presence of Nature. His leftist and pacifist stance is given body in such poems as "Autumn in California," where California's peaceful climate is held against the war in Japan: "In Nanking at the first bomb,/A moon-faced, willowy young girl runs into the street,/Leaves her rice bowl spilled and her children crying." Rexroth had long been developing his personal synthesis of East and West (as in "Another Early Morning Exercise"); and it stood threatened by this physical war between the two. In his "Toward an Organic Philosophy" he makes a strong philosophical resolution, arguing for a living sense of order echoed in his pure nature descriptions, a type of transcendental zen suggestive of American (Henry David Thoreau) and Chinese (Tu Fu) antecedents. Immediately following the U.S. declaration of war after the bombing of Pearl Harbor, the Japanese-American world began to crumble. Racist fears and attacks lead to the forced internment of West Coast Japanese-Americans. Rexroth threw himself into a campaign to preserve their culture—ideas and customs, but also paintings and libraries—and to rescue individuals being forced into the internment camps. Many of the people he saved by locating them in Midwest schools. Rexroth felt intensely the personal and universal tragedy of this violent East-West split.

Though too old for the draft, in 1941 he declared himself a conscientious objector and worked the war years in a San Francisco mental hospital: "I don't understand anybody who goes into the army. . . . I mean, any prison is better than the army . . . any prison." His second volume of poetry, *The Phoenix and the Tortoise* (1944), was dedicated to Marie. *In What Hour* was recognized for "some memorable and deeply felt articulations of the special sociological traumata of the thirties" and was more narrowly viewed by Horace Gregory as "regional verse" or nonintegrated meditations on the times. *The Phoenix and the Tortoise*, however, was received as a rare achievement and a beautifully organized progress of person and vision. The title, borrowed from Shakespeare, symbolizes the union of opposites, for Rexroth a union of human identity and social responsibility. Despite some embarrassingly self-conscious love poems, in which Rexroth seems to be posing as the D. H. Lawrence libertarian of the Pacific, the book presents an overriding intelligence that encompasses emotions and senses. It is also a book of aging, in which Rexroth, at thirty-nine, passes through the midlife rite of passage. Besides the long philosophical reverie of the title poem, the book contains fine elegies to his mother, "Delia Rexroth," and to his first wife, "Andrée Rexroth." In particular, "Un Bel Di Vedremo," which moves autobiographically from his Toledo front porch to later scenes in Milan, Italy, presents his valuable cultural perspective and breeds an intelligent understanding. William Everson finds the long poem "The Phoenix and the Tortoise" to be Rexroth's masterpiece for its very synthesis of the "manifold complexities of the modern intellectual dilemma so resonantly subsumed." In the best poems Rexroth makes his personal growth our own.

Rexroth began his long association with James Laughlin and his New Directions Publishing with *The Phoenix and the Tortoise*, and he soon put his critical talents to use by editing and writing long introductions for the New Directions books *Selected Poems of D. H. Lawrence* (1948) and *The New British Poets: An Anthology* (1949). His marriage to Marie collapsed in 1948, and a Guggenheim Fellowship for 1948 and 1949 enabled him to travel throughout Europe. *The Art of Worldly Wisdom*, for the most part a collection of his earliest poems from 1920-1930, appeared in 1949. It contains some fine love poems, "The Thin Edge of Your Pride" for Lesley Smith, and "In Memory of Andrée Rexroth" (written after her 1940 death), but chiefly it is a collection of his early literary cubist experiments. "Prolegomenon to a Theodicy," dated 1925-1927 and first published in abbreviated form in Louis Zukofsky's *An "Objectivist's" Anthology* (1932), is a long reverie in which the author seeks a mythological resolution to his philosophical questing. Other poems, such as "Fundamental Disagreement with Two Contemporaries," addressed to Dadaist Tristan Tzara and Surrealist André Breton, seek to demonstrate the superiority of his cubist methods and clear consciousness to their unconscious automatism. *The Art of Worldly Wisdom* is a fragmentary and difficult collection full of obscure though plotted juxtapositions close to the work of Gertrude Stein, yet it demonstrates early and deep awareness of the avant-garde. This is a significant recognition in light of his steady progress toward a classical and sensual clarity. While he denies membership in any Objectivist or Imagist schools, his broad awareness of them enlightens his own work.

The mid-1940s were a time of artistic and anarchistic ferment, and Kenneth Rexroth was at the center of it. On the West Coast it took the form of the Berkeley Renaissance, which Rexroth engineered. On an international scale it manifested itself in the emergence of anarchist and pacifist writers in a flourish of new magazines. In London, there was George Woodcock's *Now;* in New York Holley Cantino's *Retort: An Anarchist Review* and the *Experimental Review*, edited by Robert Duncan and Sanders Russell; in Berkeley George Leite and Bern Porter's *Circle* and Christopher and Norma Maclain's *Contour: A Resistance Magazine;* and out of the conscientious objectors' camp in Waldport, Oregon, *Illiterati.* Though Rexroth never edited any of these magazines, he solicited material for them and contributed to them all, as did such writers as Kenneth Patchen, William Everson, Robert Stock, William Stafford, Henry Miller, Robert Duncan, and others. In 1947 Rexroth's libertarian/anarchist circle brought out its single issue of the *Ark* edited by Sanders Russell, James Harmon, Robert Stock, and Philip Lamantia. It was a fine and clear

James Laughlin and Kenneth Rexroth in Wilson, Wyoming (photograph by Ann Laughlin)

distillation of the ideals of individualism, pacifism, freedom, and anarchy which Rexroth had fostered on the West Coast. The Ark Press continues this precedent as a work of Berkeley poet and critic Thomas Parkinson, and the *Ark* journal has been revived by Geoffrey Gardner.

The Berkeley Renaissance which Rexroth engineered in 1946 and 1947 was an attempt to make poetry an accepted public form and forum. Rexroth pulled together William Everson from Waldport, Thomas Parkinson and Robert Duncan from Berkeley, and Philip Lamantia and himself from San Francisco for a series of Bay-area readings. There were, however, personality disputes and diverse aspirations which caused the renaissance as well as the anarchist circle to dissolve before it reached its culmination. Rexroth went off on a Guggenheim Fellowship to Europe for 1948 and 1949, and his demands for loyalty and a clear morality were not easily accepted by his younger poetry compatriots. Rexroth's fierce individualism and dedication would not allow him to compromise his values, and his abrasive tongue often put high demands on friendships. The movement died in

birth, but its underlying values have become legendary.

Back from Europe in 1949, Rexroth married Marthe Larsen, and 1950 and 1954 saw the birth of his daughters, Mary and Katherine. His role as father became a stabilizing force in his life, and he dedicated all succeeding books of poetry to these loving companions. In San Francisco Rexroth threw himself into the activity surrounding public-sponsored radio station KPFA/FM (Pacifica Foundation). Originating in the early 1950s out of Berkeley, the station was an outgrowth of the Libertarian Circle which he had helped organize after World War II. He explained the station's goal as one "devoted to the reeducation of its audience on what you might call libertarian principles." Regular programming features included Alan Watts on Eastern and Western philosophies, Ralph Gleason on jazz, Elsa Thompson on public affairs, Pauline Kael on film, Jaime de Angulo on American Indian folktales, and Rexroth with a wide variety of book reviews. As well as featuring American poets Marianne Moore, William Carlos Williams, and Richard Eberhart, Rexroth managed to record interviews during his English tour of such progressive writers as Herbert Read, Dylan Thomas, Alex Comfort, and David Gascoyne, all of which were later aired on KPFA. In England Rexroth had become familiar with the new romantic group and the anarcho-pacifists; in France he met with surrealists Robert Desnos, Paul Eluard, and Louis Aragon; and in Italy he claims to have become intimate with Caresse Crosby, the beautiful widow of American poet and Dadaist Harry Crosby. He and Marthe became delegates to the first international anarchist conference held since the war, in Paris.

The early 1950s saw the publication of three books, *The Signature of All Things* (1950), the verse plays in *Beyond the Mountains* (1951), and *The Dragon and the Unicorn* (1952). The title poem of the first volume is taken from Jacob Boehme's "Signature of All Things" and demonstrates Rexroth's direction toward transcendence through a fuller oneness with Nature in time and place. He also developed a finer love lyric that is both sexual and grounded on a life/death awareness. The two finest achievements of *The Signature of All Things* are the Japanese seasonal sequence "Hojoki" and the richly human tribute "A Letter to William Carlos Williams." In the first, Rexroth achieves his integrated sensibility through a quiet concreteness with Nature:

> A thing unknown for years,
> Rain falls heavily in June,
> On the ripe cherries, and on
> The half cut hay.
> . . . .
> I walk on the rainy hills.
> It is enough.

This same crystalline directness is used in "A Letter to William Carlos Williams" which reaches its greatness through its honest assimilation of Williams's own humble magnificence. This letter form is a standard pattern for Rexroth as he combines precise critical insight and tribute through the poet's own medium. The book combines his sensibility to Nature and humanity with a persistent indictment against the world's system of warfare.

The verse plays of *Beyond the Mountains* achieve an integrated unit, which William Carlos Williams admired for their satiric "jolt," for their colloquial musicality, and for their philosophical roundness. *The Dragon and the Unicorn* continues Rexroth's reflective natural lyric poems, yet enhances them with the poems of his Italian travels; his deep sense of place remains a prime subject matter. In "Leda Hidden" he presents a personal

lyric set in the San Francisco Golden Gate Park in winter. His fine imagist sense is shown in such lines as, "There is nothing but night,/And the snow and the odor/Of the frosty water." Uncharacteristic of the responses to Rexroth's books that treated only subject and stance, was Richard Eberhart's review for the *New York Times Book Review* (15 February 1953), which commended Rexroth's poetic achievement: "The lines are hard and clear, precise and lean, with continuous tensile strength and nothing fuzzy." Repeated objections to Rexroth's lack of innovations do so at the neglect of his fine sensitivity to form. Whether writing in syllabics or open form, of Nature or warfare, he is uncompromisingly direct and vivid, working always for a deliberate clarity. Unity of perception is his chief method and theme as he combines an Eastern and Western sense of organic order with a daring emotional directness. He never writes of Nature or love or war, but writes of them together in his living sensibility in concrete directness and reflective lyric form. As he exclaimed, "You know where poetry is. The poetry is in song. The poetry is in direct relationship." His progress as a poet was always one of self-realization, a progress of personality and the communion of that growth.

The mid-1950s saw his emergence as a major translator with the publication of *Fourteen Poems by O. V. de L. Milosz* (1952), *One Hundred Poems from the Japanese* (1955), *One Hundred French Poems* (1955), *One Hundred Poems from the Chinese* (1956), and *Thirty Spanish Poems of Love and Exile* (1955). The Spanish poems, published as one of the earliest City Lights Books Pocket Poets series, also established an alliance with its poet-publisher, Lawrence Ferlinghetti, and with the Beat Movement that was about to blossom.

An understanding of Rexroth's relationship with the Beat Movement takes us a long way toward comprehending his often being misunderstood as a poet. By the mid-1950s he had clearly emerged as "one of the veterans of American modernist poetry" and as a central figure in the whole San Francisco Poetry Renaissance. And this is chiefly how the East Coast Beats viewed him when they migrated West. A critic as wise as Alfred Kazin must surely have been flinching under Rexroth's frequent attacks on the literary establishment of the East when he branded Rexroth an "old-fashioned American sorehead" in "Father Rexroth and the Beats" (*Reporter*, 3 March 1960). Rexroth sought neither a father nor brother relationship with the tenacious New York invaders of his home turf. Yet he would have accepted an elder's role had the Beat writers been sensitive to his position and achievement. So he (like Kenneth Patchen, William Everson, and later Lawrence Ferlinghetti, Philip Lamantia, and Gary Snyder) had to publicly disclaim the Beat label that threatened to haunt his writing as a mistaken and stereotyping categorization.

It is true that Rexroth was the man these Beat writers chose to chair their celebrated Six Gallery Reading on 13 October 1955, when Ginsberg delivered his fiery *Howl* (1956), amid Jack Kerouac's boisterous hurrahs. But Rexroth's international soirées had been going on for almost a decade and so had the Berkeley poetic, anarchistic, and libertarian circles, as well as the San Francisco Poetry Center which Rexroth had cofounded with Ruth Witt-Diamont around 1953. Rexroth was not prepared to watch the San Francisco Poetry Renaissance be swallowed up by the publicity-conscious Beats. To heighten the tension, Allen Ginsberg had voiced an insulting challenge at Rexroth in one of his meetings by shouting, "Rexroth, I'm a better poet than you are, and I'm only twenty-one years old!" Though Ginsberg later lamented the insult, attributing it to his vanity over the public reading of "Howl," he, like Jack Kerouac, who once sat on Rexroth's floor roaring with drunken laughter, was asked to leave. They had offended Rexroth's sense of artistic and human dignity in such a way that he never could forgive them. A final insult came when the Beats fostered a love affair between young poet Robert Creeley and Rexroth's estranged wife, Marthe. Though he would later step to the defense of *Howl* during the obscenity trial of summer 1957, Rexroth became an outspoken detractor of Beat writing and their early unprincipled life-style.

A closer parallel to the Beat Movement and one that directly affected them was the poetry-and-jazz movement of the late 1950s. Rexroth, Ferlinghetti, and Kenneth Patchen (who worked separately) were longtime jazz fans who took the new poetry-and-jazz form to the public in 1957. Though they all worked for a real synthesis of these brother art forms, a primary motive for Ferlinghetti and Rexroth, who performed at The Cellar Club with The Cellar Jazz Quintet, was to expand the audience for both forms. Rexroth boldly stated, "Poetry is the dying art of modern civilization. Poetry and jazz together return the poet to his audience." He had experimented with the form in early recitals at the Green Mask in Chicago during the 1920s, along with poet Langston Hughes, and in the "workers' theatre" street performances in San Francisco. Because Rexroth recognized Ferlin-

ghetti as a natural oral poet, he invited him to share the stage. They worked with the form for a couple years, performing and recording the long-playing album *Poetry Readings in "The Cellar"* (1957). Rexroth later recorded the finer *Kenneth Rexroth at the Black-Hawk* (1960). Patchen carried his concert performances up to Vancouver and to New York's celebrated Five Spot Cafe, and for a time other dedicated poets—Philip Whalen, David Meltzer, and Jack Kerouac—did poetry-and-jazz readings in and around San Francisco. However, in Rexroth's sarcastic estimation, the whole movement was destroyed by the fostering of cheap imitations throughout the country, "so that in every Greenwich Village coffee shop and bar for about two years, all kinds of bums with pawnshop saxaphones put together with scotch tape, and some other guy with something called poetry, were, like, you know, blowing poetry, man, dig? And it was absolutely unmitigated crap. It killed the whole thing."

One thing that emerged from the experiment was Rexroth's long dramatic poem "THOU SHALT NOT KILL (A Memorial for Dylan Thomas)," which appeared in his 1956 collection *In Defense of the Earth*. The poem stirred condemnation and praise, but it served the Beats chiefly as a model of revolt, a direct poetic release of anger in a fierce indictment of the sacrificed decades of young, radical artists (he lists most of them) to suicide, drink, or careers. Making ties with Saints Stephen and Sebastian, the poem bridges the modernist rebellion to that of the contemporaries and clearly targets the limited established order as the enemy. It is all the more dramatic for the irrational anger of its accusation, as David Ray concludes, " 'Thou Shalt Not Kill' is a lasting and powerful work in which the *ubi sunt* of those who have been destroyed by materialism rings as if through a hollow corridor in hell." The poem's four-part elegy, which echoes Federico García Lorca's "Lament for Ignazio Sanches Mejiás" uses Dylan Thomas's tragic death as a point of awakening.

In Defense of the Earth is a remarkably diverse collection of works—good and bad, sweet and sour, angry and wise. There are prosey lover's laments, autobiographical poems, a bestiary, epigrams, forty-five Japanese translations, and poetry statements of Rexroth's personal and poetic code. Many of the best are clear ties of self to his daughter Mary through their shared experience in nature. "The Lights in the Sky Are Stars" is a fine example, as is "A Living Pearl," which ties him to time and place as well as blood. "They Say This Isn't a Poem" is a

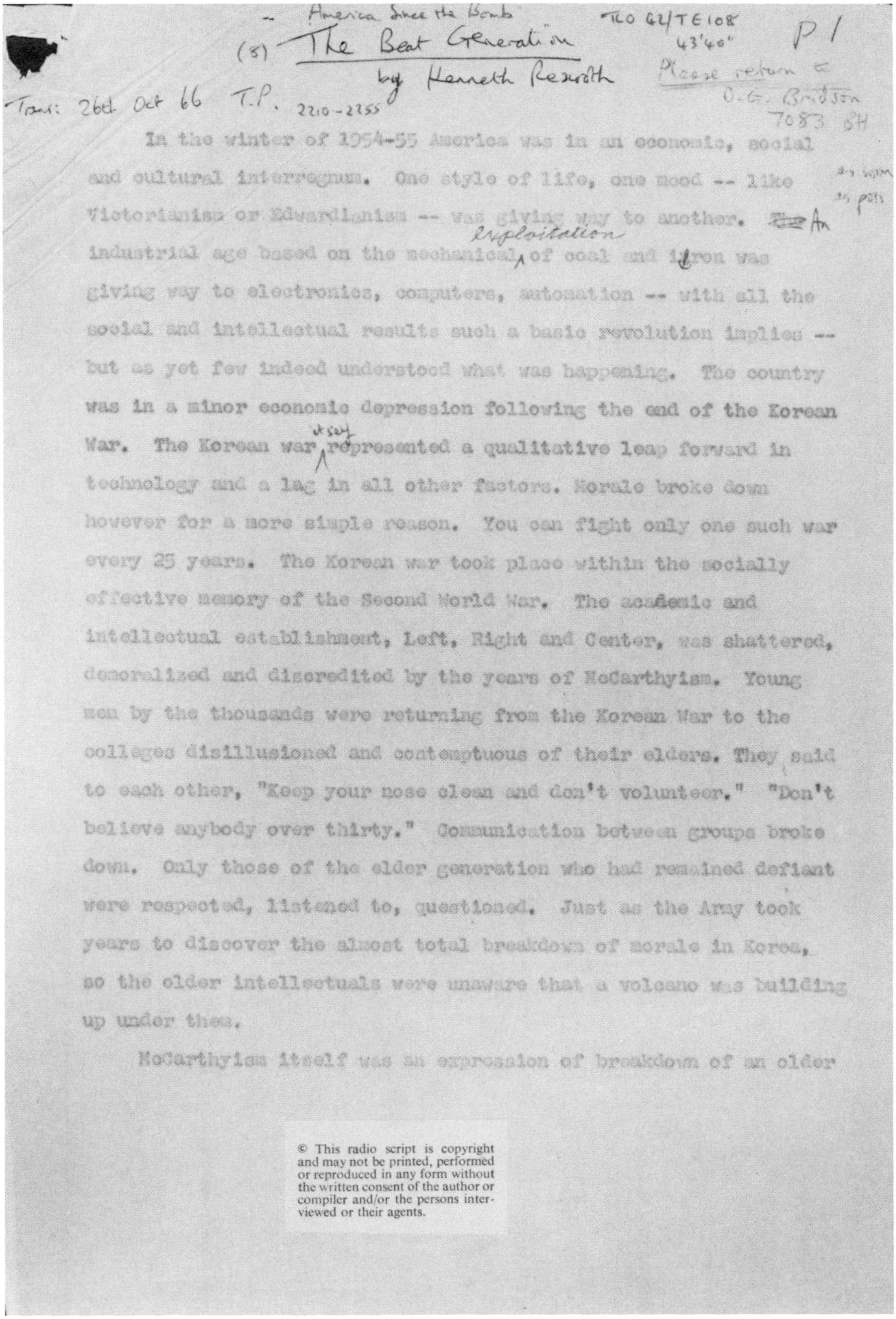

America Since the Bomb

(5) The Beat Generation

by Kenneth Rexroth

Trans: 26th Oct 66 T.P. 2210-2255

TO 62/TE108
43'40"   P 1

Please return to
D. G. Bridson
7083 BH

In the winter of 1954-55 America was in an economic, social
and cultural interregnum. One style of life, one mood -- like
Victorianism or Edwardianism -- was giving way to another. An
industrial age based on the mechanical *exploitation* of coal and iron was
giving way to electronics, computers, automation -- with all the
social and intellectual results such a basic revolution implies --
but as yet few indeed understood what was happening. The country
was in a minor economic depression following the end of the Korean
War. The Korean war *itself* represented a qualitative leap forward in
technology and a lag in all other factors. Morale broke down
however for a more simple reason. You can fight only one such war
every 25 years. The Korean war took place within the socially
effective memory of the Second World War. The academic and
intellectual establishment, Left, Right and Center, was shattered,
demoralized and discredited by the years of McCarthyism. Young
men by the thousands were returning from the Korean War to the
colleges disillusioned and contemptuous of their elders. They said
to each other, "Keep your nose clean and don't volunteer." "Don't
believe anybody over thirty." Communication between groups broke
down. Only those of the elder generation who had remained defiant
were respected, listened to, questioned. Just as the Army took
years to discover the almost total breakdown of morale in Korea,
so the older intellectuals were unaware that a volcano was building
up under them.

McCarthyism itself was an expression of breakdown of an older

*First page for a radio script (by permission of Bradford Morrow for the Trustees of the Kenneth Rexroth Trust; courtesy of the
Lilly Library, Indiana University)*

revealingly direct, though poetically flat, statement of his personal organic view, which links the harmonies of the universe to those of humankind.

Rexroth clearly sees himself as an elder statesman in this book, as his longtime friend and critic Lawrence Lipton reveals in his telling personal portrait of Rexroth in his fifties. Lipton first charts the character behind the man: "Think of him first, as an 11th century figure of a man, scholar, poet, priest, a student from the Latin Quarter out on the town. In his youth, a tramp scholar in the tradition of goliards, unchurched, unfrocked, unschooled, from whose fingers no book was safe if he needed it, no scholarly discipline too formidable to undertake, no language too arduous to study and master, no way of life too unconventional or too dangerous to sample." Then, he colors in the personal image of the present man (circa 1957): "And, today, in his middle years, a tall greying figure in ragged overcoat, with a knobbed walking stick and the look of a friendly uncaged lion who delights children and frightens their school teachers. Looks like Albert Schweitzer, talks as I imagine Gilbert K. Chesterton might have talked if he was D. H. Lawrence, lives like St. Francis, and has the reputation of Bishop Golias." Finally, Lipton closes this portrait, which accompanied the first full publication of "The Homestead Called Damascus" in the *Quarterly Review of Literature* (1957) with further character analogies: "And, by his own description, as American as Mark Twain, as simple as Robert Burns or Tu Fu, as primitive as a Bushman chant, as consecrated and maligned as Peter Abelard." Further characterization comes in Jack Kerouac's novel *The Dharma Bums* (1958) where Rexroth is presented as the bold and flamboyant raconteur in the fictionalized character Reinhold Cacoethes. Morgan Gibson reinforces this vision of the living Rexroth as one who speaks, "bluntly, sardonically, stating opinions as facts and facts as epithets." Rexroth proved himself a tenacious and outspoken man of letters who demanded of others as much as he himself gave to his art.

For a long time he had been writing reviews and criticism on a wide variety of social, political, literary, and popular culture topics, often for *Nation, Art Digest* and *New World Writing*. In 1959 he published his first collection of these writings in *Bird in the Bush: Obvious Essays* treating such diverse subjects as American jazz, Henry Miller, Kenneth Patchen, Morris Graves, D. H. Lawrence, Martin Buber, and William Butler Yeats. A second and equally provocative collection appeared in the 1961 *Assays*. Though Rexroth is often dogmatic and bla-

tantly subjective in his essays, he is always interesting and affronting, speaking authentically, whatever his bias. Like William Carlos Williams's *In the American Grain* (1925) or Edward Dahlberg's *Can These Bones Live* (1960), his essay writing always calls for a re-examination of his subject outside the conventional assimilated view. He continued to write richly anecdotal and essentially subversive essays and criticism into the 1980s, and they were collected in such books as *The Alternative Society* (1970), *American Poetry in the Twentieth Century* (1971), *The Elastic Retort* (1973), and *Communalism from Its Origins to the Twentieth Century* (1974). He is fearless before his subject.

The 1960s were in many ways a cohering period for Rexroth. Despite his divorce from Marthe in 1961, he remained ever-close to his daughters, treating their relationship in many poems. His second wife, Marie, remained close to the family serving as what Rexroth termed a "godmother" to his daughters. In 1964 he also met and became inti-

The Collected Shorter Poems of Kenneth Rexroth

Front cover for Rexroth's 1967 book, with a photograph of Rexroth with his daughters, Katherine and Mary

mate with a young poet and painter, Carol Tinker. That same year he taught for a term at San Francisco State College and then at the University of Wisconsin. In 1967 and 1968 he traveled on a Rockefeller Foundation award to Provence, Venice, through most of Europe, and to Japan. When he returned home in 1968, he lost his reviewing job with the *San Francisco Examiner* and so moved to Santa Barbara, California, where he lived and taught part-time at the University of California, Santa Barbara. In 1970 he was instrumental in fostering the antiwar demonstration which rocked that conservative campus. His poems were collected during these years in *The Collected Shorter Poems* (1967), which included the new poems of "Godol's Proof," and *The Collected Longer Poems* (1968). The publication of these volumes allowed critics and poets an opportunity to survey the Rexroth canon. One garners from a methodic reading of *The Collected Shorter Poems* a sense of the author's range and personal unity with the work. There are poems of direct statement, personal elegies, poems of love and marriage and family, profound poems which equate the process of creation with the cycle of nature in his organic vision that recognizes death and love as life's permeating forces. In a review for *Poetry* (December 1967), poet William Stafford concluded, "All his life Rexroth has apparently carried a burden that would seem quixotic to many writers with less swagger and less voiced recklessness—he has worked a tradition that puts forward poems that try to tell the truth. Even the determined imagism of many poems conveys an air of not wanting to claim more than what *is*." Placing him in the transcendental tradition of Emerson, Thoreau, and Whitman and in the modernist vein of Gertrude Stein, Ezra Pound, E. E. Cummings, and William Carlos Williams, critic Morgan Gibson concluded, "The range of thought and feeling, from some of the most passionate love poems in American literature to elegies of mass destruction, is amazing." To this statement one must add Rexroth's diverse assimilation of the classical, populist, and Eastern traditions. Like his life, his writing is homeward bound yet reaching into the world; his best poems locate the reader in time and place while drawing him into timeless universals. As critics were forced to recognize, Rexroth's writing was a finely tuned history of American poetry in the twentieth century.

The Collected Longer Poems contains philosophical reveries written approximately five to ten years apart yet providing a unity of their own. As Rexroth pointed out, "All the sections of this book now seem to me almost as much one long poem as do *The Cantos* or *Paterson*." To the direct sensuous and visionary poems of *The Homestead Called Damascus* (written 1920-1925), "Prolegomenon to a Theodicy" (written 1925-1927), "The Phoenix and the Tortoise" (1940-1944), *The Dragon and the Unicorn* (written 1944-1950), he added the contents of the volume he had written in Kyoto during his 1967 world tour, *The Heart's Garden/The Garden's Heart* (1968). This last poem, in many ways Rexroth's clearest masterpiece, takes his philosophical journeying into a visionary communion with Nature and the Tao (the Way). Wandering the Japanese forests in early summer, the poet enters into a sensual communion with nature by listening to the music of wind and water. He (and it is clearly Rexroth as personal narrator) discovers the Tao as a way of holding the world, of listening through the harmonies of human voices to an acceptance of the holiness of all things and acts. It is a richly musical poem, whose clear and simple language echo its profound theme that "The real objects are their own transcendental meaning." Critic R. D. Spector's response (*Saturday Review*, 15 March 1969) was characteristic of the re-evaluation of Rexroth as poet rather than as spokesman, "For me, Kenneth Rexroth has long appeared the American most capable of epic achievement. He possesses the necessary general knowledge, range of poetic comprehension, the varied skills requisite to the heroic poem." In the comparisons to the epics of Ezra Pound, William Carlos Williams, and Charles Olson (*Choice*, November 1969), Rexroth was given the poetic status he long deserved.

Throughout the 1970s Rexroth proved himself a prolific critic and translator. His translations of Pierre Reverdy and other French poets, as well as from the Chinese, French, and Japanese (including volumes of poems by traditional and contemporary women poets that he translated with Ikuto Atsumi), have been widely acclaimed and filled a cultural void in this country. His own poetry appeared in several volumes, the slim volume *Sky Sea Birds Trees Earth House Beasts Flowers* (1971), *On Flower Wreath Hill* (1976), and *The Silver Swan: Poems Written in Kyoto 1974-75* (1976), and *New Poems* (1974). Writing well into his sixties and seventies, Rexroth maintained a clear and wise perspective. His *New Poems*, which includes adaptations or translations of Chinese and Japanese poems, was praised for its "classic restraint and fidelity," its "lean, clear style" and finally its mellowed tone. As Herbert Leibowitz noted in the *New York Times Book Review* (13 March 1975), "This slow music exquis-

The Collected Longer Poems of Kenneth Rexroth

Front cover for the collection that lead one critic to call Rexroth "the American most capable of epic achievement"

itely suits the feeling of the people of Rexroth's poems, who are resigned to evanescence. Heartbreak is laconically stated." Rexroth returned to Japan and his beloved Kyoto in 1972, 1978, and finally in 1980. Though he went through some turbulent times with his mature daughters in the 1970s, he found some comfort in his peaceful Santa Barbara cottage with its immense library garage. With the aid of his new wife, Carol Tinker, whom he married in 1974, he continued to write, despite a long illness that often confined him to hospital care and a wheelchair. Beyond these limitations he remained a presence in the San Francisco scene, appearing frequently at poetry festivals and artists' rallies for workers' unions. His translations of contemporary Japanese poetry and his own poems continued to flow throughout the 1970s as seen in his collection, *The Morning Star* (1979). His *Selected Poems* (1984) has made him readily accessible in the 1980s.

Kenneth Rexroth was working on his autobiographical "Life" when he suffered a stroke early in 1982; he died in the back room of his Santa Barbara cottage sometime later on 6 June. *Excerpts from a Life* (1981) had already appeared, yet the entire manuscript remains unpublished. In his last years Rexroth had voiced his faith that the present ecological crisis would bring about "a scientific model for a just society." This legacy of a deep moral commitment to the laws of Nature is coupled with his advice for the young writers "to be reconnected with the avant-garde tradition of the world." In his poems, his criticism, and personal example he remains an insistent reminder that the heart of poetry is in speaking the truth. His work is appropriately characterized by his open declaration of art's ultimate value and purpose: "Because art *is* a weapon. After millions of well-aimed blows, someday perhaps it will break the stone heart of the mindless cacodemon called Things As They Are. Everything else has failed." His work and his life are testaments to this faith. Younger writers have found in him the voice of an unspoken conscience, as Daniela M. Ciani concludes, "Kenneth Rexroth is one of the outstanding personalities in contemporary American culture. He has always openly fought any threat to intellectual freedom and basic human needs. He is a man of action, a scholar, a poet and a master." Speaking as one who lived and worked alongside of Rexroth in a deeply principled revolution for human freedom and dignity, William Everson offers an appropriate epitaph, "He touched the nerve of the future and more than any other voice in the movement called it into being. Though others picked up his mantle and received the plaudits, it remains true that today we enjoy the freedom of expression and lifestyle we actually possess largely because he convinced us that it was not only desirable but possible, and inspired us to make it be." Rich and diverse, classical and visionary, transparent and committed, Rexroth's poetry of experience is a witness to the fundamental unity of life and art.

Interviews:

Cyrena N. Pondron, "Interview with Kenneth Rexroth," *Contemporary Literature*, 10 (Summer 1969): 313-331;

"Kenneth Rexroth," in *The San Francisco Poets*, edited by David Meltzer (New York: Ballantine Books, 1971), pp. 9-55.

Bibliography:

James Hartzell and Richard Zumwinkle, *Kenneth*

Broadside (by permission of Bradford Morrow for the Trustees of the Kenneth Rexroth Trust; courtesy of the Lilly Library, Indiana University)

Rexroth: A Checklist of His Published Writings (Los Angeles: Friends of the UCLA Library, University of California, 1967).

References:

Ark: For Kenneth Rexroth, edited by Geoffrey Gardner, no. 14 (1980);

Richard Eberhart, "A Voyage of the Spirit," review of *The Dragon and the Unicorn, New York Times Book Review,* 15 February 1953, p. 25;

William Everson, *Archetype West: The Pacific Coast as a Literary Region* (Berkeley: Oyez, 1976);

Lawrence Ferlinghetti and Nancy Joyce Peters, *Literary San Francisco* (San Francisco: City Lights/ Harper & Row, 1980), pp. 153-169, 174-175;

Richard Foster, "The Voice of the Poet: Kenneth Rexroth," *Minnesota Review,* 2 (Spring 1962): 377-384;

Morgan Gibson, *Kenneth Rexroth* (New York: Twayne, 1972);

Donald Hall, "Kenneth Rexroth and His Poetry," *New York Times Book Review,* 23 November 1980, p. 9;

Alfred Kazin, "Father Rexroth and the Beats," *Reporter,* 22 (3 March 1960): 54-56;

Lawrence Lipton, "Notes Toward an Understanding of Kenneth Rexroth with Special Attention to 'The Homestead Called Damascus,' " *Quarterly Review of Literature,* 9, no. 2 (1957): 37-46;

Lipton, *The Holy Barbarians* (New York: Julian Messmer, 1959);

Thomas Parkinson, "Kenneth Rexroth, Poet," *Ohio Review,* 17 (Winter 1976): 54-67;

Parkinson, "Phenomenon or Generation," *A Casebook on the Beat* (New York: Crowell, 1961);

M. L. Rosenthal, "Outside the Academy," *The Modern Poets: A Critical Introduction* (New York & London: Oxford University Press, 1960);

Robert Stock, "The Hazards of Art," review of *Collected Longer Poems, Nation,* 208 (24 March 1969): 378;

John Unterecker, "Calling the Heart to Order," review of *Collected Shorter Poems, New York Times,* 23 July 1967, p. 8;

William Carlos Williams, "Two New Books by Kenneth Rexroth," review of *One Hundred Poems from the Chinese* and *In Defense of the Earth, Poetry,* 90 (June 1957): 180-190;

Williams, "Verse with a Jolt to It," review of *Beyond the Mountains, New York Times,* 28 January 1951, p. 5.

Muriel Rukeyser

(15 December 1913-12 February 1980)

Alberta Turner
Cleveland State University

BOOKS: *Theory of Flight* (New Haven: Yale University Press, 1935);

Mediterranean (New York: Writers and Artists Committee, Medical Bureau to Aid Spanish Democracy, 1937?);

U.S. 1 (New York: Covici, Friede, 1938);

A Turning Wind: Poems (New York: Viking, 1939);

The Soul and Body of John Brown (New York: Privately printed, 1940);

Wake Island (Garden City: Doubleday, Doran, 1942);

Willard Gibbs (Garden City: Doubleday, Doran, 1942);

Beast in View (Garden City: Doubleday, Doran, 1944);

The Green Wave (Garden City: Doubleday, 1948);

Elegies (Norfolk, Conn.: New Directions, 1949);

The Life of Poetry (New York: Current Books, 1949);

Orpheus (San Francisco: Centaur Press, 1949);

Selected Poems (New York: New Directions, 1951);

Come Back Paul (New York: Harper, 1955);

One Life (New York: Simon & Schuster, 1957);

Body of Waking (New York: Harper, 1958);

I Go Out (New York: Harper, 1961);

The Colors of the Day: A Celebration for the Vassar Centennial, June 10, 1961 (Poughkeepsie, N.Y., 1961);

Waterlily Fire: Poems 1935-1962 (New York: Macmillan, 1962);

The Orgy (New York: Coward-McCann, 1965; London: Deutsch, 1966);

Bubbles (New York: Harcourt, Brace & World, 1967);

The Outer Banks (Santa Barbara: Unicorn Press, 1967);

Poetry and Unverifiable Fact: The Clark Lectures (Claremont, Cal.: Scripps College, 1968);

The Speed of Darkness (New York: Random House, 1968);

Mazes (New York: Simon & Schuster, 1970);

The Traces of Thomas Hariot (New York: Random House, 1971; London: Gollancz, 1972);

29 Poems (London: Rapp & Whiting/Deutsch, 1972);

Muriel Rukeyser, 1978 (photograph by Dixie Sheridan, Vassar Quarterly)

Breaking Open: New Poems (New York: Random House, 1973);

The Gates (New York & London: McGraw-Hill, 1976);

The Collected Poems of Muriel Rukeyser (New York & London: McGraw-Hill, 1978);

More Night (New York: Harper & Row, 1981).

PLAY PRODUCTIONS: *The Middle of the Air*, Iowa City, 1945;

The Colors of the Day, Poughkeepsie, New York, Vassar College, 10 June 1961;

Houdini, Lenox, Mass., Lenox Arts Center, 3 July 1973.

TRANSLATIONS: Octavio Paz, *Selected Poems*, translated by Rukeyser and others (Bloomington: Indiana University Press, 1963; revised edition, New York: New Directions, 1973);

Paz, *Sun Stone* (New York: New Directions, 1963);

Gunnar Ekelöf, *Selected Poems*, translated by Rukeyser and Lief Sjöberg (New York: Twayne, 1967);

Ekelöf, *Three Poems* (Lawrence, Kans.: T. Williams, 1967).

Muriel Rukeyser was one of the twentieth century's most productive and articulate poet-activists, concerned with every social and psychological issue, from Sacco and Vanzetti through Vietnam, from the disease of silicosis in miners' lungs to the dry rot in solitary souls. She saw poets as gifted leaders with a mission to encourage all human beings to realize their greatest human potential, their full reality, and she prodded them—and herself—to do it. Though she never received wholehearted and uniform critical acclaim, at least during her lifetime, the extent, quality, seriousness, and vitality of her work assure her a permanent place in the history of modern American poetry.

Born in New York City, daughter of Lawrence B. and Myra Lyons Rukeyser, Muriel Rukeyser was educated at the Fieldston Schools, and at Vassar College and Columbia University, which she briefly attended in 1930-1932. By her own choice her life was not bland or sheltered. At nineteen she caught typhoid fever in an Alabama police station during the second Scottsboro trial; she was married briefly; later she had a child by another man and raised it alone; she did time in a Washington jail for protesting the Vietnam War on the steps of the U.S. Capitol; she flew to Hanoi; and at almost sixty, nearing the end of her life and in deteriorating health, she became president of the American Center for P.E.N., a society which supports the rights of writers worldwide, and went to South Korea to intervene on behalf of poet Kim Chi-Ha, who was in prison under sentence of death. When she was not allowed to see him, she stood outside the gates of the prison and later based her last major poem, "The Gates," on that experience.

Intellectually Rukeyser was equally active. The titles of her poems indicate her interest in subjects ranging from physicist Willard Gibbs to painter Albert Ryder to composer Charles Ives to labor organizer Ann Burlack. She wrote poems on Franklin D. Roosevelt and on Wendell Willkie, Orpheus and Akiba, Herman Melville and Pablo Neruda, John Brown and Martin Luther King, Jr. In one of her published essays on the nature and craft of poetry she refers to Ernest Fenollosa on the Chinese character, Charles Pierce on semiosis, Albert Einstein on the laws of consciousness, Lu Chi and I. A. Richards on literature, Shi-Hsiang Chen on translation, Sir John Arthur Thomson and Sir Patrick Geddes on morphology, Norbert Wiener on cybernetics, the Orphic hymns, Pindar, and Marcel Proust—all as background for an explanation of the creative process, as she used it to write her own poems and as she provoked it in her students.

Rukeyser's career as a published poet began in 1935, when *Theory of Flight* won the Yale Series of Younger Poets competition and was published by Yale University Press. For the next forty-one years, until 1976, she produced a steady flow of volumes of poetry, sometimes two or three a year, and translated poetry from Swedish, French, German, and Italian. Not all her publications were poems: she wrote a novel, plays, television scripts, juvenile books, biographies, and essays. But poetry was her main interest. *The Collected Poems of Muriel Rukeyser* (1978) comprises 573 pages.

Rukeyser's work is fairly consistent in theme, tone, and technique from her twenties through her sixties. There are gradual shifts of emphasis and a clear awareness of evolving social concerns and prosodic fashions, but the poetic voice already formed in *Theory of Flight* is essentially the same voice in *The Gates* (1976).

The poems in *Theory of Flight* show that Rukeyser's vision of herself as poet-prophet-leader was formed in childhood. When her father, shaving, once asked her, "What will you be?" she answered, "Maybe : something : like : Joan : of : Arc" ("Poem Out of Childhood," part two). Her intense tone, angry but also tender, jubilant, even exalted, which was to be dominant throughout her career, is already apparent in her first book: "We pass/loud in defiance of death, the helpless lie" ("Song for Dead Children"), "Weld and prepare for action our mind's intensity" ("Metaphor to Action"), "Look! Be : leap :/paint trees in flame/bushes burning/roar in the broad sky" ("Theory of Flight"). Her anger at social injustice began in school, and so did her tendency to worship heroes with revolutionary minds: "Bruno, Copernicus, Shelley, Karl Marx,"

Muriel Rukeyser standing outside the gates of a South Korean prison to protest the imprisonment of poet Kim Chi-Ha (photograph by Roy Whang, Asia Economic News*)*

the "lynched Jesuses" ("The Lynchings of Jesus," part one). Her intense need for love appears in poems such as "Effort at Speech Between Two People":

> When I was fourteen, I had dreams of suicide,
> and I stood at a steep window, at sunset, hoping toward death :
> if the light had not melted clouds and plains to beauty,
> if light had not transformed that day, I would have leapt.
> I am unhappy.   I am lonely.   Speak to me.

But her self-pity was balanced by a tough honesty that was to temper her view of herself for the rest of her life: "When I was nine I was fruitily sentimental."

Theory of Flight also introduces Rukeyser's continuing search in the subconscious mind to discover the fullest human potential. Sometimes it is a search into the individual mind, as in these lines from "In a Dark House":

> walls close in to a shaft and blur of brown:
> out of the chaos and eclipse of mind rise stairs.
> ....

nothing in the world but the slow spiral rise, expectancy, and fear.

Sometimes, as in "Cats and a Cock," it is a search into the Jungian collective unconscious:

> The latchpieces of consciousness unfasten.
> We are stroked out of dream and night and myth.
> ....
> Never forget in legendary darkness
> the ways of the hands' turning and the mouth's ways [.]

In technique the poems in *Theory of Flight* are characterized by a combination of manners that continue into Rukeyser's later work.

A torrential fullness of expression compels the reader to accompany her while she points, ejaculates, and explains—at length. Though she often uses space on the page for emphasis (punctuation at abnormal distances from words, groups of short lines to vary the tempo of blocks of long lines, extra spaces between sentences), she makes little use of silence. She often exhorts the reader directly, as in these lines from "The Structure of the Plane," part three: "Answer with me . . . Answer the men . . . take to yourself . . . ," and she employs considerable exposition, as in "The Gyroscope":

All directions are *out*,
all desire turns outward : we, introspective,
continuing to find in ourselves the microcosm
imaging continents, powers, relations, reflecting
all history in a bifurcated Engine.

Her diction is abstract, often academic. Some of her abstractions, such as "reflecting all history" in the lines above, have become abstract because they are dead metaphors. Others, words such as *introspective, microcosm,* and *bifurcated,* seem more at home in a textbook than a poem. Yet she often personalizes this tendency toward abstract exposition by using the dramatic and journalistic technique of inserting bits of actual dialogue, detailed factual description, and brief dramatic scenes, as in these lines from "The Tunnel," part one:

"Well," says the father, "nothing comes of this,
the strippings run to weeds, the roads all mucked.
A dead mine makes dead miners.   God, but I
was a fool not to have chucked

the whole damned ruin when I was a kid."

Rukeyser's poems are most often written in long free-verse sentences whose syntax is more like prose than song, more like written platform oratory than colloquial speech. In "The Tunnel," for instance, one sentence comprises four four-line stanzas, and the twenty-two lines in part three of "Poem Out of Childhood" consist of only two sentences. Yet the sustained, oratorical rhythms of these poems combine with her abstract diction to create heightened style, which is also characteristic of her metered verse, such as the opening of "Theory of Flight," an invocation in blank verse.

Throughout most of her career Rukeyser usually preferred to write sequences of poems strung on characters, clusters of poems grouped about single situations, or gatherings of poems under a title which linked the parts thematically. In *Theory of Flight* the title poem is a cluster of seven poems (two of which are themselves clusters) centered on the theme of the human aspiration and threaded partly on the narrative of an early airman taking up his primitive machine. The first section of the book, "Poem Out of Childhood," consists of fifteen poems. While some treat various aspects of her own childhood and adolescence and others are more general, the last one appears to have been

written deliberately to fuse the others into a unit. The last section of the book, "The Blood is Justified," comprises fourteen poems, one of which consists of three separately titled parts, and another is divided into eight parts separated by slashes—all of them only loosely related to one another by the theme of integrity in particular lives and deaths implied by the section title "The Blood is Justified." This title is also the title of the last poem in the section, a rousing revolutionary challenge to the past and a resolution for the future, which brings the last section and the whole book to a crescendo of resolve. This handling of her main theme in separate, autonomous bits, varied in line length and stanza form (though more varied in appearance than in sound or emotion) is Rukeyser's characteristic method. The parts of each book roll toward the reader in a series of waves, each of which crashes firmly.

The most obvious literary influence on *Theory of Flight* is Walt Whitman, and behind him, she said, is the Bible: "We are talking about the endless quarrel between the establishment and the prophets, and I hope to be forever on the side of the prophets." For Rukeyser Milton was also a prophet. The influence of Whitman and Milton is apparent in the confluence of intensity, celebration, long lines in rhetorical rhythms, in both copious detail and copious explanation, and in the vision of personal wholeness fused with social wholeness. Yet the differences are significant too. Unlike Whitman, Rukeyser is not celebrating the realization of a dream, but its necessity. Unlike Milton, she pushes outward, but does not define her dream's conclusion.

Although no profound or startling changes took place in her choice of subjects, themes, or style during her forty-one years of publishing poetry, an examination of Rukeyser's last book of poems, *The Gates* (1976), shows how these years of study, involvement, and continuous writing firmed and refined both style and statement.

One is struck first by the continuances: poems praising young activists—"the young bearded rebels and students tearing it all away" ("For Kay Boyle"), the "students in the branches/Defending the tree" against the concrete mixers ("Boys in the Branches"), a description of a peaceful Washington demonstration for "the dead in Asia" ("How We Did It"). There are tributes to women—the woman who must have been among the prehistoric cave painters ("Painters"), Lot's daughters ("Ms. Lot"), an activist mother of an activist son ("Mother as Pitchfork"). There are tributes to the power of poetry: "Rune," "Poem White Page White Page

PLEASE BELIEVE THE PUNCTUATION

          A   L O U I S   S O N N E T

The jokes, the feuds, the puns, the punishments:

This traditional man being brave, going in grace,

Finding the structure of lives more than perfected line;

The forms of poetry are his time and space.

He's quirky, he rhymes like daily life; light wine

Is all his flavor till ~~strange and~~ *fierce* reverence

Turns delicatessen into delicatesse −

The man who anthologizes experience.

He is anthologized; a wave of the sea,

He is here, he is there, he changes; impossibly

He is blue surface, green suspended, the dark deep notes.

A stain of brilliance spreading upwards floats

In luminous air; we are luminous; he makes us be

The jokes of Job and Heine's anecdotes.

Muriel Rukeyser

A sonnet for Louis Untermeyer (by permission of the Estate of Muriel Rukeyser; courtesy of the Lilly Library, Indiana University)

Poem," "Work for the Day is Coming." There are tributes to Neruda ("Neruda, the Wine"); a love poem ("Then"); a poem celebrating physical joy—sex, music, movies, "cut in rhythms of collision" ("Song: Remembering Movies"); a journey into the collective and the personal unconscious ("Double Ode"). These are familiar subjects treated with familiar attitudes. But though the intensity is still there, the tone is less strident. In "St. Roach" she extends her reverence for the oppressed of the human race to the oppressed of the insect world, the cockroach. In "Painters" and "How We Did It" she risks understatement. In "Not to Be Printed" and "Back Tooth" she risks triviality. In other words, she took the final risk of not straining too hard.

The technical control that was an achievement in a poet of twenty-two has become second nature, and continued success has let her relax it. Her style is less rhetorical. The lines and poems are shorter, and fewer are organized in clusters. The images are in greater proportion to the abstractions. And though the poems still end firmly with clearly stated, strong opinions, they are less likely to pummel their readers. Though the title poem is a long

cluster, strung on a narrative thread with a linking refrain and a climactic, prophetic ending that reminds one of "Theory of Flight" (1935), "The Book of the Dead" (1938), "Ajanta" (1944), "Waterlily Fire" (1962), or "Akiba" (1973), the poem is more immediate, economical, and tentative. The climax is no longer a statement but a series of questions: "How shall we speak to the infant beginning to run?/All those beginning to run?" The long sentences characterized by abstract diction and pulpit rhythms have become shorter and closer to emotional, vernacular speech: "How shall we venture home?/How shall we tell each other of the poet?/ How can we meet the judgment of the poet/or his execution?" or "The gates are open. The prisoners go in." or "Fool that I am! I had not seen the ropes/ down at their wrists in the crowded rush hour bus." These lines are still rhetorical, but it is a rhetoric of emotional breathing, rather than the "high style" of oratory. The poem contains a much greater proportion of scene and dialogue than of exhortation, effusion, or explanation, and its brief introduction sets the stage as if for a play.

Critical reaction to Rukeyser's work during her lifetime was mixed. The literary temper of her

The Bollingen Prize Committee, 9 January 1955: (seated) Marianne Moore and Muriel Rukeyser; (standing) Wallace Stevens, Randall Jarrell, and Allen Tate. They awarded the prize to Léonie Adams and Louise Bogan.

times was against direct preaching and found prophetic optimism simplistic. Hence, the critics were often cool to her method, even when they respected her message. Kenneth Rexroth praised her for avoiding propaganda, for the lack of provincialism that distinguished her translations, and for avoiding assimilation by the establishment. But Randall Jarrell, reviewing *The Green Wave,* deplored her rhetoric, emotionalism, and "merely conventional" attitudinizing. Suzanne Junasz, reviewing *The Gates,* noted with approval that in this volume Rukeyser was moving away from grandiloquence and rhetorical posturing "to the colloquial and to the sharpness of sudden perception."

It is too soon to tell if Rukeyser will have any lasting influence on other twentieth-century poets. She did not become known as member or leader of a poetic sect. At her death she had received little attention from scholars, and her work was not required reading in those courses in contemporary poetry that required the works of Denise Levertov, Sylvia Plath, Adrienne Rich, and Anne Sexton— all socially conscious female poets who were her contemporaries. The feminists of the 1970s and 1980s considered her one of them, but, though always aware of woman's power and woman's needs, she seems not to have belonged to that part of the women's movement that resented woman's historical role or became hostile toward the male sex. Nor did her poetic techniques raise much enthusiasm in the writing programs. Even she herself once told her friend Louise Bernikow that she found it hard to believe that anyone read or loved her poems. But that was perhaps false modesty. She was thoroughly and passionately reviewed, positively and negatively. She had a long career of teaching young writers and readers of poetry at Vassar, the California Labor School, Sarah Lawrence, the 92nd Street Y.M.H.A. in New York, and by means of continual campus and public readings all over the country. When she died, at sixty-six, the University of Dayton had just announced that Muriel Rukeyser would read her work on its campus fifteen days later.

Muriel Rukeyser will probably not be ranked finally as one of the greatest of twentieth-century American poets—nor will she have as great an impact on the movement of American poetry as T. S. Eliot, William Carlos Williams, Wallace Stevens, or even Allen Ginsberg or Robert Lowell. She wrote too much that was intense but fuzzy, trusting intensity to create a magic rather than selecting and juxtaposing fresh powerful words or images. But at times she was able to find the right image, especially in her later books. Characteristic of her best poetry is "Resurrection of the Right Side," from *The Gates,* in which she describes the slowly returning powers of speech, movement, and sight after a major stroke:

> When the half-body dies its frightful death
> forked pain, infection of snakes, lightning, pull down the
>   voice.   Waking
> and I begin to climb the mountain on my mouth,
> word by stammer, walk stammered, the lurching deck
>   of earth.
> Left-right with none of my own rhythms.

Because she demonstrates her will and its slow success without interpreting her "stumble down corridors of self, all rhythms gone" in order to universalize it, she does universalize it; so that the final image is instantly and simultaneously a fact, a symbol, and an epiphany: "in this late impossible daybreak/all the blue flowers open."

References:
Louise Bernikow, "Muriel at 65: Still Ahead of Her Time," *MS,* 7 (January 1979): 14-16;

Bernikow, "Rare Battered She-Poet," *MS,* 2 (April 1974): 35-36;

Randall Jarrell, *Poetry and the Age* (New York: Knopf, 1953), pp. 163-166;

Louise Kertesz, *The Poetic Vision of Muriel Rukeyser* (Baton Rouge: Louisiana University Press, 1979);

David Madden, ed., *Proletarian Writers of the Thirties* (Carbondale: Southern Illinois University Press, 1968);

Kenneth Rexroth, *American Poetry in the Twentieth Century* (New York: Herder & Herder, 1971), pp. 123-124;

M. L. Rosenthal, "Muriel Rukeyser: The Longer Poems," in *New Directions in Prose and Poetry,* no. 16, edited by James Laughlin (Norfolk, Conn.: New Directions, 1953), pp. 201-229;

T. Solotaroff, "Rukeyser: Poet of Plenitude," *Nation,* 230 (8 March 1980): 277-278.

May Sarton

(3 May 1912-   )

Constance Hunting
University of Maine

See also the Sarton entry in *DLB Yearbook: 1981*.

BOOKS: *Encounter in April* (Boston: Houghton Mifflin, 1937);

The Single Hound (Boston: Houghton Mifflin, 1938; London: Cresset, 1938);

Inner Landscape (Boston: Houghton Mifflin, 1939; London: Cresset, 1939);

The Bridge of Years (Garden City: Doubleday, 1946);

The Underground River: A Play in Three Acts (New York: Play Club, 1947);

The Lion and the Rose (New York: Rinehart, 1948);

Shadow of a Man (New York: Rinehart, 1950; London: Cresset, 1951);

The Leaves of the Tree (Mount Vernon, Iowa: Cornell College, 1950);

A Shower of Summer Days (New York: Rinehart,

May Sarton (Gale International Portrait Gallery)

1952; London: Hutchinson, 1954);

The Land of Silence (New York: Rinehart, 1953);

Faithful Are the Wounds (New York: Rinehart, 1955; London: Gollancz, 1958);

The Fur Person (New York: Rinehart, 1957; London: Muller, 1957);

In Memoriam (Brussels: Presses de W. Godenne, 1957);

The Birth of a Grandfather (New York: Rinehart, 1957; London: Gollancz, 1958);

In Time Like Air (New York: Rinehart, 1958);

I Knew a Phoenix: Sketches for an Autobiography (New York: Rinehart, 1959; London: Owen, 1963);

Cloud, Stone, Sun, Vine: Poems, Selected and New (New York: Norton, 1961);

The Small Room (New York: Norton, 1961; London: Gollancz, 1962);

Joanna and Ulysses (New York: Norton, 1963; London: Murray, 1963);

Mrs. Stevens Hears the Mermaids Singing (New York: Norton, 1965; London: Owen, 1966);

Miss Pickthorn and Mr. Hare (New York: Norton, 1966; London: Dent, 1968);

A Private Mythology (New York: Norton, 1966);

As Does New Hampshire and Other Poems (Peterborough, N.H.: Smith, 1967);

Plant Dreaming Deep (New York: Norton, 1968);

The Poet and the Donkey (New York: Norton, 1969);

Kinds of Love (New York: Norton, 1970);

A Grain of Mustard Seed (New York: Norton, 1971);

A Durable Fire (New York: Norton, 1972);

As We Are Now (New York: Norton, 1973; London: Gollancz, 1974);

Journal of a Solitude (New York: Norton, 1973);

Collected Poems (1930-1973) (New York: Norton, 1974);

Punch's Secret (New York: Harper & Row, 1974);

Crucial Conversations (New York: Norton, 1975; London: Gollancz, 1976);

A Walk Through the Woods (New York: Harper & Row, 1976);

A World of Light (New York: Norton, 1976);

The House by the Sea (New York: Norton, 1977);

A Reckoning (New York: Norton, 1978; London: Gollancz, 1980);

Selected Poems of May Sarton, edited by Sue Hilsinger and Lois Brynes (New York: Norton, 1978);

Halfway to Silence (New York: Norton, 1980);

Recovering (New York: Norton, 1980);

Writings on Writing (Orono, Maine: Puckerbrush Press, 1981);

Anger (New York: Norton, 1982);

A Winter Garland (Concord, N.H.: W. B. Ewert, 1982);

At Seventy (New York: Norton, 1984);

Letters from Maine (New York: Norton, 1984);

The Magnificent Spinster (New York: Norton, 1985).

Now in her vigorous seventies, May Sarton has produced fourteen books of poetry, as well as eighteen novels, several nonfiction "journals," books for children, and autobiographical works. Her range is unusually wide, and she continues to experiment within each genre. Paradoxically, the diversity of her approaches to literature, and her broad and varied readership, may have affected the responses of major critics to her achievements. Only in the past few years has serious attention begun to be paid to what is an oeuvre in the fullest sense. But it is as a poet that Sarton would most wish to be known.

Eléanore Marie Sarton (whose name was later Anglicized to Eleanor May) was born in Wondelgem, Belgium, to George Sarton, an eminent philosopher and scientific historian, and Eleanor Mabel Elwes Sarton, a gifted furniture and fabric designer. Her father was Belgian, her mother English, and when World War I broke out, the Sartons fled to England, and thence, in 1916, to Cambridge, Massachusetts, where George Sarton obtained a part-time teaching position at Harvard University. Young May began her education at the progressive Shady Hill School, where her burgeoning love of poetry flourished (she began writing poems at the age of nine) and continued at the Institut Belge de Culture Française, where she spent a year when she was twelve, and at the Cambridge High and Latin School. Her first published poems, a group of sonnets, appeared in *Poetry* when she was seventeen. In that same year, 1929, although she had won a scholarship to Vassar College, she joined Eva Le Gallienne's Civic Repertory Theatre in New York as an apprentice. When the Civic Rep closed in 1933, Sarton founded The Apprentice Theatre, based at the New School for Social Research in New York. The company soon moved to Hartford, Connecticut, where it became

The Associated Actors Theatre with Sarton as director. In 1936 this company disbanded, and Sarton began to devote herself fully to writing. A year later, her first book, *Encounter in April* (1937), appeared to generally favorable comment. William Rose Benét, for example, noted the poems' "dignity and spiritedness." High praise indeed for a twenty-five-year-old, as Sarton then was.

The poems in *Encounter in April* were composed in the period 1930-1936, and naturally reflect Sarton's experiences and concerns during those years. She had spent the winter of 1931-1932 on her own in Paris, writing poetry, seeing plays, and exploring the city, an experience that provided a rich stimulation for the mind and senses. In 1936 she visited England and formed lasting friendships with such figures as Julian Huxley and S.S. Koteliansky, James Stephens, and Elizabeth Bowen; here, too, she met Virginia Woolf. Her experiences fertilized and focused her imagination, resulting in themes which would remain predominant in her work: the difference between physical passion, which is doomed to fade, and real love, which is permanently fulfilling; the value of the human being in the world; and the role of art in reconciling the human being to the world. The poems in *Encounter in April* are romantic, meditative, and questing, and show the purity of purpose which throughout Sarton's career has never wavered. Her skill in using multiple forms is already evident; she employs the sonnet, the short lyric, and free verse with equal competence; and her salient constellation of images—landscape, weather, music, art—is already in place. The weakest poems show the influence, almost impossible to escape at the time, of such women poets as Edna St. Vincent Millay, who allowed the note of self-pity to creep in; the strongest are those which sustain image and thought and do not permit emotion to drag them down. Most experimental among these poems is "She Shall Be Called Woman," a long, free-verse exploration of Eve's coming to accept the fact that she is a body, female, as well as a soul, essentially sexless. The effect of the short, pressured lines, whose breaks echo pauses in thought, is that of enquiry pursued to answer. Perhaps significantly, Sarton for her *Collected Poems (1930-1973)* chose to include only three from *Encounter in April:* "First Snow," "She Shall Be Called Woman," and "Strangers."

From 1937 to 1940, Sarton taught creative writing and choral speech at the Stuart School in Boston, and in 1938 her first novel, *The Single Hound,* was published. But the poetic impulse continued strong, and a second book of poems appeared in 1939. *Inner Landscape* represents an advance over her first collection in almost all respects. There is less self-pity, and the poems are less tentative; decoration is kept to a minimum; images are not superimposed but are grounded in thought. The themes of love, art, and personality are again predominant, but they are more deeply examined. There is pain in the poems, but instead of giving in to suffering, Sarton wrestles with it in lines which paradoxically give off the aura of certitude. The poet is newly confident in her stance, if buffeted by her emotions. As in *Encounter in April*, a variety of forms is employed: the Shakespearean sonnet (there are twelve of these), whose structure encouraged Sarton toward both firmness of technique and boldness of image; free verse; rhymed and carefully crafted lyrics; and the canticle, which introduces a lighter, more supple line in graceful but everyday language. The final poem of the volume, "A Letter to James Stephens," in the epistolary genre, refers to Sarton's recent London visit and replies to Stephens's criticism of her poetry as treating only of "this personal all,/The little world." He had urged her to "write for an abstracted beauty's sake . . . /The word that will endure, comfort, sustain a man," to which she rejoins, "If there are miracles we can record/They happen in the places that you curse," and goes on to set forth the concept that has become the foundation of her life and art: "to build on the quicksand of despair/A house where every man may take his ease." Here too is embedded the idea that the isolation necessary for artistic creation need not be loneliness but can be solitude, a theme which runs through Sarton's work and existence. Basil de Sélincourt, in a review of *Inner Landscape*, correctly interpreted the "solemn dedication" which "grounds the ultimate, creative personality on an ultimate renunciation, on an achieved independence, an impassioned solitariness." Sarton's later insight that the artist, having to stand in some sense apart from other human beings, constitutes a kind of monstre sacré, stems from these early observations.

The poems of *Inner Landscape* were composed in the period 1936-1938; those of Sarton's next collection, *The Lion and the Rose* (1948), spanned ten years. During the decade 1938-1948 Sarton traveled widely, lecturing at many American colleges and universities. She also wrote book reviews (but never reviewed other poets' work, disliking the power that attaches to such activity) and articles on theater and poetry. In 1944, hired by the U.S. Office of War Information as a scriptwriter for documentary films on life in America, she lived for a short while in New York; in 1945 she was poet-in-residence at Southern Illinois University. All of these experiences had their effect on her poetry, making it more public. *The Lion and the Rose* takes as subjects not only love and art and their ancillary themes but ranges out to include politics, history, Indian culture, Southern culture, war, social unrest, and feminism. The sense of the volume is of intense probing of the actual, immediate world— of fascination with the multiplicitous mundane. The variety of subjects and modes impresses with its vitality; no longer is the poet primarily a dreamer, but an active participant and an energetic observer. Of course there are poems of memory and solitude, but only one who deeply knows the condition of solitude (and of loneliness) could intuit so precisely the emotions of the concentration-camp figures of "The Tortured" or of the refugees of "To the Living." Indeed, May Sarton for many years continued to feel herself a literal exile because of the uprootings of her childhood; the violence that war wreaks on a whole populace she knew firsthand. Thus such lines from "To the Living" as "Each is an exile from the whole. The agony/Of separation is the human agony" owe their power partly to their authenticity. Turning from war to feminism, Sarton in "My Sisters, O My Sisters" sounds again the themes of exile and renunciation as she has experienced these as poet and woman. Of Emily Dickinson and Sappho she can say with authority, "Only when she renounced did Emily/Begin in the fierce lonely light to learn to be./Only in the extremity of spirit and the flesh/And in renouncing passion did Sappho come to bless." Paradoxically, Sarton knows that "nothing has to be renounced or given over": out of exile can come wholeness of being. The "marvelous skill to make/Life grow in all its forms" must be used to "let this stranger [the masculine principle]/Plough deep into our hearts his joy and anger." Not only are the overall forms of "To the Living" and "My Sisters, O My Sisters" large, thus permitting of thorough development of the themes, but within their general forms they are variously structured, so that the poems finally emerge not as didactic but as organic. At the same time, the several internal forms give the impression of conscious treatment of parts which become a unified fulfillment. In contrast, the long poem "Poet in Residence" consistently uses a rather loose, easy line, allowing rhyme but not consciously deciding on it as integral; the effect is of extended, natural, restless questioning as Sarton ponders the role of teacher and the expectations of students. Of the more "private" poems in the volume, many are set in France and use landscape or architecture as foundation for meditation or metaphor. In "What the Old Man Said," Sarton pays homage to Lugné-Poë, who established the Oeuvre Theatre in Paris and whom Sarton regarded as her mentor during the winter of 1931-1932; it was Lugné-Poë who saw that she had the face of a writer rather than of an actress, as she chronicles in her memoir *I Knew A Phoenix* (1959). "The Lady and the Unicorn" is written from the point of view of the unicorn in the Cluny tapestries; its form is unusual in that the first four stanzas are cinquains tightly rhymed in an *abbaa, baabb* pattern, giving the sense of the poet weaving sound as the tapestries weave color, and the last five stanzas consist of interlocking couplets, giving the effect that the speaker is now less the unicorn than Sarton's persona: "My wild love chastened to this history/Where I before your eyes, bow down my head."

After the rich diversity and the exhilarating perception that the poet has come into her own and knows it in *The Lion and the Rose*, the poems of *The Leaves of the Tree* (1950) seem unaccountably tamer in technique and content. Written between 1948 and 1950, they perhaps indicate the slight flagging of energy that is not uncommon after the completion of a comprehensive, sustained, and far-reaching work.

With the publication of *The Land of Silence* (1953) Sarton regained her poetical balance. Her mother had died in 1950, of cancer, and the book opens with a poem for her, "The First Autumn," whose deceptively simple lines, tender, radiant, thoughtful, set the dominant tone of the collection. The technique of these poems is intensely musical; they are songs sung against the deep silence of eternity as symbolized by landscape, sky, subterranean flow. During the early 1950s Sarton was an instructor in freshman English at Harvard University (1949-1952), a lecturer in creative writing at the Bread Loaf Writers' Conference in Middlebury, Vermont (1951-1953), a Lucy Martin Donnelly Fellow at Bryn Mawr College in Pennsylvania (1953); but she also traveled to the American West, and the sense of its immensity, "A land of work and silence, a whole land," as "Letter to an Indian Friend" puts it, permeates the majority of the poems. The "work" is often that of poetry, or prayer, or faith—of activities that require consummate concentration. The silence is not passive nor restrictive but is a kind of creative waiting, as in "Because What I Want Most Is Permanence"/"Poetry, prayer, or call it what you choose/That frees

the complicated act of will/And makes the whole world both intense and still"; or as in "Journey toward Poetry": "To be still, to be silent, to stand by a window/Where time not motion changes light to shadow,/Is to be present at the birth of creation." Mixed with the spirituality of stillness is the necessity for growth of the spirit: "Letter from Chicago," a poem for Virginia Woolf four years after her death, speaks of "A plume of smoke dissolving,/ Remaking itself, never still,/Never static, never lost," and the final poem of the book, "Now I Become Myself," of "My work, my love, my time, my face/Gathered into one intense/Gesture of growing like a plant." *The Land of Silence* is a book of acceptances—even when rebellion interrupts, as in "The Caged Bird," in which the "unrepenting rage" of the poet is equated with the "fierce wing-beat of despair" of the caged wild bird, the sense is that after the poem, after "I wept hot tears of blood," ultimate acceptance will come; in "Without the Violence," peace can come only after "a terrible and rending war." The great reconciliations take place between life and death, passion and love, with imagination the mediator. Sarton explores this theme in the sequence of eleven love sonnets significantly titled "These Images Remain," in which she deliberately yokes unlike entities: "despair" and "love," "delight" and "grief," "parting" and "return"/"But parting is return, the coming home,/ Parting in space and yet the dearest meeting;/ Where most we seem to go, there most do come/ And give each other an eternal greeting." By the final sonnet, the pairing of opposites has paradoxically become reassuring, and the lover accepts the images of past happiness as still existing in the present: "Here are the peaceful days we cannot share./ Here is our peace at last, and we not there."

The next few years saw Sarton occupied in writing novels. In 1956 her father died, and her next book of poems, *In Time Like Air* (1958), opens with "A Celebration for George Sarton" and contains "My Father's Death," in which Sarton compares herself to "the clean stripped hull" of a ship that "Glides down the ways and is gently set free." In this collection also is "After Four Years," a gentle elegy for Sarton's mother. May Sarton was unusually close to her parents, mentioning them frequently in interviews as well as devoting chapters to them in such memoirs as *I Knew a Phoenix* (1959) and *A World of Light* (1976). *In Time Like Air* shows the poet at the height of her powers. Written between 1953 and 1958, the poems are by turns philosophical, whimsical, serious, humorous, above all attuned to the human. Poem after poem is masterly

The Captain's House

In Memoriam E.M.S.

1

I stood in the unknown street;
I held in my hand the key
To the house. I had driven all day.
When the ship came in, it was twilight,
And there was a lavendar haze on the sea,
On the walls of the house, a lavendar light.
The empty windows all looked out at me.
The great door was wonderfully white.

Captain, you never came home with more need
Than I at your threshold, trembling, did.
You never waited with more tumultuous blood
Before the heavy knocker to rouse up your bride
Than I to wake the silences inside.

The church bell rang six times, ending.
I put the key in the lock. The door swung open.
In the chill house I could feel you standing
Back to the fire, watching the sun go down,
Or at the table spreading your maps again.
This is the end of every voyage, Captain.

I stood in your house and knew it would be well
In the river of memory with me and with you.
We had been lost like sand in the sandglass
Of the years, but all that love can tell
We'll tell each other now, we'll tell at last.

It's starlight and the ship is anchored fast.

2

I open my eyes to the chill April morning
And smell the sweet rain and the fresh salt wind;
Now I come back through every wave of mourning,
The wash and flow of these unplanted memories
And my mind sways and trembles like your ship.
Alone in the silent village, I am not alone.
The silences are tears, tears, tears, my own;
They people the house and make me almost human
After the long inhuman time of no returning
When work went on and on, the visits, letters, phone,
But the day's voyage never brought me home.

Captain, my mother died four months ago
And I have journeyed nearly four months now.

Typescript for one of Sarton's memorials to her mother (by permission of the author; courtesy of the Lilly Library, Indiana University)

in its sense of freedom and enjoyment in the very making; there is the impression of an almost Yeatsian loss of fear and a consequent expansion of technique. It is as though the line from "Death and the Lovers" has come true for her: "Death becomes real, and love is forced to grow." The subjects of *In Time Like Air* range from "the great Toby" ("Lament for Toby, A French Poodle") to the "serene glory" of a della Francesca painting ("Nativity") to scenes and seasons ("At Muzot," with its references to Rilke, whom Sarton reveres; "Spring Day," with its light, rippling lines such as "princes of the hour, while these green palaces/Glide into summer, where we too are going/With all the birds, and leaves, and all the kisses"). No poems of social concern appear in this collection, and no poems on writing poetry per se. It is not that the poems are private; rather, it seems that Sarton is standing on a tremendously high plateau of her art and is able to take a comprehensive view of the whole pattern of life. With this volume, Sarton's mastery of form becomes unassailable, in that she makes form seem natural, not noticeable. The title poem begins simply, "Consider the mysterious salt:/In water it must disappear." The poem is in five stanzas of tetrameter, each stanza six lines long. What makes the poem crystallize (and this image is central to it) is the accretionary power of the rhyme scheme (*abaccb, bdbeed, fgfggg, hihggi, jkjllk*). The third stanza, with its oblique but perfectly recognizable rhymes, is the stanza of questions—"What element dissolves the soul/So it may be both found and lost/ . . . /What is the element so blest/That there identity can rest"; the first two stanzas set up the scientific situation, and the last two answer the questions of the third metaphysically. Thus thought, form, music, technique are blended. *In Time Like Air* is full of such seemingly effortless poems, that repay close study.

In 1958 Sarton moved to Nelson, New Hampshire, where she restored a small house near the village green, carved a garden out of brush and stony soil, and took up active solitude in earnest. *Cloud, Stone, Sun, Vine*, poems selected from her four previous books, was published in 1961. Its title is from "At Muzot," which contains the lines, "Angels, often invoked, become a fact./And they have names, Cloud, Stone, Sun, Vine,/But the names are interchangeable." Besides work published earlier, the volume includes new poems, several about her new existence, and a sequence of twenty love sonnets, titled "A Divorce of Lovers." On the literal level, this sequence is a narrative which tells of the end of a painful affair. The language is a combi-

nation of the ordinary—"I could not reach you. You were lost and cold"—and the poetical—"Like some strong swimmer on the icy airs,/I glide and can survive the heart's own pitfall." The philosophical conflict is between Reason and Poetry, while the emotional conflict is between the protagonists' approach to life and thus to love. There is also the hint that the warring lovers are two sides of the person who speaks "A Divorce of Lovers." These sonnets are among the most thematically complex that Sarton has yet attempted, rich in implication and admirable in scope.

In 1960 Sarton was a lecturer in creative writing and a Danforth Fellow. From 1960 to 1964 she taught creative writing at Wellesley College in Massachusetts, and in 1965 she was poet-in-residence at Lindenwood College in St. Charles, Missouri; but Nelson continued as the center of her private life. In her next volume of poetry, however, she chronicles extensive travels as well as domestic incidents—having a well dug, watching the hired man scythe a field. The most poetically exciting section of *A Private Mythology* (1966) is the one in which she finds that free verse can again serve as vehicle for yet another spurt of growth—toward spiritual serenity. To celebrate her fiftieth birthday Sarton undertook her first visits to Japan, India, and Greece. Throughout the travel poems there is the sense that she is seeking a rebirth, in middle age, of poetic spontaneity. The poems of *A Private Mythology* were written between 1961 and 1966, and it is startling to move from the traditional opening poem, "The Beautiful Pauses," with its familiar musical quality and its attendant long iambic pentameter lines in completely mastered rhyme, to the extremely delicate, almost tentative strokes of such poems as "A Child's Japan" ("Paper skaters/Blown across a lacquer tray") or "Kyoko" ("Disaster/Shadows her cheek/Like the falling plum blossom"). The sequence titled "Japanese Prints" has the elegance and precision of haiku, but the poems are not just attempts at imitation; Sarton sees, in "Inn at Kyoto," that "I inhabit a marvelous world/Where every sense is taught/New ways of perceiving," and she is an eager student. In the poems about India, Sarton retains the new form, or rather, the old form that she has transformed, but what she looks at she finds disturbing: in "The Approach-Calcutta," "Here the gods themselves/Are too thick, too many"; in "Notes from India" she sees how "The pool is troubled/Again and again/By the dark bodies/That go down through the scum," and finds temple figures "Boring erotica." But in "The Sleeping God," which is, interestingly enough, in her more usual rhymed structure, she discovers in the "Young man relaxed in beauty" the power that paradoxically lies in vulnerability: "Disarmed, without a wall, without a keep . . . And so, become the master of all space." From the "dark, Edgeless and melting,/[of] the Indian ethos," as Sarton puts it in "Birthday on the Acropolis," to the "knife-clean air" of Greece is jolting for the poet. But, just as she discovered from Vishnu vulnerability's power, so she confronts "the archaic smile" of Athene herself, "The smile beyond suffering" that is the Greek essence. Sarton maintains her free-verse approach throughout the poems of Greece; then, in a virtuosic poem, "Ballads of the Traveler," returns to rhymed form, but with a clearer eye and a felt resolution to incorporate the "New ways of perceiving" in her future work. For the rest, *A Private Mythology* shows Sarton invigorated by her outward and inner journeying; from which are echoes, as in the line "A voice heard in Japan long months ago," from "Lazarus," or re-thinkings, as in "Second Thoughts on the Abstract Gardens of Japan," in which Sarton finds "too-formalized" landscape "absolutely sterile" and declares, "I want good violence to find organic form."

A Private Mythology was followed a year later by *As Does New Hampshire* (1967). This collection looks closely at nature, studying trees, stars, weather, animals, birds, flowers. It is as though Sarton is looking at and meditating on the "quaint New England wilderness" referred to in "Second Thoughts on the Abstract Gardens of Japan," in which she writes, "I have staked/My life on controlled native powers;/My garden, so untamed, still has not lacked/Its hard-won flowers." In the next year was published *Plant Dreaming Deep* (1968) which centers around her New Hampshire existence. Clearly, she is re-examining her territory.

The subjects change in *A Grain of Mustard Seed* (1971). Written during the period 1967-1971, the poems reflect the concerns of the time, and the title, taken from Christ's words on the power of faith, implies the difficulty of keeping faith in times of worldwide violence and suffering. "A Ballad of the Sixties" opens with "In the West of the country where I was/Hoping for some good news," and concludes "For only the sick are well;/The mad alone have truth to tell/ . . . /Our love has withered away." " 'We'll to the Woods No More, the Laurels Are Cut Down' " laments in pared-down language and simple rhythm the killings of "our own children/Because they hated war." In "Night Watch," which shows the poet nursing a sick neighbor in what would seem an act of ordinary mercy, and

musing on "What happens/When the baby screams,/Batters the barred cage of its bed,/Wears patience thin?/What happens/When the baby is six feet tall,/Throws stones,/Breaks windows?" Grappling with these issues does not allow beauty of language; these social poems are hard, free verse, unlike any others that Sarton has written. Interspersed with these painfully acute poems are those that permit softer, gentler techniques, such as "Girl with 'Cello," with its long-bowed lines and deep, slow tone; or "Evening Walk in France," with its leisurely couplets. But even in these the note of world worry is occasionally sounded, as in "Dutch Interior," where although "life is tempered, orderly, and calm," the poet involuntarily wonders, "How many from this quiet room have drowned?" The two most powerful poems in the collection are "The Invocation to Kali" and "A Hard Death." "The Invocation to Kali" is in five parts, the first untitled, the second titled "The Kingdom of Kali," the third "The Concentration Camps," the fourth "The Time of Burning," and the last, untitled, an invocation. In order to purge violence, Sarton seems to say, we must look directly not only at the violence in the world but we must force ourselves to look at that within us: "The beast/Is the god. How murder the god?/How live with the terrible god?" Kali, "the destroyer," must be "blest," for "She cannot be cast out (she is here for good)." The progress of the poem stems from the pun in this last phrase. The theme is that of "Without the Violence" in *The Land of Silence:* peace can come only after struggle, but "Kali" is not limited to private wars. If indeed violence is "here for good," what is that "good"? In impassioned indignation Sarton cries, "We gassed God in the ovens, great piteous eyes,/Burned God in a trash heap of images." Yet as Sarton has already seen, "Every creation is born out of the dark./Every birth is bloody. Something gets torn." In the final invocation, Sarton pleads, "Put the wild hunger where it belongs,/Within the act of creation." In contrast to the hard-edged language, the "raw images," and the varied internal forms of "The Invocation to Kali" are the smooth iambic-pentameter couplets and the comforting, flowing language of "A Hard Death." Suffused with a moving sympathy and a yearning for reconciliation with grace, the poem asks, in simple music charged with meaning, that we "at each second be aware/How God is moving always through each flower/ . . . and when the petals fall/Say it is beautiful and good, say it is well." The last stanza warns while it appeals, "Let us be gentle to each other this brief time/For we shall die in exile far from home,/

May Sarton and her dog, Tamas (photograph by Betsy Swart)

. . . /Only the living can be healed by love."

Sarton's next collection, *A Durable Fire* (1972), is aptly named. The title comes from the sequence of eleven "Autumn Sonnets," which ends, "And in this testing year beyond desire,/Begun to move toward durable fire." Once more the poet tells of the ending of a love affair, and wins through to hopeful acceptance; but this time the image of the house set amid landscaping is an integral part of the poem's scheme and development. The house whose "odd owner with madness in her head" keeps it ready "For love that has no time here or elsewhere" and places "fresh flowers on each mantel still,/And sweeps the hearth and warms the chilling air," becomes the symbol of the rejected lover, and the turning point of the sequence comes with the transformation of the house: "Home is a granite rock and two sparse trees." Sarton has often used landscape and architecture symbolically, sometimes to indicate mood, sometimes to comment on art, but here she metamorphoses architecture into landscape. The "granite rock and two sparse trees" indicate that the lover has moved into the starker air of art and has learned "for sure/My life has asked not love but poetry." The other

poems of *A Durable Fire* treat aging ("Gestalt at Sixty"), nature and the seasons ("February Days," "Composition"), memory ("After an Island"), the necessity of grace ("The Angels and the Furies"), the necessity of growth ("Fulfillment"). Sarton has of course dealt with these subjects before; the difference here is in the calmness and certainty of her approach, whether in free verse or traditional forms. Her poetic impulse has not flagged, but it is directed in *A Durable Fire,* toward assessment and re-collection.

During the 1970s and 1980s, Sarton's renown was steadily growing, and she was, and is, in great demand as lecturer and reader; the announcement of a Sarton appearance means large and enthusiastic audiences. In 1973 she moved to York, Maine, a move presaged in the poem "Gestalt at Sixty," in which she writes, "I am not ready to die,/But as I approach sixty/I turn my face toward the sea." The jacket photograph of *Halfway to Silence* (1980) shows the path through the meadow to the sea which her house fronts. Again, but freshly, these poems take joy in multiple form, going easily from the six-lined rhyme stanzas of the meditative landscape poem "In Suffolk" to—on the facing

Working draft (by permission of the author)

May Sarton (photograph © Kelly Wise)

page—the active, immediate free verse of "A Winter Notebook" with such "homely" observations as, "So many lives pour into this house,/Sometimes I get too full;/The pump wears out." Sarton had, in fact, experienced a poetic drought for several years preceding the poems of *Halfway to Silence,* and the return of the lyric flow allows the simplest subjects, such as "June Wind," "The Summer Tree," or "The Geese," to put on myth's light garments. Nor has the poetic flow halted: thirteen new poems by Sarton appeared in a 1983 issue of the *Paris Review* and were included in *Letters from Maine* (1984).

Although May Sarton became an American citizen in 1924 and has made America her home for many decades, her ethos is European, her poetic masters George Herbert, Thomas Traherne, Rainer Maria Rilke, William Butler Yeats, and it is

perhaps this richly historical ethos that not only sets her work apart from that of most contemporary American poets, who for at least a century have been straining to throw off European influences (although there are signs now that point to a change in this attitude), but also may account for the ambivalent criticism the work has received. It is the work itself that has risen above criticism to meet the demands of an ever-increasing audience. Both readers and listeners respond to her courageous, intensely human, musical voice, the voice of one who has held fast, through pain, practical difficulties, loss, to a joy in and a reverence for life. What Sarton said to Karla Hammond in a 1979 interview sums up the reasons for her acclaim: "I think that the deeper you go into the personal— the deeper you go —the more you hit the universal. . . . I have the proof of it in that whenever I've written a poem which has seemed to me extremely strange—that nobody else would ever understand, that came from very deep in my own experience, these are the poems that bring people to me to ask, 'How did you know?' " Indeed, for May Sarton, as her poem "Because What I Want Most Is Permanence" presciently declares, "These are not hours of fire but years of praise,/The glass full to the brim, completely full,/But held in balance so no drop can spill."

Interviews:

Karla Hammond, "To Be Reborn: An Interview with May Sarton," *Bennington Review,* 3 (December 1978): 16, 18-20;

Hammond, "A Further Interview with May Sarton," *Puckerbrush Review,* 2 (Spring 1979): 5-9;

Dolores Shelley, "A Conversation with May Sarton," *Women and Literature,* 7 (1979): 33-41;

Karen Saum, "The Art of Poetry," *Paris Review,* 89 (Fall 1983): 80-110.

Bibliographies:

L. P. Blouin, *May Sarton: A Bibliography* (Metuchen, N.J.: Scarecrow Press, 1978);

Blouin, "A Revised Bibliography," in *May Sarton: Woman and Poet,* edited by Constance Hunting (Orono, Maine: National Poetry Foundation, 1982), pp. 282-319.

References:

Constance Hunting, ed., *May Sarton: Woman and*

Poet (Orono, Maine: National Poetry Foundation, 1982);

Agnes Sibley, *May Sarton* (New York: Twayne, 1972).

Papers:
There is a collection of Sarton's papers in the Henry W. and Albert A. Berg Collection at the New York Public Library.

Delmore Schwartz
(8 December 1913-11 July 1966)

Craig Tapping
University of British Columbia

See also the Schwartz entry in *DLB 28, Twentieth-Century American-Jewish Fiction Writers.*

BOOKS: *In Dreams Begin Responsibilities* (Norfolk, Conn.: New Directions, 1938);

Shenandoah (Norfolk, Conn.: New Directions, 1941);

Genesis: Book One (New York: New Directions, 1943);

The World Is a Wedding (Norfolk, Conn.: New Directions, 1948; London: Lehmann, 1949);

Vaudeville for a Princess and Other Poems (New York: New Directions, 1950);

Summer Knowledge: New and Selected Poems, 1938-1958 (Garden City: Doubleday, 1959);

Successful Love And Other Stories (New York: Corinth Books, 1961);

Selected Essays of Delmore Schwartz, edited by Donald A. Dike and David H. Zucker (Chicago & London: University of Chicago Press, 1970);

In Dreams Begin Responsibilities and Other Stories, edited by James Atlas (New York: New Directions, 1978);

Last and Lost Poems of Delmore Schwartz, edited by Robert Phillips (New York: Vanguard, 1979).

OTHER: Arthur Rimbaud, *A Season In Hell*, translated by Schwartz (Norfolk, Conn.: New Directions, 1939; revised, 1940);

"The Present State of Modern Poetry," in *American Poetry at Mid-Century* (Washington, D.C.: Library of Congress, 1958), pp. 15-31;

Syracuse Poems 1964, edited, with a foreword, by Schwartz (Syracuse, N.Y.: Department of English, Syracuse University, 1965).

PERIODICAL PUBLICATIONS: "The Poet As

Poet," *Partisan Review*, 6 (Spring 1939): 52-59;

"Rimbaud In Our Time," *Poetry*, 55 (December 1939): 148-154;

"The Isolation of Modern Poetry," *Kenyon Review*, 3 (Spring 1941): 209-220;

"T. S. Eliot As The International Hero," *Partisan Review*, 12 (Spring 1945): 199-206;

"The Literary Dictatorship of T. S. Eliot," *Partisan Review*, 16 (February 1949): 119-137;

Delmore Schwartz, 1938 (photograph by Mrs. Forbes Johnson-Storey)

"Views Of A Second Violinist," *Partisan Review,* 16
       (December 1949): 1250-1255;
"The Vocation Of The Poet In The Modern
       World," *Poetry,* 78 (July 1951): 223-232.

Delmore Schwartz, hailed as "the American
Auden" even before the publication of his first collection of poetry in 1938, is now more often remembered as the inspiration for poems by John
Berryman and Robert Lowell, and as the source
for Saul Bellow's protagonist in *Humboldt's Gift*
(1975). His own poetry is sporadic and often derivative in achievement.

Schwartz defined himself as a poet throughout a career as short-story writer, dramatist, critic,
influential journalist, and teacher. For Berryman,
he was "the most underrated poet of the twentieth
century." Schwartz's early years and family background are the subject of his best writing; his disastrous final years are the basis of a literary
mythology which colors many accounts of his place
in mid-twentieth-century American literature.

The first-born son of Rumanian-Jewish immigrants Harry and Rose Nathanson Schwartz,
Delmore David Schwartz proclaimed himself "the
poet of the Atlantic migration, that made America": this event, and these new Americans dominated his imaginative and creative efforts.
Acknowledged by his biographer, James Atlas, as
"one of the most self-conscious writers who ever
lived," Schwartz saw his parents' choice of his first
name as symbolic of their aspirations for accultur-
ation, and he parodied what he felt was the oxy-
moronic linking of its establishment gentility to the
immigrant identity revealed in the family's surname through personae as variously named as
Shenandoah Fish.

The clashes which Schwartz believed his name
embodied—between social aspirations and cultural
values, old world civility and new world philistin-
ism, and generational differences between immigrants and their American-born offspring—are the
subject of much of his prose fiction and poetry.

All of Schwartz's writing attempts to evoke,
analyze, and at times transcend what he saw as the
inevitable disappointments and profound disillusionment which life forces on people. In 1934
Schwartz extended this paradigm to explain that
his work attempts to describe "the values by which
human beings exist (as distinct from their beliefs
and explicit avowals of choice) and the tragic contrast between these values and the tragic environment in which they must be brought to fruition."

Growing up in Brooklyn, Schwartz decided

early in life on his vocation as a poet, admitting
that he hoped to win power and attention through
such specialized mental and linguistic abilities. His
early years—during which he witnessed the bitter
arguments that ended in his parents' estrangement
and divorce when he was fourteen—are chronicled
with minute precision in *Genesis: Book One* (1943),
an epic poem intended to illumine contemporary
experience through carefully heightened instances
of autobiography, distilled through the double focus of Karl Marx and Sigmund Freud. These same
events are also related in short stories, verse plays,
sonnets, and various lyrics.

Though he was a bright child and perspica-
cious mimic, Schwartz's school years were marked
by mixed success. A compulsive journal keeper, he
continually recorded events, recasting them in order to test his family's daily experiences against the
forms and themes of his precociously varied, self-
imposed reading program. These chronicles are
central in his writing to his own identity and to the
culture's history. As he wrote in poem four of *In
Dreams Begin Responsibilities* (1938): "The theodicy
I wrote in my high school days/Restored all life
from infancy."

His first published poems—which appeared
in the *Poet's Pack of George Washington High School*
when he was sixteen—revealed his characteristic
persona: an overrefined modernist sensibility,
grounded through allusion to an entire European
tradition of poetry, which is seen as tedious and
limiting to the writer's uncertain quest for colloquial images and diction. This teenaged affectation
is, in large measure, a defense against the hostile
world in which he found himself after the ruin of
the family's fortunes with the stock-market crash
of 1929, and his father's subsequent death in June
1930.

His university years were uneventful academ-
ically. After a college-preparatory course at Columbia University, Schwartz was admitted to the
University of Wisconsin in 1931. He was eager to
be part of the bohemianism pervading the campus,
or as he called it, "free love and bolshevism." Student life, not necessarily studies, appealed to
Schwartz who, at seventeen, had already styled
himself a member of the avant-garde. His ambitions to literary eminence were fueled by the exposure to undergraduate dilettantism and
Marxism. He also learned that his natural resort to
arrogance and intuition would advance his popularity. Schwartz left the university in June 1932
without taking final examinations, and returned to
New York City.

In fall 1932 he enrolled at the Washington Square College of New York University, where he studied classical, analytical, and contemporary philosophy, earning a B.A. in 1935. In 1934, he and three of his classmates—Alvin Schwartz and Sigmund and Vivienne Koch—edited *Mosaic*, a magazine which sought to define "the vital question of a Marxian aesthetic." Contributions were successfully solicited from many eminent poets and critics, including R. P. Blackmur, Norman Macleod, and William Carlos Williams. Schwartz's own critical essay in the first number of the magazine, which closed with an examination of works by Louis MacNeice, Louis Zukofsky, and Paul Goodman, was praised in most notices of the issue.

Entering graduate studies in philosophy at Harvard in autumn 1935, Schwartz left without taking a degree in March 1937, returning once more to New York City. Later that year his criticism, fiction, and poetry began to appear in magazines such as *Poetry* and the *Partisan Review*. He was already singled out for high praise. To James Laughlin, who had included some of Schwartz's shorter poems in his *New Directions in Prose & Poetry* anthology for 1937, Schwartz was "the American Auden." In autumn 1938 Dwight MacDonald, of the *Partisan Review*, introduced Schwartz at a party as "the new Hart Crane." Before reaching the age of twenty-five, therefore, Schwartz had been marked for greatness as an American poet. His reputation seemed made even before the publication of his first collection of poems.

In December 1938 New Directions published Schwartz's widely acclaimed *In Dreams Begin Responsibilities*, a collection that includes a short story, a play, a group of lyrics, and an extended poem. Revealing the young poet's range and craft, the book is ambitious, varied in formal experiment, and overall an impressive achievement.

The title story is considered by many to be Schwartz's masterpiece. Taut sentences and repetitive syntax sustain a formal analogy between the prose and the silent movie which Schwartz describes. Thematically, the story is tied to all his confessional, autobiographical work in its investigation of his parents' courtship. "In Dreams Begin Responsibilities" is memorable for its nightmare-like evocation of turn-of-the-century New York, and for the son's haunted, but impotent, witnessing of an inevitable history. Seeing the early symptoms of discontent and alienation between his parents, Schwartz the narrator stands up in the cinema where the film is being projected and screams at his parents. They should separate now, he yells, on the eve of their engagement: "Don't do it! It's not too late to change your minds, both of you. Nothing good will come of it, only remorse, hatred, scandal, and two children whose characters are monstrous."

Quieted by rebukes from members of the audience and the management, the narrator resumes his seat and watches the inexorable progress of his own prehistory. He breaks social contract again, confronting the past in a vain attempt to alter the present: "I in my seat in the darkness am shocked and horrified. I feel as if I were walking a tightrope one hundred feet over a circus audience and suddenly the rope is showing signs of breaking, and I get up from seat and begin to shout once more the first words I can think of to communicate my terrible fear . . . and the shocked audience has turned to stare at me, and I keep shouting: 'What are they doing? Don't they know what they are doing?'" Evicted from the Coney Island film house for his unruly behavior, the narrator awakes, and the story ends with a Kafkaesque intimation that the nightmare was perhaps real.

The tragedy within the prosaic, so evocatively manifested in this story, and the elusive sense of any present securities are informing virtues of the poems which follow in the collection. The hallmark of Schwartz's first book is his grounding of metaphysical discourse in mundane experiences, colloquial idiom, and commonplace objects.

The section of lyrics, titled "Poems of Experiment and Imitation," is in two parts. The first, "The Repetitive Heart," contains eleven numbered poems loosely based on the fugue. In an end note, Schwartz admits the inability of language to match the contrapuntal effect of the musical form, and his poems eschew direct formal analogy to music. Instead, repetition of phrases, lines, and rhythms creates a pattern which folds in on itself, almost mirroring the complexity of his musical model. Many of the poems, however, are overwhelmed by a labored mellifluousness, and others suffer from too obvious an indebtedness to Yeats and Auden.

The fourth poem, for example, reveals both lack of control and derivativeness. After an introduction which mixes formal diction and neologism, Schwartz descends into a pastiche of Audenesque rhetoric and Yeatsian meditation:

Between the worker and the millionaire
Number provides all distances,
It is Nineteen Thirty-Seven now,
Many great dears are taken away,
What will become of you and me
(This is the school in which we learn. . .)

James Agee and Delmore Schwartz, circa 1939 (photograph by Helen Levitt)

Besides the photo and the memory?
(. . . that time is the fire in which we burn.)

The poem's syntactic labyrinth also reveals Schwartz's knowledge of, and love for, the first of T. S. Eliot's *Four Quartets* (1936-1942).

There are poems in this section, however, which transcend Schwartz's imitation of his models to achieve memorable utterance. The fifth poem, for example, with its enigmatic first line, "Dogs are Shakespearean, children are strangers," contrasts Freudian and Wordsworthian images of childhood. Its final stanza is replete with poetic flourish and rhetorical allusion to other poets:

This which we live behind our unseen faces,
Is neither dream, nor childhood, neither
Myth, nor landscape, final, nor finished,
For we are incomplete and know no future,
And we are howling or dancing out our souls
In beating syllables before the curtain:
We are Shakespearean, we are strangers.

A characteristic of all these poems is Schwartz's penchant for the pregnant first line.

Often, succeeding lines and stanzas do not match the promise of memorable imagery found, for example, in the seventh poem's first lines:

I am to my own heart merely a serf
And follow humbly as it glides with autos
And come attentive when it is too sick,
In the bad cold of sorrow much too weak,
To drink some coffee, light a cigarette
And think of summer beaches, blue and gay.

Throughout the poems which follow, Schwartz affects ordinary speech at times, in contrast to the abstract meditational thrust of his themes. Common objects and phenomena such as automobiles, street scenes, and conversations, insomnia, fairgrounds, and the cinema are used as images to embody Schwartz's philosophical concerns.

The ninth poem, "The heavy bear who goes with me," one of Schwartz's most-frequently anthologized pieces, carries an epithet from Alfred North Whitehead, under whom Schwartz had studied contemporary philosophical analysis at Harvard. The poem is a remarkable fusion of the banal and the profound:

> That inescapable animal walks with me,
> Has followed me since the black womb held,
> Moves where I move, distorting gesture,
> A caricature, a swollen shadow,
> A stupid clown of the spirit's motive,
> Perplexes and affronts with his own darkness,
> The secret life of belly and bone,
> Opaque, too near, my private, yet unknown,
> Stretches to embrace the very dear
> With whom I would walk without him near[.]

The bear suggests, through its performing abilities, the circus, which recurs as an image for daily life throughout the collection (an allusion once more to Yeats's later poetry). That allusion recedes here, however, as the bear becomes an image of the body and its heavy existence in time, its claims on the poet's spirit. Again, Schwartz contrasts aspirations with the realities of existence. Questing for a purer, more spiritual life, the poet is dragged back from such illusion by the "stupid clown" of his own physicality. The final metaphor of the football field again locates the poet's language, thought, and struggles within contemporary America. The poem is a clear demonstration of Schwartz's achievement in fusing the personal statement with philosophical meditation through images and metaphors drawn from the modern condition.

Although Schwartz avers in the end notes that "no happening related . . . has ever occurred," the poems which follow in the second section are patently autobiographical and even confessional. The first, "Prothalamion," rather than celebrating the marriage its title suggests, opens with the prophetic line, "Now I must betray myself." The image of a circus self is repeated as Schwartz recounts events from his life as both child and adult. The violence and disintegration of his parents' relationship is again central to his intention. An early incident in which his mother's anger publicly humiliated his father, and which Schwartz regarded as the single most-traumatic episode in his early life, is used to explain the poet's withdrawal from intimacy and to describe his idiomatic training:

> I will forget the speech my mother made
> In a restaurant, trapping my father there
> At dinner with his whore. . . .
> . . . .
> I will remember this. My mother's rhetoric
> Has charmed my various tongue, but now I know
> Love's metric seeks a rhyme more pure and sure.

Other poems in this section continue this ex-

ploration of his family and early environment. The Coney Island atmosphere of the title story recurs in "Far Rockaway," for example, where "The rigor of the weekday is cast aside with shoes." A few of the poems are too obviously trammeled by Schwartz's wide reading and critical championship of modernism. Some, like "For The One Who Would Take Man's Life In His Hands," are too close a pastiche of both Eliot's and Yeats's writings to merit much attention.

On the other hand, "The Ballad Of The Children Of The Czar" is remarkable for its imagistic concision and its telescopic intensity. The innocence of the imperial children at play is compared to Schwartz's own childhood, and his family's past in Eastern Europe further parallels the lost worlds of prerevolutionary Russia. The children's ball becomes the image of "another bouncing ball./The wheeling, whirling world," and Schwartz returns from the abstraction to a metaphysical law central to his scrutiny of history:

> The innocent are overtaken,
> They are not innocent.
>
> They are their father's fathers,
> The past is inevitable.

The final section of the poem is terse, and fraught with the sense of impending doom which characterizes the volume:

> And I see the ball roll under
> The iron gate which is locked.
>
> Sister is screaming, brother is howling,
> The ball has evaded their will.
>
> Even a bouncing ball
> Is uncontrollable,
>
> And is under the garden wall.

One of the last poems in the collection, "In The Naked Bed, In Plato's Cave," is assuredly one of Schwartz's finest pieces. It represents the most articulate and achieved imaginative effort in this first collection, and reveals through a taut cohesion what is best in Schwartz's intentionally philosophical poetry. At its most literal level, the poem is about the insomnia which wreaked havoc throughout Schwartz's life. There is a verbal felicity in this poem which links the bedroom in which the poet sits awake, a prisoner to the noises outside the window which continually intrude, to Plato's metaphor of the cave on the walls of which the shadows of reality flicker. The restless images of half-lit, troubled reflections tie the poem to its philosophical model while the outside pandemonium is registered with the heightened intensities of sleeplessness.

As morning approaches, the imagery captures the quality and distinction of newly lighted perceptions, and the activity in the poem is less strident. The mechanical noises of the night are replaced by natural images that are tentative and gentle, and reveal that the poet is not a prisoner behind a looking glass, but rather an organic part of the life outside his cave, the bedroom. The startling, half-line subordinate clause which ends the poem—"while History is unforgiven"—moves the poem away from the purely philosophical to the meditation on history and time which runs through the collection. The persona in this poem, a world-weary, brooding fatalist who masters his environment only through poetry and the creative confrontation with history, is difficult to equate with the poet who is so evidently young and derivative in many other poems.

Through the rest of the collection, Schwartz's rhetoric is often obviously, and sometimes unconsciously, comic: he juxtaposes passionate, absurdly philosophical flourishes with flat declarations about modern life. Yet the achieved persona, charged with its perceptions of fatalism and despair, rises frequently above the occasional bathetic failure. *In Dreams Begin Responsibilities*, as a result, has the spiritual quality often associated with a testament. Schwartz shifts from self-assertion to self-laceration in frequently startling images or metaphors. In 1962 Irving Howe wrote that Schwartz was "the poet of the historical moment quite as Auden was in England" (*New Republic*, 10 March 1962). Schwartz's first volume, as a result of such acclaim, was seen to determine the standards by which his generation of poets were judged. It was this early recognition and praise which damaged his later career.

In the succeeding years, Schwartz's public career seemed to blossom, however. A series of critical essays culminated in his becoming the poetry editor for the *Partisan Review*. Holding this position from 1943 to 1947, he used it to champion the cause of modernism and the creative efforts of his friends and other poets of his generation most generously. His marriage to Gertrude Buckman in June 1938 was followed by divorce in 1944 and a second marriage to Elizabeth Pollet in June 1949, which also ended unhappily in 1955. A career as

university professor and visiting lecturer at Harvard (1940, 1946-1947), Princeton (1949-1950, 1952-1953), the Kenyon School of English (summer 1950), the Indiana School of Letters (summer 1951), Chicago (March-June 1954), UCLA (summer 1961), and Syracuse (1962-1965) was curtailed, often by Schwartz himself, who was angered by what he saw as the mandarin demands and intrigues of academic life. Various university administrations and several friends were similarly dismayed at this time by his undisciplined and destructive bouts of alcoholism, his barbiturate dependence, and the resulting manic depression. Schwartz never again wrote so cogently and coherently as he did in 1938: his own sense of his unfulfilled and broken promises—recorded in journals and uncollected poetry and prose—filled his middle and later life with profound gloom. The American Auden could not sustain his reputation.

His 1939 translation of Arthur Rimbaud's *A Season In Hell* was condemned on publication for various, glaring verbal and grammatical misconceptions—a reception that caused Schwartz permanent humiliation. His revised translation was published in 1940.

Schwartz received Guggenheim fellowships in 1940 and 1941, the Guarantor's Prize from *Poetry* magazine in 1950, a National Institute and American Academy of Arts and Letters Award in Literature in 1953, and *Poetry*'s Levinson Prize in 1959. He was poetry editor and film critic of the *New Republic* from 1955 to 1957. During the period 1938-1958, however, his creative life suffered. His verse play *Shenandoah* (1941) and *Genesis: Book One* (1943), both of which further articulated his belief in the central significance of autobiography in the contemporary world, received negative reviews. The poor reception of *Genesis: Book One*, especially, which was intended as the first installment of a major modern epic based on his own life, damaged Schwartz's creative impulse and self-esteem.

In 1950 Schwartz published *Vaudeville for a Princess and Other Poems*, a collection of fifty-six poems, including forty sonnets. The sense of failure in these poems, when they are compared to his first collection, is overwhelming. Whether conscious of their defects or not, Schwartz himself included only three of the poems from *Vaudeville for a Princess* in *Summer Knowledge: New and Selected Poems, 1938-1958* (1959).

More than half the poems in *Summer Knowledge* are from his 1938 debut. Although Schwartz claimed to have revised most of these, the only apparent revision is in the ordering and retitling

Delmore Schwartz and Randall Jarrell, 1958 (courtesy of the Library of Congress Information Office)

of various sections. An early play, *Coriolanus and His Mother*, and an excerpt from *Genesis: Book One* are also included. Some of the new poems in *Summer Knowledge* are dauntingly labored. Walt Whitman is now Schwartz's predominant influence, and the longer lines are extravagantly mellifluous, perhaps in an attempt to rid the writing of the desolate resignation that characterized the poems in *Vaudeville for a Princess*.

Again, titles often overburden the poems, as with "Darkling Summer, Ominous Dusk, Rumorous Rain." The effect is both cloying and claustrophobic, as Schwartz depends in most of these new poems on a surfeit of internal rhyme and alliteration. Poems such as "The First Morning Of The Second World" and "Summer Knowledge" explicate this departure, the direct result of Schwartz's turning from the intellectual and introspective inspiration of urban life to the natural world and its organic cycles. His imagery too often clutters the poetry. Schwartz's earlier rhetorical intensities and passionate tautness are loosened under a welter of synesthetic clichés.

In another section of the book Schwartz ex-

periments with adapting diaries, journals, and letters of Antonio Vivaldi, Laurence Sterne, Jonathan Swift, Charles Baudelaire, and Friedrich Hölderlin to lyrics. Though these poems display a rhetorical aptness to their subjects, they are interesting only insofar as they reveal Schwartz's critical perceptions of each writer's quirks of perception and style.

"The Kingdom Of Poetry," which promises to be an *ars poetica*, is actually a catalogue of abstract absolutes, which avoids fulfilling its own terms of specific definition. The last section also includes a somewhat bizarre attempt to retell the situation of Christ's disciples when they are left behind after the ascension, unable to summon necessary inspiration or motivation. Its theme underlines the reader's confusion at the squandering of this poet's gifts.

There is one poem, however, which merits closer attention. In "Seurat's Sunday Afternoon Along The Seine" Schwartz controls his Whitmanesque use of accumulated detail and syntactical repetition, avoiding the mannerisms too prevalent elsewhere in the collection. Summer knowledge, the realm and power of all great art, and the phil-

Delmore Schwartz, 18 October 1965 (photograph by Hi-Lite Studios, Syracuse)

osophical truths which he once despaired of realizing are incarnate in Schwartz's analysis and celebration of Georges Seurat's painting, which he describes as "The kingdom of heaven on earth on Sunday summer day." Responding to the intellectual rigor of Seurat's pointillistic techniques and composition, Schwartz recognizes the gift which care, craft, and scrupulous dedication bestows on humanity. Like John Keats's "Ode On A Grecian Urn," Schwartz's poem searches for and defines the transcendent eternal moment of art. The isolated martyr as artist, a figure that fills so much of Schwartz's previous work, is here abandoned in a catalogue of artists whose works celebrate life-affirming realities. The weak, emotionally diffuse, and abstract poems which proliferate throughout earlier sections are relegated to a very minor place in his canon by Schwartz's controlled achievement in this poem.

The critical reception of *Summer Knowledge* was both magnanimous and deferential. Schwartz's position as the voice of his generation, first acclaimed twenty years earlier, was reclaimed. In

1960 he was awarded the Bollingen Prize in Poetry and the Shelley Memorial Award.

The final lines of "Seurat's Sunday Afternoon Along The Seine" were prophetic, however, about Schwartz's last years:

> Without forbears, without marriage, without heirs,
> Yet with a wild longing for forbears, marriage, and heirs:
> They all stretch out their hands to me: but they are too far away!

The final years of his life saw little creative work. A regime of liquor, barbiturates for sleep, and benzedrine for waking up debilitated Schwartz physically and mentally. Despite his initial success, the recognition of his worth had come after twenty years of his feeling slighted and failed. His position at Syracuse was often too demanding for him to fulfill its responsibilities, but he profoundly influenced many students. His public presence remained striking. His personal life, however, suffered immensely: Schwartz seemed to veer manically away from the support offered by the few friends who remained willing to cope with him in his chameleon despair. Saul Bellow's *Humboldt's Gift* records this sad, strained time and witnesses the plight of Schwartz's genius damaged and unfulfilled.

As Schwartz became more and more unstable, he was less and less able to communicate even through his personal notebooks. In and out of Bellevue, angered by friends who tried to help, he left Syracuse in January 1966 and took lodgings in a series of rundown hotels. On the morning of 11 July 1966, while in a hotel elevator he suffered a heart attack—probably from a fatal mixture of alcohol and drugs—and died on the way to the hospital. His body was taken to the New York City morgue, where it lay unclaimed for two days.

In John Berryman's *His Toy, His Dream, His Rest* (1968), dedicated "to the sacred memory of Delmore Schwartz," poems 146-159 are an impassioned, grief-stricken elegy for the patron, friend, and poet whose work suffered as the man did, and whose death, according to Berryman, challenged the remaining poets of his generation. Berryman describes Schwartz's work as "one solid block of agony" filled with "wit & passion" in its attempt to "recover & be whole." Schwartz's work and life hold "secrets . . . hidden in history & theology, hidden in rhyme" which now others must "come on to understand."

Letters:

Letters of Delmore Schwartz, edited by Robert Phillips (Princeton: Ontario Review Press, 1984).

Biography:

James Atlas, *Delmore Schwartz: The Life of an American Poet* (New York: Farrar, Straus & Giroux, 1977).

Reference:

Richard McDougall, *Delmore Schwartz* (New York: Twayne, 1974).

Papers:

The largest collection of Schwartz's papers is in the Beinecke Rare Book and Manuscript Library, Yale University.

Evelyn Scott

(17 January 1893-3 August 1963)

Robert L. Welker
University of Alabama in Huntsville

See also the Scott entry in *DLB 9, American Novelists, 1910-1945.*

BOOKS: *Precipitations* (New York: Nicholas L. Brown, 1920);

The Narrow House (New York: Boni & Liveright, 1921; London: Duckworth, 1921);

Narcissus (New York: Harcourt, Brace, 1922); republished as *Bewilderment* (London: Duckworth, 1922);

Escapade (New York: Thomas Seltzer, 1923);

In the Endless Sands: A Christmas Book for Boys and Girls, by Scott and Cyril Kay Scott (New York: Holt, 1925);

The Golden Door (New York: Thomas Seltzer, 1925);

Ideals: A Book of Farce & Comedy (New York: A. & C. Boni, 1927);

Migrations: An Arabesque in Histories (New York: A. & C. Boni, 1927; London: Duckworth, 1927);

The Wave (New York: Cape & Smith, 1929; London: Cape, 1929);

Witch Perkins, A Story of the Kentucky Hills (New York: Holt, 1929);

On William Faulkner's "The Sound and the Fury" (New York: Cape & Smith, 1929);

Blue Rum, as Ernest Souza (New York: Cape & Smith, 1930; London: Cape, 1930);

The Winter Alone (New York: Cape & Smith, 1930);

A Calendar of Sin, American Melodramas, 2 volumes (New York: Cape & Smith, 1931);

Eva Gay: A Romantic Novel (New York: Smith & Haas, 1933; London: Lovat Dickson, 1934);

Breathe Upon These Slain (New York: Smith & Haas, 1934; London: Lovat Dickson, 1934);

Billy the Maverick (New York: Holt, 1934);

Bread and a Sword (New York: Scribners, 1937);

Background in Tennessee (New York: McBride, 1937);

Evelyn Scott, 1934 (portrait by Francis Criss)

The Shadow of the Hawk (New York: Scribners, 1941).

PLAY PRODUCTION: *Love: A Play in Three Acts,* New York, Provincetown Playhouse, 19 February 1921.

OTHER: "Adventures and Incidents in Writing *The Wave,*" *Wings,* 3 (July 1929): 6-9;
"Communist Mentalities," in *America Now: An Inquiry into Civilization in the United States by Thirty-six Americans,* edited by Harold E. Stearns (New York: Scribners, 1938).

PERIODICAL PUBLICATIONS:
FICTION
"The Old Lady," *Dial,* 78 (May 1925): 369-379;
"The Lover," *Scribner's Magazine,* 88 (October 1930): 407-413;
"Home," *Scribner's Magazine,* 90 (December 1931): 634-644;
"Turnstile," *Scribner's Magazine,* 93 (February 1933): 80-88;
"Englishman," *Yale Review,* 23 (March 1934): 568-602;
"Lady Author," *American Mercury,* 31 (April 1934): 485-498;
"To Kenitra," *Yale Review,* 24 (March 1935): 555-575.
POETRY
"Rifts," *Nation,* 111 (10 July 1920): 41;
"To a Snake in Eden," *Nation,* 139 (1 August 1934): 133;
"Flight for Angels," *Poetry,* 46 (June 1935): 162-165;
"Opus Ten Billion," *North Georgia Review,* 4 (Autumn 1939): 42;
"Apocrypha: To All Negro Poets Now Alive," *Saturday Review,* 21 (17 February 1940): 8;
"To Artists of Every Land," *Saturday Review,* 31 (22 May 1948): 20;
"She Dies," *Saturday Review,* 32 (29 January 1949): 10;
"Ivory Tower," *Poetry Review* (London), 42 (September-October 1951): 283;
"Old American Stock," *Poetry Review* (London), 43 (July-September 1952): 157-159;
"Survival," *Saturday Review,* 36 (6 June 1953): 13.
NONFICTION
"From Brazil to the U.S.," *Poetry,* 15 (November 1919): 99-101;
"A Tardy Obeisance," *Egoist,* 6 (December 1919): 78-79;

"Gilbert Cannan: Inquisitor," *Dial,* 68 (February 1920): 173-186;
"A Critic of the Threshold," *Dial,* 68 (March 1920): 311-325;
"Emilio de Menezes," *Poetry,* 16 (April 1920): 40-43;
"A Divine Beachcomber," *Dial,* 68 (May 1920): 650-663;
"Argentine Drama," *Poetry,* 17 (October 1920): 52-55;
"Contemporary of the Future," *Dial,* 69 (October 1920): 353-367;
"A Philosopher of the Erotic," *Dial,* 70 (April 1921): 458-461;
"Brazilian Dance Songs," *Poetry,* 18 (August 1921): 267-271;
"Kentucky Land," *New Republic,* 68 (4 November 1931): 332-333;
"South American Rhapsody," *Nation,* 137 (30 August 1933): 244;
"When Wars End," *Nation,* 138 (21 February 1934): 225;
"A Novel of Revolution," *Saturday Review,* 10 (2 June 1934): 724;
"From a Novelist," *Saturday Review,* 11 (10 November 1934): 272, 280;
"War Between the States," *Nation,* 143 (4 July 1936): 19-20;
"Test of Maturity," *Poetry,* 50 (July 1937): 215-219;
"Black Is My True Love's Hair," *North Georgia Review,* 4 (Spring 1939): 25-26;
"Introduction to 'Books of Southern Interest,'" *Southern Literary Messenger,* 1 (July 1939): 489-491;
"How Can Intelligent Southerners Best Help the South?," *North Georgia Review,* 6 (Winter 1941): 19;
"The Doctor from New Jersey," *Poetry Review* (London), 42 (July-August 1951): 204-207;
"Dr. Sitwell and the American Genius," *Poetry Review* (London), 42 (September-October 1951): 260-266;
"Six Poets," *Poetry Review* (London), 42 (November-December 1951): 334-338.

Evelyn Scott was among the early experimenters in imagism, expressionism, stream-of-consciousness, and the "psychological" novel. An innovator in form and technique—having early developed simultaneously with James Joyce and others the poetic prose of intense inner realism, and later, along with John Dos Passos, the panoramic novel—she was widely acclaimed one of America's most important and intellectual literary figures during the 1920s and 1930s.

Until the age of twenty, Evelyn Scott was Elsie Dunn, born to Maude and Seeley Dunn, into a Clarksville, Tennessee, family with wealth and aristocratic, artistic inclinations—and a superb Greek-revival mansion. With her social background and striking physical beauty—fine bone structure, a sensuous mouth, haunting gray eyes, and a wreath of brown-gold hair—she was abundantly equipped to play the expected role of Southern belle. She revolted. Her precocious nature, exceptional intelligence, and above all the strict emotional and intellectual honesty which was to mark her for life mandated rejection of the conventional injustices, contradictions, and chauvinisms attendant on the role. Her autobiographical *Background in Tennessee* (1937) recounts her rebellion and the cultural milieu which supported it. Moving to New Orleans with her family when she was sixteen, she studied art at Sophie Newcomb College, read extensively, and, partially to escape the environment of her parents' unhappy marriage, immersed herself in avant-garde causes. She became associated with Frederick Creighton Wellman, head of the School of Tropical and Preventative Medicine at Tulane University, who—twice her age and married to his second wife—also sought escape from an incompatible marriage. On 3 December 1913, shortly before her twenty-first birthday, Elsie Dunn and Creighton Wellman secretly left New Orleans together, took the names Evelyn and Cyril Kay Scott, and sailed for England.

Evelyn Scott wrote: "Until aboard the ship at sea I was a virgin with contempt for a view of chastity as psychological rather than of the spirit. We went away knowing we could draw reprehension on ourselves. No one guessed we had gone until we were well away, and the expected *and* unexpected happened." Because Cyril Kay Scott was threatened with imprisonment under the Mann Act if they should return to the United States, the Scotts eventually went to Brazil, where for five years they endured desperate poverty and extreme hardships pioneering in the wilds of Baia. The experience, along with complications resulting from the birth of her child on 25 October 1914, affected Evelyn Scott's health for the remainder of her life but saw the emergence of Evelyn Scott as artist. In almost complete isolation, she began publishing poetry and criticism alongside the works of Eliot and Joyce in the *Egoist*, *Poetry*, the *Dial*, and *Others*. Her slightly fictionalized biography, *Escapade* (1923), details the Brazilian episode as background to the

poetic drama of the birth of an inner spirit from pain and suffering. Of her early work, Ludwig Lewisohn wrote: "By her cold acuteness of psychological observation, by peering exactness of physical vision, she succeeds in giving *The Narrow House* and *Narcissus* and above all *Escapade* a hardness of surface that seems to protect these books from decay. They have an intellectual lucidity and a powerful and bitter moral vision that keeps them fresh and memorable."

Shortly after her return to the United States in 1919, Evelyn Scott published her first collection of poetry, *Precipitations* (1920). Basically imagistic with a strong injection of the metaphysical, the poems are filled with verbal shocks, sudden shifts in meaning, and surprising images delivering a sharp tension between a childlike naivety yearning for the fanciful and an honest lost-innocence aware of a bitter but noble truth: life is a *liebstod* in which love and death are equated as creator of the fullest consciousness. It is a consciousness, Lola Ridge wrote, "that, while close to and keenly aware of instinct, has yet obtained its release; so that it watches, intent but calmly elect—impartial appraiser of its own pleasure and its own pain. The consciousness knows fear, the while it walks intrepidly forward to the pit and casts a stone at the coiled terrors within. But the fear walks unashamed and does not cloak itself in cynicism; or that chain-armor of the week, a sneer."

Evelyn Scott's poetry was widely praised, but with the publication of *The Narrow House* in 1921 she became a literary sensation. Representative of the enthusiastic reception of her art was Sinclair Lewis's comment: "Salute to Evelyn Scott! It would be an insult to speak with smug judiciousness of her 'promise.' *The Narrow House* is an event, it is one of those recognitions of life by which life itself becomes the greater." H. L. Mencken saw the novel as a landmark which would free the American novel from the constraints of convention and sentimentality. *The Narrow House*, *Narcissus* (1922), and *The Golden Door* (1925) compose a trilogy on the broad theme of modern man's tragedy of solipsism. The trilogy relates the story of three generations of a family whose members are painfully ensnared, first, in the traps of conventional morality to which their selves are meaninglessly sacrificed; and, later, in the abandon of an imaginary freedom from all restraints they are equally imprisoned in narcissistic idealism. After pain and suffering, dimly aware that love is realistically learned rather than romantically generated, the survivors emerge defeated but victorious in spiritual regeneration.

Her second trilogy—*Migrations* (1927), *The Wave* (1929), and *A Calendar of Sin* (1931)—brought her focus from the intense interior lives of her characters to the extensive drama of the development of America from 1850 to 1914. Hundreds of characters merge into the great wave of war and western expansion. Combining the minutia of the psychological novel of inner reality with the broad mythical sweep of the epic, the trilogy ranges in technique from conventional narrative to stream-of-consciousness, from a mosaic of kaleidoscopic vignettes to long interior monologues. The effect delivers simultaneously the godlike objective view and the emotional intensity of personal involvement, the individual and collective destiny in both their separateness and oneness. *The Wave* is recognized as one of the best novels written about the Civil War and, according to some critics, is the most successful war novel written by a woman. *The Wave* firmly established Evelyn Scott's reputation, and so high was her position that her critique of Faulkner's *The Sound and the Fury* (1929)—perhaps the earliest recognition of Faulkner's art published in America—went far in establishing Faulkner as a serious writer. During this most productive period of her career, she also published her second collection of poetry, *The Winter Alone* (1930), an ironic title since the solitary, unflinching peering at the world around her evolves the strong feeling for the kinship of all life. During this period, from 1925 to 1931, Evelyn Scott drifted in Bermuda, France, North Africa, and England, wherever her modest income could best support her prodigious writing. Her common-law marriage with Cyril Scott dissolved in divorce in 1928, and in New Mexico in 1930 she married the English novelist John Metcalfe.

For the next decade, Evelyn Scott resided primarily in the United States and Canada. In 1932 she received a Guggenheim Fellowship to write *Eva Gay* (1933), a novel loosely based on the interrelationships and lives of herself, Cyril Scott, and Owen Merton, father of Thomas Merton. The novel explores a woman's compelling love for two men and the conflicting philosophies of intellect and sensuality which the two men embody. After *Eva Gay,* Evelyn Scott focused her talents on the dilemma of the individual, epitomized by the artist, in a culture becoming more and more enervated by totalitarianism, propaganda, collectivism, and Communist mentalities. The decline of the bourgeoisie was examined in *Breathe Upon These Slain* (1934), and *Bread and a Sword* (1937) attacked communism from the standpoint of a libertarian.

Though her novels continued to be highly praised by critics and she continued to write poetry of high quality, her philosophical viewpoint was not popular with many left-leaning critics and her complex subject matter had little appeal to the general reader, and thus her reputation began its decline. Her last published novel, *The Shadow of the Hawk* (1941), reminiscent of Dickens's plotting and characterization, delineates the effect upon a son of his innocent father's imprisonment for murder. The book received modest attention from the reviewers.

Plagued by bureaucratic red tape and the conviction, for which there was some evidence, that she was being persecuted by hostile political agents, Evelyn Scott moved to Canada. From there, shortly before England entered World War II, she joined her husband, who was serving as a Royal Air Force officer in London. There they endured the bombings, ill health, poverty, and neglect from the literary world. Desperate but determined to reestablish their literary careers, in 1952 the couple went to California under the auspices of the Huntington Hartford Foundation and later moved to New York City, where they settled in one room of a cheap hotel. Evelyn Scott continued to write in spite of a stroke which left her with expressive aphasia. With agonizing effort she regained her powers and finished one long novel, "Escape into Living"; a collection of poetry, "The Gravestones Wept"; and a collection of poems for children, "The Youngest Smiles." She also nearly completed the rewriting of a lost manuscript, "Before Cock Crow," begun in 1929. None of these works was published. Finally, hospitalized and temporarily sent home, on the night of her return to her one-room home, she died in her sleep at her husband's side. John Metcalfe, nearly blind, returned to England and died shortly afterward as a result of a fall down stairs.

Although in the later period of Evelyn Scott's career she was all but unknown to most readers, there were always writers and critics, such as William Faulkner and Caroline Gordon, who recognized her as an important innovator and artist who opened new ground for fictional exploration. Others have recognized her keen intellect, absolute objectivity, and contribution to the honest presentation of the feminine spirit. She has the distinction of having written two works, *Escapade* and *The Wave*, which may be called classics in their two diverse forms. She also has the honor of having published first in the United States genuine recognition of the art of James Joyce and William Faulkner. *The Narrow House, Narcissus, Background in Tennes-*

see, and *On William Faulkner's "The Sound and the Fury"* have recently been reprinted, and there is expectation that *The Wave* and *Escapade* may soon be republished, evidence that perhaps Evelyn Scott is receiving wider recognition.

References:

Peggy Bach, "Melancholy Necessity: Evelyn Scott," *New Orleans Review,* 6 (September 1979): 388-395;

Joseph Warren Beach, *The Twentieth Century Novel* (New York: Appleton-Century-Crofts, 1932), pp. 481-484, 519-520, 553;

John M. Bradbury, *Renaissance in the South* (Chapel Hill: University of North Carolina Press, 1963);

Oscar Cargill, *Intellectual America: Ideas on the March* (New York: Macmillan, 1941), pp. 723-724;

D. A. Callard, "Pretty Good for a Woman: A Quest for Evelyn Scott," *London Magazine,* 21 (October 1981): 52-61;

Callard, *Pretty Good for a Woman: The Enigmas of Evelyn Scott* (New York: Norton, 1986);

Padraic Colum, "Two Women Poets," *New Republic,* 28 (2 November 1921): 304-305;

Clifton Fadiman, "Eros in America," *Nation,* 133 (11 November 1931): 521-522;

Dudley Fitts, "The Verse of Evelyn Scott," *Poetry,* 36 (September 1930): 338-343;

Harlan Hatcher, *Creating the Modern American Novel* (New York: Farrar & Rinehart, 1935), pp. 172-182;

Grant C. Knight, *American Literature and Culture* (New York: Long & Smith, 1932), pp. 445-461;

Ludwig Lewisohn, *Expressions in America* (New York: Harper, 1932), pp. 201, 402-409;

Robert Lively, *Fiction Fights the Civil War, An Unfinished Chapter in the Literary History of the American People* (Chapel Hill: University of North Carolina Press, 1957), pp. 137-138, 175;

Robert Morss Lovett, "The Evolution of Evelyn Scott," *Bookman,* 70 (October 1929): 153-156;

H. L. Mencken, *Prejudices* (New York: Knopf, 1922), pp. 203-204;

Lola Ridge, "Evelyn Scott," *Poetry,* 17 (March 1921): 334-337;

Harry Salpeter, "Portrait of a Disciplined Artist," *Bookman,* 74 (November 1931): 281-286;

Paul Snelling, "Evelyn Scott and Southern Background," *North Georgia Review,* 2 (Winter 1937-1938): 3-4, 26-31;

Carl Van Doren, *Modern American Prose* (New York: Harcourt, Brace, 1934), p. 936;

Carl Van Doren, Review of *A Calendar of Sin, Wings,* 6 (January 1932): 16-17;

Carl Van Doren, *The Roving Critic* (New York: Knopf, 1923), pp. 130-132;

Mark Van Doren, "Generations in Love," *New York Herald Tribune Books,* 11 October 1931, pp. 1-2;

Mark Van Doren, "Sapphics," *Nation,* 112 (5 January 1921): 20;

Robert L. Welker, "Evelyn Scott: A Literary Biography," Ph.D. dissertation, Vanderbilt University, 1958;

Welker, Introduction to *Background in Tennessee* (Knoxville: University of Tennessee Press, 1980), pp. v-xv;

Welker, "Liebstod with a Southern Accent," in *Reality and Myth: Essays in American Literature,* edited by Welker and William E. Walker (Nashville: Vanderbilt University Press, 1964), pp. 179-211;

Amos N. Wilder, *The Spiritual Aspects of the New Poetry* (New York: Harper, 1940), pp. 131-140.

Papers:

The Humanities Research Center at the University of Texas has approximately 500 items, including manuscripts and correspondence.

Karl Shapiro

(10 November 1913-   )

Ross Labrie
University of British Columbia

BOOKS: *Poems* (Baltimore: Privately printed at the Waverly Press, 1935);

Person, Place and Thing (New York: Reynal & Hitchcock, 1942; London: Secker & Warburg, 1944);

The Place of Love (Malvern, Australia: Bradley Printers, 1942);

V-Letter and Other Poems (New York: Reynal & Hitchcock, 1944; London: Secker & Warburg, 1945);

Essay on Rime (New York: Reynal & Hitchcock, 1945; London: Secker & Warburg, 1947);

English Prosody and Modern Poetry (Baltimore: Johns Hopkins University Press, 1947);

Trial of a Poet and Other Poems (New York: Reynal & Hitchcock, 1947);

A Bibliography of Modern Prosody (Baltimore: Johns Hopkins University Press, 1948);

The Thin Bell-Ringer (N.p.: Privately printed, 1948);

Beyond Criticism (Lincoln: University of Nebraska Press, 1953); republished as *A Primer for Poets* (Lincoln: University of Nebraska Press, 1965);

Poems 1940-1953 (New York: Random House, 1953);

The Tenor: Opera in One Act, libretto by Shapiro and Ernst Lert, score by Hugo Weisgall (Bryn Mawr, Pa.: Merion Music, 1957);

Poems of a Jew (New York: Random House, 1958);

In Defense of Ignorance (New York: Random House, 1960);

The Writer's Experience, by Shapiro and Ralph Ellison (Washington, D.C.: Library of Congress, 1964);

The Bourgeois Poet (New York: Random House, 1964);

A Maleboge of 1400 Books: Six Lectures, Carleton Miscellany, 5 (Summer 1964);

A Prosody Handbook, by Shapiro and Robert Beum (New York, Evanston & London: Harper & Row, 1965);

Randall Jarrell (Washington, D.C.: Library of Congress, 1967);

Karl Shapiro (courtesy of Information Services, University of California, Davis)

To Abolish Children and Other Essays (Chicago: Quadrangle Books, 1968);

Selected Poems (New York: Random House, 1968);

White-Haired Lover (New York: Random House, 1968);

Edsel (New York: Bernard Geis, 1971);

The Poetry Wreck: Selected Essays 1950-1970 (New York: Random House, 1975);

Adult Bookstore (New York: Random House, 1976);

399

Collected Poems 1940-1978 (New York: Random House, 1978).

OTHER: "Noun," in *Five Young American Poets: Second Series* (Norfolk, Conn.: New Directions, 1941), pp. 173-218.

In an essay first published in *The Writer's Experience* (1964) Karl Shapiro recalled a woman who came up to him just before a lecture he was about to give on anarchism and said crisply: "I don't believe a word you are going to say, and I don't think you do either." The anecdote illustrates Shapiro's reputation as a provocateur and—as far as his poetry and poetics are concerned—brings to mind his controversial attack on the poetic establishment, particularly against the hegemony of Ezra Pound, T. S. Eliot, and William Butler Yeats. The wisdom of Shapiro's iconoclastic crusade against the kind of poetry written by Pound and Eliot and of his espousal of Walt Whitman and William Carlos Williams as the true shapers of twentieth-century American poetry has been vindicated by the theory and practice of American poets during the 1950s and 1960s.

Shapiro's own poetry has been far less controversial than the critical stances he has adopted. Over the past forty years he has demonstrated a mastery of both traditionally formal and contemporary, open styles amid a broad variety of themes. In particular, in the 1940s he produced some of the best war poetry ever written by an American poet.

Karl Shapiro was born in Baltimore, Maryland, on 10 November 1913, the son of Joseph and Sarah Omansky Shapiro. His father was a businessman whose income fluctuated greatly during the 1920s and 1930s. As a senior in high school, for example, Shapiro remembers having sensed the imminent financial collapse of his family. His father and Baltimore relatives were solidly committed to commerce and the professions, and Shapiro recalled in an essay titled "A *Maleboge* of Fourteen Hundred Books" (collected in *To Abolish Children and Other Essays,* 1968) that although in his family's circle of friends there was "no literary atmosphere" his father encouraged his older brother (the more successful student of the two sons) to "write and perhaps even to become a writer." In the same essay, in what is perhaps a tracing of the origins of his own future irreverence, Shapiro also noted that his father "kept a limp scarlet leather collection of Wilde's poetry on a table in the living room" whose pages were "edged in bright gold, like a naughty Bible."

Shapiro's early, undistinguished years as a student were spent in Baltimore, Chicago, and Norfolk, Virginia. He spent part of a year at the University of Virginia (1932-1933) where he felt ostracized by both the Anglo-Saxon majority and by students of German-Jewish background who, Shapiro claims, regarded themselves as superior to Jews whose ancestors, like his own, had come from Russia. Shapiro's chagrin about this period of his life has been captured in his poem "University," where the "curriculum" is said to be to "hurt the Negro & avoid the Jew."

Due to his self-consciousness about his background, the adolescent Shapiro at one time thought of changing his name to "Karl Camden," the name Camden being drawn from a "beautiful old railway station in Baltimore called Camden Station." Although he never adopted this anglicized surname, he did legally change the spelling of his first name from Carl to the more Germanic Karl.

The consideration of a name change not only reached deeply into Shapiro's anomalous position as a Jewish southerner but also undermined his lifelong feeling that he was destined to be a poet. "Nobody in the *Oxford Book of English Verse*," he recalled in *The Poetry Wreck* (1975), "had been named Shapiro." He remembered feeling during the 1930s that it would be difficult to get a poem published unless one had an Anglo-Saxon name, "but I decided to stick to my name; that decision made me 'Jewish.' And since I had made the decision I wrote poems about Jewishness."

Although Shapiro was raised as a middle-class Jew and "underwent the formal training of a barmitzvah," he was not particularly religious. Nonetheless, his sense of identity as a Jew had been firmly rooted. In his introduction to *Poems of a Jew* (1958) he wrote: "As a third generation American I grew up with the obsessive idea of personal liberty which engrosses all Americans except the oldest and richest families. As a Jew I grew up in an atmosphere of mysterious pride and sensitivity, an atmosphere in which even the greatest achievement was touched by a sense of the comic. Isolated within my own world, like a worm in an apple, I became a poet."

Shapiro has had an equally embedded consciousness of himself as a southerner. Many of his poems focus on the South as landscape and theme, poems such as "Conscription Camp," "Alexandria," "Jefferson," "Demobilization," "Snob," and "The Southerner." While acutely aware of and alienated by the southern tradition of caste, the South remained home for Shapiro long after he had ceased to live in it. In this connection he has acknowledged the influence of H. L. Mencken, a fellow Baltimorean, feeling that the acerbic essayist might have accounted in part for his own tendency to "take the other side of almost any argument" ("A *Maleboge* of Fourteen Hundred Books"). He also felt an unsentimental affinity with that other Baltimorean, Edgar Allan Poe, as can be seen in his poem "Israfel."

During the 1930s Shapiro led a desultory life, traveling to Tahiti, working in his father's business (which had begun to prosper), and becoming attracted paradoxically both to communism and Catholicism. His poem "The Crucifix in the Filing Cabinet" reflects both his lackluster existence as a clerk in his father's firm and his fascination with Catholicism. That fascination was to last through his service in World War II, but was to wane after that. He came eventually to dislike Christian asceticism, turning with relief toward the earthier traditions of Judaism.

In 1935 Shapiro privately published *Poems*, an unremarkable collection that nonetheless won him a scholarship to Johns Hopkins University, which he attended from 1937 to 1939. His formal schooling was to remain incomplete. "I went to three high schools and two universities," he noted in *The Writer's Experience*, "and am without a degree." Eventually he studied to be a librarian at the Enoch Pratt Library School in Baltimore, but a few weeks before his examinations in 1941 he was drafted into the army. Ironically, the barrenness of army life stimulated him to write as neither before nor since, and between 1941 and 1945 he turned out four volumes of poetry as well as having a poem published in *Five Young American Poets: Second Series* (1941).

The Place of Love, which was privately printed in Australia in 1942, gives little indication of the poet Shapiro was to become. *Person, Place and Thing* (1942), on the other hand, marked a formidable beginning for Shapiro's career. Poems from the collection, which were published in *Poetry* in 1940 and 1941 while Shapiro was serving as a Medical Corps clerk in the South Pacific, were awarded the magazine's Levinson Prize and the collection itself was lauded by the critics. Allen Tate, who represented the southern cultural elite and whose praise therefore meant much to Shapiro, liked the book's honesty and its "special savagery of attack." While the word "attack" accurately mirrors the book's exposure of urban decadence, the word is even more helpful in its capturing of Shapiro's directness. He

confronts his subjects, whether they be war, love ("To Evelyn for Christmas"), southern history, or Jewish Sundays, with a bracing clarity and firmness. The effect is intensified by Shapiro's incisive use of imagistic technique—his fondness for hard, sharp surfaces—as can be seen in the much-anthologized "Auto Wreck."

The Baudelairean atmosphere of urban malaise that characterizes poems such as "The Dome of Sunday" and "Washington Cathedral" figures in the war poems as well, giving them a brooding, unsettling quality. The events of the war are set within the framework of the dehumanized technocracies that send men and women to war. The impersonal mood is underlined by Shapiro's convincing portrayal of the enervating monotony that engulfs the soldier's days. On other occasions he depicts the zeal of young recruits with mordant foreboding, as in "Scyros":

Hot is the sky and green
Where Germans have been seen
The moon leaks metal on the Atlantic fields
Pink boys in birthday shrouds
Loop lightly through the clouds
Or coast the peaks of Finland on their shields.

Shapiro's skillful use of the dramatic monologue in *Person, Place and Thing*—in poems such as the well-known "Cut Flower" and "Mongolian Idiot"—add much to the energy and richness of this volume, whose excellence in many ways he was never to surpass. While "Mongolian Idiot" might have seemed to some readers evidence of the heartlessness of Shapiro's imagination, Shapiro's sympathy for the child and its plight comes through poignantly, and the poem should not be associated with the author's admitted taste for the ugly and the obscene.

V-Letter and Other Poems (1944), published when Shapiro was serving in New Guinea, was awarded a Pulitzer Prize. The title refers to the correspondence of overseas military personnel; letters from abroad were censored and sent on microfilm to the United States, where they were reprinted in smaller format (V-letters) and mailed. (Letters from the United States to military personnel overseas were treated in the same way though they were not censored.) Thus, Shapiro's soldier's letter home symbolized the overlapping of personal feeling and public exposure in the life of the U.S. serviceman. The distanced perspective, which one finds in many of Shapiro's war poems, reminds one of Randall Jarrell, whose poetry he much admired.

Karl Shapiro in New Guinea, 1944

The war poems in *V-Letter*, such as "Hill at Paramatta," "Sydney Bridge," "Christmas Eve: Australia," and the memorable sonnet "Full Moon: New Guinea" exhibit both a contemplative openness to experience and a relentless detachment, the effect being the dramatization of men forced to stare at the horror of their situation without their being in any way able to control it:

> The small burr of the bombers in our ear
> Tickles our rest; we rise as from a nap
> And take our helmets absently and meet,
> Prepared for any spectacle or mishap.

Characteristically in *V-Letter*, the machinery of war overshadows and mesmerizes the men who attend it, as in the unexpectedly elegant "Ballet Mécanique" in which the "wheel forgets the hand that palpitates/The danceless power." The tautness of the poems is everywhere sustained by their opposed elements; the romantic flood of moonlight in "Full Moon: New Guinea," for example, serves as a backdrop for a night air attack.

Shapiro's long poem *Essay on Rime* (1945) was written in the heat of New Guinea, where Shapiro had no access to a library, a fact which makes his sustained poetic consideration of the problems facing contemporary verse all the more remarkable. William Van O'Connor, who was also stationed in New Guinea, had lent Shapiro a copy of Yeats's *The Oxford Book of Modern Verse* (1936) and other than that Shapiro had only his own copy of Baudelaire. Obviously written with Pope's *An Essay on Criticism* (1711) in mind, the *Essay on Rime*, which, written in a loose blank verse—but with some occasional rhymes—and divided into three cantos, assesses the position of twentieth-century poetry after the collapse of those traditional values that had served as a basis for centuries of poetic themes. In a similar vein Shapiro reflects on the demise of a formalism that had been succeeded by an apparently structureless free verse. *Essay on Rime* was the first major occasion on which Shapiro attacked the ponderous influence of modern criticism on the making of poetry. He called here, and later in his controversial book *In Defense of Ignorance* (1960), for a direct reading of experience through the poet's senses and emotions, forsaking the sort of reflexive intellectualizing which Shapiro believed had drained contemporary poetry of vitality. Moreover, he argued for a personal voice in poetry as opposed to the impersonality prescribed by Eliot.

While some commentators reacted caustically to *Essay on Rime*, accusing Shapiro of oversimplification, the book received praise from eminent critics such as Conrad Aiken and F. O. Matthiessen. While the versification of the *Essay on Rime* is often pedestrian and even clumsy at times and while the poem does contain oversimplifications and inconsistencies, it nonetheless conveys a fundamental outlook which Shapiro has never renounced and for which there is much to be said. Shapiro was principally attacking the calcification and narrowness which had overtaken modern poetry in the wake of the dogmatism of Eliot, Pound, and the New Critics. What he wanted for poetry was the sort of provisional tone and openness that he saw in contemporary science, which he later characterized in "A *Maleboge* of Fourteen Hundred Books" as the "poetry of our time." Above all, Shapiro set himself against the sort of criticism that reduced "all experience to abstract ideas" (*In Defense of Ignorance*). What he was after was a poetry not of ideas, but of "what ideas feel like," as he put it in *The Bourgeois Poet* (1964): "Ideas on Sunday, thoughts on vacation."

Largely because of his winning a Pulitzer Prize, Shapiro was named Consultant in Poetry to the Library of Congress, a position which he held 1947-1948. On 25 March 1945 he married Evalyn Katz, who as literary agent had shepherded his poetry to press during the war years. They subsequently had three children. In 1948 while serving on the committee for the Bollingen Prize, at that time sponsored by the Library of Congress, he found himself surrounded by controversy after he voted against awarding the prize to Ezra Pound and declared publicly that Pound's questionable political and moral philosophy, including a pronounced anti-Semitism, vitiated his poetry.

Some of the poems in *Trial of a Poet and Other Poems* (1947) had been written in the South Pacific, while others were written on the troopship home and in New York. The book evocatively conveys a sense of aftermath, as in "Homecoming":

The mighty ghoul-ship that we ride exhales
The sickly-sweet stench of humiliation
And even the majority, untouched by steel
Or psychoneurosis, stare with eyes in rut.

Deepening the mood of aftermath, Shapiro foresaw the moral consequences of the awesome weapon that had permitted America to end the war, darkly depicting America's invention of the A-bomb as a Faustian pact: "He hid, appearing on the sixth to pose/In an American desert at War's end/Where, at his back, a dome of atoms rose" ("The Progress of Faust").

In 1948 Shapiro became an associate professor of writing at Johns Hopkins University, another windfall brought about by his Pulitzer Prize. From 1950 to 1956 he was editor of *Poetry,* and from 1953 to 1955 he was also editor of the *Newberry Library Bulletin.* He ironically found himself in the case of both august journals upholding the critical values of the poetic establishment in spite of his previously chosen role as anticritic.

Poems 1940-1953 (1953) includes a selection of previously published material as well as eighteen new poems. Some of the images, as in "The Minute" in which an "office building treads the marble dark," recall the fine, burnished surfaces of *Person, Place and Thing.* Other poems, such as "Going to School," show a merging of visual detail and metaphysical resonance.

In 1956 Shapiro accepted a position as professor in the department of English at the University of Nebraska. At the same time he became editor of the *Prairie Schooner,* a position which he held until 1966 when he resigned his professorship and his editorship because the university administra-

tion and staff of the journal, according to Shapiro, refused to let him publish a short story involving a homosexual. He had already felt ostracized by the reception given *In Defense of Ignorance* (1960), a book whose acerbic views he subsequently said in a 1978 interview in the *Tri-Quarterly* made him lose "practically all" of his friends.

In the meantime he had published two volumes of poetry, *Poems of a Jew* (1958) and *The Bourgeois Poet* (1964). In *Poems of a Jew,* which includes a number of his earlier poems in addition to some new ones, Shapiro both embraces his Jewishness and on occasion strikes out at Christianity. Objecting particularly to what he saw as Christianity's repression of sexuality, he titled a poem about a boy's first masturbation, "The Confirmation." On the other hand, in poems such as "The Alphabet" he asserted the formative role of Judaism in the creation of Christianity, and in other poems, such as "Teasing the Nuns" and "The Jew at Christmas Eve," his tone was conciliatory. Shapiro attempted to naturalize the term *Jew,* to offset the stinging effect of the word in North American culture, as can be felt in the poem "The First Time." The best poem in *Poems of a Jew* is probably "Messias": A Jewish middle-class boy is suddenly met on his doorstep by an ancient, scholarly-looking Jew with a patriarchal face and beard who inescapably confronts the boy with his heritage. The poem illuminates Shapiro's strength as a poet—his fine sense of narrative situation and his deft and inventive use of commonplace experience: "Between the poetry of language or symbol and that of situation," he said in "A *Maleboge* of Fourteen Hundred Books," "I chose the situation."

Because of its open-endedness and prosiness *A Bourgeois Poet* signalled a radical new direction for Shapiro. He became attracted to the Beat poetry of Allen Ginsberg and Lawrence Ferlinghetti, and had come to view Whitman as the father of American poetry, a poetry he took pains to point out *was* rather proselike. His method in *The Bourgeois Poet* was that of free association and montage. At the foreground of the sequence is Shapiro's Nebraska house in summer from which he drifted back over earlier stretches of his life and thought. *The Bourgeois Poet* is thus Shapiro's song of himself. The poem emphasizes self-analysis and reveals Shapiro's conspicuous attempt to be candid with himself—as in his admission that in his minor intellectual vanities he was not all that morally different from his midwestern neighbors.

The title of the collection came from Theodore Roethke, who teasingly called Shapiro a

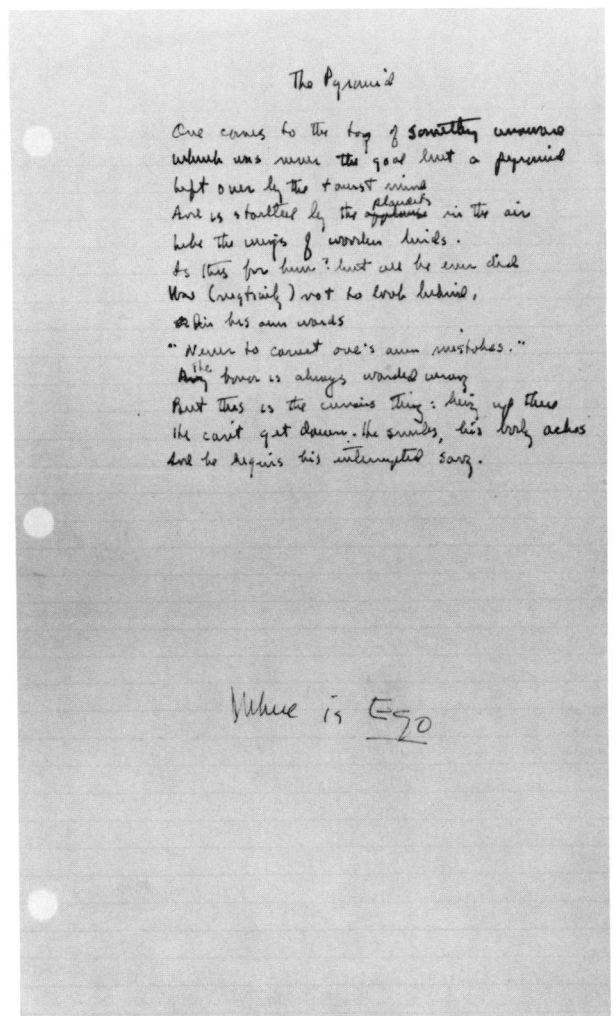

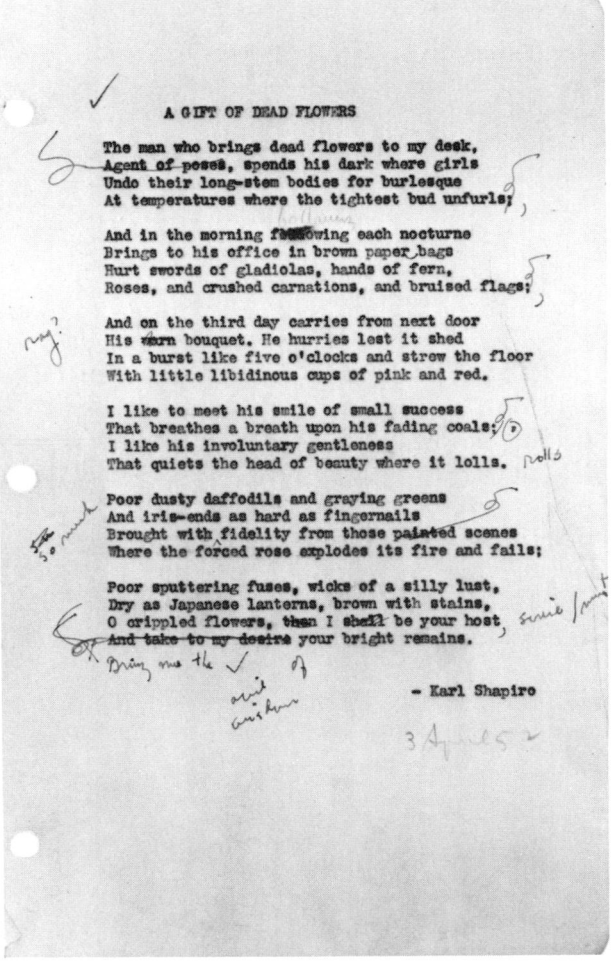

Manuscript and revised typescript for two poems in the Shapiro Collection at the Lilly Library, Indiana University (by permission of the author)

"bourgeois poet" at a party in Seattle in 1955. Shapiro accepted the term, conceding that he could not, after all, free himself from middle-class aspirations in the way that Henry Miller had succeeded in doing: "You go from the pogroms of Russia to the East Side of New York. Your father becomes a businessman so you can get an education and become a writer. You don't want to give up those material things that you just got." Thus, at one point in *The Bourgeois Poet* he wonders with faintly masochistic, though wry, self-consciousness what "kind of notation is in my *Time* file for my life, especially my death? Will they say I died, O God? If they don't say I died how can I die?" While not one of Shapiro's stronger works, *The Bourgeois Poet* is a fertile source of autobiographical information. Furthermore, the book is a watershed of sorts since it expanded Shapiro's range of themes to include the everyday, relaxed round of his existence.

After a two-year stint at the University of Chicago from 1966 to 1968 Shapiro joined the faculty of the University of California at Davis, where he still teaches. About this side of his life he has said: "I have a sort of special status around English departments—I'm not really a professor, but sort of a mad guest." After having been divorced from his first wife in January 1967, he married Teri Kovach on 31 July 1967. She is the focus of *White-Haired Lover* (1968), a cycle of twenty-nine love poems in which Shapiro returns to traditional forms, principally the sonnet. The quality of these poems is uneven, and a few, such as "Epithalamium, the Second Time Around," "I Swore to Stab the Sonnet," and "Now Christ is Risen," are somewhat banal. Others, however, such as "You Played Chopin" and the Petrarchan sonnet, "You Lay Above Me," from which the title of *White-Haired Lover* is taken, are fresh and moving. For both the *Selected Poems* (1968) and *White-Haired Lover*, Shapiro received the 1969 Bollingen Prize for Poetry, sharing the award that year with John Berryman.

In *Adult Bookstore* (1976), published when he was sixty-two, Shapiro wrote some of his most polished verse. There is no hint, for example, of the awkwardness of *White-Haired Lover*. Poems such as "My Father's Funeral," which might have elicited such writing, are firm and tight on both a technical and emotional level. In poems such as "Garage Sale" and "Girls Working in Banks" Shapiro adapts his earlier imagistic precision to the quotidian flow

of experience, including some evocative poems about his California surroundings. The social satires, such as "Flying First Class" and "Sestina: of the Militant Vocabulary," are marked by artfulness and panache, as is the conclusion to "Sestina," which parodies the vocabulary of the militant activists of the late 1960s and early 1970s: "While pigs perpetuate the power structure,/Baby, be relevant to the revolution/Till we experience the Establishment."

The high standard of these poems is continued in the handful of new pieces that were included in Shapiro's *Collected Poems 1940-1978* (1978), indicating that age has apparently not diminished his powers. Whatever his future output, Shapiro has established himself as a poet who managed to free himself from the constraints of many of the cultural and poetic dogmas of his time. In the end he will probably be remembered for his dispassionately vivid war poems and for the sometimes painful but memorable lyrics in which he struggled with the polarities of his identity as a Jewish American.

Bibliographies:

William White, *Karl Shapiro: A Bibliography* (Detroit: Wayne State University Press, 1960);

Ralph J. Mills, Jr., "Karl Shapiro," in his *Contemporary American Poetry* (New York: Random House, 1965), pp. 101-121;

Stephen Stepanchev, "Karl Shapiro," in his *American Poetry Since 1945* (New York: Harper & Row, 1965), pp. 53-68;

Karl Malkoff, "The Self in the Modern World: Karl Shapiro's Jewish Poems," in *Contemporary American-Jewish Literature*, edited by Irving Malin (Bloomington: Indiana University Press, 1973), pp. 213-228;

Michael Anania and Ralph J. Mills, Jr., "Karl Shapiro: An Interview on *Poetry*," *Tri-Quarterly*, 43 (Fall 1978): 197-215;

Lee Bartlett, *Karl Shapiro: A Descriptive Bibliography 1933-1977* (New York: Garland, 1979);

Joseph Reino, *Karl Shapiro* (Boston: Twayne, 1981).

Papers:

The Charles Feinberg Collection at Wayne State University, the Lilly Library at Indiana University, and the Library of Congress have important collections of Shapiro's papers.

Hy Sobiloff
(16 December 1912-August 1970)

Nicki Sahlin
Dean Junior College

BOOKS: *When Children Played as Kings and Queens* (N.p.: Privately printed, 1948);
Dinosaurs and Violins (New York: Farrar, Straus & Young, 1954);
In the Deepest Aquarium (New York: Dial Press, 1959);
Breathing of First Things (New York: Dial Press, 1963);
Hooting Across the Silence (New York: Horizon Press, 1971).

SCREENPLAYS: *Montauk,* Sobiloff, 1959;
Central Park, Sobiloff, 1960;
Speak to Me Child, Sobiloff, 1962;
Market to Market, Sobiloff, 1968.

Hy Sobiloff (photograph by Oscar Williams)

OTHER: Oscar Williams, ed., *The New Pocket Anthology of American Verse from Colonial Days to the Present,* includes poems by Sobiloff (Cleveland: World, 1955).

Hy Sobiloff, whose poetry was respected by many of his better-known contemporaries for its fresh, honest, unpretentious qualities, was also widely known as a filmmaker, industrialist, and philanthropist. Despite his other activities, Sobiloff was more than a part-time poet. He was constantly writing and associating with other poets. Introductions to his books were written by highly regarded figures: Anatole Broyard, Conrad Aiken, Allen Tate, James Wright, and Edwin Honig. He contributed to *Poetry* and was represented in a number of anthologies, including Oscar Williams's *The New Pocket Anthology of American Verse from Colonial Days to the Present* (1955).

Born Hyman Jordan Sobiloff, the son of Israel and Fannie Gollub Sobiloff, he grew up with an older brother, Myer, and two sisters, Sara and Ruth, in Fall River, Massachusetts. He was plagued by allergies, an affliction occasionally mentioned in his poems and one of the factors which influenced his completing high school in Tucson, Arizona, and then electing to attend the University of Arizona for undergraduate studies. He later attended Boston University, from which he received his bachelor's degree, and New York University. Sobiloff married Adelaide Goldstein, and they had one son, Stephen. In 1955 he was named an honorary chancellor of Florida Southern College, which awarded him a Doctor of Laws degree in 1956.

If Sobiloff had not been a poet, his accomplishments as a businessman would have been impressive in themselves. At the time of his death, he was chairman of the Larchfield Corporation in New York, of Marshall-Wells International in Nassau, of the Johnson Stores of Raleigh, North Carolina, and of the Auto-Lec Stores of New Orleans.

The ways in which he used the resources made available to him by his success in business suggest a great concern for others, a concern which becomes explicit in certain of his poems. Sobiloff was a founder of the Albert Einstein College of Medicine and the Technion-Israel Institute of Technology, both in New York, and the Edward Adaskin Educational Foundation in Fall River. He was also a founder and trustee of the National Foundation for Research of Allergies. Many of his charitable donations were undertaken jointly with his brother Myer. On a more personal level, Hy Sobiloff was known for his expansive gestures of good will, such as throwing large and lavish parties for friends on special occasions. His townhouse on 77th Street in New York City was visited by poets and other writers—including such members of the Beats as Jack Kerouac and Allen Ginsberg, celebrities from the film industry, and internationally known businessmen.

His four highly successful short films illustrate his desire to enrich the lives of others through poetry. Commenting on these experimental films, Sobiloff expressed the conviction "that an experiment should be made to develop poetry in three dimensions through the mass media of motion pictures and television. My aim was to add meanings to poetry by combining the visual and auditory appeal of film with the emotional appeal of words thereby bringing poetry to a wider audience."

The first film, *Montauk* (1959), a color short narrated by Ed Begley, concerns Montauk Point, Long Island, the setting for a number of Sobiloff's poems and the site of a house he owned. The film was nominated for an Academy Award and received a citation for its color photography at the First Boston International Film Festival. In 1960, a second film, *Central Park*, narrated by Jason Robards, Jr., was a United States entry to the International Film Festival in Venice. Filmed in and around Central Park in New York City, it is closely related to Sobiloff's city poems and street vignettes.

Speak to Me Child (1962) is narrated by David Wayne, who presents some of the poet's most characteristic poems, those dealing with childhood and children. The film's title is also the title of the first section of *Breathing of First Things* (1963), Sobiloff's fourth book. *Market to Market* (1968) was filmed in the predawn hours at New York City's Washington Market shortly before it was demolished; the film now stands as a historical document.

Though Sobiloff achieved recognition in several distinct areas of endeavor, among poets he was a fellow poet, conscious of his limitations, humble about the status of his poetry, yet unafraid to make direct statements on occasion. Edwin Honig later remembered Sobiloff's forthright behavior at a small party where John Berryman was giving an informal reading of a series of poems he had written on the John F. Kennedy assassination. As Berryman pronounced, "Part Three: 'I am an automobile,' " Sobiloff interrupted loudly and without hesitation: "That's ridiculous, John, you're *not* an automobile, you're John Berryman." Berryman, far from taking offense, paused and then burst out, "Hy, goddammit, you're right," and threw the poem to the floor.

Other poets have perceived the truthfulness of observation in Sobiloff's poetry. Conrad Aiken, in the introduction to *Dinosaurs and Violins* (1954), praised the "lyric immediacy" and what he termed the "metropolitan 'folk' " of the poetry, as well as "an apparent simplicity which is deceptive." In particular, he stressed Sobiloff's "newness of eye and language" and his "gift for seeing the ordinary as if it had never been looked at before." Allen Tate, introducing *In the Deepest Aquarium* (1959), referred to this characteristic simplicity less overtly, but commented that Sobiloff did not bother playing the " 'role of the poet' "; rather, "he has his eye on the object." Tate also noted that Sobiloff had received little critical attention (a fact which never changed) and that he belonged to no particular school: "Mr. Sobiloff owes allegiance to no one; this is not an act of defiance, the stance of the lone wolf; he is merely unaware."

While praising his work, both Aiken and Tate come close to representing the poet as a primitive, particularly by their use of words such as "folk" or "unaware." James Wright, in a lengthy introduction to *Breathing of First Things* (1963), a piece which does a great deal toward compensating for the lack of critical attention to Sobiloff's work, specifically denied that the poet is "primitive" or "anti-intellectual." Instead, Wright argued convincingly, Sobiloff is exploring a central theme, "the search for the child within the self," which is more complex than it appears and which also manifests itself in "the struggle to be true to one's own self." It is not just the rediscovery of childhood innocence that Sobiloff undertook but also a quest that is both psychological and spiritual. Wright's valuable perceptions are based upon only one collection, Sobiloff's longest; yet they also apply to the entire body of his work.

Wright's observations on the quest motif suggest the possibility of viewing each new volume of poetry as one phase of a cycle, a cycle which perhaps ends in joy, which as Edwin Honig points out in his introduction to *Hooting Across the Silence*

(1971), is the most recurrent word in Sobiloff's poetry. The tone of each volume is refined and developed by a process of careful selection, rearrangement, minor revisions, and, frequently, a renewal of earlier poems by their placement in a fresh context.

In the first volume, the privately printed *When Children Played as Kings and Queens* (1948), there are poems which might be termed metaphysical, yet they do not stand out as such in context of that volume. There is a random quality to the volume, a lack of direction which Sobiloff seemed eager to correct, since he often asked fellow poets for advice on revision, urging them to be as harsh as the poems warranted and not to spare his feelings. An untitled poem in the first volume defines a stick by comparison to the wood itself, by the influence of wind on its shape, and by its uses. The poem ends:

> Compare a stick with the wood,
> Compare a man to his child,
>   Yourself to yourself;
> Compare a stick to the wind,
>   to a flower stalk half bruised,
> Frightened by family screams.
>   Compare a stick to memory.

Sobiloff is demonstrating that while the essence of an object is unchangeable, there is a certain relativity in the object's connections with its origins, its history, and its uses. The stick is not "just" a stick, and though one can be nothing more nor less than oneself, there is still a point to indulging in just that comparison: "Yourself to yourself." That this poem is also a playful justification of psychoanalysis cannot be inferred from the poem itself, yet when the same poem appeared in *In the Deepest Aquarium* (1959) eleven years later, with the penultimate line excised and with the fresh title, "Family Screams," the context had caused the meaning to expand to include Freudian theory. Still, a stick remains simple, just as—no matter what its origins, no matter how it has been shaped—the poem must also retain its simplicity, an air of not having been tampered with too much. Early on Sobiloff was well aware of the complex nature of an outwardly playful poem. The technique that made the expression of such awareness possible still needed development, however, and some of the earliest poems possess an air of sophistication at odds with the poet's relatively immature poetic technique. "Compounding Immortality," from *When Children Played as Kings and Queens*, begins:

> In gardens of prophecy, forgiving our inheritance,
> In front of the sky, near the looking glass
> Where exhausted objects converge to exist
> My forgotten prayers froth at my mouth.

Here an attitude of profound world-weariness and a stab at a universal theme are obscured by abstraction and overly formal language, tendencies which Sobiloff gradually overcame.

Dinosaurs and Violins (1954), the first volume to be published commercially, draws heavily on the previous collection but is dominated by poems of personal experience, making the concern with personal identity clearer. In "Rapping on My Own Windows," a poem which had appeared untitled in *When Children Played as Kings and Queens*, the poet combines private emotion with the issue of how to develop his work, almost as if setting a directive for himself. The poem begins:

> Rapping on my own windows,
> Remembering Whitman's words
> ("I contradict myself")
> And aware of my own questions,
> What do I say?

The need to objectify personal emotion sufficiently to give it poetic form is already partially satisfied by the poem itself, but it does not reach the level of refinement achieved in later work. The phrase "Rapping on my own windows" shows the poet's keen awareness that not turning away from the self, but approaching it as if from outside, will be the way to conduct his poetic quest. Sobiloff refers to other poets infrequently, so it is significant that here he invokes Walt Whitman, a poet to whom he would later be compared, most extensively by James Wright. Later in the poem, the speaker refers to himself as "My poor mechanic": to deal with his own experience the poet must be a technician. He realizes that the task can be confusing: "I shuffled chaos,/Looked around and yelled for help...." The end of the poem, however, asserts that staying power is as important as immediate success:

> Still, my rude patience believes me
> And my hope stays,
> Like a small boy looking up there,
> Rapping on my own windows.

The appearance of outright naïveté, even confusion, combined with a complex concept, in this case the poet's proper attitude, is representative of a large proportion of Sobiloff's poetry.

From this volume, however, no clear pattern emerges. There are some lively city poems, a few descriptive nature poems, and some poems about the poet's own past, including "My Mother's Table," from the first volume. Several poems form a sort of psychological series, most notably "The Process of a Dream" and "The Stream of Unconsciousness." As Sobiloff's poetry continued to develop, he apparently abandoned the explicitly psychological exploration in favor of poems that were directed at the simpler level of childlike perception. The minor theme of the dream in this early volume may indicate that the poet was still grappling with an assortment of elements in which he as yet had found no unity. The poems in *Dinosaurs and Violins* have great clarity, but it is a clarity of the moment, of the object, or of the past, more than a clarity of poetic voice.

Five years later, with the poems of *In the Deepest Aquarium*, there is the sense of the poet's artistic concerns being worked out in a deeper, more consistent way than before. The poem "Intimation of a City" hints that the poet is discovering his own territory, not yet fully formed, as its last lines describe: "Tiptoeing to a shore/To a shape unknown, a shape to be." Sobiloff's art was not becoming self-conscious, for he was still capable of writing thoroughly playful poems, some of them, such as "Sex at El Morocco," reminiscent of Wallace Stevens's more whimsical poems. The title poem of *In the Deepest Aquarium*, which ends the volume, is an ambitious, moving poem about an ocean voyage. As Allen Tate points out, "the sea is in some sense the Unconscious"; however, it is a naturally realized symbol, in no sense contrived, and "In the Deepest Aquarium" is certainly a more mature poem than the earlier, more explicit poem "The Stream of Unconsciousness."

Though Sobiloff was developing his own poetic voice through his first several volumes, there is no doubt that in his fourth volume, *Breathing of First Things* (1963), he combined a fully developed voice with a sense of purpose stronger than ever before. The book is divided into four sections: "Speak to Me Child," "Oddballs," "Love Poems," and "Nature Poems." The first section informs the entire volume, its many perspectives on the natural wisdom of the child in turn expanding the sense

Oscar Williams, Robert Frost, Richard Eberhart, Carl Sandburg, L. Quincy Mumford, and Hy Sobiloff at the Library of Congress, May 1960 (courtesy of the Library of Congress)

of newness and freshness in the sections that follow. "There is no expiration to childhood," states a short poem called "Fragment," and in the poems in this section there is an easy blend of adult and childlike language. Sobiloff does not disguise his poetic goal in associating with children, and in "The Child's Sight" he makes a typically straightforward statement:

> The child's wisdom is in saying
> They say what they see when they see it
> I am beginning to remember how
> When I don't say it when I see it
> I remember it differently[.]

Later in the poem, with lines such as, "The child is a little inspector when it crawls/It touches and tastes the earth," and "I am learning the child's way," he emphasizes the necessity of seeing things as if for the first time. In themselves, perhaps such blunt statements of purpose would become tedious, even pedantic, but they are placed among other poems which present the phenomena of childhood without such comments. "Jump Rope," for example, explains the difficulty of coordinating both legs in that seemingly easy activity (even though it could also be interpreted as a metaphor for the Zen concept of self-forgetting, it is still totally unself-conscious). "The Soft Guard," about a two-and-a-half year old comforting her injured one-year-old sister, is a wise, gentle poem, ending: "The soft guard pulled her up to a sitting position/And with small talk she mothered her own hurt lullaby."

In the first section's childhood panorama the poet justifies his use of "the child's sight" and "the child's way," so that the childlike observations of other poems, already convincing in their own right, gain force by echoing the more explicit statements and ring truer. "Science Obese," in the "Oddballs" section, pokes fun at science, but also gives the sense that a child would be wiser than scientists. The love poems are simple but full of genuine emotion. The nature poems especially seem part of the continuum which begins with the child poems, and "Weather Wisdom" makes the creation of poetry seem as natural as the weather, in which ". . . birds sing early at dream's window/Breathing of first things." This last line, with its brilliant connection of birds' singing with their breathing, gives the profound impression that poetry, too, is more than song, more than artful contrivance: it is essential to life, as undeniable as breathing.

Breathing of First Things gained part of its strength from the grouping of the poems into categories, but in *Hooting Across the Silence* (1971), his last volume, Sobiloff's new, stronger voice is evident without such grouping and labeling. There are more than a dozen animal poems, which seem a continuation of the child sequence, a number of love poems, and a few explicitly about poetry. Most notably, there are poems about personal emotion which surpass any in previous volumes in terms of their directness of language and imagery. In "Under My Skin," for example, enormous poetic strength is gained from emotional weakness:

> Baking home-style anxiety pies,
> Cross-bordered, out-territoried,
> . . . .
> Startled, I saw stars on earth
> Twinkle with wan-worn wisdom[.]

Hooting Across the Silence was published posthumously, the year after Sobiloff's death from a heart attack. Despite his demanding business career, and in spite of periods of great emotional uncertainty, the man had always been a poet. In the earliest poems, he had written well, and from a number of angles, about what it means to be a poet, and then he began to explore what it means to be a child. The last volume brings such themes to their fullest development, at a time when the poet's voice, refined but fresher than ever, was just getting around to addressing, for better or worse, exactly what it meant to be Hy Sobiloff.

Jesse Stuart
(8 August 1906-17 February 1984)

J. R. LeMaster
Baylor University

See also the Stuart entries in *DLB 9, American Novelists, 1910-1945,* and *DLB Yearbook: 1984.*

BOOKS: *Harvest of Youth* (Howe, Okla.: Scroll Press, 1930);

Man with a Bull-Tongue Plow (New York: Dutton, 1934; abridged and revised, 1959);

Head O' W-Hollow (New York: Dutton, 1936);

Beyond Dark Hills (New York: Dutton, 1938; London: Hutchinson, 1938);

Tim (Cincinnati: Little Man, 1939);

Trees of Heaven (New York: Dutton, 1940);

Men of the Mountains (New York: Dutton, 1941);

Jesse Stuart at home in W-Hollow, 28 June 1955 (photograph by Maurice Kaplan)

Taps for Private Tussie (New York: Dutton, 1943); republished as *He'll Be Coming Down the Mountain* (London: Dobson, 1947);

Mongrel Mettle (New York: Books, Inc./Dutton, 1944);

Album of Destiny (New York: Dutton, 1944);

Foretaste of Glory (New York: Dutton, 1946);

Tales from the Plum Grove Hills (New York: Dutton, 1946);

The Thread That Runs So True (New York: Scribners, 1949);

Hie to the Hunters (New York, London & Toronto: Whittlesey House/McGraw-Hill, 1950);

Clearing in the Sky & Other Stories (New York, London & Toronto: McGraw-Hill, 1950);

Kentucky Is My Land (New York: Dutton, 1952);

The Beatinest Boy (New York, Toronto & London: Whittlesey House/McGraw-Hill, 1953);

The Good Spirit of Laurel Ridge (New York, Toronto & London: Whittlesey House/McGraw-Hill, 1953);

A Penny's Worth of Character (New York, Toronto & London: Whittlesey House/McGraw-Hill, 1954);

Red Mule (New York, Toronto & London: Whittlesey House/McGraw-Hill, 1955);

The Year of My Rebirth (New York, Toronto & London: McGraw-Hill, 1956; London: Gollancz, 1958);

Plowshare in Heaven (New York, Toronto & London: McGraw-Hill, 1958);

Huey, The Engineer (St. Helena, Cal.: James E. Beard, 1960);

The Rightful Owner (New York, Toronto & London: Whittlesey House/McGraw-Hill, 1960);

God's Oddling (New York, Toronto & London: McGraw-Hill, 1960); abridged by Elinor Chamberlain as *Strength from the Hills* (New York: Pyramid Books, 1968);

Andy Finds a Way (New York, Toronto & London: Whittlesey House/McGraw-Hill, 1961);

Hold April (New York, Toronto & London: McGraw-Hill, 1962);

A Jesse Stuart Reader (New York, Chicago, San Francisco & Dallas: McGraw-Hill, 1963);

Save Every Lamb (New York, Toronto & London: McGraw-Hill, 1964);

Daughter of the Legend (New York, Toronto & London: McGraw-Hill, 1965);

A Jesse Stuart Harvest (New York: Laurel Leaf Library/Dell, 1965);

My Land Has a Voice (New York, Toronto, London & Sydney: McGraw-Hill, 1966);

A Ride With Huey the Engineer (New York, Toronto, London & Sydney: McGraw-Hill, 1966);

Mr. Gallion's School (New York, Toronto, London & Sydney: McGraw-Hill, 1967);

Rebels With a Cause (Murray, Ky.: Murray State University, 1967);

Stories by Jesse Stuart (New York: McGraw-Hill, 1968);

Come Gentle Spring (New York, St. Louis, San Francisco & Toronto: McGraw-Hill, 1969);

Old Ben (New York, Toronto, London, Sydney, St. Louis, San Francisco, Mexico & Panama: McGraw-Hill, 1970);

To Teach, To Love (New York & Cleveland: World, 1970);

Come Back to the Farm (New York, St. Louis, San Francisco, Dusseldorf, London, Mexico, Sydney & Toronto: McGraw-Hill, 1971);

Autumn Lovesong (Kansas City, Mo.: Hallmark Editions, 1971);

Come to My Tomorrow Land (Nashville & London: Aurora, 1971);

Dawn of Remembered Spring (New York, St. Louis, San Francisco, Dusseldorf, Mexico & Toronto: McGraw-Hill, 1972);

The Land Beyond the River (New York, St. Louis, San Francisco, Dusseldorf, London, Mexico, Sydney & Toronto: McGraw-Hill, 1973);

32 Votes Before Breakfast (New York, St. Louis, San Francisco, Dusseldorf, London, Mexico, Sydney & Toronto: McGraw-Hill, 1974);

Seven by Jesse (Terre Haute: Indiana Council of Teachers of English, Indiana State University, 1974);

The World of Jesse Stuart: Selected Poems, edited by J. R. LeMaster (New York, St. Louis, San Francisco, Dusseldorf, London, Mexico, Sydney & Toronto: McGraw-Hill, 1975);

My World (Lexington: University Press of Kentucky, 1975);

Up the Hollow from Lynchburg, text by Stuart and photographs by Joe Clark (New York, St. Louis, San Francisco, Dusseldorf, London, Mexico, Sydney & Toronto: McGraw-Hill, 1975);

The Seasons of Jesse Stuart: An Autobiography in Poetry 1907-1976, selected by Wanda Hicks (Danbury, Conn.: Archer Editions Press, 1976);

Honest Confession of a Literary Sin (Detroit: W-Hollow Books, 1977);

Dandelion on the Acropolis: A Journal of Greece (Danbury, Conn.: Archer Editions Press, 1978);

The Kingdom Within (New York: McGraw-Hill, 1979);

Lost Sandstones and Lonely Skies and Other Essays (Danbury, Conn.: Archer Editions Press, 1979);

If I Were Seventeen Again and Other Essays (Danbury, Conn.: Archer Editions Press, 1980);

Land of the Honey-Colored Wind, edited by Jerry A. Herndon (Moorhead, Ky.: Jesse Stuart Foundation, 1982);

The Best-Loved Short Stories of Jesse Stuart, edited by H. Edward Richardson (New York: McGraw-Hill, 1982).

In a career of more than half a century Jesse Stuart produced nearly sixty books. He is still being read, in English or in translation, in England, Ireland, Denmark, Sweden, Norway, Iceland, Germany, Holland, Switzerland, France, Poland, Czechoslovakia, Russia, Italy, Saudi Arabia, Kuwait, Pakistan, Korea, South Africa, Australia, New Zealand, Canada, Brazil, and throughout much of South America. He traveled over much of the world as a goodwill ambassador for the U.S. Department of State. He also taught and lectured abroad, and in 1937 he received a Guggenheim Fellowship in order to travel to Scotland and study the literary origins of the Appalachian region from which he came. Recipient of fourteen honorary degrees, Stuart has been known primarily as a popular writer and has enjoyed a large readership. Since World War II he has been more widely known for his prose than for his poetry, but he first established his literary reputation as a poet, and over his long career he produced a significant body of poetry which deserves more critical attention than it has heretofore received.

Jesse Hilton Stuart was born in a log cabin in Greenup County, Kentucky, on 8 August 1906, and, except for brief periods when he attended college, served in the U.S. Navy, and studied or lectured abroad, he lived within a few miles of where he was born. He was the second child in a family of seven. His father, Mitchell Stuart, was a coal miner, tenant farmer, and railroad worker. His mother, Martha Hilton (sometimes spelled Hylton) Stuart, who viewed education as a means for her children to escape the hard life of the hills, encouraged him "to learn" from the time he was old enough to understand. Stuart first attended Plum Grove School, where a young teacher named Calvin Clarke taught him to read and write. The family moved frequently, however, and he missed school so often to help his father on the farm that he finally dropped out altogether. When he was fifteen and working for a contractor paving the streets of Greenup, Kentucky, he quit his job and entered Greenup High School. Because he had gone to school only twenty-two months previously, he was required to take an entrance exam and he scored barely well enough to enter.

He walked to and from school, which was five miles from his home. While he played on the school football team for four years and also played baseball, he worked on weekends wherever he could to help pay for his books and clothes. Encouraged by Mrs. Harriet Lewis MacFarland Hatton, an English teacher, he fell in love with literature and writers, especially with Robert Burns, who would become the "patron saint" of his early writing career. When he completed high school in 1926, he sold tickets for carnival rides and worked in a steel mill, but throughout this time he was writing and wanting desperately to return to school. He looked for a college, knowing that his chances of being accepted were slim, but in the fall of 1926 he was accepted by Lincoln Memorial University in Harrogate, Tennessee.

Stuart published some of his poems in the *Blue and the Gray*, the student newspaper at Lincoln Memorial, as early as 1927 and served as editor in 1928 and 1929. By the end of his senior year, in 1929, his poems had begun to appear in such periodicals as *American Poet, Sonnet Sequences, Kentucky Folk-lore* and *Poetry Magazine*. Lincoln Memorial was a landmark in Stuart's development as a poet, and in a short time after his graduation with an A.B. in August of 1929 he published his first collection of poems.

Harvest of Youth (1930), an experiment in verse, contained poems Stuart had been writing since turning sixteen. Written during a time in which being a poet meant being a craftsman, the poems in this collection show obvious resemblances to the poems of numerous other writers, including practitioners of vers libre, the imagists, and the symbolists, as well as traditionalists. Trying different modes and working out different effects, Stuart allowed himself considerable latitude in exploring idiom.

Stuart said many times that by the time *Harvest of Youth* was published, he was ashamed of it, and, in fact, he tried to suppress it, destroying most,

but not all, copies. Yet poet Lee Pennington—at one time a student of Stuart's—felt the juvenilia valuable enough to have it reprinted by the Council of Southern Mountains in 1964. As Pennington knows, however, what is valuable about *Harvest of Youth* is not the quality of its poetry. Rather, its value lies in the locale treated, Stuart's Appalachia, and in the experiments in sonnet writing in the third section, "Sonnets: Juvenilia." Nearly everything Stuart wrote is about Appalachia, and he has cultivated the sonnet form throughout his writing career.

After Stuart graduated from Lincoln Memorial University in the summer of 1929, he went home to become principal of Warnock High School, and in 1930 he went on to become the principal of Greenup High School. Dissatisfied with his education, however, he enrolled for graduate work in English at Vanderbilt University in 1931. While at Vanderbilt he took courses under Robert Penn Warren, Donald Davidson, John Wade Hall, and Edwin Mims, but his efforts at a thesis on John Fox, Jr., were destroyed when the dormitory he was living in burned in February of 1932 and he left without earning an M.A. degree. He wrote extensively while he was at Vanderbilt. He met such writers as Allen Tate, John Crowe Ransom, and Walter Clyde Curry, and he also wrote a 310-page autobiography for Edwin Mims in lieu of a research paper. Donald Davidson advised him to go home and write about his people, and he did just that. Except for one more summer of study at Peabody College in 1936 (he had attended summer school there in 1930 and 1931), he never returned to the classroom as a student.

During the 1932-1933 academic year, Stuart was superintendent of Greenup County schools. In autumn 1933 he became principal of McKell High School in South Shore, Kentucky, where he worked until 1937, at which time he received a Guggenheim Fellowship to travel to Scotland. He later returned to McKell High School as principal for the 1956-1957 academic year. Throughout his career as a writer Stuart wrote many stories and articles, as well as three significant books—the autobiographical volumes *The Thread That Runs So True* (1949), *To Teach, To Love* (1970), and a novel, *Mr. Gallion's School* (1967)—about his roles as student, teacher, and administrator.

In October 1934 Dutton published Stuart's *Man with a Bull-Tongue Plow*, a collection of 703 sonnets. Both damned and praised by the critics, *Man with a Bull-Tongue Plow* established the Kentucky writer as a poet. Robert Frost found the set-

Jesse Stuart, 1935

ting for his poetry in the country north of Boston; William Faulkner created his mythical Yoknapatawpha County; and with *Man with a Bull-Tongue Plow* Jesse Stuart began creating a mythical Appalachia which he would continue to shape throughout his career as a writer. He developed a system of parallels and phonic reiterations reminiscent of those found in Walt Whitman's *Leaves of Grass* and for which Whitman appears to be the model. That he would persist in writing sonnets while using Whitman's prosodic techniques seems strange, but the style he achieved was peculiarly his own. The sonnet proved to be a convenient form— a canvas on which he could paint his scenes of life in W-Hollow (the name of the hollow where Stuart lived in Greenup County) and its surroundings. He used a large number of voices, and by having each name into existence a small segment of the composite locale he succeeded in lifting his part of Appalachia to a literary level.

After his initial success, *Man with a Bull-*

Tongue Plow, Stuart turned more toward fiction writing. He did not publish another collection of poems for ten years, but in the meantime he established a reputation as a significant writer of fiction. Dutton published his first two collections of stories, *Head O' W-Hollow,* in 1936, and *Men of the Mountains,* in 1941. On the basis of the second collection he received awards from the National Institute of Arts and Letters and the American Academy of Arts and Sciences. Dutton also published his first autobiographical book, *Beyond Dark Hills,* in 1938, and his first novel, *Trees of Heaven,* in 1940. In 1939 Stuart left teaching to become a sheep farmer, and on 14 October 1939 he married Naomi Deane Norris, whom he had known since his high-school days. They settled down in the house where they lived until Stuart's death in 1984. In 1942 their only child, Jessica Jane, was born. Even the birth of a daughter did not lessen the pace at which Stuart was writing and publishing. In 1943 Dutton published *Taps for Private Tussie,* a novel which proved to be the writer's greatest literary success.

Stuart wrote the sonnets for *Man with a Bull-Tongue Plow* (1934) in about ten months, but the sonnets for his third collection of poetry, *Album of Destiny* (1944), took him ten years. While looking at a family photograph album, he conceived of the plan for the book: a picture gallery containing five groups of paintings. As he wrote in "Why I Think *Album* Is My Best," published in a 1956 issue of *Prairie Schooner:* "This was the idea for my book. Take these people whose photographs had been made in the springtime of their lives and write portraits of them in verse." Dividing the book into four albums that contain pictures of the same people and a final album devoted to their children, he represented the stages in man's life, the seasons of the year, and ultimately the ancient archetypal pattern of life-death-resurrection. *Album of Destiny* became a "moving picture" of the comings and goings of generations—something of a modern American epic.

The portraits in *Album of Destiny* are often vivid, and combined they create the kind of chronicling effect which one finds in *Man with a Bull-Tongue Plow.* The major weakness of *Album of Destiny,* however, is that it is much like *Man with a Bull-Tongue Plow.* Its publication the year after the appearance of his enormously popular *Taps for Private Tussie* also proved to be a disadvantage. From the publication of *Taps for Private Tussie* until the end of his career, Stuart's readers viewed him primarily as a fiction writer, even though he continued to write and publish poems after *Album of Destiny*.

In March 1944 Stuart entered the U.S. Navy, and, after basic training at the Great Lakes Naval Station, he was commissioned a lieutenant j.g. and sent to Washington, D.C., to write navy training pamphlets. He spent most of the war in Washington, joining the staff of *Naval Aviation News* in March 1945. After his discharge in late December 1945, he returned with his wife and daughter to W-Hollow. He continued to devote most of his creative energy to writing fiction, and his next volume of poetry did not appear until 1952. The thin volume *Kentucky Is My Land* (1952) seemed a bit too jingoistic for most readers, and there is no advancement in prosodic technique beyond that of *Album of Destiny*. What *Kentucky Is My Land* did represent, however, was a loosening up accompanied by a proclivity for prose, as indicated by the fact that long prose poems begin and end the collection. Written in free-verse paragraphs, the title poem to

Kentucky Is My Land is a prosaic tribute to the poet's native state. The poems in the second part of the collection, including "The Cities," "Mountain Funeral," "Deserted Coal-Mine Camp," "Elegy for Mitch Stuart," "By Sandy Waters," and "The Ballad of Lonesome Waters," were first published in the 1930s. The third part, "Songs for Naomi," is a group of sonnets, which echo Elizabeth Barrett Browning. The fourth part, "Songs for My Daughter," is overly sentimental and is given to moralizing. Parts five and six consist of random impressions on various topics, but the last section of *Kentucky Is My Land*, consisting of a long prose poem entitled "The Builder and the Dream," is genuinely impressive. Written in free verse, "The Builder and the Dream" is Stuart's version of a postwasteland America. In October of 1954, Stuart had the first in a series of heart attacks, and two months later his father, Mitchell Stuart, died.

Stuart spent the 1960-1961 academic year as

Jesse, Jane, and Naomi Stuart in Washington, D.C., 9 December 1945 (photograph by Lt. Art Schoni)

The Stuarts in Egypt, spring 1961

visiting lecturer at American University in Cairo, Egypt. In 1961 he was presented with an Academy of American Poets Fellowship in the amount of $5,000; in 1962 he served as American representative to the Asian Writers Conference; and from September 1962 until February 1963 he conducted a world lecture tour, which was sponsored by the United States Information Service of the state department. In 1962 he also published *Hold April*, another thin volume of verse, in which he came closer to a modern sound than he had in any of his previous collections. Most of the poems were written in the late 1950s following his first heart attack, and the pessimistic naturalism of previous collections gives way in these poems to religious optimism. Marked by quietude, *Hold April* contains proportionately more good verse than anywhere else in the Stuart canon. A few poems from early in the poet's career, such as "Desolation," "House in the Wind," and "The Ballad of the Bride," are far too regular in meter and rhyme and the diction is faulty (in "Desolation" in particular one has to question the poet's seriousness). On the other hand,

Hold April contains many poems possessing vitality and movement, especially "Song," "Time Passes," "Autumn Poem," "Green River," "Spring Voices," "Autumn Sequence," "Come Gentle Snow," "Sandy Will Flow Forever," "The Snow Lies Patched," "Soliloquy of the Wild Rose in the Rock," "World of Springtimes Past," "Hold April," "Voices of Spring," and "Be in a Joyful Mood."

Still in Stuart's possession at the time of his death was an unpublished manuscript entitled "Songs of a Mountain Plowman," dating from the period when he wrote *Man with a Bull-Tongue Plow*. While the prosodic technique is similar in both books, "Songs of a Mountain Plowman," as a more recent arrangement of old material, is helpful in understanding Stuart's interest in satire. Rejecting contemporary values, the poet in "Songs of a Mountain Plowman" has searched the past for values which can endure. Viewing himself in a modern wasteland, the poet celebrates his ancestry and admonishes others to sing because art is the only surviving means of creating values worth bothering about. Having watched the decay of his country—

suggested in part by the daughters of strong pioneer stock who have taken to whoring and drinking wine—the poet is desperate, feeling trapped in this wasteland and reduced to making vain boasts. How best to deal with the future becomes the central concern of "Songs of a Mountain Plowman."

"Birdland's Golden Age," another unpublished collection of satirical poems, which had its inception around 1965, constitutes a direct attack upon social, moral, and political ineptitude in America. Stuart's metaphorical birdland likely had its origin in Aristophanes' play "The Birds," but its subject matter is the present madness of the world. The birdland poems began out of anger over the way President Lyndon Johnson was handling the war in Vietnam, but the madness, Stuart discovered, did not stop with the Johnson administration: "In a way, we're still living in Birdland. Wallace now shot. Wilt (the Stilt) Chamberlain, a millionaire because he's seven feet three inches tall. This could only happen in Birdland," he wrote in a letter dated 16 May 1972. Stuart satirizes President Johnson, President Eisenhower, President Truman, evangelist Billy Graham, Lady Bird Johnson, Billy Sol Estes, and others, but "Four Maidens and a King," part four of "Birdland's Golden Age," contains the most effective satire as well as the most effective poetry. Directed at President Truman's decision to drop atomic bombs on Nagasaki and Hiroshima, this group of four poems presents four Japanese maidens (one in each poem) who tell how the bombings ruined their lives.

In 1975 McGraw-Hill published *The World of Jesse Stuart: Selected Poems*, edited by J. R. LeMaster, which contains work from all earlier Stuart collections, poems from journals and magazines, and previously unpublished poems, including some from "Songs of a Mountain Plowman" and "Birdland's Golden Age." Avoiding the chronological approach that characterizes most selections of poets' work, *The World of Jesse Stuart* is dedicated to displaying the range of Stuart's work as poet. The volume assumes the poet's home in W-Hollow as a geographical center, and moves outward through each successive section, emphasizing the fact that Stuart's concerns are ultimately anything but provincial. His poems are about the human condition in America in particular and in the world in general.

A second collection of selected poems, *The Seasons of Jesse Stuart* (1976), edited by Wanda Hicks, is an autobiography in verse that employs the structural plan of *Album of Destiny*. Containing a foreword by Stuart and illustrated with photo-

graphs of Stuart and his family, as well as the manuscript for each of the poems, *The Seasons of Jesse Stuart* is divided into seven sections, each introduced by a short biographical essay written by the editor, and it succeeds in chronicling the poet's life.

In assessing Jesse Stuart's stature as a poet, one must acknowledge that he made the past of his locale available for new generations of readers, and his history of Appalachia will continue to prove important to cultural historians. Jesse Stuart stubbornly and persistently held before us an alternative to life as we know it. He lifted his beloved Appalachia to the level of literature, and he attempted to create a model for a habitable world.

Always a powerful man, Stuart drove himself mercilessly. As poet, fiction writer, lecturer, educator, world traveler, and farmer, he maintained a rigorous schedule that took its toll. After his first heart attack in 1954, he suffered many more before he had his first stroke in 1978, which left him paralyzed on the left side. In the spring of 1982 he suffered three more strokes, the last of which left him unconscious until his death in February 1984. He will survive in his readers' memories, however. His house and thousand-acre farm are to be preserved by the Jesse Stuart Foundation, and more important, he will survive through his poetry and fiction, which constitute one of the most thorough chronicles ever written about a single place.

Bibliographies:
Hensley C. Woodbridge, *Jesse and Jane Stuart: A Bibliography* (Murray, Ky.: Murray State University, 1979);
J. R. LeMaster, *Jesse Stuart: A Reference Guide* (Boston: G. K. Hall, 1979).

Biography:
H. Edward Richardson, *Jesse: The Biography of an American Writer, Jesse Hilton Stuart* (New York, St. Louis, San Francisco, Toronto, Hamburg & Mexico: McGraw-Hill, 1984).

References:
Everetta Love Blair, *Jesse Stuart: His Life and Works* (Columbia: University of South Carolina Press, 1967);
Mary Washington Clarke, *Jesse Stuart's Kentucky* (New York: McGraw-Hill, 1967);
Ruel E. Foster, *Jesse Stuart* (New York: Twayne, 1968);
J. R. LeMaster, *Jesse Stuart: Kentucky's Chronicler-Poet* (Memphis: Memphis State University Press, 1980);

LeMaster, ed., *Jesse Stuart: Selected Criticism* (St. Petersburg, Fla.: Valkyrie Press, 1978);

LeMaster and Clarke, eds., *Jesse Stuart: Essays on His Work* (Lexington: University Press of Kentucky, 1977);

Lee Pennington, *The Dark Hills of Jesse Stuart* (Cincinnati: Harvest Press, 1967);

Dick Perry, *Reflections of Jesse Stuart* (New York: McGraw-Hill, 1971);

John Howard Spurlock, *He Sings for Us: A Socio-* *linguistic Analysis of the Appalachian Subculture and of Jesse Stuart as a Major American Author* (Lanham, Md.: University Press of America, 1980).

Papers:

Murray State University in Murray, Kentucky, is the official depository for Stuart's papers.

Melvin B. Tolson
(6 February 1898-29 August 1966)

Robert M. Farnsworth
University of Missouri, Kansas City

BOOKS: *Rendezvous with America* (New York: Dodd, Mead, 1944);

Libretto for the Republic of Liberia (New York: Twayne, 1953);

Harlem Gallery: Book I, The Curator (New York: Twayne, 1965);

A Gallery of Harlem Portraits, edited by Robert M. Farnsworth (Columbia & London: University of Missouri Press, 1979);

Caviar and Cabbage: Selected Columns by Melvin B. Tolson from the Washington Tribune, 1937-1944, edited by Farnsworth (Columbia & London: University of Missouri Press, 1982).

In his introduction to *Harlem Gallery* (1965), Karl Shapiro called Melvin B. Tolson "a great poet . . . living in our midst . . . almost totally unknown, even by the literati." Mindful that Allen Tate, in his earlier introduction to *Libretto for the Republic of Liberia* (1953), had praised Tolson generously for his proper concern with poetry as "the main thing"—presumably as opposed to racial issues—Shapiro emphatically declared Tolson's greatness was based on his ability to write "in Negro," thus sparking a critical controversy about the cultural implications of Tolson's complex style that distracted critics for some time from the demanding task of reading his poetry in the broader context it deserves. In more recent years a new generation of scholars and writers have examined Tolson's challenging late poetry with more diligent and

Melvin B. Tolson

more curious eyes and in the process are also discovering the full range of Tolson's achievement.

Melvin Beaunorus Tolson was born in Moberly, Missouri, to the Reverend Alonzo Tolson and

Lera Hurt Tolson. As a Methodist minister, his father was reassigned frequently, moving his family, which included four children, to a variety of small-town parishes in northern Missouri and central Iowa. A morally earnest, self-disciplined, and intellectually ambitious man, who had taught himself Latin and Greek, Alonzo Tolson was an important influence on his literary son. At the age of fourteen young Tolson published his first poem, on the sinking of the Titanic, in an Oskaloosa, Iowa, newspaper. In 1916 the family moved to Kansas City, Missouri, where Melvin Tolson attended his junior and senior years of high school. In 1918 he was elected senior-class poet.

Tolson entered Fisk University in autumn 1918, but a year later he transferred, as a freshman, to Lincoln University in Pennsylvania, where he earned a B.A. with honors in June 1923. On 29 January 1922, during his junior year at Lincoln, he married Ruth Southall, and his first son, Melvin B. Tolson, Jr., was born during the month of his graduation. Thus his writing ambitions took second priority to the needs of providing for a family, which by the end of 1928 included three more children, Arthur, Wiley Wilson, and Ruth Marie. In 1923 when other young black writers were discovering Harlem and its bright cultural promises, Tolson accepted a teaching position in the English department of Wiley College in Marshall, Texas. Having won several prizes as a speaker and debater at Lincoln, he built on this success at Wiley. In 1924 he organized the Wiley Forensic Society, which achieved legendary success by the late 1930s. His debate teams challenged the color line throughout the South, West, and Midwest and probably reached their climactic triumph in defeating the University of Southern California in 1935. His personal reputation as a fearless and provocative speaker grew in tandem with his renown as a debate coach. He also wrote a novel, "Beyond the Zaretto," during these busy years at Wiley but the manuscript has been lost.

The years 1931-1932 proved a turning point in his career. With the aid of a fellowship he took leave from Wiley to spend that academic year in Harlem and to study for an M.A. in comparative literature at Columbia University, completing his thesis in 1940, after returning to Wiley. He used

The Tolson family, 1930: (front) Arthur, Wiley Wilson, and Melvin, Jr.; (back) Ruth Marie, Ruth, and Melvin B. Tolson

the occasion to expand his personal and professional acquaintance with the writers of the Harlem Renaissance and wrote a thesis about their achievement. He was stimulated to mark out a role for himself built upon the legacy of the Renaissance. In 1932 he began his first book of poems, *A Gallery of Harlem Portraits,* which was published posthumously in 1979. Impressed with the popular success of Edgar Lee Masters's poetic representations of Spoon River, he attempted an epic representation of Harlem in a collection of poetic portraits which was to emphasize a sense of community emerging out of great diversity. In consonance with the racial and economic politics of the 1930s Tolson gave to the "race-welding" prophecy, which Alain Locke had found in Harlem, a stronger emphasis on class.

Though *A Gallery of Harlem Portraits* did not find a publisher during Tolson's lifetime, poems from the collection were published in V. F. Calverton's *Modern Monthly* and its successor *Modern Quarterly.* Calverton became a staunch supporter and friend. Langston Hughes had already become an influential model as a poet. Tolson admired the use Hughes made of the blues in his poetry, and he shared his strong proletarian convictions. In a 1933 article for the *Pittsburgh Courier,* Tolson defended Hughes's religious and social statement in his controversial poem "Good-Bye Christ." From 1937 through 1944 Tolson wrote a weekly column, "Caviar and Cabbage," for the *Washington Tribune* in which he outlined his view of the needs and interests of black people during the Great Depression and World War II.

The strong religious beliefs of Tolson's father and of the community in which Tolson lived were modified, but not essentially contradicted, by his awareness of the class politics of the 1930s and of the international drama of World War II. Holding a toughly optimistic apocalyptic vision, Tolson believed that God might be stern, but he was just, and that righteousness would eventually prevail. The Great Depression dramatized the division of class interests, but, Tolson believed, the meek—or the proletariat—would inevitably prevail if they were willing to organize and to assert their God-given rights. Tolson saw hope in the breakdown of racial barriers and he believed that the greed of the industrialists would lead to their own destruction. World War II amplified this lesson to the international scene. Because the so-called superior European civilization had made a mockery of the very culture it pretended to represent, its downfall was imminent, and the "meek" nations, abused and ex-

ploited by colonialism, would hold the key to the future and inherit the earth.

In 1939 Tolson's poem, "Dark Symphony," won the national poetry contest sponsored by the American Negro Exposition in Chicago. Its later publication in *Atlantic Monthly* opened the way for the publication of his first book of poems. *Rendezvous with America* appeared in 1944, when World War II was making rubble of many of the world's cities, the symbols of man's cultural aspirations. Tolson arranged his poems to shape a message to a nation and a world at war. The long opening poem, "Rendezvous with America," reminds the reader of the strength America draws from being a nation of peoples from widely different national, social, and racial experiences. "Dark Symphony" celebrates specifically the historic contribution of black Americans and their struggle to gain recognition for their achievements, ending with a proud and defiant prediction of black accomplishment

Melvin B. Tolson, 1941

and cultural realization. "Of Men and Cities" takes an apocalyptic view of world history as a drama of human aspiration and its many failures. "The Idols of the Tribe" focuses on the corruption of man's dreams by his prejudices, his creation and worship of false gods. The final poem, "Tapestries of Time," threads a sturdy faith in human progress through the wreckage of man's history, particularly through the chaos and destruction of World War II, amid which the poem was conceived and meant to be read. The American attempt to realize one nation of many peoples coalesces with a worldwide attempt to achieve a new democracy of nations, and the potential success of both in the poem promises the realization of new possibilities for mankind.

For Tolson, the poet was most insistently a namer and a seer. His was the responsibility to announce and identify the forces and aspirations which determine man's historical destiny. Like Abba Micah Soudani, the "Bard of Addis Ababa," he must "Cry the heroes to wake up the dead."

Rendezvous with America was reviewed widely and surprisingly well considering its present neglect. Margaret Walker, Richard Wright, and Langston Hughes praised it, and it was reviewed favorably in the *New York Times, Saturday Review, Christian Science Monitor, Crisis,* and *Phylon.* Frank Marshall Davis, however, sounded a theme which would be repeated even more emphatically after Tolson's later books: "His first volume reveals strength, maturity, and mastery of technique. Most of his poetry is in rhyme, but it is a rhyme as modern as tomorrow. He also has a remarkable gift for epigram. Mr. Tolson lives in no ivory tower. . . . Unfortunately, he is yet too complex for the masses."

In January 1947, as a tribute to what he had thus far achieved and to the promise of his future work, Tolson was named Poet Laureate of Liberia. President William V. S. Tubman commissioned him to write a poem and Duke Ellington to write a musical composition to commemorate Liberia's 1956 centennial. Also in 1947, Tolson was persuaded to make a midcareer academic move. He left Wiley College after twenty-four years to join the faculty of Langston University in Oklahoma and thus began another seventeen years of continuous academic service. It was a time for new beginnings and he faced them with a confidence based on substantial achievement and recognition.

By the late 1940s Tolson, and other black writers such as Ralph Ellison, Robert Hayden, and Gwendolyn Brooks, recognized the modernist revolution in literature as an accomplished fact. *Libretto*

for the Republic of Liberia (1953) became Tolson's ambitious initial effort to build on this assumption and to translate his continuing faith in the need for the realization of the democratic dream throughout the world into a newly challenging idiom.

Invoked as "the quicksilver sparrow that slips/ The Eagle's claw!," Liberia is an extension of American history, a smaller bird that attempts to fly higher, an effort by Americans white and black to establish a new nation by sailing east instead of west, to a continent of ancient human habitation—perhaps the most ancient in the world. Tolson develops many of the particular historical paradoxes associated with returning to the old to begin anew later in the poem, but beyond these historical facts he sees Liberia, as its name implies, as the offshoot of a dream of democratic freedom. It is the "*Mehr licht* for the Africa-to-be," which is itself a part of an emerging universal brotherhood that makes a mockery of the divisive idols of the tribe—race, caste, and class. The quicksilver sparrow is to extend the flight of the eagle.

In *Libretto for the Republic of Liberia,* drawing on ideas he discussed in his "Caviar and Cabbage" column for 19 October 1940, Tolson puts forth analogies for the world as it is—the Ferris wheel—and the world as it ought to be—the merry-go-round. The rise and fall of nations is now like a Ferris wheel. When a nation becomes powerful, he explained in his column, it characteristically becomes deluded with a sense of its innate superiority, a vanity that leads to its fall. This sort of world, where the haves and have-nots change but the class structure remains, should be replaced with a world that operates like a merry-go-round, a world based on both economic and racial brotherhood: "On the merry-go-round all seats are on the same level. Nobody goes up; therefore, nobody has to come down. . . . Racial superiority and class superiority produce the hellish contraption called the Ferris-Wheel of history. Democracy will produce the Merry-Go-Round of History."

This image recurs in the "Ti" section of his libretto:

> The ferris wheel
> of race, of caste, of class
> dumped and alped cadavers till the ground
> fogged the Pleiades with Gila rot. . . .

In contrast the new day dawning is a triumph of the world's previously despised—the *vile canaille,* the *Gorii,* the *Bastard-rasse,* the *uomo-qualyque,* the *hoibarbaroi*, the *vsechelovek*, the *descamisados*, the *hoi polloi*—all of these "Unparadised nobodies with maps of Nowhere/ride the merry-go-round!"

Tolson is well aware that the weight of man's history makes distressingly difficult the emergence of utopian order. In *Libretto for the Republic of Liberia* he cites instance after instance of man's barbarism and self-destructiveness, his witting or unwitting worship of the false idols of race, caste, and class, all of which are the product of the lust for money that leads to competition for economic power. The tragic history of human failure only redoubles the need to project man's dreams for a better world and to increase the effort to get off the Ferris wheel and onto the merry-go-round, to make even the patched and troubled history of a nation like Liberia into a new vision of universal democracy, "the *Mehr licht* for the Africa-To-Be."

Thus Tolson closes his poem with a surreal tour—by auto (the Futurafrique), by train (The United Nations Limited), and by plane (*Le Premier des Noir*)—which ends at the Parliament of African Peoples, where the "Iscariot cuckolded four freedoms" are given new life, and the axiom *unto each according as any one has need*, is brought out of storage and made ready for use. The economic and cultural dominance of Europe ultimately gives way to a liberated and fruitfully peaceful universal order of mankind. Man's imagination is freed from the self-inhibiting restrictions with which generations of history have shackled it.

In his introduction Allen Tate praised Tolson highly: "there is a great gift for language, a profound historical sense, and a first-rate intelligence at work in this poem from first to last." Another of his compliments proved invidious: "For the first time, it seems to me, a Negro poet has assimilated completely the full poetic language of his time and, by implication, the language of the Anglo-American tradition." Other reviews were mixed, with many clearly uncertain how to evaluate such an ambitiously esoteric poem. Lorenzo Turner was one of the few who immediately recognized Tolson's message and praised the poem unstintingly: "In its breadth, in the subtlety and richness of its allusions, and in the force and suggestiveness of its language, it is a triumph of poetry on the grand scale." While Arthur P. Davis found that "it doesn't quite come off as a poem," he nevertheless concluded, "Because of its word-magic, because of its astounding versatility and energy, and because of its endorsement by Allen Tate, it will become a landmark in Negro literature." John Ciardi reserved final judgment but was much impressed:

"This is obviously a book to return to. The blast of language and vision is simply too overwhelming for first judgments. It seems a reasonable guess, however, that Tolson has established a new dimension for American Negro poetry."

In 1951 Tolson's "E. & O. E." won *Poetry* magazine's Bess Hokin Prize, and in 1952 Tolson was also elected Mayor of Langston, one of several all-black communities in Oklahoma. He was reelected three times, in 1954, 1956, and 1958, and his family had difficulty persuading him not to run for a fifth term. Tolson wrote and directed a dramatic version of Walter S. White's *Fire in the Flint* (1924), which was performed at the national convention of the NAACP in Oklahoma City on 28 June 1952. In 1954 Tolson was admitted to the Knighthood of the Order of the Star of Africa and about the same time Lincoln University awarded Tolson an honorary Doctor of Letters degree. Also in 1954 he was appointed permanent fellow in poetry and drama at Bread Loaf Writers' Conference and thus began a much prized friendship with Robert Frost. In 1956 Tolson was an honored guest at the cer-

Melvin B. Tolson and Walter White after the premiere of Fire in the Flint, *28 June 1952*

emonies inaugurating William V. S. Tubman for his third term as President of Liberia in Monrovia. On his return trip from Monrovia, he stopped in Paris where Melvin Tolson, Jr., was studying at the Sorbonne. During that stopover Tolson and Richard Wright spent a long afternoon sharing experiences in a local café.

During the years he was writing *Libretto for the Republic of Liberia,* the idea for his last and best book was forming in his mind. The challenge of an epic representation of Harlem still remained. The manuscript for *A Gallery of Harlem Portraits* was buried in a trunk and its mode seemed passé, but the problems of representing the prophecy of Harlem in poetry now assumed new proportions for Tolson. The representation of Harlem was to serve as the climax for an epic poem on the history of black America from its African origins to its present. This epic, which was to be divided into five books, begins in the present, the chronological end of the story, with the first book—the only one Tolson completed—set in Harlem. Instead, however, of representing a diverse citizenry of Harlem as poetic portraits hanging in a fictional gallery as in the original *A Gallery of Harlem Portraits,* Tolson created a literal art gallery functioning within the Harlem community. The Curator of the gallery provides the central point of view, but three major characters, all practicing artists, dramatically amplify the reader's view of the black artist's dilemma and achievement.

John Laugart's painting *Black Bourgeoisie* is in keeping with Tolson's view that the artist, the true ape of God, must cleanse this world with his searing portrayal of the enervating prejudices of the tribe. The Curator sees himself and Laugart as "The Castor and Pollux of St. Elmo's fire,/on Harlem's Coalsack Way." Mister Starks—*Mister* is his given name—is a former jazz pianist and now conductor of the Harlem Symphony Orchestra and composer of *Black Orchid Suite,* dedicated to his wife, whose infidelity causes him to choose suicide in a Hardyesque beau geste, which raises questions about the value of what he has achieved. Starks is also a poet, however, and his "Harlem Vignettes," reminiscent of Tolson's *A Gallery of Harlem Portraits,* give penetrating insight into the other characters of *Harlem Gallery.* Hideho Heights, the bold and popular "Redskin beatnik bard of Lenox Avenue," also has a hidden self, which the Curator discovers when he comes across the manuscript of Hideho's "E. & O. E.," a private poem in the modern vein, a dramatically ironic reference to Tolson's own earlier poem.

The Curator, who is both professionally and personally interested in the lives and achievements of these artists, shares his views and concerns with Dr. Obi Nkomo, an alter ego whose challenging observations sometimes carry more authority than the Curator's. Nkomo is a native African, educated in the West, at sophisticated ease in Harlem, although still retaining an authentic African perspective. The Curator and Dr. Nkomo carry on a running debate on the relation of the artist to his milieu. It is through this debate and its extension in the lives of the artists, Laugart, Starks, and Heights, that Tolson attempts to depict the achievements and dilemmas of contemporary black American culture.

Their world is marked by thwarted ambition and absurd conflict as the inevitable collapse of the idols of the tribe brings confusion and chaos in its wake. Yet it also carries the seeds of new beginnings. The Curator opens the poem by observing that "The Harlem Gallery, an Afric pepper bird,/ awakes me at a people's dusk of dawn." The echo of W. E. B. Du Bois's *Dusk of Dawn* (1940) is meant to remind the reader of Du Bois's prophecy that the twentieth century is the century of the color line. The Curator closes the poem by asserting that the paintings in the gallery "chronicle/a people's New World odyssey,/from chattel to Esquire!" Art is a touchstone by which culture is measured, and Tolson sees black American culture as having come a long way down "that lonesome road." Amid the absurd moral confusion of this transitional century in history "the white heather/and the white almond grow" in the black ghetto while "the hyacinth and the asphodel blow/in the white metropolis!" The flowers of hope for the future grow in Harlem, while the flowers most often associated with death grow in the white world.

In the introduction to *Harlem Gallery* Karl Shapiro argued that Tolson was a great poet because he "writes in Negro," thus challenging Tate's high praise for Tolson as the first Negro poet to assimilate the full poetic language of the Anglo-American tradition. Shapiro, however, was in turn rebuked by Sarah Webster Fabio: "Melvin Tolson's language is most certainly not 'Negro' to any significant degree." Fabio saw Tolson as "victimized by the cultural lag that is common between the white and Negro worlds. . . . while Tolson busied himself out-pounding Pound, his fellow poets forgot to send him the message that Pound was out." Fabio's judgment was echoed by others. But these judgments were bandied about by critics who usually admitted considerable uncertainty about what

Tolson was saying. Fifteen years after the publication of *Harlem Gallery*, Mariann Russell published the first extensive and detailed analysis of Tolson's epic poem in her book-length *Melvin B. Tolson's Harlem Gallery* (1980). In 1958 in the *Saturday Review of Literature* John Ciardi distinguished between the "horizontal audience," for a poem, which consists of everybody alive at the moment of the poem's publication, and the "vertical audience," which consists "of everyone, vertically through time who will ever read a given poem." Tolson believed, with Ciardi, that the true poet writes for the "vertical audience." That audience may finally be forming.

Nevertheless 1965 brought Tolson much recognition. His alma mater, Lincoln University, granted him a second honorary degree. He was elected to the *New York Herald Tribune* book-review board. In October he gave a reading at the Library of Congress under the auspices of the Gertrude Clark Whittall Poetry and Literature Fund and the District of Columbia gave him a Citation and Award for Cultural Achievement in the Fine Arts. Upon his retirement from Langston University, he became the first appointee to the Avalon Chair in humanities at Tuskegee Institute for the academic year, 1965-1966.

However, all this gratifying public recognition came against a backdrop of concern for his physical health. In 1964 Tolson had two operations for abdominal cancer. His recovery at times seemed almost miraculously complete, as he thrived on the public attention that now seemed lavish compared to that of previous years. In 1966 he added to his laurels a grant of $2500 from the National Institute and American Academy of Arts and Letters. But in June he entered St. Paul's Hospital in Dallas, Texas, for the first of three more operations over the next three months, which regrettably proved vain efforts to save his life. He died on 29 August 1966. During those final months of his life the Rockefeller Foundation granted him an award which he did not live to accept.

References:

Robert M. Farnsworth, *Melvin B. Tolson, 1898-1966: Plain Talk and Poetic Prophecy* (Columbia: University of Missouri Press, 1984);

Joy Flasch, *Melvin B. Tolson* (New York: Twayne, 1972);

Mariann Russell, *Melvin B. Tolson's Harlem Gallery* (Columbia: University of Missouri Press, 1980).

Papers:

The principal collection of Tolson's papers is in the manuscript division at the Library of Congress.

Robert Penn Warren

Victor Strandberg
Duke University

See also the Warren entries in *DLB 2, American Novelists Since World War II,* and *DLB Yearbook: 1980.*

BIRTH: Guthrie, Kentucky, 24 April 1905, to Robert Franklin and Ruth Penn Warren.

EDUCATION: B.A., Vanderbilt University, 1925; M.A., University of California at Berkeley, 1927; Yale University, 1927-1928; B.Litt., Oxford University, 1930.

MARRIAGES: 12 September 1930 to Emma Brescia (divorced). 7 December 1952 to Eleanor Clark; children: Rosanna, Gabriel Penn.

AWARDS AND HONORS: Rhodes Scholarship, 1928; Houghton-Mifflin Literary Fellowship for *Night Rider,* 1936; Guggenheim Fellowships, 1939-1940, 1947-1948; Shelley Memorial Award, 1943; Consultant in Poetry, Library of Congress, 1944-1945; Pulitzer Prize for *All the King's Men,* 1947; D. Litt, University of Louisville, 1949; L.H.D., Kenyon College, 1952; D.Litt., University of Kentucky, 1955; D.Litt., Colby College, 1956; Edna St. Vincent Millay Memorial Award (American Poetry Society), 1958; National Book Award for *Promises,* 1958; Pulitzer Prize for *Promises,* 1958; D.Litt., Swarthmore College, 1958; D.Litt., Yale University, 1959; LL.D., University of Bridgeport, 1965; Bollingen Prize in Poetry, 1966-1967; D.Litt., Fairfield University, 1969; Van Wyck Brooks Award for Poetry, 1970; National Medal for Literature, 1970; D.Litt., Wesleyan University, 1970; D.Litt., Harvard University, 1973; D.Litt., Southwestern College at Memphis, 1974; D.Litt., University of the South, 1974; D.Litt., University of New Haven, 1974; Emerson-Thoreau Award (American Academy of Arts and Sciences), 1975; D.Litt., Johns Hopkins University, 1975; Copernicus Award (American Academy of Poets), 1976; Pulitzer Prize for *Now and Then,* 1979; Harriet Monroe Award for Poetry, 1979; Common Wealth Award, 1980; Presidential Medal of Freedom, 1980; Prize Fellowship, MacArthur Foundation, 1981; Poet Laureate of the United States, 1986.

Robert Penn Warren (photograph by Robert A. Ballard, Jr.)

BOOKS: *John Brown: The Making of a Martyr* (New York: Payson & Clarke, 1929);
Thirty-Six Poems (New York: Alcestis Press, 1935);
An Approach to Literature, by Warren, Cleanth Brooks, and John Thibault Purser (Baton Rouge: Louisiana State University Press, 1936);
Night Rider (Boston: Houghton Mifflin, 1939; London: Eyre & Spottiswoode, 1940);
Eleven Poems on the Same Theme (Norfolk, Conn.: New Directions, 1942);

At Heaven's Gate (New York: Harcourt, Brace, 1943; London: Eyre & Spottiswoode, 1943);

Selected Poems, 1923-1943 (New York: Harcourt, Brace, 1944; London: Fortune Press, 1951);

All the King's Men (New York: Harcourt, Brace, 1946; abridged edition, London: Eyre & Spottiswoode, 1948);

Blackberry Winter (Cummington, Mass.: Cummington Press, 1946);

The Circus in the Attic and Other Stories (New York: Harcourt, Brace, 1947; London: Eyre & Spottiswoode, 1952);

Modern Rhetoric, by Warren and Brooks (New York: Harcourt, Brace, 1949);

World Enough and Time: A Romantic Novel (New York: Random House, 1950; London: Eyre & Spottiswoode, 1951);

Fundamentals of Good Writing, by Warren and Brooks (New York: Harcourt, Brace, 1950; London: Dobson, 1952);

Brother to Dragons: A Tale in Verse and Voices (New York: Random House, 1953; London: Eyre & Spottiswoode, 1954; new version, New York: Random House, 1979);

Band of Angels (New York: Random House, 1955; London: Eyre & Spottiswoode, 1956);

Segregation: The Inner Conflict in the South (New York: Random House, 1956; London: Eyre & Spottiswoode, 1957);

To a Little Girl, One Year Old, In a Ruined Fortress (New Haven: Yale School of Design, 1956?);

Promises: Poems 1954-1956 (New York: Random House, 1957; London: Eyre & Spottiswoode, 1959);

Selected Essays (New York: Random House, 1958; London: Eyre & Spottiswoode, 1964);

Remember the Alamo (New York: Random House, 1958);

How Texas Won Her Freedom (San Jacinto Monument, Tex.: San Jacinto Museum of History, 1959);

The Cave (New York: Random House, 1959; London: Eyre & Spottiswoode, 1959);

The Gods of Mount Olympus (New York: Random House, 1959; London: Muller, 1962);

All the King's Men (A Play) (New York: Random House, 1960);

You, Emperors, and Others: Poems 1957-1960 (New York: Random House, 1960);

The Legacy of the Civil War: Meditations on the Centennial (New York: Random House, 1961);

Wilderness: A Tale of the Civil War (New York: Random House, 1961; London: Eyre & Spottiswoode, 1962);

Flood: A Romance of Our Time (New York: Random House, 1964; London: Collins, 1964);

Who Speaks for the Negro? (New York: Random House, 1965);

A Plea in Mitigation: Modern Poetry and the End of an Era (Macon, Ga.: Wesleyan College, 1966);

Selected Poems: New and Old, 1923-1966 (New York: Random House, 1966);

Incarnations: Poems 1966-1968 (New York: Random House, 1968; London: Allen, 1970);

Audubon: A Vision (New York: Random House, 1969);

Homage to Theodore Dreiser: August 27, 1871-December 28, 1945, On the Centennial of His Birth (New York: Random House, 1971);

Meet Me in the Green Glen (New York: Random House, 1971; London: Secker & Warburg, 1972);

Or Else: Poem/Poems 1968-1974 (New York: Random House, 1974);

Democracy and Poetry (Cambridge: Harvard University Press, 1975);

Selected Poems: 1923-1975 (New York: Random House, 1977; London: Secker & Warburg, 1977);

A Place to Come To (New York: Random House, 1977; London: Secker & Warburg, 1977);

Now and Then: Poems 1976-1978 (New York: Random House, 1978);

Being Here: Poetry 1977-1980 (New York: Random House, 1980; London: Secker & Warburg, 1980);

Jefferson Davis Gets His Citizenship Back (Lexington: University Press of Kentucky, 1980);

Rumor Verified: Poems 1979-1980 (New York: Random House, 1981; London: Secker & Warburg, 1982);

Chief Joseph of the Nez Perce (New York: Random House, 1983);

New and Selected Poems 1923-1985 (New York: Random House, 1985).

OTHER: "The Briar Patch," in *I'll Take My Stand: The South and the Agrarian Tradition*, by Twelve Southerners (New York: Harper, 1930);

A Southern Harvest: Short Stories by Southern Writers, edited by Warren (Boston: Houghton Mifflin, 1937);

Understanding Poetry: An Anthology for College Students, edited by Warren and Cleanth Brooks (New York: Holt, 1938; fourth edition, New York: Holt, Rinehart & Winston, 1976);

Understanding Fiction, edited by Warren and Brooks (New York: Crofts, 1943; third edition, Englewood Cliffs, N.J.: Prentice-Hall, 1976);

"A Poem of Pure Imagination: An Experiment in Reading," in *The Rime of the Ancient Mariner*, by Samuel Taylor Coleridge (New York: Reynal & Hitchcock, 1946), pp. 59-117;

An Anthology of Stories from the Southern Review, edited by Warren and Brooks (Baton Rouge: Louisiana State University Press, 1953);

Short Story Masterpieces, edited by Warren and Albert Erskine (New York: Dell, 1954);

Six Centuries of Great Poetry: From Chaucer to Yeats, edited by Warren and Erskine (New York: Dell, 1955);

A New Southern Harvest, edited by Warren and Erskine (New York: Bantam, 1957);

The Scope of Fiction, edited by Warren and Brooks (New York: Appleton-Century-Crofts, 1960);

Dennis Devlin, *Selected Poems*, edited by Warren and Allen Tate (New York: Holt, Rinehart & Winston, 1963);

Faulkner: A Collection of Critical Essays, edited by Warren (Englewood Cliffs, N.J.: Prentice-Hall, 1966);

Randall Jarrell: 1914-1965, edited by Warren, Robert Lowell, and Peter Taylor (New York: Farrar, Straus & Giroux, 1967);

Selected Poems of Herman Melville: A Reader's Edition, edited by Warren (New York: Random House, 1970);

John Greenleaf Whittier's Poetry, edited by Warren (Minneapolis: University of Minnesota Press, 1971);

American Literature: The Makers and the Making, 2 volumes, edited by Warren, Brooks, and R. W. B. Lewis (New York: St. Martin's Press, 1973).

Until recent years, the popularity of Robert Penn Warren's fiction, crowned by the ascendancy of *All the King's Men* (1946) to the status of a classic, has somewhat obscured his achievement as a poet. His development as a poet, however, antedated his first novel (*Night Rider*, 1939) by almost two decades, and over nearly sixty years he has published some fourteen volumes of verse interspersed with eleven books of fiction, a dozen books of nonfiction prose, and numerous essays and textbooks. This prolific creativity has arguably made Warren his nation's foremost living man of letters—"America's Dean of Letters," according to a 25 August 1980 *Newsweek* essay.

Far from imagining such a future, Warren grew up in the small town of Guthrie, Kentucky, wanting to be a sea captain. After dividing his boy-hood years between his grandfather's farm in summer and his family home during school terms, he actually obtained an appointment to enroll as a naval cadet at Annapolis. While he was waiting for the appointment to become active, however, a serious eye injury changed his plans, and he instead matriculated at Vanderbilt University in 1921 with the intention of becoming an electrical engineer.

During his freshman year, an English course with John Crowe Ransom combined with the influence of Allen Tate, an older student whom he met early in 1923, to kindle Warren's passion for literature, leading him to become part of Nashville's Fugitive group, so named after their literary magazine of the mid-1920s. During these formative years, Tate and Ransom helped shape Warren's poetic style both through their own examples (Ransom's verse being especially instructive) and through their respective affinities. Ransom's taste for traditional poets from the metaphysical school to A. E. Housman and Thomas Hardy left its mark on many of Warren's earlier poems. "The Garden," for example, shows Andrew Marvell's strong influence in its imagery, style, and tone; and "Love's Parable" develops a central metaphor as elaborately as a conceit of John Donne's while using consciously archaic diction: "As kingdoms after civil broil,/ Long faction-bit and sore unmanned,/Unlaced, unthewed by lawless toil. . . ."

Likewise, Allen Tate's affinities with modern experimenters such as Hart Crane and T. S. Eliot proved influential early on. After *The Waste Land* was published late in 1922, Warren drew its scenes on his dormitory wall (Tate was most impressed by the rat crawling through vegetation); he later claimed in a 1970 interview that he and most of his college literary circle had soon learned the poem by heart. "To a Face in a Crowd," the earliest of his poems to survive into later volumes (it terminates all four of the *Selected Poems*), clearly displays the influence of Eliot in its theme of alienation (implicit in the title), its imagery of the futile quest for meaning ("we . . . weary nomads in this desert"), its dread of mortality ("I was afraid"), and its mood of world-weariness rendered in memorable sound play: "how black and turbulent the blood/Will beat through iron chambers of the brain." Within a few years, Warren's two most ambitious early poems were to show a more sophisticated level of apprenticeship to Eliot: "Kentucky Mountain Farm" for its form (in five segments) and imagery (including a death by water), and "The Return: An Elegy" for its mood and prosody.

After graduating summa cum laude from

including Adam Stanton in *All the King's Men* and Lilburne Lewis in *Brother to Dragons* (1953).

Returning from Oxford in 1930 to marry Emma Brescia and take up a teaching career, Warren found positions as an assistant professor at Southwestern Presbyterian College (now Southwestern College at Memphis; 1930-1931) and as an acting assistant professor at Vanderbilt (1931-1934). In autumn 1934 he went on to Louisiana State University, where, with Cleanth Brooks and Charles W. Pipkin, he founded the *Southern Review* in 1935 and where his collaboration with Brooks also produced several textbooks of landmark importance for their propagation of the so-called New Criticism—an approach to literature stressing analysis of the formal elements making up the work of art. The most important of these books was *Understanding Poetry* (1938), which brought the New Criticism into thousands of college classrooms over the next several decades.

Despite his outstanding success in letters, Warren was not promoted to full professor at Louisiana State University, and so he accepted a position as professor of English at the University of Minnesota in 1942. Here, after completing his *Selected Poems, 1923-1943* (1944), he devoted the remainder of the decade to writing several major prose works, including the novels *All the King's Men* and *World Enough and Time* (1950), as well as important essays in literary criticism such as his classic book-length interpretation of Coleridge, "A Poem of Pure Imagination: An Experiment in Reading" (published in a 1946 edition of *The Rime of the Ancient Mariner*), and pioneering studies of Joseph Conrad, Ernest Hemingway, William Faulkner, Robert Frost, Herman Melville, Katherine Anne Porter, and Eudora Welty. In addition to their many penetrating and original insights, these essays furnish significant revelations concerning Warren's own practice as a creative writer. His essay on Conrad (collected in *Selected Essays*, 1958), for example, contains a statement of purpose applicable to every particle of Warren's own literary creation: "The philosophical novelist, or poet, is one for whom the documentation of the world is constantly striving to rise to the level of generalization about values, for whom the image strives to rise to symbol, for whom images always fall into a dialectical configuration, for whom the urgency of experience, no matter how vividly and strongly experience may enchant, is the urgency to know the meaning of experience." The essays on Porter and Welty have an even more direct relevance to Warren's poetry in that Welty's "A Still Moment,"

Robert Penn Warren, 1924

Vanderbilt in 1925, Warren went for graduate study to the University of California at Berkeley, where he met his wife-to-be Emma Brescia but found the program of literary studies unfulfilling compared with the excitement of his Fugitive circle at Vanderbilt. He therefore headed East, first to Yale and then on a Rhodes Scholarship to Oxford University in England, where he worked on his first book, *John Brown: The Making of a Martyr* (1929). This portrayal of Brown as a bloody fanatic who had coldly slaughtered several entire families in the name of the abolitionist ideal prior to Harper's Ferry was the precursor to a memorable series of similar characters in Warren's fiction and poetry, together with a word of advice from Porter, combined to form the genesis of Warren's *Audubon: A Vision* (1969), published some twenty-five years later.

In 1950 Warren's acceptance of a professorship at Yale University coincided shortly thereafter with divorce from Emma Brescia (1951) and marriage to the writer Eleanor Clark (1952), by whom he fathered his only two children, Rosanna (1953) and Gabriel (1955). Since then, Warren has divided his habitation between his home in Fairfield, Connecticut, a former barn in which he personally did much of the renovation in carpentry and stone work, and his summer home in Stratton, Vermont. These settings, together with his frequent sojourns with his family in France and Italy, have provided a vital stimulus to much of Warren's verse since *Brother to Dragons* in 1953.

Brother to Dragons, the most ambitious long poem in Warren's fourteen volumes of poetry, is generally seen as a watershed separating his traditional, formally disciplined earlier verse from the later volumes, which display the loosening effects that were becoming generally prevalent in American poetry of the 1950s. Among those loosening effects was a more open use of his own persona in the later poetry, once he had broken away from the "impersonality of art" doctrine by installing

Eleanor Clark (photograph by Ellen Levine)

"R. P. W." as a major character in *Brother to Dragons*. It should be remarked, however, that the loosening effects in Warren's later style, though extending far enough to encompass free verse, generally coexist with a continuing respect for traditional forms. From first to last, Warren's verse comprises a virtual catalogue of modified conventions, from the epic grasp of *Brother to Dragons* to the nursery rhymes in *You, Emperors, and Others* (1960). Sonnets, terza rima, iambic couplets, rhyming quatrains, sestinas, quasi-Spenserian stanzas, and various combinations thereof characterize Warren's style in virtually all his volumes of poetry.

Within this great range of styles, however, a fundamental coherence in the development of Warren's themes gives his poetic opus an underlying unity reminiscent of William Faulkner's remark that "not only each book had to have a design but the whole output or sum of an artist's work had to have a design." In Warren's verse this total design may in the end justify reference to another eminent quotation, T. S. Eliot's assertion that "We must know all of Shakespeare's work in order to know any of it." Something similar may be said of the poetry of Robert Penn Warren.

The master theme that unifies Warren's fourteen volumes of verse published over six decades is the neoromantic trauma of the Fall—considered as a philosophical and psychological phenomenon—along with a gradually evolving set of redemptive possibilities. In retrospect, it can be seen that this subject matter has extended across Warren's poetic opus within the frame of three overlapping phases. Using mainly lyrical form, the poetry of the first phase—the 1920s and 1930s—depicts the Fall in the usual fashion: original innocence, characterized by delight in one's being within the kingdom of nature, yielding to a forced, one-way passage into a world ruined by time, loss, and evil, the naturalistic Waste Land promulgated in the writings of Eliot and Hemingway. At times, Warren employs a frankly Wordsworthian manner, as in "Letter from a Coward to a Hero" (*Thirty-Six Poems*, 1935): "The scenes of childhood were splendid,/And the light that there attended,/But is rescinded:/The cedar,/The lichened rocks,/The thicket where I saw the fox,/And where I swam, the river." Elsewhere, somewhat like Robert Frost, he makes nearly obsessive use of an autumnal setting as a seasonal pun for the theme of losses—in "Late Subterfuge" and "Garden Waters," for example, as well as "The Garden" and "Aged Man Surveys Past Time" (all in *Thirty-Six Poems*). And as these poems of passage proliferate, T. S. Eliot continues to manifest his spectral presence; for example, a phrase lifted from "Gerontion"—"fractured atoms"—appears in the *Kentucky Mountain Farm* segment entitled "At the Hour of the Breaking of the Rocks" (*Thirty-Six Poems*).

To the irony and regret of this "Paradise Lost" perspective, Warren adds still deeper trauma through bringing the Fall to bear upon the inner psyche. Repeatedly in his verse the lapsarian experience precipitates a bifurcation within the psyche between a fleeing anima figure, representing the lost child-self, and a fallen persona that is left behind to cope as best it can with its inner vacancy and its ruined environment. In "Man Coming of Age" (*Thirty-Six Poems*) the lost self is "That frail reproachful *alter ego*" who, harking back toward "a season greener and of more love," flees the approach of his lapsed, autumn-bound doppelgänger as the poem ends. In other poems, the fleeing anima takes a nonhuman form, like the doe escaping the hunt in "Eidolon" and the hawk sailing into the sunset (Warren's most frequent version of this motif) at the end of "Picnic Remembered." The often anthologized poem "Bearded Oaks" (*Eleven Poems on the Same Theme*, 1942), which portrays the state of being dead in terms of undersea imagery (like Eliot's "Death by Water" in *The Wasteland*), illustrates the bankrupt condition of the fallen self without its anima. Here, pursuing their intent to "spare an hour's term/To practice for eternity," the two lovers maintain absolute silence and total stasis in a sea-bottom setting, where "Dark is unrocking, unrippling, still." To this scene, the upper, living world contributes just so much sediment: "Passion and slaughter, ruth, decay/Descend, minutely whispering down,/Silted down swaying streams."

Further exacerbating this postlapsarian sense of fragmentation—of being separated from one's deepest self, from nature, from the world of the living—is the motif of broken relationships that extends through these poems. Portrayed at times in terms of society at large, as in two poems in *Thirty-Six Poems*—"Pondy Woods" (where a killer flees the manhunt) and "History" (whose present generation disgraces the noble dream of its pioneer ancestors)—this theme of alienation most commonly affects intimate relationships, such as that between mother and son in "The Return: An Elegy" (*Thirty-Six Poems*) and "Revelation" (*Eleven Poems on the Same Theme*). Most often, it dissolves the bond between lovers, thereby promoting an ultimate expression of the "Paradise Remembered" sensibility. In their depictions of this subject, poems such as "Monologue [as opposed to Dialogue] at Midnight," "Love's Parable," and "Picnic Remembered" (all in *Eleven Poems on the Same Theme*) anticipate the broken romance between Anne Stanton and Jack Burden after their one Edenic summer in *All the King's Men*—itself a title whose reference to Humpty Dumpty implies the "Great Fall" from innocence suffered by all the book's main characters.

Extending its ruinous sway in this fashion, the first phase of Warren's verse culminates at last in the five-poem sequence, "Mexico Is a Foreign Country: Five Studies in Naturalism" (*Selected Poems, 1923-1943*). Like his predecessor John Brown, or like the bloody ideologues who were precipitating global war at the time the poem was written, the political fanatic in poem one, "Butterflies Over the Map," seeks relief from his intolerable inner vacancy by committing slaughter while "robed in the pure/Idea." By comparison, the ragged beggar sitting passively in poem two, "The World Comes Galloping: A True Story," is a figure of wisdom and dignity. For the speaker of these poems, the world's fragmentation widens from the human dimension in poem three, "Small Soldiers with Drum in Large Landscape" (their drumbeat accentuates his solitude: "And I and I, and they are they,/And *this* is *this*, and *that* is *that*"), to the theological level in poem five, "The Mango on the Mango Tree," where God the "Great Schismatic" is to blame for "the Babel curse by which we live." To the craving for communion in this poem there is no answer but fantasy—"And I could leap and laugh and sing . . . and everything/Take hands with us and pace the music in a ring."

Reversing the biblical analogue, the second phase of Warren's verse—that of the 1940s and 1950s—moves from the theme of the Fall to that of "Original Sin," which Warren defines (in his essay on Coleridge) as "original with the sinner and . . . of his will." Here the bifurcation of the psyche precipitated by the lapsarian experience brings on a crisis of identity that necessitates the addition of dramatic and narrative elements to Warren's earlier elegiac-lyric mode. Extending from *Eleven Poems on the Same Theme* (1942) through "The Ballad of Billie Potts" (in *Selected Poems, 1923-1943*), *Brother to Dragons* (1953), *Promises* (1957), and *You, Emperors, and Others* (1960), this phase of Warren's verse dramatizes the lost alter ego of prelapsarian innocence being supplanted by a fearsome new identity, a figure of innate evil rising up with hatchet in hand—like Big Billie Potts or Lilburne Lewis—to answer the fallen self 's yearning for definition. In terms of Jungian archetypes, the "undiscovered self" or "shadow" (comparable to Freud's id) thus replaces the lost child-self, or anima; and the poems of Warren's middle period become a sort of psychodrama in which a sanctimonious surface ego (whom Warren calls "you") attempts to repudiate any consanguinity with its polluted Jungian shadow.

In the most original of the *Eleven Poems on the Same Theme*—"End of Season," "Original Sin: A Short Story," "Crime," "Pursuit," and "Terror"—"you" is portrayed in headlong flight from this bestial doppelgänger, but the pursuit is relentless. Hence the "Terror" of that last title: there is no preserving of "innocence." In "End of Season" the persona takes refuge in a beach resort whose quasi-baptismal rites of play offer a cleansed new identity. (John the Baptist, Ponce de Leon, and Dante add to the ironic "new life" motif in this stanza.) The undersea realm renders protection in lines of rich sound texture—"deep and wide-eyed, dive/Down the glaucous glimmer where no voice can visit"—but the past self is a relentless pursuer: "But the mail lurks in the box at the house where you live." In "Crime" another passage of arresting aural effects describes the polluted self as a corpse showing alarming signs of resurrection from the secret place where "you" had buried it: "though the seasons stammer/Past pulse in the throat of the field-lark,/Still memory drips, a pipe in the cellar-dark,/And in its hutch and hole . . ./The cold heart heaves like a toad, and lifts its brow. . . ." In "Terror" the "clean" part of the self strives mightily to maintain its sanctity, as "you now, guiltless, sink/To rest in lobbies, or pace gardens. . . ," but the worldwide outpouring of depravity in this poem, embodied in the figures of Mussolini, Hitler, Stalin, and Franco, makes innocence an increasingly untenable concept, as "you" admit in the closing comparison between "you" (vis-à-vis the shadow) and Macbeth "the criminal king" (vis-à-vis Duncan): "the conscience-stricken stare/Kisses the terror; for you see an empty chair."

This effort of "you" to escape or renounce its fallen shadow self creates the central drama of Warren's subsequent four volumes. In "The Ballad of Billie Potts" Little Billie's "original sin"—his attempt to ambush and murder a wayfarer—precipitates first his loss of Eden ("the green/World, land of the innocent bough"—a reference to Eden's Tree) and then his loss of the anima, whose departure "like the cicada had left . . ./The old shell of self, thin, ghostly, translucent, light as air." Flight to the West gives Billie "another name and another face," but the insufficiency of this new identity imposes the vacancy of "you" upon the runaway, bringing him home at last in search of the missing anima:

> Though the letter always came and you lovers were always true,
> Though you always received the respect due to your position,
> Though your hand never failed of its cunning and your glands always
>   thoroughly knew their business,
> Though your conscience was easy and you were assured of your innocence.
>
> You became gradually aware that something was missing from the picture,
> And upon closer inspection exclaimed: "Why, I'm not in it at all!"
> Which was perfectly true.
>
> Therefore you tried to remember when you last had
> Whatever it was you had lost,
> And you decided to retrace your steps from that point[.]

So Billie returns home and drinks at the spring where his ghostly reflection in the dark may yet harbor the child-self that was lost so long ago:

> But perhaps what you lost was lost in the pool long ago
> When childlike you lost it and then in your innocence rose to go
> After kneeling, as now, with your thirst beneath the leaves:
> And years it lies here and dreams in the depth and grieves,
> More faithful than mother or father in the light or dark of the leaves.

For the fallen psyche, what rises up from the dark is not the innocent child-self, however, but rather the father "Who is evil and ignorant and old." After the hatchet stroke of Big Billie—"What gift—oh, father, father—from that dissevering hand?"—Little Billie's death ("the patrimony of your crime") leaves "you" to carry the search for true selfhood to its momentous conclusion.

For its visionary power, its vividness of image, and its appeal to the ear, that conclusion (in the closing lines of "The Ballad of Billie Potts") marks a pinnacle of achievement rarely equalled and never surpassed in Warren's other poetry:

> The bee knows, and the eel's cold ganglia burn,
> And the sad head lifting to the long return,
> Through brumal deeps, in the great unsolsticed coil,

Carries its knowledge, navigator without star,
And under the stars, pure in its clamorous toil,
The goose hoots north where the starlit marshes are.
The salmon heaves at the fall, and, wanderer, you
Heave at the great fall of Time, and, gorgeous, gleam
In the powerful arc, and anger and outrage like dew,
In your plunge, fling, and plunge to the thunderous
    stream:
Back to the silence, back to the pool, back
To the high pool, motionless, and the unmurmuring
    dream.

As though to illustrate the Coleridgean reconciliation of opposites, "you" (the lapsarian ego) are here reconciled with the shadow self represented in the multitude of animal faces—faces that call up such precursors as the "old horse" and "old hound" that "you" locked out in "Original Sin: A Short Story." In their compulsive movement homeward, driven by intuitions of subhuman or prehuman origin, they manifest Carl Gustav Jung's insight that the collective unconscious is "the only accessible source of religious experience." Using expressly religious diction and imagery, the coda to "The Ballad of Billie Potts" opens up two specific religious possibilities: the lapsarian ego's recovery of "innocence" through a shared identity with these questing creatures ("Brother to pinion and the pious fin that cleave/Their innocence of air and the disinfectant flood"); and—a crucial tenet in any religious attitude—the sacramental acceptance of one's mortality:

The hour is late,
The scene familiar even in shadow,
The transaction brief,
And you, wanderer, back,
After the striving and the wind's word,
To kneel
Here in the sacramental silence of evening
At the feet of the old man
Who is evil and ignorant and old[.]

Because this moment is so crucial in Warren's total poetic vision—it initiates the third major phase in his design, that which postulates a kind of redemption from the Fall—its philosophical groundwork requires some exposition from two of Warren's seminal prose writings. The first of these is Warren's essay on *The Rime of the Ancient Mariner*, which he had already begun to contemplate at the time he was writing this poem. While speaking of Coleridge, Warren defines the nature and purpose of poetry in terms directly applicable to his own practice. Calling poetry "a myth of the unity of being" and "a glorious synthesis in which all breaches would be healed and all malice reconciled," he quotes Coleridge's celebrated definition of the Imagination for confirmation of his inferences: "It dissolves, diffuses, dissipates in order to recreate: . . . at all events it struggles to idealize and to unify." This unification may begin on the psychological level—"We know by creating, and one of the things we create is the Self "—but ultimately it entails theological consequences. The "imagination shows us how Nature participates in God," Warren says; and the poet who apprehends this truth—whether Coleridge or Warren—then promulgates "the theme of sacramental vision," which is "the sense of the 'One Life' in which all creation participates." From such a sacramental vision, the wanderer in "The Ballad of Billie Potts" derives a sense of final identity that transcends the fragmentation, the "original sin," and the fear of mortality which the Fall had precipitated.

Further illumination of this central design of Warren's poetry may be found in "Knowledge and the Image of Man," an essay whose publication date (1955) suggests that it is the poet's retrospective on his mythopoeic construction. "Man eats of the tree of knowledge, and falls," Warren writes. "But if he takes another bite, he may get at least a sort of redemption." For Warren this redemption does not postulate a convert's withdrawal from the world of the "unclean," as orthodoxy teaches; it rather requires an opposite process of union between oneself and the whole of reality: "[Man is] in the world with continual and intimate interpenetration, an inevitable osmosis of being, which in the end . . . affirms his identity." From the reconciliation of opposites that this vision permits, merging "the ugly with the beautiful, the slayer with the slain," Warren's figures of grace may derive "such a sublimation that the world which once provoked . . . fear and disgust may now be totally loved." Moreover, as against the unconscious innocence of the Eden period, the redemptive knowledge that is attained through this osmosis of being is the more precious for being willed and earned: "Man can return to his lost unity, and if that return is fitful and precarious, if the foliage and flower of the innocent garden are now somewhat browned by a late season, all is the more precious for the fact, for what is now achieved has been achieved by a growth of moral awareness. . . ."

Although Warren's system of ideas was essentially complete with "The Ballad of Billie Potts," he has renewed and reinvigorated his fundamental themes in his later poetry by bringing on vast

Peter Taylor, Robert Lowell, Robert Penn Warren, and Marc Friedlaender in Greensboro, North Carolina, 1948 (courtesy of the University Archives, Walter Clinton Jackson Library, University of North Carolina at Greensboro)

stretches of freshly imagined material—"willing," as he says in his tribute to Conrad, "to go naked into the pit, again and again, to make the same old struggle for his truth." About half of Warren's total body of verse, written over six decades, relates to the theme of the Fall, or forced passage into a ruined world; against this background he has played off the other two themes—reconciliation between the ego and its shadow, and between the self and the whole of reality—in a continuous dialectical tension.

In *Brother to Dragons* (1953), it is Thomas Jefferson and his nephew Lilburne Lewis who act out this drama of reconciliation between the "innocent" surface ego and its bestial shadow. Drawn from the Book of Job—the story of another "innocent" character who eventually comes to say, "Behold, I am vile"—the poem's title refers primarily to Lilburne's vivisection of a slave in retaliation for a minor transgression, an actual incident in the family history that Jefferson was never known to mention in speech or writing. In the poem, Jefferson's disillusion at this betrayal of his humanistic idealism generates variations upon the "brother to dragons" motif such as his cacophonous description of the minotaur: "In the blind dark, hock-deep in ordure, its beard/And shag foul-scabbed, and when the hoof heaves—/Listen! the foulness sucks like mire./ /The beast waits. He is . . ./Our brother, our darling brother." That this president, probably the only genius ever to hold the office, should state such sentiments bespeaks a national Fall from innocence appropriate to the poem's biblical analogue. But here again, as in "The Ballad of Billie Potts," the shadow self offers redemptive affinities with the whole of reality which are inaccessible to the surface ego. Thus, as Jefferson downgrades the human image toward these bestial archetypes, dragon and minotaur, R. P. W. in contrary fashion upgrades the beastly toward the human level. The giant snake that rears up "taller/Than any man" from the ruins of the Lewis home thereby assumes a demeanor more humane than reptilian in R. P. W.'s view of it: "then/The bloat head sagged an inch, the tongue withdrew,/And on the top of that strong stalk the head/Wagged slow, benevolent and sad and sage,/As though it understood our human pitifulness/And forgave all, and asked forgiveness, too." Likewise, the Mississippi catfish, though its "brute face/Is the face of the last torturer," enjoys an immersion in nature of quasi-religious dimensions: "The catfish is in the Mississippi and/The Mississippi is in the catfish and/Under the ice both are at one with God./Would that we were!"

Described by Hyatt Waggoner in his *American Poets: From Puritans to the Present* (1968) as "certainly a central *document* in American poetry," *Brother to Dragons* has elicited responses ranging from encomiastic to contemptuous. When it first appeared, Parker Tyler complained that the poem is "full . . . of ideological axes" (*Poetry*, December 1953), and Hugh Kenner said its style "resembles that of a Kentucky preacher hypostatizing Sin" (*Hudson Review*, Winter 1954). But other poets found it admirable. Robert Lowell, saying he had read the work three times through without stopping, found it "superior to any of the larger works of Browning" (*Kenyon Review*, Autumn 1953); Delmore Schwartz thought it "most remarkable as a sustained whole" (*New Republic*, 14 September 1953); and Randall Jarrell called it "an event, a great one" (*New York Times Book Review*, 23 August 1953). In 1979 Warren published a rewritten version of *Brother to Dragons*, revising the characterization (Jefferson, for one thing, is less vitriolic), recasting the form (in five segments), and generally doing away with "the blank verse trap," as the poet later called it. Although the later version is more economical than, the first, it retains the most skillful passages, like the coming of the annus mirabilis and R. P. W.'s long closing meditation, virtually intact.

In his prizewinning volume *Promises* (1957), Warren's belated experience of fatherhood revives a lyric strain, as he fills the two sequences dedicated to his son and daughter with sonnets, ballads, lullabies, and other harmonic forms. In substance, however, his theme of the Fall is still very much in evidence. The five-poem sequence dedicated to Rosanna, "To a Little Girl, One Year Old, in a Ruined Fortress," creates a dialectic tension between the melancholia of the narrator, thinking of "The malfeasance of nature or the filth of fate" ("The Child Next Door"), and the prelapsarian delight of his daughter: "And you sing as though human need/Were not for perfection" ("The Flower"). The "Promises" sequence addressed to Gabriel includes episodes of "Original Sin," such as a father's slaughter of all his children ("School Lesson Based on Word of Tragic Death of Entire Gillum Family")

and a grandfather's culpability in a legalized lynching ("Court-Martial"). Probably Warren's most obsessive image of a fallen soul is the tragically rootless wandering bum in "Dark Night of the Soul," a character transposed into poetry from his most widely admired short story, *Blackberry Winter* (published in 1946). But in "Dragon Country: To Jacob Boehme," the poet argues the "fortunate fall" idea that the world's evil—the dragon—gives life its truest meaning: "in church fools pray only that the Beast depart.//But if the Beast were withdrawn now, life might dwindle again/To the ennui, the pleasure, and the night sweat, known in the time before/Necessity of truth had trodden the land. . . ." Also counteracting the Fall are the epiphanies in *Promises* emanating from the world's beauty ("Gold Glade") and from a boy's first experience of shared work ("Boy's Will, Joyful Labor Without Pay, and Harvest Home—1918).

For its visionary power, the most original and momentous poem in *Promises* is "Ballad of a Sweet Dream of Peace," a sequence of seven lyrics in which a brash young fellow (resembling "you") is forcibly initiated into the next world through the ministrations of a skeletal granny. Reminiscent of Cass Mastern's cosmic web in *All the King's Men*, the guide's assertion that "all Time is a dream, and we're all one Flesh, at last" promulgates the Osmosis of Being in this setting, as do the spectral hogs that embody the "one Flesh" principle.

You, Emperors, and Others (1960) concludes the poems about "you" that had commenced two decades earlier in *Eleven Poems on the Same Theme*. In the "Garland for You" sequence, a new intensity is manifest in the postlapsarian psychodrama. "Man in the Street," for example, portrays a young man with "eyes big as saucers" who simply can not accept the fallen world: "I see facts I can't refute—/Winners and losers,/Pickers and choosers . . ./And my poor head, it spins like a top." Although the poem's headnote relates Jesus to this world ("Raise the stone, and there thou shalt find me"), the young man prefers the Christianity of the flight reflex: "And I go to prepare a place for you,/For this location will never do." Another notable instance of the flight reflex is "The Letter About Money, Love, or Other Comfort, If Any," in which "you" first revert to the anima-self of childhood ("crooning among the ruined lilies to a teddy bear, not what a grown man ought//To be doing past midnight") and finally lapse back into primal bestiality ("you, like an animal,/will crouch among the black boulders . . .//waiting for hunger to drive you down to forage . . ."). The emperors—two of the worst,

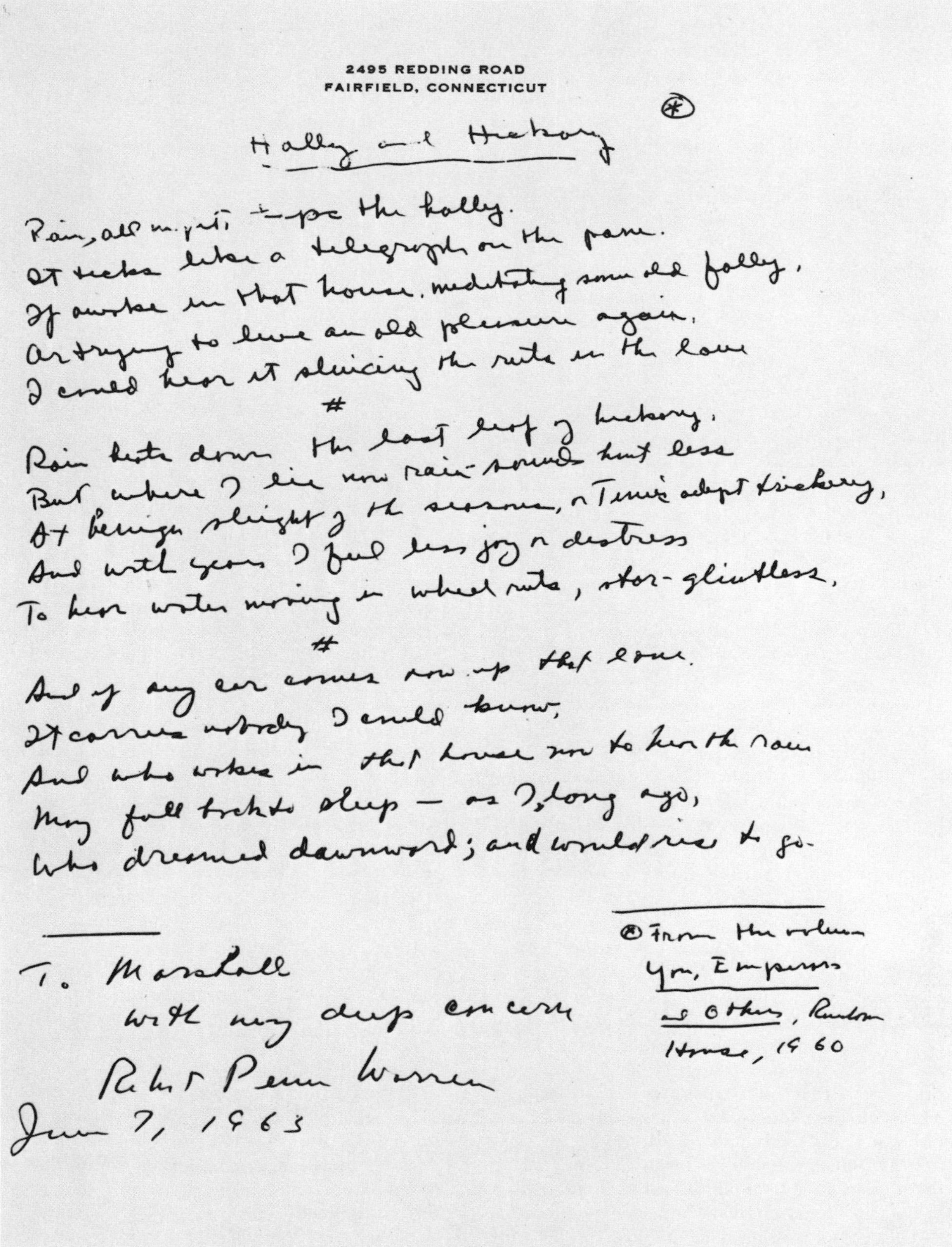

2495 REDDING ROAD
FAIRFIELD, CONNECTICUT   ⊛

Holly and Hickory

Rain, all night, *type* the holly.
It ticks like a telegraph on the pane.
If I awoke in that house, meditating some old folly,
Or trying to live an old pleasure again,
I could hear it sluicing the ruts in the lane

\#

Rain beats down the last leaf of hickory,
But where I lie now rain sounds hurt less
At bringing plight of the seasons, or Time's adept trickery,
And with years I feel less joy or distress
To hear water moving in wheel ruts, star-glintless.

\#

And if any ear comes now up that lane,
It carries nobody I could know,
And who wakes in that house now to hear the rain
May fall back to sleep — as I, long ago,
Who dreamed dawnward; and would rise to go.

———

To Marshall
     with my deep concern

Robert Penn Warren
Jun 7, 1963

⊛ From the volume
You, Emperors
and Others, Random
House, 1960

Fair copy (by permission of the author; courtesy of the Clifton Waller Barrett Library, University of Virginia)

Domitian and Tiberius—add further instruction to "you" about innate depravity ("Let's stop horsing around—it's not Domitian, it's you/We mean . . .").

The most moving poems in this volume are the "Mortmain" sequence about the death of the poet's father. Here, poised between his small son's and his father's life spans, the speaker stares "Down the tube and darkening corridor of Time" to glimpse a scene from his father's boyhood: "The boy,/With imperial calm, crosses a space, rejoins/ The shadow of woods, but pauses, turns, grins once,/And is gone . . ." ("A Vision: Circa 1880"). Poem four of this sequence, "In the Turpitude of Time: N.D.," recalls the "One Life" theme at the end of "The Ballad of Billie Potts" while also anticipating later poems such as "Trying to Tell You Something" (*Selected Poems: 1923-1975*, 1977): "Can we—oh, could we only—know/What annelid and osprey know,/And the stone, night-long, groans to divulge?/If only we could, then that star/ That dawnward slants might sing to our human ear. . . ."

The 1966 *Selected Poems* opens with a section entitled "Tale of Time: New Poems 1960-1966." Here Warren's growing preference for poem sequences—a reminder of his comment that he stopped writing short stories because they kept turning into poems—resulted in six such arrangements that subsume nearly the whole collection. (The only separate poem is "Shoes in the Rain Jungle," an early protest against the war in Vietnam.) Through five of the six sequences, the Tale of Time is the familiar story of the Fall retold as individual history. "Notes on a Life to be Lived," somewhat like *Promises*, juxtaposes the postlapsarian narrator's fear ("Stargazing"), grief ("Blow, West Wind"), and regret against various anima figures: the prelapsarian lad in "Little Boy and Lost Shoe," the fetus rapt in its "pulse and warm slosh of/. . . unbreathing bouillon" in "Vision under the October Mountain," the eagle "climbing/The light above the mountain" in "Composition in Gold and Red-Gold," and the speaker's small son in "Ways of Day": "I watch you at your sunlight play./Teach me, my son, the ways of day." "Tale of Time," the title sequence, recalls that supreme trauma in any man's life, the death of a mother—in this case amplified by the additional death of an ancillary mother figure, the family's black servant. Tracing the mother's life from an Edenic girlhood ("What Were You Thinking, Dear Mother?") to her funeral ("What Happened?"), "Tale of Time" fashions for this occasion a new formulation of the Osmosis of Being concept, reminiscent of the hogs' feast in

"Ballad of a Sweet Dream of Peace": "the solution: You/Must eat the dead./You must eat them completely, bone, blood, flesh, gristle. . . ." The "Homage to Emerson, On Night Flight to New York" sequence juxtaposes the great figure of transcendentalist prophecy—who said that there was no Fall, that man is an incarnation of God living in nature, the divine kingdom—against a series of postlapsarian images: "The Wart," "The Spider," masturbation, drunkenness, fear of flying, urban filth, the inhuman immensity of nature. "The Day Dr. Knox Did It"—committed suicide—uses its setting of August 1914 as a paradigm of lost innocence reaching from the boy-witness to the Western world. The discovery of "original sin" on the narrator's part—his confession that "I have lied, . . . committed/adultery, and for a passing pleasure/. . . inflicted death on flies"—completes the experience of the Fall: "for there is//no water to wash the world away./We are the world, and it is too late/to pretend we are children at dusk watching fireflies." In the "Holy Writ" sequence Warren's theme of "original sin" informs the first poem, "Elijah on Mount Carmel," in that the slaughter of the priests of Baal precipitates psychopathic frenzy—suggestive of Warren's first murderous fanatic, John Brown—in God's prophet: "he screamed,/Screaming in glory/ Like/A bursting blood blister." The other biblical episode, "Saul at Gilboa," is probably the grimmest instance of postlapsarian trauma in all Warren's poetry. Here the prophet Samuel anoints Israel's first king only to witness, later, the anointed head lying severed from its torso, which, with "a stake/ Thrust upward to twist the gut-tangle, towered/ Above the wall of Beth-shan." Saul's prelapsarian innocence during the anointing—"How beautiful are the young, walking!"—is all the more unbearable in this hindsight: "through/The enormous hollow of my head, History/Whistles like a wind. . . ." Yet the "Tale of Time" section ends in "Delight," a sequence of seven short, exquisitely musical lyrics about the world's redemptive beauty.

Two remaining books of the 1960s, *Incarnations* (1968) and *Audubon: A Vision* (1969), counterbalance morbidity versus delight. *Incarnations*, as its title implies, takes up the "One Flesh" theme of "The Ballad of Billie Potts" and *Promises*, drawing support for the concept from a biblical epigraph: "Yet now our flesh is as the flesh of our brethren.— *Nehemiah* 5.5" The flesh in *Incarnations* is greatly various: animal ("The Red Mullet"), human ("Internal Injuries," about a dying convict and an old woman struck by an automobile), and even vegetable ("The Ivy"). What binds most of these poems into unity is the premise of limitation: to be incarnated as a man is to be conscious of time, death, and separation from the "One Flesh" ideal. "Myth on Mediterranean Beach: Aphrodite as Logos" is particularly effective in its portrayal of Aphrodite as a humpbacked old crone whose fleshly decay represents the Logos (Truth) principle: "The breasts hang down like saddle-bags,/To balance the hump the belly sags. . . ." Rising from the sea "In Botticellean parody," she "passes the lovers, one by one,//And passing, draws their dreams away,/And leaves them naked to the day." Several poems of "delight" counteract this mood, including "The Faring" (in a style reminiscent of Old English poetry), "The Enclave," and "Skiers," but *Incarnations* ends with two images of limitation: fog, a recurring image of being dead in Warren's later verse; and, in the fog, a crow call, evoking the problem of solipsism: "crow,/Come back, I would hear your voice://That much, at least, in this whiteness."

Initially, *Audubon* too seems morbid, describing an attempted murder that is punished by the hanging of the perpetrators. But, as Allen Shepherd has shown, Warren departed sharply from John James Audubon's *Ornithological Biography* (1831-1839), where the great naturalist, saved from murder by a band of vigilantes, was "well-pleased" at seeing the "infernal hag" who tried to kill him hanged for her turpitude. The poem instead imputes to Audubon a profound empathy with the old woman, whose willfulness during her hanging evokes something close to a mystical experience in the observer: "The face,/Eyes, a-glare, jaws clenched, now growing black . . . had achieved,/It seemed to him, a new dimension of beauty." This beauty of human character, like the beauty of Audubon's birds, has the effect of reversing the Fall, imparting to Audubon that perfected contentedness with himself ("Simply . . . as he was/. . . The blessedness!") and with the surrounding world that is normally reserved to prelapsarian innocence. Even his own mortality is easily accepted in this spirit, and the Osmosis of Being becomes immanent ("Thinks/How thin is the membrane between himself and the world"). In the end, the poem's narrator (Warren's persona) takes instruction from this figure of grace, emulating Audubon's life-joy as he hears the geese flying North (the anima returning): "Tell me a story of deep delight."

Warren's remarkable late-flowering of creativity, compared by George Palmer Garrett, Jr., to that of Pablo Picasso, Igor Stravinsky, and William Butler Yeats, produced four more volumes in the 1970s, as the poet was settling into his eighth dec-

ade. Subtitled *Poem/Poems 1968-1974, Or Else* takes as its epigraph a verse from Psalm 78 that identifies Jehovah's succor of Israel with the modern poet-prophet's mission: "He clave the rocks in the wilderness, and gave them drink as out of the great depths." The dialectic between rocks/wilderness and drink in *Or Else* begins in poem one with the ominous image of Time the Devourer: "the sun,/ Beyond the western ridge of black-burnt pine stubs like/A snaggery of rotten shark teeth, sinks. . . ." Poem two, "Natural History," counteracts this mood with a visionary portrayal of death as a benign absorption into nature. Here the spectral old couple's nakedness implies a return to Edenic innocence, and their embodiment in rain and flowers signifies the Osmosis of Being perfectly: "In the rain the naked old father is dancing. . . ./Her breath is sweet as bruised violets, and her smile sways like daffodils reflected in a brook." A similar counterpoint juxtaposes the two artists in "Homage to Theodore Dreiser"—a soul damned by his knowledge of his own and the world's evil—and "Flaubert in Egypt," in which Gustave Flaubert's life is redeemed by his intense experience of the world's beauty: "his heart/burst with a solemn thanksgiving to God for/the fact he could perceive the worth of the/world with such joy.//Years later, death near, he remembered the palm fronds—/ how black against a bright sky!" At the close of *Or Else*, two verbal paintings represent the terminal instance of this juxtaposition. In "Birth of Love" a man, "all/History dissolving from him, is/Nothing but an eye. Is an eye only. Sees," as he is absorbed totally into the spectacle of his beloved bathing, "A white stalk from which the face flowers gravely toward the high sky." This epiphany yields in the next poem, however, to a description of death as "A Problem in Spatial Composition." Here Warren's long-standing image of the anima as a hawk disappearing into darkness at sunset occurs in a newly pictographic fashion, with the patterning of words on the page providing a visual image of the bird's descent:

All is ready.

    The hawk,
Entering the composition at the upper left frame
Of the window, glides,
In the pellucid ease of thought and at
His breathless angle,
Down.

    Breaks speed.
       Hangs with a slight lift and hover.

Makes contact[.]

Though few in number, the new poems in *Selected Poems: 1923-1975* (1977) include several memorable achievements. Gathered under the title, "Can I See Arcturus From Where I Stand?—Poems 1975," these ten poems subserve that collective title in their recurring reach toward transcendence ("Arcturus") from a generally postlapsarian environment ("Where I Stand"). The opening poem, "A Way to Love God," depicts the dialectical conflict between the world's immanent beauty and its appalling turpitude through sudden contrast in sound and image patterns: "the sea's virgin bosom unveiled/To give suck to the wavering serpent of the moon; and/In the distance, in *plaza, piazza, place, platz,* and square,/Boot heels, like history being born, on cobbles bang." The closing memory of sheep standing in fog ("Their eyes/Stared into nothingness") amplifies the poem's title: waiting quietly for death is A Way to Love God. "Evening Hawk" recalls a familiar anima image—the bird "climbing the last light/Who knows neither Time nor error"—and sharply contrasts its inaccessible realm of transcendence ("The star/Is steady, like Plato, over the mountain") against the fallen world, where one might "hear/The earth grind on its axis, or history/Drip in darkness like a leaking pipe in the cellar." Two other poems about loss and fragmentation, "Answer to Prayer" (a "paradise past" poem about a lost romance) and "Brotherhood in Pain" (a paradox defining loneliness as the deepest human bond), add resonance to perhaps the finest postlapsarian poem in this collection, "Loss, of Perhaps Love, in Our World of Contingency." Trying to isolate the exact lapsarian moment, when the "Loss, of Perhaps Love" of the world occurred, this poem moves backward from the present moment, epitomized in the image of a ruined bum sliding shoe soles on the pavement, and forward from the prelapsarian memory of "the dapple/Of sunlight on the bathroom floor while your mother/Bathed you."

This poem's concluding line, "We must learn to live in the world," states simply enough the prevailing issue of Warren's postlapsarian poetry. Total immersion in the world's beauty, like that portrayed in "Trying to Tell You Something," is one way of addressing this issue; but Warren's most distinctive and, in the "Arcturus" collection, most ambitious response to the problem is the final and longest poem of the group, "Old Nigger on One-Mule Cart Encountered Late at Night When Driving Home from Party in the Back Country." Like

Audubon, the Old Nigger becomes in the end a figure of grace and an alter ego for Warren's persona, despite the barriers imposed by race, class, age, education, and—since their near-collision—time and distance. "Brother, Rebuker, my Philosopher past all/Casuistry," the Old Nigger reconciles "Arcturus" and "Where I Stand" within the vast embrace of his final attitude: "Between cart and shack,/[he] Pauses to make water, and while/The soft, plopping sound in deep dust continues, his face/Is lifted into starlight, calm as prayer."

Now and Then: Poems 1976-1978 (1978), the volume that earned Warren his second Pulitzer Prize for poetry, adumbrates the theme of the Fall in its title—the *Now* of lapsarian consciousness being played off against the *Then* of Edenic memory. In general, the *Then* motif occurs in the opening ("Nostalgic") cluster of poems, while the *Now* preoccupies the second ("Speculative") collection, but several of the finest poems weave the *Now* and *Then* together. The book's opening poem, "American Portrait: Old Style," accomplishes this design by juxtaposing the youth and the old age of "K," a boyhood friend who had figured into one of Warren's early short stories, "Goodwood Comes Back." The paradise past of K.'s youth, now resembling "a vision still clinging to plaster/Set by Piero della Francesca," allowed him to "float/With a singular joy and silence,/In his cloud of bird dogs, like angels,/With their eyes on his eyes like God,/And the sun on his uncut hair bright. . . ." Later a big-league pitcher, until ruined by booze, K. now, "some sixty/Years blown like a hurricane past," has deteriorated into a pathetic ruin of a man, illustrating "How the teeth in Time's jaw all snag backward/And whatever enters therein/Has less hope of remission than shark-meat." The poem's closing summation, "And I love the world even in my anger," suggests the dialectic of moods that the rest of the volume amplifies.

The biblical epigraph of *Now and Then*—". . . let the inhabitants of the rock sing. . ." (Isaiah 42:11)—also announces this dialectical pattern through its contrast between the noun "rock" (a Waste Land analogue) and the verb "sing." Among the poems that sing most lyrically of nature's beauty are "Star-Fall," "Code Book Lost," and "Dream of a Dream": "Moonlight stumbles with bright heel/In the stream, and the stones sing. . . ." The poems of the contrary "rock" mentality, such as "Waiting," "Sister Water," and "Last Laugh," lead to a deepening of the speaker's hunger for his lost anima. In "Ah, Anima!," where a storm's ruinous aftermath is "a metaphor for your soul . . . in the hurricane of Time," the vacancy of the fallen self prompts the vain wish "that you, even in the wrack and pelt of gray light,//Had run forth, screaming . . . to leave//The husk behind, and leap/Into the blind and antiseptic anger of air." "Heart of Autumn"—a notably imagistic postlapsarian title—closes *Now and Then* with an extraordinary expression of this anima-hunger in a speaker who stands watching a flock of geese fly South:

> and I stand, my face lifted now skyward,
> Hearing the high beat, my arms outstretched in the
> tingling
> Process of transformation, and soon tough legs,
>
> With folded feet, trail in the sounding vacuum of
> passage,
> And my heart is impacted with a fierce impulse
> To unwordable utterance—
> Toward sunset, at a great height.

Being Here: Poetry 1977-1980 (1980), dedicated to Warren's grandfather, begins with three epigraphs about Time, the last of which is Warren's own formulation: "Time is the dimension in which God strives to define His own Being." For the poet, memory is the dimension of Time in which the attempt to define *his* Being occurs, creating most of these poems in the process. This gathering of memories begins with a prefatory poem, "October Picnic Long Ago," that portrays the poet-persona as a seven-year-old safely ensconced within his nuclear family. As against this fragile prelapsarian moment, section one counterposes early episodes of lost innocence. Death and funerals—including his mother's funeral in "Grackles, Goodbye"—are landmarks of initiation here, but almost as traumatic is the first awareness of solipsism. In the opening poem, "Speleology," the solitude of self in the cave—"I dared not move in darkness so absolute./I thought: *This is me*. Thought: *Me—who am I?*"—precipitates a wish for self-transcendence ("to be, in the end, part of all"), a motif that recurs in "Boyhood in Tobacco Country" ("I . . . try/To forget my own name and be part of the world") and in "Platonic Drowse" ("your body began to flow/On every side into distance,/. . .//Leaving only the steady but pulsing/Germ-flame of your Being. . . .") Section two portrays the emergence of the poet's artistic purpose, which in "Youthful Truth-seeker, Half-Naked, at Night, Running down Beach South of San Francisco," evokes a strong biblical analogy: "You dream that somewhere, somehow, you may embrace/The world in

its fullness and threat, and feel, like Jacob, at last/ The merciless grasp of unwordable grace." Skillful appeals to the eye and ear characterize this section ("the glutted owl makes utterance," "Scraggle and brush broken through, snow-shower jarred loose/ To drape shoulders. . . ."), but not all its poems record Nature's beauty; "Sila" concludes section two with the remembered mercy killing, by knife blade, of a wounded deer. Section three focuses upon the religious imagination, beginning and ending with the imagery of the Cross—the speaker mounting a cross in the first instance and erecting a grave marker for a drowned monkey in the other. Guilt, like that of Warren's "Original Sin" poems, proves a recurrent theme here, linking together the callous decapitation of kittens in "Dream, Dump-Heap, and Civilization," the killing of snakes for sport in "Deep—Deeper Down," a clandestine romance in "Vision," a giant boulder poised to overrun a valley "like God's wrath" in "Globe of Gneiss," and the color white as a cover for guilt in "Function of Blizzard." And the summoning of the dead—"Each wants to know if you remember a name"—adds another religious dimension in "Better Than Counting Sheep." Section four, focusing on the inadequacy of communication, begins with a similar seance ("Truth is the long soliloquy/Of the dead all their long night"), and goes on to counterpose the silence of Nature in "No Bird Does Call" and "Language Barrier" against indecipherable or fragmentary speech in "What Is the Voice That Speaks?" and "Lesson in History." Section five concludes *Being Here* by gathering up the book's themes in a dialectical configuration. "Eagle Descending," an anima poem dedicated "To a Dead Friend," evokes a vision of mortality that advances upon the persona himself in "Acquaintance with Time in Early Autumn." Here, watching a leaf "Release/Its tiny claw-hooks, and trust/A shining destiny," he sees it instead "descend to water I know is black." This less-than-benign paradigm of his own death leads to a moment of theomachy—"and I hate God"—which appears to be strengthened by other postlapsarian poems such as "Ballad of Your Puzzlement" ("He picks the scab of his heart"), "Trips to California" (during the Dust Bowl disaster), and "Auto-da-Fé" ("stench of meat burned:/ Dresden and Tokyo, and screams/In the Wilderness . . ."). On the other hand, the Osmosis of Being transpires in "Antimony: Time and Identity," where, in a canoe at night, "As consciousness outward seeps, the dark seeps in./As the self dissolves . . ./. . . .//I wonder if this is I." And the epiphanies in "Synonyms" and "Night Walking" affirm that "beauty is one word for reality" ("Synonyms"). In "Passers-By on Snowy Night," the last poem of *Being Here* (1980), the lyrically rhyming quatrains restate earlier themes (such as *"the moon, skull-white"* evoking nature's beauty and threat) while balancing the theme of isolation against its motif of the encounter. Here the essential purpose of poetry seems implicit in this partial release from solipsism: *"Alone,/I wish you well in your night/As I pass you in my own."*

Rumor Verified: Poems 1979-1980 (1981) derives its distinctive unity and power from the intensity of its meditations on mortality—a natural theme in the poet's eighth decade. The ramifications of the subject include the expiring of a day in "Sunset Scrupulously Observed" ("The evening slowly, soundlessly, closes. Like/An eyelid."); a bird smashed bloodily in "Going West" (it is going West on a car windshield); a horse being devoured by crows and vultures in "Dead Horse in Field," its missing eyes enabling it to "more readily see/Down the track of pure and eternal darkness"; the deaths of friends in "Minneapolis Story" and "Small Eternity"; the obituary of an old girl friend, "photo-

graph unrecognizable," in "Afterward"; and the death of the poet's father in "One I Knew," and "Questions You Must Learn to Live Past." In this last poem, the memory of father's deathbed (played off against seeing "your own child, that first morning, wait//For the school bus") calls forth a prospect of the speaker's own impending future, "when/After the fable of summer, a lithe sinuosity//Slips down to curl in some dark, wintry hole, with no dream."

In relating this central subject of *Rumor Verified* to himself, the Warren persona retains a characteristically dialectical range of responses. "Rumor Verified," the book's title poem, appears to imply some mode of death as the subject of its "rumor"— the death of an old identity if not physical death. "Since the rumor has been verified, you can, at least,/Disappear," the poem begins; "you" can now abandon the carefully cultivated persona of public life in favor of some new possibilities, such as becoming a guerilla fighter in a Third World country. But in the end, there is no escaping "the terror/Of knowledge"—in this instance, a knowledge of limitations sufficient to transform an old idiom into

At the Fugitive Reunion in Nashville, 4 May 1956: Allen Tate, Merrill Moore, Robert Penn Warren, John Crowe Ransom, and Donald Davidson (photograph by Rob Roy Purdy)

an ominous pun: "you are simply a man, with a man's dead reckoning, nothing more." The dead reckoning of "Convergences" somewhat resembles Edwin Arlington Robinson's "The Man Against the Sky" in its portrayal of a distant figure disappearing into a railroad tunnel: "Now I saw him a half-mile back,//A dot in the distance of sun/Where two gleaming rails became one//To impale him in the black throat/Of a tunnel that sucked all to naught." Another poem, "Immanence," has the persona foreseeing his own death even more nihilistically; he "will, into//The black conduit of Nature's Re-packaging System, be sucked./But that possibility is simply too distressing//To—even—be considered." Yet other poems, in the "But Also" section, conceive of death as a welcome absorption into larger being reminiscent of the son's return "home" at the end of "The Ballad of Billie Potts." "What Voice at Moth-Hour" depicts its twilight scene in such tones of invitation: *It's late! Come home.*" Likewise, "Gasp-Glory of Gold Light" evokes the osmosis of being through a quasi-romantic apprehension of Nature so annealing that "The Self flows away into the unbruised/Guiltlessness of no-Self," and one may "try to think, at the same moment,/Of the living and the dead." And "English Cocker: Old and Blind" describes the blind creature's descent of the stairs—"At the edge of each step one paw suspended in air"—as representing the One Flesh concept impinging against mortality: "But you remember how you last saw/Him hesitate in his whirling dark, one paw//Suspended above the abyss at the edge of the stair,/And . . . you knew in him/The kinship of all flesh defined by a halting paradigm."

"Fear and Trembling," the concluding section of *Rumor Verified*, begins, in "If Ever," with a formulation of this dialectical tension: "Do contradictory/Voices now at midnight utter/Doom—or promise?" One of the contradictory voices, in "Have You Ever Eaten Stars?," describes how a field of wild mushrooms suddenly—like Wordsworth's daffodils—entrances the speaker: "There, by a deer trail, by deer dung nourished,/Burst the gleam, rain-summoned,/Of bright golden chanterelles./However briefly, however small and restricted, here was/A glade-burst of glory." Gathered to be eaten, these starlike plants also nourish, metaphorically, the poet's appetite for epiphanies: "What can you do with stars, or glory?/ . . . Eat. Swallow. Absorb. . . ./Let brain glow/In its own midnight of darkness,/. . . let the heart/Rejoice." The contrary voice, in "Afterward," fastens with Melvillean brooding upon the "polar/Icecap

stretching forever in light of gray-green ambiguousness,/And, lulled by jet-hum, [you] wondered if this/Is the only image of eternity." A "nameless skull"—suggesting the final meaning of the title "Afterward"—poses the riddle of mortality in a radically stoic question: the skull, "In the moonlit desert, smiles, having been/So long alone. After all, are you ready/To return the smile?" Set off by itself in a "Coda" to *Rumor Verified*, "Fear and Trembling" recalls the two poems that began the book by comprising its "Prologue." The first of these, "Chthonian Revelation: A Myth," is a strikingly Edenic love poem set against a Mediterranean seacoast. The other poem, "Looking Northward, Aegeanward: Nestlings on Seacliff," describes the tenacity of new life in a harsh environment: "From huddle of trash, dried droppings, and eggshell, lifts/. . . The pink corolla of beak-gape, the blind yearning lifeward." In "Fear and Trembling," those earlier seasons of love and vitality give way to autumnal meditation, not only about the speaker's impending transition—"The gold leaf—is it whirled in anguish or ecstasy skyward?"—but also about the efficacy of turning one's past life into poems. "It is time to meditate on what the season has meant," the first stanza posits; but it is hard to meditate as the seasonal metaphor takes a more ominous coloring: "Can one, in fact . . . find his own voice in the towering gust now from northward?" In the end, a sacrifice of self ("the death of ambition") precipitates the new life of poetic resurrection: "only at death of ambition does the deep/Energy crack crust, spurt forth, and leap//From grottoes, dark—and from the caverned enchainment."

In 1983 Warren's abiding interest in American history was manifested in a new book-length narrative poem, *Chief Joseph of the Nez Perce* (subtitled *Who Called Themselves the Nimipu "The Real People"*). Focusing on the War of 1877, in which Chief Joseph resisted efforts, in violation of several treaties, of the U.S. government to relocate his people, the poem recreates the long trek of the Indians through Idaho and Montana until their valiant and resourceful band was overcome by superior force. Told partly by the poet and partly in the native eloquence of Chief Joseph's own voice, the narrative also draws upon a broad range of contemporary documents for added resonance. Thus the sympathy of Presidents Jefferson and Grant for the Indians is set against Charles Dickens's contempt for these "savages" and the satisfaction expressed in an Oregon newspaper when a party of miners returned from an expedition "with twenty scalps and some plunder. The miners are well." The Indians' achievement of glory despite military defeat is nicely encompassed in two quotations from General William Tecumseh Sherman, whose words at the outset serve as an epigraph: "The more we can kill this year, the less will have to be killed the next war." In the end he wrote: "The Indians throughout have displayed a courage and skill that elicited universal praise; they abstained from scalping; let captive women go free . . . they fought with almost scientific skill."

Wallace Stevens's remark that a poet reveals his personality in his choice of a subject has interesting implications in this instance. Warren's life-long effort to revise Americans' perception of their past frequently has taken the form of reversing the traditional assignment of guilt and innocence: John Brown, in Warren's first book, was a murderous fanatic, while the Secession's leader, in the recent *Jefferson Davis Gets His Citizenship Back* (1980), was a high-minded gentleman. But Warren's purpose is not merely to expose, once again, the moral turpitude of the victorious Northern politicians and generals; his deeper interest lies in his affinities with the aging Indian leader. Chief Joseph's devout attitude toward nature (reminiscent of Warren's Audubon), his strong loyalty to the father figure ("I prayed/That my father . . ./Might find some worth in a act of mine,/However slight"), and his posture in facing old age ("A dying animal humped with no motion under/Darkness of skies that reach out forever")—these are deeply felt themes of Warren's later poetry. And perhaps the quest for religious meaning is the final affinity between Chief Joseph and his commemorator: "But what is a man? An autumn-tossed aspen,/Pony-fart in the wind, the melting of snow-slush?/Yes, that is all. Unless—unless—/We can learn to live the Great Spirit's meaning. . . ."

On 24 April 1985—the poet's eightieth birthday—Random House published Warren's fourth volume of selected poems (*New and Selected Poems 1923-1985*). Although too few poems are republished here from his earlier volumes, this book's new poems—gathered in a section entitled "Altitudes and Extensions 1980-1985"—are an important addition to Warren's poetic oeuvre. The "Extensions" of his title encompass large horizons in both geography and time, represented by poems such as "Minnesota Recollection," "Arizona Midnight," "Far West Once," "Winter Wheat: Oklahoma," and "Old-Time Childhood in Kentucky." This last poem, evoking the octogenarian poet's octogenarian grandfather, indicates the great range of personally felt time in this collection (which is dedicated to Warren's infant granddaughter). Perhaps the most striking achievement of this collection relates to the other key word in its title, "Altitudes." From the first poem, "Three Darknesses," to the terminal "Myth of Mountain Sunrise" a dialectical pattern of images gradually produces an extraordinary final effect of rejuvenation. At one pole of the dialectic are numerous intimations of mortality in such poems as "Mortal Limit," "Old Dog Dead," "Rumor at Twilight," "Last Walk of Season," and "Sunset." At the other pole are the poems of virtually pantheistic affinities with nature (reminding us of Chief Joseph and Audubon yet again), such as "Caribou," "Hope," "Why You Climbed Up," and "First Moment of Autumn Recognized." Initially rejuvenation appears hopelessly remote as the speaker (at the end of "Three Darknesses") compares his stay in the hospital to "A dress rehearsal/. . . for/The real thing. Later. Ten years? Fifteen?" Even here the "Altitudes" suggest a presence, however, in the miniature form of a background image in the television movie the patient is watching: "Far beyond/All the world, the mountains lift. . . ./. . . They float/In that unnamable altitude of white light." Reappearing with increasing imminence at various points in the collection (in "Last Walk of Season," "If Snakes Were Blue," "Wind and Gibbon," "Delusion—No!"), the mountains are animate in the end, infused by the poet's vitalistic vision: "The mountain dimly wakes, stretches itself on windlessness. Feels its deepest chasm, waking, yawn." Ending the poem ("Myth of Mountain Sunrise") and the collection is one of the most striking images in all Warren's verse as the mountain birch assumes an erotic stance toward the rising sun, her lover:

> Think of a girl-shape, birch-white sapling, rising now
> From ankle-deep brook-stones, head back-flung, eyes closed in first beam,
> While hair—long, water-roped, past curve, coign, sway that no geometries know—
> Spreads end-thin, to define fruit-swell of haunches, tingle of hand-hold.
> The sun blazes over the peak. That will be the old tale told.

For its originality, its visionary power, and its technical virtuosity, poetry such as this seems to justify Warren's comment in the *Georgia Review* for Summer 1982 that "I've done some of my best poems in the last few years." Concerning his work as a whole, perhaps the best summary of Warren's poetic career is his own statement of purpose from his Jefferson Lecture in the Humanities, published as *Democracy and Poetry* in 1975. Beginning in his foreword with "the notion of the self as the central fact of 'poetry.'" Warren later explains that "only insofar as the work [of art] establishes and expresses a self can it engage us." Ultimately, "the work itself represents the author's adventures in selfhood," he goes on to observe; and in the end Warren's concept of creating selfhood serves to describe the design of his sixty years of poetic practice: "we may declare that the self is a style of being, continually expanding in a vital process of definition, affirmation, revision, and growth, a process that is the image, we may say, of the life process. . . ." The shelf of books in which Warren has recorded that life process has now become, by general consensus, a major document in American poetry. Given the magnitude and excellence of his achievement, it seems singularly appropriate that in February 1986 the Librarian of Congress, Daniel J. Boorstin, designated Robert Penn Warren the first official Poet Laureate of the United States of America.

Interviews:

Robert Penn Warren Talking: Interviews 1950-1978, edited by Floyd C. Watkins and John T. Hiers (New York: Random House, 1980);

David Farrell, "Reminiscence: A Conversation with Robert Penn Warren," *Southern Review,* new series 16 (Autumn 1980): 782-798;

Farrell, "Poetry As a Way of Life: An Interview with Robert Penn Warren," *Georgia Review,* 36 (Summer 1982): 314-331.

Bibliographies:

Mary Nance Huff, *Robert Penn Warren: A Bibliography* (New York: David Lewis, 1968);

Neil Nakadate, *Robert Penn Warren: A Reference Guide* (Boston: G. K. Hall, 1977);

James A. Grimshaw, Jr., *Robert Penn Warren: A Descriptive Bibliography 1922-1979* (Charlottesville: University Press of Virginia, 1981).

References:

Charles Bohner, *Robert Penn Warren* (New York: Twayne, 1964; revised edition, 1981);

John M. Bradbury, *The Fugitives: A Critical Account* (Chapel Hill: University of North Carolina Press, 1958), pp. 172-255;

Cleanth Brooks, *Modern Poetry and the Tradition* (Chapel Hill: University of North Carolina Press, 1939);

Robert Buffington, "The Poetry of the Master's Old Age," *Georgia Review,* 25 (Spring 1971): 5-16;

Leonard Casper, *Robert Penn Warren: The Dark and Bloody Ground* (Seattle: University of Washington Press, 1960);

William Bedford Clark, "A Meditation of Folk-History: The Dramatic Structure of Robert Penn Warren's 'The Ballad of Billie Potts,'" *American Literature,* 49 (January 1978): 635-645;

Clark, ed., *Critical Essays on Robert Penn Warren* (Boston: Twayne, 1981);

A. L. Clements, "Sacramental Vision: The Poetry of Robert Penn Warren," *South Atlantic Bulletin,* 43 (November 1978): 47-65;

George Core, "In the Heart's Ambiguity: Robert Penn Warren as Poet," *Mississippi Quarterly,* 22 (Fall 1969): 313-326;

Louise Cowan, *The Fugitive Group: A Literary History* (Baton Rouge: Louisiana State University Press, 1959);

Donald Davidson, "The Thankless Muse and Her Fugitive Poets," *Sewanee Review,* 66 (Spring 1958): 201-228;

D. M. Dooley, "The Persona RPW in Warren's *Brother to Dragons," Mississippi Quarterly,* 25 (Winter 1971-1972): 19-30;

Four Quarters, Robert Penn Warren Issue, edited by John J. Keenan, 21 (May 1972);

George P. Garrett, Jr., "The Recent Poetry of Robert Penn Warren," in *Robert Penn Warren: A Collection of Critical Essays,* edited by John L. Longley, Jr. (New York: New York University Press, 1965), pp. 223-236;

Richard Gray, ed., *Robert Penn Warren: A Collection of Critical Essays* (Englewood Cliffs, N. J.: Prentice-Hall, 1980);

Frank Graziano, ed., *Homage to Robert Penn Warren* (Durango, Col.: Logbridge-Rhodes, 1982);

James A. Grimshaw, Jr., ed., *Robert Penn Warren's Brother to Dragons: A Discussion* (Baton Rouge: Louisiana State University Press, 1983);

James H. Justus, *The Achievement of Robert Penn Warren* (Baton Rouge: Louisiana State University Press, 1981);

John L. Longley, Jr., ed., *Robert Penn Warren: A Collection of Critical Essays* (New York: New York University Press, 1965);

F. O. Matthiessen, "American Poetry Now," *Sewanee Review,* 55 (January-March 1947): 24-55;

Frederick P. W. McDowell, "Psychology and Theme in *Brother to Dragons, PMLA,* 70 (September 1955): 565-586;

Neil Nakadate, ed., *Robert Penn Warren: Critical Perspectives* (Lexington: University Press of Kentucky, 1981);

Sister Bernetta Quinn, "Warren and Jarrell: The Remembered Child," *Southern Literary Journal*, 8 (Spring 1976): 24-40;

Sona Raiziss, *The Metaphysical Passion: Seven Modern American Poets and the Seventeenth-Century Tradition* (Philadelphia: University of Pennsylvania Press, 1952);

Guy Rotella, " 'One Flesh': Robert Penn Warren's *Incarnations*," *Renascence*, 31 (Autumn 1978): 25-42;

Rotella, "Robert Penn Warren's *Tale of Time*," *Essays in Arts and Sciences*, 8 (May 1979): 45-61;

Louis D. Rubin, Jr., *The Faraway Country: Writers in the Modern South* (Seattle: University of Washington Press, 1963), pp. 105-130;

Allen Shepherd, "Warren's *Audubon*: 'Issues in Purer Form' and 'The Ground Rules of Fact,' " *Mississippi Quarterly*, 24 (Winter 1970-1971): 47-56;

W. P. Southard, "The Religious Poetry of Robert Penn Warren," *Kenyon Review*, 7 (Autumn 1945): 653-676;

Monroe K. Spears, "The Latest Poetry of Robert Penn Warren," *Sewanee Review*, 78 (Spring 1970): 348-358;

Peter Stitt, "Robert Penn Warren, the Poet," *Southern Review*, new series 12 (Spring 1976): 261-276;

Victor Strandberg, *The Poetic Vision of Robert Penn Warren* (Lexington: University Press of Kentucky, 1977);

Strandberg, "Warren's Osmosis," *Criticism*, 10 (Winter 1968): 23-40;

Strandberg, "Warren's Poetic Vision: A Reading of *Now and Then*," *Southern Review*, new series 16 (Winter 1980): 18-45;

Marshall Walker, *Robert Penn Warren: A Vision Earned* (Edinburgh: Paul Harris, 1979);

William Wasserstrom, "Robert Penn Warren: From Paleface to Redskin," *Prairie Schooner*, 31 (Winter 1957-1958): 323-333;

Floyd C. Watkins, "Billie Potts at the Fall of Time," *Mississippi Quarterly*, 11 (Winter 1958): 19-28;

Watkins, *Then & Now: The Personal Past in the Poetry of Robert Penn Warren* (Lexington: University Press of Kentucky, 1982).

Papers:

Most of Warren's manuscripts and letters are on deposit in the Beinecke Library at Yale University; the Margaret I. King Library, Special Collections and Archives, at the University of Kentucky in Lexington; and the *Southern Review* files at Louisiana State University in Baton Rouge.

Yvor Winters
(17 October 1900-25 January 1968)

Tom Zaniello
Northern Kentucky University

BOOKS: *The Immobile Wind* (Evanston, Ill.: Monroe Wheeler, 1921);

The Magpie's Shadow (Chicago: Musterbookhouse, 1922);

The Testament of a Stone, Being Notes on the Mechanics of the Poetic Image, Secession, no. 8 (April 1924);

The Bare Hills: A Book of Poems (Boston: Four Seas, 1927);

The Proof (New York: Coward-McCann, 1930);

The Journey And Other Poems (Ithaca, N.Y.: Dragon Press, 1931);

Before Disaster (Tryon, N.C.: Tryon Pamphlets, 1934);

The Case of David Lamson: A Summary, prepared by Winters and Frances Theresa Russell (San Francisco: Lamson Defense Committee, 1934);

Primitivism and Decadence: A Study of American Experimental Poetry (New York: Arrow, 1937);

Maule's Curse: Seven Studies in the History of American Obscurantism (Norfolk, Conn.: New Directions, 1938);

Poems (Los Altos: Gyroscope Press, 1940);

The Anatomy of Nonsense (Norfolk, Conn.: New Directions, 1943);

The Giant Weapon (Norfolk, Conn.: New Directions, 1943);

Edwin Arlington Robinson (Norfolk, Conn.: New Directions, 1946; revised edition, New York: New Directions, 1971);

The Brink of Darkness (Denver: Alan Swallow, 1947);

In Defense of Reason (New York: Swallow Press & William Morrow, 1947; London: Routledge & Kegan Paul, 1960);

Three Poems (Cummington, Mass.: Cummington Press, 1950);

Collected Poems (Denver: Alan Swallow, 1952; revised, 1960; London: Routledge & Kegan Paul, 1960);

The Function of Criticism (Denver: Alan Swallow, 1957; London: Routledge & Kegan Paul, 1962);

On Modern Poets (Cleveland & New York: Meridian/World, 1959; London: Mayflower, 1960);

Yvor Winters (courtesy of the Department of Special Collections, Research Library, University of California at Los Angeles)

The Poetry of W. B. Yeats (Denver: Alan Swallow, 1960);

The Poetry of J. V. Cunningham (Denver: Alan Swallow, 1961);

The Early Poems of Yvor Winters, 1920-28 (Denver: Alan Swallow, 1966);

Forms of Discovery: Critical and Historical Essays on the Forms of the Short Poem in English (Chicago: Alan Swallow, 1967);

Uncollected Essays and Reviews, edited by Francis Murphy (Chicago: Swallow Press, 1973);

The Collected Poems of Yvor Winters (Manchester: Carcanet New Press, 1978); republished as *The Poetry of Yvor Winters* (Athens, Ohio: Swallow, 1980).

RECORDING: *Twentieth Century Poetry in English,* (Library of Congress, PL7, 1949).

OTHER: *Quest for Reality,* edited by Winters and Kenneth Fields (Chicago: Swallow Press, 1969).

PERIODICAL PUBLICATIONS: "More Santa Clara Justice," *New Republic,* 80 (10 October 1934): 239-241;

"The 16th Century Lyric in English," *Poetry,* 53 (February 1939): 258-272; 53 (March 1939): 320-335; 54 (April 1939): 35-51.

When Yvor Winters's publisher and friend Alan Swallow hailed him in 1940 as the "sage of Palo Alto," he accurately touched on the paradox of Winters's career: the isolation in which he became admired as a poet, a teacher, and critic of poetry. For Winters, who adopted California early in his career as his permanent home, participated in the major poetic and critical movements of the twentieth century—imagism, the expatriate *transition* scene, and new criticism—from afar: "In the 'twenties," he wrote in an autobiographical introduction to *The Early Poems of Yvor Winters, 1920-28* (1966), "I was not in Paris, nor even in Harvard." Nevertheless he became well known as a poet in the 1920s, as a strong moralistic critic in the 1930s, and, in his long career as a professor of English at Stanford University, as an advocate of neglected poets both living and dead, and as a teacher of poetry and critical thinking.

The son of Harry and Faith Winters, Arthur Yvor Winters was born in Chicago but grew up in Eagle Rock, California, near Pasadena. Although Eagle Rock is now a suburb of Los Angeles, in the early 1900s this southern California town was the rural landscape Winters celebrated in his poem, "On a View of Pasadena from the Hills":

> The hills so dry, so dense the underbrush,
> That where I pushed my way the giant hush
> Was changed to soft explosion as the sage
> Broke down to powdered ash, the sift of age,
> And fell along my path, a shadowy rift.

In 1917-1918 he attended the University of Chicago, where he continued his early acquaintance with contemporary poetry, especially Wallace Stevens and the imagists, with avid purchases of little magazines and by joining the Poetry Club with Glenway Wescott, Elizabeth Madox Roberts, and Monroe Wheeler (who published Winters's first book in 1921). He also met Harriet Monroe, whose editorship of *Poetry* in Chicago and whose wide contacts provided Winters important early links with other poets, such as Marianne Moore, with whom Winters corresponded.

At the end of the fall quarter in 1918, the discovery that Winters had tuberculosis brought about the most dramatic change in his early life. He was sent to a sanatorium in Santa Fe, New Mexico, where he stayed until 1921, and—because of enforced isolation and bedrest—he absorbed contemporary poetry from the little magazines, including back issues of *Poetry* supplied by Harriet Monroe and books sent from New York City by Marianne Moore. Locally, he became absorbed in the Santa Fe Movement, which championed Indian culture (both songs and paintings).

Translations of songs from Indian languages and of Japanese poems, as well, the spare lyrics of both Emily Dickinson and the now virtually unknown Adelaide Crapsey, influenced the style of his first books, *The Immobile Wind* (1921) and *The Magpie's Shadow* (1922), both collected in *The Early Poems of Yvor Winters, 1920-28.* In "Hawk's Eyes," from *The Immobile Wind,* Winters used Indian-like perceptions to present not only the speaker's perception of the hawk but also the hawk's perception of the speaker. The second book, *The Magpie's Shadow,* consists of poems which record perceptions of the Indian's Southwest in lines such as "My door frame smells of leaves," from "Spring Rain." Some of the poems are closer to intuitions than sense perceptions, as he describes "fields" where he "did not pick/a flower." This precision of sense perception and intuition was part of Winters's poetic theory in the early 1920s. In *The Testament of a Stone, Being Notes on the Mechanics of the Poetic Image* (1924), he defined the poet as one who perceives "The poet moving in a world that is largely thought, so long as he regards it curiously and as a world, perceives certain specific things, as the walker in a field perceives a grassblade. These specific things are the material of the image, of art."

The Indian belief in the real physical presence of the spiritual world forms the background to Winters's only published short story, "The Brink of Darkness" (*Hound and Horn,* July/September

1932). As Winters wrote in a 1928 *transition* review of books of Indian songs, "all phenomena, personal or objective" have an "immediacy" to the Indian perceiver; and such phenomena provide his protagonist, a rural schoolteacher, with trials of courage and patience. Winters described the story as "a study of the hypothetical possibility of a hostile supernatural world, and of the effect on the perceptions of a consideration of this possibility." The story may be autobiographical, in that it reflects Winters's life after he left the Santa Fe sanatorium in 1921: the continued isolation in which he lived and worked for two years as a schoolteacher in Madrid and Los Cerilos, New Mexico, and the setting of the University of Colorado, which he entered as an undergraduate in 1923 (he earned B.A. and M.A. degrees in Romance languages in 1925) and the University of Idaho at Moscow, where he was a language instructor in 1925-1927. The story also points to one of the themes of his later poetry and essays—the fear of loss of control, a surrender to irrational forces. Winters's touchstone for this fear was Robert Bridges's "Low Barometer," a poem he regarded as one of the finest in the English language. In a review of Bridges's poems for a 1932 issue of *Hound and Horn,* Winters quoted the stanza which dramatizes this fear:

> On such a night, when air has loosed
> Its guardian grasp on blood and brain,
> Old terrors then of god or ghost
> Creep from their caves to life again.

On 22 June 1926 Winters married Janet Lewis, who had also been a member of the University of Chicago Poetry Club and had also gone to Santa Fe to recover from tuberculosis. They had two children, Joanna and Daniel. Janet Lewis went on to become an accomplished poet, as well as the author of a number of distinguished novels and short stories with both historical and contemporary settings. Like Winters, her early poems and one of her novels (*The Invasion,* 1932) were heavily influenced by Indian culture. Although Winters later turned to different themes and forms, he felt the presence of American Indian culture throughout his life. In his poem "To the Painter Polelonema," first collected in *The Proof* (1930), he celebrated the power of Indian art:

> You wring life
> from the rock
> from gold air
> violent with odors
> smoking wrath.

Thirty-five years after leaving Santa Fe he would still recite a Chippewa song to his Stanford students as he paused on the threshold of the classroom: "Whenever I pause/The noise of the village."

At the end of the 1920s Winters abandoned imagism and free verse and turned toward traditional English meter and rhyme. This shift began in the three years between his third and fourth books of poetry. In "April," from his third book, *The Bare Hills* (1927), the perceived details—of the "little goat" who "crops/new grass"—are almost exclusively the poem. But in "Simplex Munditiis," from *The Proof,* the goat now evokes the poet's extended comments on the humbling and difficult quality of learning from nature. In spring the goat "nips yellow blossoms/shaken loose from rain," and, as these falling "blossoms/drown the air with sorrow," man must approach the earth with humility and keep his mind clear "to face the sod beside his door,/to wound it as his own flesh." He must:

> bow his head and take
> with roughened hands
> sweet milk at dusk,
> the classic gift of earth.

Two related events may account for Winters's shift from sensory to moral perception in his poetry and critical creed: his arrival at Stanford as a graduate student in 1927, which led to his greater knowledge of traditional English verse, and his controversial friendship with Hart Crane, which lasted four years, from 1926 to 1930.

Winters's friendship with Crane was mainly by correspondence, although they did meet briefly at Christmas in 1927. Each man admired the other's work, although they were temperamentally quite different: Crane was flamboyant, public, a man of city life and riotous behavior; Winters was more steady, less outwardly dramatic, a man of California country life. Early in their correspondence, Winters praised Crane's work-in-progress, *The Bridge* (1930), and Crane reciprocated by recognizing the strengths of Winters's own multi-poem series, "The Fire Sequence" (first published in *The American Caravan* in 1927). Crane admired Winters's grasp of foreign languages, his erudition, and his discovery of the poems of the "unknown" Gerard Manley Hopkins, whose poems Winters loved to declaim. Winters admired the "steely tangible imagery that crystallizes an infinitude of meta-

Yvor Winters, 1928 (courtesy of Janet Lewis Winters)

physical and nervous implications" in Crane's early poetry, and even later, when criticizing *The Bridge*, he wrote that he was pointing out "flaws in a genius of a high order."

Well before Winters wrote negatively of *The Bridge* in a 1930 issue of *Poetry* their friendship was strained: Winters had begun, in 1927, to champion the idea that the poet had a special ethical relationship to society. Crane disagreed: "I write damned little because I am interested in recording certain sensations, very rigidly chosen, with an eye for what according to my taste and sum of prejudices seem suitable to—or intense enough—for verse." Winters's review of *The Bridge* marked the beginning of his mature critical position: perception, in itself, was too limiting. Winters's shift from sensory to moral perception represented a sharp critique of the imagist tendency to regard natural details as self-sufficient (a tendency Winters had himself shared). *The Bridge*, Winters concluded,

had lines "perceived with great precision"—"A cyclone threshes in the turbine crest,/Swooping in eagle feathers down your back"—but there is "no fluid experience bathing the perceptions and giving them a significant relation."

Crane could not accept the direction of Winters's comments. Crane's personal instability and his acceptance of "Whitmanian" inspiration and Emersonian "impulse" became for Winters a symbol of the failure of the poet's ethical role: fifteen years after Crane's suicide in 1932 Winters—in a controversial essay, "The Significance of 'The Bridge' by Hart Crane, or What are We to Think of Professor X?," published in *In Defense of Reason* (1947)—called Crane a "saint of the wrong religion," but favored his position over that of academics, like the prototypical Professor X who teaches Ralph Waldo Emerson and Walt Whitman but who does not accept their doctrines. Winters concluded that he would rather "emulate Odysseus

. . . and go down to the shadows for another hour's conversation with Crane on the subject of poetry" than "discuss poetry with Professor X."

Stanford University also provided Winters with a crucial context for his mature critical position. He began his doctoral studies in English in 1927, became an instructor the following year, and took his Ph.D. in 1934: he stayed at Stanford until his retirement in 1966, becoming an assistant professor in 1937, an associate professor in 1941, a full professor in 1949, and Albert Guerard Professor of Literature in 1961. His growing acquaintance with the large body of traditional English verse may have influenced—or at least paralleled—his shift to traditional meter and rhyme in his own poetry. The culmination of his research in the English lyric was an important essay published in the February, March, and April 1939 issues of *Poetry*, "The 16th Century Lyric in English," which upheld the "plain style" of George Gascoigne, Barnabe Googe, and George Turberville as a worthy competitor to the ornate Petrarchan style of Philip Sidney and Edmund Spenser.

In the 1930s Winters began scholarly work in earnest, and the next twenty years were marked by his polemical critical studies of poetry and the American novel. A crucial event early in the 1930s established the tone and direction of Winters's career at Stanford. This event, in the national news as a scandal, was the David Lamson case.

Winters joined—and was a principal figure in—a defense committee formed to help clear David Lamson, a Stanford University Press employee who had been convicted, on the basis of circumstantial evidence and a dubious judicial atmosphere, of murdering his wife; Lamson was eventually released after spending three years behind bars, including a year on death row at San Quentin, awaiting execution. Although Winters was throughout his life an undramatic but serious supporter of such organizations as the ACLU and NAACP and an opponent of the Japanese-American concentration camps in the 1940s, the Lamson case was the only social issue on which his public involvement was sustained. The theme of Winters's critical philosophy in general—the arrogance of the academic world, or, more precisely, its pretensions to absolute knowledge, and the fragile hold of reason in human affairs—was the basis for Winters's work on this case: out of this experience came an essay in the *New Republic*, an extended pamphlet based on the appeal, and three powerful poems. The reputation of Winters as a sharp-tongued absolutist was no doubt strengthened by such remarks

as this one from the *New Republic* essay: "Lamson . . . was the victim of an accident and of the irreducible ugliness and irrationality of the human mind." The poems on the Lamson case—"To Edwin MacKenzie," "To a Woman on her Defense of her Brother Unjustly Convicted of Murder," and "To David Lamson," all published in 1940—are ultimately optimistic. Three individuals—Lamson's lawyer, the condemned man, and his sister—stand for the triumph of the human spirit over the prejudices of a legal machine and the follies of intellectuals who became (in the words of the third poem) "county politicians' tools." Winters's commitment to this struggle was fierce. Stanford colleagues remembered that even twenty years later he would rehearse the details of the Lamson defense and actually restage the accident which caused Mrs. Lamson's death.

After the Lamson case Winters always remained a strong advocate of rational judgment in matters of life and art—a position he advocated in his critical works of the late 1930s and early 1940s. Extensive examinations of American literature, past and present, these three books were eventually collected in one volume with the revealing title of *In Defense of Reason* (1947). In the first, *Primitivism and Decadence* (1937), Winters continued his earlier studies of imagism and free verse; yet, despite his thorough and to a certain extent sympathetic explication of contemporary experimentation, he concluded that "experimental meter loses the rational frame which alone gives its variations the precision of true perception." The third, *The Anatomy of Nonsense* (1943), is also a critique of contemporary poetry, concentrating on what he regarded as the morally limiting ideas of Wallace Stevens, T. S. Eliot, and John Crowe Ransom. The second book, *Maule's Curse* (1938), surveyed earlier great writers of the American tradition—Nathaniel Hawthorne, James Fenimore Cooper, Herman Melville, Edgar Allan Poe, Emily Dickinson, and Henry James—especially attacking what he saw as their adherence to the romantic principle of taking impulse or emotion as the central guide to human activity.

The climax of Winters's career as a poet came with his *Collected Poems* (1952; revised edition, 1960), on the basis of which he was granted the Bollingen Prize for Poetry in 1961, one of several awards he won for his poetry. The revised *Collected Poems*, Winters wrote in 1960, "represents . . . a kind of definition by example of the style which I have been trying to achieve for a matter of thirty years." An important aspect of this style is Winters's

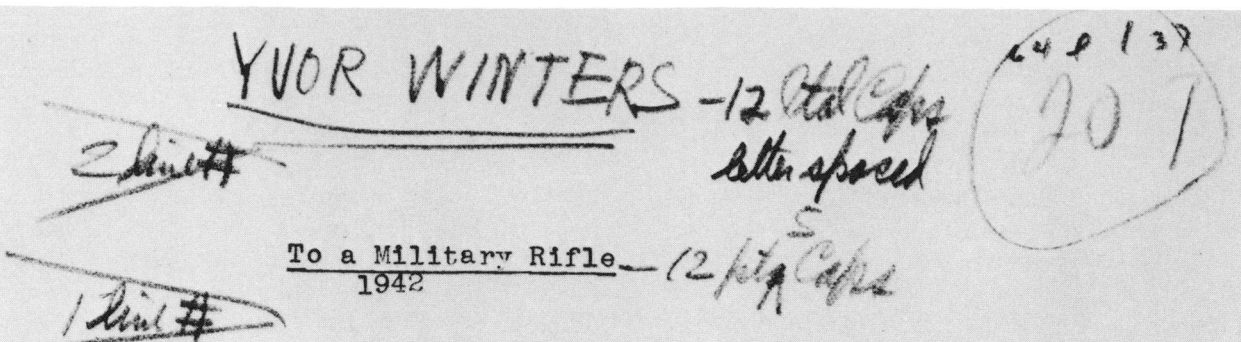

To a Military Rifle
1942

The times come round again;
The private life is small;
And individual men
Are counted not at all.
Now life is general,
And the bewildered Muse,
Thinking what she has done,
Confronts the daily news.

Blunt emblem, you have won:
With carven stock unbroke,
With core of steel, with crash
Of mass, and fading smoke;
Your fire leaves little ash;
Your balance on the arm
Points whither you intend;
Your bolt is smooth with charm.
When other concepts end,
This concept, hard and pure,
Shapes every mind therefor.
The time is yours, be sure,
Old Hammerheel of War.

I cannot write your praise
When young men go to die;
Nor yet regret the ways
That ended with this hour.
The hour has come. And I,
Who alter nothing, pray
That men, surviving you,
May learn to do and say
The difficult and true,
True shape of death and power.

Yvor Winters.

Setting copy for a poem published in New Poems 1943, *edited by Oscar Williams (by permission of Janet Lewis Winters; courtesy of Princeton University Library)*

skillful handling of metrics, a subject he discusses in "The Audible Reading of Poetry," an important essay in his fourth book of criticism, *The Function of Criticism* (1957). The range of subject matter in his poems is wide; besides occasional and very public poems—on the Lamson case, university events, life during the war—there are epigrams in the plain style, including a biting two-line poem to "Saint Herman" Melville, asking salvation "from the worms who have infested thee," and a number of California poems, where precise description of the landscape moves toward moral statement. In "To the Holy Spirit," for example, a visitor to an old graveyard describes "stones/Pushed here and there," commenting that they are "the seat/Of nothing" and concluding that beneath them are:

Relics of lonely men,
Brutal and aimless, then,
As now, irregular.

Perhaps "On Teaching the Young" best sums up his experience of teaching and writing poetry, which he saw as a demanding and severe craft, with its only reward—a "cold certitude" sustained by traditional poets for centuries. This poem epitomizes his theoretical statements about poetry as well. "A poem," he wrote in a foreword to *In Defense of Reason*, "is a statement in words about a human experience." While many may agree with such a formulation, his definition of the poet in *Primitivism and Decadence* is characteristically Wintersian—morally evaluative, conscious of tradition: "the poet, in striving toward an ideal of poetic form at which he has arrived through the study of other poets, is actually striving to perfect a moral attitude toward that range of experience of which he is aware."

The final books of Winters's career, *Forms of Discovery* (1967), an integrated collection of essays "on the forms of the short poem in English," and *Quest for Reality* (1969, which he edited with Kenneth Fields), an anthology of short poems, were related acts of scholarship and criticism. Both books celebrate what Winters regarded as the two great eras of English poetry—the sixteenth and seventeenth centuries (from Wyatt to Dryden) and the late-nineteenth and twentieth centuries. This anthology contains numerous surprises (and "omissions") to most readers trained in the canon of *The Norton Anthology of English Literature*, for Winters and Fields excluded all eighteenth-century, romantic, and Victorian poets, with only one exception (Charles Churchill). They included, from

England, Thomas Hardy, Robert Bridges, T. Sturge Moore, Elizabeth Daryush, and Thom Gunn, and, from the United States, such relatively unknown poets as Jones Very and Frederick Tuckerman in the nineteenth century, and Adelaide Crapsey, Mina Loy, Janet Lewis, J. V. Cunningham, and Edgar Bowers from the twentieth century. He accepted some of the poems of Emily Dickinson and Wallace Stevens with reservations, because of their tendency to rely on undeveloped sensuous detail. There are no poems by T. S. Eliot, Ezra Pound, Hart Crane, or Marianne Moore. *Forms of Discovery* defends these choices. The reason for Winters's omission of the bulk of the established eighteenth- and nineteenth-century poets has been one of the most controversial features of his career. He argued that the vast majority of these poets he excluded were imbued with a romantic aesthetic which was based on the faulty assumption that since all ideas came from sense perceptions, then all ideas in poetry could be expressed through sense perceptions. The early Winters may have accepted this assumption, but not the later. Only in the "controlled association" of such powerful poems as Stevens's "Sunday Morning" or the "post-symbolist" method of Emily Dickinson did he find sense perception and concept successfully joined.

Winters had reasonable success in retrieving unknown poets and poems. His preference for serious and direct plain-style poems is evident in his championing of Philip Pain, an Anglo-American of the seventeenth century whose lyric "Scarce do I pass a day . . . ," from his only book, *Daily Meditations* (1668), received little attention until Winters, in his lectures and in *Forms of Discovery*, argued for its perfect insight into the "human predicament, whether Christian or other."

Whatever notoriety his opinions earned him in nearly fifty years of writing, Winters had a notable career as poet, critic, and teacher. In *The Armed Vision* (1948) Stanley Edgar Hyman called him an "excessively irritating and bad critic of some importance." But others have gone beyond even Winters's self-evaluation in "Two Old Fashioned Songs" (1957-1958), the last poems in the 1960 *Collected Poems*: "What I did was small but good." Allen Tate, in a *New Republic* review (2 March 1953) of the first *Collected Poems*, gave Winters high praise: "among American poets who appeared soon after the first war he is, Crane being dead, the master." Since part of Winters's legacy has been rebellion against the dictates of critical and poetic fashion, his admirers may yet secure him a place in the company of his better-known peers. In terms of his critical work, R. P. Blackmur's remarks in *Poetry* (November 1940) set a respectful but circumspect tone: Winters's "intimacy with the matter-and-form of poetry and imaginative prose . . . is genuine and complete and stirring," but the rigor of his principles and his drive for order, Blackmur concluded, disturbs many readers.

Although Winters discouraged would-be biographers, a few revealing reminiscences have appeared, such as David Levin's essay in the summer 1978 issue of the *Virginia Quarterly Review* as well as a special issue of the *Southern Review* devoted to his contributions to poetry and criticism. A number of his students who have had successful writing careers have attested to the friendly and demanding nature of his teaching; poet Thom Gunn remembered him as speaking "of poetry with a peculiar intimacy and dedication for the art about which he had more to tell than anyone else." He may also be remembered as a special kind of new critic, one who believed the text was integral, but who also argued that understanding its context was morally and philosophically necessary.

Bibliographies:

Kenneth A. Lohf and Eugene P. Sheehy, *Yvor Winters: A Bibliography* (Denver: Alan Swallow, 1959);

Grosvenor Powell, *Yvor Winters: An Annotated Bibliography, 1919-1982* (Metuchen, N.J.: Scarecrow Press, 1983).

References:

Charles L. Crow, *Janet Lewis,* Western Writers Series (Boise: Boise State University, 1980);

Kenneth Fields, "The Free Verse of Yvor Winters and William Carlos Williams," *Southern Review,* new series 3 (Summer 1967): 764-775;

Elizabeth Isaacs, *An Introduction to the Poetry of Yvor Winters* (Chicago: Swallow Press, 1981);

David Levin, "Yvor Winters at Stanford," *Virginia Quarterly Review,* 54 (Summer 1978): 454-473;

Thomas Parkinson, *Hart Crane and Yvor Winters: Their Literary Correspondence* (Berkeley: University of California Press, 1978);

Grosvenor Powell, *Language as Being in the Poetry of Yvor Winters* (Baton Rouge: Louisiana State University Press, 1980);

Southern Review, Yvor Winters Issue, new series 17 (October 1981).

Papers:

Winters destroyed most of the correspondence in his possession; those letters in private or public collections (such as Stanford University and Princeton University) may not, according to the provisions of Winters's will, be quoted until 1993 (twenty-five years after his death).

Books for Further Reading

Ackroyd, Peter. *Notes for a New Culture: An Essay on Modernism.* New York: Barnes & Noble, 1976.

Aiken, Conrad. *A Reviewer's ABC: Collected Criticism of Conrad Aiken from 1916 to the Present.* New York: Meridian Books, 1958.

Aiken. *Scepticisms: Notes on Contemporary Poetry.* New York: Knopf, 1919.

Aiken. *Ushant: An Essay.* New York: Duell, Sloan & Pearce/Boston: Little, Brown, 1952.

Aldington, Richard. *Life for life's Sake: A Book of Reminiscences.* New York: Viking, 1941.

Alvarez, A. *The Shaping Spirit: Studies in Modern English and American Poets.* London: Chatto & Windus, 1958.

Anderson, Margaret. *My Thirty Years' War: the Autobiography: Beginnings and Battles to 1930.* New York: Covici-Friede, 1930.

Antheil, George. *Bad Boy of Music.* Garden City: Doubleday, Doran, 1945.

Baker, Houston A., Jr. *Blues, Ideology, and Afro-American Literature: A Vernacular Theory.* Chicago: University of Chicago Press, 1984.

Barnard, Mary. *Assault on Mount Helicon: A Literary Memoir.* Berkeley: University of California Press, 1984.

Beach, Sylvia. *Shakespeare and Company.* New York: Harcourt, Brace, 1959.

Berman, Marshall. *All That is Solid Melts into Air: The Experience of Modernity.* New York: Simon & Schuster, 1982.

Bigsby, C. W. E., ed. *The Black American Writer,* volume 2, *Poetry and Drama.* De Land, Fla.: Everett Edwards, 1969.

Blackmur, R. P. *Anni Mirabiles, 1921-1925: Reason in the Madness of Letters.* Washington, D.C.: Library of Congress, 1956.

Blackmur. *Language as Gesture: Essays in Poetry.* New York: Harcourt, Brace, 1952.

Bogan, Louise. *Achievement in American Poetry, 1900-1950.* Chicago: Regnery, 1951.

Bogan. *Selected Criticism: Prose, Poetry.* New York: Noonday, 1955.

Bornstein, George. *Transformations of Romanticism in Yeats, Eliot and Stevens.* Chicago: Chicago University Press, 1976.

Borroff, Marie. *Language and the Poet: Verbal Artistry in Frost, Stevens, and Moore.* Chicago: University of Chicago Press, 1979.

Bradbury, Malcolm, and James McFarlane, eds. *Modernism*. Harmondsworth, U.K.: Penguin, 1976.

Brooks, Cleanth. *Modern Poetry and the Tradition*. Chapel Hill: University of North Carolina Press, 1939.

Brooks, Gladys. *If Strangers Meet: A Memory*. New York: Harcourt, Brace & World, 1967.

Brooks, Van Wyck. *Scenes and Portraits: Memories of Childhood and Youth*. New York: Dutton, 1954.

Bruns, Gerald L. *Modern Poetry and the Idea of Language. A Critical and Historical Study*. New Haven: Yale University Press, 1974.

Bryher (Winifred Ellerman). *The Heart to Artemis: A Writer's Memoirs*. New York: Harcourt, Brace & World, 1962.

Burke, Kenneth. *Counterstatement*. Berkeley: University of California Press, 1968.

Butler, Christopher. *After the Wake: An Essay on the Contemporary Avant-garde*. Oxford & New York: Oxford University Press, 1980.

Butterfield, R. W., ed. *Modern American Poetry*. Totowa, N.J.: Barnes & Noble, 1984.

Cambon, Glauco. *The Inclusive Flame: Studies in Modern American Poetry*. Bloomington: Indiana University Press, 1963.

Christ, Carol T. *Victorian & Modern Poetics*. Chicago: University of Chicago Press, 1984.

Coffman, Stanley K., Jr. *Imagism: A Chapter for the History of Modern Poetry*. Norman: University of Oklahoma Press, 1951.

Cook, Albert. *Prisms: Studies in Modern Literature*. Bloomington: Indiana University Press, 1967.

Cork, Richard. *Vorticism and Abstract Art in the First Machine Age*, 2 volumes. Berkeley: University of California Press, 1976.

Cowan, Louise. *The Fugitive Group: A Literary History*. Baton Rouge: Louisiana State University Press, 1959.

Cowley, Malcolm. *The Dream of the Golden Mountains: Remembering the 1930s*. New York: Viking, 1980.

Cowley. *Exile's Return: A Literary Odyssey of the 1920's*, revised edition. New York: Viking, 1951.

Cowley, ed. *Writers at Work: The Paris Review Interviews*, series 1. New York: Viking, 1958.

Crosby, Caresse. *The Passionate Years*. New York: Dial, 1953.

Cunard, Nancy. *These Were the Hours: Memories of My Hours Press, Réanville and Paris, 1928-1931*, edited by Hugh Ford. Carbondale & Edwardsville: Southern Illinois University Press, 1969.

Davenport, Guy. *The Geography of the Imagination: Forty Essays*. San Francisco: North Point Press, 1981.

Davidson, Donald, ed. *Fugitives: An Anthology of Verse*. New York: Harcourt, Brace, 1928.

Davie, Donald. *The Poet in the Imaginary Museum. Essays of Two Decades*. Manchester: Carcanet Press, 1977.

Dembo, L. S. *Conceptions of Reality in Modern American Poetry*. Berkeley: University of California Press, 1966.

Deutsch, Babette. *Poetry in our Time: A Critical Survey of Poetry in the English-Speaking World 1900 to 1960*, revised and enlarged edition. Garden City: Doubleday, 1963.

Donoghue, Denis. *Connoisseurs of Chaos: Ideas of Order in Modern American Poetry*. New York: Macmillan, 1965.

Donoghue. *Seven American Poets from MacLeish to Nemerov. An Introduction*. Minneapolis: University of Minnesota Press, 1975.

Duffey, Bernard. *The Chicago Renaissance in American Letters: A Critical History*. East Lansing: Michigan State College Press, 1954.

Ehrenpreis, Irwin, ed. *American Poetry*. Stratford-Upon-Avon Studies, no. 7. London: Arnold, 1973.

Eliot, T. S. *The Sacred Wood: Essays on Poetry and Criticism*. London: Methuen, 1920.

Eliot. *Selected Essays, 1917-1932*. London: Faber & Faber, 1932.

Ellman, Richard, and Charles Feidelson, Jr., eds. *The Modern Tradition: Backgrounds of Modern Literature*. New York: Oxford University Press, 1965.

Feder, Lillian. *Ancient Myth in Modern Poetry*. Princeton: Princeton University Press, 1971.

Fender, Stephen. *The American Long Poem: An Annotated Selection*. London: Arnold, 1977.

Fitch, Noel Riley. *Sylvia Beach and the Lost Generation: A History of Literary Paris in the Twenties and Thirties*. New York: Norton, 1983.

Ford, Hugh. *Published in Paris: American and British Writers, Printers, and Publishers in Paris, 1920-1939*. New York: Macmillan, 1975.

Ford, ed. *The Left Bank Revisited. Selections from the Paris Tribune, 1917-1934*. University Park & London: Pennsylvania State University Press, 1972.

Forrest-Thomson, Veronica. *Poetic Artifice: A Theory of Twentieth-Century Poetry*. Manchester: Manchester University Press, 1978.

Foster, Richard. *The New Romantics: A Reappraisal of the New Criticism*. Bloomington: Indiana University Press, 1962.

Fowlie, Wallace. *The Clown's Grail: a Study of Love in its Literary Expression*. London: Dobson, 1948; republished as *Love in Literature: Studies in Symbolic Expression*. Bloomington: Indiana University Press, 1965.

Frank, Joseph. *The Widening Gyre: Crisis and Mastery in Modern Literature*. New Brunswick: Rutgers University Press, 1963.

Frankenberg, Lloyd. *Pleasure Dome: On Reading Modern Poetry*. Boston: Houghton Mifflin, 1949.

Fredman, Stephen. *Poet's Prose: The Crisis in American Verse*. Cambridge: Cambridge University Press, 1983.

Frye, Northrop. *The Modern Century*. Toronto: Oxford University Press, 1967.

Fussell, Edwin. *Lucifer in Harness: American Meter, Metaphor and Diction.* Princeton: Princeton University Press, 1973.

Gaines, James R. *Wit's End: Days and Nights of the Algonquin Round Table.* New York & London: Harcourt Brace Jovanovich, 1977.

Gefin, Laszlo K. *Ideogram: History of a Poetic Method.* Austin: University of Texas Press, 1982.

Gould, Jean. *American Women Poets: Pioneers of Modern Poetry.* New York: Dodd, Mead, 1980.

Gould. *Modern American Women Poets.* New York: Dodd, Mead, 1984.

Greenbaum, Leonard. *The Hound and Horn: The History of a Literary Quarterly.* The Hague: Mouton, 1966.

Gregory, Horace, and Marya Zaturenska. *A History of American Poetry, 1900-1940.* New York: Harcourt, Brace, 1946.

Gross, Harvey, ed. *Sound and Form in Modern Poetry: A Study of Prosody from Thomas Hardy to Robert Lowell.* Ann Arbor: University of Michigan Press, 1964.

Guggenheim, Peggy. *Out of this Century: Confessions of an Art Addict.* New York: Universe Books, 1979.

Hall, Donald. *Remembering Poets: Reminiscences and Opinions.* New York, Hagerstown, San Francisco & London: Harper & Row, 1978.

Halpert, Stephen, and Richard Johns. *A Return to Pagany: The History, Correspondence, and Selections from a Little Magazine 1929-1932.* Boston: Beacon Press, 1969.

Hamburger, Michael. *The Truth of Poetry: Tensions in Modern Poetry from Baudelaire to the 1960s.* New York: Harcourt, Brace & World, 1970.

Hamovitch, Mitzi Berger, ed. *The Hound & Horn Letters.* Athens: University of Georgia Press, 1982.

Harriman, Margaret. *The Vicious Circle: the Story of the Algonquin Round Table.* New York: Rinehart, 1951.

Hartman, Charles O. *Free Verse: An Essay on Prosody.* Princeton: Princeton University Press, 1980.

Hoffman, Frederick J. *The Twenties: American Writing in the Postwar Decade,* revised edition. New York: Collier, 1962.

Hoffman, Charles Allen, and Carolyn F. Ulrich. *The Little Magazine: A History and a Bibliography.* Princeton: Princeton University Press, 1946.

Hollander, John, ed. *Modern Poetry: Essays in Criticism.* London, Oxford & New York: Oxford University Press, 1968.

Huggins, Nathan. *Harlem Renaissance.* New York: Oxford University Press, 1971.

Hughes, Glenn. *Imagism and the Imagists: A Study in Modern Poetry.* Stanford: Stanford University Press, 1931.

Isaacs, J. *The Background of Modern Poetry.* London: Bell, 1951.

Jackson, Blyden, and Louis Rubin. *Black Poetry in America: Two Essays in Historical Interpretation.* Baton Rouge: Louisiana State University Press, 1974.

Janssens, G. A. M. *The American Literary Review: A Critical History, 1920-1950.* The Hague: Mouton, 1968.

Jarrell, Randall. *Poetry and the Age.* New York: Knopf, 1953.

Jarrell. *The Third Book of Criticism.* New York: Farrar, Straus & Giroux, 1969.

Johnson, Carol. *The Disappearance of Literature.* Amsterdam: Rodopi, 1980.

Johnson, W. R. *The Idea of Lyric: Lyric Modes in Ancient and Modern Poetry.* Berkeley: University of California Press, 1982.

Jones, Peter, ed. *Imagist Poetry.* Harmondsworth, U.K.: Penguin, 1972.

Joost, Nicholas. *Scofield Thayer and The Dial: An Illustrated History.* Carbondale & Edwardsville: Southern Illinois University Press, 1964.

Josephson, Matthew. *Life Among The Surrealists. A Memoir.* New York: Holt, Rinehart & Winston, 1962.

Juhasz, Suzanne. *Metaphor and the Poetry of Williams, Pound, and Stevens.* Lewisburg: Bucknell University Press, 1974.

Kenner, Hugh. *Gnomon: Essays on Contemporary Literature.* New York: McDowell Obolensky, 1958.

Kenner. *A Homemade World: The American Modernist Writers.* New York: Knopf, 1974.

Kenner. *The Pound Era.* Berkeley: University of California Press, 1971.

Kermode, Frank. *Romantic Image.* London: Routledge & Kegan Paul, 1957.

Kramer, Dale. *Chicago Renaissance: the Literary Life in the Midwest, 1900-1930.* New York: Appleton-Century, 1966.

Kreymborg, Alfred. *Our Singing Strength: An Outline of American Poetry.* New York: Coward-McCann, 1929.

Kreymborg. *Troubadour: An Autobiography.* New York: Boni & Liveright, 1925.

Krieger, Murray. *The New Apologists for Poetry.* Bloomington: Indiana University Press, 1963.

Kronick, Joseph G. *American Poetics of History: From Emerson to the Moderns.* Baton Rouge: Louisiana State University Press, 1984.

Langbaum, Robert. *The Mysteries of Identity: A Theme in Modern Literature.* New York: Oxford University Press, 1977.

Langbaum. *The Poetry of Experience: The Dramatic Monologue in Modern Literary Tradition.* New York: Random House, 1957.

Langford, Richard E., and William E. Taylor, eds. *The Twenties: Poetry and Prose. 20 Critical Essays.* De Land, Fla.: Everett Edwards, 1966.

Locke, Alain. *Four Negro Poets.* New York: Simon & Schuster, 1927.

Loeb, Harold. *The Way It Was*. New York: Criterion, 1959.

Lowell, Amy. *Tendencies in Modern American Poetry*. New York: Macmillan, 1917.

Lutyens, David Bulwer. *The Creative Encounter*. London: Secker & Warburg, 1960.

MacLeish, Archibald. *Poetry and Experience*. Boston: Houghton Mifflin, 1960.

Mariani, Paul. *A Usable Past: Essays on Modern and Contemporary Poetry*. Amherst: University of Massachusetts Press, 1984.

Martz, Louis L. *The Poem of the Mind: Essays on Poetry, English and American*. New York: Oxford University Press, 1966.

Mazzaro, Jerome, ed. *Modern American Poetry: Essays in Criticism*. New York: McKay, 1970.

McAlmon, Robert. *Being Geniuses Together 1920-1930*, revised edition, with additional material by Kay Boyle. Garden City: Doubleday, 1968.

McMillan, Dougald. *Transition: The History of a Literary Era, 1927-1938*. New York: Braziller, 1976.

Mellow, James R. *Charmed Circle: Gertrude Stein & Company*. New York & Washington, D.C.: Praeger, 1974.

Miles, Josephine. *The Primary Language of Poetry in the 1940s*, University of California Publications in English, volume 19, no. 3. Berkeley: University of California Press, 1951.

Miller, James E., Jr. *The American Quest for a Supreme Fiction: Whitman's Legacy in the Personal Epic*. Chicago: University of Chicago Press, 1979.

Miller, J. Hillis. *Poets of Reality: Six Twentieth-Century Writers*. Cambridge: Harvard University Press, 1965.

Monroe, Harriet. *A Poet's Life: Seventy Years in a Changing World*. New York: Macmillan, 1938.

Moore, Marianne. *Predilections*. New York: Viking, 1955.

Morgan, A. E. *The Beginnings of Modern American Poetry*. London: Longmans, Green, 1946.

O'Connor, William Van. *Sense and Sensibility in Modern Poetry*. Chicago: Chicago University Press, 1948.

Paz, Octavio. *The Bow and the Lyre*, translated by Ruth L. C. Simms. Austin: University of Texas Press, 1973.

Paz. *Children of the Mire; Modern Poetry from Romanticism to the Avant-Garde*, translated by Rachel Phillips. Cambridge: Harvard University Press, 1974.

Pearce, Roy Harvey. *The Continuity of American Poetry*. Princeton: Princeton University Press, 1961.

Perkins, David. *A History of Modern Poetry from the 1890's to the High Modernist Mode*. Cambridge: Harvard University Press, 1976.

Perloff, Marjorie. *The Poetics of Indeterminacy: Rimbaud to Cage*. Princeton: Princeton University Press, 1981.

Pinsky, Robert. *The Situation of Poetry: Contemporary Poetry and its Tradition.* Princeton: Princeton University Press, 1976.

Plimpton, George, ed. *Writers at Work: The Paris Review Interviews,* series 2-5. New York: Viking, 1963-1981.

Poggioli, Renato. *The Theory of the Avant-Garde,* translated by Gerald Fitzgerald. Cambridge: Harvard University Press, 1968.

Pound, Ezra. *Literary Essays of Ezra Pound,* edited, with an introduction, by T. S. Eliot. London: Faber & Faber, 1954.

Pound. *Make It New: Essays.* London: Faber & Faber, 1934.

Pound. *Selected Prose, 1909-1965,* edited by William Cookson. New York: New Directions, 1973.

Pratt, William, ed. *The Fugitive Poets; Modern Southern Poetry in Perspective.* New York: Dutton, 1965.

Pratt, ed. *The Imagist Poem: Modern Poetry in Miniature.* New York: Dutton, 1963.

Press, John. *The Chequer'd Shade. Reflections on Obscurity in Poetry.* London: Oxford University Press, 1958.

Pritchard, William H. *Lives of the Modern Poets.* New York: Oxford University Press, 1980.

Putnam, Samuel. *Paris Was Our Mistress.* New York: Viking, 1947.

Quinn, Sister M. Bernetta. *The Metamorphic Tradition in Modern Poetry: Essays on the Work of Ezra Pound, Wallace Stevens, William Carlos Williams, T. S. Eliot, Hart Crane, Randall Jarrell and William Butler Yeats.* New Brunswick: Rutgers University Press, 1955.

Raiziss, Sona. *The Metaphysical Passion: Seven Modern American Poets and the Seventeenth Century Tradition.* Philadelphia: University of Pennsylvania Press, 1952.

Rajan, B., ed. *Modern American Poetry,* Focus 5. London: Dobson, 1950.

Ransom, John Crowe. *Beating the Bushes; Selected Essays, 1941-1970.* New York: New Directions, 1972.

Ransom. *The New Criticism.* Norfolk, Conn.: New Directions, 1941.

Ransom. *The World's Body,* revised edition. Baton Rouge: Louisiana State University Press, 1968.

Ransom, Allen Tate, Donald Davidson, and others. *I'll Take My Stand: The South and the Agrarian Tradition, By Twelve Southerners.* New York & London: Harper, 1930.

Revell, Peter. *Quest in Modern American Poetry.* Totowa, N.J.: Barnes & Noble, 1981.

Rexroth, Kenneth. *American Poetry in the Twentieth Century.* New York: Herder & Herder, 1971.

Rosenfeld, Paul. *Port of New York: Essays on Fourteen American Moderns.* New York: Harcourt, Brace, 1924.

Rosenthal, M. L. *The Modern Poets: A Critical Introduction.* New York: Oxford University Press, 1960.

Rubin, Louis D. *The Wary Fugitives: Four Poets and the South.* Baton Rouge: Louisiana State University Press, 1978.

Schwartz, Delmore. *Selected Essays,* edited by Donald A. Dike and David H. Zucker. Chicago: University of Chicago Press, 1970.

Scully, James, ed. *Modern Poetics.* New York: McGraw-Hill, 1965.

Sergeant, Howard. *Tradition in the Making of Modern Poetry,* volume 1. London: Britannicus Liber, 1951.

Shapiro, Karl. *In Defense of Ignorance.* New York: Random House, 1960.

Shapiro, ed. *Prose Keys to Modern Poetry.* New York & London: Harper & Row, 1962.

Smoller, Sanford. *Adrift Among Geniuses: Robert McAlmon, Writer and Publisher of the Twenties.* University Park & London: Pennsylvania State University Press, 1975.

Spears, Monroe K. *Dionysus and the City: Modernism in Twentieth-Century Poetry.* New York: Oxford University Press, 1970.

Stanford, Donald E. *Revolution and Convention in Modern Poetry: Studies in Ezra Pound, T. S. Eliot, Wallace Stevens, Edwin Arlington Robinson and Yvor Winters.* Newark: University of Delaware Press, 1983.

Stauffer, Donald. *A Short History of American Poetry.* New York: Dutton, 1974.

Stepanchev, Stephen. *American Poetry Since 1945: A Critical Survey.* New York: Harper & Row, 1965.

Stewart, John L. *The Burden of Time: The Fugitives and Agrarians; the Nashville Groups of the 1920's and 1930's, and the Writing of John Crowe Ransom, Allen Tate, and Robert Penn Warren.* Princeton: Princeton University Press, 1965.

Sutton, Walter. *American Free Verse: The Modern Revolution of Poetry.* New York: New Directions, 1973.

Tashjian, Dickran. *Skyscraper Primitives: Dada and the American Avant-Garde, 1920-1925.* Middletown, Conn.: Wesleyan University Press, 1975.

Tate, Allen. *Essays of Four Decades.* Chicago: Swallow, 1968.

Tate. *The Man of Letters in the Modern World, Selected Essays: 1928-1955.* New York: Meridian/London: Thames & Hudson, 1955.

Tate. *Memoirs and Opinions, 1926-1974.* Chicago: Swallow, 1975.

Tate. *Reactionary Essays on Poetry and Ideas.* New York & London: Scribners, 1936.

Tate. *Reason in Madness: Critical Essays.* New York: Putnam's, 1941.

Taylor, Carole A. *A Poetics of Seeing: The Implications of Visual Form in Modern Poetry.* New York & London: Garland, 1985.

Turner, Darwin. *In a Minor Chord: Three Afro-American Writers and Their Search for Identity.* Carbondale & Edwardsville: Southern Illinois University Press, 1971.

Untermeyer, Louis. *American Poetry Since 1900.* New York: Holt, 1923.

Van Doren, Mark. *Autobiography.* New York: Harcourt, Brace, 1958.

Vendler, Helen. *Part of Nature, Part of Us: Modern American Poets.* Cambridge: Harvard University Press, 1979.

Vickery, John. *The Literary Impact of the Golden Bough.* Princeton: Princeton University Press, 1973.

Waggoner, Hyatt H. *American Poets, from the Puritans to the Present.* Boston: Houghton Mifflin, 1968.

Waggoner. *The Heel of Elohim: Science and Values in Modern American Poetry.* Norman: University of Oklahoma Press, 1950.

Wald, Alan M. *The Revolutionary Imagination: The Poetry and Politics of John Wheelwright and Sherry Mangan.* Chapel Hill: University of North Carolina Press, 1983.

Warren, Robert Penn. *A Plea in Mitigation: Modern Poetry and the End of an Era.* Macon, Ga.: Wesleyan College, 1966.

Weatherhead, A. Kingsley. *The Edge of the Image: Marianne Moore, William Carlos Williams, and Some Other Poets.* Seattle: University of Washington Press, 1967.

Weaver, Mike. *William Carlos Williams: The American Background.* Cambridge: Cambridge University Press, 1971.

Wees, William C. *Vorticism and the English Avant-Garde.* Toronto: University of Toronto Press, 1972.

Welsh, Andrew. *Roots of Lyric: Primitive Poetry and Modern Poetics.* Princeton: Princeton University Press, 1978.

Wertheim, Arthur Frank. *The New York Little Renaissance: Iconoclasm, Modernism, and Nationalism in American Culture, 1908-1917.* New York: New York University Press, 1976.

Wheelwright, Philip. *Metaphor & Reality.* Bloomington: Indiana University Press, 1962.

Wickes, George. *Americans in Paris.* Garden City: Doubleday, 1969.

Williams, Ellen. *Harriet Monroe and the Poetry Renaissance: The First Ten Years of* Poetry *1912-1922.* Urbana: University of Illinois Press, 1977.

Williams, Jonathan. *The Magpie's Bagpipe. Selected Essays.* San Francisco: North Point Press, 1982.

Williams, William Carlos. *The Autobiography of William Carlos Williams.* New York: Random House, 1951.

Williams. *The Embodiment of Knowledge,* edited by Ron Loewinson. New York: New Directions, 1974.

Williams. *Selected Essays.* New York: Random House, 1954.

Wilson, Edmund. *Axel's Castle: A Study in the Imaginative Literature of 1870-1930.* New York & London: Scribners, 1931.

Winters, Yvor. *In Defense of Reason.* Denver: University of Denver Press, 1947.

Winters. *On Modern Poets.* Cleveland & New York: Meridian/World, 1959.

Wolff, Geoffrey. *Black Sun: The Brief Transit and Violent Eclipse of Harry Crosby.* New York: Random House, 1976.

Wright, George T. *The Poet in the Poem: The Personae of Eliot, Yeats, and Pound.* Berkeley: University of California Press, 1960.

Contributors

George F. Butterick ....University of Connecticut
Lisa Pater Faranda ....Pennsylvania State University, Berks Campus
Robert M. Farnsworth ....University of Missouri, Kansas City
Donald W. Faulkner ....Yale University
Suzanne Ferguson...Wayne State University
Philip L. Gerber ....State University of New York College at Brockport
John Griffith.. University of Washington
Minrose C. Gwin ....Virginia Polytechnic Institute and State University
John Haffenden...University of Sheffield
John A. Harrison.. University of Arkansas
Paula L. Hart.. University of British Columbia
Marie Hénault .... Saint Michael's College
Michael Hennessy ....Southwest Texas State University
Constance Hunting...University of Maine
Ross Labrie .... University of British Columbia
J. R. LeMaster ....Baylor University
Vernon H. Liang...New York, New York
Thomas E. Lucas.. Seton Hall University
Shirley Lumpkin...Marshall University
Joanne McCarthy...Tacoma Community College
Joseph Miller ....Vancouver, British Columbia
R. Baxter Miller .... University of Tennessee
Robert H. O'Connor .... North Dakota State University
Jenny Penberthy...University of Cape Town
Tony N. Redd ....The Citadel
Peter Revell...Westfield College, London
Joel Roache ....University of Maryland, Eastern Shore
Karen L. Rood...Columbia, South Carolina
Nicki Sahlin.. Dean Junior College
Larry R. Smith.........................Firelands College, Bowling Green State University
Victor Strandberg ....Duke University
Craig Tapping.. University of British Columbia
Alberta Turner.. Cleveland State University
Robert L. Welker.................................... University of Alabama in Huntsville
Joyce Wexler...Loyola University
Joseph Wilson .... Anna Maria College
Don Wood .... State University of New York at Buffalo
Melody M. Zajdel...Montana State University
Tom Zaniello ....Northern Kentucky University
David Zucker ....Quinnipiac College

Cumulative Index

Dictionary of Literary Biography, Volumes 1-48
Dictionary of Literary Biography Yearbook, 1980-1985
Dictionary of Literary Biography Documentary Series, Volumes 1-4

Cumulative Index

DLB before number: *Dictionary of Literary Biography*, Volumes 1-48
Y before number: *Dictionary of Literary Biography Yearbook*, 1980-1985
DS before number: *Dictionary of Literary Biography Documentary Series*, Volumes 1-4

B

C

D

E

H

K

N

S

T